EMERGING EUROPEAN FINANCIAL MARKETS
INDEPENDENCE AND INTEGRATION
POST-ENLARGEMENT

INTERNATIONAL FINANCE REVIEW

Series Editor: J. Jai Choi

INTERNATIONAL FINANCE REVIEW   VOLUME 6

EMERGING EUROPEAN FINANCIAL MARKETS
INDEPENDENCE AND INTEGRATION POST-ENLARGEMENT

EDITED BY

JONATHAN A. BATTEN
Macquarie University, Sydney

and

COLM KEARNEY
Trinity College, Dublin

ELSEVIER
JAI

Amsterdam – Boston – Heidelberg – London – New York – Oxford
Paris – San Diego – San Francisco – Singapore – Sydney – Tokyo

ELSEVIER B.V.
Radarweg 29
P.O. Box 211
1000 AE Amsterdam,
The Netherlands

ELSEVIER Inc.
525 B Street, Suite 1900
San Diego
CA 92101-4495
USA

**ELSEVIER Ltd
The Boulevard, Langford
Lane, Kidlington
Oxford OX5 1GB
UK**

ELSEVIER Ltd
84 Theobalds Road
London
WC1X 8RR
UK

First edition 2006

British Library Cataloguing in Publication Data
A catalogue record is available from the British Library.

ISBN-10:   0-7623-1264-5
ISBN-13:   978-0-7623-1264-1
ISSN: 1569-3767 (Series)

∞ The paper used in this publication meets the requirements of ANSI/NISO Z39.48-1992 (Permanence of Paper).
Printed in The Netherlands.

CONTENTS

**PART C: FINANCIAL INNOVATION
AND LIBERALIZATION**

PART D: EQUITY MARKET INTEGRATION

PART E: FDI AND ENLARGEMENT

INTERDEPENDENCE AND INTEGRATION IN EMERGING EUROPEAN FINANCIAL MARKETS

Jonathan A. Batten and Colm Kearney

The history and prospects of European integration are both fascinating and exciting. Analysts of every aspect of this process, including its cultural, economic, financial, historical, political, and social dimensions, should recall that its main rationale remains as it has always been, to permanently end conflict and to secure peace and prosperity for all Europeans. As the European Union's (EU's) own website (see http://europa.eu.int) points out Europe has been the scene of many and frequent bloody wars throughout the centuries. In the 75-year period between 1870 and 1945, for example, France and Germany fought each other three times with huge loss of life. The history of modern European integration commenced in earnest with the realization in the early 1950s that the best way to prevent future conflict is to secure more economic and political integration. This led to the establishment of the European Coal and Steel Community in 1951, followed shortly by the European Economic Community (EEC) in 1957. Since then, the process of integration and enlargement has progressed at varying speeds, but always moving forwards. In 1967, the founding institutions of the EEC were merged to form today's European Commission (EC), the Council of Ministers, and the European Parliament. The members of the European Parliament were initially chosen by the member governments of the EEC,

Emerging European Financial Markets: Independence and Integration Post-Enlargement
International Finance Review, Volume 6, 1–14
Copyright © 2006 by Elsevier Ltd.
ISSN: 1569-3767/doi:10.1016/S1569-3767(05)06001-2

but direct elections commenced in 1979, and have continued every 5 years since then. The Treaty of Maastricht created the EU in 1992 and established the process of economic and monetary union (EMU) that culminated in the introduction of the euro in 12 of the 15 Member States in 2002.

The founding six members of the EEC in 1957 were Belgium, France, Germany, Italy, Luxembourg, and the Netherlands. Alongside the process of enhanced cooperation and integration that has ensued ever since, there has been a spectacular process of expansion and enlargement. There has been a number of enlargements of the initial EEC to form today's EU comprising 25 countries. In 1973, Denmark, Ireland, and the United Kingdom joined the EEC, followed by Greece in 1981. These countries were joined by Portugal and Spain in 1986. In 1995, Austria, Finland, and Sweden joined the EU. In 2004, the largest ever enlargement took place when the EU welcomed 10 new countries: Cyprus, the Czech Republic, Estonia, Hungary, Latvia, Lithuania, Malta, Poland, Slovakia, and Slovenia. Future enlargements are already envisaged, with Bulgaria and Romania expected to join in 2007, and with Croatia and Turkey due to commence negotiations in late 2005.

The economic consequences for the incumbents of previous EU enlargements pale in comparison to the likely consequences of the accession of the 10 Central and Eastern European (CEE) countries. This is not just because of the scale of the recent enlargement and the number of countries involved, but because of the income differences that exist between the incumbent and candidate countries. The recent enlargement has increased the land area of the EU by 34 per cent, the EU population has grown by 105 millions (28 per cent), and EU gross domestic product (GDP) (evaluated at purchasing power parity or PPP) has expanded by 11 per cent. The population increase compares to the 1973 enlargement of 31 per cent. The GDP increase of 11 per cent compares to the 1986 enlargement of 12 per cent, and the land mass increase compares to each of the previous enlargements. A major difference in the recent enlargement, however, is the much lower level of development of the CEE countries. The per capita PPP-based GDP of these countries is 39 per cent of that of the EU-15, compared to an equivalent figure of 61.5 per cent for the smaller accessions (in population terms) of the 1980s. By contrast, the enlargements of the 1970s and 1990s barely affected average incomes.

This volume is concerned with contributing to the growing body of literature that examines the extent of, and the implications of enhanced independence and integration that will result from the recent EU enlargement for the development of emerging European financial markets.[1] The objective is to provide a perspective on the nature and complex problems associated with financial market development in the emerging European economies and their relationships with the EU (and other major regions) in the post-EU enlargement environment. The volume is divided into five parts. Part A focuses on the important implications for fiscal policy, Part B deals with monetary policy and banking, Part C explores issues concerned with financial innovation and liberalization, Part D examines recent developments in equity market integration, and Part E looks at the implications of enhanced independence and integration for foreign direct investment (FDI). The latter is of particular interest because the ability to attract significant amounts of foreign capital will have potentially profound consequences for both the overall level of economic growth in the region, and its geographical distribution (UNCTAD, 2000).

In introducing the chapters in Part A which deals with fiscal policy, it is useful to recall that the structural differences between the new CEE entrants and the prior EU-15 Member States has led to hard bargaining over how the EU budgetary programmes will be extended to the new accession countries. Some commentators have suggested that the scale and effects of the CEE-10 enlargement might be gauged by reflecting on the experience of German reunification, implying that enlargement might involve substantial deficit spending and rising interest rates. This is most unlikely to happen, however, because the incumbent EU-15 Member States have worked hard to keep down the budgetary costs of enlargement, and the scale of budgetary support offered will be much less than in the case of German reunification. While the budgetary implications loom large in the general European policy debate, however, the welfare consequences over the longer term are likely to be dominated by the increased trade and factor flows that the enlargement will give rise to. Due to the relative sizes of the two groups of economies, the consequences will be much more profound for the CEE countries than for the new members during any of the previous enlargements.

In Chapter 2, Nico Groenendijk looks at fiscal policy surveillance in the enlarged EU, and considers what form it should take in the new EU Member States during the run-up to EMU membership. In a thorough review of the important issues, Groenendijk first reviews the commitment and the delegation approaches to fiscal discipline through centralization of the budgetary decision-making process. He then describes current fiscal surveillance practice in the EU, including the excessive deficit procedure (EDP) of the stability and growth pact (SGP) and the multilateral surveillance that is part of the Broad Economic Policy Guidelines (BEPGs). Groenendijk points to a number of deficiencies in current EU fiscal surveillance practices, and outlines the September 2004 Commission proposal for an enriched common fiscal framework to better cater for differences in the fiscal deficit and debt situation across the new Member States. He argues that the fore-casting and early warning activities that are now in the hands of the EC should be transferred to an independent body of experts, and that the ruling authority that is part of the SGP sanction mechanism should be taken from the Ecofin Council and given to the European Court of Justice that will act on the initiative of the independent fiscal body. He concludes that in order to enhance the ability of the new Member States to finance their transition processes, a temporary mechanism should be established to exclude public infrastructure investments from the calculations of government deficits.

In Chapter 3, Dalia Grigonytė examines the impact of fiscal policy on risk premia in the CEE countries. He points out that if a country runs a balanced budget, there will be no linkage between fiscal variables and interest rates, but in the case of fiscal expansion, foreign investors will absorb the deficit only in the presence of a higher risk premium. Grigonytė shows that after 10 years of transition, the risk premia of CEE government bonds have declined considerably, and his econometric analysis focuses on the impact of fiscal variables on interest rate differentials in the transition economies. His results are consistent with the literature that higher public debt and deteriorating fiscal positions lead to higher risk premia, while healthy GDP growth rates and higher tax to debt ratios lead to reduced premia. The results suggest that investors pay careful attention to expected future fiscal balances as well as to historical positions, and that they reward fiscal adjustment with lower risk premia. Taken together with the analysis by Groenendijk in Chapter 2, the picture that emerges is that responsible fiscal management by the CEE countries in the context on improved and more flexible institutional arrange-ments for the conduct of fiscal policy should deliver favourable interest rate outcomes.

In introducing the chapters in Part B that deals with monetary policy and banking, it is useful to note that despite substantial improvement since the mid-1990s, the financial markets of emerging Europe are underdeveloped relative to their peers in Western Europe. This is hardly surprising given the significant gap between the two regions in terms of economic development. Their markets have been little used until recently as a source of finance in the region, although it is acknowledged that it is essential to do so to provide long-term economic benefits. Market development has often been hindered by the fact that many of the region's economies have sometimes failed to provide the necessary environment, including macroeconomic stability, low inflation, and credible commitment to modern regulation and governance. The limited market activity of the CEE-10 governments has, for example, curtailed the development of public bond markets and the related market infrastructure which is a prerequisite to building viable private markets. Even today, only the bond markets of the Czech Republic, Hungary, Poland, Turkey, and to a lesser extent Russia, play some role in the region (Szilagyi, Fetherston, & Batten, 2003). A general discussion of trends in individual markets in Europe is also provided in the edited volume by Batten, Fetherston, and Szilagyi (2004).

In Chapter 4, Orazio Mastroeni compares the monetary policy operational frameworks in the euro area with some of the frameworks that exist in non-euro area countries. He points out two central banks of the non-euro area Member States operate under a currency board system. Although the monetary policy implementation frameworks in these countries are broadly similar to those in the euro area, differences in the minimum reserve systems relate to the remuneration of required reserves, the determination of maintenance and calculation periods, and the level of the reserve ratio. All central banks of non-euro area Member States operate under a structural liquidity surplus, as opposed to only a few in the Eurosystem, and this influences the operational frameworks in a number of ways. As a result of excess liquidity in the banking systems, most open market operations are liquidity absorbing, the most frequently used being repurchase agreements (repos), the issuance of short-term paper, and the collection of deposits. Liquidity-providing open market operations and marginal lending facilities are collateralized in the non-euro area Member States, with the list of eligible assets including almost solely public debt instruments. Measured against GDP, the total outstanding amount of eligible assets is considerably lower than in the euro area. This may be due to the fact that large pools of eligible assets are not necessary in a market with a structural liquidity surplus.

In Chapter 5, Richard Werner suggests some aspects of the operations of the European Central Bank (ECB) that should be of significance to the CEE countries. He questions whether the current institutional framework of the ECB and its control over the euro follows best practice that empirical evidence suggests, based on the experience of a successful central bank such as Germany's. In doing so, he first defines "successful" monetary policy, and then engages in comparative institutional analysis in order to identify the true lessons of the German central banking experience and whether these have been heeded in the design of the ECB. His conclusion is controversial. He suggests that the ECB does not follow the best practice as suggested by the experience of the Bundesbank. Instead, it is in line with the institutional design of one of the least successful central banks in history, the German Reichsbank. This author sounds a note of caution, as a number of important issues require further research before a country hands over control of its monetary policy to the ECB.

In Chapter 6, Peter Zajc examines bank efficiency in six CEE countries during the period from 1995 to 2000. He addresses three issues: first, whether there are differences in efficiency between domestic and foreign banks; second, whether the difference in foreign and domestic bank efficiency has changed over time; and third, whether the extent of foreign bank presence affects the efficiency of the domestic banks. In doing so, Zajc begins by outlining the theory of efficiency and discussing the relevant estimation techniques and functional forms of production functions that are used in extant studies. He presents two models for testing the relative efficiency of the CEE banks. He finds that there are indeed differences in the efficiency of domestic and foreign banks, and that a change in ownership from domestic to foreign tends to be associated with a decline in efficiency that might reflect the need for upgrading expenditures and market penetration expenses that will produce greater efficiency over longer time spans than can be analysed with currently available data. He also identifies other factors that drive bank efficiency in the CEE countries.

In Chapter 7, Ilko Naaborg and Bert Scholtens perform a comparative analysis of banks' balance sheets in the EU and in the new EU CEE countries over the period from 1995 to 2003. Although banking in relation to GDP in the EU-15 countries is about twice as large as in the CEE-10 countries, the composition of their assets and liabilities appears to be quite similar. This similarity disappears, however, when we consider the composition of the asset side. In their loan portfolio, banks in the former EU-15 have relatively more loans with longer maturities. Furthermore, the diversity of loans on banks' balance sheets is much higher in the former EU-15 than in the CEE-10 countries, and in this respect the latter are still underdeveloped. When looking at the liabilities of banks, they find that those in the former EU-15 have much significantly higher leverage than those in the CEE countries. Contrary to the general trend, foreign bank size in the former EU-15 became smaller after 1998. Due to merger and acquisition (M&A) in the CEE countries, foreign banks are on average three times larger than their domestic counterparts. Foreign banks in all regions are better capitalized than their domestic counterparts. The authors conclude that in the course of their economic development, banks in the CEE transition countries are beginning to catch up on those in the EU-15 countries.

We conclude Part B with a case study of financial reform in Turkey. In Chapter 8, Caner Bakir provides a very interesting analysis of the process of monetary and financial reform in Turkey. He argues that the current situation in which Turkey finds itself can best be understood in terms of the pressures emanating the International Monetary Fund (IMF) and the World Bank with their financial support and technical assistance, and from the necessity for reform as part of the accession process towards future membership of the EU. Bakir explains that Turkey is proceeding along a long time path of "Europeanization", and that it has made remarkable progress in economic and financial restructuring since the crises of 2000 and 2001. Turkey's transition programme aimed at achieving macroeconomic stability, and its banking sector restructuring programme aimed at strengthening the monetary and financial governance of the banking sector, were both introduced following the crises, and have benefited from substantial financial and technical assistance from the "twin" organizations of the IMF and the World Bank. In essence, Bakir argues that the EU accession process and the "twin" sisters with their financial and technical support have served as an effective external anchor for financial and monetary governance by supranational interdependence. With regards to good governance in the financial services industry, Bakir argues that Turkey faces a few major challenges. The Turkish Government still seems to be reluctant to adopt a sufficiently proactive approach to the financial services industry, and more proactive policies incorporating best practice governance with appropriate accountability and transparency will be needed to lock in future progress.

In introducing the chapters in Part C, which focuses on financial innovation and liberalization, it is appropriate to note that international financial markets throughout the world have developed rapidly throughout the past four decades. Watson et al. (1988) document this development in terms of internationalization, securitization, and liberalization. In terms of internationalization, the pace of activity in financial markets has grown faster than real output in the major industrial countries, but this has been accompanied by even faster growth in offshore financial market activity. Concerning securitization, there has been a move away from indirect finance through intermediaries to direct finance through international bond markets. Liberalization has resulted in the removal of domestic quantity and price restrictions, greater international participation in domestic financial markets, more cross-border capital flows, and new financial instruments. It is universally accepted that the net effect of these developments has been to expand the set of states of nature against which market operators can insure and/or upon which they can speculate. Recent analyses and reviews of this process, such as those by Bracker, Docking, and Koch (1999), Bekaert, Harvey, and Lumsdaine (2003), and Kearney and Lucey (2004a) are plentiful, and the reader is referred to these and to many other studies and the references therein. This area promises to remain an active research topic for many years to come.

In Chapter 9, Jing Chi and Martin Young describe the process of the development of financial derivatives markets in the expanded EU. They begin by describing the history of the development of financial derivative markets in the EU-15 countries along with the current state of development of these markets in the 10 new EU Member States and other countries of Europe outside of the EU. Chi and Young proceed to conjecture about the likely alliances that will be formed, the appropriate product developments, and the benefits to be gained through the development of financial derivatives trading in these countries. They conclude that the rationalization of the derivative markets that has occurred recently within the established EU Member States will continue within the expanded EU. Financial derivatives trading within the new EU Member States will develop from their home equity markets or through alliances to be formed with the exchanges of the established EU Member States. They foresee that the main area for derivatives market growth within these markets will be with individual stock and equity index products.

In Chapter 10, Lúcio Vinhas de Souza conducts an interesting study of the relation between the process of financial liberalization and the pattern of business cycles in the new EU Member States. In doing so, de Souza effectively extends the prior work of Kaminsky and Schmukler (2003) to a group of countries that has not thus far been studied in this way. He points out that whereas financial liberalization can play a fundamental role in increasing economic growth and welfare, it can also be risky, as has evidenced by many past, banking, currency, and financial crises. Using business cycles defined by the Bry-Boschan algorithm to locate cyclical turning points, de Souza finds weak evidence that financial liberalization generates short- and long-run benefits measured by the extension of the amplitude of upward cycles and the reduction of downward cycles of stock market indexes. He also finds that participation in the EU enlargement process seems to reduce volatility in the CEE countries. This is a promising area for further research.

In Chapter 11, Patrick McGuire and Martijn Schrijvers search for the existence of common factors in euro-denominated emerging market bond spreads. Their approach, based on factor analysis, differs markedly from other recent work that applies regression-based techniques (see Wagner, Hogan, & Batten, 2005; Batten, Hogan, & Jacoby, 2005). They begin by describing the development of euro-denominated emerging market debt as an asset class, and they proceed to employ principal factor analysis to investigate the degree to which common sources of variation have the power to explain daily changes in their spreads. Whereas a single common factor characterizes the variation in US-dollar-denominated spreads, they identify two factors underlying this variation in euro-denominated spreads. These two factors seem to capture the differences in spread movements for investment grade and non-investment grade sovereign bonds. While any interpretation of the common factors is subjective, McGuire and Schrijvers point out that the countries rated as investment grade tend to load highly on the first factor, while non-investment grade countries tend to load highly on the second. They show that this interpretation is supported by separate analysis of countries grouped by rating class. They conclude that although it is impossible to attach precise meaning to the common factors, there is evidence that they reflect changes in investors' tolerance for risk.

As in Part B, we conclude Part C with another case study in emerging CEE financial markets. In Chapter 12, Michael Skully and Kym Brown provide a thorough overview, history, and assessment of Romania's financial reform process that commenced in 1990. They begin by providing an overview of Romania's macroeconomic performance, and follow this with a description of developments within the financial institutions including the banks, the credit cooperatives, leasing companies, and insurance companies. They then discuss capital market developments including the main stock exchanges. Further sections examine developments in Romania's money and bond markets, including its mutual funds and venture capital funds. A further section provides an overview of the sweeping programme of privatization. Skully and Brown conclude that with the possibility of EU accession, and with the sustainable programme of reform now occurring, the potential for growth and development is very significant. Equity has been trading more frequently and market capitalization has increased rapidly in the past few years. Moves are now in place to amalgamate the stock exchanges and to de-list thinly traded firms. Further confidence in the Romanian economy is illustrated with increased maturity dates for bond markets with limited secondary trading.

In introducing the chapters in Part D on the topic of equity market integration, it suffices to say that this area of study has blossomed enormously in recent years. The expansion in available datasets together with exciting developments in financial time series econometrics, such as the dynamic conditional correlation model of Engle (2002), has led to a veritable explosion in the quantity and quality of empirical studies of both developed market integration and the enhanced integration amongst emerging markets and between these and the developed markets. Readers who are interested in exploring developments related to European market integration are referred to Dockery and Vergari (2001), Bekaert and Harvey (2002), Fratzschler (2002), Bekaert et al. (2003), Kearney and Lucey (2004b), Voronkova (2004), and Kearney and Poti (2006), and, indeed, to the chapters in Part C of this volume and the references therein.

In Chapter 13, Seppo Pynnönen examines the determinants of the contemporaneous correlations among European emerging markets. The markets included are the Czech Republic, Estonia, Hungary, Latvia, Lithuania, Poland, Slovakia, and Slovenia, and the main European developed markets (Germany and the United Kingdom) as well the United States are also included. Pynnönen suggests modelling the time-varying contemporaneous correlations as a function of conditional volatilities, and in an insightful generalization, he also includes possible additional explanatory variables using logit-type regressions. The advantage of the model is that it allows studying explicitly besides the own volatilities also the contribution of external volatilities to the correlation, that is, volatilities that are not directly involved in the definition of the basic correlation. The results of the chapter indicate that, like among the more developed markets, higher world volatility tends to raise many of the emerging European correlations, particularly those between the developed and emerging markets. This is an intuitive result that should be of interest to practioners as well as researchers.

In Chapter 14, Roy Kouwenberg and Albert Mentink use weekly data on stock and bond returns over the period of February 1997 to November 2004 from Western European markets, treated as a single market, and from three CEE markets and the Czech Republic, Hungary and Poland, Russia, and Turkey to calculate the correlations between the equity and bond market returns. Although they find clear links between the equity markets of Western Europe, and CEE, there remains ample opportunity for risk reduction through portfolio diversification. Kouwenberg and Mentink report no evidence of long-term cointegration relationships between the equity markets. For the euro-denominated government bond markets, however, their finding is different. Here, the short-term return correlation between Western Europe and two CEE countries' bond markets is over 90 per cent. Diversification of euro-denominated government bond portfolios is still possible, however, through investments in East European bond markets. Finally, they report that no security market clearly dominates all others in causality, and the best opportunities for diversification are contained in stock–bond portfolios.

In Chapter 15, Lucey and Voronkova examine the relationship between Russian and other CEEs and European developed equity markets over the period from 1995 to 2004. The application of traditional multivariate cointegration and vector-error correction analysis indicates that the strength of the relationships differs markedly before and after the Russian crisis of 1998. When structural breaks are permitted in the relationships, the authors then find that the effect of the Russian crisis is quite complex. The Russian market shows significantly more evidence of integration with developed markets since the crisis, albeit the extent of interdependencies differs in case of the European and United States markets. Analysis of conditional correlations also indicates that the conditional relationships between the Russian and the main developed markets have strengthened after the crisis. Interestingly, Lucey and Voronkova find virtually no evidence of regional equity market integration.

In Chapter 16, Uri Ben-Zion and Niklas Wagner use daily returns from January 1999 to December 2000 to study trading and non-trading overnight returns in Russia and the United Kingdom. The authors argue that the relation between trading and non-trading return periods has been insufficiently studied to date, although it has significant potential to assist our understanding of trading, the transmission of information into prices, and the formation of asset price illiquidity premiums. They find that expected returns are higher during non-trading periods, and that an overnight risk premium exists in both markets. The latter does not seem to be attributable to volatility risk only, and Ben-Zion and Wagner argue that it may in part reflect the risk of large overnight price declines. The results for Russia indicate a lower trading to non-trading variance ratio and a relatively high overnight return expectation. Taking higher overnight volatility into account yields a per unit time return to volatility ratio very similar to that of the United Kingdom. Amongst their most interesting conclusions is that overnight shocks unrelated to trading may in part be responsible for fat tails in return distributions, and non-normality in daily close-to-close returns may persist in empirical models that include volume or the number of trades. Overall, this chapter provides an interesting example of how the study of emerging markets can lead to greater understanding of the microstructure of developed markets.

In introducing Part E, which examines the role of FDI in the European integration process, it is important to be aware of the considerable build up in expectations that EU enlargement will significantly enhance the attractiveness of the CEE countries as a location for FDI. EU accession removes all intra-European customs frontiers and trade barriers associated with differing technical standards, it allows full access to government procurement contracts, it enhances transparency in the legal and business environment because of the EU's *acquis communautaire,* and it raises the confidence of foreign investors by allowing for the possibility of appeal beyond the courts of the associated countries to those of the EU in the event of legal disputes arising. For all of these reasons, EU accession promises a dramatic change in the CEE climate for foreign investors that will allow the CEE countries to compete more effectively for FDI. As Dunning (1997a, b) shows, previous episodes of trade liberalization in Europe have increased the pool of FDI both from within Europe and from outside. As Gorg and Strobl (2001, 2002), and Barry (2002) show, the potential benefits of attracting enhanced FDI flows are considerable, and Barry (2004), and Barry and Kearney (2006) show how successful FDI policies can greatly transform an economy.

In Chapter 17, Steven Globerman, Daniel Shapiro, and Yao Tang examine the determinants of inward and outward FDI in 20 emerging and transition economies in Europe over the period from 1995 to 2001. They adopt a comparative perspective to their work by explicitly comparing the determinants of FDI samples of both developed and developing countries. In doing so, they pay particular attention to measures of governance and institutional change such as privatization as potential determinants of both inward and outward FDI. They find that the determinants of FDI in the region are generally similar to those for other developing and developed countries. In addition to highlighting the importance of good governance, they verify that joining the EU, or even the prospect of joining the EU, promotes inward FDI. They interpret this as suggesting the importance of a "locking in effect" with respect to governance that provides long-term assurance to potential foreign investors that institutional changes undertaken by the transition economies will not be reversed.

Chapter 18 by Yusaf Akbar, Heather Elms, and Tej Dhakar examine the relationship between economic development, inward FDI, and local stock exchange development (LSED) in a group of CEE countries. The literature on economic development suggests that economic development is associated with FDI and LSED since capital formation is central to the growth potential of economies. Through a statistical analysis of data for the period from 1990 to 2002, they find evidence of this link for some countries in their sample. This is a very interesting and insightful piece of research that will surely foster more work as more data becomes available.

In Chapter 19, Kálmán Kalotay examines the impact of EU enlargement on FDI flows to the new members from beyond the former Iron Curtain. He points out that the competitive advantage of the new members is derived mostly from their labour productivity rather than from lower taxes or large potential transfers from the EU budget. Compared to available opportunities, the FDI inflows and outflows of the new members have been small to date and growing slowly due to the wrapping up of privatization and the slow take-off of large greenfield projects. Part of the explanation, however, is also to be found in the protectionist pressures in the old members of the Union, prompted by fears of massive relocation of FDI to the new members. On the outward side, the low level of FDI reflects the nascent stage of capitalism in the new Member States. In the near future, both inward and outward FDI is expected to rise in these countries.

In conclusion, this volume offers a comprehensive perspective of issues concerning the independence and integration of European financial markets. Chapters in a number of critical areas including fiscal policy, money and banking, financial innovation and liberalization, equity market integration, and finally FDI and enlargement, offer valuable insights into experiences to date, while also identifying some of the important challenges ahead. In this way, the analyses presented also highlight further opportunities to be explored, while the results offer hypotheses, which, however tentative, may be subject to further work.

NOTES

1. The Bank for International Settlements includes the following countries in the emerging European economies category: Albania, Belarus, Bosnia and Herzegovina, Bulgaria, Croatia, Cyprus, the Czech Republic, Estonia, Gibraltar, Hungary, Latvia, Lithuania, Macedonia, Malta, Moldova, Poland, Romania, Russia, Serbia and Montenegro, the Slovak Republic, Slovenia, Turkey, and the Ukraine.

REFERENCES

Barry, F. (2002). EU accession and prospective FDI flows to CEE countries. In: R. Lipsey (Ed.), *Foreign Direct Investment in the Real and Financial Sector of Industrial Countries*. Frankfurt: Deutsche Bundesbank.

Barry, F. (2004). Export platform FDI: The Irish experience. *European Investment Bank EIB Papers*, 9, 8–37.

Barry, F., & Kearney, C. (2006). MNEs and industrial structure in host countries: A portfolio analysis of FDI in Irish manufacturing. *Journal of International Business Studies* (forthcoming).

Batten, J. A., Fetherston, T. A., & Szilagyi, P. G. (Eds) (2004). *European fixed income markets: Money, bond and interest rate derivatives*, (pp. xx–484). England: John Wiley & Sons Ltd, (part of the Wiley Finance Series). ISBN 0-470-85053-1.

Batten, J. A., Hogan, W. P., & Jacoby, G. (2005). Measuring credit spreads: Evidence from Australian eurobonds. *Applied Financial Economics*, 15(9), 651–666.

Batten, J. A., Hogan, W., & Wagner, N. (2005). Interest rates, stock market returns, and variations in German credit spreads. *Economic Notes*, 34(1), 35–50.

Bekaert, G., & Harvey, C. R. (2002). Research in emerging market finance: Looking to the future. *Emerging Market Review*, *3*, 429–448.

Bekaert, G., Harvey, C., & Lumsdaine, R. (2003). Dating the integration of world equity markets. *Journal of Financial Economics*, *65*, 203–248.

Bracker, K., Docking, D. S., & Koch, P. D. (1999). Economic determinants of international stock market integration. *Journal of Empirical Finance*, *6*, 1–28.

Dockery, D., & Vergari, F. (2001). An investigation of the linkages between European Union equity markets and emerging capital markets: The East European connection. *Managerial Finance*, *27*, 24–39.

Dunning, J. (1997a). The European internal market programme and inbound foreign direct investment, Part 1. *Journal of Common Market Studies*, *35*(1), 1–30.

Dunning, J. (1997b). The European internal market programme and inbound foreign direct investment, Part 2. *Journal of Common Market Studies*, *35*(2), 189–223.

Engle, R. F. (2002). Dynamic conditional correlation: A simple class of multivariate generalised autoregressive conditional heteroskedasticity models. *Journal of Business and Economic Statistics*, *20*, 339–350.

Fratzschler, M. (2002). Financial market integration in Europe: On the effects of EMU on stock markets. *International Journal of Finance and Economics*, *7*, 165–193.

Gorg, H., & Strobl, E. (2001). Multinational companies and productivity spillovers: A meta analysis. *Economic Journal*, *111*, F723–F739.

Gorg, H., & Strobl, E. (2002). Multinational companies and indigenous development: An empirical analysis. *European Economic Review*, *46*, 1305–1323.

Kaminsky, G., & Schmukler, S. (2003). *Short-run pain, long-run gain: The effects of financial liberalization*. IMF Working Papers no. WP/03/34, IMF.

Kearney, C., & Lucey, B. (2004a). Equity market integration – an overview. *International Review of Financial Analysis*, *13*, 571–583.

Kearney, C., & Lucey, B. (2004b). International equity market integration. Special Issue. *International Review of Financial Analysis*, *13*, 5.

Kearney, C., & Poti, V. (2006). Correlation dynamics in European equity markets. *Research in International Business and Finance* (forthcoming).

Szilagyi, P. G., Fetherston, T. A., & Batten, J. A. (2003). Disintermediation and the development of bond markets in emerging Europe. *International Journal of the Economics of Business*, *10*(1), 69–84.

UNCTAD (2000). World Investment Report. *United Nations conference on trade and development*, Palais des Nations, CH-1211, Geneva 10, Switzerland.

Voronkova, S. (2004). Equity market integration in central European emerging markets: A cointegration analysis with shifting regimes. *International Review of Financial Analysis*, *13*, 633–647.

Watson, M., et al. (1988). *International capital markets: Developments and prospects. World economic and financial surveys*. Washington, DC: International Monetary Fund.

PART A:
FISCAL POLICY

FISCAL POLICY SURVEILLANCE IN THE ENLARGED EUROPEAN UNION: PROCEDURAL CHECKS OR SIMPLE ARITHMETIC?

Nico Groenendijk

1. INTRODUCTION

In its recommendation on the 2004 update of the Broad Economic Policy Guidelines (BEPGs), the European Commission (2004) issued country-specific recommendations for fiscal policy in the Central and Eastern European (CEE) countries that have recently joined the European Union (EU) (henceforth the EU-10 countries). All countries except Estonia and Slovenia were urged to reduce their general government deficits, or to pursue low budget deficits in a credible and sustainable way within the multi-annual framework of EU budgetary surveillance. Some countries have received additional recommendations (the Czech Republic to reform its health care and pension systems, Estonia and Lithuania to avoid pro-cyclical policies, and Poland to reform its pension system). Most new Member States will consequently have to reduce their fiscal deficits and/or will have to avoid pro-cyclical fiscal policies to comply with the BEPGs, but also because of the required convergence within the Economic and Monetary Union (EMU). Bearing in mind that the government balance for the new Member

Emerging European Financial Markets: Independence and Integration Post-Enlargement
International Finance Review, Volume 6, 17–45
Copyright © 2006 by Elsevier Ltd.
ISSN: 1569-3767/doi:10.1016/S1569-3767(05)06002-4

States was −5.7 per cent of gross domestic product (GDP) in 2003, the required reduction of fiscal deficits will not be easy. This has been acknowledged by the Commission, which has argued that the need to reach and maintain sound budgetary positions will require an appropriate time path between the necessary consolidation and the appropriate fiscal stance supporting the transition. Particular attention will also need to be given to country-specific circumstances, in particular to initial budgetary positions, to ongoing structural shifts in the new Member State economies, and to the possible risks resulting from current account imbalances and strong credit growth.

This chapter overviews the upcoming budgetary surveillance procedure and the balancing act that will be required to ensure the consolidation of public finances in a sustainable way. The main question we pose is as follows: What should the fiscal surveillance of the new EU Member States look like in the run-up to EMU membership in the light of the recent debate on reform of the stability and growth pact (SGP)? This chapter is structured as follows. In Section 2 the literature on fiscal discipline is discussed. Following the distinction often made between rules and discretion, two approaches can be used to ensure fiscal discipline; setting numerical targets or establishing adequate fiscal procedures. Both approaches have their pros and cons, which will be reviewed. In Section 3, we first provide a brief description of the current fiscal surveillance practice in the EU (i.e. both the fiscal surveillance that is part of the excessive deficit procedure (EDP), the SGP, and the multi-lateral surveillance that is part of the BEPGs). We will discuss the literature that deals with the deficiencies of EU fiscal surveillance, especially of the SGP, in some detail, and we will review the Commission's (2004) proposal for an enriched common fiscal framework with a stronger emphasis on the economic rationale for its rules to better cater for differences in economic situations across the EU. Section 4 deals with fiscal policy in the new CEE Member States, focusing on fiscal policy and fiscal convergence, and will set aside the other convergence issues. This section also includes the discussion on fiscal surveillance at the domestic and EU level. Section 5 summarises and concludes.

2. FISCAL DISCIPLINE: NUMERICAL TARGETS VERSUS PROCEDURAL RULES

Following Alesina and Perotti (1996), budgetary institutions refer to the rules and regulations according to which budgets are drafted, approved, and implemented. These rules can be numerical targets like expenditure ceilings or a balanced-budget rule, or procedural rules which regulate the preparation, the legislative approval, and the execution of the budget, or rules regarding budget transparency. Budgetary or fiscal rules is a generic term referring to rules concerning the way government budgets are prepared and arranged, as well as to rules guiding budgetary behaviour.[1] The statutory underpinning of these rules can vary from international treaties to constitutional amendments, and from laws and regulations to policy guidelines, as can the different semantics: budgetary norms, reference values, guidelines, principles, and fiscal frameworks. Fiscal rules can also vary in terms of stringency and enforcement. There are ex ante rules (which apply only in the budget approval phase) and ex post rules (budget execution), and the sanction for non-compliance can be judicial, financial, and/or reputational (see Kopits & Symansky, 1998).

The function of fiscal rules is to ensure fiscal discipline, which in a broad sense encompasses macroeconomic stability, the assistance of other financial policies, fiscal sustainability, avoidance of negative spillovers, and credibility of government policy over time. In most studies, a more narrowly defined set of rules have been put forward. von Hagen and Harden (1994) mention two main sources of inefficiency that fiscal rules have to deal with: the deficit bias and the common pool problem. The deficit bias is the inclination to finance too large a part of current public spending by issuing debt, caused by the under-representation of future taxpayers in current decisions. The common pool problem refers to the systematic bias in favour of excessive spending which arises if the marginal cost of financing a public activity is not fully accounted for in the decision over the volume of that activity. If the expenditure proposed by each agent in the majority can be closely targeted to the group he or she represents, while revenues with their distortionary costs can be spread over a large number of groups, there will be a lack of internalisation of the costs of aggregate expenditure (see von Hagen & Harden, 1994, 1995; Kontopolous & Perotti, 1999; von Hagen, Hallett, & Strauch, 2001). Essentially, this is the idea of focused gains and diffused losses. The common pool problem is of course influenced by the number of parties involved, or the degree of fragmentation. Fragmentation arises when several agents or groups participate in the fiscal decision-making process, each with its own interests and constituency to satisfy, and each with some weight in the final decision. To participate in the majority, each group demands a share in the budget, and as all groups do this, the end result is a high level of expenditure or a large deficit. The more decision-makers, the less internalisation of the costs of policies takes place. Kontopolous and

Perotti (1999) have shown that for many Organization for Economic Cooperation and Development (OECD) countries in the period 1960–1995, the number of parties as well as the number of spending ministers has an impact on fiscal performance. Both kinds of fiscal inefficiencies (i.e. the deficit bias and the common pool problem) result from a lack of adequate mechanisms to resolve conflicts in the budget process and from the inability to strengthen the collective interest of the government over the individual incentives of the spending ministers.

How can excessive fiscal deficits be prevented? The answer to this question has been discussed in the well-known *rules-versus-discretion* debate, which stems from monetary policy but has been expanded to fiscal policy. In that latter realm, it deals with the question whether it is necessary to have a priori budgetary rules, or whether budgetary matters should be left at the discretion of the budgetary authorities. The difference between a rule on the one hand and discretion on the other hand can be discerned by taking into account three aspects (see de Haan, 1989), viz. pre-commitment versus no pre-commitment, state contingent policy versus non-state contingent policy, and the formulation of policy in terms of instruments or outcomes. Geared to fiscal disciplinary issues in nation states, the rules-versus-discretion issue has been rendered into a choice between two basic methods to ensure fiscal discipline. *First*, commitment throughout the budgetary cycle by all parties to numerical targets. According to Kopits and Symansky (1998), there are three major types of such numerical rules: balanced-budget or deficit rules, borrowing rules, and debt or reserve rules. To this can be added rules on total expenditure or revenue, or on categories of expenditure or revenue. *Second*, procedural strategic dominance of a party (like a finance minister) that is sympathetic to the efficient use of public resources.

Both of these methods aim to centralise the budget process and to reduce the impact of fragmentation of the budgetary decision-making process. Each approach has its pros and cons. As far as *effectiveness* is concerned, both methods have been shown to be effective in some cases but not in all. Both commitment to rules and the procedural approach as such do not have an unambiguous impact on fiscal performance. There is some evidence that balanced-budget rules have been effective in restraining the ability of US state governments to run large deficits (see Poterba, 1995; Alesina & Bayoumi, 1996; Knight & Levinson, 2000). Similar results have been found by Alesina, Hausmann, Hommes, and Stein (1999) for Latin American countries in the 1980s and early 1990s, and by von Hagen and Harden (1994) for EU Member States. On the other hand, balanced-budget rules can vary in stringency, depending on whether a balanced-budget must be submitted and/or approved and whether ex post deficits can be carried over to next year or not. If these rules are really effective, we would expect the stringency of balanced-budget rules to influence the average fiscal perform-ance of these states. This is not the case: Stringency does not affect fiscal performance, other than the choice of debt instruments. Tager and van Lear (2001) are also rather sceptical about the general effectiveness of the numerical approach, even when it is underpinned by constitutional arrangements.

Hallerberg et al. (2001) have shown that some countries in the EU are relatively successful in using the commitment approach to centralise the budget process. Within the commitment approach, the following aspects of fiscal rules are conducive to greater fiscal discipline:

- Clear multi-annual budget plans written into coalition agreements.
- Relatively high connectedness of the stability or convergence programme with the annual budget process.
- The existence of fiscal rules to deal with unexpected shocks during the implementation of the budget.
  Within the delegation approach, there are also some best practices:
- A finance minister with rules that guarantee him a privileged position in the setting of the yearly budget.
- A finance minister with broad discretion during the implementation of the budget.
- Fiscal rules that establish a ceiling on personnel cost and on those ex-penditures, which, in some Member States, are not included in the central government, such as welfare costs.

The conclusion is that both methods can be effective if implemented properly, and the choice between the two methods may then be a matter of cost minimisation. If we focus on the costs of both methods, some important differences between the two methods come to the fore. *First*, balanced-budget rules or other rules restraining deficits may have significant mac-roeconomic costs by not allowing the necessary fiscal flexibility required to respond to transitory output shocks in the economy (see Alesina & Perotti, 1996; Corsetti & Roubini, 1996; Milesi-Ferretti, 1997). Such a loss of flexibility due to numerical rules on the budget is important within a neoclassical framework (tax smoothing) as well as within a Keynesian framework (anti-cyclical policies). Alesina and Bayoumi (1996) have found that balanced-budget rules do not have any impact on output variability in the case of the US states. This is in line with the earlier findings of von Hagen and Harden (1994) for EU Member States. For the US context,

Alesina and Bayoumi (1996) also argue that tax smoothing and Keynesian anti-cyclical policy arguments may be much more relevant to the national level than to the state and local levels.

Second, numerical targets like a balanced-budget rule may lead to a systematic resort to dubious accounting practices (Corsetti & Roubini, 1996; Milesi-Ferretti, 2000, 2003), including the creative and strategic use of what is kept on and off budget. Alesina and Perotti (1996) list a variety of tricks: optimistic predictions on key economic variables, optimistic forecast of the effects on the budget of various new policies, creative use of off-budget expenditures, and strategic use of budget projections and multi-year budgeting. Such window-dressing has been widely experienced in the run-up to EMU (see Milesi-Ferretti, 2000, for many examples). In the long run, lack of transparency in the budget process can become a critical obstacle for achieving budget consolidation and expenditure control.

Third, and highly related to the former issue, both methods involve monitoring costs by the finance minister. These are especially relevant to the contracts approach, in which the finance minister must ensure that all parties live up to the contract and that they do not get engaged in window-dressing. In this respect, the size of the economy is relevant, as, according to von Hagen and Harden (1994), the size of economies correlates with complexity of administrations. The greater the degree of complexity, the more opportunities exist for individual players in the budget process to circumvent numerical targets through administrative gimmicks, and the larger the monitoring costs turn out to be.

Fourth, the use of numerical targets at an aggregate level may lead to the use of analogue targets and detailed allocation rules at the micro-level, resulting in what Hanushek (1986) has called formula budgeting, or what Tager and van Lear (2001) have called "policy on autopilot". Formula budgeting is simple, it requires little information, and has an apparent fairness. However, it is lacking in refined judgement and it avoids clear budgetary choices. What may be desirable from a macroeconomic perspective may be counterproductive from a microeconomic perspective. von Hagen and Harden (1994) have also warned that the budget process should not be reduced to a mere record of prior commitments.

Finally, there is the aspect of dealing with multi-party preferences. The delegation approach is not suitable for multi-party governments because it gives too much power to a representative (the finance minister) of one party. The necessary hierarchical procedural rules are less respectful of the rights of the minority than collegial rules, and are more likely to generate budgets that are tilted in favour of the interests of the majority (see Alesina

& Perotti, 1996). For coalition governments, the contracts approach is generally is to be preferred, not only because of the danger with the delegation method of a finance minister promoting the political interests of his own party, but also because of differences in credibility and enforcement mechanisms between one-party and coalition governments (see von Hagen, 2002).

Table 1 lists both methods and their score on the criteria discussed above. Of course, all these aspects are related and can be traded off. To give an example: The margin for window-dressing in the budget may be used for real fiscal adjustment in the presence of a strict numerical budget rule (see Milesi-Ferretti, 2000, 2003), thereby reducing macroeconomic costs. To give another example, Hallerberg et al. (2001) have shown that countries like Austria, France, Germany, Greece, Italy, and the UK have opted for the delegation approach. These are countries with one-party or one-block governments. Small countries, often with coalition governments, like Belgium, Finland, Ireland, Luxembourg, and the Netherlands, use a commitment system. It is clear that the choice of system is related to a country's composition of government (single-party government, party-block government, coalition government), which is in its turn largely determined by the electoral system (proportionality rule, plurality rule), and to size (due to

Table 1.   Commitment Approach and Delegation Approach Compared.

Criteria/Approach	Commitment Approach (Numerical Targets)	Score	Delegation Approach (Procedural Rules)	Score
Effectiveness	OK, if implemented properly (best practices)	+	Idem	+
Macroeconomic policy	Limits possibilities	−	OK	+
Incentive to shirk rules, corresponding monitoring costs	High	−	Low	+
Danger of formula budgeting	Yes	−	No	+
Symbolic use, electoral use	Yes	+	No	−
Suitability for coalition government, dealing with minorities	OK	+	Not really suited	−

Note: +: positive; −: negative.

Table 2. Use of Fiscal Approaches by EU Member States.

Commitment Approach	Delegation Approach	Mix/Hybrid System
Belgium	Austria	Denmark
Czech Republic	France	Portugal
Estonia	Germany	Spain
Finland	Greece	Sweden
Hungary	Italy	
Ireland	UK	
Latvia		
Lithuania		
Luxembourg		
The Netherlands		
Poland		
Slovakia		
Slovenia		

Notes: Based on Hallerberg et al. (2001); von Hagen (2002, referring to Gleich (2002)); and Dában, Detragiache, di Bella, Milesi-Ferretti, and Symansky (2003). The table includes all Member States except Cyprus and Malta.

complexity of administrative systems and corresponding level of monitoring costs).

To conclude this section, Table 2 provides an overview of the approaches used currently by the old EU-15 and the new EU/CEE-8. From that table it becomes clear that all CEE-8 have opted for centralisation of the budget procedure following the commitments approach. This does not come as a surprise, as most of the CEE-8 are small countries with coalition governments.

3. CURRENT FISCAL SURVEILLANCE PROCEDURES IN THE EU

How does the discussion in the previous section relate to EU fiscal surveillance? Basically, there are two aspects at issue.[2] The *first* issue is which approach is most suited for the EU in ensuring fiscal discipline at the domestic level throughout the EU area. In making that choice, all the elements discussed above (and some more) play a part, including monitoring costs, symbolic value, and the danger of window-dressing. The *second* issue is the impact that EU fiscal surveillance might have on domestic choices regarding the two different approaches. In the concluding section, we will come back to these key problems; in this section we will briefly describe fiscal surveillance as it is currently in use within the EU. Current fiscal surveillance within the EU is made up of two parts. The first part is the surveillance that is part of the EDP as laid down in the Maastricht Treaty, supplemented by the surveillance on the basis of the SGP. For those Member States that are not yet part of EMU, the EDP surveillance serves as convergence procedure into EMU. The second part is the surveillance within the framework of the BEPGs. These two parts will be described in more detail below, followed by a discussion of the main deficiencies of the current fiscal framework, and of the recent Commission proposal to reform the SGP.

3.1. EDP and SGP Fiscal Surveillance

The EU Treaty and the SGP contain a number of fiscal rules. The central rule is the prohibition against excessive government deficits, viz. deficits exceeding 3 per cent GDP. This rule is applicable to all Member States whether in or out of EMU (except for the UK which is subject to a special derogation, and only has "to endeavour" to avoid excessive deficits). If an excessive deficit exists and is not put right in conformance with Council recommendations, sanctions can be imposed, but only on euro area Member States (so-called "participating Member States"). The SGP furthermore stipulates that all EU Member States (i.e. participating and non-participating Member States) must commit themselves to a medium-term budgetary position close-to-balance or in surplus, in order for automatic stabilisers to work freely, within the 3 per cent GDP ceiling. Non-compliance with the medium-term objective may result in verbal criticism by peers, but not in sanctions, because the latter are exclusively linked to the 3 per cent limit.

At the heart of the actual surveillance are the stability and convergence programmes. Stability programmes are drafted by participating Member States, convergence programmes by non-participating Member States. In the run-up to accession, as from 2001, pre-accession economic programmes and fiscal (i.e. debt and deficit) notifications were drafted by the candidate countries, which served the same purpose as the current convergence programmes. Stability and convergence programmes contain information on the medium-term objective for the budgetary position, actual budgetary position and expected path (for the upcoming 3 years, of both deficit and debt), main assumptions about expected economic developments, and description of budgetary and other economic policy measures.[3] (Updated) programmes are submitted to the Commission and Council annually. Based on assessments by the Commission, the Council examines the medium-term position and the targeted adjustment path towards the medium-term budgetary objective of "close-to-balance or in surplus". In the event that the Council identifies significant divergence, it gives a recommendation, either warning the Member State concerned or urging it to take prompt corrective measures (in the latter case the recommendation can be made public).

The recommendation/sanction procedure that is part of the EDP is different and follows a rather tight schedule.[4] First, the Commission has to establish whether an excessive deficit exists (or whether there is clear danger of an excessive deficit occurring) or whether the excess is exceptional and temporary. The excess of a deficit over the reference value is considered to be exceptional when resulting from an unusual event outside the control of the Member State concerned and which has a major impact on the financial position of the general government, or when resulting form a severe economic downturn (i.e. an annual fall of real GDP of at least 2 per cent). It is considered to be temporary if budgetary forecasts indicate the deficit will fall below the reference value following the end of the unusual event or severe economic downturn. If real GDP falls less than 2 per cent, it is up to the Council to decide whether the excessive deficit is nevertheless exceptional or not. As a rule, Member States are to take an annual fall of at least 0.75 per cent as a reference point in evaluating whether the economic downturn is severe. If a (non-exceptional and non-temporary) deficit exists, the Council gives a recommendation establishing, *first*, a 4-month deadline for effective action to be taken by the Member State concerned and, *second*, a deadline for the correction of the excessive deficit (as a rule to be completed in the year following its identification, unless there as special circumstances). If effective action does not take place, the Member State is given final notice, after which the sanction procedure starts (with a deposit, which can later be turned into a fine). If the Member State concerned acts in compliance with recommendations or notices, the EDP will be held in abeyance.

3.2. BEPGs Surveillance

The BEPGs lay down the EU's medium-term economic policy strategy, concentrated around growth and stability-oriented macroeconomic policies, economic reforms to raise Europe's growth potential, and strengthening sustainability (the Lisbon strategy). BEPGs surveillance is different from the

EDP/SGP surveillance in two respects. *First*, although the BEPGs also deal with budgetary policies, as part of macroeconomic policies, the focus is not solely on deficits but on sustainable government finances at large. As far as deficits are concerned the BEPGs build on the SGP framework. Member States should avoid excessive deficits, and should – over the cycle – achieve budgetary positions close-to-balance or in surplus. However, when assessing compliance with the close-to-balance requirement, the BEPGs take into account country-specific circumstances, especially:

- Sufficiency of the safety margin under the 3 per cent GDP ceiling, and coherence between the evolution and quality of the public finances in the stability and convergence programmes and the close-to-balance requirement.
- Long-term sustainability of public finances, with the emphasis on government debt and the impact of ageing populations. Member States should ensure a further decline in debt ratios, and reform their pension systems.

Second, the BEPGs do not involve sanctions. The BEPGs make both general and country-specific recommendations, without any obligation on the addressees' side to live up to these recommendations. The BEPGs are supplemented by an annual report by the Commission on the state of public finances in EMU.

Since 1999 a number of amendments and refinements have been made during implementation of the SGP. Besides that BEPGs and EDP/SGP fiscal surveillance have become more and more integrated. The main element of the SGP that has been clarified and refined is the medium-term objective of budgetary balance or surplus. *First*, the Commission has come up with benchmarks for each Member State for the cyclically adjusted budget balances (CABBs). These benchmarks reflect how far individual Member States' CABBs should be from the 3 per cent GDP ceiling in order to avoid an excessive deficit, given the nature of the business cycle and the sensitivity of the Member State's government budget to that cycle.[5] To a certain extent the SGP has been individualised by means of these CABBs. *Second*, "medium term" had to be interpreted. In 2002 (that is to say 3 years after the SGP came into force), most Member States had not reached a budgetary position close to their benchmark. It was decided by the Ecofin Council in October 2002 that those Member States should reduce their cyclically adjusted deficits by at least 0.5 per cent of GDP annually. *Third*, when assessing the margin between the benchmarks and the actual CABB, and the efforts made by a Member State to close that gap, the long-term sustainability of the Member States' public finances were taken into concern. The SGP is interpreted slightly more flexible for Member States with a relatively low government debt.

Another important development is the establishment and expansion of a framework for data supply by Member States to the Commission and the Council. In 1996 a reference framework of common standards, definitions, classifications, and accounting rules was adopted (European System of Accounts, ESA 95), supplemented by regulations on quarterly non-financial and financial accounts for general government (2002 and 2003, respectively).

3.3. Deficiencies

An extensive recent literature[6] has emerged on the deficiencies of specially the SGP. Following and amending that literature, these deficiencies can be listed as follows: (1) On the most fundamental level the whole rationale for the SGP is questioned. The SGP is meant to ensure sound budgetary positions as a means to strengthen the conditions for price stability. The actual economic logic between monetary union and the SGP has always been somewhat shaky and inconsistent (Hefeker, 2003). It is not clear what repercussions excessive deficits do precisely have on monetary policy, if any at all (Eichengreen & Wyplosz, 1998).[7] (2) Assuming there is some sort of need to protect the European Central Bank (ECB) from "fiscal profligacy" (Crowley, 2003) in a single Member State or group of Member States, the choice of the key variable, government deficits, has been questioned. From a monetary perspective government debt (the stock variable) is relevant and should be the key variable of the SGP.[8] In the run-up to EMU both deficits and debt were taken into account. Actually, the 3 and 60 per cent GDP ceilings for deficits and debt, respectively, were not chosen arbitrarily, as is often thought, but were stipulated against the background of an average debt level in the EU of 62 per cent GDP in 1992, and an assumption of a nominal growth rate of 5 per cent and an inflation target of 2 per cent. But with changing growth perspectives, with changing average debt levels, and with debt levels having been taken out of the framework, the 3 per cent deficit rule has indeed become arbitrary. (3) Assuming there is a need to focus on budget deficits, the current definition and use of deficits can be criticised. First, rather than focusing on the deficits of individual Member States the focus should be on the aggregate deficit of all EU Member States or on the aggregated euro area deficit. Following this line of reasoning, Casella (2001) has advocated a system of tradable deficit permits within the

EMU. (4) The current definition of the government deficit conflates current expenditure and capital expenditure (public investment expenditure). According to some, the 3 per cent GDP limit has exactly been chosen to incorporate capital expenditure (for the euro area currently amounting to approximately 2.5 per cent GDP), and the 3 per cent rule should be considered to be a de facto current account budgetary balance rule.

Obviously, this is at odds with the 3 per cent margin being used for the free operation of automatic stabilisers. Serving public investment purposes and automatic stabilisation purposes, at one and the same time, would – under the current ceiling – require a structural position in surplus (of 2.5–3.0 per cent GDP) rather than close-to-balance, or would necessitate a shift upwards of the excessive deficit ceiling to 5.5–6.0 per cent GDP. As both these conditions are not met at this moment, we would expect some serious trade-offs between public investment and automatic stabilisation. Turrini (2004) has found that in the convergence to EMU (phase II) public investment has indeed come under pressure (due to fiscal retrenchment in general rather than automatic stabilisation), whereas under the SGP (phase III) the share of public investment on GDP rose on average in the EU area, but the increase was concentrated in a small number of Member States.

Application of the golden rule (current expenditure to be funded from current revenues, capital expenditure financed via public indebtedness) would require a major revision of the SGP. The basic idea behind the golden rule is that budget deficits associated with productive public investment do not pose a problem, as such investment yields future income and tax receipts for government. Buti, Eijffinger, and Franco (2003) have listed a number of arguments against incorporation of the golden rule into the SGP. For example, fiscal measures other than public investment may have similar effects, like a well-devised tax reform. Dual budgets may discriminate against human capital and may work on favour of physical assets. A general difficulty with the golden rule is how to identify productive public investment, and this difficulty provides ample opportunities for creative budgeting (Eichengreen, 2004). (5) Another issue is whether to change over to a primary budgetary balance, that is, a balance measure that takes out debt service payments. Under the current SGP, falling or rising interest rates will automatically lead to lower/higher expenditure to service the debt, especially for highly indebted Member States. If changes in the CABB are to be seen as reflecting the effort of discretionary fiscal policy, in order to correct for changes in the budget balance due to interest rate changes (which are out of control of national governments) cyclically adjusted primary balances should be used. (6) The SGP relies exclusively on automatic stabilisers and does not allow for additional discretionary anti-cyclical fiscal policies, even though the need to pursue such policies is felt by some Member States. Whether such policies can be considered wise is questionable. Discretionary anti-cyclical policies are prone to leaks and lags; in the best case they are not very effective, in the worst case they are pro-cyclical. On the other hand, fiscal measures to correct excessive deficits, which have to be rapidly implemented, can also work pro-cyclically. Anyhow, it is important to make the best use possible of automatic stabilisers.[9] (7) The current framework works asymmetrically as it does not really deal with fiscal policy during upswings. In good times, the SGP does not give sufficient incentives for budgetary consolidation ("rainy day funds", "reloading the fiscal cannon"). (8) The fiscal framework is prone to forecast errors (see von Hagen, Hallerberg, & Strauch, 2004; Gros, Mayer, & Ubide, 2004). Forecast errors can be found in the stability programmes submitted by Member States but also in the estimates made by the Commission, especially of the CABBs (which are "moving targets"). Errors are systematic (i.e. optimistic) and in the range of 0.7 per cent GDP. In the case of Germany and France the Commission in 2002 underestimated the 2003 deficits by two full percentage points. Without proper forecasting the whole SGP decision-making process simply becomes a farce. Larch and Salto (2003) have put forward suggestions to improve the calculation of CABBs as indicators of discretionary fiscal policy, Gros et al. (2004) have argued in favour of more forecasting resources within the Commission, and Jonung and Larch (2004) in favour of independent forecasts (rather than forecasts made in-house) at the national level, to be incorporated into stability programmes. (9) Finally, there is the weak enforceability of the SGP, even when – as in the case of Germany and France – there was no doubt whatsoever about the excessiveness of their deficits. These excessive deficits originated from 2002, and recommendations were issued in January 2003 (Germany) and June 2003 (France). According to the SGP these excessive deficits should have been corrected in 2004. In the autumn of 2003 the European Commission proposed a recommendation, in which it –acrobatically – suggested that the necessary tightening measures could be spread over 2004 and 2005. Adoption of that recommendation would have meant that non-compliance by Germany and/ or France would have signalled the beginning of the SGP sanction procedure. The majority at the Ecofin Council recoiled, and the Council came up with non-binding Council conclusions urging Germany and France to take appropriate measures. In July 2004 the Court of Justice ruled that the Council should have acted upon the Commission's recommendation rather than issue Council conclusions.

The breakdown of the SGP procedure in November 2003 has seriously affected the credibility of the entire fiscal framework, but this breakdown obviously is related to the previous deficiencies: It is hard to enforce a framework that lacks clear economic rationale, does not take into account circumstances that Member States consider to be important, and is prone to forecasting errors. Enforceability is also weakened by the fact that for the current EMU-12 non-compliance has hardly any consequences, in contrast with the period up to the introduction of the euro where the convergence criteria served as exclusion device. Under the SGP the carrot of entry into EMU has been eaten while the stick of exclusion has been replaced by half-hearted recommendations and vague threats of sanctions.

3.4. The Commission's Proposals for Reform

The proposals made by the Commission (2004)[10] build on the Council Report of March 2003 on strengthening the co-ordination of budgetary policies, and at the heart of which was the view that when assessing a Member State's compliance with the SGP attention should be paid to country-specific circumstances, including the long-term sustainability of public finances.[11] The objective of the reform, according to the Commission, is to enhance the economic underpinnings of the existing framework and thus strengthen credibility and enforcement. The aim is not to increase rigidity or flexibility of current rules but rather to make them more effective. The main elements of the September 2004 Commission Communication are as follows:

- Placing more focus on government debt and sustainability in the surveillance of budgetary positions, but as a complement to continued rigorous attention to deficit developments. Specifically, the debt criterion in the Treaty (debt reduction at a "satisfactory pace") is to be rendered operational, taking into account country-specific initial debt levels, potential growth conditions and actual growth, and – possibly – additional factors related to ageing and contingent liabilities.
- Allowing for more country-specific circumstances in defining the medium-term deficit objective of close-to-balance or in surplus. Given the increased economic diversification in an EU of 25 Member States, uniform objectives for all countries do not appear appropriate and lack economic rationale.
- Considering economic circumstances and developments in the implementation of the EDP. *First*, the Commission mentions catering for prolonged

periods of sluggish growth through the exceptional circumstances clause. Slow but positive growth is currently not taken into account in the current EU fiscal framework, only (substantial) negative growth. A redefinition of the exceptional circumstances clause may be called for. *Second*, the Commission argues in favour of allowing for country-specific elements in the enforcement of the correction of excessive deficits, specifically with regard to the deadlines. One-size-fits-all deadlines have basic limitations because they do not permit distinguishing between countries with different cyclical developments and with different debt levels, possibly resulting in too stringent pro-cyclical adjustments. The deadlines for exercising surveillance should be brought more in line with national budgetary processes.
- Ensuring earlier actions to correct inadequate budgetary developments, aimed at prudent and symmetric-over-the-cycle policies, including the achievement of surpluses in good times.

In order to improve the effectiveness of the framework the link between the BEPGs, the SGP, and the national budgetary processes should be reinforced, as well as the role of the stability and convergence programmes.

4. FISCAL POLICY IN THE CEE-8

In the Commission's (2004) proposal, a general reference is made to the fact that the SGP is a pre-enlargement design, and that the EU of 25 is characterised by considerable heterogeneity and diversity. The question that is central to this section is whether the difficulties Member States generally have in complying with the fiscal framework will be increased or supplemented because of special characteristics of the CEE-8. Table 3 lists selected economic indicators for the new EU-10. The main differences and similarities between the CEE-8 (we will set aside Cyprus and Malta) relative to the EU-15 are: low-income per capita, high growth rates, equally low inflation, high current account deficits, high government deficits, and relatively low government debt. However, the CEE-8 form a rather diverse group, with growth rates being especially high in the Baltic states, and inflation being relatively high in Hungary, Slovenia, and Slovakia. CEE countries with high growth rates also tend to have large current account deficits. Figures on government deficits and debt are quite mixed, ranging from Estonia's exemplary fiscal conduct to Hungary that has both a considerable deficit and debt.

Table 3. Selected Economic Indicators, New EU Member States (2003).

	GDP % (PPS, EU-15 = 100)	Real GDP Growth	Inflation	Current Account Balance as % GDP	Government Balance as % GDP	Government Debt as % GDP
Cyprus	76	2.0	4.0	−4.4	−6.3	72.2
Czech Republic	62	2.9	−0.1	−6.5	−12.9	37.6
Estonia	40	4.8	1.4	−13.7	2.6	5.8
Hungary	53	2.9	4.7	−5.7	−5.9	59.0
Latvia	35	7.5	2.9	−9.1	−1.8	15.6
Lithuania	39	8.9	−1.1	−6.1	−1.7	21.9
Malta	69	0.4	1.3	−3.4	−9.7	72.0
Poland	41	3.7	0.8	−2.0	−4.1	45.4
Slovakia	47	4.2	8.5	−0.9	−3.6	42.8
Slovenia	69	2.3	5.7	0.2	−1.8	27.1
New Member States	47	3.6	2.1	−3.7	−5.7	42.2
EU-15	100	0.8	2.0	0.5	−2.6	64.0
Euro area		0.4	2.1	0.4	−2.7	70.4

Note: PPS: purchasing power standards.
Source: Commission service.

To what extent is the current fiscal framework relevant to the CEE-8? Upon joining the EU in May 2004, the 10 new Member States became members with derogation as regards the EMU. They must comply with the SGP rules, and if necessary EDP will be started, but they cannot be subject to an imposition to take actions to reduce excessive deficits nor can formal sanctions be imposed on them, which should be a relief to four countries (the Czech Republic, Hungary, Poland, and Slovakia) that currently have excessive deficits. On the other hand, as all CEE-8 want to join the EMU (in some cases as soon as possible, in other cases, like Poland, at a far later stage), there is a huge incentive to get deficits in check even though the SGP sanction mechanism does not apply.

At first sight, none of the CEE countries is likely to have any real problems with the 60 per cent GDP debt reference value, that is part of the fiscal convergence criteria of Maastricht. Yet, as Table 4 shows, government debt is on the rise in most CEE Member States, due to increases in deficits in earlier years. Especially Poland, Hungary, and the Czech Republic have debt dynamics that pose a threat to compliance with the 60 per cent debt rule. The Maastricht Treaty offers two ways out of the debt rule: substantial decline towards the 60 per cent reference value and temporary exceeding of the reference value. The first way out was relevant to the EU-15 but it is not relevant to the CEE-8. Still, as their debt rates are still below the euro area average, exclusion of these countries on the basis of non-compliance with

Table 4.   Government Finances, New EU Member States (2002, 2003).

	Government Balance as % GDP				Government Debt as % GDP	
	1997	2000	2002	2003	2002	2003
Czech Republic	−1.2	−3.5	−6.4	−12.9	28.9	37.6
Estonia	2.2	−1.1	1.8	2.6	5.7	5.8
Hungary	−4.8	−3.5	−9.3	−5.9	57.1	59.0
Latvia	0.2	−1.9	−2.7	−1.8	15.5	15.6
Lithuania	−1.0	−2.8	−1.4	−1.7	22.8	21.9
Poland	−1.3	−2.4	−3.6	−4.1	41.2	45.4
Slovakia	−1.8	−2.1	−5.6	−3.6	43.3	42.8
Slovenia	−1.2	−1.0	−1.9	−1.8	27.8	27.1
New Member States			−4.9	−5.7	39.4	42.2
EU-15			−2.0	−2.6	62.5	64.0
Euro area			−2.3	−2.7	69.2	70.4

Source: ECFIN/441/00-EN and Commission service.

the debt criterion will be hard to sell politically. Besides, some of the increase in recent years in public debt in countries like Poland and the Czech Republic is due to cleansing of their banking sectors (see Gros, Castelli, Jimeno, Mayer, & Thygesen, 2002). The fiscal impact of ageing (a factor currently taken into account to assess the sustainability of public finances in the EU) is broadly similar to that in the EU-15.

Although we disregard the non-fiscal convergence criteria, as explained in the introductory section, we need to establish what macroeconomic risks the CEE-8 run that might have an impact on the compliance with the fiscal criteria. As far as economic growth is concerned, the CEE-8 have followed a path of almost uninterrupted and fast growth after the initial collapse of output due to the transition. These higher growth rates reflect the catching-up process and are likely to persist in the medium term, but they will gradually fall. As can be deduced from Table 3, growth rates are already relatively low (but still far above the euro area average) for those countries that have partly caught up with the EU-15, that is, the Czech Republic, Hungary, and Slovenia. Output volatility may also pose a considerable problem. For the 1995–2003 period, the average standard deviation of real GDP growth was 2.2 percentage points for the new EU-10 compared to an (unweighted) average of 1.6 in the euro area.[12] Moreover, business cycles in some CEE countries tend to be out of sync with the euro area, especially in the case of Latvia and Lithuania (due to their specific trade and economic structures). Unfortunately, up till now, the Commission has not come up with CABBs and benchmarks for the CEE-8. Tentative research (by Kattai, Kangur, Liiv, & Randveer, 2003) done in the case of Estonia shows that the magnitude of automatic stabilisers is rather limited; Estonia could afford a structural budget deficit in the range of 1 per cent GDP without running the risk of the actual deficit going through the 3 per cent ceiling.

Inflation currently is low in the CEE-8. Inflationary pressures are likely to increase in the short run, due to the (in)famous Balassa–Samuelson effect whereby catching-up countries tend to have higher inflation due to higher productivity growth differentials between tradables and non-tradables sectors. Wage pressures, completion of price liberalisation, and factors related to EU accession (especially the introduction of various indirect taxes and adjustment of agricultural prices) may also have a temporary upward effect on inflation. To counter these pressures, the exchange rate instrument is not really an option, especially not for those countries that have chosen to hard-peg their currency to the euro. Whether curbing inflation really becomes an issue, and whether EMU-candidates will have to accept lower growth rates in order to temporarily reduce inflation also depends on the way the inflation criterion will be applied. With inflation being low in the euro area as well as in the area of CEE euro candidates, but even lower in the non-EMU-3, the formula prescribed in the Maastricht Treaty may well render perverse outcomes (see Gros et al., 2002).

Current account deficits may pose another risk. As long as these deficits can easily be financed by the inflow of foreign direct investment (FDI), there is not really a problem. Table 5 shows that FDI inflow is far from sufficient to cover the current account deficit in Estonia, Hungary, and Latvia. From the fiscal perspective, it is important to keep budget deficits low because large budget deficits contribute to wide external imbalances. Moreover, fiscal prudence contributes to attracting FDI. In the near future the CEE-8 especially need to attract FDI that is associated with regular business activities rather than with privatisation operations (as much of the FDI in the last 5–10 years was).

Considerable public investment needs are also characteristic of the CEE-8. As became clear in the previous section, in the run-up to EMU public investment in the EU-15 very likely has been crowded out by the need for fiscal consolidation. It is important that in the CEE-8 public investment does not lag behind economic development (and thus forms an impediment to growth), but on the other hand major investments in especially infrastructure may well be overdone, given the state of economic development. Public infrastructure investment and economic development should keep up

Table 5. Current Account Balance and FDI Inflow (2002), CEE-8.

	Current Account Balance as % GDP	Total FDI Inflow as % of GDP
Czech Republic	−5.8	12.7
Estonia	−12.2	4.4
Hungary	−4.0	1.3
Latvia	−7.6	4.8
Lithuania	−5.4	5.3
Poland	−2.6	2.1
Slovakia	−8.2	16.3
Slovenia	1.7	8.4

Source: Commission service.

with each other, and the level of public investment should not be determined by external restraints due to fiscal consolidation.

Finally, there is the fiscal shock of accession that puts pressure on the budgets of the CEE-8. Transfers from the EU budget have been limited within the framework of the revised 2000–2006 EU Financial Perspectives. The CEE-8 will only get their full share as from 2007, and their contributions to the EU have to be paid in full from the moment of accession. These contributions not only include the regular transfers of EU own resources (value-added tax (VAT) share, custom duties, GDP share) but also a contribution to the UK rebate and contributions to buy oneself into the European Investment Bank, into the European Development Fund, and into the Research Fund of Coal and Steel. Moreover, transfers from Brussels accrue to the economies of the CEE at large, and not specifically to government budgets. More than that, budgets will have to bear the burden of co- and pre-financing that is part of most EU support programmes, especially within the EU Cohesion Policy and the Common Agricultural Policy (CAP). EU membership will make (increasing) demands on the administrative capacity of the public sector that will also have fiscal implications. The all-over fiscal impact of accession has been estimated by a number of authors, and by the CEE-8 themselves. Kopits and Székely arrive at an estimate of a negative fiscal effect in the range of 3–4.75 per cent GDP for the Czech Republic, Estonia, Hungary, Poland, and Slovenia. Backé makes similar estimates (of up to −2.0 per cent GDP), Antczak foresees fiscal deficits deteriorating by up to 3 per cent GDP in the first few years after accession. Table 6 shows estimates by Funck of the magnitude of the net fiscal costs of accession for individual Member States.[13]

In Section 3, two issues were put forward for final discussion in this concluding section. The first is the impact EU fiscal surveillance may have

Table 6. Net Fiscal Cost of EU Accession, Annual Average in % GDP.

Czech Republic	3.2
Estonia	n.a.
Hungary	2.1
Latvia	3.3
Lithuania	1.7
Poland	1.0
Slovakia	3.6
Slovenia	2.6

Source: Funck, based on 2003 pre-accession economic programmes (Hallet, 2004, p. 14).

on domestic choices regarding the two different approaches to centralisation of fiscal decision-making. The second issue is which approach is most suited for the EU itself in ensuring fiscal discipline at the domestic level throughout the EU area, in light of the recent discussion on SGP reform. Below, we will deal with these aspects, putting special emphasis on the position of the CEE-8 Member States.

4.1. Centralisation at the Domestic Level Within the Larger EU Framework

One of the basic features of the EU fiscal surveillance system is that it leaves actual fiscal conduct within the authority of Member States. It is still up to Member States to choose between the two approaches to enhance fiscal discipline, and all CEE-8 Member States have opted for the commitment approach with its inherent drawbacks (limited possibilities for active fiscal "activism", high monitoring costs due to shirking, though depending on size of the economy and complexity of the administrative structure, danger of formula budgeting at the lower budget levels). The advantages of a commitment system apparently have dominated: Suitability for multi-party coalition government and symbolic value. Governments of the CEE Member States not only have to build fiscal credibility on the domestic level, but also on the international financial level and vis-à-vis the EU.

In this regard an important aspect of the choice between the two approaches, discussed by von Hagen (2002), is the level of congruency between the approach used at the domestic level and the approach used within the EU fiscal framework. One should expect procedures that are part of the

EDP and the SGP, which strongly resemble the contract approach, to be more effective in countries whose institutional environment is favourable for this approach, and less effective in environments where the delegation approach is appropriate. Hallerberg et al. (2001) have confirmed this empirically. In the broader context of the EU, the choice for a commitment system on the domestic level is also a matter of effectiveness. Furthermore, choices made regarding EU fiscal surveillance clearly have an impact on the domestic level: The more the EU system relies on commitment and numerical rules, the more difficult it becomes for individual Member States to operate a delegation system. In that sense, it comes as no surprise that the majority of countries that have recently clashed with the SGP are countries following the delegation approach (France, Germany, Greece, Italy, and Portugal). On the other hand, as Corsetti and Roubini (1996, p. 412) have argued, European policy-makers probably considered nominal targets to be neutral and hence more in line with political sovereignty of Member States. An EU system based on procedures would require institutional convergence rather than nominal fiscal convergence. Evidently, the EU did not want to meddle with domestic fiscal institutions. But by choosing an EU-wide numerical targets system, and thereby creating differences in effectiveness between systems used on the domestic level, the EU is indeed meddling with domestic fiscal institutional issues.

As part of the ongoing discussion on fiscal discipline within the EMU Wyplosz (2001) and Calmfors (2003) have put forward a more far-reaching application of the delegation approach at the domestic level that would render EU surveillance obsolete. They propose to delegate fiscal policy to a council of independent experts, similar to a central bank regarding monetary policy. The independent council would have the authority to make sure that the budget is kept in balance or the deficit within a prescribed range. Decisions on the composition of expenditure and revenues can be kept in the domain of government and parliament. If all EU Member States were to introduce such expert councils, there would not be any need for further EU fiscal surveillance. Unfortunately, the ideas by Wyplosz and Calmfors disregard the special character of fiscal policy. We may be able to distinguish between stabilisation, allocation, and distribution on an analytical level, but each budgetary decision involves all three budgetary functions that cannot be separated within the decision-making process. Moreover, compared to monetary policy, fiscal policy is extremely political (Tager & van Lear, 2001, p. 70) and should, in a democracy, not be taken out of the hands of elected politicians.

4.2. EU Fiscal Surveillance

The Commission has proposed to supplement the deficit rules of the SGP with rules regarding the reduction of public debt. It has argued in favour of more over-the-cycle-symmetric rules. It also wants to redefine the circumstances that constitute acceptable excessive deficits, especially in the case of sluggish growth. In spite of these changes in and amendments to the current fiscal rules, and giving the usual rhetoric the go-by, the recent proposals for SGP reform made by the Commission clearly signify a move away from a rules-based system towards a system with more discretion. The original SGP was thought to be an example of a set of budgetary rules with only a small discretionary element, namely the assessment by the Ecofin Council of the legitimacy of an excessive budget deficit due to exceptional circumstances. Discretion turned out to be far greater than expected, and will increase even more if the Commission's proposals become reality. Discretion is increased in order to increase both the economic rationale of the whole system, its acceptability to participants, and hence its enforceability. The key question then is whether this increase in discretion is accompanied by sufficient centralising elements regarding decision-making procedures, and the Commission's proposal does not really deal with this issue.

There are various ways to strengthen the centralisation in EU fiscal surveillance by means of procedures, rather than by numerical rules. The central issue is to bring on to the EU scene a single independent authority that has the collective fiscal interests at heart. We could think of "beefing-up" the Ecofin Council and/or the Euro Group (the group of finance ministers of the EMU-12); for instance, by giving considerable authority to its president. It is unclear whether the recent appointment of Jean-Claude Juncker as Semi-Permanent President of the Euro Group must be regarded as the introduction of such a centralising element within the fiscal surveillance procedure. Will "Mr Euro" really be a dominant player who will bang heads together? Or will he be a mere chairman of meetings, a liaison with the ECB, and representative of the Euro Group at international finance events? There is also the idea by Fatás et al. (2003) of a Stability Council for EMU. Such a council could be entrusted with the application of the EDP and SGP as well as with the admission of new Member States into EMU. The role of such an independent board could vary from a strong single authority, independent from the Ecofin Council, on the one hand, to a mere advisory agency on the other hand. Such an independent council could also be put in charge of the independent forecasting of relevant fiscal variables (Jonung & Larch, 2004).

A similar but more specific proposal has been made by the European Economic Advisory Group (EEAG, 2004) to transfer decisions concerning sanctions in connection with the EDP from the Ecofin Council to the European Court of Justice. The feasibility of these proposals is limited. The stronger the version of such an independent fiscal body, the less acceptable it will be for the Ecofin Council. Still, a lot of the monitoring activities that are currently executed by the Commission could easily be transferred to a council of independent experts, including forecasting, calculation of bench-marks, and the issuing of early warnings. The credibility of independent experts in these matters is probably higher than the Commission's. A trans-fer of ruling authority to the European Court of Justice could accompany such transfers of authority, with such rulings exclusively being made by the European Court of Justice on the initiative of the independent board. This would leave the better part of discretion in the hands of the Ecofin Council and/or Euro Group, but it would improve the quality of the surveillance process and would introduce a realistic new "threat" to the Member States. If necessary, to this end the European Court of Justice could be expanded with a special Fiscal Policy Chamber. Finally, there is the idea of Eichen-green (2003, 2004) to exempt those Member States from the EDP and SGP that are not prone to chronic fiscal deficits and unsustainable debt. Eichengreen suggests that countries that have shown to have the right institutional fiscal framework (either following the commitment approach or the delegation approach) have limited future pension liabilities, and have put through adequate labour market reforms are left in peace. If a Member State does not fulfil these three criteria, it is subject to the warnings, sanc-tions, and fines of the SGP. The exact definition and application of the exemption index should be put into the hands of an independent committee or council. Eichengreen's ideas can easily be combined with the previous one.

4.3. Special Rules for the CEE-8?

Finally, do we need special rules for the CEE-8 regarding their convergence to EMU? It is tempting to refrain from any changes in the framework for EMU entry, as the convergence process of (eventually) 12 EU Member States into EMU is often portrayed as a huge success. According to Buti and Giudice (2002, pp. 840–841) among the main ingredients of Maastricht's success were the public visibility of the criteria, their political ownership, the clear structure of incentives and effective monitoring, and the constraining calendar with clear deadlines for moving into EMU. It is not likely that this success story will repeat itself, as the CEE-8 differ markedly from the EU-15 in their run-up to EMU. We may have clear rules and a clear incentive, but the entry rules are probably far less accepted at the domestic level than in the 1990s. Public visibility of the criteria was especially important for domestic use in the 1990s, as almost all the countries involved at that time were in desperate need of fiscal consolidation. The EMU was used as a device for collective fiscal retrenchment (McKinnon, 1997). The CEE-8 are fiscally in far better shape than the EU-15 were in the early 1990s, especially regarding public debt, and the pressures against budgetary consolidation are far more substantial. The Maastricht criteria are not politically owned by the CEE-8 as they are part of the *acquis* decided on before their accession. Regardless of the formal Council decision rules in this matter, the "ins" will now apply the criteria to the "outs", rather than apply "among equals" as was done in 1998. Finally, contrary to the 2004 EU accession, and contrary to the first EMU wave, there will not be a clear collective time path for accession to EMU. In brief, the entry procedure in the Maastricht Treaty was written for the EU-15 in the 1990s, and not for the CEE-8 a decade later.

The main difference for CEE Member States as far as fiscal surveillance is concerned, between being part of the EMU and not being part, is the possibility of imposition of EDP/SGP sanctions. This difference could be an incentive to postpone EMU entry. Countries that have public debt well below the 60 per cent reference value can freely run excessive deficits for a number of years, yielding to their fiscal needs as they are trying to catch up. This seems to be the strategy chosen by Poland. We take the view that such postponement of EMU entry on fiscal grounds only is not desirable, and that the EMU entry rules should right away, but temporarily, take into consideration the legitimate budgetary pressures of the CEE-8 stemming from public investment needs, including co-financing of infrastructure as part of the EU Cohesion Policy. Rather than raising the 3 per cent GDP ceiling, and calculating a general extra margin for investment and relevant co-financing expenditure, and rather than by introducing a complicated golden-rule system, two deficits should be calculated, one including and one excluding such expenditure, the latter one being relevant to the 3 per cent GDP rule. Public debt increases due to public investment, even if debt exceeds the 60 per cent GDP reference value, should not be held against the countries concerned. If necessary, and to prevent dubious accounting practices, an exhaustive list of relevant public capital expenditure could be drawn up. As soon as the country concerned has caught up in income measurement terms, the correction for public investment needs should be brought to an end. Furthermore, up to and including 2006, all transfers to and from the EU budget should be excluded from calculating the deficit.[14] As from 2007, under the new 2007–2013 Multi-Annual Financial Framework (MAFF), such transfers could be re-incorporated, provided the new MAFF is more balanced than the current revised 2000–2006 Financial Perspectives. Other budgetary pressures, like the ones resulting from output volatility and inflation, should be dealt with within the 3 per cent GDP ceiling.

5. SUMMARY AND CONCLUSIONS

Our purpose in this chapter has been to outline the budgetary surveillance procedure that will be required to ensure the consolidation of public finances in a sustainable way in the enlarged EU. The main question we posed concerned what fiscal surveillance procedure for the new EU-10 countries will look like in the run-up to EMU membership in the light of the recent debate on reform of the SGP? To answer this question, we first reviewed the literature on fiscal discipline, distinguishing between rules and discretion, and discussing the setting of numerical targets or establishing adequate fiscal procedures. We then provided a description and assessment of the current fiscal surveillance practice in the EU. This was followed by a discussion of fiscal policy in the new CEE Member States, focusing on fiscal policy and fiscal convergence, and on the procedures to ensure fiscal discipline. We argued that the main difference for CEE Member States between being part of the EMU and not being part is the possibility of imposition of EDP/SGP sanctions. This difference could be an incentive to postpone EMU entry. We argue that such postponement is not desirable, and that the EMU entry rules should take account of the budgetary pressures of the CEE-8 stemming from their public investment needs.

NOTES

1. This broad definition of fiscal rules is common to most of the literature, with a few exceptions like Kopits and Symansky (1998), who define fiscal (policy) rules as permanent constraints on fiscal policy, typically defined in terms of an indicator of overall fiscal performance, often expressed as a numerical ceiling or target. In their view procedural rules are different from fiscal rules (Kopits & Symanski, 1998, p. 4), in our view procedural rules are a subset of fiscal rules.

2. Groenendijk (2002) deals with a third issue, the application of the two approaches to the EU general budget and Brussels' budgetary discipline.

3. Council Regulation on the strengthening of the surveillance of budgetary positions and the surveillance and co-ordination of economic policies (EC) No. 1466/97, 9 July 1997.

4. Council Regulation on speeding up and clarifying the implementation of the EDP (EC) No. 1467/97, 7 July 1997.

5. See Andersen (2002) for a discussion of the calculation of these CABBs.

6. See for instance Buti and Giudice (2002), Buti et al. (2003), Eichengreen (2003, 2004), Eijffinger (2003), and Jensen and Larsen (2004). See Buti et al. (2003, p. 13) for an overview of the main arguments and proposals.

7. Theoretically the case for prudent fiscal policies to preserve price stability can easily be made: Prevention of spillovers in a currency area and insulation of the ECB from national interests. See for instance Buti and Giudice (2002, p. 824) and the literature mentioned there. It is however much harder to make that case empirically.

8. Gros (2003) has come up with a simple way to introduce a numerical rule on public debt into the SGP, starting from the Maastricht Treaty reference value of 60 per cent GDP.

9. See Buti and Van den Noord (2004, pp. 12–23) for a discussion of automatic stabilisers.

10. Commission (2004) 581, final.

11. According to the Commission, it also builds on the July 2004 ruling of the Court of Justice. Strangely enough, in its Communication the Commission argues that the Court of Justice ruling has confirmed that a rules-based system is the best guarantee for commitments to be enforced and for all Member States to be treated equally. However, the ruling did not deal with that broader issue.

12. European Commission, ECFIN. *EMU after 5 years.* Unrevised manuscript 15 July 2004, downloadable from http://europa.eu.int/comm/economy_finance/publications/eespecialreports_en.htm, p. 150.

13. See Hallet (2004) for an overview of these estimates and corresponding references.

14. The inclusion or exclusion of transfers between EU Member States' budgets and the EU budget in calculating deficits used in EU fiscal surveillance does not only pertain to the CEE-8 but is a matter of more general concern.

REFERENCES

Alesina, A., & Bayoumi, T. (1996). *The costs and benefits of fiscal rules: Evidence from U.S. states.* Cambridge, Mass: NBER Working Paper.

Alesina, A., & Perotti, R. (1996). Fiscal discipline and the budget process. *American Economic Review, Papers and Proceedings, 86*, 401–407.

Alesina, A., Hausmann, R., Hommes, R., & Stein, E. (1999). Budget institutions and fiscal performance in Latin America. *Journal of Development Economics, 59*, 253–273.

Andersen, A. B. (2002). Cyclically adjusted government budget balances. *Monetary Review*, 3rd quarter. Copenhagen: Danmarks Nationalbank.

Buti, M., & Giudice, G. (2002). Maastricht's fiscal rules at ten: An assessment. *Journal of Common Market Studies, 40*, 823–848.

Buti, M., & van den Noord, P. (2004). *Fiscal policy in the EMU: Rules, discretion and political incentives.* Economic Papers no. 206.

Buti, M., Eijffinger, S., & Franco, D. (2003). *Revisiting the stability and growth pact: Grand design or internal adjustment.* Economic Papers no. 180.

Calmfors, L. (2003). Fiscal policy to stabilise the domestic economy in the EMU: What can we learn from monetary policy? *CESifo Economic Studies, 49,* 319–353.

Casella, A. (2001). Market mechanisms for policy decisions: Tools for the European Union. *European Economic Review, 45,* 995–1006.

Corsetti, G., & Roubini, N. (1996). European versus American perspectives on balanced-budget rules. *American Economic Review, 86,* 408–413.

Crowley, P. (2003). Stupid or sensible? The future of the stability and growth pact. *EUSA Review 2003,* 9–11.

Dában, T., Detragiache, E., di Bella, F., Milesi-Ferretti, G. M., & Symansky, S. (2003). *Rules-based fiscal policy in France, Germany, Italy, and Spain.* IMF Occasional Paper no. 225.

Eichengreen, B. (2003). *What to do with the stability pact?* Intereconomics, *38,* 7–10.

Eichengreen, B. (2004). Institutions for fiscal stability. *CESifo Economic Studies, 50,* 1–25.

Eichengreen, B., & Wyplosz, C. (1998). The stability pact: More than a minor nuisance? *Economic Policy, 26,* 65–114.

Eijffinger, S. C. W. (2003). How can the stability and growth pact be improved to achieve both stronger discipline and higher flexibility? *Intereconomics, 38,* 10–15.

European Commission. (2004). 238 final.

Fatás, A., Hallet, A. H., Sibert, A., Strauch, R., & von Hagen, J. (2003). *Stability and growth: Towards a better pact.* London: CEPR.

Gleich, H. (2002). *The evolution of budget institutions in Central and Eastern European countries.* Bonn: Rheinischen Friedrich-Wilhelms-Universität.

Groenendijk, N. S. (2002). Budgetary discipline in Brussels: Numerical targets of procedural strategic dominance? *Current Politics and Economics of Europe, 11,* 205–224.

Gros, D. (2003). *A stability pact for public debt?* CEPS Policy Brief no. 30, Brussels.

Gros, D., Castelli, M., Jimeno, J., Mayer, T., & Thygesen, N. (2002). *The euro at 25.* Brussels: Special Report of the CEPS Macroeconomic Policy Group.

Gros, D., Mayer, Th., & Ubide, A. (2004). *The nine lives of the stability pact.* Brussels: Special Report of the CEPS Macroeconomic Policy Group.

de Haan, J. (1989). *Public debt: Pestiferous or propitious? On the economic consequences of the creation and existence of government debt.* Groningen: University of Groningen.

von Hagen, J. (2002). Fiscal rules, fiscal institutions, and fiscal performance. *Economic and Social Review, 33*(3), 263–284.

von Hagen, J., & Harden, I. J. (1994). National budget processes and fiscal performance. *European Economy, Reports and Studies, 3,* 311–418.

von Hagen, J., & Harden, I. J. (1995). Budget processes and commitment to fiscal discipline. *European Economic Review, 39,* 771–779.

von Hagen, J., Hallerberg, M., & Strauch, R. (2004). *Budgetary forecasts in Europe – the track record of stability and convergence programmes.* Working Paper no. 307, European Central Bank.

von Hagen, J., Hallett, A. H., & Strauch, R. (2001). *Budgetary consolidation in the EMU.* Brussels: EC DG Economic and Financial Affairs, Economic Papers no. 148.

Hallerberg, M., Strauch, R., & von Hagen, J. (2001). *The use and effectiveness of budgetary rules and norms in EU member states, ZEI.* Bonn: Report prepared for the Dutch Ministry of Finance by the Institute of European Integration Studies.

Hallet, M. (2004). *Fiscal effects of accession in the new member states.* Brussels: EC DG Economic and Financial Affairs. Economic Papers no. 203.

Hanushek, E. A. (1986). Formula budgeting: The economics and analytics of fiscal policy under rules. *Journal of Policy Analysis and Management, 6,* 3–19.

Hefeker, C. (2003). Credible at last? Reforming the stability pact. *Intereconomics, 38,* 15–18.

Jensen, Th. H., & Larsen, J. A. K. (2004). The stability and growth pact – status in 2004. *Monetary Review.* Copenhagen: Danmarks Nationalbank.

Jonung, L., & Larch, M. (2004). *Improving fiscal policy in the EU: The case for independent forecasts.* Brussels: EC DG Economic and Financial Affairs.

Kattai, R., Kangur, A., Liiv, T., & Randveer, M. (2003). Automatic fiscal stabilisers in Estonia: The impact of economic fluctuations on general government budget balance and fiscal policy decisions. Paper presented at the *Eurofaculty conference on tax policy in EU candidate countries.* 12–14, September, Riga, Latvia.

Knight, B., & Levinson, A. (2000). Fiscal institutions in US states. In: R. R. Strauch & J. von Hagen (Eds), *Institutions, politics and fiscal policy* (pp. 167–187). Boston, Dordrecht: Kluwer Academic Publishers.

Kontopolous, Y., & Perotti, R. (1999). Government fragmentation and fiscal policy outcomes: Evidence from OECD countries. In: J. Poterba & J. von Hagen (Eds), *Fiscal institutions and Fiscal performance* (pp. 81–102). Chicago, Ill: University of Chicago Press.

Kopits, G., & Symansky, S. (1998). *Fiscal policy rules.* IMF Occasional Paper.

Larch, M., & Salto, M. (2003). *Fiscal rules, inertia and discretionary fiscal policy.* Brussels: EC DG Economic and Financial Affairs, Economic Papers no. 194.

McKinnon, R. I. (1997). EMU as a device for collective fiscal retrenchment. *American Economic Review, 87,* 227–229.

Milesi-Ferretti, G. M. (1997). *Fiscal rules and the budget process.* London: Centre for Economic Policy Research, Discussion Paper no. 1664.

Milesi-Ferretti, G.M. (2000). *Good, bad or ugly? On the effects of fiscal rules with creative accounting.* IMF Working Paper.

Milesi-Ferretti, G. M. (2003). Good, bad or ugly? On the effects of fiscal rules with creative accounting. *Journal of Public Economics, 88,* 377–394.

Poterba, J. (1995). Balanced budget rules and fiscal policy: Evidence from the states. *National Tax Journal, 48,* 329–337.

Tager, M., & van Lear, W. (2001). Fiscal and monetary policy rules revisited. *Social Science Journal, 38,* 69–83.

Turrini, A. (2004). *Public investment and the EU fiscal framework.* Brussels: EC DG Economic and Financial Affairs, Economic Papers no. 202.

Wyplosz, C. (2001). *Fiscal policy: Institutions vs. rules.* Unpublished manuscript. Graduate Institute for International Studies.

THE IMPACT OF FISCAL VARIABLES ON RISK PREMIUMS IN CENTRAL AND EASTERN EUROPEAN COUNTRIES

Dalia Grigonytė

1. INTRODUCTION

Theory suggests that as long as a country runs a balanced budget regime, there is no linkage between fiscal variables and the interest rates. In the case of fiscal expansion that is not sufficiently covered by government revenues, however, the government has two options to finance its deficit: printing money or additional borrowing. Both options lead to an increase in the risk premia on government bonds. One strand of literature focuses on a currency crisis that emerges as a necessary outcome in light of contradictions between fixed exchange rate, and fiscal and financial fundamentals. If government bonds are denominated in domestic currency, the government can reduce their real value by higher inflation or by devaluation of the national currency. In order to bear this risk foreign investors require a currency risk premium. Governments can eliminate the risk of currency devaluation by issuing bonds denominated in foreign currencies, but the default risk remains and it depends on public finances. Another strand of the literature

Emerging European Financial Markets: Independence and Integration Post-Enlargement
International Finance Review, Volume 6, 47–68
Copyright © 2006 by Elsevier Ltd.
ISSN: 1569-3767/doi:10.1016/S1569-3767(05)06003-6

looks at the relation between fiscal variables and government bond yields in the framework of portfolio balance model.

Ten Central and Eastern European (henceforth CEE) countries started their transition process with high levels of inflation and outstanding fiscal imbalances. After the transition period, these countries have achieved considerable macroeconomic stabilisation reflected in the greater credibility of their currencies and the declining risk premia of their bonds. This chapter investigates the extent to which their fiscal discipline has reduced the risk premium in the CEE economies. The chapter is structured as follows. Section 2 reviews the literature related to currency and default risk premia. This is followed by discussion of the model put forward by Uribe (2002) that explains the impact of markets expectations on fiscal discipline on the development of risk premium and default rate in the price-targeting economy. Section 3 presents the empirical analysis of the influence of fiscal variables on the risk premium in the 10 transition economies: Bulgaria, Czech Republic, Estonia, Hungary, Latvia, Lithuania, Poland, Romania, Slovak Republic and Slovenia. The final section summarises the results and draws together our conclusions.

2. LITERATURE REVIEW

This section explains the influence of fiscal policy on currency and default risk premiums. First, in the framework of currency crisis literature we look at the interaction between fiscal variables and currency risk premium under fixed exchange rates. Next, we briefly discuss the role of fiscal discipline for the effectiveness of inflation targeting regime. Finally, concentrate on portfolio balance models and default risk when bonds are denominated in foreign currency.

2.1. Currency Risk

Kopits (2000) summarises previous research efforts that explain the impact of fiscal policies on risk premium and currency crisis. First – generation models (Krugman, 1979) emphasise the inconsistency between fiscal policy fundamentals and the exchange rate peg that leads to the abandonment of the peg. A large monetised deficit is accompanied by declining foreign reserves that the government might try to counteract by increasing government bonds' yields and attracting higher capital inflows into the country.

Increasing government debt causes a higher debt service, so at some point foreign reserves are exhausted, and the government has to give up defending the peg by increasing interest rates. This basic model can be developed to include not only recorded fiscal deficits, but also those related with quasi – fiscal activities or potential imbalances associated with the gathering of contingent government liabilities, especially if such deficits are expected to be covered by printing money in the future. Thus the net public assets can be considered as a key indicator of speculative attacks.

In second – generation models (Obstfeld, 1994), large – scale capital in-flows (often provoked by a speculative bubble) result in pre – crisis outflows that may be forecasted on a policy inconsistency. Compared to the first generation models, the government has more alternatives to defend the peg: borrowing foreign exchange reserves, increasing domestic interest rate, cut-ting budget deficit or introducing exchange controls. Defending fixed exchange rates has its costs. The government's readiness to accept these costs depends on the state of the economy. Whether the economy is in good or bad state depends on public expectations. A shift in investors sentiment from a good to a bad equilibrium triggers the actual attack on the currency. The unfavourable change in sentiment can be induced by a new perception about likely policy inconsistencies related to future budget deficits resulting from quasi – fiscal activities or contingent liabilities such as a likely bailout of failing banks. In general, vulnerability to a crisis is enhanced not only by a large existing fiscal imbalance but also by a expected lack of fiscal sustainability.

The link between public finance and risk premium is even more trans-parent under floating exchange rates. Here a monetisation of fiscal deficits provokes an immediate devaluation of domestic currency and increases the stock of public debt which in emerging markets is typically denominated in foreign currency. High debt levels make market participants to expect de-valuation in the future, so the investors will be willing to accept a new emission of domestic bonds if these bonds offer a higher risk premium and compensate for the expected devaluation.

In this context Favero and Giavazzi (2004) analyse the inflation targeting regime in Brazil over 1999 – 2003. The response of risk premium to an international financial shock and thus the effectiveness of inflation targeting are influenced by domestic fiscal policy. For example, a country is hit by an external shock to the risk premium which depreciates the exchange rate and increases inflationary expectations. The bonds of developing countries often have short maturity, so a rise of domestic interest rates raises the costs of debt service. If the government runs restrictive fiscal policies, the debt ratio remains stable and inflation targeting works: higher domestic interest rates compensate for the initial exchange rate depreciation. Non-adjustment of primary surpluses provokes three effects that lead to a higher stock of public debt. First, the debt grows because government deficits must be covered by new borrowing. Second, financing public deficits by borrowing raises the spreads of new government bonds and leads to higher costs of debt service. Finally, a depreciation of the exchange rate raises the value of bonds denominated in foreign currency. The exchange rate depreciation has also an impact on inflation expectations and inflation itself. In order to counteract rising inflation expectations, the central bank increases the domestic interest rates further, the risk premium explodes so do the costs of debt service. Lacking fiscal adjustment weakens the effectiveness of inflation targeting and intensifies the response of risk premium to the international financial shock.

Using the frameworks of a general equilibrium asset pricing model and a balance portfolio model Giorgianni (1997) analyses empirically if fiscal policy variables affect the risk premium, and if so, how much of their impact on the risk premium can be explained by the changes in fiscal policy.

Giorgianni criticises the asset pricing model as in this model financial instruments are perfect substitutes, investors have forward – looking expectations and Ricardian equivalence is taken for granted. Risk premium depends on the development of the exogenous home and foreign state variables: output, money, and government expenditure. So under these conditions (i.e. the assumption of perfect substitutable financial assets and of Ricardian equivalence), higher supply of government bonds does not change their expected return. It is impossible to test whether a rising domestic budget deficit financed with sales of new bonds has any impact on the risk premium of bonds issued in the domestic currency. The only effect of fiscal policy on the risk premium comes from the volatility of future government expenditure. A higher expected volatility of government expenditure at home should lead to a larger risk premium on domestic currency denominated securities.

According to the portfolio balance model approach, the portfolio assets issued in different currencies are regarded as imperfect substitutes. A rise in the supply of particular securities implies a higher return on that asset. Given that Ricardian equivalence is not always satisfied, an expansionary domestic fiscal policy financed with bonds sales results in a higher stock of domestic currency denominated assets in circulation that leads to a higher home currency premium. This framework seems to reflect the reality of emerging markets much better, as highly indebted economies have to offer higher interest rates so that foreign investors would buy their bonds.

Testing the risk premium data for the Italian lira over the period 1987 – 1994 confirms the predictions of portfolio balance model. The empirical results suggest that Italian net government borrowing requirement has a positive effect on the risk premium, implying that an expected higher public deficit, which is considered of being covered by additional sales of government bonds, is related to the higher risk premiums on Italian lira assets.

2.2. Default Risk

Based on the foundations of the Tobin's Portfolio Theory, Flavin and Limosani (2001) develop a model which identifies a set of macroeconomic factors that influence short – term interest rate differentials. The portfolio theory implies a risk – return trade – off: investors will be willing to buy risky bonds if they are rewarded by earning a higher return. The riskiness of the asset depends on the volatility of its return, which might be influenced by the volatility in the wider economic environment. Contagion effects induce potential investors to ask for a larger compensation in terms of a higher risk premium.

Short – term interest rate differentials are affected not only by the volatility of the differential itself but also by some macroeconomic variables: domestic inflation rate, public debt to GDP ratio and the expected rate of depreciation of the exchange rate. The first two variables stand for changes in monetary and fiscal policy while the exchange rate is supposed to control for international effects.

Empirical testing of the influence of above mentioned macroeconomic variables on short – term interest rates differentials is performed with the data of nominal interest rates on 3 month Eurocurrency deposits on the London market for Italy, France, Belgium, UK and Germany covering the period from 1978 to 1996. Germany is a benchmark country. Their main result is that the macroeconomic variables do not have a direct impact on short – term interest rate differential. However, they still exert an important influence on the conditional volatility of the interest rate differential, which is itself an important indicator of the level of risk premium.

Bernoth, von Hagen and Schuknecht (2003) develop a static portfolio model which explains long run government bond yields' spreads and test it

with the data from EU countries. According to their model, the yield
spreads between the bonds issued by two countries depend on (1) default
risk premium; (2) liquidity risk premium and (3) country specific risk premium which grows with the total supply of domestic bonds. The empirical
results show that the interest rate differentials of EU countries between 1991
and 2002 versus Germany and the USA were positively influenced by the
debt and debt service ratios of the issuer country. This suggest that credit
markets observe fiscal performance of the issuer countries and this induces a
disciplining pressure on sovereign borrowers.

An important input to modelling the relation between the equilibrium
default rate, expected future fiscal deficits, and initial public debt comes
from Uribe (2002). We use his model as a theoretical underpinning for our
research, because its specifications are relevant for the reality of emerging
markets that have to pay high risk premiums for their bonds more
frequently than developed economies. The fiscal theory of sovereign risk and
default describes the equilibrium processes of the country risk premium and
the default rate in the setting under which the government cannot fulfil its
public obligations without surrendering price stability. Fiscal policy is 'active' by assumption[1], i.e. fiscal authority does not pay attention to the state
of government debt and is free to set its fiscal surplus or deficit as it wishes.
A passive authority (i.e. monetary authority) has to react to government
debt shocks. So, real primary surpluses are exogenous and random. In the
price targeting economy the central bank fixes the price level, so nominal
public debt is equal to real public debt. Given that primary surpluses are
exogenous and random, a key result is that in this economy current and past
fiscal deficits determine future default rates. Thus fiscal variables exert a
significant influence on the sovereign risk premium and the rate of default.
The price targeting environment is relevant for CEE economies because
their public debt to a large extent is denominated in foreign currencies, and
the government cannot inflate it away. In the following section we proceed
with the exposition of the model using the original notation.

2.3. Fiscal Theory of Sovereign Risk

This section introduces the basic features of Uribe (2002) model that
illustrate the impact of fiscal variables on nominal interest rates. There are
two assumptions: (1) the government always respects its financial commitments if it can; and (2) there is no indexation on public debt. The government collects lump-sum taxes, τ_t, which follow an exogenous, stationary,

stochastic AR(1) process:

$$\tau_t - \bar{\tau} = \varphi(\tau_{t-1} - \bar{\tau}) + \varepsilon_t \tag{1}$$

where $\bar{\tau}$ stands for the unconditional mathematical expectation of taxes, the parameter $\varphi \in [0,1)$ measures the serial correlation of taxes, and $\varepsilon_t \approx N(0, \sigma_\varepsilon^2)$ is an iid random tax innovation. In period t, the fiscal authority finances its deficits by issuing bonds B_t, that pay a gross nominal interest rate R_t in the next period, $t+1$. It is risky to purchase government's bonds because in response to a negative fiscal shock the government may repudiate on a fraction δ_t of its total obligations. With P_t denoting the price level, the public debt evolves as follows:

$$B_t = R_{t-1}B_{t-1}(1 - \delta_t) - \tau_t P_t \qquad t \geq 0. \tag{2}$$

In the price targeting economy price level is constant and normalised to one:

$$P_t = 1; \qquad t \geq 0. \tag{3}$$

This implies that nominal public debt is equal to real public debt. The risk-free interest rate is constant and depends only on the subjective discount factor:

$$R_t^f = \beta^{-1} \tag{4}$$

With pegged price level, the government cannot inflate away the real value of its liabilities in periods of low tax realisations. Thus it follows that in response to a negative fiscal shock the government has to default. The equilibrium default rate is given by:

$$\delta_t = 1 - \frac{\sum\limits_{h=0}^{\infty} \beta^h E_t \tau_{t+h}}{R_{t-1}B_{t-1}} \tag{5}$$

where E_t is a mathematical operator conditional on information available in period t. Equation (5) offers a straightforward interpretation. When the present discounted value of primary surpluses equals to the real value of total initial government liabilities, δ_t is zero, i.e. there is no default. If the present value of primary surpluses is zero, then δ_t is equal to one, and there is a 100% default on government liabilities. The government has to default on its debt when the present discounted value of primary surpluses is smaller than total real initial liabilities. The higher is a gap between discounted primary surpluses and initial real public debt, the higher is a default fraction δ_t.

2.4. Default Rule

The government could follow a certain default rule whereby it defaults if the tax-to-debt ratio falls below a given threshold α:

$$\text{defaultrule}: \delta_t \begin{cases} <0 & \text{if} \quad \tau_t/B_{t-1} > \alpha \\ =0 & \text{if} \quad \tau_t/B_{t-1} = \alpha \\ >0 & \text{if} \quad \tau_t/B_{t-1} < \alpha \end{cases} \quad t = 1, 2, \ldots \quad (6)$$

The threshold α is set by the fiscal authority. In periods of low tax realisations, when the tax-to-debt ratio τ/B_{t-1} is below the chosen benchmark α, the government repudiate on its debt obligations. If the tax-to-debt ratio is higher than the threshold α, the government has to remunerate the investors by giving them a subsidy relative to the size of their portfolios.

Under this default rule, the nominal interest rate is given by

$$R_t = \alpha + \frac{\beta\varphi(1-\beta)(\alpha B_t - \bar{\tau}) + \beta(1-\beta\varphi)\bar{\tau}}{B_t(1-\beta)(1-\beta\varphi)}; \quad t = 0, 1, \ldots \quad (7)$$

This expression defines interest rate as a function of fiscal variables: debt and taxes. Nominal interest rate increases with higher stock of public debt and with a higher value of selected default benchmark α. As far as the risk free interest rate is constant (equation (4)), the country risk premium, R_t/R_t^f, is proportional to R_t. Thus, a deterioration in fiscal variables induces a continuing growth of sovereign risk.

To illustrate the given default rule, equation (6), Uribe (2002) performs a numerical simulation which yields the following results for the equilibrium dynamics of taxes, public debt, the interest rate after a negative tax shock. In response to the 20 percent negative tax innovation, there is a default of about 2.5 percent of the public debt in the same period. Since the tax-to-debt ratio is lower than its long run level during the entire transition period there are additional defaults in the next periods. The cumulative default makes about 23 percent. In the period of a negative tax shock, the interest rate increases to 3.6 percent and then declines monotonically to its steady-state level of 1.5 percent.

3. EMPIRICAL ANALYSIS

Eq. (7) expresses nominal interest rate as a function of fiscal variables. In a price–level-targeting economy the risk-free interest rate is constant[2] thus the sovereign risk premium is proportional to the nominal interest rate. Given this relation, we can generally express the risk premium on government bonds as a function of fiscal variables:

$$RP_t = f(B_t, \tau_t - \bar{\tau})$$

Thus we test the impact of fiscal variables on the risk premium by estimating the following model:

$$RP_{it} = \beta_0 + \beta_1 * F_{it} + \beta_2 * K_{it} + \beta_3 * C_t + \varepsilon_t \tag{8}$$

where RP_{it} is the yield spread of a bond issued by the CEE country i over a benchmark country j for an analogue bond denominated in the same currency. F_{it} denotes several fiscal variables: tax-to-debt ratio, public debt/GDP, general government balance/GDP and government debt service to its total revenues ratio. The first variable is motivated by the theory. The higher the gap between tax revenues and debt, the higher is the risk premium and the probability of default. This variable controls for government's ability to raise taxes in response to increasing debt levels. Public debt and general government balance to GDP ratios reflect the impact of fiscal discipline on bond spreads. The last variable controls for the constraint imposed by a high debt burden on budgetary flows. K_{it} denotes a vector of control variables like GDP growth rate, CR index and inflation. Control variables (GDP growth, inflation, CR) reflect general economic and political conditions of a country. The CR index is derived from Standard an Poor's bond ratings which depend on the four following criteria: (1) economic factors related to the GDP growth, its sustainability and diversification; (2) debt factors focusing on maturity and composition of the debt as well as the debt's coverage by foreign reserves; (3) governmental/administrative/political factors concentrating on the rule of law and stability of democracy and (4) fiscal and financial performance factors looking at the health of public finance and banking system. In times of economic slowdown the government revenues usually decline which increases the probability of default. A CR index is a composite indicator, and its correlation with other explanatory variables does not exceed 50 per cent. C_t is a dummy variable for the years 1998 and 1999 that controls for contagion effects of the Russian crisis.

4. DATA DESCRIPTION

The data of yield spreads come from the Capital DATA Bondware. The sample contains 10 EU accession countries: Bulgaria, Czech Republic,

Estonia, Hungary, Latvia, Lithuania, Poland, Romania, Slovak Republic and Slovenia for the period 1990–2002. The interest rate differential for foreign currency (US dollar, German mark, euro, etc.) denominated bonds of CEE countries is measured as the difference in the yield to maturity at the time of issue between a national bond and an equivalent bond issued by a benchmark country. For example, the Lithuanian government issues a bond denominated in US dollars with 10 years maturity and pays 9 per cent per annum. At the same time the USA issues an analogue bond but pays 4 per cent per annum. Thus a risk premium for the Lithuanian bond is 500 basis points. Comparing national bonds denominated in foreign currency is preferred to national bonds denominated in their national currencies as we do not have to account the exchange rate risk. The comparison of yields' spreads at issue is more precise than the average yields on debt outstanding because (1) at the point of issue the residual maturity of a bond is equal to its full maturity and (2) the bonds are actively traded when the record of yield is taken. The sample has 80 observations.

The data on public debt, general government balance, debt service, GDP growth rate, inflation are taken from the statistics provided (Table 1) by the European Bank for Reconstruction and Development (EBRD). The tax–to-debt ratio is calculated from International Monetary Fund (IMF) statistics. The country ratings of Standard and Poor's are summarised by a CR index which obtains a value of 1 if a country has triple A-rating (AAA) and a value of 17 if a country has a B-rating. Table 1 presents summary statistics.

First intuition about the development of risk premium from 1991 to 2002 can be gleaned from Fig. 1. In Hungary, Czech Republic and Poland the risk premia considerably declined, while in Slovenia, the country with the lowest risk premium at the beginning of transition, the spreads increased in the last years. In 2001 the spreads of Slovenian government bonds were slightly above the spreads of Poland or Hungary.

After a negative shock from Russian and Commonwealth of Independent States (CIS) markets in 1998–1999, the spreads on government bonds experienced an upward jump in Latvia, Lithuania and the Slovak Republic. However, due to improving macroeconomic performance after the crisis in these countries, the risk premium had a declining trend over the last years. There was also a fall of risk premium in Bulgaria, but compared to other countries it remains quite high in absolute levels. The outlier case of 1999 in Bulgaria is explained by the financial and banking crisis of 1997. Failing macroeconomic stabilisation in Romania is reflected by the highest risk premium among transition economies which considerably increased over the time.

Table 1. Data Description.

Variable	Description	Average	Standard Deviation	Maximum	Minimum
Spread *(in basis points)*	Difference between the yield of CEE government bond and a comparable government bond issued in the same currency related to the gross nominal return of the government bond issue	247.8	150.5	700	43
Tax-to-debt ratio	Tax revenues divided by general government debt	1.04	0.67	4.64	0.30
Debt	General government debt to GDP ratio	49.7	28.2	98.7	8
General government balance	General government balance to GDP ratio includes the state, municipalities and extra-budgetary funds	−4.5	2.5	0.5	−10.4
Debt service	Interest payments to the total revenues of general government	8.7	5.0	19.6	0.8
GDP growth	Percentage change in real terms	2.6	2.6	7.9	−6.1
CPI	Percentage change, annual averages	16.9	19.4	154.8	0.3
CR	Index variable summarising the S&P ratings	9.0	2.8	15	6

Figure 2 presents the relation between tax-to-debt ratio and bond spreads. Low tax-to-debt ratio signals tax collecting problems or exploding debt ratio. Bonds of such countries are probably perceived as risky by foreign investors, so they would accept the bonds in the presence of a higher risk premium. The lowest tax-to-debt ratio among the CEE countries is in Bulgaria that explains its high spreads. In Slovenia, Poland, Hungary and the Slovak Republic there is a negative relationship between the tax-to-debt ratio and the risk premium. In two Baltic countries, Latvia and Lithuania, this relationship is positive: Declining tax-to-debt ratio was accompanied by a falling risk premium.

The portfolio balance model predicts that highly indebted economies should offer higher risk premia so that investors would accept their bonds. A positive relationship between high stock of public debt and high spreads at launch are clearly observable in Hungary and Bulgaria in Fig. 3. These two economies have the highest stocks of public debt among the CEE countries. A positive correlation between debt and spreads is also present in the Czech Republic, Slovenia and Poland. However, the situation in Latvia

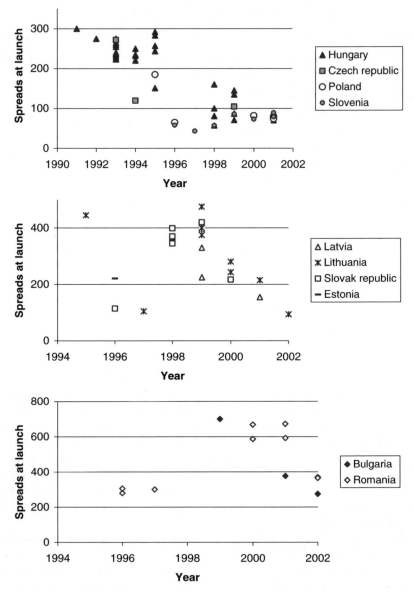

Fig. 1. Spreads in CEE in 1991–2002.

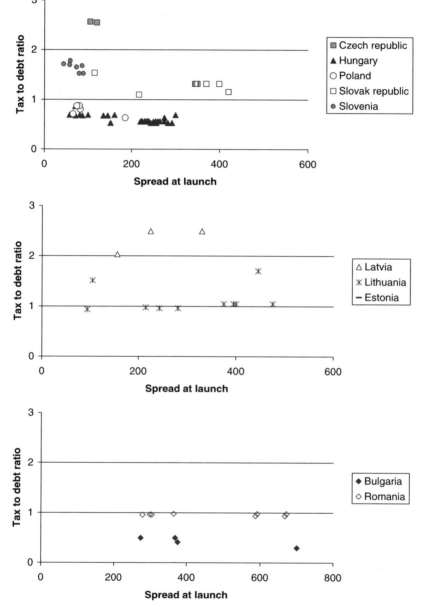

Fig. 2. Spreads in Relation to Tax-to-Debt Ratio.

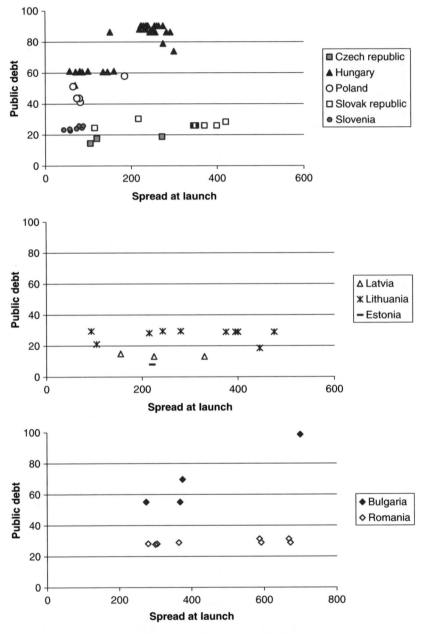

Fig. 3.   Spreads in Relation to Public Debt.

in Lithuania is different. Although the public debt in the Baltic countries has increased in the last years, progress with structural reforms and macroeconomic stabilisation led to lower risk premiums. The public debt is relatively low in Romania, but its risk premium is much higher than the premium of other CEE countries with a similar stock of public debt.

A relatively high burden of debt service in Romania gives a better explanation of its risk premium than its moderate debt level (Fig. 4). A positive influence of higher debt service on spreads at launch can be observed in Slovenia, Hungary, the Czech Republic, Bulgaria and Poland. There is no positive correlation between debt service and risk premium in Latvia and Lithuania. This can be explained by the fact that the Baltic States started their transition with no public debt at all. Although during first years of transition their debt increased, it remained at quite low levels, while the improving macroeconomic performance resulted in declining risk premia in the Baltic States.[3]

Finally, Fig. 5 presents the relationship between general government balance and bond spreads. General government deficit is a volatile number. In general, high and persistent public deficits should promote an increase in the risk premium. There is a clear negative relationship between these two variables in Bulgaria, Hungary, Latvia and Lithuania. The Baltic States switched to restrictive fiscal policies after the Russian crisis, while Bulgaria had to tighten its fiscal policies after the financial crisis of 1997 and the introduction of currency board. Foreign investors granted their efforts to enhance fiscal discipline by a lower risk premium. In Poland, Romania and Slovenia this relationship is positive.

Descriptive evidence suggests that in Latvia and Lithuania the relationship between fiscal variables and risk premium is somewhat different from the other transition economies. Thus in the econometric analysis we first estimate joint regressions for all 10 CEE countries and then perform a robustness check by excluding the two Baltic economies.

5. EMPIRICAL RESULTS

The estimates of Eq. (6) are summarised in the Table 2. In all estimations we have used ordinary least squares (OLS) with White corrected standard errors that are robust to heteroscedasticity. As far as all bonds in the sample are denominated in foreign currency, the inflation turned out to be insignificant in all estimations. Thus in the estimations reported below this variable is excluded. In all estimations yield spreads are significantly and

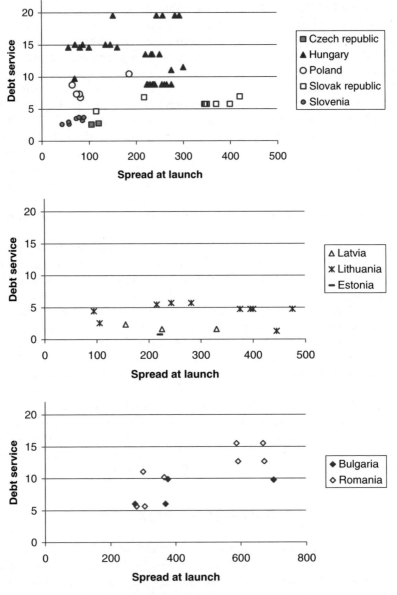

Fig. 4. Spreads in Relation to Debt Service.

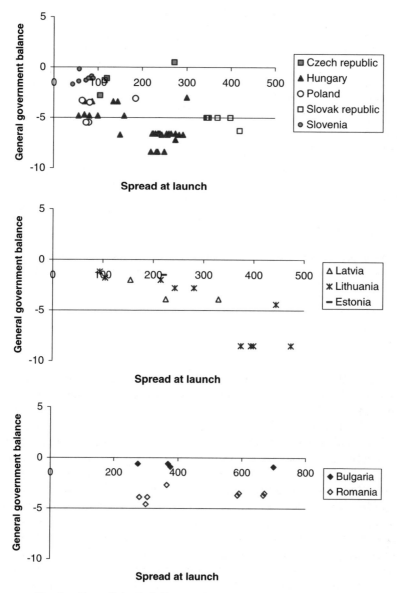

Fig. 5. Spreads in Relation to General Government Balance.

Table 2.   Estimation Results.

Dependent Variable	Yield Spreads of CEE Governments			
	I	II	III	IV
Country risk	44.4 (5.86)***	46.4 (5.54)***	45.4 (5.46)***	44.9 (5.56)***
Tax-to-debt	−4.14 (16.1)			
Public debt		0.92 (0.47)**		
Debt service			5.05 (2.10)**	
Government balance				−14.9 (4.92)***
GDP growth	−12.6 (5.30)**	−11.4 (5.18)**	−11.5 (5.26)**	
Crisis	57.0 (24.2)**	59.9 (23.4)***	59.4 (25.1)**	46.5 (28.8)
Intercept	−149.8 (54.3)***	−215.3 (54.5)***	−210.4 (50.9)***	−252.0 (47.8)
Time dummies	Yes	Yes	Yes	Yes
R^2	0.65	0.67	0.68	0.65
Number of observations	80	80	79	80

Note: We include time dummies for the years 1993–1994. The first years of transition process were quite volatile that is reflected by considerably higher risk premia than in the following years.
Significance levels at:
**5%; and
***1%.

positively influenced by CR ratings that reflect general economic and political conditions of a country. The higher is the rating, the riskier is considered a bond. An investor agrees to buy a risky bond if he is compensated by a higher risk premium. Increasing GDP growth rates have a negative effect on bond spreads. A rapidly growing economy should be able to honour its debt obligations. A tax-to-debt ratio has a positive but statistically insignificant effect on the risk premium (regression I). A coefficient of public debt to GDP ratio is positive and significant (regression II). A large stock of outstanding public debt increases the probability of default, which consequently raises the risk premium. Similarly in regression III, the yield spreads of CEE governments' bonds are positively affected by a higher burden of debt service. The dummy crisis has a positive and significant coefficient in the regressions I through III indicating contagion effects on Central and Eastern European countries (CEEC) bonds' spreads after the Russian crisis. In regression IV general government balance exerts a negative impact on the spreads, that is, if the country runs a deficit the government bonds' spread will grow while a surplus tends to diminish the spread.[4] So far the empirical results suggest that CEE government bonds yields' spreads are significantly influenced by fiscal variables.

Next step in our empirical analysis is to check if the results obtained are robust to a possible problem of endogeneity. We estimate the Eq. (6) with country dummies but excluding the variable *rating*. Now in the first column of Table 3 we obtain a result as predicted by the model. A higher tax-to-debt ratio shows the government's capacity to collect taxes and reduces the risk premium. Coefficients on debt and debt service ratios are positive and statistically significant as in the previous estimations, while the impact of general government balance remains negative. The numerical values of all four fiscal variables are considerably higher than those in Table 2. As before, GDP growth rates affect the risk premium negatively while the Russian crisis provoked an increase of CEE governments' bond spreads.

Since the descriptive evidence suggests that Latvia and Lithuania might be different from the other transition economies, we perform some robustness analysis and estimate the Eq. (6) after dropping the two Baltic States. The most important change in the results of Tables 4 and 5 comparing them to previous findings is that the coefficient of GDP growth turns out to be statistically insignificant. This might explain why the risk premium of the

Table 3. Estimation Results with Country Dummies.

Dependent Variable	Yield Spreads of CEE Governments			
	I	II	III	IV
Tax-to-debt	−67.6 (34.3)**			
Public debt		5.98 (1.22)***		
Debt service			22.3 (5.33)***	
Government balance				−21.6 (8.48)***
GDP growth	−13.1 (5.67)**	−8.29 (5.29)	−14.1 (5.92)**	
Crisis	51.6 (28.1)*	64.8 (21.6)***	54.6 (25.9)**	35.8 (32.9)
Country dummies	Yes	Yes	Yes	Yes
Time dummies	Yes	Yes	Yes	Yes
R^2	0.91	0.93	0.93	0.91
Number of observations	80	80	79	80

Note: For time dummies refer to footnote of Table 2.
Significance levels at:
*10%;
**5%; and
***1%.

Table 4.   Estimation Results Excluding Latvia and Lithuania.

Dependent Variable	Yield Spreads of CEE Governments			
	I	II	III	IV
Country risk	44.7 (6.55)***	46.5 (6.01)***	45.1 (5.99)***	45.4 (6.01)***
Tax-to-debt	−9.39 (18.6)			
Public debt		1.07 (0.51)**		
Debt service			6.19 (2.09)***	
Government balance				−11.9 (5.18)**
GDP growth	−9.77 (6.78)	−8.07 (6.51)	−8.06 (6.77)	
Crisis	46.9 (30.9)	44.4 (28.9)	40.6 (33.8)	36.8 (32.6)
Intercept	148.4 (58.9)***	−228.6 (54.9)***	−224.9 (49.7)***	−237.2 (51.7)***
Time dummies	Yes	Yes	Yes	Yes
R^2	0.66	0.68	0.69	0.66
Number of observations	67	67	66	67

Note: For time dummies refer to footnote of Table 2.
Significance levels at:
**5%; and
***1%.

Table 5.   Estimation Results Excluding Latvia and Lithuania with Country Dummies.

Dependent Variable	Yield Spreads of CEE Governments			
	I	II	III	IV
Tax-to-debt	−94.8 (32.1)***			
Public debt		6.76 (1.03)***		
Debt service			24.5 (5.09)***	
Government balance				−12.2 (13.4)
GDP growth	−9.32 (7.37)	−2.97 (6.84)**	−11.4 (8.35)	
Crisis	34.5 (41.4)	43.2 (26.1)	44.5 (36.7)	19.7 (43.6)
Country dummies	Yes	Yes	Yes	Yes
Time dummies	Yes	Yes	Yes	Yes
R^2	0.91	0.94	0.94	0.90
Number of observations	67	67	66	67

Note: For time dummies refer to footnote of Table 2.
Significance levels at:
**5%; and
***1%.

Baltic countries has declined despite the increase of their public debt ratios. During the first decade of transition the Baltic economies enjoyed quite high GDP growth rates. Although the public debt rose, increasing tax revenues kept the debt service ratio at reasonably low levels. Healthy growth rates and sustainable public finances have enhanced the credibility of foreign investors in Latvia and Lithuania, and led to lower spreads of the Baltic governments' bonds. The dummy crisis turns out to be statistically insignificant as well. This might be explained by the fact that among CEE economies the Baltic countries were the hardest affected by the Russian crisis.

Similarly to previous results, the spreads of CEE government bonds are significantly affected by fiscal variables. A tax-to-debt ratio has a negative impact on the bond spreads which is statistically significant only in Table 5. Higher debt to GDP and debt service ratios as well as deteriorating general government balance tend to increase the risk premium. The magnitude of coefficients on all fiscal variables except the general government balance in Table 5 increase compared to the coefficients of Table 3. This suggests that the risk premium in Latvia and Lithuania is more responsive to changes in general government budget position than to changes in debt.

6. CONCLUDING REMARKS

The portfolio balance model suggests that increasing public debt levels lead to a higher risk premium. A large debt stock increases the probability of default so that foreign investors would buy new bonds only in the presence of higher bond spreads. However, experiences of developed and emerging markets have demonstrated that investors' preparedness to accept new bonds is influenced not only by recorded but also by expected fiscal imbalances. A hike in bonds' spreads might be triggered by the expectations of contingent liabilities and future deficits.

This chapter looks at the impact of fiscal variables on bond spreads in the 10 CEE EU accession countries. The empirical results are consistent with the literature. Increasing public debt and debt service ratios as well as deteriorating fiscal position lead to a higher risk premium. An opposite effect on the spreads is exerted by healthy GDP growth rates and higher tax-to-debt ratio. The results suggest that investors do care for the present value budget constraint and reward fiscal adjustment with lower risk premia.

NOTES

1. See Leeper (1991).
2. For empirical work we proxy the risk-free interest rate by foreign interest rate that is exogenous for CEE.
3. General government debt of Estonia is les than 10% of GDP. Our sample includes only one observation for Estonia.
4. GDP growth rates are strongly correlated with general government balance, so the former are excluded from the fourth regression.

REFERENCES

Bernoth, K., von Hagen, J., & Schuknecht, L. (2003). *Sovereign risk premia in the European government bond market.* ZEI Working Paper no. B26.
Favero, C.A., & Gavazzi, F. (2004). *Inflation targeting and debt: Lessons from Brazil.* NBER Working Paper no. 10390.
Flavin, T. J., & Limosani, M.G. (2001). *Explaining European short-term interest rate differentials: An application of Tobin's portfolio theory.* National University of Ireland, NUI Maynooth Working Paper no. 100–05–00.
Giorgianni, L. (1997). *Foreign exchange risk premium: Does fiscal policy matter? evidence from Italian data.* IMF Working Paper no. 97–39.
Kopits, G. (2000). *How can fiscal policy help avert currency crisis?* IMF Working Paper no. 00–185.
Krugman, P. (1979). A model of balance-of-payments crises. *Journal of Money, Credit and Banking, 11*(3), 311–325.
Leeper, E. M. (1991). Equilibria under "active" and "passive" monetary and fiscal policies. *Journal of Monetary Economics, 27*, 129–147.
Obstfeld, M. (1994). *The logic of currency crises.* NBER Working Paper no. 4640.
Uribe, M. (2002). *A fiscal theory of sovereign risk.* NBER Working Paper no. 9221.

FURTHER READING

Berk, J.M., & Knot, K.H.W. (1999). *Co-movements in long-term interest rates and the role of PPP-based exchange rate expectation.* IMF Working Paper no. 99–81.
Caballero, R., & Krishnamurthy, A. (2004). *Fiscal policy and financial depth.* NBER Working Paper no. 10532.
Calvo, G., & Mishkin, A.F.S. (2003). *The mirage of exchange rate regimes for emerging market countries.* NBER Working Paper 9808.
Cote, D., & Graham, C. (2004). *Convergence of government bond yields in the Euro zone: The role of policy harmonization.* Bank of Canada Working Paper no. 2004–2023.

PART B:
MONETARY POLICY AND BANKING

MONETARY POLICY OPERATIONAL FRAMEWORKS COMPARED: EURO AREA VERSUS SOME NON-EURO AREA COUNTRIES

Orazio Mastroeni

1. INTRODUCTION

This chapter analyses the operational framework for monetary policy implementation in some central European countries that have recently joined the European Union (EU).[1] For the sake of simplicity, they will be referred to as "non-euro area countries" in the rest of the chapter (although such a classification also includes Denmark, Sweden and the United Kingdom) which are not analysed here. The analysis is based on public information collected for 2001; since then, the operational framework of these central banks has not changed substantially. Most of the recent changes in the operational framework have taken place in the Eurosystem (or euro area, as it is also commonly known). For this reason, more recent euro area data is reported for 2003 and 2004, and a detailed analysis is made wherever appropriate. The study therefore presents an uptodate comparison of operational frameworks across the

Emerging European Financial Markets: Independence and Integration Post-Enlargement
International Finance Review, Volume 6, 71–97
Copyright © 2006 by Elsevier Ltd.
ISSN: 1569-3767/doi:10.1016/S1569-3767(05)06004-8

countries. The remainder of the chapter is organised as follows. Section 2 examines the characteristics of the minimum reserve system in the euro area. Section 3 examines open market operations, Section 4 examines the standing facilities and Section 5 looks at counterparties. Finally, chapter 6 describes at eligible collateral.

2. ON MINIMUM RESERVE SYSTEMS AND THE LEVEL OF RESERVE REQUIREMENTS

The minimum reserve system is a monetary policy instrument whose characteristics can be defined independently by the central bank. In the past, minimum reserve systems were often seen as a tool to control the growth of broader monetary aggregates (deposits) through the so-called money multiplier mechanism. At that time the emphasis was given more on the quantitative side of bank reserves held with the central bank, not so much on their price (the rate of interest). More recently, minimum reserve systems have often been applied in order to stabilise the shortest money market rates around the level that corresponds to the key policy rate. This stabilising function is normally achieved by setting the level of required reserves higher than the level of required working balances for payment purposes and by applying the so-called averaging mechanism to the fulfilment of reserve requirements.

Currently all central banks of the euro area and the non-euro area countries that recently joined the EU apply a minimum reserve system. Table 1 summarises the main purposes for applying a minimum reserve system.

Table 1. Purposes of the Minimum Reserve Systems.

	Euro Area	CY	CZ	EE	HU	LV	LT	MT	PL	SK	SI
Stabilise money market rates through the creation of a liquidity buffer	X	X	X	X	X	X	X	X	X	X	X
Absorb structural liquidity surpluses					X				X		
Create liquidity needs	X					X					
Control monetary growth								X			

2.1. Characteristics of the Minimum Reserve Systems

The Eurosystem's minimum reserve system primarily pursues the following monetary functions:

- Stabilisation of money market interest rates: The "averaging" provision of the Eurosystem's minimum reserve system aims to contribute to the stabilisation of money market interest rates by giving institutions an incentive to smooth the effects of temporary liquidity fluctuations.
- Creation or enlargement of a structural liquidity shortage: The Eurosystem's minimum reserve system contributes to creating or enlarging a structural liquidity shortage. This may be helpful in order to improve the ability of the Eurosystem to operate efficiently as a supplier of liquidity.

The European Central Bank (ECB) requires credit institutions to hold minimum reserves on accounts with the national central banks within the framework of the Eurosystem's minimum reserve system. The amount of minimum reserves to be held by each institution is determined in relation to its reserve base (Box 1). The Eurosystem's minimum reserve system enables counterparties to make use of averaging provisions, implying that compliance with reserve requirements is determined on the basis of the average of the end-of-calendar-day balances on the counterparties' reserve accounts over a maintenance period. Institutions' holdings of required reserves are remunerated at the rate on the Eurosystem's weekly main refinancing operations (MRO). Reserve holdings exceeding the required reserves are not remunerated.

2.2. Minimum Reserve Systems in the Non-Euro Area Countries

In the non-euro area countries the most often mentioned function of the minimum reserve system is the stabilisation of money market rates through the creation of a liquidity buffer in the banking system. Minimum reserve systems are also used for the absorption of structural liquidity surpluses and for the creation of liquidity needs. Some countries use the minimum reserve system also to control monetary growth. In addition to reserve requirements in domestic currencies, Lithuania and Malta have reserve requirements also for foreign currencies (USD or EUR). With the exceptions of Slovenia, all the central banks of the non-euro area member states have a lagged reserve requirement accounting procedure

---

Box 1. Reserve Base and Reserve Ratios.

A: Liabilities included in the reserve base and to which the positive
       reserve ratio (currently 2%) is applied
       Overnight deposits
       Deposits with agreed maturity up to 2 years
       Deposits redeemable at notice up to 2 years
       Debt securities issued
       Debt securities with agreed maturity up to 2 years
B: Liabilities included in the reserve base and to which a zero reserve
       ratio is applied €4,741 billion
       Deposits with agreed maturity over 2 years
       Deposits redeemable at notice over 2 years
       Repos
       Debt securities issued
       Debt securities with agreed maturity over 2 years
C: Liabilities excluded from the reserve base
       Liabilities vis-à-vis other institutions subject to the Eurosystem's
          minimum reserve system
       Liabilities vis-à-vis the ECB and the national central banks
Total reserve base (A + B) €11,369 billion

---

in place, where the maximum lag between the start of the reserve maintenance period and the end of the calculation period of the reserve base is
1 month.

Table 2 shows that reserve ratios are relatively high in non-euro area
countries. High reserve ratios imply that the average level of required reserves will fall considerably when non-euro area countries start to harmonise their reserve ratios closer to the Eurosystem level. With the exceptions
of Latvia, Lithuania and Poland, required reserves are remunerated.

In all non-euro area countries credit institutions have the possibility to use
averaging provisions in fulfilling the reserve requirements, in some countries, however, with certain limitations. Overdrafts are not allowed. Four
non-euro area countries also accept vault cash in the fulfilment of reserve
requirements. In Estonia, credit institutions can also use high-quality euro-
denominated assets in the fulfilment of reserve requirements.

Table 2. Characteristics of Minimum Reserve Systems, Reserve Maintenance Periods and the Fulfilment of Reserve Requirements.

	Euro Area	CY	CZ	EE	HU	LV	LT	MT	PL	SK	SI
Reserve requirement in domestic currency	Y	Y	Y	Y	Y	Y	Y	Y	Y	Y	Y
Reserve requirement in foreign currency	N	N	N	N	N	N	Y	Y	N	N	N
Ratio (%)	2	6.5	2.0	13	6	5	8	4	4	4	Depends on maturity of deposits
Remuneration of required reserves	Y[a]	Y[a]	Y[b]	Y[c]	Y	N	N	Y[d]	N	Y	Y
Averaging during the maintenance period	Y	Y	Y	Y	Y	Y	Y	Y	Y	Y	Y
Negative balances at end of day	N	N	N	N	N	N	Y	Y	N	N	N

[a]Linked to marginal lending rate.
[b]Repo rate.
[c]ECB deposit rate is reference rate.
[d]Fixed rate.

2.3. Reserve Requirements in Non-Euro Area Countries

In relative terms, minimum reserve systems and reserve requirements play a bigger role in non-euro area countries than in the euro area. Whereas the size of the aggregate reserve requirements in the euro area as a percentage of gross domestic product (GDP) is 1.9 per cent, the corresponding figure in non-euro area countries that recently joined the EU is 2.7 per cent (taking required reserves in domestic and foreign currencies together). The absolute figures give a different picture due to generally lower liability bases of credit institutions in non-euro area countries. The two biggest non-euro area countries, Hungary and Poland, have a reserve requirement comparable to the two smallest national reserve requirements in the euro area (Finland and Greece) (Fig. 1).

Around 1,200 credit institutions were subject to reserve requirements in non-euro area countries at the end of 2001. Poland and Hungary account for roughly 80 per cent of all these credit institutions. In the Eurosystem by comparison, approximately 7,000 institutions were subject to reserve

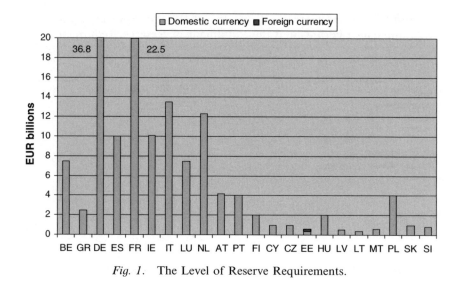

Fig. 1.   The Level of Reserve Requirements.

Table 3.   Average Reserve Requirements per Institution (Aggregate).

	Euro Area	New EU Countries
Reserve requirements	123.7	11.0
Average requirement per institution (€ billions)	16.8	8.6

requirements in the same period. The levels of reserve requirement in the euro area and in non-euro area countries are not wide apart when observed at the level of credit institutions. Whereas the total reserve requirement in the euro area exceeds the total reserve requirement of non-euro area countries that recently joined the EU by 11 times, the average requirement per institution is only twice as high (Table 3). This naturally reflects the fact that in the euro area more institutions are subject to reserve requirements than in non-euro area countries that recently joined the EU on average. From Fig. 2 it can be inferred from looking at reserve requirements per credit institution that non-euro area countries and the euro area countries do not differ significantly. For example, comparing the lowest figures of the euro area (Austria and Finland) to the lowest figures of non-euro area countries (Poland and Slovenia) shows that they stood at €5 million.

Figs. 2 and 3 shows that when assessed against GDP figures, institution's reserve requirements are on average higher in non-euro area countries than in the euro area. This highlights the relative importance of this monetary policy instrument and of the fact that higher reserve ratios are applied in

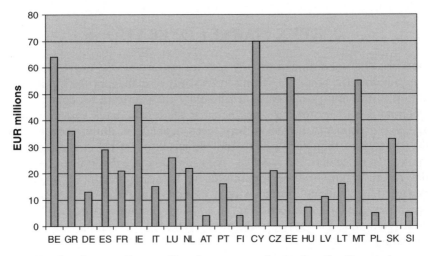

Fig. 2. Average Reserve Requirements per Institution (by Country).

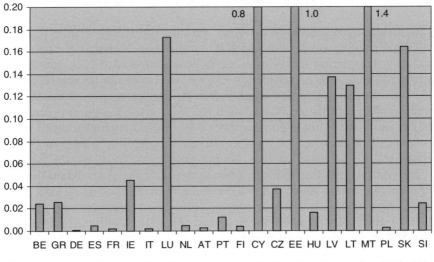

Fig. 3. Average Reserve Requirements per Institution Relative to the GDP (%).

non-euro area countries. Moreover, small non-euro area countries tend to have relatively high reserve requirements per credit institution whereas the largest non-euro area countries have usually lower reserve requirements per credit institution.

3. OPEN MARKET OPERATIONS

Open market operations normally play an important role in monetary policy, pursuing the aims of steering interest rates, managing the liquidity situation in the money market and signalling the stance of monetary policy. Open market operations are conducted at the central bank's own initiative, and the instruments and procedures used depend on, among other things, the strategy of monetary policy and the structure of the domestic money market. In particular, the types of operations used are determined largely by the structural liquidity position and the net liquidity demand of the banking system. In a banking system with a liquidity surplus, the main types of operations are liquidity absorbing. In a system running a structural liquidity deficit like the Eurosystem, the main types of operations are liquidity providing.

3.1. Open Market Operations in the Euro Area

Eurosystem open market operations can be divided into four categories: main refinancing operations (MRO), longer-term refinancing operations (LTRO), fine-tuning operations and structural operations. As for the instruments used, reverse transactions are the main open market instrument of the Eurosystem and can be employed in all four categories of operations, whereas debt certificates may be used for structural absorption operations. In addition, the Eurosystem has three other instruments available for the conduct of fine-tuning operations: outright transactions, foreign exchange swaps and the collection of fixed-term deposits.

Reverse transactions[2] refer to operations where the Eurosystem buys or sells eligible assets under repurchase agreements or conducts credit operations against eligible assets as collateral. Reverse transactions are used for MRO and LTRO. These are the two most commonly conducted operations. The MRO provides approximately three quarters of the regular refinancing to the banking systems, whereas the LTRO provides the remaining 25 per cent. Reverse transactions are also used for structural and fine-tuning operations: The outstanding quantities of these operations are negligible. The Eurosystem may execute reverse transactions either in the form of repurchase agreements (i.e. the ownership of the asset is transferred to the creditor, while the parties agree to reverse the transaction through a re-transfer of the asset to the debtor at a future point in time) or as collat-eralised loans (an enforceable security interest is provided over the assets but, assuming fulfilment of the debt obligation, the ownership of the asset is retained by the debtor).

From the beginning of 1999 to June 2000, the Eurosystem conducted its MRO as fixed rate tenders. Since 27 June 2000, the MRO have been con-ducted as variable rate tenders with a minimum bid rate using a multiple rate procedure. The reason for the change was the severe overbidding ex-perienced in the fixed rate MRO, which resulted from the existence of a wide and persistent spread between money market interest rates and the fixed rate applied to the MRO in early 2000. This spread was, in turn, largely driven by market expectations of further increases in ECB interest rates, especially in the spring of 2000. The spread between market rates and the ECB's main refinancing rate made it very attractive for banks to obtain funds from the central bank. However, a problem arose with variable rate tenders with a minimum bid rate. In a few cases, the aggregate of all bids submitted in the tender was lower than the amount needed for the smooth fulfilment of reserve requirements ("underbidding"). As these episodes also stemmed from significant interest rate speculation, the ECB Governing Council de-cided to adjust its operational framework as of March 2004. Upon switching to variable rate tenders, the Eurosystem also started to announce, each week, the estimated liquidity needs of the banking system for the period until the day before the settlement of the next MRO. The publication of this estimate assists counterparties in preparing their bids for the forth-coming MRO.

3.2. Open Market Operations in Non-Euro Area Countries

Table 4 shows the types of open market operations that are in use in non-euro area countries. The two non-euro area countries that recently joined the EU that have a currency board system, Estonia and Lithuania, do not normally conduct any open market operations.[3] The other eight non-euro area countries tend to use more than one type of open market operations, unlike the Eurosystem, which uses only reverse repo in all of its operations. It can also be inferred from the table that, similarly to the euro area, the

Table 4. The Types of Open Market Operations Conducted in Non-Euro Area Countries.

	Euro Area	CY	CZ	EE	HU	LV	LT	MT	PL	SK	SI
Liquidity-absorbing repos		X				X					
Liquidity-providing repos	X	X				X	X				X
Forex swaps						X					
Outright transactions in public securities						X			X		
Issue of short-term paper			X		X				X	X	X
Collection of fixed-term deposits		X				X		X			
Other						X		X			

most commonly used liquidity-providing open market operation in non-euro area countries that recently joined the EU was the reverse repo. In three non-euro area countries that recently joined the EU, Latvia, Malta and Slovenia, this type of operation was the most used in terms of volume. In Cyprus, repos are seldom conducted.

The other types of open market operations used for providing liquidity to the banking system in non-euro area countries are foreign exchange swaps and outright transactions. There is no single most used type of operation for liquidity absorption, but the reverse repo, the issuance of short-term papers, and the collection of fixed-term deposits are used equally commonly in terms of volume. Due to structural liquidity surpluses and the excess supply in the banking systems on average, non-euro area countries conduct more liquidity-absorbing than liquidity-providing operations.

4. STANDING FACILITIES

4.1. Standing Facilities in the Euro Area

The Eurosystem also implements monetary policy by setting the interest rates on its standing facilities. Standing facilities provide or absorb liquidity with an overnight maturity on the initiative of counterparties. Two standing facilities are available to eligible counterparties: the marginal lending facility and the deposit facility. There is little incentive for banks to use standing facilities, as the interest rates applied to them are normally unfavourable when compared with market rates. Fig. 4 shows the daily use of the standing facilities from January 1999 to December 2004. This mostly remained below €1 billion, and only occasionally there have been massive recourses to the

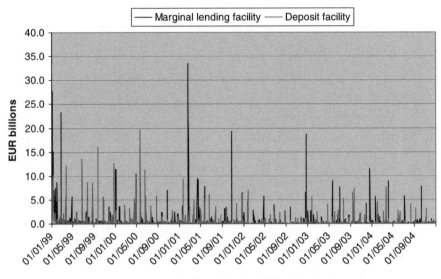

Fig. 4. Daily Use of the Standing Facilities in the Euro Area.

facilities when the provision or absorption of liquidity in exceptional circumstances occurred. The introduction of the euro at the beginning of 1999 and the transition to 2000 were examples of such exceptional circumstances, and explain the relatively high level of recourse to the marginal lending facility in the initial maintenance periods (Fig. 5). The trend towards a reduction in the use of facilities has continued throughout this period.

The use of the standing facilities is largest at the end of the reserve maintenance period. This is due to the averaging mechanism of the minimum reserve system, which allows credit institutions to run daily liquidity deficits and surpluses, and either bring forward the fulfilment of reserve requirements or postpone it until the end of the maintenance period. As previously noted, reserve requirements become binding only on the last day of the maintenance period when liquidity deficits or surpluses can no longer be compensated by opposite imbalances within the same maintenance period.

4.2. Standing Facilities in Non-Euro Area Countries that Recently Joined the EU

Apart from the countries that operate under a currency board system, all non-euro area countries have both liquidity-providing and -absorbing overnight

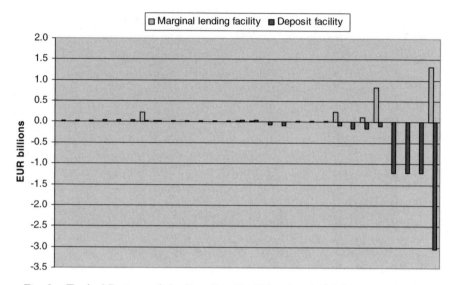

Fig. 5.   Typical Pattern of the Standing Facilities Over a Maintenance Period.

Table 5.   Overnight Standing Facilities and Their Main Purposes in
Non-EuroArea Member States.

	Euro Area	CY	CZ	EE	HU	LV	LT	MT	PL	SK	SI
Marginal lending facility	X	X	X		X	X	X	X	X	X	X
For temporary liquidity needs	X	X	X		X	X		X	X	X	X
As ceiling for o/n rate	X	X	X		X	X		X	X		X
Signalling stance of monitory policy	X	X									
Deposit facility	X	X	X		X	X		X	X	X	X
Withdraw temporary liquidity excesses	X	X	X		X	X		X	X	X	X
–As floor for o/n rate	X	X	X		X	X		X	X		X
–Signalling stance of monetary policy	X										

standing facilities in place. Lithuania, which runs a currency board system,
also has a marginal lending facility, but this is seldom used. Table 5 shows the
main purposes for having standing facilities in non-euro area countries. The
most often mentioned purposes for the standing facilities are to satisfy temporary liquidity management needs and to bind overnight market interest

rates, which are also the main purposes for the Eurosystem standing facilities. No potential role to signal the general stance of monetary policy is commonly given to standing facilities in non-euro area countries that recently joined the EU.

Tables 6 and 7 show the characteristics of, respectively, the marginal lending facility and the deposit facility in non-euro area countries. In general terms, the characteristics do not differ that much from the Eurosystem's standing facilities, which is not surprising since the purposes of the standing facilities are similar. Concerning the marginal lending facility, both reverse repos and collateralised loans are technically used. Apart from Lithuania, which runs a currency board system, the interest rates applied to both marginal lending and deposit facilities are pre-specified. Eligible collateral for overnight loans are the same as accepted in open market operations.

Apart from collateral, there are normally no other major limitations to the use of standing facilities in non-euro area countries. In Czech Republic and Hungary, minimum amounts for accessing the deposit facility are set, and in Lithuania a shortage of funds for settlement is required for accessing the marginal lending facility. In Hungary, Latvia and Malta, both automatic and on-demand loans are available. Generally speaking, it can be said that when the average usage of standing facilities are observed relative to average reserve requirements, in 2001 the standing facilities were used comparatively more in non-euro area countries than in the euro area countries.

5. COUNTERPARTIES

5.1. Counterparties in the Euro Area

Counterparties to Eurosystem monetary policy operations must fulfil certain eligibility criteria. These criteria are defined with a view to giving a broad range of institutions access to Eurosystem monetary policy operations, enhancing equal treatment of institutions across the euro area and ensuring that counterparties fulfil certain operational and prudential requirements:

- Only institutions subject to the Eurosystem's minimum reserve system are eligible to be counterparties. Institutions exempted from minimum reserve system are not eligible to be counterparties.
- Counterparties must be financially sound: They should be subject to at least one form of EU/European economic area (EEA) harmonised

supervision by national authorities. However, financially sound institutions subject to non-harmonised national supervision of a comparable standard can also be accepted as counterparties (e.g. branches established in the euro area of institutions that have their head office outside the EEA).

- Counterparties must fulfil any operational criteria specified in the relevant contractual or regulatory arrangements applied by the respective national central bank (or the ECB), so as to ensure the efficient conduct of Eurosystem monetary policy operations.

These general eligibility criteria are uniform throughout the euro area. Institutions fulfilling these eligibility criteria may access the Eurosystem's standing facilities, and participate in Eurosystem open market operations based on standard tenders.

5.2. Counterparties in Non-Euro Area Countries

The right to be a counterparty for open market operations and standing facilities in non-euro area countries is usually connected with the obligation to hold required reserves. The group of institutions that is subject to the minimum reserve system, therefore, also defines the group of counterparties for open market operations and standing facilities. Table 8 summarises the general and additional criteria used to select counterparties for open market operations and standing facilities. The most common general criteria are that the institution should be subject to the minimum reserve system and licensed under the prevailing legal agreements. The additional criteria seem to differ considerably between non-euro area countries. Sometimes the criteria are defined in detail, and in other cases the criteria are of a more general nature. Table 9 gives details on the average number of counterparties that actually participated to open market operations in non-euro area countries. The purely liquidity-absorbing operations and reserve repos have the highest total numbers.

6. ELIGIBLE COLLATERAL FOR CREDIT OPERATIONS

The main purpose of collateralising central bank credit is to protect the central bank from incurring losses, should a counterparty happen to default

Table 6. The Marginal Lending Facilities in Non-Euro Area Countries.

	Euro Area	CY	CZ	EE	HU	LV	LT	MT	PL	SK	SI
Type of instrument	Reverse repo/ collateralised loan	Reverse repo	Reverse repo		Collateralised loan	Collateralised loan	Collateralised loan	Collateralised loan	Collateralised loan	Reverse repo	Collateralised loan
Interest rate	Pre-specified	Pre-specified	Pre-specified		Pre-specified	Pre-specified	Variable	Pre-specified	Pre-specified	Pre-specified	Pre-specified
Collateral	Yes, same as for open market operations	Yes, same as for open market operations	Yes, same as for open market operations		Yes, same as for open market operations	Yes, same as for open market operations	Yes, same as for open market operations	Yes, same as for open market operations	Yes, same as for open market operations	Yes, same as for open market operations	Yes, same as for open market operations
Other characteristics					Automatic loan for overdraft at e-o-d/on demand during business hours	Automatic loans are o/n/ demand loans maturity from o/n to 30 days		Both automatic and on-demand loans			Separate loans of last resort available

Table 7. The Deposit Facilities in Non-Euro Area Countries.

	Euro Area	CY	CZ	EE	HU	LV	LT	MT	PL	SK	SI
Interest rate	Pre-specified		Pre-specified		Pre-specified	Pre-specified			Pre-specified	Pre-specified	
Major limits or controls			Minimum size necessary		Minimum size necessary						

Table 8. Eligibility Criteria of Counterparties for Monetary Policy Operations.

Country	General Criteria	Additional Criteria
Euro area	Financially sound institutions subject to the minimum reserve system	Any operational criteria specified in the relevant contractual or regulatory arrangements applied by the respective NCB or the ECB
CY	Institutions subject to the minimum reserve system	Operational criteria specified in the regulatory arrangements applied by the central bank
CZ	Banks are accepted as counterparties on request	Repo tenders and Lombard credits are only available for banks which have signed the repo agreement with the central bank
EE		
HU	Credit institutions, central clearinghouse and depository as well as primary dealers may become counterparties. Different operations involve different counterparties	Institutions should accept "business conditions" by signing the "letter of acceptance" with the central bank
LV	All banks and foreign bank branches registered in Latvia	Participation to the securities settlement system and the signing of respective agreements with the central bank
LT	Banks that hold their required reserves with the central bank	Operational, prudential and solvency requirements
MT	Credit institutions licensed under the Banking Act to conduct business denominated in Maltese liri	
PL	Two groups of criteria for banks. Looser criteria are applied to standing facilities and stricter to open market operations	A number of detailed operational criteria for counterparties to access standing facilities and open market operations. Only selected money market dealers and the Banking Guarantee Fund can be counterparties for open market operations
SK	Every bank established under the Banking Act has the right to be a counterparty	For repo operations the General Master Agreement should be signed with the central bank
SI	Banks and savings banks subject to the minimum reserve system and prudential supervision	Savings banks can only access the deposit facility and 60-day Tolar bills. Banks can participate to repos, liquidity loans and central bank foreign currency bills. A specific agreement has to be signed by banks to participate to 27-days Tolar bills and foreign exchange swaps

Table 9. Number of Counterparties Normally Participating in Open Market Operations.

	Euro Area (2004)	New EU Members	CY	CZ	EE	HU	LV	LT	MT	PL	SK	SI
Liquidity-absorbing operations (repos)	MRO 350 LTRO 150 Fine tuning: 30	39	5	13	n/a		1	n/a			16	
Liquidity-providing operations (repos)		20	5			4	2		4			
Forex swaps		3					2					
Outright transactions (absorbing and providing)		16					2					
Issue of short-term paper (absorbing)		50				14				13	10	12
Collection of short-term deposits (absorbing)		26	5			13			4	14		

on its debt with the central bank. In this respect, collateral is actually a second, the first being a careful choice of solid counterparties. The collateral framework of a central bank also aims to ensure the equal treatment of counterparties and enhancing operational efficiency.

6.1. Eligible Collateral in the Euro Area

The collateral framework of the Eurosystem is based on a number of guiding principles stemming from the treaty establishing the EU as well as from operational guidelines developed in the course of the preparatory work for Stage 3 of economic and monetary union. The collateral framework was developed in such a way as not to depart substantially from the established market practices prevailing prior to the introduction of the euro. Due regard was given to the existing differences in central bank practices and financial structures across EU Member States. The harmonisation of eligibility criteria throughout the euro area has contributed to ensuring equal treatment and operational efficiency. As a result, the list of eligible assets in the Eurosystem consists of a very broad range of different types of assets (Table 10).

6.2. Eligible Collateral in Non-Euro Area Countries

Similar to the euro area, lending through open market operations and the marginal lending facility is collateralised in non-euro area countries (Table 11). With the exception of Malta, intra-day credit is also collateralised

Table 10. Main Categories of Eligible Assets for Eurosystem Credit Operations.

Type of Asset	Tier One (EEA)	Tier Two (Euro Area)
Marketable	• ECB debt certificates (at present not issued) • Debt issued by foreign and supranational institutions • Central, regional and local government securities • Uncovered credit institution bonds • Pfandbrief-type securities • Corporate bonds	• Central, regional and local government securities • Credit institution bonds • Corporate bonds • Certificates of deposit • Medium-term notes • Commercial paper • Equities • Marketable private claims
Non-marketable	None	• Bank loans • Mortgage-backed promissory notes • Trade bills

where such a facility is available. In Cyprus, Slovakia and Slovenia, intra-day credit is not available for counterparties. Estonia does not offer credit through open market operations and the marginal lending facility.

Treasury bills and government bonds are accepted as eligible collateral in all non-euro area countries (Table 12), and central bank debt certificates are the next most common type of eligible assets. Only Cyprus and Latvia accept private debt instruments (corporate or credit institution) as eligible collateral in their credit operations, and Cyprus accepts some additional assets as eligible collateral. Normally there are no limitations on eligible assets for different credit operations. The exceptions to this rule are Czech Republic, Lithuania and Slovenia. Czech Republic and Slovenia have restrictions relating to the type of asset, and Lithuania's restrictions concern the remaining maturity of the assets.

There are, of course, also certain general criteria for the eligible assets in non-euro area countries. For example, it is common to accept only those eligible assets whose remaining maturity exceeds the maturity of credit

Table 11. The Use of Collateral in Credit Operations.

	Euro Area	CY	CZ	EE	HU	LV	LT	MT	PL	SK	SI
Open market operations	Y	Y	Y		Y	Y	Y	Y	Y	Y	Y
Marginal lending facility	Y	Y	Y		Y	Y	Y	Y	Y	Y	Y
Intra-day credit		Y	Facility not available		Y	Y	N	Y	Y	Facility not available	Facility not available

Table 12. The Types of Eligible Assets.

	Euro Area	CY	CZ	EE	HU	LV	LT	MT	PL	SK	SI
Central bank debt certificates	X		X		X			X		X	X
Government bills/bonds	X	X	X		X	X	X	X	X	X	X
Municipal bonds	X	X									
Corporate bonds	X	X				X					
Equities	X										
Bank loans	X										
Other assets	X	X									

operation. Another common requirement is that the assets should be registered and held at the Central Depository in a dematerialised form. Moreover, in some cases additional requirements are in place: that possible coupons do not fall due during the operation, that the assets should not be issued by the counterparty receiving the credit and that the assets should be owned by the counterparty receiving the credit. However, these criteria are not applied by all the central banks of the non-euro area countries.

6.3. Risk Control Measures

Risk control measures are applied to the assets underlying Eurosystem monetary policy operations in order to protect the Eurosystem against the risk of financial loss if underlying assets have to be realised owing to the default of a counterparty. The risk control measures at the disposal of the Eurosystem are described in Box 2.

The Eurosystem applies specific risk control measures according to the types of underlying assets offered by the counterparty. The appropriate risk control measures for tier one assets are determined by the ECB. Risk control measures for tier one assets are broadly harmonised across the euro area. The risk control framework for tier one assets includes the following main elements:

- Eligible tier one assets are allocated to one of four categories of decreasing liquidity, based on issuer classification and asset type. The allocation of eligible assets to the four liquidity categories is described in Box 3.
- Individual debt instruments are subject to specific "valuation haircuts". The haircuts are applied by deducting a certain percentage from the market value of the underlying asset. The haircuts differ according to the residual maturity and coupon structure of the debt instruments as described in Box 4.
- No valuation haircuts are applied in liquidity-absorbing operations. The assets are subject to daily valuation.

6.4. Risk Control Measures for Eligible Assets in Non-Euro Area Countries

Risk control measures are in place to protect the central bank against the risk of financial losses if underlying assets have to be realised owing to the default of a counterparty. The most common risk measures that are

---

Box 2. Risk control measures.

The Eurosystem currently applies the following risk control measures:

- *Valuation haircuts*
  The Eurosystem applies "valuation haircuts" in the valuation of underlying assets. This implies that the value of the underlying asset is calculated as the market value of the asset less a certain percentage (haircut).
- *Variation margins (marking to market)*
  The Eurosystem requires the haircut-adjusted market value of the underlying assets used in its liquidity-providing reverse transactions to be maintained over time. This implies that if the value, measured on a regular basis, of the underlying assets falls below a certain level, the national central bank will require the counterparty to supply additional assets or cash (i.e. a margin call). Similarly, if the value of the underlying assets, following their revaluation, exceeds a certain level, the counterparty may retrieve the excess assets or cash.

The following risk control measures are currently not applied by the Eurosystem:

- *Initial margins*
  The Eurosystem may apply initial margins in its liquidity-providing reverse transactions. This would imply that counterparties would need to provide underlying assets with a value at least equal to the liquidity provided by the Eurosystem plus the value of the initial margin.
- *Limits in relation to issuers/debtors or guarantors*
  The Eurosystem may apply limits to the exposure vis-à-vis issuers/debtors or guarantors.
- *Additional guarantees*
  The Eurosystem may require additional guarantees from financially sound entities in order to accept certain assets.
- *Exclusion*
  The Eurosystem may exclude certain assets from use in its monetary policy operations.

Box 3. Liquidity categories for tier one assets.

Category I	*Category II*	*Category III*	*Category IV*
Central government debt instruments	Local and regional government debt instruments	Traditional Pfandbrief-style debt instruments	Asset-backed securities
Debt instruments issued by central banks	Jumbo Pfandbrief-style debt instruments	Credit institution debt instruments	
	Agency debt instruments	Debt instruments issued by corporate and other issuers	
	Supranational debt instruments		

---

potentially available to a central bank for this purpose are initial margins, valuation haircuts, variation margins and limits in relation to certain issuers.

Table 13 shows the risk control measures applied by the central banks of the non-euro area countries currently. Initial margins and valuation haircuts are used in six central banks. The other non-euro area countries apply only one of these measures. The size of initial margins and valuation haircuts vary considerably.

6.5. Overall Amounts of Eligible Collateral

Table 14 reports the amount of debt instruments issued by the government and the central bank of these states. Overall, these issuers accounted for 99.6 per cent of assets. As a comparison, in the euro area these issuers accounted

Box 4. Levels of valuation haircuts (%) applied to eligible tier one assets in relation to fixed coupon and zero coupon instruments.

Liquidity categories

Residual Maturity (years)	Category I		Category II		Category III		Category IV	
	Fixed Coupon	Zero Coupon	Fixed Coupon	Zero Coupon	Fixed Coupon	Zero Coupon	Fixed Coupon	Zero Coupon
0–1	0.5	0.5	1	1	1.5	1.5	2	2
1–3	1.5	1.5	2.5	2.5	3	3	3.5	3.5
3–5	2.5	3	3.5	4	4.5	5	5.5	6
5–7	3	3.5	4.5	5	5.5	6	6.5	7
7–10	4	4.5	5.5	6.5	6.5	8	8	10
>10	5.5	8.5	7.5	12	9	15	12	18

Table 13. Risk Control Measures Concerning Eligible Assets in Non-Euro Area Countries.

Country	Initial Margins	Valuation Haircuts
Euro area	1% for intra-day and overnight transactions 2% for longer transactions	Depends on the type of instrument and varies between 0% and 20%
CY	10% for the marginal lending facility	10% for repo operations
CZ	2% for repo operations	7% from the nominal value in intra-day credit
EE		
HU		Depends on the type of instrument, the remaining maturity of the asset and the maturity of the operation. Varies between 1% and 6%
LV	25% for the marginal lending facility	In repo operations haircuts depend on the type and the remaining maturity of the asset. Haircuts are set weekly
LT	20% for the marginal lending facility	For repo operations the haircuts are pre-announced in the operation announcement
MT	0% for the marginal lending facility 1% for repo operations	
PL		20% for the marginal lending facility
SK	n/a	n/a
SI	For the majority of instruments 10% initial margin is applied	

only for around 58 per cent of the total outstanding amount of eligible assets, emphasising the importance of the private sector issuers in the Eurosystem collateral framework.

The total outstanding amount of eligible assets in non-euro area countries was 2.3 per cent of the corresponding amount in the euro area. The low absolute amounts in non-euro area countries can be only partly explained by their size. Looking at the amounts relative to GDP, it is only 21 per cent on average in non-euro area countries, compared to 55 per cent in the euro area. The low percentages of Estonia, Latvia, Lithuania and Poland particularly stand out. On the other hand, the percentages of Czech Republic, Hungary, Malta and Slovakia are rather close to the euro area average. It is likely that the relatively low figures result partly from the fact that non-euro area countries primarily conduct liquidity-absorbing operations, and there are therefore no compelling reasons for extending the list of eligible assets.

Table 14. Outstanding Amounts of Eligible Assets (€ billion).

Non-euro area

	Total Non-Euro Area	CY	CZ	EE	HU	LV	LT	MT	PL	SK	SI
Debt instruments issued by the government and the central bank	84.9	1.7	24.2	0.2	20.8	0.5	0.4	2.4	18.6	9.7	4.7
As a per cent of GDP	21	20	45	4	43	7	4	64	11	47	24

Euro area

	Total Euro Area	BE	DE	GR	ES	FR	IE	IT	LU	NL	AT	PT	FI
Debt instruments issued by the government and the central bank	3625	240.1	112.6	790.1	307.3	704.6	21.6	1050.1	18.0	173.8	107.4	53.5	46.0
As a per cent of GDP	55	97	93	39	51	50	21	90	88	43	52	47	35

NOTES

1. The countries under review are Cyprus (CY), Czech Republic (CZ), Estonia (EE), Hungary (HU), Latvia (LV), Lithuania (LT), Malta (MT), Poland (PL), Slovakia (SK) and Slovenia (SI). Bulgaria and Rumania will join the EU later on. Also the acronyms of the euro area countries are indicated here: Belgium (BE), Germany (DE), Greece (GR), Spain (ES), France (FR), Ireland (IE), Italy (IT), Luxembourg (LU), Holland (NL), Austria (AT), Portugal (PT) and Finland (FI). The frameworks of Denmark, Sweden and the United Kingdom are beyond the scope of this article and are thus not analysed.

2. Under a currency board system no open market operations are conducted in domestic currency, but the most important monetary policy instrument is usually a foreign exchange facility, which allows buying and selling of reserve currency at a fixed exchange rate. Similarly, normally no standing facilities in domestic currency exist under a currency board system.

3. A reverse transaction (or reverse repo) is a liquidity-providing or -absorbing operation conducted on the initiative of a central bank; in a liquidity-providing operation the central bank sells funds against collateral. The delivery of collateral by the central bank does not take place in a liquidty-absorbing operation.

WHAT ACCESSION COUNTRIES NEED TO KNOW ABOUT THE ECB: A COMPARATIVE ANALYSIS OF THE INDEPENDENCE OF THE ECB, THE BUNDESBANK AND THE REICHSBANK

Richard A. Werner[1]

1. INTRODUCTION

The popular rejection of the European constitution in France and the Netherlands triggered much debate in and around the European Central Bank (ECB) concerning the long-term viability of the euro. The region of European Monetary Union (EMU) member countries has suffered from economic strains for several years: while Germany has been in a severe economic downturn since 2001, and thus its government has implored the ECB to adopt more stimulatory monetary policy, other countries, such as Ireland and Spain, have been in the midst of an economic boom. With the prospect of a slowdown in the political process of forming a United States of Europe, a number of observers and policy-makers have begun to review the long-term viability of the European currency system. In early June 2005,

Emerging European Financial Markets: Independence and Integration Post-Enlargement
International Finance Review, Volume 6, 99–115
ISSN: 1569-3767/doi:10.1016/S1569-3767(05)06005-X

politicians in Italy even publicly contemplated the possibility of leaving the euro-system and re-introducing their domestic currency, thus enabling Italy to conduct its own monetary policy, suitable for its own policy goals. Meanwhile, policy-makers in a large number of East European and Asian countries continue to favour joining the EMU and adopting the euro at the earliest possible date. Given the most recent events and discussions, and after several years of experience with the euro, it may be a suitable time to reconsider some of the potential benefits and disadvantages for new accession countries to join the euro system in the future.

A comprehensive cost–benefit analysis of joining the euro would include many aspects of monetary union, including the ability to achieve domestic policy goals such as stable prices, stable growth and low unemployment, as well as an assessment of whether the proposed currency union meets the recognized criteria for optimal currency areas. Before engaging in such a comprehensive exercise, however, potential accession countries need to be certain that the current institutional set-up of the ECB is appropriate and likely to achieve its self-declared goals. The question potential new entrants to the European monetary system (EMS) need to ask is whether, given the empirical record (i.e. the relevant historical experience), we can expect the present institutional and legal framework of the ECB to provide a suitable incentive structure for achieving the officially declared goals of stable prices, stable growth and low unemployment. This is the question considered in this chapter. Only if one can answer this question in the affirmative should accession to the euro be contemplated and a full-blown cost–benefit analysis be conducted. It is thus the purpose of this chapter to focus on the institutional design of the ECB in order to reconsider whether the lessons of historical experience have been learned.

2. CENTRAL BANK INDEPENDENCE NOT A REQUIREMENT FOR LOW INFLATION

The Bundesbank is commonly considered one of the most successful central banks in the world, and usually the most successful in Europe. Before introduction of the euro, the Deutsche Mark was the anchor currency of the EMS. After the US dollar, it was the second most widely used currency in the world. After the collapse of the Iron Curtain, it had quickly become the common currency for international trade in Eastern Europe. Several

Eastern European countries adopted explicit currency boards linked to the Mark, while some even adopted the Mark outright as their currency.[2]

Given its generally acknowledged success, it is therefore little wonder that the officially declared goal of a common European currency has been to emulate the Deutsche Mark, and likewise, for the ECB to be modelled on the Bundesbank. The question asked in this chapter is therefore more specifically whether the lessons of the Bundesbank have indeed been learned and reflected appropriately in the structure of the ECB.

The main policy mistake made by central banks is usually considered to be inflation. Many economists have therefore reduced the definition of successful central bank policy to the requirement that there be little inflation. Indeed, during much of the postwar era, German inflation has been modest by international comparison. Defining the success of the Bundesbank solely by inflation, the next step is to identify the reasons for the success of the Bundesbank to achieve low inflation.

A substantial literature makes the claim that the Bundesbank – and indeed any other central bank – mainly achieved low inflation due to its legal independence. This is the reported result of research on the link between central bank independence and inflation (Cukierman, Webb & Neyapti, 1992; Alesina & Summers, 1993; Eijffinger, Schaling, & Hoeberichts, 1998), which often claims that there is significant empirical evidence for a negative correlation between independence and inflation. From this it would appear that the less influence governments can exert over central banks, the more stable the currency.[3] The scientific evidence in favour of central bank independence that was relied upon in the Maastricht Treaty derives from a study commissioned by the European Commission itself (Emerson & Gros, 1992). Published under the name "*One market, one money*," the study purported to demonstrate that central bank independence leads to low inflation.

However, these findings have been subjected to severe criticism by a number of scholars. Forder (1998) finds a large number of severe problems with Emerson and Gros (1992). The study arbitrarily selects a number of countries, then arbitrarily determines the degree of independence of their central banks and then finds that this is correlated with the past inflation performance of the country concerned. There were no robustness tests to determine whether the results vary if a different time period is used for average inflation or if a different selection of countries is chosen.[4] The methodology employed to determine the degree of central bank independence of the countries that were examined is also subject to criticism, such as subjectivity bias. Even leaving aside these criticisms, Forder (1998) confirmed whether the researchers followed their own definitions of independence and hence were at least consistent in their argument – the most basic, necessary but not sufficient requirement for scientific research. Correcting for apparent mistakes made by the studies used in Emerson and Gros (1992), Forder finds that some of the data points from the countries most crucial for obtaining the result suddenly differ. After correction, no statistically significant correlation could be detected between independence and inflation. The conclusion: The data and method used by the economists commissioned by the European Commission do not provide evidence of any apparent relationship between central bank independence and inflation.

Other studies have since confirmed Forder's conclusion. Mangano (1998) shows that the most commonly used indices of central bank independence are subject to a rather large subjectivity bias. It is also often argued (Posen, 1998; Forder, 1998; Hayo, 1998) that central bank independence and the commitment to a low inflation rule is determined jointly and endogenously by social attitudes. Thus independent central banks may be successful in implementing low and stable inflation merely because their independence reflects a social attitude that supports low inflation. Other researchers conducted multi-country tests of the relationship between central bank independence and inflation and concluded that there is no evidence that greater central bank independence results in lower inflation and price stability (Daunfeldt & de Luna, 2003). It must therefore be concluded that central bank independence is not shown to be consistently linked to low inflation.

3. OTHER DEFINITIONS OF SUCCESSFUL CENTRAL BANK POLICY

While it is commonly argued that the success of the Bundesbank is described by its inflation record, it is not clear that this statement has been established scientifically. Inflation is not the only example of central bank policy mistakes. Japan's inflation rate has been lower than German inflation for much of the post-war era. Hence if success is solely defined by low inflation, then the Bank of Japan beat even the highly respected Bundesbank at its game. Japanese consumer price inflation averaged 1.5 per cent in the last 20 years, compared to 2.5 per cent in Germany. Consumer price inflation in the late 1990s even turned negative in Japan, averaging 0.8 per cent during the 1990s (compared to 2.3 per cent in Germany). Yet, few economists would consider Japanese monetary policy a success over the last two decades. Especially for the past 15 years Japan's economy has operated below its potential growth rate, resulting in unemployment. Hence the Bank of Japan is not usually considered a highly successful central bank. This demonstrates that low inflation cannot be the sole requirement to measure the success of central bank policy.

Apart from inflation, there appear to be other serious problems that central bank policy can create – such as recessions. In this case, inflation may be low, but the economy may suffer from large-scale unemployment. Central banks can also create deflation, which increases the debt burden of borrowers, such as house owners with mortgages. Again, by the measure of absence of inflation, a central bank would have been successful.

Central bank policy can also provide fertile grounds for speculative booms and asset inflation. Many economists would argue that central bank policy has been a factor in the rise of equity prices in the Nasdaq market, or the movement of real estate prices in countries as diverse as the USA, UK, Spain, Australia, the Scandinavian countries, Japan and much of Asia. These asset booms are often followed by busts and financial crises.

Systemic banking sector crises, involving significant corporate and financial distress and economic dislocation have occurred in many countries during the past two decades. Caprio and Klingebiel (1999) identified 93 countries in which a systemic financial crisis occurred during the 1980s and 1990s, of which five were in industrial countries and the remainder in the developing world. Well-known examples include the crises among Scandinavian countries in the 1990s, the prolonged Japanese crisis of the 1990s, the Mexican crisis of 1994, the so-called Asian financial crisis, involving Thailand, Korea, Indonesia and Malaysia and crises in transition economies. In all these instances, consumer price inflation may have been low or stable, yet many observers would be reluctant to classify central bank policy as "successful". It is apparent that the mainstream definition of successful central bank policy is derived from an excessively [on] focus on one area of potential central bank error – probably based on the experience of the early 1970s, when expansionary central bank policy was a significant cause of inflation in many countries (Barsky & Kilian, 2000; IMF, 2000; Werner, 2003).

In all these cases, central bank policy must be considered unsuccessful. Returning to the main focus of attention – the success of the Bundesbank – it becomes apparent that its success was not merely characterized by low inflation (as there are other countries, such as Japan, with lower inflation), but by the successful avoidance of boom–bust cycles, asset inflation and deflation. In general, the Bundesbank not only achieved stable prices (including asset prices), but also stable economic growth, with a reasonably high capacity utilization (and hence reasonably close to potential).

German economic growth was fairly high throughout the post-war era, recording 6 per cent in real terms in the 1950s and 1960s, and averaging 2.7 per cent in the 1970s, the 1980s and again the 1990s. Unemployment, while rising especially in the mid-1980s and late 1990s, remained significantly below that of other European countries.[5] This placed Germany among the best performers of all industrialized countries. Moreover, there has neither been a deflationary credit crunch, nor a nationwide asset bubble based on excessive speculation in financial investments in Germany – as happened in so many other countries the world over.

It is this broader definition of success that is relevant in order to identify the institutional features that may have been responsible for this success, and in order to confirm whether these lessons have been learned in the establishment and conduct of the ECB. When defining success more broadly to include stable growth and the avoidance of cycles and financial crises, what have been the institutional features that ensured the Bundesbank's success?

4. INDEPENDENCE AND SUCCESSFUL CENTRAL BANK POLICIES

There is no evidence that the central bank policies leading to asset inflation, financial crises or deflationary recessions over the past twenty years were mainly due to the influence by other players, such as governments. Instead, the relevant monetary policies were taken by central banks that were already largely independent from government interference concerning their credit quantity policies. This suggests that central bank independence alone does not guarantee economic success of monetary policy. For instance, no author in the literature suggests that the US central bank leadership was influenced by political pressure when it increased credit creation steadily throughout the 1990s, thus contributing to asset inflation. Meanwhile, research has indicated that the central banks of Thailand and Korea independently encouraged the commercial banks to increase lending to the real estate sector and set policies that encouraged the corporate sector to borrow from abroad.[6] These independent policy mistakes were followed by excessively tight credit policies, triggering deep recessions.[7] The case study that has been researched in greatest detail is the central bank of the second largest economy in the world: here the latest literature shows that the Bank of Japan acted independently when it forced the Japanese banks to create the 1980s asset bubble (via its informal "window guidance" credit controls) and when it maintained excessively tight quantitative credit policies throughout the 1990s, triggering a prolonged economic slump.[8]

An appropriate analysis of the determinants of the success of German central banking must include the question of when this success began. Abstracting from the temporary "Bank der deutschen Laender", the predecessor of the Bundesbank was the Reichsbank. Unlike the Bundesbank, this German central bank is not generally credited with successful policies. Therefore, a comparative analysis of the institutional design and degree of independence of the Reichsbank and the Bundesbank should yield some insights into the relevance of legal independence for successful monetary policy and the potential identification of other relevant institutional features.

Like the Bundesbank, the Reichsbank was legally independent from the government. This independence existed to a great extent de facto since its foundation in 1875, because the central bank was largely privately owned and accountable to the shareholders.[9] Independence was explicitly written into law in May 1922, and lasted until 1939.[10] In August 1924, a new Banking Law again confirmed the Reichsbank's independence from the government – "but greatly increased the influence over the central bank of Germany's foreign creditors".[11] Thus unlike the Bundesbank, the Reichsbank was also legally independent from any other German institution, including the democratically elected parliament. While the Reichsbank was totally independent from German democratic institutions, it was under the control of the Reparations Commission, which was dominated by Wall Street banks.[12]

Thus we find that the Reichsbank was far more independent than the Bundesbank ever was. Indeed, at the time the Reichsbank was the most independent central bank in history. It is therefore relevant to examine the policy track record of this unprecedently independent central bank. As is well known, this track record is not impressive. The Reichsbank was responsible for one of the world's greatest inflations, namely the hyperinflation of 1922 and 1923 (in the latter year consumer prices rose 2 billion-fold). Subsequently, from the mid-1920s until 1933, the Reichsbank adopted highly restrictive policies and implemented a regime of direct credit controls, which forced banks to implement credit quotas imposed by the central bank. The first phase of credit tightening, between 1924 and 1926, was followed by an even worse credit crunch in 1931. Between 1924 and 1930, the decision-making power over Reichsbank policy was in the hands of one central banker, who therefore also became a politically powerful figure in German history, the economist Dr. Hjalmar Schacht. While Schacht set interest rates, the true monetary policy tool used by him was the quantity of credit, which he used to engage in structural policy, as well as regional policy. In other words, the highly independent Reichsbank used its powers over the creation and allocation of purchasing power in order to pursue political goals which went beyond what would normally be considered the mandate of a central bank's monetary policy. During the phase of tight control over the quantity of credit, from 1924 to 1930, Schacht pursued the goal to accelerate "rationalization", a process referred to by today's central bankers as "restructuring" and structural change.[13]

When US banks withdrew their deposits from German banks in the aftermath of the US credit crunch that began in 1929, the Reichsbank insisted that the banks call in their loans to German industry to pay the US depositors. As had been expected, industry had invested the funds in plant and equipment. The policies of the independent Reichsbank meant that firms had to close down and sell their assets. Overnight, mass unemployment was triggered. Germany was thrown into the great depression. For those who trust that such disastrous policies will not be repeated, it may instructive that the central banks of Thailand, Korea and Indonesia virtually followed the extraordinary policies of the Reichsbank 70 years earlier. In a further parallel to events of the 1920s, international bankers, this time represented by the International Monetary Fund (IMF), not the Reparations Committee, demanded deep structural changes from these Asian nations.

The economic instability that doomed the Weimar Republic was not only due to the substantial separation demands of the victors of the First World War. It was at least as much due to an unaccountable central bank that had excessive powers. Germany's first democracy had little chance, since the powers of the government were severely limited by the fact that an independent and unaccountable central bank set the policies that determined economic growth. Economists concluded that the Reichsbank had become a "second government" (*Nebenregierung*) that acted independently from the elected government.[14] The democratically elected government was the less powerful one.

Being independent from the German government did not prevent the Reichsbank from adopting the misguided policies of the 1920s and early 1930s that ultimately proved fatal for Germany and the world, as they set the stage for the arrival of a pro-growth party, the NSDAP. It remains to be added that the key central banker, having become so powerful due to the institutional design of the Reichsbank, become the single most influential person supporting the candidacy of Adolf Hitler as Chancellor of Germany. This lesson in the benefits of central bank independence serves to remind ourselves that arguing in favour of independent central banks effectively is to say that politicians cannot act in the national interest. Only central bankers, neutral and objective technical experts as they are, can take decisions for the benefit of the people.

No doubt this is a cynical view of democracy as a system. It was also the view taken by the NSDAP, which argued that politicians could not be trusted. It is a view that is not without dangers, as it effectively proposes technocratic totalitarianism. The evidence suggests that this approach is also naïve. The highly acclaimed monetary technician Hjalmar Schacht, for one, used his skills and legal powers to actively and purposely hand Germany over to Adolf Hitler. He was rewarded for his services by being reappointed as head of the Reichsbank from 1933 to 1939 and as powerful minister in Hitler's cabinet.[15]

5. THE INSTITUTIONAL FEATURE RESPONSIBLE FOR THE SUCCESS OF THE BUNDESBANK

This analysis of the legal predecessor of the Bundesbank helps in the quest to identify the institutional features that rendered the Bundesbank successful. Considering the official goal of monetary policy, it must be recognized that legally the Bundesbank was not just required to work towards price stability. In 1967, 10 years after the founding of the Bundesbank, parliament passed the Stability and Growth Act, which clearly set out the objectives of Bundesbank policy as "price stability, a high level of employment, external equilibrium, steady and adequate economic growth". Put simply, the law mandated the Bundesbank to produce low inflation and stable growth. This was also what the Bundesbank had in mind when it made its policies. Bundesbank President Klasen, for instance, is said to have "accorded economic growth equal priority to monetary stability" (Holtfrerich, 1999, p. 194).

The Bundesbank is often thought to have been the most independent central bank in the world. In reality, the independence of the Bundesbank was clearly limited. Firstly, central bank independence was not enshrined in the constitution and was thus not irrevocable. Moreover, the Bundesbank was only given "independence from government instructions". When this was formulated, the law makers, presumably remembering the lessons from

Weimar, explicitly warned that this phrase "of course must not be interpreted to mean that the central bank become a state within the state".[16] While being independent from direct instruction from the government, the Bundesbank was *not* independent from Parliament, which could pass laws or give instructions if it so wished. Moreover, it was not independent from other institutions of the Federal Republic, but was subject to German laws, was accountable to the federal audit agency (*Bundesrechnungshof*) and the decisions of German law courts.

But even the independence from the government was limited, for the Bundesbank Law also said explicitly that "it is the duty of the Bundesbank ... while fulfilling its tasks to support the general economic policy of the Federal Government". And there is virtually no time period when the government's main policy aim was not to achieve satisfactory economic growth. Despite the inability to give direct instructions to the central bank, government representatives could join the policy board meetings of the Bundesbank and expect the bank to support their policy objectives of near-full employment. As legal experts point out, if the government placed a different emphasis among the goals of the Stability and Growth Act than the Bundesbank – for instance by pursuing economic and employment growth – then as long as price stability was not neglected, the Bundesbank was obliged to follow the policies of the government. Ignoring the goals of the Stability and Growth Act would have been illegal.[17]

There were other incentives embedded in the legal structure that helped make the Bundesbank successful. For instance, the Bundesbank had a decentralized structure that included representatives of the German states in the policy decision-making, which were appointed by the Bundesrat. Moreover, each regional representative was in turn advised by representatives of the various occupations, including trade unions.[18] As a result, the decision-making process of the Bundesbank was usually well balanced, reflected the various parts and regions of society, had to take government policy into consideration and was subject to legal checks and balances.

This multi-faceted accountability and consensus orientation produced the Bundesbank's successful monetary policy. There are many instances where the government would have liked it to stimulate the economy more, but the Bundesbank refused. The downfall of three chancellors – Ludwig Erhard in 1966, Kurt Georg Kiesinger in 1969 and Helmut Schmidt in 1982 – was directly or indirectly linked to tight Bundesbank policies.[19] Often the government, not the Bundesbank turned out to be right.[20] But ultimately there were political limits on the Bundesbank to act alone against the interests of the population.[21]

Ironically, it must therefore be concluded that the success of the Bundesbank was less due to its independence, but instead to its subtle *dependence* on the other elements of the democratic system. The legal design rendered the central bank highly accountable for its policies, and it was always clear that these policies could not solely consist of producing low inflation, but had to reflect the goal of stable economic growth. By contrast, the Reichsbank's failure was due to its excessive independence without accountability and recourse. Thus comparing the Reichsbank and the Bundesbank, we find that the *reduction* in central bank independence and the introduction of accountability and dependence on democratic institutions that was undertaken in the post-war period greatly enhanced the performance of central bank policy. Contrary to popular opinion, the Bundesbank's success was due to its comparative *lack* of independence. Thus in order to determine whether the ECB's institutional setting provides for the ingredients of success, as identified from German monetary history, one must determine whether the ECB is similarly accountable to the people to implement the twin goals of low inflation and stable growth.

6. RESURRECTION OF THE REICHSBANK

With the introduction of the ECB system, the German government has lost its influence over monetary policy. With the creation of the ECB, the Bundesbank Law was also revised. In the new Bundesbank Law, the German central bank not only became subject to the ECB instructions, but it is also no longer required to support the general policies of the government.[22] Neither is the ECB required to support the policies of the German government. It is, however, required to support the "general policy goals of the European Union (EU)". The Maastricht Treaty, which defines the role of the ECB, says that the ECB has a primary mandate to maintain stable prices. It also says that, "where it is possible without compromising the mandate to maintain price stability", the ECB will also support the "general economic policy of the EU", which includes, among others, "steady, non-inflationary and environmentally friendly growth" and "a high level of employment".[23]

This could be interpreted to mean that the ECB, like the Bundesbank, has to work towards the twin goals of low inflation and stable economic growth. However, the emphasis is explicitly on price stability. Moreover, unlike in the case of the Bundesbank, there are virtually no checks and balances on the actions of the ECB. It is therefore practically impossible for anyone, for instance a government, parliament or even the (unelected) EU Commission to enforce goals besides price stability. Unlike the Bundesbank, the ECB is not only independent from the government, but also from parliaments, democratically elected assemblies or other institutions of or within the EU. Moreover, the Maastricht Treaty, defining the ECB's status, includes the unprecedented clause that no democratic institution within the EU is even allowed to *attempt* to influence the policies of the ECB, without acting illegally.[24] This is unprecedented among contemporary democracies.

In addition, the ECB is far less transparent than the Bundesbank was. For instance, the deliberations of its decision-making bodies are secret.[25] It is not required to publish the detailed information about its transactions (this requirement was also abandoned for the Bundesbank with the establishment of the ECB). While it has the power to obtain data from any bank or company in the EU, the ECB is not obliged to publicize such or any specific statistics.

Not surprisingly, the ECB's statutes are already being interpreted as virtually exclusively aimed at price stability. Wim Duisenberg, when he was head of the ECB's predecessor organization, the EMI, told us that he favours "a single monetary policy which strictly aims at price stability in the euro area as a whole".[26]

7. CONCLUSIONS

The ECB is far more independent than the Bundesbank has ever been. It is also far more independent than the US central bank, the Federal Reserve, whose legal status is far weaker and which is directly accountable to Congress and the government.[27] We find that the ECB is the least accountable central bank among advanced nations. Its degree of independence has only one precedence: the Reichsbank, a central bank with one of history's most disastrous records.

One must conclude that there is a danger that the incentive structure of the staff at the ECB is not sufficient to guarantee optimal economic policies. This is worrying. It suggests that the lessons of German history were not interpreted correctly and the ECB was created on the wrong foundations. Instead of adopting those features that made the Bundesbank successful – accountability and interdependence with other democratic institutions – the creators of the ECB revived the corpse of the unaccountable

Reichsbank. The "human wisdom nurtured by history" (cited by Bank of Japan governor Mieno (1994) to support central bank independence, see Bank of Japan, 1994) tells us that it is dangerous to hand vast powers without checks and accountability into the hands of a few unelected officials. Human wisdom is not to revive the Reichsbank. But the creation of the ECB seems to have done that. These are the issues that any country considering accession to the euro must debate and analyse appropriately before coming to a final decision.

Another issue that remains under-researched concerns the details of monetary policy implementation of the ECB. While officially monetary policy is set via interest rates, it is apparent that despite the same interest rate for all member countries of euroland, very diverse quantity policies are implemented under the instruction of the ECB by the various national central banks. For instance, in 2001 and 2002 the Bundesbank, under orders the ECB, reduced its credit creation by a record amount, thereby precipitating a recession in Germany, while at the same time the central banks in Ireland and Spain increased their credit creation. While interest rates are identical, information value is gained from scrutiny of the quantitative credit policies. Furthermore, recent research in macroeconomics suggests that due to imperfect information and consequent pervasive market rationing, quantities may in any case be more relevant for observers, forecasters and policy-makers (Werner, 2005). Given these open questions, potential entrants would be well advised to engage in further research concerning these issues, before giving up economic control to the ECB.

Economic theory suggests that for potential new entrants to the EMU a comprehensive assessment of the costs and benefits is advisable. Before such comprehensive analysis can be conducted, it is necessary to determine whether the current institutional design of the ECB and control over the euro follows the best practice that empirical evidence would suggest, based on the experience of a successful central bank, such as Germany's. This paper first considered the definition of "successful" monetary policy, and then engaged in comparative institutional analysis in order to identify the true lessons of German central banking experience and whether these have been heeded in the design of the ECB. The conclusion is devastating: the ECB does not follow the best practice suggested by the experience of the Bundesbank. Instead, it is in line with the institutional design of one of the least successful central banks in history, the German Reichsbank. This sounds a strong note of caution, as a number of important issues require further research, before a hasty decision is made by any country about handing over monetary policy control to the ECB.

NOTES

1. The author is grateful to Dirk Bezemer and James Forder for valuable comments and active contribution to this research program. Research assistance by Jim Mac-Donald and support by the Profit Research Center Ltd., Tokyo, are gratefully acknowledged. This paper draws heavily on an older version reported in Werner (2003).

2. The success of the Bundesbank was so obvious that many observers called its planned abolition a "puzzle": "The Deutsche Mark became the key currency of the EMS and one of the world's major currencies; by the 1980s it was second to the US dollar in terms of the proportion of world trade that was invoiced in it. That so much was achieved in such a relatively short time makes the history of the currency remarkable. What is perhaps even more remarkable is its future. That a currency which achieved so much, and which was for that reason so popular with the citizens of the country which used it is to disappear into EMU in 2002 is, at the least, surprising. An observer who simply saw what had happened ... would be as at a loss to understand ... One could not but be surprised that a currency at once a cause and a symbol of Germany's recovery should be abandoned in a democracy." Capie and Wood (2001).

3. Klaus Stern argues that it is "right" to give independence to central banks, for "never has a central bank destroyed a currency on its own volition" (Stern, 1998, p. 183). See also other contributors to Baltensperger and Deutsche Bundesbank (1999), such as Neumann, who asserts that "monetary stability cannot be maintained unless governments are prevented from gaining access to the country's money supply", p. 275.

4. For instance, the study failed to include many members of the EU, such as Austria, Luxembourg, Portugal, Ireland and Greece.

5. German unemployment averaged 5.3 per cent between 1975 and 1997, compared to 9.1 per cent for France, 7.1 per cent in Italy and 8.7 per cent in the UK. Data according to the US Bureau of Labour Statistics.

6. See Werner (2000a, b).

7. This time they were influenced – by the IMF. See the letters of Intent.

8. Werner (1998, 2002a, 2005).

9. Rudolf von Havenstein, for instance, became President of the Reichsbank in 1908 and strongly defended the principle of central bank independence. See Stern (1998).

10. In January 1939, the Reichsbank Law was changed, the central bank renamed Deutsche Reichsbank, and made directly accountable and subordinate to the Reich government.

11. Marsh (1992). Article 1 of the Banking Law said that "The Reichsbank is a bank independent form the Reich government".

12. Article 14 gave half of the seats on the Reichsbank's 14 strong general council to foreign members from Britain, France, Italy, Belgium, America, Holland and Switzerland. Article 19 established a Commissioner for the note issue, who was required to be a foreigner. The appointment of all of the members, including the German ones, fell under the sway of the Reparations Commission and the banks that controlled it (Marsh, 1992). This commission had no mandate to operate in the interest of the German people. To the contrary, its job was to efficiently extract the Reparations imposed on Germany by the Treaty of Versailles. Officially the payments were to the UK and France. But Britain had been vastly indebted to US Wall Street banks. Thus the Reparations Commission was staffed with members from JP Morgan and other US banks and the reparations payments were dollar denominated.

13. For details, see Werner (2002b).

14. See, for instance, Bosch (1927); Dalberg (1926); Mueller (1973).

15. For an introduction to Schacht's activities to help Hitler into power, see, for instance, Marsh (1992); Weitz (1997); Werner (2003).

16. Stern (1998), p. 186.

17. See, for instance, Stern (1998), ibid.

18. The Bundesbank had two decision-making bodies, the Zentralbankrat, consisting of the Direktorium and the Presidents of the state central banks, which decides policy; and the Direktorium, consisting of the President, Vice-President and up to six other members, which is responsible for implementing this policy. While the Direktorium is suggested by the government, the Presidents of the state central banks are proposed by the Bundesrat.

19. Marsh (1992).

20. For instance, in 1972, when Economics and Finance Minister Karl Schiller correctly argued that the excessive credit creation by the USA and massive flight from the dollar should be countered by revaluing the Deutsche Mark, the Bundesbank under President Klasen refused. The highly popular and hitherto successful minister was forced out of the government and resigned. A year later the Bundesbank took exactly his advice. See, for instance, Marsh (1992).

21. As was clearly seen with German monetary union, the details of which the Bundesbank clearly disagreed with. With Karl-Otto Poehl's resignation it seemed that, for once, a Bundesbank president was the one to resign as a result of a disagreement with the government, not the chancellor or finance minister.

22. The new paragraph in the Bundesbank Law says that the Bundesbank will only support the general economic policy of the government as far as this is possible with its task as part of the European System of Central Banks (ESCB).

23. Protocol no. 3 on the ESCB and the ECB, as well as the Maastricht Treaty, Article 105, says that "the primary objective of the ESCB shall be to maintain price stability. Without prejudice to the objective of price stability, the ESCB shall support the general economic policies in the Community with a view to contributing to the achievement of the objectives of the Community as laid down in Article 2. The ESCB shall act in accordance with the principle of an open market economy with free competition, favoring an efficient allocation of resources, and in compliance with the principles set out in Article 3a." The goals mentioned in Article 3a of the Maastricht Treaty are: stable prices, healthy public finances and general monetary conditions, as well as a sustainable current account balance. Article 2 lists as purpose of the EU, the harmonious and balanced development of the economy, steady, non-inflationary and environmentally friendly growth, a high degree of convergence of economic performance, a high level of employment, a high degree of social security, the raising of the standard of living and the quality of life and the economic and social cohesion and solidarity between member states.

24. Article 107 establishes an independent and unaccountable apparatus: "When exercising the powers and carrying out the tasks and duties conferred upon them by this Treaty and the Statute of the ESCB, neither the ECB, nor a national central bank, nor any member of their decision-making bodies shall seek or take instructions from Community institutions or bodies, from any government of a Member State or from any other body. The Community institutions and bodies and the governments of the Member States undertake to respect this principle and not to seek to influence

114   RICHARD A. WERNER

the members of the decision-making bodies of the ECB or of the national central banks in the performance of their tasks.

25. Article 108a, 2 says: The ECB may decide to publish its decisions, recommendations and opinions. It does not mention the possibility of publicizing the content of the deliberations itself, only the results.

26. "... I am convinced that the risks [of Monetary Union] can be contained, if not fully avoided, by a high degree of sustainable convergence of those countries which participate in Monetary Union, by a single monetary policy which strictly aims at price stability in the euro area as a whole, by stability-oriented economic and fiscal policies and by sound wage developments in Stage Three." There is no hint that monetary policy will aim at both price stability and stable economic growth, as the Bundesbank did. He also said that he interpreted the mentioning of the "general economic policies" of the EU as an opportunity, but not an obligation for the ECB to give advice. He makes no mention of active support. "Furthermore, one may argue that Article 105.1 of the Treaty gives the ESCB the opportunity, if not the obligation, to support the general economic policies in the Community also by giving appropriate advice to those responsible for these policies and that this advice should be given with a view to supporting price stability and an open market economy with free competition, favouring an efficient allocation of resources." (Duisenberg, 1998).

27. Since the US constitution explicitly assigns the right to issue money to the government, a number of scholars even dispute the constitutionality of the Federal Reserve itself. This line of reasoning is also supported by well-known US economists. See, for instance, the writings of the economist Murray Rothbard, members of the so-called Austrian School of Economics and the Ludwig von Mises Institute (http://www.mises.org/).

REFERENCES

Alesina, A., & Summers, L. (1993). Central bank independence and macroeconomic performance: Some comparative evidence. *Journal of Money, Credit and Banking, 25*, 151–162.
Baltensperger, E., & Deutsche Bundesbank (Eds) (1999). *Fifty years of the Deutsche Mark: Central bank and the currency in Germany since 1948*. Oxford: Oxford University Press.
Barsky, R. B., & Kilian, L. (2000). *A monetary explanation of the great stagflation of the 1970s*. Mimeographed. University of Michigan. NBER Working Paper no 7547.
Bosch, W. (1927). *Die Epochen der Kreditrestriktionspolitik der Deutschen Reichsbank 1924/26*. Stuttgart.
Capie, F., & Wood, G. (2001). The birth, life and demise of a currency: 50 years of the Deutsche Mark. *The Economic Journal, 111*, F449–F461.
Caprio, J., & Klingebiel, D. (1999). *Episodes of systemic and borderline financial crises*. Mimeographed. World Bank, October, Washington, DC.
Cukierman, A., Webb, S. B., & Neyapti, B. (1992). Measuring the independence of central banks and its effects on policy outcomes. *World Bank Economic Review, 6*, 353–398.
Dalberg, R. (1926). *Deutsche Währungs- und Kreditpolitik, 1923–26*. Berlin: R. Hobbing.
Daunfeldt, S.-O., & de Luna, X. (2003). Central bank independence and price stability: Evidence from 23 OECD-countries. Paper presented at the *Eighth international conference*

on macroeconomic analysis and international finance. 27–29 May 2004, University of Crete, Crete, Greece. Available at: http://www.econ.umu.se/ues/ues589.pdf

Duisenberg, W. F. (1998). EMU – *How to grasp the opportunities and avoid the risks.* Speech delivered by the President of the European Monetary Institute, at the Forum de l'Expansion, Paris, 22 January 1998. See http://www.ecb.int/emi/key/key18.htm

Eijffinger, S., Schaling, E., & Hoeberichts, M. (1998). Central bank independence: A sensitivity analysis. *European Journal of Political Economy, 14,* 73–88.

Emerson, M., & Gros, D. (1992). *One market, one money.* Oxford: Oxford University Press.

Forder, J. (1998). The case for an independent European central bank: A reassessment of evidence and sources. *European Journal of Political Economy, 14,* 53–71.

Hayo, B. (1998). Inflation culture, central bank independence and price stability. *European Journal of Political Economy, 14,* 241–263.

Holtfrerich, C.-L. (1999). In: E. Baltensperger & Deutsche Bundesbank (Eds), *Fifty Years of the Deutsche Mark: Central Bank and the Currency in Germany since 1948.* Oxford: Oxford University Press.

IMF (2000). *The impact of higher oil prices on the global economy, staff report.* Available at: http://www.imf.org/external/pubs/ft/oil/2000/oilrep.PDF

Mangano, G. (1998). Measuring central bank independence: A tale of subjectivity and of its consequences. *Oxford Economic Papers, 50,* 468–492.

Marsh, D. (1992). *The Bundesbank: The bank that rules Europe.* London: Heinemann.

Mieno, Y. (1994). The conduct of monetary policy by the Bank of Japan. *Bank of Japan Quarterly Bulletin,* August, Bank of Japan, Tokyo, pp. 6–12.

Mueller, H. (1973). *Die Zentralbank als eine Nebenregierung.* Westdeutscher Verlag Opladen.

Posen, A. (1998). Central bank independence and disinflationary credibility: A missing link? *Oxford Economic Papers, 50,* 335–359.

Stern, K. (1998). In: Deutsche Bundesbank (Ed.) (1998). *Fuenfzig Jahre Deutsche Mark. Notenbank und Waehrung in Deutschland seit 1948.* Muenchen: Verlag C. H. Beck.

Weitz, J. (1997). *Hitler's banker.* Boston: Little, Brown and Company.

Werner, R. A. (1998). Bank of Japan window guidance and the creation of the bubble. In: F. Rodao & A. Lopez Santos (Eds), *El Japon Contemporaneo.* Salamanca: University of Salamanca Press. Also available from www.profitresearch.co.jp

Werner, R. A. (2000a). Indian macroeconomic management: At the crossroads between government and markets. In: *Rising to the challenge in Asia: A study of financial markets, Vol. 5, India.* Manila: Asian Development Bank, September. Also available from www.profitresearch.co.jp

Werner, R. A. (2000b). Macroeconomic management in Thailand: The policy-induced crisis. In: Ghon S. Rhee (Ed.), *Rising to the challenge in Asia: A study of financial markets, Vol. 11, Thailand.* Manila: Asian Development Bank, September. Also available from www.profitresearch.co.jp

Werner, R. A. (2002a). Monetary policy implementation in Japan: What they say vs. what they do. *Asian Economic Journal, 16*(2), 111–151.

Werner, R. A. (2002b). A reconsideration of the rationale for bank-centered economic systems and the effectiveness of directed credit policies in the light of Japanese evidence. *The Japanese economy, 30*(3), 3–45. New York: M.E. Sharpe.

Werner, R. A. (2003). *Princes of the Yen, Japan's central bankers and the transformation of the economy.* New York: M.E. Sharpe.

Werner, R. A. (2005). *New paradigm in macroeconomics.* Basingstoke: Palgrave Macmillan.

A COMPARATIVE STUDY OF BANK EFFICIENCY IN CENTRAL AND EASTERN EUROPE: THE ROLE OF FOREIGN OWNERSHIP

Peter Zajc

1. INTRODUCTION

The processes of liberalisation, globalisation and integration have brought new dynamics into banking markets. In an increasingly competitive environment, banks have been forced to refocus their strategies and examine their performance, because their survival in the 21st century will depend on efficiency (Denizer & Tarimcilar, 2001). In recent years, therefore, bank efficiency has received wide attention, and researchers have developed an extensive array of sophisticated methods and tools to estimate efficiency.

Research on the role of foreign bank entry and its impact on bank efficiency is of interest not only to academics, but also to policy makers, bank creditors and owners and managers.[1] In general, bank efficiency studies address two major issues (Lovell, 1993): the cost (and profit) efficiency of banks, and the identification of variables that can explain differences in efficiency across banks. In this chapter, I concentrate on the

Emerging European Financial Markets: Independence and Integration Post-Enlargement
International Finance Review, Volume 6, 117–156
Copyright © 2006 by Elsevier Ltd.
All rights of reproduction in any form reserved
ISSN: 1569-3767/doi:10.1016/S1569-3767(05)06006-1

link between bank efficiency and bank ownership in Central and Eastern European countries (henceforth the CEECs). In contrast to the European Union (EU) countries where bank ownership is relatively stable and the share of foreigners is low, bank ownership has changed dramatically in the CEECs in the last decade, and foreigners have aquired a majority share of the banking sector in most of the CEECs.

The objective of this chapter is to estimate the cost efficiency of banks in six CEECs during the period 1995–2000: the Czech Republic, Estonia, Hungary, Poland, Slovakia and Slovenia. In particular, I focus on exploring differences in average efficiencies between domestic and foreign banks where the groups of domestic and foreign banks change over time, whether changes in ownership affect average efficiency, and whether the magnitude of foreign bank presence in the banking sector has an impact on efficiency.

The remainder of the chapter is structured as follows. Section 2 is a short literature overview that highlights the development of the efficiency framework and discusses the body of literature on bank efficiency. The latter is organised along three lines: bank efficiency studies for CEECs, cross-country studies of bank efficiency, and studies of bank efficiency and ownership. In Section 3, I outline the theory of efficiency, discuss the relevant estimation techniques and functional forms of production functions, and present the two models used in my study in detail. This is followed in Section 4 by a discussion of the hypothesis testing to be conducted. Finally, estimation results for cost efficiency as well as for an extensive set of efficiency correlates are presented in Section 5. In Section 6, I summarise and conclude.

2. LITERATURE REVIEW

Studies of the performance of banks often focus on the presentation of financial ratios and the analysis of scale and scope economies.[2] Molyneux, Altunbas, and Gardener (1996) note that there are other aspects of efficiency such as technical and allocative efficiency. These two components of efficiency were first identified by Farrell (1957). The concept of X-efficiency encompasses both allocative and technical efficiency.[3] X-efficiency was introduced by Leibenstein (1966), and reflects differences in managerial ability to control costs and/or maximise profits (Molyneux et al., 1996). The dominance of X-inefficiency over scale and scope inefficiency in banking has been recognised for quite some time, but researchers have only recently turned their focus to studying X-inefficiency. This new direction of research has brought about several approaches and methods of analysis. Molyneux et al. (1996) indicate that there is no agreement on how to measure and model X-inefficiency. The key issue is how to measure or determine the efficiency frontier.

Although the body of literature on bank efficiency is substantial, it is heavily geared towards studies of US banks, followed by European banks as a distant second. There are some studies of bank efficiency in less developed countries, but their number is relatively small. In their survey, Berger and Humphrey (1997) list only eight efficiency studies for developing countries, of which none deals with the CEECs. Efficiency studies for CEEC banks, still small in number, have predominantly been published as working papers, mimeos and dissertations, and very few have appeared in refereed journals.

Another area of bank efficiency research that has not been intensively explored yet is bank efficiency across countries. In their survey, Berger and Humphrey (1997) list only five inter-country comparisons at the time of their study. They note that cross-country studies are difficult to perform and interpret because regulatory and economic environments differ, and because there are differences in the quality of banking services across countries that are difficult to account for. The first cross-country study was the comparative analysis of bank efficiency in Finland, Norway and Sweden by Berg, Forsund, Hjalmarsson, and Suominen (1993), who found Swedish banks to be the most efficient in the pooled sample.

As to cross-country studies for transition economies, Grigorian and Manole (2002) estimate bank efficiency using the data envelopment analysis (DEA) technique, and include a dummy variable for foreign ownership. They divide the countries included in the study into three groups: Central Europe, South-Eastern Europe and the Commonwealth of Independent States. Overall, banks from Central Europe are found to be most efficient. Another study on transition economies by Yildirim and Philippatos (2002) uses stochastic frontier analysis (SFA) as well as the distribution-free approach (DFA) to estimate bank efficiency for 12 CEECS. They find cost efficiency to be higher than profit efficiency in CEECs on average.

A branch of bank efficiency literature focuses on the effect of ownership on bank efficiency. One aspect of ownership that these studies consider is the effect of different organisational forms. Cebenoyan, Cooperman, and Register (1993) study US saving and loan associations (S&Ls) in 1988 and expect to find stock S&Ls more efficient than mutual S&Ls because under the general agency theory, stock companies have better monitoring characteristics. They find, however, that S&L efficiency is not significantly related to the form of ownership. Mester (1993) also investigates efficiency of US mutual and stock S&Ls, and finds that on average stock S&Ls are less efficient than mutually owned ones. A second aspect of ownership is foreign versus domestic ownership, which in recent years has received increasing attention. Hasan and Hunter (1996) study the cost and profit efficiency of Japanese and domestic banks in the US. For the 1984–1989 period they find that Japanese banks operating in the US were less cost and profit efficient that their US-owned counterparts. Chang, Hasan, and Hunter (1998) perform a comparative study of efficiency of foreign and US-owned commercial banks operating in the USA. Their results indicate that in the US foreign banks are less cost efficient than domestic ones. In one of the few studies analysing the role of foreign ownership in a cross-country comparison, Berger, DeYoung, Genay, and Udell (2000) undertake an efficiency analysis of foreign and domestic banks in 13 countries. The average cost and profit efficiency of domestic banks is higher than foreign banks, which are found to be less efficient.

Once again, the body of literature on the effects of bank ownership on efficiency for CEECs is quite limited. Hasan and Marton (2000) study bank efficiency in Hungary and the performance of foreign banks based on the extent of foreign involvement. Banks with a higher percentage of foreign ownership turn out to be more efficient than those with a lower percentage. Nikiel and Opiela (2002) analyse the performance of domestic and foreign banks in Poland. Domestic private- and state-owned banks have on average higher profit and lower cost efficiency than foreign banks. This may seem unusual at first glance, but the authors explain it by the fact that many domestic banks operate in niche markets in which they enjoy a degree of market power.

This short literature overview reveals three aspects of bank efficiency that deserve further research. First, there is ample room for bank efficiency research in the transition CEECs. Second, comparisons of bank efficiency across countries call for and warrant further research (Berger & Humphrey, 1997; Maudos, Pastor, Perez, & Quesada, 2002). Third, the link between foreign ownership and bank efficiency deserves more attention. An analysis encompassing these three dimensions remains to be done.

3. THEORY

There are two types of *efficiency*: technical and allocative. *Technical efficiency* is based on input and output quantities and reflects the ability of a firm to obtain the maximum output from given inputs. *Allocative efficiency* incorporates prices as well, and reveals whether a firm is using inputs in optimal proportions given their relative prices and the production technology. Technical and allocative efficiency combined provide a measure of *total* or *overall economic efficiency*.[4] Although the concept of X-efficiency was introduced by Leibenstein in 1966, it has been used in bank efficiency research only since the 1990s. Several authors applied the concept of X-efficiency in respect of banks without using the term explicitly (e.g. Ferrier & Lovell, 1990; Berger & Humphrey, 1991). The term X-efficiency was first explicitly introduced in bank efficiency research by Berger, Hunter, and Timme (1993).

3.1. Estimation Techniques

The analysis of efficiency assumes that the production function of the fully efficient bank is known, which is never the case in practice (Coelli, Rao, & Battese, 1998). Farrell (1957) proposed that the production function could be estimated from the sample data applying either a non-parametric (mathematical programming) or a parametric (econometric) approach.[5] Berger and Humphrey (1997) surveyed 130 studies on the efficiency of financial institutions, and found that approximately half of the studies apply non-parametric estimation techniques while the other half apply one of the parametric techniques.

The two most commonly used non-parametric efficiency estimation techniques are the DEA and the free disposable hull (FDH); the latter being a special case of DEA. DEA is a linear programming technique in which the DEA frontier is constructed as piecewise linear combinations that connect the set of best practice observations. Although non-parametric approaches have been widely applied, these techniques have some drawbacks. They focus on technological optimisation rather than economic optimisation, they ignore prices and they provide information on technical efficiency while ignoring allocative efficiency. Non-parametric techniques generally do not allow for random error in the data; that is, they do not consider measurement error and luck as factors affecting efficiency estimates (Berger & Mester, 1997). Thus, any deviation from the frontier is assumed to reflect inefficiency. If measurement errors are present, they would be reflected in a change of measured efficiency, and as pointed out by Berger and Humphrey (1997), any of these errors in one of the banks on the efficient frontier may change the measured efficiency of all banks. On the other hand, DEA does not require an explicit specification of the functional form of the underlying production function, and it therefore imposes less structure on the frontier.

The three major parametric techniques are the SFA, the DFA and the thick frontier approach (TFA). These methods focus on the difference or distance from the best practice bank (efficient frontier); that is, this distance reflects the inefficiency effect u_i. For example, if costs are higher than those of the best practice bank, then the bank is cost inefficient. The key characteristic of the non-parametric techniques is that they a priori impose an assumption on how random errors can be separated from inefficiency. Thus, they make an arbitrary distinction between randomness and inefficiency, which is the main drawback and criticism of the parametric techniques (Schure & Wagenvoort, 1999). The estimation techniques differ in the way they handle the composite error term $v_i + u_i$; that is, in the way they disentangle the inefficiency term u_i from the random error term v_i. The SFA is based on the assumption that the random error v_i is symmetrically distributed (usually normal standard distribution), and that the inefficiency term u_i follows an asymmetric (one-sided) distribution (usually a half-normal distribution). Further details on the SFA are presented later in the chapter.

3.2. Functional Forms

The analysis of bank efficiency based on one of the parametric techniques requires a selection of an appropriate functional form for the cost function. Ideally, a functional form should be sufficiently flexible to accommodate different production structures, and should permit the imposition of constraints or properties consistent with the assumed optimising behaviour (Coelli et al., 1998). Although a variety of functional forms have been used in efficiency analyses, three forms stand out as the most frequently applied: the Cobb–Douglas, the translog and the Fourier-flexible functional forms. The *Cobb–Douglas form* is a simple functional form and is easy to estimate. However, it imposes restrictive properties such as constant returns to scale. Schure and Wagenvoort (1999) apply the Cobb–Douglas form in their analysis of efficiency of European banks. The *transcendental logarithmic functional form*, for short the *translog functional form*, belongs to the group of flexible forms. It is less restrictive than the Cobb–Douglas form, but is mathematically more demanding and leads to potential problems with multicolinearity and degrees of freedom. It is linear in parameters and a good second-order Taylor approximation of a general cost (production) function. The *Fourier-flexible form* is more flexible than the translog form and it is a global approximation to many cost and profit functions. The specification of the Fourier-flexible form is, however, more complex.

Some authors suggest that applying a single translog function to a sample of banks varying substantially in size and product mix might create a specification bias (Yildirim & Philippatos, 2002). However, Berger and Mester (1997) report that the use of the Fourier-flexible form does not produce results significantly different from those obtained using a translog form. In the empirical analysis that follows, I use the translog functional form of the cost function.

3.3. Stochastic Frontier Estimation Technique[6]

The concept of efficiency measurement assumes that the production function of the fully efficient firm or firms is known. As this is not the case in practice, one has to estimate the production function. There is a general distinction between deterministic and stochastic frontier production functions (Kaparakis, Miller, & Noulas, 1994). The deterministic frontier, presented in Eq. (1) envelops all sample observations:

$$y_i = x_i \beta - u_i \quad i = 1, \ldots, N \tag{1}$$

where y_i is the logarithm of the maximum output obtainable from x_i, x_i is a vector of logarithms of inputs used by the ith firm, β is an unknown parameter vector to be estimated, and u_i is a non-negative random variable associated with inefficiency.

The observed output y_i is bounded above by the non-stochastic (deterministic) quantity $\exp(x_i\beta)$. The main drawback of the deterministic frontier is that it does not account for measurement errors and statistical noise problems, so all deviations from the frontier are assumed to reflect inefficiency. This can seriously distort the measurement of efficiency. For an application of the deterministic frontier to bank efficiency analysis see English, Grosskopf, Hayes, and Yaisawarng (1993).

The stochastic frontier production function avoids some of the problems associated with the deterministic frontier. Aigner, Lovell, and Schmidt (1977), and Meeusen and van den Broeck (1977) independently proposed a stochastic frontier function with a composite error term, which allows the production function to vary stochastically:

$$y_i = x_i \beta + e_i \quad i = 1, \ldots, N \tag{2}$$

where y_i is the logarithm of the maximum output obtainable from x_i, x_i is a vector of logarithms of inputs used by the ith firm, β is the unknown parameter vector to be estimated, and e_i is the error term.

The error term e_i is composed of two parts:

$$e_i = v_i - u_i \quad i = 1, \ldots, N \tag{3}$$

where v_i is the measurement error and other random factors, and u_i is the inefficiency component.

The v_i component captures the statistical noise; that is, measurement error and other random or uncontrollable factors (e.g. luck, machine performance and labour strikes). Aigner et al. (1977) assume that the v_i are independently and identically distributed normal random variables with mean zero and a constant variance: $v_i \sim$ i.i.d. $N(0, \sigma_v^2)$. The u_i component is a non-negative random variable accounting for technical inefficiency in production. It measures technical inefficiency in the sense that it measures the shortfall of output from its maximal possible value given by the stochastic frontier $x_i\beta + v_i$ (Jondrow, Knox Lovell, Materov, & Schmidt, 1982). This shortfall, or (more generally) deviations from the frontier, is due to the factors that are under control of management, as opposed to the v_i, which are not under control of the management (Chang et al., 1998). u_i are distributed either i.i.d. exponential or half-normal.

The model presented in Eqs. (2) and (3) is called the stochastic frontier production function because the output values are bounded above by the stochastic variable $\exp(x_i\beta + v_i)$.[7] As the random error v_i can take positive as well as negative values, the stochastic frontier outputs vary around the deterministic frontier $\exp(x_i\beta)$. The stochastic frontier model has been widely used by economists, but has its shortcomings. The main problem is the a priori distributional assumption of u_i.[8] This assumption is necessary in order to use the maximum likelihood method to solve for the parameters. In general, the stochastic frontier model can be estimated by using the corrected ordinary least squares (OLS), but maximum likelihood is asymptotically more efficient.

To estimate stochastic cost frontiers, I use the computer programme FRONTIER Version 4.1, developed by Tim Coelli.[9] The programme executes a three-step procedure to estimate the maximum likelihood estimates of parameters of the stochastic frontier function. First, it estimates the parameters of the frontier function (production or cost function) using OLS. Second, it evaluates the likelihood function for a number of values of gamma (γ) between 0 and 1 (see Eq. (4) below for the definition of γ), and it sets the frontier function parameters to OLS values. All other parameters are set to zero at this stage. Third, the best values from the second step are used as starting values for a Davidon–Fletcher–Powell Quasi-Newton iterative maximisation routine, which gives the final maximum likelihood estimates. These estimates are further used to calculate efficiency.

The mean of the distribution of the u_i (the mean technical inefficiency) is easy to compute by calculating the average of e_i estimates, and the statistical noise component v_i averages out (recall that it is assumed to be distributed with mean zero). However, the more interesting aspect is to compute technical inefficiency for individual firms. The decomposition of the error term into its two components, v_i and u_i, remained unresolved until Jondrow et al. (1982) proposed how to calculate observation (firm) specific estimates of inefficiency conditional on the estimate of the error term e_i.[10] The best predictor for u_i is the conditional expectation of u_i given the value of $e_i = v_i - u_i$. The predictor for efficiency is obtained by subtracting the inefficiency from 1.

Battese and Coelli (1988) show that the best predictor of technical efficiency, $\exp(-u_i)$, is obtained by using:

$$E[\exp(-u_i)|\, \varepsilon_i] = \frac{1 - \Phi\left(\sigma_A + \frac{\gamma\varepsilon_i}{\sigma_A}\right)}{1 - \Phi\left(\frac{\gamma\varepsilon_i}{\sigma_A}\right)} \exp\left(\gamma\varepsilon_i + \frac{\sigma_A^2}{2}\right) \quad (4)$$

where $\Phi(.)$ is the cummulative density function of a standard normal random variable:

$$\sigma_A = \sqrt{\gamma(1-\gamma)\sigma_S^2}$$

$$\gamma \equiv \frac{\sigma^2}{\sigma_S^2} \quad \sigma_S^2 \equiv \sigma^2 + \sigma_V^2$$

σ^2 is the variance of u_is
σ_V^2 is the variance of v_is.

Early stochastic frontier models were developed for cross-sectional data and production functions only. Over time, they were extended to accommodate cost and profit inefficiencies, and panel data. The model to estimate profit efficiency is the same as the production model; that is, it is based on (profit) maximisation. The model for cost efficiency is slightly modified to accommodate cost minimisation. In Eq. (2), the error term is $e_i = v_i + u_i$, the plus sign on u_i indicating that inefficient banks have costs above those of the maximum efficient (frontier) bank.

I use panel data on banks from CEECs to estimate cost efficiency. To implement this analysis, several model specifications are available. I use two models proposed by Battese and Coelli (1992, 1995) because their specifications fit well the nature of the issues being addressed. These models are labelled Models 1 and 2.

3.3.1. Model 1

Battese and Coelli (1992) proposed a stochastic frontier model with time-varying inefficiency effects. This model can be written as

$$\ln(y_{it}) = x_{it}\beta + v_{it} - u_{it} \quad i = 1, 2, \ldots, N \quad t = 1, 2, \ldots, T \tag{5}$$

where y_{it} is the output of ith firm in the tth time period, x_{it} is a K-vector of values of logarithms of inputs and other appropriate variables associated with the suitable functional form, β is a K-vector of unknown parameters to be estimated, v_{it} are random errors assumed to be i.i.d. $N(0, \sigma_v^2)$ independent of u_{it} and u_{it} are technical inefficiency effects.

Different distributions of u_{it} have been assumed for this panel data model (see Coelli et al., 1998, for a short overview of the evolution of this model). The model permits unbalanced panel data and u_{it} are assumed to be an exponential function of time, involving only one unknown parameter:

$$u_{it} = \{\exp[-\eta(t - \mathrm{T})]\}u_i \quad i = 1, 2, \ldots, N \quad t = 1, 2, \ldots, T \tag{6}$$

where u_i are assumed to be i.i.d. generalised truncated normal random variables and η is a unknown scalar parameter to be estimated.

In period $T(t = T)$, the exponential function $\exp[-\eta(t-T)]$ has value of 1 and thus the u_i is the technical inefficiency for the ith firm in the last period of the panel. Inefficiency effects in all previous periods of the panel are the product of the technical inefficiency for the ith firm in the last period of the panel and the value of the exponential function $\exp[-\eta(t-T)]$. The value of the exponential function is determined by the parameter eta (η) and the number of periods in the panel. Inefficiency effects can decrease, remain constant or increase as time increases (i.e. $\eta > 0$, $\eta = 0$ and $\eta < 0$, respectively).

3.3.2. Model 2

Model 1 gives estimates of efficiency, but it does not allow for the exploration of potential correlates; that is, factors or variables that might explain some of the differences in predicted efficiencies among banks.[11] To include efficiency correlates into the analysis, one can perform a two-stage estimation procedure in which efficiency estimates from the first stage are regressed on a vector of potential correlates (stage two). This two-stage approach has been used in several bank efficiency studies such as Allen and Rai (1996), Berger and Hannan (1998), Berger and Mester (1997), Chang et al. (1998), and Mester (1993, 1994). Hasan and Marton (2000) performed a two-stage efficiency analysis for Hungary, and Nikiel and Opiela (2002) for Poland.

This approach, however, has the drawback of being inconsistent with regard to the assumption of identical distribution of efficiency effects in the two steps of the estimation (Coelli, 1996).[12] In the first stage, inefficiency effects are assumed to be independently and identically distributed in order to be able to use the approach of Jondrow et al. (1982) to predict efficiency values. In the second stage, the inefficiency effects are assumed to be a function of the number of bank-specific correlates, which implies that they are not identically distributed, unless the correlates are jointly insignificant. This inconsistency was first noted by Kumbhakar, Ghosh, and McGuckin (1991) and Reifschneider and Stevenson (1991). They specified a stochastic frontier model where inefficiency effects are explicit functions of some firm-specific factors. All parameters are estimated using a single-stage maximum likelihood procedure.

Along these lines, Battese and Coelli (1995) proposed a model in which the parameters of the stochastic production function (Eq. (7)) and the inefficiency model (Eq. (8)) are estimated simultaneously. This model assumes inefficiency effects to be independently, but not identically, distributed non-negative random variables. It therefore does not suffer from inconsistency in assumptions, as is the case with the two-stage approach.

The model allows the use of panel data and can be expressed as:

$$\ln\left(y_{it}\right) = x_{it}\beta + v_{it} - u_{it} \quad i = 1, 2, \ldots, N \quad t = 1, 2, \ldots, T \quad (7)$$

where y_{it} is the output of ith firm in the tth time period, x_{it} is a K-vector of values of logarithms of inputs and other appropriate variables associated with the suitable functional form, β is a K-vector of unknown parameters to be estimated, v_{it} are random errors assumed to be i.i.d. $N(0, \sigma_v^2)$ independent of u_{it}, and u_{it} are technical inefficiency effects assumed to be independently (but not identically) distributed as truncations at zero of the $N(m_{it}, \sigma_u^2)$.

And

$$m_{it} = z_{it}\delta \quad (8)$$

where z_{it} is a p-vector of logarithms of efficiency correlates, and δ is a vector of parameters to be estimated.

The model presented by Eq. (8) is specified for the stochastic production frontier, and can also be directly applied to a stochastic profit function. To specify a stochastic cost function, one has to change the error term specification from $v_{it}-u_{it}$ to $v_{it}+u_{it}$. As mentioned before, efficiencies measured relative to the cost and profit function are referred to as cost and profit efficiencies, respectively. Model 2 is simultaneously estimated using the maximum likelihood method.

4. HYPOTHESIS TESTING IN MODELS 1 AND 2

4.1. Testing for the presence of inefficiency effects

One way to test for no inefficiency effects is to see whether parameter γ is statistically significantly different from zero (see Eq. (6.4)). This can be performed using several test statistics, but, according to Coelli (1995), the one-sided generalised likelihood ratio (LR) test should be performed when maximum likelihood estimation is used because this test has the correct size.[13] To use the generalised LR test one has to estimate the model under the null and the alternative hypotheses. The test statistic is calculated as:

$$LR = -2\{\ln[L(H_0)] - \ln[L(H_1)]\} \tag{9}$$

where $L(H_0)$ and $L(H_1)$ are the values of the likelihood function under the null and the alternative hypotheses.

Under the null hypothesis this statistic is asymptotically distributed as a Chi-square random variable with the number of degrees of freedom equal to the number of restrictions. Since the value of γ under the null hypothesis lies on the parameter space boundary, the LR test has an asymptotic distribution, which is a mixture of Chi-square distributions. Critical values for the mixed Chi-square distribution are provided in Table 1 in Kodde and Palm (1986). The number of degrees of freedom is somewhat different to those in the general LR test. In Model 1, three degrees of freedom are used to test whether γ is zero (i.e. $q+1$, where q is the number of parameters specified to be zero but are not boundary values, η and μ—see below for definitions of η and μ). In Model 2, q is the number of correlates and the constant (Battese & Brocca, 1997). The LR statistic to test for γ being zero is already reported in the FRONTIER 4.1 output, but not the critical value.

Testing for time-varying inefficiency effects (Model 1): The null hypothesis of time-invarying inefficiency effects captured by parameter η, can be tested by applying the same procedure as in the case of the generalised LR test. In this case the restricted (η restricted to zero) and the unrestricted model have to be estimated to calculate the LR statistic, which has one degree of freedom.

Testing the distribution of inefficiency effects (Model 1): Model 1 specifies the inefficiency effects distribution to be a truncated normal distribution. If the parameter mu (μ) equals zero, then the half-normal distribution is preferred, otherwise a more general truncated normal distribution is appropriate. To test for μ being zero, one performs the LR test as described for parameter η above.

Testing the functional form of the frontier (Models 1 and 2): To test the null hypothesis of Cobb–Douglas functional form being the appropriate representation of the data given the translog specification, one estimates the Cobb–Douglas (null model) and translog model (alternative model), and calculates the LR statistic from the estimated log-likelihood functions. LR statistic is distributed as Chi-square and the degrees of freedom are equal to the number of restrictions.

Testing for technical change (Models 1 and 2): The test for technical change can be performed in a similar way to the test for functional form. Under the null hypothesis there is no technical change. Again, one has to estimate two models (i.e. with and without technical change) to obtain the LR statistics.

Testing the explanatory power of correlates (Model 2): In Model 2, one can test if the efficiency correlates are jointly equal to zero. If the efficiency correlates are jointly equal to zero (all δ are zero), then this model reduces to the panel data version of Aigner et al. (1977). To test whether the deltas (δ) are zero, one proceeds as described above with the procedure for the functional form or for technical change. The number of degrees of freedom is equal to the number of restrictions (number of correlates).

5. EFFICIENCY ESTIMATION RESULTS

As my objective is to compare bank efficiency across the six CEECs and between the two ownership groups (domestic and foreign), I have to pool all the data and estimate a pooled efficiency frontier. Deviations from a pooled frontier are directly comparable; that is, I can present efficiency differences among the countries. I can also present differences between foreign and domestic banks from various perspectives.

5.1. The Dataset

Although there are differences among the banking sectors of the countries in the sample, they nevertheless form a relatively homogeneous group which makes it possible to perform an efficiency analysis and compare the estimated efficiencies across countries. To construct the sample, I use the information from the financial statements of individual banks provided by the BankScope database for the period 1995–2000 (Table 1).

The three main approaches to measuring foreign bank penetration are the number of foreign banks in a banking system, foreign bank participation and foreign control. *Number of foreign banks* is simply the number of banks in which foreigners own a certain percentage of equity. The most frequently used threshold is 50 per cent. *Foreign participation* is calculated as bank assets multiplied by the share of equity held by foreigners, expressed as a percentage of total assets. The sum of this ratio over all banks gives the total foreign bank participation in the banking sector. *Foreign control* is the sum of total assets of banks in which foreigners hold more than 50 per cent of equity as a percentage of total bank assets.

Although the number of foreign banks is a very simplistic concept, which may not provide adequate information on the importance on foreign banks in a country, it has nevertheless often been used as a rough indicator of foreign presence in the banking sector. The foreign participation measure assumes that foreign control over bank assets is directly linked to the share that foreigners hold in a bank's equity. Foreign control, on the other hand, assumes that a share in equity of 50 per cent or even less is generally enough to ensure effective control over the bank. If banks had homogeneous ownership (they were owned solely either by domestic or foreign owners) then both measures (foreign participation and foreign control) would be identical.

The BankScope database provides information on bank ownership. There are, however, two problems with this information. First, no ownership information is available for some banks, especially banks that ceased to exist, or were merged with or taken over by other banks. Second,

Table 1. Number of Domestic and Foreign Banks in the Sample.

	1995	1996	1997	1998	1999	2000	Period Total
Domestic	59	67	64	53	48	36	327
Foreign	20	25	32	33	46	38	194
Total	79	92	96	86	94	74	521

BankScope classifies banks as foreign or domestic at the time the database was last updated. Many authors use the built-in filter to separate domestic from foreign banks, but this is not the best approach. Although it is a very time-consuming and difficult procedure, one should gather ownership data for every bank for every year. I use a wide array of sources, including annual reports, home pages, daily and weekly financial publications, as well as direct contact with banks to compile precise and up-to-date data (Bol, de Haan, de Haas, & Scholtens (2002) apply a similar approach to construct their database).[14] I classify a bank as foreign (ownership dummy equals one) when non-residents hold more than 50 per cent of its equity. If foreigners acquire a majority share during a year, the bank remains domestic (ownership dummy equals zero) until the end of the respective year and becomes foreign at the beginning of the next year. Thus, bank ownership can change during the sample period.

In specifying input prices and outputs of the cost function, I follow the intermediation approach as suggested by Sealey and Lindley (1977). Three inputs (labour, funds and physical capital) are used to produce two outputs (loans and securities) (Table 2). The three inputs reflect the three key groups of inputs in the bank production process: bank personnel and management expertise necessary for the provision of bank services (*labour*), funds collected on the liabilities side (*funds*), and offices, branches and computer hardware (*physical capital*).

BankScope does not provide data on the *price of labour* (PL) directly. There is no information of the number of employees that would enable the

Table 2. Input and Output Variables.

	Variable	Name	Description
Dependent variable	TC	Total cost	Sum of labour, interest, physical capital and other costs
Input prices	PL	Price of labour	Personnel expenses over total assets
	PF	Price of funds	Interest expenses over the sum of deposits, other funding
	PC	Price of physical capital	Depreciation over fixed assets
Output quantities	TL	Total loans	Sum of short- and long-term loans, mortgages and other
	TS	Total securities	Sum of government and investment securities

construction of the ratio of personnel expenses to the number of employees as the unit PL. Instead, I use the ratio of personnel expenses over total assets, which is a common approach in bank efficiency studies based on BankScope (Yildirim & Philippatos, 2002). *Price of funds* (PF) was constructed as the ratio of the interest expense over funding (customer and short-term funding, and other funding). *Price of physical capital* (PC) also cannot be directly taken from BankScope and was constructed as depreciation over fixed assets. The two outputs, loans and securities, are proxies for banking services provided. *Total loans* (TL) is the total customer loans item from BankScope, and *total securities* (TS) is the sum of government and investment securities. The dependent variable, *total cost* (TC), is the sum of total operating expenses and interest expenses. *Total profit* (TP) is profit before tax.

All data were taken from BankScope in euro. To make them comparable, all data are in 2000 prices (Table 3 provides descriptive statistics). Following Berger and Mester (1997), cost and input prices were normalised by the PL in order to impose homogeneity of the cost function. Cost and output quantities were normalised by equity to control for potential heteroskedasticity.

I do not require a bank to have existed throughout the sample period to be included in the sample. Thus, in the unbalanced panel, the number of banks across the years varies for all countries (Table 4). Poland has the largest number of banks, followed by the Czech Republic and Slovenia. Estonia has the smallest number of banks, which reflects the small and specific Estonian banking sector. There are no foreign banks for Estonia in the sample for the period 1995–1998, and only two in the last 2 sample years.

Model 2, as described above in Eqs. (7) and (8), includes *correlates* – factors that are at least partially exogenous and might explain some of the

Table 3. Descriptive Statistics of Dependent Variables, Inputs and Outputs for the Cost function for Model 2[21].

Variable	Units	Mean	Standard Deviation	Minimum	Maximum
Total assets	€ million	1460.7	2467.8	11.4	16007.7
TL	€ million	693.6	1167.9	2.9	9254.4
TS	€ million	237.9	430.2	0.1	4520.5
PL	%	1.65	0.96	0.22	7.02
PF	%	8.28	4.04	1.26	30.05
PC	%	79.80	121.29	0.15	885.71
TC	€ million	156.1	270.5	1.4	2028.4

Notes: 481 observations, 132 banks. Figures in € million are in 2000 prices.

Table 4. Total Number of Banks per Country (Model 1).

Country	1995	1996	1997	1998	1999	2000
Czech Republic	11	12	17	16	16	10
Estonia	9	11	11	3	4	4
Hungary	14	16	14	9	13	11
Poland	24	28	26	31	31	27
Slovakia	9	12	11	10	13	9
Slovenia	12	13	17	17	17	13
Total	79	92	96	86	94	74

differences in predicted efficiencies among banks and across countries. Potential correlates have been tested in various studies (e.g. Allen & Rai, 1996; Berger & Mester, 1997; Casu & Molyneux, 2000). I compiled a list of 18 correlates. Table 5 provides an overview and description of these correlates, and Table 6 provides their descriptive statistics. There are 10 bank-specific and eight country-specific correlates. The 10 bank-specific correlates are bank ownership, share of equity in total assets, share of net loans in total assets, return on average assets (ROAA), return on average equity (ROAE), net interest margin (NIM), individual bank's share in TL and deposits, share of securities in total assets, and total assets. Data on individual bank's ownership, as noted before, were collected from different sources such as bank internet sites, annual reports and direct contact with the particular bank. Country-specific variables reflect the influence of the environment in which banks operate on their performance. The eight bank-specific correlates are stock market capitalisation, GDP per capita, bank claims on the private sector, market shares of the five largest banks, state-owned banks and foreign banks, the stock of non-performing loans and legal effectiveness. They were obtained from different sources, including central bank publications, International Monetary Funds (IMFs) International Financial Statistics and from various issues of the European Bank for Reconstruction and Development (EBRD) Transition Reports (for details see Table 5). These correlates can be grouped into five categories: bank characteristics and size (ownership, total assets, share of equity, share of net loans and share of securities), market power (share in TL and in total deposits, share of five largest banks, NIM), performance (ROAA and ROAE), characteristics of the economy (stock market capitalisation, GDP per capita and legal effectiveness) and characteristics of the banking sector (bank claims on the private sector, the stock of non-performing loans, market shares of state-owned banks and foreign banks).

Table 5.   Description of Correlates.

Variable	Source	Description
Share of equity	BankScope	Equity divided by total assets
Share of net loans	BankScope	Net loans divided by total assets
ROAA	BankScope and IFS	Net income divided by average assets, inflation adjustment
ROAE	BankScope and IFS	Net income divided by average equity, inflation adjustment
NIM	BankScope and IFS	Net interest income divided by earning assets, inflation adjustment
Stock market capitalisation	Standard and Poor's	Total market value of domestic listed companies
GDP per capita	IFS (GDP) and CIA	GDP divided by number of inhabitants
Bank claims on private sector	IFS	Bank claims on all private entities
Share of five largest banks	Central banks[a]	Assets of five largest banks divided by total assets
Share of state-owned banks	EBRD	Assets of state-owned banks divided by total assets
Share of foreign banks	Central banks[a]	Assets of foreign banks divided by total assets
Non-performing loans	EBRD	Non-performing loans divided by TL
Legal effectiveness	EBRD	EBRD rating of legal effectiveness[b]
Share in TL	BankScope	Bank's TL divided by TLs of all banks
Share in total deposits	BankScope	Bank's total deposits divided by TL of all banks
Share of securities	BankScope	Bank's securities divided by bank's total assets
Total assets	BankScope	Total bank assets
Ownership	Author	Foreign bank if $>50\%$ of equity owned by foreigners

Source: Various publications by central banks; CIA Factbook 2001 (http://www.cia.gov/cia/publications/factbook/); EBRD Transition Reports, various years; Fitch IBCA's BankScope database; IMF's International Financial Statistics (IFS) CD-Rom 2001; S&P Emerging Stock Markets Factbook 2001.
[a]For Slovakia: BankScope.
[b]Scale from 1 to 4, 1 being the lowest rating.

5.2. Cost Efficiency: Model 1

I first estimate Model 1 to check the robustness of efficiency estimates for domestic and foreign banks calculated with Model 2. Model 1 is a stochastic frontier cost function model for panel data as specified in Battese and Coelli

Table 6. Descriptive Statistics of Correlates.

Variable	Units	Mean	Standard Deviation	Minimum	Maximum
Share of equity	% total assets	11.28	8.87	−0.7	79.09
Share of net loans	% total assets	44.69	13.92	4.39	83.01
ROAA	%	−11.42	11.06	−80.11	1.40
ROAE	%	−5.72	38.91	−371.18	287.78
NIM	%	−7.99	11.21	−79.07	9.28
Stock market capitalisation	% GDP	15.14	10.08	0	37.37
GDP per capita	€	4927.86	1814.20	3040.63	9765.89
Bank claims on private sector	% GDP	30.49	13.92	11.91	65.15
Share of five largest banks	% total assets	60.04	11.53	42.90	99.36
Share of state-owned banks	% total assets	34.62	19.81	0	71.7
Share of foreign banks	% total assets	29.50	24.54	2.04	97.36
Non-performing loans	% TL	15.37	9.57	1.53	44.31
Legal effectiveness	Index	3.64	0.55	2	4.3
Share in TL	% TL	7.43	11.06	0.045	71.61
Share in total deposits	% total deposits	7.43	10.95	0.081	71.29
Share of securities	% total assets	16.91	11.84	0.039	66.06
Total assets	€ million	1460.7	2467.8	11.4	16007.7
Ownership	Dummy	0.40	0.49	0	1

Notes: 481 observations, 132 banks. Figures in € million are in 2000 prices.
Source: Exchange rates (national currency/euro) provided by Eurostat's NewCronos database. For other data sources refer to Table 5.

(1992). I estimated the following translog cost function:

$$\ln\left(\frac{TC}{PL}\right) = \beta_0 + \beta_1 \ln\left(\frac{PF}{PL}\right) + \beta_2 \ln\left(\frac{PC}{PL}\right) + \beta_3 \ln(TL) + \beta_4 \ln(TS)$$

$$+ \frac{1}{2}\beta_5 \left(\ln\left(\frac{PF}{PL}\right)\right)^2 + \frac{1}{2}\beta_6 \left(\ln\left(\frac{PF}{PL}\right)\right)^2 + \frac{1}{2}\beta_7 \left(\ln(TL)\right)^2$$

$$+ \frac{1}{2}\beta_8 \left(\ln(TS)\right)^2 + \beta_9 \ln\left(\frac{PF}{PL}\right) \ln\left(\frac{PC}{PL}\right)$$

$$+ \beta_{10} \ln\left(\frac{PF}{PL}\right) \ln(TL) + \beta_{11} \ln\left(\frac{PF}{PL}\right) \ln(TS)$$

$$+ \beta_{12} \ln\left(\frac{PF}{PL}\right) YR + \beta_{13} \ln\left(\frac{PC}{PL}\right) \ln(TL)$$

$$+ \beta_{14} \ln\left(\frac{PC}{PL}\right) \ln(TS) + \beta_{15} \ln\left(\frac{PC}{PL}\right) YR$$

$$+ \beta_{16} \ln(TL) \ln(TS) + \beta_{17} \ln(TL) YR$$

$$+ \beta_{18} \ln(TS) YR + \beta_{19} YR + \frac{1}{2}\beta_{20} YR^2 + v + u \qquad (10)$$

where TC is total cost, PL is price of labour, PF is price of funds, PC is price of physical capital, TL is total loans, TS is total securities, YR is year of observation, v is random error, and u is inefficiency term.

The time and the bank index (t and i) are omitted from Eq. (10) for ease of exposition. To analyse efficiency and technical change, I estimated the translog cost function including time trend. The estimates of the cost function for Model 1 are presented in Table 7. I test several hypotheses, the results of which are presented in Table 8. The first hypothesis tests whether the Cobb–Douglas specification is appropriate. The null hypothesis ($\beta_5 = \ldots = \beta_{18} = \beta_{20} = 0$) is rejected by the data; the translog specification is preferred to the Cobb–Douglas specification. The second hypothesis tests if technical change is present in the model. The null hypothesis of no technical change ($\beta_{12} = \beta_{15} = \beta_{17} = \ldots = \beta_{20} = 0$) is rejected by the data at the 10 per cent significance level. The third hypothesis specifies that cost inefficiencies are not present ($\gamma = 0$). The data reject this hypothesis as well, which indicates that cost inefficiencies exist. The null hypothesis of time invariant inefficiency effects ($\eta = 0$) is also rejected. The negative coefficient on η in Table 7 suggests that inefficiency effects tend to become larger over time. Finally, I test the distributional assumption of inefficiency effects. If $\mu = 0$, then the half-normal distribution is preferred, otherwise a more general truncated normal distribution is appropriate. The null hypothesis of $\mu = 0$ is accepted with the log-likelihood ratio of 1.4 and a critical value of 3.84 (5 per cent significance level). The half-normal distribution is therefore preferred.

Estimates of cost efficiency for the six CEECs in the 1995–2000 period are presented in Table 9.[15] All reported figures are weighted averages with total assets as weights. The average cost efficiency for the entire sample period is 0.74. In other words, an average bank had costs that were 35 per cent higher than necessary, or 35 per cent above the potential minimum cost faced by the best practice bank operating under the same conditions. Turning to the six CEECs in the study, Slovenia has the highest cost efficiency (0.83), followed by Poland and Slovakia (0.80 and 0.79, respectively). Somewhat surprisingly, Hungary has the lowest cost efficiency. Over time, the average cost efficiency for the six CEECs declined by 10 percentage points, from 0.78 in 1995 to 0.68 in 2000. This result is somewhat unexpected as the CEECs underwent banking sector consolidation and stabilisation in the second half of the 1990s. The last part of Table 9 shows a comparison across countries and time. The downward trend in cost efficiency is present in all countries. The Czech Republic had the largest decline in cost efficiency of more than 20 percentage points.

Table 7. Maximum Likelihood Estimates for Parameters of the Stochastic Cost Frontier with Time-Varying Inefficiency Effects and Technical Change; Pooled Sample.

Variable	Parameter	Coefficient	Standard-error	t-ratio[a]
Stochastic frontier				
Constant	β_0	1.172***	0.316	3.708
PF	β_1	1.136***	0.145	7.806
PC	β_2	−0.131*	0.070	−1.865
TL	β_3	0.618***	0.120	5.133
TS	β_4	0.319***	0.077	4.144
PF^2	β_5	0.162***	0.062	2.618
PC^2	β_6	−0.005	0.012	−0.414
TL^2	β_7	0.111***	0.031	3.552
TS^2	β_8	0.092***	0.014	6.424
PF × C	β_9	0.043*	0.023	1.919
PF × TL	β_{10}	−0.141***	0.035	−4.016
PF × TS	β_{11}	0.028	0.025	1.121
PF × YR	β_{12}	0.023	0.015	1.531
PC × TL	β_{13}	0.036**	0.016	2.271
PC × TS	β_{14}	−0.023*	0.012	−1.863
PC × YR	β_{15}	−0.005	0.007	−0.721
TL × TS	β_{16}	−0.080***	0.019	−4.272
TL × YR	β_{17}	0.002	0.011	0.134
TS × YR	β_{18}	−0.011	0.009	−1.255
Yr	β_{19}	−0.056	0.059	−0.948
YR^2	β_{20}	0.071	0.012	0.634
Variance parameters				
Sigma squared	σ^2	1.199	0.752	1.594
Gamma	γ^2	0.926	0.050	18.510
Mu	μ	−2.107	1.635	−1.286
Eta	η	−0.073	0.029	−2.534
Log-likelihood		−201.5		

Notes: Dependent variable is TC; numbering of β refers to translog cost equation with trend. Statistically significant levels at, *10%, **5% and ***1%.
[a]Two-sided t-test. Critical value at 1% significance level 2.57, at 5% 1.96 and at 10% 1.64 (∞ degree of freedom).

How do these results compare to other studies? Recall that efficiency estimates obtained from different cost functions are not comparable. Nevertheless, one may look at the range of results. Yildirim and Philippatos (2002) estimate the average cost efficiency for 12 transition economies of 76 per cent, which is very close to my result. Altunbas, Gardener, Molyneux, and Moore (2001) find cost efficiencies for EU countries in the range of 67

Table 8. Generalised Likelihood-Ratio Tests of Hypotheses for
Parameters of the Stochastic Frontier Cost function for Pooled Sample.

	Null Hypothesis	Log-likelihood[a]	LR[b]	Critical Value[c]	Decision
1	$\beta_5 = \ldots = \beta_{18} = \beta_{20} = 0$	−239.3	75.6	24.99* (15)	Reject H_0
2	$\beta_{12} = \beta_{15} = \beta_{17} = \ldots = \beta_{20} = 0$	−206.9	10.8	10.64** (6)	Reject H_0
3	$\gamma = 0$	−264.8	126.6	7.05*** (3)	Reject H_0
4	$\eta = 0$	−203.7	4.4	3.84* (1)	Reject H_0
5	$\mu = 0$	−202.2	1.4	3.84* (1)	Accept H_0

Chi-squared at:
*5% significance level and
**10% significance level,
***Mixed Chi-squared from Table 1 in Kodde and Palm (1986).
[a]Log-likehood of the unrestricted model is −201.5.
[b]Likelihood ratio.
[c]Degrees of freedom in parentheses.

per cent (Luxembourg) and 87 per cent (Germany). They report an EU
average of 82 per cent, which is higher than my average for CEECs.
Dividing the sample into domestic and foreign banks reveals some
interesting results. For the 1995–2000 period, the weighted average cost
efficiency for domestic banks is higher than the average for foreign banks
(Table 10).[16] The average cost efficiency of domestic banks was 16
percentage points higher than that of foreign banks. Over time, the average
cost efficiency of foreign banks first increased and then decreased. Domestic
banks experienced decreasing efficiency throughout the sample period. A
breakdown by ownership and country shows that Hungary was the only
country in which foreign banks had a higher cost efficiency average for the
sample period than domestic banks. The largest difference between domestic
and foreign banks was in the Czech Republic and Slovakia. Hasan and
Marton (2000) find different results for Hungary. They report that foreign
banks had higher cost efficiency (79 per cent) than domestic banks (75 per
cent). Nikiel and Opiela (2002) come to a similar conclusion for Polish banks.

5.3. Cost Efficiency: Model 2

Model 2 allows simultaneous estimation of efficiency as well as the
inefficiency effects model in which efficiency is regressed on a set of
explanatory variables (correlates). Thus, with Model 2 I explore the
association of an extensive set of potential efficiency correlates, of which the

Table 9. Cost Efficiency Estimates 1995–2000 (Model 1).

1995–2000 Average for All Countries: 0.74

1995–2000 Average by Countries		Yearly Averages for All Countries	
Country	Cost Efficiency	Year	Cost Efficiency
Czech Republic	0.67	1995	0.78
Estonia	0.69	1996	0.77
Hungary	0.66	1997	0.76
Poland	0.80	1998	0.74
Slovakia	0.78	1999	0.72
Slovenia	0.83	2000	0.68

Average by Years and Countries

Year	Czech Republic	Estonia	Hungary	Poland	Slovakia	Slovenia
1995	0.73	0.73	0.72	0.85	0.85	0.87
1996	0.73	0.70	0.70	0.82	0.82	0.86
1997	0.72	0.71	0.67	0.80	0.78	0.84
1998	0.69	0.69	0.63	0.79	0.75	0.83
1999	0.64	0.68	0.61	0.78	0.75	0.81
2000	0.52	0.65	0.61	0.77	0.72	0.79

Note: Weighted averages (total assets as weights).

ownership dummy and the share of foreign banks in total assets are of particular interest. The cost function in Model 2, presented in Eq. (11), in which the time and bank index (*t* and *i*) are omitted for ease of reference, is specified as in Model 1.

$$
\ln\left(\frac{TC}{PL}\right) = \beta_0 + \beta_1 \ln\left(\frac{PF}{PL}\right) + \beta_2 \ln\left(\frac{PC}{PL}\right) + \beta_3 \ln(TL)
$$

$$
+ \beta_4 \ln(TS) + \frac{1}{2}\beta_5\left(\ln\left(\frac{PF}{PL}\right)\right)^2 + \frac{1}{2}\beta_6\left(\ln\left(\frac{PC}{PL}\right)\right)^2
$$

$$
+ \frac{1}{2}\beta_7(\ln(TL))^2 + \frac{1}{2}\beta_8(\ln(TS))^2 + \beta_9 \ln\left(\frac{PF}{PL}\right)\ln\left(\frac{PC}{PL}\right)
$$

$$
+ \beta_{10}\ln\left(\frac{PF}{PL}\right) + \ln(TL) + \beta_{11}\ln\left(\frac{PF}{PL}\right)\ln(TS)
$$

$$
+ \beta_{12}\ln\left(\frac{PF}{PL}\right)YR + \beta_{13}\ln\left(\frac{PC}{PL}\right)\ln(TL)
$$

$$
+ \beta_{14}\ln\left(\frac{PC}{PL}\right)\ln(TS) + \beta_{15}\ln\left(\frac{PF}{PL}\right)YR + \beta_{16}\ln(TL)\ln(TS) \quad (11)
$$

Table 10.   Cost Efficiency Estimates (Model 1) and Bank Ownership.

Average by Bank Ownership	
Ownership	Cost Efficiency
Domestic	0.78
Foreign	0.62

Averaged by Bank Ownership and Year			Average by Bank Ownership and Country		
Year	Domestic	Foreign	Country	Domestic	Foreign
1995	0.80	0.59	Czech Republic	0.75	0.52
1996	0.79	0.64	Estonia	0.72	0.65
1997	0.78	0.66	Hungary	0.65	0.68
1998	0.76	0.65	Poland	0.81	0.72
1999	0.77	0.63	Slovakia	0.82	0.59
2000	0.76	0.60	Slovenia	0.84	0.64

Note: Weighted averages (total assets as weights).

where TC is total cost, PL is price of labour, PF is price of funds, PC is price of physical capital, TL is total loans, TS is total securities, YR is year of observation, v is random error, and u is inefficiency term.

An inefficiency effects model with 18 correlates is added in Eq. (12), giving this efficiency study an additional perspective on which factors drive differences in efficiency estimates.

$$ineff = \delta_0 + \sum_{i=1}^{18} \delta_i z_i + w \tag{12}$$

where z_1 is share of equity; z_2 is share of net loans; z_3 is ROAA; z_4 is ROAE; z_5 is NIM; z_6 is stock market capitalisation; z_7 is GDP per capita; z_8 is bank claims on private sector; z_9 is share of five largest banks; z_{10} is share of state-owned banks; z_{11} is share of foreign banks; z_{12} is non-performing loans; z_{13} is legal effectiveness; z_{14} is share in TL; z_{15} is share in total deposits; z_{16} is share of securities; z_{17} is total assets; z_{18} is ownership dummy, and w is the error term.

As with Model 1, cost and profit optimisation theory implies linear homogeneity in input prices. Thus, cost and input prices are normalised by the PL to impose linear homogeneity (Berger & Mester, 1997). Also, second-order parameters must be symmetric. Model 2 is estimated using a translog cost function including a time trend. The estimates are presented in Table 11. With Model 2, I test four hypotheses in Table 12. First, the null hypothesis of the Cobb–Douglas specification ($\beta_5 = \ldots = \beta_{18} = \beta_{20} = 0$) is rejected; that is, the translog functional form is preferred. Second, the data show that there is technical change (the null hypothesis of no technical change $\beta_{12} = \beta_{15} = \beta_{17} = \ldots = \beta_{20} = 0$ is rejected by the data at the 5 per cent significance level). Third, the null hypothesis of the correlates (explanatory variables) in the inefficiency model being jointly equal to 0 ($\delta_1 = \ldots = \delta_{18} = 0$) is rejected by the data at the 5 per cent significance level. Finally, the fourth hypothesis tests whether cost inefficiencies are present in the model. The null hypothesis of no inefficiencies ($\gamma = 0$) is rejected. Inefficiencies are not random and they are present in the model.

The sample average cost efficiency is 0.73, which is approximately the same as the average efficiency obtained by Model 1. The efficiency estimate of 73 per cent indicates that the average bank had costs that are 37 per cent above the potential minimum cost of the best practice bank producing the same output mix and operating under the same conditions. The movement of the average for all six countries across the years is relatively small. There is an initial improvement in the average cost efficiency in 1995–1997, followed by a decline. Overall, cost efficiency is just above 70 per cent. Country averages for the sample period show larger differences across countries than the results of Model 1. The Czech Republic had the lowest cost efficiency (0.53). Poland has the highest cost efficiency (0.92), followed by Slovenia (0.89). These two countries have the best efficiency scores in Model 1 as well.

Cost efficiencies were also averaged according to ownership in Table 14. In line with the results of Model 1, efficiency estimates obtained by Model 2 confirm that domestic banks have on average higher cost efficiency than foreign banks (Table 13). The difference between cost efficiency of domestic (0.77) and foreign banks (0.62) is substantial and approximately the same as the difference in Model 1. Looking at the time dimension, domestic and some foreign banks improved their average bank efficiency in the 1995–2000 sample period. Finally, a breakdown by ownership and country shows that in the Czech Republic, Poland and Slovakia the average domestic bank have higher cost efficiency than the average foreign bank.

The inefficiency effects model includes correlates – the factors that are at least partially exogenous and might explain some of the differences in predicted efficiencies among banks and across countries. Most of the bank efficiency studies perform a two-stage analysis to include correlates. As mentioned above, the two-stage approach has the drawback of being

Table 11. Maximum Likelihood Estimates of Parameters of the Stochastic Cost Frontier.

Variable	Parameter	Coefficient	Standard Error	t-ratio[a]
Stochastic frontier				
Constant	β_0	1.413***	0.184	7.668
PF	β	0.543***	0.078	6.944
PC	β_2	0.118***	0.034	3.495
TL	β_3	0.449***	0.057	7.853
TS	β_4	0.538***	0.044	12.248
PF^2	β_5	0.233***	0.030	7.707
PC^2	β_6	0.009	0.006	1.466
TL^2	β_7	0.208***	0.016	13.037
TS^2	β_8	0.120***	0.008	14.155
PF × PC	β_9	−0.036***	0.011	−3.460
PF × TL	β_{10}	−0.092***	0.017	−5.553
PF × TS	β_{11}	0.063***	0.013	4.897
PF × YR	β_{12}	0.021**	0.010	2.118
PC × TL	β_{13}	0.011	0.007	1.481
PC × TS	β_{14}	−0.009	0.006	−1.535
PC × YR	β_{15}	−0.010***	0.004	−2.721
TL × TS	β_{16}	−0.159***	0.010	−15.608
TL × Yr	β_{17}	−0.015**	0.006	−2.462
TS × YR	β_{18}	0.011**	0.005	2.207
Yr	β_{19}	0.034	0.041	0.821
YR^2	β_{20}	−0.003	0.008	−0.349
Variance parameters				
Sigma squared	σ^2	0.027	0.002	13.876
Gamma	γ^2	0.234	0.035	6.776
Log-likelihood		208.1		

Notes: Dependent variable is TC; numbering of β refers to translog cost equation with trend. Statistically significant levels at *10%, **5% and ***1%.
[a]Two-sided t-test. Critical value at 1% significance level 2.57, at 5% 1.96 and at 10% 1.64 (∞ degree of freedom).

inconsistent in respect of the assumptions regarding the identical distribution of the inefficiency effects in the two steps of the estimation (Coelli et al., 1998). Battese and Coelli (1995) propose a model that overcomes this problem. The cost function and the inefficiency model are simultaneously estimated. This approach is expected to give better estimates.

In the literature on banking in the CEECs, there are more arguments in favour of foreign banks than against them. However, Konopielko (1999)

Table 12. Generalised Likelihood-ratio Tests of Hypotheses for Parameters of the Stochastic Frontier Cost Function and Inefficiency Model for the Pooled Sample.

	Null Hypothesis	Log-likelihood[a]	LR[b]	Critical Value[c]	Decision
1	$\beta_5 = \ldots = \beta_{18} = \beta_{20} = 0$	102.1	212.0	24.99* (15)	Reject H_0
2	$\beta_{12} = \beta_{15} = \beta_{17} = \ldots = \beta_{20} = 0$	165.6	85.0	12.59* (6)	Reject H_0
3	$\delta_1 = \ldots = \delta_{18} = 0$	−163.7	743.6	28.86* (18)	Reject H_0
4	$\gamma = 0$	−195.9	808.1	30.81** (20)	Reject H_0

[a]Log-likehood of the unrestricted model is 208.1.
[b]Likelihood ratio.
[c]Degrees of freedom in parentheses.
*Chi-squared at 5% significance level.
**Mixed Chi-squared at 5% from Table 1 in Kodde and Palm (1986).

notes that this is the view of (mainly) authors from outside the region. Therefore, and because there is no theoretical model for correlates, I believe that it would be inappropriate to a priori expect a positive or a negative relation between the ownership dummy and efficiency estimates. Table 5 provides an overview and description of these correlates and Table 6 provides their descriptive statistics. Estimates of the coefficients on the correlates are presented in Table 15. Note that these are maximum likelihood estimates of parameters of the inefficiency effects model.

As the focal point of this analysis is the role of foreign banks in the CEECs, two correlates deserve priority: the ownership dummy and the share of foreign banks in total assets. The *ownership* dummy (δ_{18}) is not a standard dummy because it may change over time for the same bank. It addresses the second question of my analysis: What impact does the change in a bank's ownership have on its cost efficiency? The ownership dummy measures the change in the conditional mean of inefficiency if a bank undergoes a change of ownership in any given year, averaged over all years. It therefore measures the impact of ownership change on inefficiency, rather than the average difference between domestic and foreign banks, as would be the case in a cross-section or panel in which ownership was constant over time. The coefficient on the ownership dummy shows a negative correlation with cost efficiency and is significant at the 10 per cent level. The negative correlation means that if the average bank changed ownership from domestic to foreign, then its cost efficiency will decline. A sensitivity analysis checking for robustness of the model (by excluding some z's) shows a very weak relation between the ownership dummy and the estimated cost efficiency.

Table 13. Cost Efficiency Estimates 1995–2000 (Model 2).

1995–2000 Average for All Countries: 0.73

1995–2000 Average by Countries		Yearly Averages for All Countries	
Country	Cost Efficiency	Year	Cost Efficiency
Czech Republic	0.53	1995	0.69
Estonia	0.73	1996	0.72
Hungary	0.65	1997	0.75
Poland	0.92	1998	0.73
Slovakia	0.73	1999	0.74
Slovenia	0.89	2000	0.72

Average by Years and Countries					
Year	Czech Republic	Estonia	Hungary	Poland	Slovakia	Slovenia
1995	0.61	0.61	0.60	0.90	0.79	0.82
1996	0.62	0.75	0.62	0.95	0.79	0.78
1997	0.58	0.78	0.65	0.95	0.70	0.93
1998	0.48	0.67	0.69	0.95	0.60	0.91
1999	0.41	0.70	0.63	0.92	0.74	0.91
2000	0.42	0.77	0.76	0.87	0.81	0.93

Notes: Weighted averages (total assets as weights); *Means for domestic and foreign are not statistically different.

Table 14. Cost Efficiency Estimates (Model 2) and Bank Ownership.

Average by Bank Ownership	
Ownership	Cost Efficiency
Domestic	0.77
Foreign	0.62

Averaged by Bank Ownership and Year			Average by Bank Ownership and Country		
Year	Domestic	Foreign	Country	Domestic	Foreign
1995	0.71	0.52	Czech Republic	0.59	0.41
1996	0.75	0.52	Estonia	0.69	0.76
1997	0.79	0.59	Hungary	0.64	0.66
1998	0.74	0.69	Poland	0.95	0.85
1999	0.82	0.65	Slovakia	0.78	0.56
2000	0.90	0.60	Slovenia	0.86	0.93

Note: Weighted averages (total assets as weights).

In the literature on banking sectors in the developing countries, there is a general belief that foreign banks are more efficient than their domestic counterparts because they capitalise on their access to better risk management, information technology and other resources of their mother banks (e.g. Wachtel, 1995; Sabi, 1988; IMF, 2000; Mathieson & Roldos, 2001). However, foreign banks, especially in the early years of operation, have to put up substantial amounts of money to sort out the problems of the acquired banks, introduce new technology, and invest in expansion and marketing. This result may imply that banks under foreign ownership do not pay special attention to costs in the sample period. Perhaps new entrants via greenfield investments have high costs to establish their local presence, enhance brand recognition, attract adequate personnel and possibly build a branch network to increase market share. Multinational banks that have taken over domestic banks may concentrate on dealing with inherited problems, and invest in installing and/or overhauling information systems. As noted before, my sample period is relatively short and future results might be different. In addition, since these changes are relatively recent, their full effect may not yet be evident. Foreign banks may also be expected to improve their cost efficiency. As these are broad-brush results for all six CEECs, they may not be representative for each country individually, especially for the smaller countries.

The second correlate reflecting the presence of foreign banks is the *share of foreign banks* in total assets (δ_{11}). In the CEECs, the share of foreign banks in total assets is very high compared to the EU and also to other developing countries. The share of foreign banks addresses the third question of the empirical analysis: What influence did the extent of foreign bank penetration have on cost efficiency? It shows whether the presence of foreign banks in the banking sector influences the cost efficiency of the average bank. The estimated coefficient δ_{11} is not statistically significant. The presence of foreign banks in the banking sector, measured as the share of foreign banks in total assets, does not seem to influence the cost efficiency of the average bank. In other words, in the six CEECs a high share of foreign banks in total assets is not associated with higher cost efficiency, at least for the second half of the 1990s.

The *share of equity* captures safety and soundness of a bank. It reflects the effect of capitalisation on bank efficiency. Higher capital ratios imply lower leverage and thus lower risk, which may lead to lower borrowing costs.[17] Grigorian and Manole (2002) suggest that well-capitalised banks carry implicit deposit insurance and are better positioned to attract deposits. A higher share of equity implies a smaller share of other liabilities (deposits

Table 15. Maximum Likelihood Estimates of Parameters of Cost Inefficiency Effects Model Including Bank and Country-Specific Variables (Model 2).

Inefficiency Model	Parameter	Coefficient	Standard Error	t-ratio[a]
Constant	δ_0	1.134***	0.151	7.476
Share of equity	δ_1	−0.005***	0.001	−5.396
Share of net loans	δ_2	−0.019***	0.001	−17.464
ROAA	δ_3	−0.031***	0.004	−6.411
ROAE	δ_4	−0.001***	0.0003	−2.884
NIM	δ_5	0.028***	0.005	6.176
Stock market capitalisation	δ_6	0.001	0.002	0.504
GDP per capita	δ_7	0.00003**	0.00001	2.473
Bank claims on private sector	δ_8	0.002	0.002	1.287
Share of five largest banks	δ_9	0.009***	0.001	6.093
Share of state-owned banks	δ_{10}	−0.001	0.002	−0.861
Share of foreign banks	δ_{11}	−0.0001	0.001	−0.088
Non-performing loans	δ_{12}	0.003	0.003	1.206
Legal effectiveness	δ_{13}	−0.057**	0.025	−2.285
Share in TL	δ_{14}	−0.029***	0.004	−7.095
Share in total deposits	δ_{15}	0.023***	0.004	5.533
Share of securities	δ_{16}	−0.031***	0.002	−19.111
Total assets	δ_{17}	−0.000001	0.00001	−0.135
Ownership	δ_{18}	0.049*	0.026	1.860

Notes: Dependent variable is cost inefficiency (u_i); numbering of δ refers to translog cost equation with trend.
Statistically significant levels at: *10%, **5% and ***1%.
[a]Two-sided t-test. Critical value at 1% significance level 2.57, at 5% 1.96 and at 10% 1.64 (∞ degrees of freedom).

and issued securities). The bank therefore has lower interest expenses, which are the largest component of TC. Košak (2000) notes that the higher the stake of owners (equity), the more they are motivated to choose the best management and to monitor them. Managers of banks close to bankruptcy (low-capital ratios) are inclined to concentrate on their benefits and perks (Mester, 1993). The statistically significant positive relation between the share of equity and cost efficiency is in line with my expectations. This is also the general finding of most bank efficiency studies that include correlates (see, e.g. Hasan & Marton, 2000; Nikiel & Opiela, 2002; Yildirim & Philippatos, 2002).

Another proxy for risk is the *share of net loans*, defined as net loans over total assets, where net loans are TL minus loan loss reserves. The ratio indicates what percentage of a bank's assets is tied up in loans, and thus reflects liquidity. The coefficient in my analysis is highly significant and shows a positive correlation. This is in line with Allen and Rai (1996), who suggest that higher loans-to-assets ratios indicate more aggressive banks (more lending activity), which tend to be operated more efficiently. Nikiel and Opiela (2002) find a statistically significant positive relation between the share of loans and cost efficiency for Polish banks. Yildirim and Philippatos (2002) confirm this result for 12 CEECs. However, the literature also presents an opposing view, which seems to hold for developed countries. More risk – higher share of loans in total assets – is expected to be negatively correlated with cost efficiency. That is, banks with more risk are under less pressure to control their costs (Maudos et al., 2002). Berger and Mester (1997) report a statistically significant negative relation between cost efficiency and the share of loans for US banks. Similar results are found by Mester (1996) and Hasan and Marton (2000). Maudos et al. (2002) do not find a statistically significant relation between the share of loans and efficiency for European banks.

The coefficient on the *share of fixed-income securities* is also statistically significant and shows a positive association with cost efficiency; that is, a higher share of securities in total assets implies lower cost. This is in contrast with the result for the share of net loans. Capital markets are not well developed in the CEECs. Government and municipal securities dominate the market for corporate securities. Returns on government securities are relatively high, and these securities do not require a high use of human and IT resources by banks. This may explain why a higher share of securities is positively related to cost efficiency.

Total assets measures the size of the bank. There is no agreement in the literature on the correlation between bank assets and efficiency. On the one hand, portfolios of larger banks might be more diversified and allow banks to benefit from economies of scale and scope. On the other hand, as banks grow larger they inherently become more difficult to control and more complex, which brings about additional costs (Košak, 2000). I do not, therefore, have an a priori expectation on the coefficient δ_{17}. It turns out to be statistically insignificant, suggesting that bank size does not matter for cost efficiency. There is no evidence that larger banks are more (or less) cost efficient than smaller banks. This result is in line with Berger and Mester (1997), who find that cost efficiency does not vary significantly with bank size. Cebenoyan et al. (1993) and Mester (1996) come to similar conclusions.

Market power is an important determinant of efficiency. It is reflected by four correlates: share of five largest banks in total assets, a bank's share in total deposits in the banking sector, NIM and a bank's share in TL in the banking sector. Again, it is difficult to formulate an a priori expectation on the sign of these relationships. If a high market share in the respective banking segment is a result of an efficient production process and professional management, then there may be a positive relation with cost efficiency. However, if a bank's market share is a result of its (inherited) dominant position, then there might be a negative correlation with cost efficiency. In a less competitive environment, banks are expected to be under less pressure to control costs and thus are likely to be less cost efficient. The latter turns out to be the case with three out of four market power correlates. *Share of five largest banks* is a measure of market concentration.[18] As described above, a high market share of the five largest banks can be a reflection of a highly competitive environment (positive correlation with cost efficiency) or of the high market power of these banks (negative correlation with cost efficiency). The share of the five largest banks is statistically negatively correlated with cost efficiency. This suggests that a high market share is a result of a low degree of competition, and is thus related to low cost efficiency. Berger and Mester (1997) and Yildirim and Philippatos (2002) find the same correlation, while Grigorian and Manole (2002) report a statistically significant positive association between market concentration and cost efficiency.

Share of total deposits has a statistically significant negative correlation with cost efficiency. The larger the market share in deposits, the less cost efficient is the bank. This accords with previous findings that a high market share, which is a result of market power and the absence of competition, is associated with poorer efficiency performance. *NIM* is negatively correlated with cost efficiency. A high NIM indicates a higher margin (difference between lending and deposit rates) – low efficiency and/or high market power. A bank charging a high margin is either in poor condition and needs a larger margin to cover its cost, or it has enough market power to be able to sustain a relatively high margin over some period. In both cases, one would expect a negative correlation between NIM and cost efficiency. The data confirm a statistically significant correlation between these variables.

The fourth and last market share correlate is the *share in TL*. It reflects a bank's market share in TL of the banking sector. In contrast to the other three, a higher share in TL is statistically significantly linked to higher cost efficiency. This could be explained by a competitive loan market where not only locally present foreign banks extend loans in the host country, but local companies also get loans directly abroad (cross-border lending). The supply of loans may therefore be larger than demand, and in light of a relatively competitive environment, a bank can increase its market share in TL only by offering favourable and competitive conditions.

Higher efficiency is expected to be correlated with better performance (Mester, 1993). Both standard profitability indicators, *ROAA* and *ROAE*, are statistically positively correlated with cost efficiency.[19] This confirms that higher cost efficiency is directly reflected in higher profitability in terms of return on assets (equity), and is in line with the general findings of bank efficiency studies such as Berger and Mester (1997), Mester (1996), Pastor, Lozano, and Pastor (1997), and Yildirim and Philippatos (2002).

Turning to characteristics of the economy, *stock market capitalisation* is a proxy for the role of the banking sector in the economy. A small and under-developed stock market indicates that banks play a major role in providing funds to companies. But in the case of a well-developed stock market, companies have more choice in financing, which implies that banks must try harder and be more efficient in order to keep existing and win new clients.[20] I expected to find a positive relation with cost efficiency, but the coefficient turns out to be statistically insignificant. Stock market capitalisation does not seem to influence the cost efficiency of the banks in my sample.

GDP per capita is a proxy for the development of the banking sector. Higher GDP per capita indicates a better-developed financial system, higher wealth and demand for more sophisticated bank products. In general, a higher degree of development is expected to be positively correlated with bank efficiency. This is confirmed by the estimation results, which show a statistically significant and positive relation between GDP per capita and cost efficiency. Grigorian and Manole (2002) and Yildirim and Philippatos (2002) find the same relation.

The *legal effectiveness* index captures the institutional environment in which banks operate. A developed legal and regulatory system is positively correlated with economic growth and financial development. Higher legal effectiveness is therefore expected to be positively correlated with bank efficiency. In accordance with my expectations, the analysis shows a statistically significant and positive relation between legal effectiveness and cost efficiency. Interestingly, Manole and Grigorian (2002) do not find a statistically significant relation. In the CEECs, the design and implementation of a sound legal system was perhaps the key task in establishing these countries' banking systems. Although most of the bank regulation and legislation in these countries has been de jure aligned with those of the EU, the de facto implementation is still lagging behind. This relation between legal effectiveness and bank efficiency suggests that these countries should further enhance their efforts to secure legal effectiveness in terms of the efficiency with which collateral is seized and sold to repay defaulted debt.

Finally, the analysis of correlates addresses the three proxies for the general characteristics of the banking sector. *Bank claims on the private sector* indicate the involvement of banks in servicing private clients as opposed to non-private (state) clients. Private clients are more sensitive to cost and quality of bank products, and change their banks more readily. This might imply that banks having more private clients are more efficient. However, the coefficient on bank claims on the private sector is statistically insignificant. The *share of state-owned banks* was expected to be negatively linked to efficiency. In the CEECs, state-owned banks are often regarded as remnants of the past, and in most countries were privatised during the last decade. The coefficient on the share of state-owned banks is statistically insignificant. A high level of *non-performing loans* suggests that a bank is poorly run; it might have inadequate screening procedures in loan origination or it may not control its loan portfolio effectively. Non-performing loans was expected to be negatively correlated with efficiency, but it turns out to be statistically insignificant.

6. COMMENTS AND CONCLUSION

Models 1 and 2 give similar but somewhat different results. In Model 1, cost efficiency is determined by the cost frontier, so that efficiency estimates reflect only cost minimisation. However, one might want to know if other factors also affect efficiency. These other correlates can be incorporated into the analysis in two ways. First, in a two-step procedure, efficiency estimates are obtained as in Model 1, and these efficiencies are then regressed on potential correlates. This approach has econometric pitfalls. Second, a one-step approach can be used, in which efficiency is simultaneously determined by the cost frontier and other explanatory variables. With this technique, used in Model 2, the estimated inefficiencies are a better approximation of actual inefficiencies.

The key finding of my study is the relation between efficiency and ownership. Overall, foreign banks are less cost efficient than domestic banks in both models. Looking at individual countries, with Model 1 in all countries except Hungary, foreign banks have lower cost efficiency than domestic banks. With Model 2, this is the case in Estonia, Hungary and Slovenia. There is some inconclusiveness, therefore, regarding the relation between cost efficiency and bank ownership at the level of individual countries. In the literature, foreign banks in developed countries are generally less cost efficient than domestic banks, while the converse holds for developing countries. Berger et al. (2000) find that in developed countries, foreign banks have lower cost efficiency than domestic banks. Hasan and Hunter (1996) analyse Japanese banks operating in the USA and also find that they are less cost efficient than the domestic banks, and Chang et al. (1998) confirm that foreign-owned banks are less cost efficient than the US banks. On the other hand, Nikiel and Opiela (2002) and Hasan and Marton (2000) show that foreign banks in Poland and Hungary, respectively, are more cost efficient than their domestic peers.

There may be a plausible explanation for the lower cost efficiency of foreign banks in the CEECs. Foreign banks that entered the market as greenfield investments had to set up their operations from scratch. Establishing a branch network, recruiting and training staff, and building up a reputation and recognition are very expensive undertakings, the costs of which are spread over several years. Also, in the initial years of existence, concentrating on gaining market share may have resulted in cost control being relegated to a position of secondary importance. Banks that entered through takeovers acquired both the good domestic banks and the troubled banks that were put up for sale at attractive discounts. At first glance, the takeover approach to entry may appear to entail lower cost, but to reconstruct and refurbish an old house is in many cases more expensive than building a new one. Many foreign parent banks had to invest substantial sums in dismantling the old and setting up new organisational structures. In some cases, they also had to deal with non-performing loans. All these efforts could have led to relatively high costs, resulting in low cost efficiency compared to domestic banks. Another potential explanation may be that foreign banks in some countries may have adapted their business strategy to local market conditions; in banking markets in which there is a low degree of competition, banks are inclined not to pay much attention to the cost side. To sum up, my results seem to be consistent with the results of studies for developed countries that domestic banks are more cost efficient than their foreign counterparts.

The analysis of correlates provides some additional insights into the effect of ownership on efficiency. The ownership dummy is negatively correlated with cost efficiency, suggesting that for an average bank, a change of ownership from domestic to foreign leads to a reduction in cost efficiency. The explanation may be that, as discussed above, new foreign owners face substantial initial outlays to dismantle the old and set up a new organisational structure and deal with inherited non-performing loans. The share of foreign banks in the banking sector's total assets is not statistically significantly correlated with cost efficiency; that is, the share of foreign banks in the sector does not seem to matter for the cost efficiency of an average bank. The share of foreign banks in the banking sector's total assets is negatively correlated with the profit efficiency. This suggests that the higher the share of foreign banks, the lower the profit efficiency. When foreign banks enter a new market, they seem to increase competition, and to capture market share they must offer competitive pricing for their products. Foreign banks may therefore be keener to enter countries in which the presence of foreign banks is lower.

What future developments are to be expected? The share of foreign banks will probably increase further, and eventually foreign banks are likely to dominate the banking sectors in all of the CEECs. Remaining domestic banks may be left to service small- and mid-sized companies, and will likely remain relatively cost efficient. The efficiency of foreign banks may improve further, for two reasons. First, the need for investment will decrease as they complete their reorganisation and modernisation. Second, in light of globalisation and new technologies, several functions may be transferred to the parent banks, reducing the number of highly trained and expensive local employees, as well as reducing the cost per transaction.

NOTES

1. See Berger and Humphrey (1997).
2. DeYoung (1997, p. 21) notes that "accounting-based expense ratios can be misleading and that statistics-based efficient cost frontier approaches, although far from flawless, often provide more accurate estimates of cost efficiency".
3. Terms *X-efficiency* and simply *efficiency* are not used consistently in the literature and in this chapter. They both refer to frontier efficiency.
4. In economic literature, the terms *efficiency* and *inefficiency* are used inconsistently as both terms address the same issues from different perspectives.
5. See Bauer et al. (1998) for a discussion of parametric and non-parametric estimation techniques.
6. As the initial stochastic frontier estimation technique was developed for the production function, I use the production function version of the technique to illustrate the concept of stochastic frontier estimation. This technique can easily be applied to cost and profit functions as well. Also, I use the term technical efficiency because it relates to the production function. Cost efficiency relates to the cost function, respectively.
7. See Bauer (1990) for frontier literature review and assumptions of stochastic frontiers.

8. According to Battese and Broca (1997), these problems have been partially alleviated by the introduction of the truncated normal and the two parameter gamma distributions.

9. FRONTIER 4.1 is available at http://www.une.edu/econometrics/cepa.htm. See also Coelli (1996) for a description of the programme.

10. Berger and Hannan (1998) note that the difficulty in estimating efficiency is in disentangling the two elements of the error term.

11. There is no theoretical model on which correlates to include in the analysis. Maudos et al. (2002, p. 53) note that "… in the absence of a theoretical model, we will speak of potential correlates of efficiency rather than explanatory variables".

12. Berger and Mester (1997) identify two econometric problems with the two-stage estimation procedure: (i) efficiency as the dependent variable in the second stage is an estimate but its standard error is not accounted for in the second-stage regression analysis, and (ii) generally none of the second-stage variables is completely exogenous, thus endogeneity may make conclusions about causation problematic.

13. Probability of Type I error; that is, probability of rejecting the null hypothesis when it holds.

14. I am grateful to Ralph de Haas for letting me use his data on bank ownership in Hungary and Poland to check my data and to partly complement it.

15. I cannot test for statistical significance of differences in means between two countries (ownership groups) with the standard test because the means are averages of estimates and not data.

16. It is important to note that these observations are based on the sample period and one cannot draw inferences about future developments from them.

17. However, bank clients other than financial institutions (or governments) generally do not take into account the riskiness of the bank. Thus, lower deposit interest rates may not necessarily reflect the lower risk of the bank. However, in the interbank market a bank's risk is more closely linked to its cost of funding.

18. Share of five largest banks can be a misleading measure of market concentration if one does not know the share of each of the five banks.

19. ROAA and ROAE are accounting ratios and can, to a certain extent, be influenced by the bank's management. For example, banks may be pursuing a strategy of profit smoothing to prevent excessive increases and declines in these ratios (e.g. variations in loan loss provisioning according to the state of the economy). Another issue is transfer pricing, as a result of which profitability ratios might not reflect the actual performance of a bank.

20. See Grigorian and Manole (2002) for a discussion of the link between stock market capitalisation and bank efficiency.

21. For Model 1 there are more observations (521) but the descriptive statistics are very similar (not reported).

REFERENCES

Aigner, D., Lovell, C. A. K., & Schmidt, P. (1977). Formulation and estimation of stochastic frontier production function models. *Journal of Econometrics, 6*, 21–37.

Allen, L., & Rai, A. (1996). Operational efficiency in banking: An international comparison. *Journal of Banking and Finance, 20*, 655–672.

Altunbas, Y., Gardener, E. P., Molyneux, P., & Moore, B. (2001). Efficiency in European banking. *European Economic Review, 45*, 1931–1955.

Battese, G. E., & Broca, S. S. (1997). Functional forms of stochastic frontier production functions and models for technical inefficiency effects: A comparative study for wheat farmers in Pakistan. *Journal of Productivity Analysis, 8*, 395–414.

Battese, G. E., & Coelli, T. J. (1988). Prediction of firm-level technical efficiencies with a generalised frontier production function and panel data. *Journal of Econometrics, 38*, 387–399.

Battese, G. E., & Coelli, T. J. (1992). Frontier production functions, technical efficiency and panel data with application to paddy farmers in India. *Journal of Productivity Analysis, 3*, 153–169.

Battese, G. E., & Coelli, T. J. (1995). A model of technical inefficiency effects in a stochastic frontier production function for panel data. *Empirical Economics, 20*, 325–332.

Bauer, P. (1990). Recent developments in the econometric estimation of frontiers. *Journal of Econometrics, 46*, 39–56.

Bauer, P. W., Berger, A. N., Ferrier, G. D., & Humphrey, D. B. (1998). Consistency conditions for regulatory analysis of financial institutions: A comparison of frontier efficiency methods. *Journal of Economics and Business, 50*, 85–114.

Berg, S. A., Forsund, F. R., Hjalmarsson, L., & Suominen, M. (1993). Banking efficiency in the Nordic countries. *Journal of Banking and Finance, 17*, 371–388.

Berger, A. N., & Hannan, T. H. (1998). The efficiency cost of market power in the banking industry: A test of the "quiet life" and related hypotheses. *Review of Economics and Statistics, 80*, 454–465.

Berger, A. N., & Humphrey, D. B. (1991). The dominance of inefficiencies over scale and product mix economies in banking. *Journal of Monetary Economics, 28*, 117–148.

Berger, A. N., & Humphrey, D. B. (1997). Efficiency of financial institutions: International survey and directions for future research. *European Journal of Operational Research, 98*, 175–212.

Berger, A. N., & Mester, L. J. (1997). Inside the black box: What explains differences in the efficiencies of financial institutions? *Journal of Banking and Finance, 21*, 895–947.

Berger, A. N., Hunter, W. C., & Timme, S. G. (1993). The efficiency of financial institutions: A review and preview of research past, present, and future. *Journal of Banking and Finance, 17*, 221–249.

Berger, A. N., DeYoung, R., Genay, H., & Udell, G. F. (2000). Globalization of financial institutions: Evidence from cross-border banking performance. *Brookings–Wharton Paper on Financial Services, 3*, 23–158.

Bol, H., de Haan, J., de Haas, R., & Scholtens, B. (2002). How important are foreign banks in European transition countries? A comparative analysis. In: T. Kowalski, R. Lensink & V. Vensel (Eds), *Papers of the 5th Conference on financial sector reform in central and eastern Europe: The impact of foreign banks' entry* (pp. 21–40). Tallinn: Faculty of Economics and Business Administration, Tallinn Technical University.

Casu, B., & Molyneux, P. (2000). *A comparative study of efficiency in European banking*. Wharton Financial Institutions Center Working Paper no. 17.

Cebenoyan, A. S., Cooperman, E. S., & Register, C. A. (1993). The relative efficiency of stock versus mutual S&Ls: A stochastic cost frontier approach. *Journal of Financial Services Research, 7*, 151–170.

Chang, E. C., Hasan, I., & Hunter, W. C. (1998). Efficiency of multinational Banks: an empirical investigation. *Journal Applied Financial Economics, 8*, 689–696.

Coelli, T. J. (1995). Estimators and hypothesis tests for a stochastic frontier function: A monte carlo analysis. *Journal of Productivity Analysis, 6*, 247–268.

Coelli, T. J. (1996). *A guide to FRONTIER Version 4.1: A computer program for stochastic frontier production and cost function estimation.* Centre for Efficiency and Productivity Analysis Working Paper no. 7-96.

Coelli, T. J., Rao, D. S. P., & Battese, G. E. (1998). *An introduction to efficiency and productivity analysis.* Boston: Kluwer Academic Publishers.

DeYoung, R. (1997). Measuring bank cost efficiency: Don't count on accounting ratios. *Financial Practice and Education, 7*, 20–31.

English, M., Grosskopf, S., Hayes, K., & Yaisawarng, S. (1993). Output allocative and technical efficiency of banks. *Journal of Banking and Finance, 17*, 349–366.

Farrell, M. J. (1957). The measurement of productive efficiency. *Journal of the Royal Statistical Society, 120*, 253–281.

Ferrier, G. D., & Lovell, C. A. K. (1990). Measuring cost efficiency in banking: Econometric and linear programming evidence. *Journal of Econometrics, 46*, 229–245.

Grigorian, D. A., & Manole, V. (2002). *Determinants of commercial bank performance in transition: an application of data envelopment analysis.* IMF Working Paper no. 146.

Hasan, I., & Hunter, W. C. (1996). Efficiency of Japanese multinational banks in the United States. In: A. H. Chen (Ed.), *Research in finance* (pp. 157–173). Greenwich: JAI Press.

Hasan, I., & Marton, K. (2000). *Development and efficiency of the banking sector in a transitional economy: Hungarian experience.* Bank of Finland's Institute for Economies in Transition (BOFIT) Discussion Paper no. 7.

IMF. (2000). *International Capital Markets.* Washington: International Monetary Fund.

Jondrow, J., Knox Lovell, C. A., Materov, I. S., & Schmidt, P. (1982). On the estimation of the technical inefficiency in the stochastic frontier production function model. *Journal of Econometrics, 19*, 233–238.

Kaparakis, E. I., Miller, S. M., & Noulas, A. G. (1994). Short-run cost inefficiency of commercial banks: A flexible stochastic frontier approach. *Journal of Money, Credit, and Banking, 26*, 875–893.

Kodde, D. A., & Palm, F. C. (1986). Wald criteria for jointly testing equality and inequality restrictions. *Econometrica, 54*, 1243–1248.

Konopielko, L. (1999). Foreign banks' entry into central and east European markets: motives and activities. *Post-Communist Economies, 11*, 463–485.

Košak, M. (2000). *Učinkovitost in tržna struktura v bančništvu – Primer Slovenije.* Doctoral dissertation, Ekonomska fakulteta, Ljubljana.

Kumbhakar, S. C., Ghosh, S., & McGuckin, J. T. (1991). A generalized Production frontier approach for estimating determinants of inefficiency in US dairy farms. *Journal of Business and Economic Statistics, 9*, 279–286.

Leibenstein, H. (1966). Allocative efficiency vs. "x-efficiency". *American Economic Review, 56*, 392–415.

Lovell, C. A. K. (1993). Production frontier and productive efficiency. In: H. O. Fried, C. A. K. Lovell & S. S. Schmidt (Eds), *The measurement of productive efficiency* (pp. 3–67). Oxford: Oxford University press.

Mathieson, D. J., & Roldos, J. (2001). Foreign banks in emerging markets. In: R. E. Litan, P. Masson & M. Pomerleano (Eds), *Open doors – foreign participation in financial systems in developing countries* (pp. 15–55). Washington, DC: Brookings Institution Press.

Maudos, J., Pastor, J. M., Perez, F., & Quesada, J. (2002). Cost and profit efficiency in European banks. *Journal of International Financial Markets, Institutions and Money, 12*, 33–58.

Meeusen, W., & van den Broeck, J. (1977). Efficiency estimation from Cobb–Douglas production functions with composed error. *International Economic Review, 18*, 435–444.

Mester, L. J. (1993). Efficiency in the savings and loan industry. *Journal of Banking and Finance, 17*, 267–286.

Mester, L. J. (1994). How efficient are third district banks? *Federal Reserve Bank of Philadelphia Business Review, 3–18.*

Mester, L. J. (1996). A study of bank efficiency taking into account risk-preferences. *Journal of Banking and Finance, 20*, 1025–1045.

Molyneux, P., Altunbas, Y., & Gardener, E. (1996). *Efficiency in European Banking.* Chichester: John Wiley & Sons Ltd.

Nikiel, E. M., & Opiela, T. P. (2002). Customer type and bank efficiency in Poland: Implications for emerging market banking. *Contemporary Economic Policy, 20*, 255–271.

Pastor, J. T., Lozano, A., & Pastor, J. M. (1997). *Efficiency of European banking systems: A correction by environment variables.* Instituto Valeniano de Investigaciones Economicas Working Paper no. Ec97-12.

Reifschneider, D., & Stevenson, R. (1991). Systematic departures from the frontier: A framework for the analysis of firm inefficiency. *International Economic Review, 32*, 715–723.

Sabi, M. (1988). An application of the theory of foreign direct investment to multinational banking in LDCs. *Journal of International Business Studies, 19*, 433–447.

Schure, P., & Wagenvoort, R. (1999). *Economies of scale and efficiency in European banking: New evidence.* Economic and Financial Reports 99/01. EIB, Luxembourg.

Sealey, C. W., Jr., & Lindley, J. T. (1977). Inputs, outputs, and a theory of production and cost at depository financial institutions. *Journal of Finance, 32*, 1251–1266.

Wachtel, P. (1995). *Foreign banking in the central European economies in transition.* Issue paper. Institute for EastWest Studies.

Yildirim, H. S., & Philippatos, G. C. (2002). *Efficiency of banks: Recent evidence from the transition economies of Europe 1993–2000.* University of Tennessee.

A COMPARATIVE STUDY OF BANKS' BALANCE SHEETS IN THE EUROPEAN UNION AND EUROPEAN TRANSITION COUNTRIES, 1995–2003

Ilko Naaborg and Bert Scholtens

1. INTRODUCTION

The banking sector in the new European Union Member States (NMS)[1] has changed dramatically since the transition from centrally planned to market-based economies.[2] In 1993, the ratio of average banking assets to gross domestic product (GDP) was 53 per cent, and this had increased to 72 per cent by 2000. However the banking sector in NMS is, however, still relatively small compared to the former European Union 15 (EU-15), for which the same ratio was 140 per cent in 2000. In NMS the level of bank intermediation is also low. In 2000, the ratio of private sector credit to GDP was less than 40 per cent, whereas in the euro area it was 100 per cent. A third distinguishing feature of NMS banks is that foreign investors now dominate ownership. In 1995, 8 per cent of banking assets were in foreign hands, and by 2002 this had increased to 88 per cent.[3] In contrast, banks in

Emerging European Financial Markets: Independence and Integration Post-Enlargement
International Finance Review, Volume 6, 157–178
ISSN: 1569-3767/doi:10.1016/S1569-3767(05)06007-3

the former EU-15 are mainly domestically owned or are traded on national stock markets.

In this chapter, we compare bank balance sheets in the former EU-15 countries with their counterparts in NMS, and South-Eastern Europe and the Commonwealth of Independent States (SEE/CIS).[4] Our data comprise information from the balance sheets of commercial banks for the period 1995–2002. We first examine the asset side – the various types of loan products and their maturity. We then analyse the composition of the banks' liabilities. A special feature of this study is that we differentiate between domestically owned banks and foreign banks in all three regions.[5] Most of the existing literature on banking in the transition economies focuses on bank efficiency and performance, on banks' impact on the domestic economy, and on differences between domestic and foreign banks with respect to these issues (for a review of this literature, see Zajc, 2003). We examine the composition of banks' balance sheets to see what is behind the conventional aggregate measures that are used when analysing financial development.

We find that there are substantial differences between the three regions, but that the balance sheet structure of banks in the NMS is converging to that of banks in the former EU-15. With respect to the impact of foreign ownership on financial intermediation, we find that foreign banks are better capitalised than domestic banks, and that customer deposits comprise a larger proportion of their funding base. Foreign banks also make less use of alternative funding sources than their domestic counterparts. Further, in all countries, foreign banks are more likely to be involved in leasing operations and loans to the corporate sector than domestic banks.

The structure of the chapter is as follows. In Section 2 we introduce the data, and in Section 3, bank size is discussed. Sections 4 and 5 present the analysis on assets, and liabilities and equity, respectively. Section 6 summarises and concludes.

2. DATA

We use 31,319 observations from the balance sheets of commercial banks, savings banks and cooperative banks provided by BankScope, for the period 1995–2003. Table 1 shows the number of banks in our sample on a regional basis. It is clear from the table that as the number of banks in 2003 is considerably lower than in previous years, we are not always able to include data from 2003 in the analysis. Using previous issues of BankScope we are able to provide yearly ownership data (if available).[6] Appendix A

Table 1. Banks in Sample by Ownership.

Group	Class	1995	1996	1997	1998	1999	2000	2001	2002	2003
Former EU-15	All banks	2,780	3,253	3,543	3,702	3,735	3,645	3,632	3,233	402
	Domestic banks	144	200	206	205	203	212	346	303	65
	Foreign banks	107	130	132	132	145	135	240	217	29
NMS	All banks	148	212	235	226	230	251	243	225	54
	Domestic banks	9	15	16	17	14	6	47	44	9
	Foreign banks	8	14	18	19	23	36	95	89	22
SEE/CIS	All banks	82	114	148	149	223	272	301	243	32
	Domestic banks	0	1	1	1	7	8	39	34	7
	Foreign banks	2	2	3	3	3	5	26	26	3

presents the number of banks in each country, and Table 1 summarises the number of majority-owned domestic banks and majority-owned foreign banks in the three regions. Where our analysis involves comparing foreign banks and domestic banks, we include only those that can clearly be identified as majority domestic owned or majority foreign owned.

3. BANK SIZE

Appendix B gives the bank assets in each country as a percentage of total bank assets in their region. In the former EU-15, banks in France, Germany and the UK hold 60 per cent of all EU banking assets, and Poland, the Czech Republic and Hungary together account for almost 70 per cent of bank assets in the NMS. In the SEE/CIS group Russia clearly dominates, with approximately three-quarters of the region's assets. Appendix C shows average bank size. In the former EU-15, banks are largest in the Netherlands, Finland and the UK, and German and Austrian banks are the smallest. Czech and Polish banks are the largest in the NMS banking sector.

Table 2 shows the changing median size in each region for the period 1995–2002. Banks in the three regions differ considerably in size. In 1995, the median bank size in the former EU-15 was more than 8 times that of NMS banks, and over 50 times that of SEE/CIS banks, and these ratios remain about the same in 2002. Although the levels of bank size do not seem to converge, Fig. 1 shows that banks in each region grew at about the same pace on average, tripling in size over the period.

Table 2. Median Bank Size in Million Euro's.

	1995	1996	1997	1998	1999	2000	2001	2002
Former EU-15	3.303	6.663	6.870	7.432	9.096	9.892	11.075	10.533
NMS	387	348	316	655	712	780	1.102	1.221
SEE/CIS	291	262	360	261	372	356	328	309

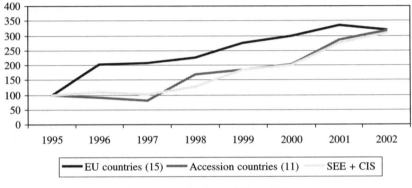

Fig. 1. Bank Size (1995 = 100).

3.1. Foreign versus Domestic Banks

Fig. 2(a)[7] depicts bank size in the former EU. It is clear that foreign banks are smaller than domestic banks. Domestic banks increased in size over the period 1995–2002, but foreign bank size saw no particular trend. In the NMS (Fig. 2(b)) a different picture is apparent. Foreign banks' size increased steadily over the period and domestic banks reduced in size. This trend might be explained by foreign acquisitions of large privatised state-owned banks in the region. Fig. 2(c) shows that in CIS/SEE countries, domestic banks are generally larger than foreign banks, but foreign banks grew substantially in size over the period.

4. BANK ASSETS

Table 3 shows the composition of assets in four categories: total loans, total other earning assets, total non-earning assets and total fixed assets. In all three regions, total loans increased gradually over the period 1995–2002 to

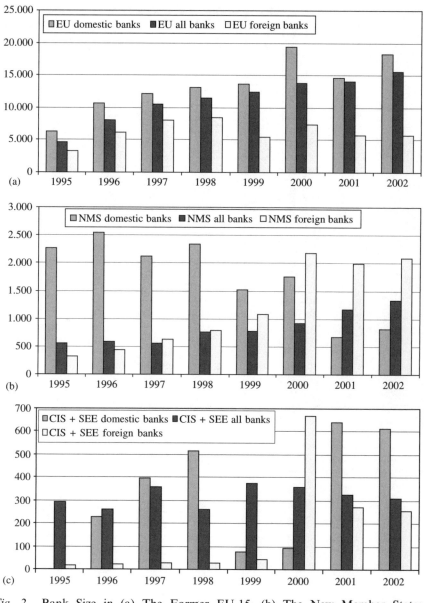

Fig. 2. Bank Size in (a) The Former EU-15. (b) The New Member States.
(c) SEE/CIS Countries (Averages, in € Million, 1995–2002).

Table 3. Composition of Assets.

Year	Total Loans – Net			Total Other Earning Assets			Total Non-Earning Assets			Total Fixed Assets		
	EU-15 (%)	NMS (%)	CIS/SEE (%)	EU-15 (%)	NMS (%)	CIS/SEE (%)	EU-15 (%)	NMS (%)	CIS/SEE (%)	EU-15 (%)	NMS (%)	CIS/SEE (%)
1995	46.3	44.0	31.6	46.8	41.7	43.6	5.5	9.3	17.3	1.5	5.0	7.5
1996	47.1	40.7	40.3	45.9	44.5	37.2	5.6	9.0	13.7	1.4	5.8	8.8
1997	48.1	40.0	42.5	44.4	45.4	35.6	6.1	9.0	13.6	1.4	5.6	8.3
1998	48.9	42.6	44.1	43.1	43.1	36.1	6.7	8.8	12.3	1.3	5.6	7.6
1999	50.2	43.1	45.3	41.4	43.0	36.2	7.2	8.2	11.1	1.2	5.6	7.5
2000	51.1	43.4	43.7	40.4	44.3	38.4	7.4	7.5	11.6	1.1	4.8	6.3
2001	51.4	42.0	46.4	39.4	45.7	35.6	8.0	8.1	12.6	1.1	4.1	5.4
2002	52.3	46.9	48.0	38.7	42.8	36.5	8.0	6.6	10.5	1.0	3.7	5.0
2003	51.5	55.4	53.5	38.5	34.1	31.7	9.0	6.7	9.6	1.0	3.7	5.2

around 50 per cent of assets. Total "other earning" assets have fallen as a proportion of assets in the former EU-15, while in the NMS and the CIS/SEE this ratio has been relatively stable. With respect to non-earning assets, the three regions have converged as the ratio rose in the former EU-15 and fell in the two other regions. Fixed assets as a proportion of total assets is considerably higher in NMS and CIS/SEE than in the former EU-15, and the trend is clearly downward in all three regions.

4.1. Loan Portfolio

Figures 3(a)–3(c) show that the composition of the banks' loan portfolio maturity is quite different in each region. In the former EU-15 (Fig. 3(a)) long-term lending clearly dominates. For example, loans maturing 5 years from now make up more than 30 per cent of the banks' assets. In general, this maturity structure does not change over the period. EU-15 banks also lend a substantial amount short term: 30 per cent of total loans have a maturity of less than 3 months. Banks in the NMS (Fig. 3(b)) have more than 50 per cent of their loans maturing in 1–5 years. The average maturity of loans in NMS banks rose steadily over the period 1995–2003, as the share of loans maturing within 1 year dropped from 60 to 45 per cent. However, the share of loans maturing in more than 5 years decreased as well. In the CIS and SEE countries, at least two-thirds of all loans mature within 1 year, and this percentage has changed little over the period.

Table 4 details the loan products that banks offer. The table shows the decreasing importance of loans to municipalities and governments in the former EU-15 and the Baltics.[8] In the former EU-15, mortgage lending increased. Banks in NMS do not report on this loan type. Hire-purchase contracts[9] and lease contracts[10] increased in both regions, especially in the Baltics. While "other loans" are substantial in the former EU-15, "loans to other corporate" are substantial in the Baltics.[11]

5. EQUITY AND LIABILITIES

5.1. Equity

Table 5(a) presents the equity ratio. The equity ratio of banks in the former EU-15 has remained about 5 per cent over the period, while the equity ratio for NMS banks has risen from about 8 per cent of total assets to over 10 per

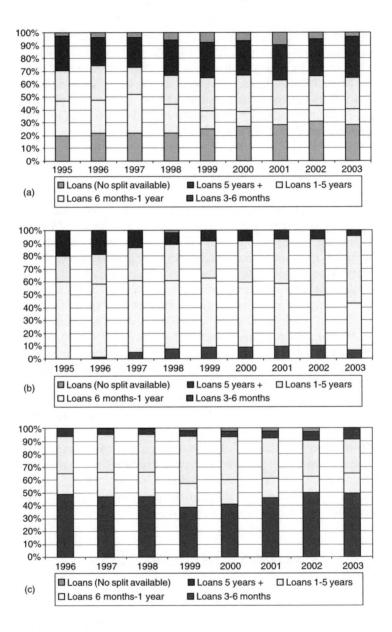

(a)

(b)

(c)

cent. The equity ratio is highest for banks in the SEE/CIS countries at around 14 per cent. This may reflect these banks' high levels of risk, as equity acts as a buffer against unexpected losses. A more appropriate measure of strength is the BIS capital ratio, but this, unfortunately, was not available for most of the banks outside the former EU-15.

5.2. Liabilities

Table 5(b) details the main categories of non-equity funding: deposits, money market funding, other funding, loan loss and other reserves, and other liabilities. The table reveals that banks in the former EU-15 have a more diversified funding base than banks in NMS and SEE/CIS. Although for all three groups deposits are by far the dominant source of funding, this

Table 4. Customer Loans, Product Specification.

Year	Loans to Municipalities/ Government		Mortgages		Hire Purchase/ Lease		Other Loans		Loans to Other Corporate	
	EU-15 (%)	NMS (%)	EU-15 (%)	NMS (%)	EU-15 (%)	NMS (%)	EU-15 (%)	NMS (%)	EU-15 (%)	NMS (%)
1995	9.0	10.9	6.5	0.0	1.3	0.0	80.9	59.6	2.1	26.9
1996	3.7	6.2	13.3	0.0	1.4	0.3	79.2	46.9	2.1	41.1
1997	3.4	4.9	10.2	0.0	1.6	1.9	82.3	26.6	2.1	58.9
1998	3.2	3.9	11.3	0.0	2.0	4.3	80.2	21.4	3.0	61.4
1999	3.1	2.3	12.2	0.0	2.0	3.9	79.1	22.1	3.3	65.3
2000	3.0	3.3	13.2	0.0	2.3	4.3	78.8	20.4	2.6	63.0
2001	2.7	4.0	13.4	0.0	2.5	8.2	78.8	15.1	2.6	58.0
2002	2.7	1.9	15.9	0.0	2.7	9.1	75.9	25.4	2.8	49.6

Source: Authors' calculations based on data from France, Italy, Luxembourg, the Netherlands, Spain, Latvia and Lithuania.

Fig. 3. Customer Loans in (a) The Former EU-15 (by Maturity). *Source:* Authors' calculations based on data from Denmark, Finland, Ireland, Italy, Luxembourg and Sweden. (b) The NMS (by Maturity). *Source:* Authors' calculations based on data from the Czech Republic, Hungary, Poland, Romania, Slovenia. (c) SEE/CIS Countries (by Maturity). *Source:* Authors' calculations based on data from Armenia, Azarbadijan, Belarus, Bosnia-Herzegovina, Kazachstan, Moldova, Russia and Uzbekistan.

Table 5(a). Liabilities and Equity.

Year	Former EU-15		NMS		SEE/CIS	
	Liabilities (%)	Equity (%)	Liabilities (%)	Equity (%)	Liabilities (%)	Equity (%)
1995	95.1	4.9	91.8	8.2	79.9	20.1
1996	95.2	4.8	92.7	7.3	87.7	12.3
1997	95.4	4.6	90.0	10.0	84.6	15.4
1998	95.2	4.8	90.0	10.0	85.4	14.6
1999	94.8	5.2	89.2	10.8	85.6	14.4
2000	94.8	5.2	89.5	10.5	85.6	14.4
2001	94.9	5.1	89.8	10.2	86.2	13.8
2002	95.1	4.9	89.7	10.3	86.4	13.6
2003	94.8	5.2	89.9	10.1	85.9	14.1

Source: Authors' calculations.

category is of decreasing importance in the former EU-15. However, deposits are increasingly dominating the liability side for SEE/CIS banks, while banks in NMS see little relative change in deposits. Money market funding and other funding is rising in former EU-15 banks, but it plays a relatively insignificant role in NMS and SEE/CIS banks.

Deposits are clearly the main source of funding. Figures 4(a)–4(c) depict deposit maturity in the former EU-15, the NMS and CEE/CIS, respectively. Deposits in the former EU-15 are highly liquid – about 50 per cent are in the form of demand and savings deposits, which can be withdrawn at call, another 20 per cent of deposits have a maturity within 3 months. The proportion of liquid deposits is slightly lower in the NMS with 60 per cent having a maturity of less than 3 months, and it is much lower in the SEE/CIS where only 35 per cent of deposits is available on an immediate basis. Deposits with a maturity of 6–12 months are dominant in the SEE/CIS, constituting about two-thirds of all deposits.[12] In the former EU-15, the maturity of the deposit portfolio changed little over the period 1995–2003, whereas in the NMS there was a gradual increase in the relative size of long-term maturing deposits (1–5 years) from 1 per cent in 1995 to around 11 per cent in 2003. In the SEE/CIS countries long-term deposits seem to be non-existent.

5.3. Foreign Versus Domestic Banks: Operations and Funding

Do foreign banks differ from domestic banks with respect to their balance sheet composition? With respect to assets, Table 6 shows that foreign banks

Table 5(b). Composition of Banks' Liabilities.

Year	Deposits			Money Market Funding			Other Funding			Loan Loss and Other Reserves			Other Liabilities		
	EU-15 (%)	NMS (%)	SEE/CIS (%)	EU-15 (%)	NMS (%)	SEE/CIS (%)	EU-15 (%)	NMS (%)	SEE/CIS (%)	EU-15 (%)	NMS (%)	SEE/CIS (%)	EU-15 (%)	NMS (%)	SEE/CIS (%)
1995	78.8	87.2	72.4	7.0	1.3	4.0	8.1	1.9	5.4	0.2	0.0	1.6	5.8	6.3	16.6
1996	76.7	85.3	78.3	6.4	1.9	3.9	9.9	3.7	7.9	0.3	0.0	0.1	6.7	5.3	9.8
1997	74.9	88.4	82.5	6.8	0.8	3.7	10.6	3.5	6.3	0.3	0.0	0.1	7.4	4.8	7.4
1998	74.1	90.4	75.9	7.0	1.7	4.6	10.4	2.0	7.8	0.4	0.1	0.0	8.1	4.7	11.7
1999	72.1	91.9	80.7	8.1	2.0	3.5	11.1	3.9	10.2	0.6	0.1	0.1	8.0	4.4	5.4
2000	69.8	90.6	83.4	8.7	1.6	2.1	11.9	3.3	10.0	1.1	0.1	0.1	8.5	5.1	4.5
2001	69.3	90.8	87.9	8.8	0.8	1.5	12.6	2.6	6.9	1.1	0.2	0.0	8.3	4.7	3.6
2002	68.0	89.6	88.8	8.7	0.9	1.7	13.1	3.0	6.7	1.1	0.3	0.1	9.1	3.9	2.8
2003	65.9	87.7	88.7	9.2	0.7	3.3	13.0	4.3	5.9	1.2	0.1	0.0	10.7	3.8	2.1

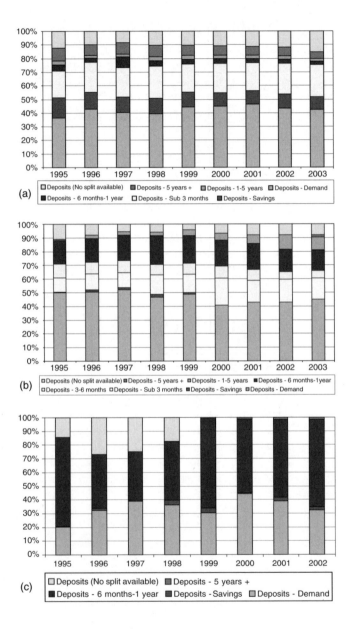

(a)

(b)

(c)

in the former EU-15 generally have fewer loans on their balance sheet and more "other earning" assets than domestic banks. In the NMS, foreign-owned banks' asset has a different structure, with more loans and fewer "other earning" assets than domestic banks. The composition of loans differs for foreign banks depending on whether they operate in the former EU-15 or the NMS. In the former EU-15, "other loans" dominate foreign bank lending whereas NMS foreign banks predominantly lend to "other corporate". Foreign banks in both regions share the fact that they lend more in the form of hire-purchase and leasing than domestic banks. As to the maturity of the loan portfolio, foreign banks are similar in all three regions, lending more long term than domestic banks. Domestic banks lend more in the mid-term segment of the maturity spectrum (6 months to 5 years). Liabilities are similar for foreign banks in the three regions, as they rely more on deposits than domestic banks for which money market and other funding are important. Equity comprises more of the total funding of banks in the NMS and SEE/CIS, and in all three regions foreign banks have more equity than domestic banks.

6. SUMMARY AND CONCLUSION

Using data from bank balance sheets, we analyse the banking sectors of the former EU-15, the NMS and SEE/CIS in terms of size, operations and funding. In the former EU-15, the banking sector in relation to GDP is about twice the size of banking in the NMS (including those that will soon join). Although bank size still differs substantially between the regions, median growth has been similar between 1995 and 2002.

The composition of assets and liabilities of banks in the three regions appears to be quite similar. This similarity vanishes, however, when we focus on the asset side of the balance sheet. Banks in the former EU-15 have more loans with longer maturities than bank in the NMS and SEE/CIS, and there is greater diversity of loans amongst the former EU-15 banks. From

---

Fig. 4. Customer Deposits in (a) The Former EU-15 (by Maturity). *Source:* Authors' calculations based on data for Denmark, Finland, Ireland, Italy, Luxembourg, the Netherlands, the UK and Sweden. (b) The NMS (by Maturity). *Source:* Authors' calculations based on data for the Czech Republic, Croatia, Hungary, Lithuania, Latvia, Poland. Romania and the Slovak Republic. (c) SEE/CIS Countries (by Maturity). *Source:* Authors' calculations based on data for the Ukraine and Albania, Belarus, Georgia, Macedonia when available.

Table 6.   Operations and Funding: Domestic and Foreign Banks
(Averages, 1995–2002).

	Former EU-15		NMS		SEE/CIS	
	DB	FB	DB	FB	DB	FB
Assets						
Total loans–net	47.4	45.9	40.7	42.9	53.9	34.7
Total other earning assets	45.4	47.9	47.9	42.9	26.8	42.9
Total non-earning assets	5.9	5.0	6.8	9.5	13.2	14.1
Total fixed assets	1.3	1.2	4.7	4.7	6.0	8.4
	100.0	100.0	100.0	100.0	100.0	100.0
*Customer loans (product)**						
Loans to municipalities/government	4.9	1.0	0.1	2.3		
Mortgages	14.1	3.5	0.0	0.0		
Hire purchase/lease	2.2	2.8	1.3	6.4		
Other loans	75.9	82.0	45.0	5.9		
Loans to other corporate	2.8	10.6	37.7	78.4		
	100.0	100.0	84.1	93.0		
*Customer loans (maturity)***						
Loans sub–3 months	31.7	29.3	0.0	0.0	0.0	0.0
Loans 3–6 months	0.3	0.3	0.0	6.0	44.7	49.4
Loans 6—12 months	21.6	18.8	49.2	46.2	21.4	35.1
Loans 1–5 years	21.9	21.6	41.6	30.1	29.1	8.3
Loans 5 + years	19.7	26.9	9.2	15.8	0.0	3.1
Loans (no split available)	1.6	1.5	0.0	0.0	0.5	0.0
	96.8	98.4	100.0	98.1	95.7	95.9
*Liabilities****						
Total deposits	74.2	80.9	86.1	89.2	80.6	87.5
Total money market funding	8.8	5.0	2.0	1.8	5.8	3.3
Total other funding	9.8	7.1	6.5	2.7	9.8	2.3
Total loan loss and other reserves	0.6	0.3	0.4	0.2	0.2	0.0
Other liabilities	6.7	6.7	5.1	6.2	3.6	6.9
	100.0	100.0	100.0	100.0	100.0	100.0
Equity						
Liabilities	94.6	93.8	90.2	88.7	80.3	74.3
Equity	5.4	6.2	9.8	11.3	19.7	25.7
	100.0	100.0	100.0	100.0	100.0	100.0

Notes: DB: domestic bank; FB: foreign bank.

*NMS data are based on Latvia and Lithuania. Loan product specification of banks in SEE/CIS countries are not sufficiently available. Customer loan product category average per group was calculated based only on those countries for which at least 73% of all loans could be categorised by product.

**SEE/CIS averages are based on 2000–2002 data. Customer loan maturity category average per group was calcultated based only on those countries for which at least 78% of all loans could be categorised by maturity.

***SEE/CIS averages are based on 1996–2002.

this perspective, therefore, the NMS banks are still underdeveloped. Further, when examining the banks' deposit base, liquidity is much higher for the clients of EU-15 banks than for those in transition countries. In combination with the maturity composition of the loan portfolios, we can conclude that banks in the former EU-15 are much more involved in maturity transformation than those in the transition countries.

Contrary to the general trend, foreign bank size in the former EU-15 became smaller after 1998. Due to continued merger and acquisition activity in the NMS, foreign banks are on average three times larger than domestic banks. In all regions, foreign banks are more involved in leasing operations and in loans to the corporate sector than domestic banks. In addition, foreign banks tend to be funded more with deposits and have less well-diversified liabilities than domestic banks. Foreign banks in all regions also are better capitalised than their domestic counterparts. Whether this means that they incur more risk is a matter for future research.

We conclude that in the course of their development, the NMS and transition countries are catching up. Banks in the former EU-15 are much more involved in credit and maturity risk transformation than those in the NMS and even more so than those in SEE/CIS. However, in the NMS we detect a trend towards more credit risk and maturity/liquidity risk transformation – a trend that is not apparent in banks operating in the SEE/CIS region.

NOTES

1. Croatia, Czech Republic, Estonia, Hungary, Latvia, Lithuania, Poland, Romania, Slovenia and Slovak Republic. Romania is expected to join the EU in 2007. Negotiations concerning EU accession of Croatia will start in 2005.

2. See for example Scholtens (2000) and Zajc (2003).

3. Data from Naaborg, Bol, de Haan, Scholtens and de Haas (2004).

4. Albania, Armenia, Azarbadijan, Belarus, Bosnia-Herzegovina, Georgia, Kazakhstan, Kyrgystan, Macedonia, Moldova, Russia, Serbia and Montenegro, Tadjikstan, Turkmenistan, Ukraine and Uzbekistan.

5. A foreign bank is defined as one in which more than 50 per cent of the assets are in hands of non-domestic investors.

6. One of the drawbacks of BankScope is that bank ownership information is given only for the most recent update. We thank Mark Wessels and Bob Vaanhof (BvDEP) for making previous versions available to us.

7. In Fig. 1 median values are shown, and Figs. 2(a)–2(c) show average values.

8. Loan product data of banks in the SEE/CIS region are not sufficiently available in BankScope.

9. Hire purchase: A method of buying goods in which the purchaser takes possession of them as soon as he has paid an initial instalment of the price (a deposit)

and obtains ownership of the goods when he has paid all the agreed number of subsequent instalments. A hire purchase agreement differs from a credit-sale agreement and sale by instalments (or a deferred payment agreement) because in these transactions ownership passes when the contract is signed. It also differs from a contract of hire, because in this case ownership never passes. Hire purchase agreements were formerly controlled by government regulations stipulating the minimum deposit and the length of the repayment period. These controls were removed in 1982. Hire purchase agreements were also formerly controlled by the Hire Purchase Act (1965), but most are now regulated by the Consumer Credit Act (1974). In this Act a hire purchase agreement is regarded as one in which goods are bailed in return for periodical payments by the bailee; ownership passes to the bailee if he complies with the terms of the agreement and exercises his option to purchase. A hire purchase agreement often involves a finance company as a third party. The seller of the goods sells them outright to the finance company, which enters into a hire purchase agreement with the hirer (Financial Glossary, UK).

10. A lease is a contract by which the owner of property allows another to use it for a specified time, usually in return for payment (Financial Glossary, UK).

11. Currently Bureau van Dijk has no data definition guide. Data provider Fitch is currently working on a guide. The difference between "other loans" and "loans to other corporate" remains unclear.

12. Please note that in fact the public usually does not withdraw all demand and savings deposits but leaves a substantial part of these funds on a semi-permanent basis with their bank.

REFERENCES

Naaborg, I. J., Bol, H., de Haan, J., Scholtens, B., & de Haas, R. A. (2004). How important are foreign banks in the financial development of European transition countries? *Journal of Emerging Markets Finance, 3*, 99–123.

Scholtens, B. (2000). Financial regulation and financial system architecture in Central Europe. *Journal of Banking and Finance, 24*, 525–553.

Zajc, P. (2003). *The role of foreign banks in Central and Eastern Europe*. PhD thesis: University of Lljubliana.

APPENDIX A

Numbers of Banks in Each Country.

	1995	1996	1997	1998	1999	2000	2001	2002	2003
Austria	54	70	119	133	141	163	177	166	24
Belgium	67	74	69	60	57	54	53	41	5
Germany	1651	1822	1804	1988	1942	1825	1700	1457	109
Denmark	35	90	90	93	93	100	93	88	57
Spain	67	126	141	134	122	133	144	140	58
Finland	4	8	9	9	9	10	9	8	8
France	320	333	319	309	332	333	331	275	25
UK	104	145	142	146	139	134	136	129	31
Greece	4	11	17	15	15	15	15	16	7
Ireland	15	25	27	29	31	33	34	35	11
Italy	275	336	598	585	651	651	682	636	34
Luxembourg	107	118	120	114	120	110	98	89	13
The Netherlands	42	52	47	44	43	39	39	37	8
Portugal	29	32	33	33	28	27	22	19	3
Sweden	6	11	8	10	12	18	99	97	9
Total	2780	3253	3543	3702	3735	3645	3632	3233	402
Bulgaria	12	16	18	21	20	24	24	23	5
Czech Republic	22	25	24	21	22	24	24	22	2
Estonia	5	9	9	4	4	5	5	5	3
Croatia	24	33	40	35	34	37	36	32	4
Hungary	16	22	24	23	27	29	25	23	4
Lithuania	3	6	8	8	8	9	9	9	7
Latvia	9	16	21	18	18	19	21	21	12
Poland	28	37	40	38	40	42	41	35	11
Romania	4	5	8	21	24	27	25	24	1
Slovenia	12	25	24	19	19	19	17	15	5
Slovak Republic	13	18	19	18	14	16	16	16	
Total	148	212	235	226	230	251	243	225	54
Albania			2	2	7	6	5	5	
Armenia		3	6	6	7	6	5	4	
Azarbadijan	1	5	7	8	8	11	11	10	1

APPENDIX A (*Continued*)

	1995	1996	1997	1998	1999	2000	2001	2002	2003
Belarus	3	6	6	7	11	11	14	13	1
Bosnia-Herzegovina	3	5	9	14	17	17	17	13	1
Georgia	1	4	5	6	10	9	5	4	
Kazakhstan	1	4	10	18	16	17	19	16	12
Kyrgystan	1	1	2			6	6	3	
FYR of Macedonia	6	7	7	7	11	11	12	10	
Moldova	3	6	7	6	10	10	10	10	2
Russia	41	45	46	38	76	114	131	104	12
Serbia and Montenegro	10	14	14	10	11	14	23	18	3
Tadjikstan	1	1							
Turkmenistan					1	1	1	1	
Ukraine	10	11	24	23	30	32	32	24	
Uzbekistan	1	2	3	4	8	7	10	8	
Total	82	114	148	149	223	272	301	243	32

APPENDIX B

Percentage of Banking Assets per Country.

	1995	1996	1997	1998	1999	2000	2001	2002
France	23.2	26.8	23.2	22.7	27.4	25.1	25.1	25.6
Germany	24.2	15.7	21.1	18.9	19.5	21.5	21.5	18.9
UK	10.8	12.8	11.3	12.6	12.5	13.7	13.7	15.0
Italy	14.2	13.0	13.7	12.8	10.8	9.5	9.5	9.7
The Netherlands	2.0	6.2	6.0	6.9	7.0	7.1	7.1	7.2
Spain	4.9	8.2	7.5	7.1	5.6	5.9	5.9	6.0
Belgium	8.8	6.0	6.1	6.7	4.7	4.3	4.3	4.0
Austria	2.8	1.3	1.0	2.0	2.0	2.4	2.3	2.4
Luxembourg	4.3	2.9	2.7	2.5	2.7	2.5	2.5	2.3
Ireland	0.7	0.8	1.0	1.2	1.4	1.6	1.6	2.0
Sweden	0.4	2.2	1.9	1.8	1.9	1.8	1.8	1.9
Denmark	0.5	1.1	1.2	1.3	1.3	1.6	1.6	1.8
Finland	1.1	0.9	1.4	1.2	1.2	1.4	1.4	1.3
Portugal	2.1	1.4	1.4	1.4	1.3	1.1	1.1	1.1
Greece	0.1	0.6	0.6	0.7	0.7	0.7	0.7	0.7
Total	100.0	100.0	100.0	100.0	100.0	100.0	100.0	100.0
Poland	24.3	29.6	34.2	33.3	36.9	39.4	38.2	32.6
Czech Republic	35.7	33.4	27.1	27.0	20.4	21.3	21.7	23.0
Hungary	11.0	10.7	11.5	11.9	13.7	12.4	11.1	12.8
Croatia	3.8	6.9	7.4	6.2	5.9	5.9	6.7	7.5
Slovenia	1.5	5.7	5.4	6.5	6.7	5.6	5.8	6.3
Slovak Republic	13.2	9.2	8.3	6.9	6.5	5.3	5.6	6.0
Romania	4.6	2.3	0.6	2.8	4.0	4.0	4.1	3.8
Estonia	0.4	1.0	1.8	1.6	1.7	1.6	1.9	2.2
Latvia	0.2	0.5	1.0	0.7	1.0	1.5	1.8	2.1
Bulgaria	4.7	0.2	1.9	1.9	1.9	1.7	1.8	2.1
Lithuania	0.5	0.6	0.9	1.1	1.2	1.2	1.3	1.4
Total	100.0	100.0	100.0	100.0	100.0	100.0	100.0	100.0

APPENDIX B   (*Continued*)

	1995	1996	1997	1998	1999	2000	2001	2002
Russia	50.2	43.2	38.2	19.9	57.1	70.6	71.9	74.0
Kazachstan	0.1	1.9	2.2	5.0	2.7	3.7	5.0	5.9
Ukraine	7.5	5.4	6.9	6.8	3.4	4.0	4.8	4.5
Uzbekistan	4.9	9.3	5.8	9.9	6.6	5.1	4.7	3.2
Serbia and Montenegro	32.7	33.9	21.5	33.1	15.7	5.4	3.3	2.9
Belarus	2.1	2.5	22.1	18.9	6.2	2.6	2.6	2.5
Albania			0.1	0.1	2.1	2.0	1.9	1.7
Bosnia-Herzegovina	0.5	0.7	0.9	2.7	1.1	1.0	1.5	1.6
Turkmenistan					2.4	2.6	1.8	1.3
FYR of Macedonia	1.6	1.5	0.8	1.6	1.3	1.2	1.2	1.1
Azarbadijan	0.0	0.8	0.6	0.8	0.5	0.8	0.5	0.5
Moldova	0.3	0.5	0.5	0.5	0.3	0.4	0.4	0.4
Armenia		0.2	0.2	0.4	0.3	0.2	0.2	0.2
Georgia	0.1	0.2	0.2	0.3	0.3	0.3	0.1	0.1
Kyrgystan	0.0	0.0	0.0			0.0	0.0	0.1
Tajikstan	0.0	0.0						
Total	100.0	100.0	100.0	100.0	100.0	100.0	100.0	100.0

APPENDIX C

Average Bank Size: € billion in 2002.

	1995	1996	1997	1998	1999	2000	2001	2002
The Netherlands	3.103	14.640	20.085	26.392	31.283	40.360	43.753	46.540
Finland	18.127	13.597	23.639	23.161	25.981	29.840	36.566	39.842
UK	6.642	10.886	12.484	14.634	17.215	21.595	24.182	27.838
Belgium	8.413	9.970	13.771	18.988	15.667	17.645	19.569	23.293
France	4.649	9.916	11.405	12.407	15.780	16.410	18.275	22.277
Ireland	2.919	3.884	5.859	7.265	8.564	9.892	11.075	13.886
Portugal	4.670	5.501	6.870	6.987	9.096	9.390	12.160	13.470
Greece	1.170	6.663	5.618	7.432	9.558	10.477	11.343	10.533
Spain	4.648	8.039	8.306	8.974	8.724	9.785	9.852	10.181
Luxembourg	2.555	3.020	3.482	3.695	4.232	4.843	6.027	6.281
Denmark	866	1.473	2.053	2.407	2.668	3.586	4.034	4.761
Sweden	4.105	25.138	37.117	31.128	30.517	23.494	4.497	4.726
Italy	3.303	4.769	3.589	3.700	3.180	3.544	3.349	3.652
Austria	3.273	2.260	1.280	2.595	2.659	3.296	3.102	3.489
Germany	941	1.063	1.832	1.606	1.920	2.936	3.050	3.098
Czech Republic	1.591	2.029	1.811	2.458	1.860	2.356	2.908	3.383
Poland	849	1.214	1.372	1.675	1.849	2.484	2.991	3.013
Hungary	676	736	767	985	1.015	1.133	1.425	1.801
Estonia	71	165	316	765	852	858	1.243	1.419
Slovenia	125	348	361	655	712	780	1.102	1.360

APPENDIX C   (Continued)

	1995	1996	1997	1998	1999	2000	2001	2002
Slovak Republic	996	774	705	729	924	879	1.125	1.221
Croatia	155	320	295	340	350	423	594	761
Romania	1.115	686	118	258	338	391	526	515
Lithuania	174	151	183	260	312	364	455	514
Latvia	24	47	75	76	113	208	275	324
Bulgaria	387	18	173	172	195	193	242	292
Turkmenistán					1.819	2.492	2.051	1.483
Russia	400	346	466	172	568	588	631	805
Uzbekistán	1.590	1.678	1.089	805	627	693	542	453
Kazakhstan	25	168	121	90	128	207	300	420
Albania			23	22	226	309	443	394
Belarus	225	148	2.061	882	423	224	216	220
Ukraine	245	179	160	96	84	119	172	210
Serbia/Montenegro	1.071	874	859	1.080	1.081	369	163	184
Bosnia-Herzegovina	59	48	59	62	50	56	101	140
FYR Macedonia	87	75	62	76	90	103	119	119
Azarbadijan	452	55	48	34	47	71	53	53
Moldova	37	32	44	30	23	34	45	50
Armenia		22	19	21	28	39	44	43
Georgia	20	15	20	18	19	29	29	36
Kyrgystan	12	9	14			6	8	36
Tajikstan	12	17						23

GOVERNANCE BY SUPRANATIONAL INTERDEPENDENCE: DOMESTIC POLICY CHANGE IN THE TURKISH FINANCIAL SERVICES INDUSTRY

Caner Bakir[1]

1. INTRODUCTION

The 17 December 2004 was a turning point in both Turkish and European history: The European Council followed the European Commission's recommendation and approved the opening of accession negotiations with Turkey, which commenced on 3 October 2005. The goal of accession to the European Union (EU) has become one of the main driving forces for broadly defined legal, political, economic, and financial reforms in Turkey.[2]

This chapter argues that the current policy outcomes of the Turkish financial system are largely the products of "governance by supranational interdependence". The policy outcomes can be understood in terms of the pressures emanating from the international political economy and from efforts to harmonize national monetary governance and financial governance arrangements.[3] Specifically, the EU, with the accession process, the International Monetary Fund (IMF) and the World Bank with their

Emerging European Financial Markets: Independence and Integration Post-Enlargement
International Finance Review, Volume 6, 179–211
Copyright © 2006 by Elsevier Ltd.
ISSN: 1569-3767/doi:10.1016/S1569-3767(05)06008-5

financial support and the technical assistance for reforms, serve as the external anchors for institutionalization and harmonization of the Turkish financial regulatory regime.[4] As such, both the National Economic Convergence Program with the EU *Acquis* adopted following the EU Summit of Helsinki in 1999 and the IMF stand-by agreements made between Turkey and the IMF since 1999 required major regulatory and legal changes in monetary and financial governance. Most of the microeconomic and macroeconomic reforms needed for convergence in Turkey towards EU standards were already embedded in the IMF/World Bank – supervised economic and financial reforms. In evaluating the responses to external pressures, the paper focuses mainly on the role of policy entrepreneurship, financial policy outcomes (e.g., rules, regulations, and policy decisions enforced by state) and degree to which they conform to the norms promoted by transnational actors.

This chapter has two main parts. The first part overviews the key features of the governance arrangements in the financial services. It argues that recent policy decisions were effectively domestic responses to external pressures. The Commission of the European Communities (CEC) notes that "sustainable integration of Turkey's financial sector will to a large extent depend on achieving macroeconomic stability, as well as on strengthening the legal and supervisory framework in this sector" (CEC, 2004a, p. 17). Accordingly, the second part of the chapter outlines the main features of the pre-accession economic program (PEP), current capital market structure, the role of the financial system in allocating resources, and its normative properties.

2. GOVERNANCE ARRANGEMENTS IN THE TURKISH FINANCIAL SERVICES

2.1. Governance by State Control: The Period Prior to the 1980s

John Zysman (1983) offered a typology of financial systems in his analysis of how national economies responded to the common external shocks of the 1970s. He found "state-directed, price-administered" financial systems in France and Japan; a "private bank organized credit market" in Germany; and "capital market-based" financial systems in the UK and the USA.[5] Today, his work still serves as a useful starting point in the comparative political economy of financial systems.

With regards to European banking, Pagoulatos (1999, p. 68) argues that "five competing and mutually complementary modes of governance define

European banking policy and policy making: governance by state control; governance by the market; governance by regulation; governance by sectoral co-ordination; and governance by supranational interdependence."[6] Governance by state control has dominated the EU banking systems, from the embedded liberalism of postwar monetary order established after Bretton Woods negotiations in 1944 to the worldwide market liberalization and European integration of the 1980s (Pagoulatos, 1999, pp. 69–72). This "model [was] identified with the banking systems of France and Southern Europe (Italy, Spain, Portugal and Greece)" (Pagoulatos, 1999, p. 69).

Following Pagoulatos (1999) Turkish banking before the 1980s fits into this "governance by state control" or what Zysman would label a "bank-based" financial system.[7] Initially, state banks were established to promote state-led industrialization in Turkey, from the 1920s onwards until the de-regulatory 1980s.[8] State intervention in banking was part of the protectionist import substitution policy which was maintained until 1980. The regulatory interventionism and direct government control over banking ownership and management were main features of state control over the banking sector during this period.

The 1960s and the 1980s in Turkey also witnessed the emergence of the family controlled conglomerate groups which established or acquired already-existing banks to fund their own operations (Akguc, 1992, pp. 66–69). The repressive financial and regulatory practices were visible before the mid-1980s. This included interest rate controls, the direct involvement of the state in the allocation of credit mainly through state banking (e.g., directed credit programs and subsidized lending), barriers on foreign bank entry, and high liquidity and reserve requirements (see Akyuz, 1990, p. 98, see also Onder, Turel, Ekinci, & Somel, 1993). Not surprisingly, repressive financial policies "coupled with the exit of a significant number of banks [i.e., 23] between 1960 and 1980 gave rise to a concentrated market dominated by public and private banks owned by industrial groups with excessively large branch networks and high overhead costs" (Denizer, 1997, p. 1).

2.2. The Era of Lack of Effective Governance in Banking: The "Crony Capitalism" of the Late 1980s and the 1990s Embedded in the Bank-Based Financial System

The lack of legal rules, accountability and transparency for money sources financing politicians and political parties have provided the larger institutional structure for the Turkish "crony capitalism" embedded in the bank-based financial system.[9] A few wealthy individuals who dominated political campaign financing were active in acquiring or establishing private banks and did this with the help of the party that they had supported during the elections (see Tartan, 2003). In a similar vein, especially during the 1990s, the state banks had largely been the instruments of channeling deposits into political rent distribution. They were controlled by political parties and abused during this period through channeling cheap loans to corporate and individual donors as well as farmers, and other electoral constituencies (see *Euromoney*, April 1998, p. 138; *Economist*, 19 May 2001, p. 48). In this environment, both state and some of the private banks had been indirect sources financing political system in Turkey. Further, the "crony capitalism" also manifested itself in a "corruption triangle" formed among politicians, businessman, and the mafia. Rigging the privatization of a state-owned bank, Turkbank, in favor of the eventual winner in 1998 was a major case illustrating this "corruption triangle" (see Sener, 2004a).[10] At least in this instance, the mafia has been one of the non-regulatory entry barriers to the bank-based financial system in Turkey.

In the 1990s, Turkey witnessed huge budget deficits which necessitated an extensive reliance on domestic and foreign borrowing. The Turkish government adopted a "hot money" policy of high real interest rates for treasury bills and domestic currency appreciation to attract short term, unproductive and speculative capital to compensate for increasing growth in government expenditure; the annual real interest rate for government securities averaged 32 percent between 1992 and 1999 (Treasury, 2001, p. 3). Not surprisingly, during the same period, both public and private banks channeled most of their funds to the government debt market rather than to corporate lending; the share of total bank loans in total assets decreased from 36 to 24 percent.[11] In this environment, the public banks also became the instruments of government deficit funding, whilst private banks increasingly preferred high yield but safer government securities to commercial lending. The share of government securities in total bank deposits increased from 10 percent in 1990 to 23 percent in 1999 (Treasury, 2001, p. 6). The private sector version of the state banking behavior in the 1990s had been to direct public deposits and profits derived from arbitrage into group financing (i.e., connected lending)[12] and "bad loans to good friends"[13] (see Organization for Economic Cooperation and Development (OECD), 2002, pp. 78–79). Not surprisingly, six banks which were granted entry following the 1991 general elections failed in less than a decade. They were all insolvent due to connected lending and were taken over by the Savings

Deposit and Insurance Fund (SDIF) in 1999 (see Banking Regulation and Supervision Authority (BRSA), 2003, p. 17).[14] Between 1997 and 2003, 20 banks were taken over by the SDIF. Majority shareholders of these 20 banks used US$9.1 billion from their own banks (BRSA, 2003, Table 11, p. 25).[15] Further, they also used loans from state banks and other SDIF banks which later became part of non-performing loans (see BRSA, 2003, pp. 72–101; Tartan, 2003, pp. 72–74). The legacy of the crony capitalism in the financial system has been devastating: The share of non-performing loans in the gross loans reached 29.3 percent in 2001 (SPO, 2004, p. 72).

In December 1999, in the face of the above-mentioned structural problems in fiscal, monetary, and financial governance, the Turkish government agreed to an exchange rate-based "Disinflation Program" sponsored by the IMF and World Bank (hereafter the "twin organizations"). In return for the financial support of the IMF, the government promised to implement the economic and financial policies of the program. The stand-by agreement of US$15 billion was approved on 22 December 1999 and expired on 4 February 2002 (IMF, 2004a). The IMF program was based on tight fiscal and monetary targets aimed at reducing the real interest rates and inflation. Monetary policy stability is regarded by the IMF as a function of the central bank's independence from political authority. Paradoxically, the Central Bank of Turkey (hereafter the Central Bank) lost its independence with regards to monetary policy instruments due to the IMF's conditions. Specifically, the program imposed limits on the Central Bank's balance sheet items, in line with a pre-announced targeted currency basket. Apparently, the Central Bank independence in Turkey has domestic and international dimensions. The former is about the independence of the central bank from the government, whilst the latter refers to that of from the twin organizations which do not have any accountability to the public in Turkey for their policy mistakes. As such, the monetary pillar of the program had tied the Central Bank's liquidity creation to foreign capital inflows. However, the program was too foreign to take the fragility of the domestic financial system into account. During the implementation of the disinflation program, the banking sector was highly vulnerable to the program due to its dependence on high real interest bearing government securities funded largely by open foreign exchange positions, making the sector vulnerable to the foreign exchange risk. For example, the banking sector's open position increased to US$20.6 billion in November 2000 (Central Bank of Republic of Turkey (CBT), 2002, p. 113) up from US$12.6 billion at the end of 1999 (Kaplan, 2002, p. 22). Further, the share of short-term foreign debt in the Central Bank's international reserves increased from 112 percent in June 2000 to 147 percent in December 2000 (Cizre & Yeldan, 2002, p. 11).

In this environment, the program "failed to meet its inflation targets despite full implementation of its monetary and fiscal policy targets" (Akyuz & Boratav, 2003, p. 1550). This reinforced "expectations of a sharp depreciation at the time of pre-announced exit date [from the crawling peg], [causing] an earlier attack on the currency" (Akyuz & Boratav, 2003, p. 1553). The increased capital outflows resulted in an increase in interbank money market interest rates. The result was a liquidity crisis as the Central Bank initially could not provide liquidity to the market due to its commitment to the program.[16] The IMF provided US$7.3 billion in December 2000. However, tight monetary and fiscal policies implemented subsequently via the IMF intervention caused the financial crisis of 2001 and "served to deepen recession" (Akyuz & Boratav, 2003, p. 1550). Not surprisingly, the stabilization program and its sponsors were rightly criticized by academics and observers from various ideological persuasions for creating the "twin crises". The criticisms were directed at the design of the program which led to the liquidity crisis of November 2000 and the mismanagement in crisis intervention which led to the subsequent February 2001 financial crisis (Akyuz & Boratav, 2003, p. 1549; see also Egilmez & Kumcu, 2003; Alper & Onis, 2004).[17] Apparently, there were problems in the diffusion of information and learning between the twin organizations and the domestic financial policy community in Turkey. However, not only the IMF but also the domestic policy community shares the responsibility for the "twin crises." For example, the implementation of banking reforms and the Banks Act of 1999 by the domestic policy community was poor. Specifically, BRSA, which was established due to the direct pressure of the IMF in June 1999, became fully operational only in September 2000 – 2 months prior to the liquidity crisis (for a detailed discussion, see Alper & Onis, 2004, pp. 41–47). Evrensel (2004, p. 5) also concludes that "the primary targets of stabilization programs are not implemented during the program years."

To sum up, the Turkish version of "crony capitalism" and the lack of effective governance – that is, the inability of the financial policy community (i.e., key regulators and regulated firms) to find collective solutions to market, government, and regulatory failure – marked the country's major step away from its integration into the European financial area during the period between the late 1980s and the 1990s. As will be detailed in the next section, the result has been the powerful penetration of extraterritorial actors into domestic policy-making in Turkey.

2.3. Governance by Supranational Interdependence, Policy Entrepreneurship, and Policy Change

The financial crisis of 2001 was triggered by the dispute between the then Prime Minister Bulent Ecevit and President Ahmet Necdet Sezer, after the president, on 19 February 2001, criticized the government for failing to fight corruption. The result was the largest economic recession in Turkey's history; real gross domestic product (GDP) contracted by 7.5 percent, whilst the consumer price index (CPI) realized at 68.5 percent in 2001 (CBT, 2003, p. 12). The Turkish lira depreciated by 115.3 percent against the US dollar and 111.3 percent against the euro (CBT, 2002, p. 16). Following the crisis, Turkey returned to floating exchange rate regime with the central bank having control over short-term interest rates.

In addition to the mistakes of the twin organizations prior to and during the crises and the government's poor implementation of the banking reforms,[18] it also became clear that "corruption cancer" had destabilized Turkish financial markets by breeding financial/economic crises, by undermining the rule of law and sustainable economic development, and by jeopardizing good governance in the public and private sectors. Consequently, the legacy of "crony capitalism" has been devastating for the Turkish financial system. The SDIF held the biggest portfolio of nonperforming loans in Turkey. As of December 2004, 21 banks have been transferred to the SDIF (also known as the SDIF banks) since 1997. The cost of the financial restructuring program has been US$47 billion in taxpayer's money, with capital support provided to banks to rehabilitate the banking sector in 2004 (SPO, 2004, p. 72). The amount of funds injected into the SDIF banks reached US$27.8 billion in 2004 (SPO, 2004, p. 73).[19] The CEC (2004b, p. 62) also reported in 2001 that "bailing out the banking sector and taking account of the costs of agricultural support resulted in a deficit of 29.8 percent of GDP".

Three parties in the ruling coalition government were accused of corruption and of obstructing a 3-year disinflation reform program backed by the twin organizations since 1999. Following the devastating financial crisis, there was strong public distrust and anger towards the government, as evidenced by opinion polls.[20] With this as background, Ecevit called a well-respected and highly influential transnational bureaucrat for a rescue mission: in March 2001, Kemal Dervis, the World Bank's vice president for poverty reduction and economic management at the time, became an *unelected* member of the Turkish Parliament and a Minister of State in charge of Treasury.[21] This was the first time that the relations between Turkey and the twin organizations moved beyond bilateral agreements between the parties. As will be detailed below, governance by supranational interdependence in financial and economic realms was institutionalized with Dervis and his team. Here, governance by supranational interdependence refers to the significant role played by extraterritorial actors (e.g., individuals and supranational organizations) and institutions (e.g., norms, rules, regulations) on domestic policy change in financial and monetary governance.[22] In the Turkish context, governance by supranational interdependence came with effective carrot and stick policies linked to: (1) the EU accession process which requires Turkey to adopt and implement the complete EU legislation and standards – the *acquis communautaire*; (2) "IMF conditionality" where IMF lending is conditional on the adoption of IMF policy prescriptions; (3) The World Bank "Programmatic Financial and Public Sector Adjustment Loans (PFPSAL)" which require implementation of financial and public sector reform program in Turkey. As such, Turkey's satisfactory progress in microeconomic and macroeconomic reforms serves as "collateral" for the prospect of EU accession and IMF/World Bank loans.

Dervis was part of an epistemic community – a "network of professionals with recognized policy expertise and competence in a particular domain and an authoritative claim to policy-relevant knowledge within that domain or issue area" (Haas, 1992, p. 3). He was an influential actor with joint memberships of the domestic and transnational policy communities (for a theoretical framework, see Coleman & Perl, 1999). As such, both the government and the twin organizations needed Dervis as a "mediator", moving between the parties in the intergovernmental negotiations environment (see *Economist*, 24 March 2001, p. 58). The government needed him not only because it had lost its domestic and international credibility[23] but also because it needed a mediator to effectively administer relations with the twin organizations. Similarly, the twin organizations also needed him following the crisis, not only because he would effectively translate policy ideas and policy paradigms into domestic policy but also because he would facilitate *policy formulation* and *implementation* which would prevent both a debtor moral hazard and a road accident similar to one that happened in the design and implementation of the previous program imposed by the twin organizations for Turkey. In spite of Turkey's lack of political will to implement the IMF's conditionality, the IMF had been providing financial support which led to a debtor moral hazard (see Evrensel, 2004).[24] With regards to the debtor moral hazard problem, Dervis was the right person who could satisfy the IMF's expectation on the implementation of the economic and financial reforms. Indeed, Dervis through the Treasury Department gathered monthly data regarding the implementation of the economic program (*Milliyet*, 18 May 2001). Highly influential Turkish Industrialists' and Businessmen' Association, the peak association of big business, also supported Dervis and pressured strongly for the implementation of the economic program (*Cumhuriyet*, 18 May 2001). With regards to the policy design, Dervis effectively translated the financial system fragility in Turkey to the "twin organizations". For example, the IMF traditionally opposes direct public financing by the Central Bank. However, the IMF did not oppose the exceptions in the new Central Bank enacted in 2001 that permitted the Central Bank to finance government expenditures on banks taken over by the SDIF.[25]

There had been widespread consensus among the key actors of this epistemic community that one of the major problems was "crony capitalism" embedded in the Turkish bank-based system. Policies to tackle this problem had already been out there due to a process of a gradual accumulation of knowledge and solutions among specialists in the financial/economic policy area. The particular problems of the Turkish political and economic system came to the fore due to both the crisis and the change in the national mood. As Kingdon notes policy change occurs when influential individuals (i.e., "policy entrepreneurs") can "couple" problems, policies, and politics. However, according to Kingdon (1995), this is possible only when a short-run opportunity (i.e., a "policy window") is opened for entrepreneurs to push certain policies, solutions, or just bring attention to a particular problem. In Turkey, a "window of opportunity" for a radical economic restructuring opened following the crisis which exposed "crony capitalism" as being embedded in the Turkish financial system. Dervis, as a "policy entrepreneur", used this window of opportunity, and combined problems, policies (e.g., solutions), and politics. He identified problems and solutions in a "Transition Program to a Strong Economy" (see Treasury, 2001). For example, he declared that "[t]he current crisis has stemmed from the problems of the banking sector" (Dervis, 2001). The banking sector was "the most urgent problem" (quoted in *WallStreet Journal*, 15 , p. A.15). With regards to solutions, the program had both macroeconomic (e.g., tax reforms, fiscal restructuring, and the removal of extra-budgetary funds) and microeconomic reform agenda (e.g., reform of the prudential and disclosure regulations and supervision; the rationalization and privatization; the restructuring and eventual sale of state-owned banks). The program also included legal reforms including new commercial and central banking laws, and the introduction of good governance principles.

Economic, financial and legal reforms, agreed on with the twin organizations were accepted by the coalition government in March 2001. Specifically, financial and public sector reform program received financial and technical support from the World Bank (World Bank, 2002).[26] The banking sector reform legislation aimed to: "incorporate market risk into capital adequacy requirements (CAR); clarify definitions for reporting and accounting purposes; include repurchase agreements on the balance sheet; improve monitoring the supervision of the banking system; and adopt international accounting standards between 2001 and 2002" (Bakir & Brown, 2004, p. 433; see also BRSA, 2001a, b).

These reforms were "part and parcel of a national program that will prepare the country for accession talks with the EU" (*WallStreet Journal*, 20, p. A.17). As such, most of the microeconomic and macroeconomic reforms needed for convergence in Turkey towards EU standards were already embedded in the twin organizations – supervised reforms.[27] As Dervis noted "the economic program is prepared in full compliance with the National Program to the EU … Indeed, our economic program represents the economic dimension of the National Program to the EU" (Dervis, 2001).[28] As such, both the EU Term President at the time and his successor declared their strong support for the new economic program and Dervis (*Cumhuriyet*, 18 May 2001). Instead of supervising the economic reforms directly, the EU offered feedback through regular reports on Turkey's progress towards accession.[29]

The IMF required the implementation of the program in return for the release of US$8 billion in May 2001. Dervis years (March 2001–August 2002) witnessed major structural reforms including amendments to the Central Bank Law in 2001, the institutionalization of banking supervision system that involved the BRSA and the SDIF in 2000, "Law on Public Sector Banks" between 2000 and 2001, "Private Banking Sector Restructuring Program" in 2001, "Istanbul Approach" for corporate loan restructurings in 2001, "Public Financing and Debt Management Law" in 2002 (for details, see OECD, 2004, Table 4.1, pp. 115–117). The IMF (2002) declared that Turkey has maintained the strong implementation of its economic program. As a result, on 4 February 2002, the IMF approved a new stand-by agreement of US$12.8 billion which expired on 3 February 2005 (IMF, 2004a).

However, the three-party coalition government was too weak to initiate further reforms and their successful implementation. Political and economic instability was largely created by weak coalition governments in Turkey.[30]

Dervis resigned in August 2002. Following the early general elections on 3 November 2002, the first single party government in 15 years was formed with 34 percent of the vote and 66 percent of majority in the Grand National Assembly under the aegis of the Justice and Development Party (hereafter the Adalet ve Kalkinma Partisi (AKP)). This was also the first time in 40 years that there was only one opposition party in the new parliament.[31] As the *Economist* noted "[a] wave of hope has swept a nation long hostage to economic mismanagement, repressive laws and corrupt politicians" (*Economist*, 9 November 2002, p. 39). The new and untested AKP had promised a strong commitment to fight corruption, to implement structural economic reforms sponsored by the twin organizations, and to continue political and legal reforms to meet the Copenhagen criteria for EU membership (*WallStreet Journal*, 4–5 November 2002). The AKP gained domestic and international credibility and experience quickly, and managed to translate parliamentary stability into political and economic stability. The Transition Program designed jointly by Dervis and "twin organizations" was fully adopted by the AKP. Indeed, the AKP government successfully implemented the program which was revised in early 2002 to cover the 2002–2004 periods. New Prime Minister, Recep Tayyip Erdogan, has been the key domestic individual actor moving towards to the discursive construction of the EU accession process which is about "how [state] elites form their identities, define their interests, and legitimate both the European integration process in general and specific policies by framing them in convincing ways" (Dyson, 2000, p. 646).

Further, the AKP did not fully adopt the previous government's "inaction" policy in enforcement.[32] The Ministry of Justice drafted new bankruptcy and foreclosure laws in consultation with the World Bank. Empowered by the World Bank sponsored laws, the SDIF effectively seized control of companies and personal property of insolvent bank owners who failed to propose a plan to pay the debts due to the collapse of their banks in 2004. The SDIF's move towards enforcement of rules and laws to recoup the tax payer's money *may be* the end of a "light touch" approach that prevailed during the previous decade.[33]

This progress, however, should be interpreted with cautious optimism. Turkey's overall international ranking in corruption,[34] and economic[35] and political freedom[36] is far from being satisfactory. As such, any improvements in financial and monetary governance arrangements would be ineffective without broader democratic, judicial, and legal consolidation in Turkey.

2.4. The Post-2001 Era: Financial Governance and Monetary Governance by Supranational Interdependence?

Financial market governance is about systemic stability. Therefore, it is essentially about "the regulation of competitive conditions and prudential control" (Moran, 2002, p. 258). Similarly, "governance by regulation" in banking is about "efficiency and safety" (Pagoulatos, 1999, p. 76). Accordingly, regulation and supervision plays a pivotal role in financial market governance (or governance by regulation). This section will argue that partial financial regulatory and supervisory consolidation and increased central bank legal independence in Turkey were the domestic responses to the IMF pressures.

Financial governance in banking can be analyzed with special reference to a *supervisory structures*, "whether there should be one or multiple supervisory authorities, and whether the central bank should be involved in bank supervision", the *scope of supervision*, "whether bank supervisor authorities should supervise other financial service industries, including in particular securities and insurance", and the *independence of supervisory authorities*, "the degree to which bank supervisors should be subject to political and economic policy pressure and influence" (Barth, Nolle, Phumiwasana, & Yago, 2003, p. 67).[37]

With regards to the financial supervisory structure, Turkey has been characterized by fragmentation and a lack of coordination and institutionalized consensus building among supervisors. Before 2000, Turkey had multiple supervisors with the Central Bank involved in off-site bank supervision. However, the Central Bank was not the only agency involved in banking supervision. The Banks Act of 1985 authorized the Treasury and Sworn Banks Auditors with on-site inspection in bank regulation and/or supervision, whilst the Council of Ministers had power to replace the boards of troubled banks. The SDIF which was established in 1983 to insure savings deposits was incorporated into the Central Bank. The Capital Markets Board of Turkey (CMB) has been responsible for disclosure regulation/supervision and investor protection. The Insurance Supervisory Office at the Treasury Undersecretariat was responsible for insurance supervision.

Apart from this fragmented state apparatus in financial services industry, there were also conflict of interest problems and the lack of adequate co-operation among financial supervisors. For example, the Treasury had no incentive to push for tight financial regulation and supervision of banks which were essentially funding government deficits, and/or beef-up the capital of the state banks, which would worsen the fiscal deficit. The CMB also failed to introduce Chinese walls between banking and non-banking activities (see OECD, 2002, n. 45, p. 79).

With regards to the scope of supervision, there has been a move towards partial consolidation since 2000. A new agency, the BRSA, was established in June 1999 following the ratification of the IMF sponsored Banks Act no. 4389 (IMF, 1999). It took responsibility for banking supervision and regulation from the Central Bank and became operational in September 2000. The BRSA was empowered with on-site and off-site supervisory powers. The BRSA also incorporated the Sworn Banks Auditors. The SDIF has become both the deposit insurance fund and agency responsible for the liquidation of the insolvent banks. It was also incorporated into the BRSA in 2001. Further, the regulation and supervision of non-bank financial institutions has been transferred from the Treasury to the BRSA in 2005.

With regards to the supervisory independence, the BRSA, however, does not have a strong institutional independence from the government; its president and senior executives are appointed by the Council of Ministers which has also final authority on cancellation of the banking and deposit taking licenses. In 2002, the BRSA failed to demonstrate competence and independence when it took over the administration of Pamukbank, the sixth largest bank at the time and a member of the Cukurova Group. The deal made between the group and the BRSA was tragic; the bank's debt of US$6 billion was postponed for 15 years at Libor + 0.5 with no payment requirement in the first 3 years (Tartan, 2003, p. 140).

The failure of Imarbank in 2003 also exposed regulatory and supervisory failure in banking (Fort & Hayward, 2004). The bank hid the real amount of deposits, sold non-existing treasury bonds and channeled funds into off-shore accounts (see Sener, 2004b). It became clear that the BRSA failed to detect misreporting in Imarbank and to conduct on-site inspections effectively.[38]

The financial regulatory and supervisory arrangements also demonstrated weaknesses in financial regulation and supervision. Specifically, there was a regulatory capture and lack of coordination and cooperation among the government regulatory agencies. For example, the CMB canceled Imarbank's license to participate in the government debt market in 1996 but the bank, through massive public advertisements, continued to sell non-existent treasury bills to the public until 2002; this should have been examined properly by the banking supervisors and the bank's license for collecting deposits should have been canceled.

Nevertheless, the Banking Sector Restructuring Program, like the European Banking Legislation Program, aimed to strengthen systemic stability through enhancing the efficacy of financial regulation and supervision through reforms in prudential regulation (see BRSA, 2001a). Improved transparency, profitability, risk management, and capital structure in the sector were among the key results of financial restructuring. In particular, the banks' capital strengthened following the Bank Capital Strengthening Program introduced in 2001. The result has been spectacular; the CAR of the banking sector increased dramatically from 9.3 percent in 2000 to 30.9 percent in December 2003 (BRSA, 2004, p. 38). This improvement was due to a move from CAR calculations based on non-inflation-adjusted financial statements in 2000 to that of inflation-adjusted financial statements, increased profitability, fund injections, and the banks' capital beef-up. Further, blanket deposit insurance, which had caused a moral hazard problem and unfair competition between banks,[39] ended in July 2004 and aligned with EU-15 average level (see Table 2). However, a deposit coverage of €27,027 is high for Turkey, as the country's per capita income is about one-fifth that of EU-15.

The restructuring, along with strong economic growth generated improvements in terms of asset and profitability growth, and improved asset quality and capital adequacy. Total bank assets increased from US$130.1 billion in December 2002 to US$184.9 billion in June 2004, whilst net profits increased from US$1.8 billion in 2002 to US$4 billion in December 2003 (SPO, 2004, p. 72). However, it should be noted that the main source of asset growth and bank profitability was the banks' securities portfolio and repo transactions, which generated high real interest income rather than the expansion of commercial lending and/or fees and commissions. The share of non-performing loans in gross loans decreased from 29.3 percent in 2001 to 6.3 percent in June 2004 (SPO, 2004, p. 72).

The EU accession process, the supervision of the twin organizations, and Turkey's need for adherence to internationally acceptable regulatory standards in a world of global finance created a pressure for financial regulatory convergence. As the head of the BRSA put it:

> For strengthening the regulatory and supervisory framework, the BRSA's regulatory activities aiming at meeting the needs of the sector continue in accordance with the European Union regulations primarily and with other international practices. The new Draft Banks Act prepared within this framework aims at both strengthening the regulatory and supervisory framework and achieving compliance with the EU legislation in the light of the realities, needs of our country and the sector as well as experiences gained. Besides, the BRSA continues its effort for preparing [sic.] the banking sector to [sic.] international competition.
>
> (BRSA, 2004, p. v)

Monetary governance is about price stability where an independent central bank plays a pivotal role. Central bank independence has been promoted by international organizations (e.g., the EU and the IMF) and regarded as a condition for entry into Economic and Monetary Union (EMU) by the EU. The monetary governance in the EU is administered by the European Central Bank (ECB) which is guided by a strong cultural and ideological commitment to price stability. The EMU is shaped by the ECB and its strong commitment to price stability. The Central Bank is responsible for monetary governance in Turkey. Over the last 5 years, between 2001 and 2005, progress has been made in strengthening the independence of the Central Bank. The new Central Bank Law of 25 April 2001 which was part of the IMF conditionality increased the legal independence of the Bank; price stability is stated as a primary objective, and the Bank shall not lend to the public sector with the exception permitting the Central Bank to finance government expenditures on banks taken over by the SDIF. The Law has also been an important step in the process of harmonizing Turkish laws with the EU's legal standards (for a comparative analysis, see Bakir, 2005a). Further, the Central Bank will adopt explicit inflation targeting in 2006. Parallel to this, the transparency of the central bank has also been increasing, as the bank reports to the Council of Ministers twice a year, and publishes interest rate decisions within 2 days of their public announcement (with special reference to the minutes of the meeting of the Monetary Policy Board).

The EU, with its accession process, and the twin organizations, with their stand-by agreements and technical assistance for reforms, serve as the external anchors for financial governance and monetary governance. Direct manifestations of a move towards such governance arrangements can be increasingly seen in improvements via reform of regulatory/supervisory processes and of institutions in the financial services industry in Turkey (see OECD, 2004, Table 4.1, pp. 115–117). For example, increased central bank legal independence, financial reporting rules and corporate governance guidelines, prudential and disclosure regulation, regulation on accounting, bank establishment rules and ownership, and deposit insurance, etc. have been increasingly aligned with international standards via amendments to relevant laws.[40] As the EU Commission puts it:

> Turkey's institutional and regulatory setup underwent substantial modernization. Key regulatory and supervisory institutions, such as the Turkish Central Bank and the Banking Regulation and Supervision Agency, gained independence. In addition, the regulatory framework of important markets, such as the financial sector [sic], was

aligned with international standards. State interference has been reduced, for example, by winding down political influence on the state banks.

(CEC, 2004b, p. 58)

3. AN OVERVIEW OF THE PEP, THE BANKING SECTOR, CAPITAL MARKETS, AND CORPORATE GOVERNANCE

3.1. PEP: A Roadmap Towards the Maastricht Criteria

An analysis of the financial system of any accession country will be incomplete without a reference to her Pre-accession Economic Program (PEP). An analysis of Turkey's current shape in this context also enables the assessment of key challenges in 2005 and beyond. Turkey submitted her PEP to the European Commission on 1 December 2004. The PEP shows macroeconomic targets and the structural reform agenda needed for EU membership (Table 1). The ultimate objective of this ambitious but quite feasible program is to meet the Maastricht criteria for Turkey (for a comparative analysis, see Bakir, 2005b). It should be noted that the PEP program is based on the policy prescriptions of the IMF stand-by agreements since 2001, and serves as the basis for Turkey's new stand-by agreement with the IMF in February 2005 (see Babacan, 2004).

With regards to inflation criterion, Turkey currently overshot the Maastricht CPI criterion that states that inflation should not be higher than 1.5 percentage points above that of the average of the three lowest Euroland inflation figures. However, inflation fell by 18.4 percent in 2003, and an average of 77.5 percent in the 1990s, to a better than expected 9.3 percent, the lowest since 1975.[41] Turkey expects to bring the CPI down to 4 percent in 2007, aligning inflation with the Maastricht criterion. Tight monetary policy coupled with the operational independence of the Central Bank with the new Central Bank Law of 2001 played a significant role in this spectacular success. On 1 January 2005, this also enabled the Central Bank to drop six zeroes from the Turkish lira, the world's largest denomination banknote, to the new redenominated currency, Yeni Turk Lirasi (YTL), in a million-to-one conversion (1 YTL is approximately €0.55).

With regards to the public finance criteria of having a government deficit of no greater than 3 percent of GDP and a national debt of 60 percent GDP, Turkey needs to improve; the public sector borrowing requirement (PSBR) is projected at 6.3 percent of GDP in 2004 while the government targets a

Table 1. The PEP.

	2003	2004E	2005E	2006E	2007E
GDP (US$, billion)	247	298	300	317.6	350
Real GDP growth (%, YoY)	5.8	9.6	4.8	5.1	5.1
CPI (%, end year)	18.4	10	8	5	4
Exports (US$, billion)	47.3	62.0	71.0	79.7	88.9
Imports (US$, billion)	69.3	95.5	104.0	114.2	125.2
Current account balance	−7.9	−14.6	−11.1	−10.8	−10.5
Current account balance/GDP (%)	−3.2	−4.9	−3.7	−3.4	−3
PSBR/GDP (%)	−10.1	−6.3	−4.4	−2.1	−0.5
Primary surplus/GDP (%)	6.7	7.8	7.5	7.2	7
Internal debts/GDP (%)	54.8	54.3	52.7	52.1	50
External debts/GDP (%)	25.4	24	22.7	20.1	18.3
Gross public debt stock/GDP (%)	80.2	78.4	75.3	72.2	68.3
Employment (thousand people)	21,147	21,649	22,182	22,741	23,304
Unemployment (%)	10.5	10	9.8	9.6	9.3
FDI (US$, billion)	1.1	2.0	3.7	3.8	3.9

Source: SPO (2004).
PSBR: public sector borrowing requirements

0.5 percent government deficit by 2007. Parallel to this, gross public debt stock is projected to decline to 68.3 percent of GDP in 2007 (down from an estimated 78.4 percent in 2004). As such, Turkey is far from meeting the 60 percent Maastricht debt ceiling for general government gross debt. However, Turkey may have the potential to reduce its public debt due to a primary surplus (over 6.5 percent of GDP) and high privatization revenues which are expected to increase in the short term.[42]

Convergence in long-term (10-year) domestic bond yields is another Maastricht criterion. The achievement of a primary budget surplus helped the government lower real domestic interest rates to 11 percent in 2004 (from an average of 33 percent in 2001).[43] The 3-year average for Turkey's 30-year Eurobond yields averaged about 10.63 percent against a reference value of 6.4 percent (Deutsche Bank, 23 December 2004, p. 4). The attainment of the interest rate criterion is directly related to Turkey's future progress in monetary and fiscal consolidation.

In terms of the exchange rate stability criterion, Turkey is vulnerable to unwanted exchange rate adjustments due to large external imbalances in the high levels of the current account deficit and external debt, which are expected to be 4.9 and 24 percent of GDP in 2004, respectively. Projected growth in the foreign direct investment (FDI), coupled with tourism receipts and an improving export capacity, may reduce external imbalances to sustainable levels in the medium term.

The PEP program served as the basis for Turkey's new US$10 billion 3 years stand-by deal agreed with the IMF on 13 December 2004. The IMF program requires reform in three key areas: (1) the social security system which is in deficit at about 4.5 percent of GDP; (2) the harmonization of the Banking Law with the EU in bank ownership, management and licensing, and connected lending; and (3) the implementation of tax reform. The EU accession process keeps Turkey anchored with an economic and financial restructuring program supported by the twin organizations. This is coupled with strong public support for the AKP government (i.e., a 55 percent approval rating in November 2004) and the prospect of EU membership (i.e., a 79 percent approval rating) in the opinion polls, strengthening the government's position to implement new institutional frameworks for fiscal, monetary, and financial governance.

3.2. The Banking Sector in a Comparative Perspective

The Turkish financial system had been dominated by a weak and inefficient banking sector which did not play a significant role in economic development. Financial intermediation indicators, such as the share of assets, deposits, and loans of GDP, show that the sector is still underdeveloped (Table 2). It is over branched, and the share of state banks and government debt securities in total banking assets is high. The share of bank loans of GDP is a fraction of the EU-15 countries.

Table 3 provides a brief comparison of some of the key indicators of the Turkish financial system with four central and eastern European countries (i.e., the Czech Republic, Hungary, Poland, and Slovak Republic – hereafter referred to collectively as CEC4). Although both Turkey and CEC4 countries have underdeveloped financial services industries, Turkey contrasts with CEC4 in that she has the lowest share of loans to GDP and the highest share of government securities in total banking assets (Table 3). In Turkey, banks channel most of their funds to the government debt market rather than to corporate lending. The analysis of three major items in the consolidated bank balance sheet reveals the underdeveloped role of the banking sector in economic development. As of September 2003, deposit items constituted a major source of funding with a 65 percent share in total liabilities. However, loans constituted only 27 percent of total assets, whilst securities constituted 43 percent of total assets (Bankers Association of Turkey

Table 2. The Turkish Banking Sector in a Comparative Perspective (2001).

	EU-15 Countries	EU-10 Countries	Turkey
Assets/GDP	474	117	97
Deposits/GDP	186	83	61
Loans/GDP	167	57	19
Average bank size (total assets/number of banks, million euro)	4,494	1,025	2,472
Number of branches per bank	36	33	113
Debt securities/total assets (Government's crowding-out)	21.68	N/A	34.5
Concentration ratio of five largest banks (%)	59	75.8	57.7
Share of state banks (public share, %)	10	24	33
CAR	12.04	16.24	16.5
Deposit insurance (in euro)	30,667	11,939	27,027

Source: Pazarbasioglu (2003).

Table 3. The Main Indicators of the Financial System (%).

	End-year Total Assets/GDP		Loans/GDP		Securities/ GDP		Capital and Reserves/GDP		Non-bank Deposits/GDP	
	1999	2001	1999	2001	1999	2001	1999	2001	1999	2001
Czech Republic	124	119	46	40	24	32	10	7	59	69
Hungary[a]	64.5	64	29	35	12	13	6	7	41	41
Poland	58	62	27	28	13	13	5	6	37	41
Slovak Republic	91	92	43	27	13	27	12	8	60	66
Turkey	89	92	24	18	20	36	5	8	56	61

Source: OECD (2003).
[a]For only commercial banks.

(BAT), 2004a, p. 81). Private deposit banks provided 71.3 percent of total loans in 2003 (CBT, 2004, Table III.1.5, p. 87). The same figure for state deposit banks and foreign deposit banks was 23.2 and 5.5 percent, respectively. Not surprisingly, the banking sector was unable to channel funds to the real sectors. The share of loans in total assets was only 28 percent in 2003, below the pre-crisis level of 32 percent in 2000 (BAT, 2004a, p. 24). The banking assets have been dominated by high real interest bearing government securities; 90 percent of these securities were government debt instruments. For example, the share of the securities portfolio in total assets increased from 35 percent in 2001 to 41.5 percent in June 2004. Further, the major source of bank profitability has been the securities portfolio due to high real interest rates: "Turkish banks have been among the most profitable in the world despite low efficiency" (see also OECD, 2002, Fig. 5, p. 66). Further, weak competition is "suggested by high interest margins alongside high operating costs" (OECD, 2002, p. 67).

Foreign bank entry and cross-border mergers and acquisitions, along with government-led restructuring, played a significant role in the bank consolidation process in emerging market banking sectors (Gelos & Roldos, 2004). For example, foreign banks dominate commercial bank assets and registered bank capital in CEC4 countries (Mero & Valentinyi, 2003). In contrast, despite highly liberal financial regimes, developed technological infrastructure and skilled labor in the banking sector, the presence of foreign banks (which mainly operate in foreign trade and corporate finance) has been limited in Turkey. As of December 2003, 13 foreign banks had 209 branches. Their share in total bank assets, loans, and deposits was 2.8, 4.1 and 2.0 percent, respectively (BRSA, 2004, pp. 14–15).[44]

Bank consolidation in CEC4 countries has been mainly due to both a legacy of the privatization of large state-owned banks and the entry of a large number of domestic and foreign banks into their respective markets; this followed the financial deregulation of the mid-1990s (Gelos & Roldos, 2004). In contrast these countries, the main feature of bank consolidation in Turkey has been bank failures rather than foreign bank entry. Not surprisingly, bank failures led to state-led consolidation and a drop in the number of banks in Turkey following the Financial Restructuring Program of 2001 that followed the twin crises. As a result of a blanket deposit guarantee, the BRSA and the SDIF played a pivotal role in this consolidation process in dealing with market and regulatory failures following the financial crisis. Nineteen out of 21 insolvent banks transferred to the SDIF. Banks have been dissolved, sold and/or merged with other banks. The total asset size of mergers and acquisitions in the sector was around US$26.5 billion (BRSA, 2003, p. 53). The total number of banks has declined from 81 in December 1999 to 49 in December 2004. The reduction in the number of banks translated into an increase in market concentration in the sector. For example, the share of the largest five banks in total assets increased 12 percentage points, from 48 percent in 2000 to 60 percent in 2004 (BAT, 2004a, p. 82). This concentration rate, however, is close to the EU average (see Table 2). During the same period, the total number of bank branches declined from

173,988 to 126,970, whereas the number of bank employees declined from 7,691 to 6,050 (BAT, 2004b).

3.3. Capital Markets

In Turkey, capital markets are undiversified and underdeveloped (Bakir & Brown, 2004). Table 4 shows the percentage distribution of total financial assets in Turkey by the end of September 2003. The bank-based system also evidenced 41.1 percent share of deposits in total financial assets. The public and private sector securities together make only 58.9 percent of total financial assets. Government bonds and treasury bills had a 47.3 and 9.9 percent share of total public securities, respectively (Table 4). The debt market is mainly dominated by government debt instruments. For example, outstanding government securities had a 91.7 percent share of total securities issued, whilst that of private sector securities was 8.3 percent in October 2003 (CBT, 2004, Table iv.2.1, p. 124). Stocks are the only private sector securities issued and have a 4.9 percent share of total financial assets, illustrating the low degree of market depth in the financial system.

Table 4. Total Financial Assets (% Share).

	1999	2000	2001	2002	2003[b]
Total deposits[a]	59.7	56.2	43.7	44.7	41.1
Total loans deposits	32.3	30.8	18.9	19.5	21.5
Saving deposits	19.8	17.9	11.5	11.7	12.5
Other	12.4	12.8	7.4	7.9	9
Fixed deposits	27.4	25.4	24.8	–	19.7
Securities	40.3	43.8	56.3	55.3	58.9
Public	34.7	36.9	51.8	50.9	53.9
Treasury bills	4.8	2.1	8.4	–	9.9
Government bonds	29.3	34.5	43.1	–	43.7
Other	0.6	0.4	0.3	–	9.9
Private	5.6	6.9	4.4	4.4	4.9
Stocks	5.6	6.9	4.4	4.4	4.9
Asset-backed securities	0	0	0	–	0
Other	0	0	0	0	0
Total	100	100	100	100	100

Sources: CMB, CBT, Treasury various tables.
[a]Excluding interbank deposits.
[b]Provisional figures by the end of September.

The corporate sector raised US$12.7 billion in the corporate debt market until the mid-1990s (Turkiye Sermaye Piyasasi Araci Kuruluslari Birligi (TSPAKB), 2004, p. 115); then, for over 8 years, the corporate debt market did not exist in Turkey. Between 1990 and 2004, funds raised by the private sector in the share market totaled about US$2 billion. The OECD noted that "[t]he stock of bank deposits exceeds that of total private securities by a factor of 10 ... and the use of non-bank savings vehicles lags far behind the rest of the OECD" (OECD, 2002, p. 67). The share of domestic debt stock in M2Y (i.e., the sum of currency in circulation, sight deposits, time deposits, and fixed deposits held by residents) increased from 112 percent in December 2002 to 125 percent in October 2003 (SPO, 2004). This high ratio illustrates both a crowding-out effect of government deficit funding in the loanable funds market and a lack of financial market depth. The rate of dollarization (i.e., the ratio of foreign exchange deposits to total deposit of residents) decreased from 56.7 percent in 2001 to 49.3 percent in 2004, showing a slow improvement in confidence in the Turkish lira (see CBT, 2004, Table III.1.4, p. 84).

Over the course of 15 years, between 1990 and 2004, only US$22 billion was raised in Turkish capital markets (TSPAKB, 2004, p. 113). The private sector raised a total of US$15 billion during this period. In 2003, the share of public sector security stocks in GDP was 54.3 percent, whereas that of the private sector was only 5 percent (Table 5). In the same year, total capital market capitalization was 26.7 percent of GDP, whilst total equity issues had 0.48 percent share in GDP. Not surprisingly, retained earnings rather than banks or capital markets play a pivotal role as domestic sources of corporate finance in Turkey. However, Turkey's steps towards becoming a member of the EU facilitates overseas funding for long-term corporate borrowers.[45] It should also be noted that high real interest rates have two paradoxical consequences for large firms; total interest expenditures of the top 500 firms reached 45 percent of total value added between 1997 and

Table 5. Main Indicators of Capital Markets in Turkey (%).

	2001	2002	2003
Total capital market capitalization/GDP	38.5	20.4	26.7
Stock market total transaction volume/GDP	52.2	38.5	40.8
Total equity issues/GDP	0.94	0.57	0.48
Total public sector securities stocks/GDP	69	55	54.5
Total private sector securities stocks/GDP	5.9	4.8	5.0

Source: CMB (2004). Compiled from Tables 4.2, 4.3, 4.5, and 4.6.

2001, whilst their interest income exceeded their operating income between 1999 and 2002 (see Boratav, 2003, p. 197).

3.4. Corporate Governance

Separation of management and ownership is at the core of good corporate governance. However, in most emerging market economies, domestic banks are owned by family businesses under family controlled conglomerates. Family control is generally strengthened through pyramid ownership, cross-shareholdings, and interlocking directorates. Turkey is no exception.

In Turkey, capital markets do not provide a market for corporate control.[46] This is not only because of the bank-based financial system but also because of the pyramidal ownership structure. Specifically, the family owned holding companies through pyramidal structures are the dominant corporate model in Turkey (Demirag & Serter, 2003).[47] A pyramid ownership corporate structure embedded in the bank-industrial cross-holding system in Turkey is a significant obstacle for good corporate governance. Such an ownership structure, coupled with still less than perfect prudential and disclosure regulation/supervision, has encouraged a lack of information, transparency, and accountability in corporate practices. This is one of the major obstacles to good corporate governance practices and market-driven consolidation processes in the Turkish financial services industry. Apparently, the family ownership, the low utilization of capital markets and the bank-dominant financial system are interrelated phenomena.

4. SUMMARY AND CONCLUSIONS

The crony capitalism version of the bank-industrial cross-holding system, the use of both state and some of the private banks as instruments of rent distribution and deficit funding, along with poor fiscal, financial, and monetary governance in the Turkish national context, marked the country's major step away from its integration into the European financial area during the 1990s. However, Turkey has made remarkable progress via economic and financial restructuring programs following the crises of 2000 and 2001. "Turkey's Transition Program", which aimed to achieve macroeconomic stability, and "The Banking Sector Restructuring Program", which aimed to strengthen monetary and financial governance in the banking sector, were introduced following the crises. These reform programs, which benefited from substantial financial and technical assistance from the "twin organizations", were institutionalized due largely to the policy entrepreneur, and carried out effectively by the AKP government following the early elections in November 2002. The EU, with its accession process, and the twin organizations, with their financial and technical support, serve as the external anchors for financial and monetary governance by supranational interdependence.

Turkey is in the long process of Europeanization, embedded in new policy processes, organizations, and institutional arrangements. There are a number of untouched areas; how political parties are funded is unknown in Turkey and "[a]s regards to fight against money laundering no progress can be reported" (CEC, 2004a, p. 87). The alignment of political funding, and money laundering legislation with the EU is not yet on the agenda. However, there is an urgent need for convergence towards EU norms.

With regards to good governance in the financial services industry, Turkey faces a few major challenges. The regulatory state, which can adopt a proactive approach in the financial services industry by steering and coordinating policy community, does not exist (for theoretical frameworks, see Coleman, 1996). The degree of centralization of the state apparatus (or regulatory/supervisor consolidation), and the existence of institutional arrangements, which ensure a balance between the perspectives of the BRSA, Treasury and the Central Bank, are needed. As such, the Turkish state is weak and cannot adopt a proactive approach in the financial services industry by steering and coordinating policy community. "Governance with government" in the financial services industry will be a function of the government's political entrepreneurialism and skill of setting and implementing its *own* agenda. As such, the fundamental issue for Turkey is "how to develop institutions with the capacity to determine appropriate policies, implement them and stick to them until circumstances change" (Eichengreen, 2002, p. 59). Enhancing the state's "transformative capacity" – to use Weiss' term (1998, 2003) – to manage change and to steer institutional adjustment in a world of global finance may be a credible answer. The policy-making in Turkey should be open, transparent and accountable to the public. The negotiation process between the relevant state actors (which must be also sufficiently insulated against sectoral interest groups) and business and labor organizations representing regulated sectors (which must have membership coherence to represent the whole of the sector) must be institutionalized and regularized, rather than being ad hoc in character.

NOTES

1. The author thanks Korkut Boratav and Ziya Onis for their encouragement and valuable comments.

2. As Bakir and Brown (2004, fn. 1, p. 24) summarized, Turkey's relations with the EU had basically governed by the stipulations of the Association Agreement of 1964 (Ankara agreement) which was supplemented and specified by an Additional Protocol in 1973. Its basic goal was the establishment of a customs union between Turkey and the EU. The European Parliament ratified the customs union on 13 December 1995. Turkey was recognized as a candidate for accession at the Helsinki European Council in December 1999. This marked a new era in relations between Turkey and the EU. Accordingly, the EU has been the major external actor supervising political reforms in Turkey since December 1999. Further, on 13 December 2002, the Copenhagen European Council decided that "if the European Council in December 2004, on the basis of a report and a recommendation from the [European] Commission, decides that Turkey fulfils the Copenhagen political criteria, the EU will open negations without delay" (Anatolian Agency, 2002). The Copenhagen criteria led the Turkish government to commit itself to political reforms. As a result, the EU has been increasingly effective in its carrot-and-stick policy.

3. Of course, governance by supranational interdependence is by no means the only source of domestic policy change, but, as will be detailed below, it has been an important one in the Turkish context.

4. The IMF stand-by agreements and the World Bank Programmatic Financial and Public Sector Adjustment Loans are the examples of such financial assistances (see IMF, 2001, 2004a; World Bank, 2002, 2004).

5. It should be noted that the major weakness of Zysman's typology is its focus on external sources of corporate finance (e.g., bank-based and market-based finance) ignoring the significant role of internal sources of funding (e.g., retained earnings). For example, net internal sources of corporate finance between 1984 and 1994 averaged 92.1 percent in France (Cobham & Serre, 1996), 71.8 percent in Germany, 71.2 percent in Japan, 81.2 percent in the UK and 109.8 percent in the USA (Corbett & Jenkinson, 1997). The same figure for Italy averaged 83.7 percent between 1983 and 1993 (Cobham, Cosci, & Mattesini, 1996). The general conclusion for external sources of corporate finance derived from these studies shows that market-based finance is always small, and when external sources of finance relatively large, it is banks rather than markets that dominate funding.

6. Governance here is defined as "collective problem solving within the public realm" (Caparaso, 1996, p. 32, cited in Pagoulatos, 1999, p. 69).

7. Demirguc-Kunt and Levine (2003) are mistaken in their identification of the Turkish financial system as "market-based".

8. For example, T.C. Ziraat Bankasi, the biggest state-owned bank provided loans to farming, T. Halk Bankasi funded small–medium-sized businesses, Etibank financed and owned mines, Sumerbank offered loans to textiles and other household goods, Sekerbank provided loans for sugar farming, and T. Emlak Bankasi contributed to real estate finance.

9. Turkish version of the "crony capitalism" has flourished under the following conditions: (1) "Public banks have created major distortions in the sector because of their large size and their abuse for political rent distribution purposes" (OECD, 2002, p. 80); (2) "Bank entry and exit was highly politicized. The granting of bank licenses was based primarily on political criteria during the 1990s" (OECD, 2002, p. 80); (3) "Tax policies and accounting procedures reinforced the channeling of resources to government, while preventing corporate governance practices which underpinned distortions in the allocation of private sector credit" (OECD, 2002, p. 78); (4) "An ineffective bankruptcy law and court system also were not conducive to quick restructuring efforts (it took 8 years to liquidate the banks taken over after the 1994 crisis)" (OECD, 2002, p. 80); (5) "Deficiencies in internal control and risk management in banks are compounded by weakness in the supervisory and regulatory framework" (OECD, 2002, p. 79); (6) "[The Savings Deposit and Insurance Fund's] ineffectiveness was highly constrained *inter alia* by an inefficient asset recovery process [coupled with the creation of a Banking Regulation and Supervision Agency] which became operational too late to prevent the banking crisis from erupting late 2000" (OECD, 2002, p. 80); (7) "... failure to limit moral hazard problems arising from full deposit insurance imposed after the 1994 crisis" (OECD, 2002, p. 80).

10. Korkmaz Yigit, a leading contractor and real estate developer at the time, won a US$600 million bid for the privatization of Turkbank on 4 August 1998. However, the sale was suspended on 22 October, after the leak of a tape recording proving a deal between Yigit and the Turkish Al Capone, Alaattin Cakici, a deal which eliminated rivals in the privatization bid. The Turkbank scandal led to the collapse of the government in 1998.

11. For example, three state-owned banks, T.C. Ziraat Bankasi, T. Halk Bankasi and T. Emlak Bankasi, were forced by politicians to "hide bad debts [i.e., duty losses] of about US$20 billion, or nearly [13]% of Turkey's entire annual economic output in 2001" (*WallStreet Journal*, 30 April 2001, p. A13).

12. Following the banking reform in 1999, regulatory limits on connected lending were reduced to 25 from 75 percent, whilst that of open positions was tightened to 20 from 50 percent (OECD, 2002, n. 44, p. 154).

13. This expression is borrowed from Kang (2002, p. 177).

14. The SDIF banks were provided with bonds against their losses. As a result, Turkey's domestic debt stock deteriorated significantly.

15. There were 12 banks out of 20 which "were taken over on the grounds that their financial positions were seriously distorted and on that banks' resources were used in favor of the majority shareholders thereby creating losses on the part of the banks" (BRSA, 2003, p. 17).

16. The result was the collapse of Demirbank which used to fund its government securities portfolio in short-term money market.

17. As Akyuz and Boratav notes, [s]uch programs typically use the exchange rate as a credible anchor for holding down inflationary expectations, often leading to currency appreciations and relying on capital inflows attracted by arbitrage opportunities to finance growing external deficits. The consequent build-up of external financial vulnerability eventually gives rise to self-fulfilling expectations of sharp currency depreciations and a rapid exit of capital, resulting in an overshooting of the

exchange rate in the opposite direction and hikes in interest rates (Akyuz & Boratav, 2003, pp. 1549–1550).

18. As will be detailed below, the combination of liberalization process and weak state apparatus and financial institutions made Turkey vulnerable to speculative capital movements. Turgut Ozal's, who dominated the Turkish politics as Prime Minister between 1983 and 1989, neo-liberal policy paradigm that privileged market liberalization over state-led industrialization came with "the creation of totally new layers of bureaucracy which often resulted in a serious intra-bureaucratic conflicts ... the implementation of the reform process in Turkey was associated with a weakening of the bureaucratic or the state apparatus, arguably with costly consequences" (Onis, 2004, p. 114). During Ozal years, as Boratav, Turel, and Yeldan (1996, p. 378) note "Decision making and implementation on rent-allocating activities definitely shifted into the prerogative of the political layer of the state structure as the upper bureaucracy was pushed increasingly into a passive position."

19. However, the SDIF has so far collected only US$2.2 billion as of the end of 2004.

20. For example, according to a poll, two-thirds of respondents indicated that they did not trust the government and 55 percent thought it had to resign. It has been shown that voters preferred the opposition parties far more than the three parties in the ruling coalition (*WallStreet Journal*, 5 March 2001, p. A.18).

21. Between 1973 and 1976, Dervis served Ecevit as an advisor on economic issues and international relations. He was strong advocate of trade liberalization and integration of the Turkish economy with the international economy (e.g., see Dervis & Robinson, 1978). Dervis became the new head of the United Nations Development Programme, the UN's global development network, on 15 August 2005.

22. Pagoulatos (1999, p. 84) uses term "supranational interdependence" in the EU context. The term "denote[s] all the stages of policy making at the EU level, that is, the initiation, formulation, negotiation, and adoption of EU legislation".

23. For example, within a month's time following his arrival on the Turkish political scene, unelected Dervis had "63 percent approval rating which is three times more than the next most popular political leader" (Euromoney, April 2001, p. 38).

24. This was mainly due to Turkey's geo-strategic importance to the USA. As the *Financial Times* (16 May 2001) commented on the IMF bailout, "[t]he main reason for supporting Turkey once again is political rather than economic. A debt default would destabilize an important US ally in a vital and sensitive region." Turkey became the second biggest borrower with a total of US$23 billion outstanding loans in 2004 (IMF, 2004a).

25. According to the CEC, however, the central bank should not have this exception which is regarded as "direct public financing by the central bank" (CEC, 2004a, p. 105). This perspective certainly reflects the lack of understanding of the financial system fragility in Turkey.

26. The World Bank approved the first PFPSAL for US$1.1 billion in July 2001 to support the reform program. In April 2002, a US$1.35 billion (PFPSAL II) was approved. The PFPSAL III of US$1 billion was approved in July 2004.

27. Indeed, as Amin (1995, p. 17) notes, "[the IMF is] merely the executive of strategies defined by the G7 – strategies that are defined by the least common denominator among the positions of the United States, Japan and the [EU]."

28. Similarly, IMF managing director, Rodrigo de Rato recently said that "[i]n the banking sector, the goal over the next three years will be to align Turkey's supervisory framework more closely with EU standards" (Rato, 2004).

29. The EU, however, played a pivotal role in political and legal reforms in Turkey as the extraterritorial source of influence.

30. There have been 16 different governments in the past 25 years.

31. Nine out of 10 political parties of the previous parliament were pushed out of the legislature by the electorate.

32. For example, only 6 years after the Turkbank scandal, on 27 October 2004, the then Prime Minister and Minister for Economic Affairs were sent by the Turkish parliament to the High Tribunal to stand trial over Turkbank privatization scandal. The number of the former ministers who were sent by the Turkish Parliament to the Supreme State Court due to corruption charges reached eight in 2004. The 2004 also witnessed the imprisonment of corrupt bank owners and the mafia leaders (see BBC Monitoring Service, 24 December 2004; *Turkish Daily News*, 15 October 2004).

33. Not surprisingly, "[t]he owners of bankrupt banks have started to line up in front of the [SDIF], fearing the same fate as the Uzan Group and asking for a payment plan for their debts to be drawn up" (*Turkish Daily News*, 20 February 2004).

34. On 20 October 2004, Turkey was ranked the 77th most corrupt country among 145 countries in the world, behind four central and eastern European countries Poland, Slovak Republic, Czech Republic, and Hungary, which ranked 67, 57, 51, 42, respectively (Transparency International, 2004). Turkey's corruption perception index score worsened from 4.5 in 1995 to 3.2 in 2004. More significantly, her score has not changed since 2001, in spite of the EU-induced legal reforms.

35. A comprehensive index of the Economic Freedom of the World (EFW) shows that Turkey increased its EFW rating, measured by chain-linked index, from 3.5 in 1980 to 4.8 in 1990 and to 5.8 in both 1995 and 2000 (Gwartney & Lawson, 2004, p. 19). However, Turkey's rating fell to 5.3 in 2001 and 5.5 in 2002, which was substantially below the mean summary rating of 6.5 in 2002.

36. According to the 2004 Freedom in the World survey, Turkey's "partly free" country status has not changed since 1994 (Freedom House, 2004). However, Turkey's combined average of Political Rights and Civil Liberties ratings improved from 4.5 that prevailed from 1996 to 2001 to a score of 3.5 in 2002/2003.

37. There is no single financial market governance model in the EU (see Barth et al., 2003).

38. For example, the Imarbank's actual amount of deposits was 10 times higher than its official balance sheet deposit figures (see Fort & Hayward, 2004, p. 4). Most recently, the report of the Inspection Board of the Prime Ministry blamed the then heads of the BRSA and Sworn Bank Auditors for negligence and wrongful acts in recognizing under-reporting of deposits and keeping false accounting books (*Radikal*, 4 January 2005).

39. Those banks which did take excessive risks with less liquidity and capital gained advantage over other banks which observed prudential guidelines and adopted a conservative approach to risk and capital management.

40. A letter of intent of the government of Turkey on 15 July 2004 indicated that: We have completed a comprehensive review of the Banking Act and prepared a new

draft Law on Credit Institutions to bring the legal framework more closely in line with EU standards. The law will place particular emphasis on strengthening the legal framework in the following areas: (i) "fit and proper" criteria for bank owners; (ii) on-site inspections; (iii) lending to related parties; (iv) legal protection for BRSA and, SDIF board members and staff for actions taken in good faith during the course of their duties; and (v) delineating the responsibilities of BRSA and SDIF respectively and providing for their effective coordination (IMF, 2004b).

41. Morgan Stanley notes that "coupled with sound macroeconomic policies, productivity gains and investment growth are behind this phenomenal performance. Labor productivity in the manufacturing sector, for example, surged by 30% in the post-crisis period, raising the country's potential growth rate and lowering unit labor costs by 38.5% in the same period" (Morgan Stanley, 21 December 2004, p. 2).

42. The primary surplus, fiscal surplus before interest payments, target was agreed with the IMF in 2001 to tackle a debt load of more than US$200 billion.

43. The compounded real interest rate for domestic debt stock was 11.9 percent in 2003 (Treasury, 2004, p. 48).

44. Foreign bank entry into the Turkish banking sector was prohibited until 1980. There were only four foreign banks operating in 1980. Between 1981 and 1990, 16 new foreign-owned banks started wholesale banking in Turkey. They specialized in foreign trade and corporate finance. Foreign banks gradually entered into retail banking: HSBC bought Demirbank following its seizure by the SDIF in December 2000, Unicreditor had a 49 percent partnership with Kocbank, BNP Paribas bought a 50 percent share in TEB, whilst already established Deustchebank recently received authorization to collect deposits. The number of foreign banks decreased from 15 in 2002 to 13 in 2003. This was due to Credit Suisse First Boston and ING Bank N.V. which ceased their activities. However, foreign interest in the Turkish banking sector accelarated throughout 2005 due to political and macroeconomic stability. Recent foreign transactions included Koc Financial Services's purchase of Yapi Kredi, Fortis Bank's purchase of an 89 percent stake in Disbank and Rabobank's purchase of a 36.5 percent stake in Sekerbank. Following the formal approval of these deals, the share of foreign banks in total Turkish banking assets will increase to 16 percent.

45. For example, in October 2004, Finansbank, Turkey's fifth largest privately owned bank, issued the longest-dated bond, a subordinated debt with a 10-year maturity. However, special features and a high price were attached to the debt. As the *Financial Times* (7 October 2004) notes "[a] special feature was the inclusion of a political risk insurance that would protect coupon payments to investors for two years if the government were to deny lira conversions or transfers abroad. The bond, rated Ba1 by Moody's Investors Service, pays a coupon of 9 per cent, which increases to 11.79 per cent after five years if it is not bought back."

46. In particular, the possibility of (hostile) takeovers in capital markets is assumed to be a device for disciplining managers.

47. A study on ownership concentration, structure and control in the top 100 companies traded on the Istanbul Stock Exchange (ISE) as at the end of 1999 showed that "families own 68 of the largest traded 100 companies; 53 of these companies families have majority control with over 50 per cent of voting rights" (Demirag & Serter, 2003, p. 47). Specifically, seven of the eight traded banks on the ISE "are ultimately owned by families. Family owned banks serve as the main bank of a group

companies organized around a holding company [which incorporates other financial and non-financial firms]."

REFERENCES

Akguc, O. (1992). *100 soruda Turkiye'de Bankacilik*. Istanbul: Gercek Yayinevi.
Akyuz, Y. (1990). Financial system and policies in Turkey in the 1980s. In: T. Aricali & D. Rodrik (Eds), *The political economy of Turkey: Debt, adjustment and sustainability* (pp. 98–198). London: Palgrave Macmillan.
Akyuz, Y., & Boratav, K. (2003). The making of the Turkish financial crisis. *World Development, 31*, 1549–1566.
Alper, E., & Onis, Z. (2004). The Turkish banking system, financial crises and the IMF in the age of capital account liberalization: A political economy perspective. *New Perspectives on Turkey, 30*, 25–54.
Amin, S. (1995). Fifty years is enough!. *Monthly Review, 46*, 8–50.
Anatolian Agency. (2002). *EU Copenhagen summit ends*, 13 December.
Babacan, A. (2004). Speech delivered by Mr. Ali Babacan at the Press Conference.
Bakir, C. (2005a). Merkez Bankasi Bagimsizligi, Hesap verebilirligi ve Saydamligi: TCMB Uygulamasi ve Uluslararasi bir Karsilastirma. *Iktisat, Isletme ve Finans, 233*, 20–36.
Bakir, C. (2005b). Turkey: En route to meet the challenging maastricht criteria? *Studia Europaea* (forthcoming).
Bakir, C., & Brown, K. (2004). Turkey. In: J. A. Batten, T. A. Fetherston & P. G. Szilagyi (Eds), *European fixed income markets* (pp. 431–448). West Sussex: John Wiley and Sons.
Bankers Association of Turkey. (2004a). Bankacilik Sektoru. *Bankacilar Dergisi, 49*, 68–99.
Bankers Association of Turkey. (2004b). Turk Bankacilik Sisteminde Banka, Sube ve Personel Bilgileri. http://www.tbb.org.tr
Banking Regulation and Supervision Authority. (2001a). Banking sector restructuring program progress report (IV). http://www.bddk.org.tr/english/publicationsandreports/brsareports/BSRP_102003.pdf
Banking Regulation and Supervision Authority. (2001b). *Towards a sound Turkish banking sector*. http://www.bddk.org.tr/english/publicationsandreports/brsareports/annex_report_towards_a_sound_turkish_banking_sector percent20.doc
Banking Regulation and Supervision Authority. (2003). *Banking sector restructuring program – Progress report*. http://www.bddk.org.tr/english/publicationsandreports/brsareports/BSRP_102003.pdf
Banking Regulation and Supervision Authority. (2004). *2003 Annual report*. http://www.bddk.org.tr/english/publicationsandreports/brsareports/annual_report_2003.doc
Barth, J. R., Nolle, D. E., Phumiwasana, T., & Yago, G. (2003). A cross-country analysis of the bank supervisory framework and bank performance. *Financial Markets, Institutions and Instruments, 12*, 67–120.
Boratav, K. (2003). *Turkiye Iktisat Tarihi 1908–2002*. Ankara: Imge Kitabevi.
Boratav, K., Turel, O., & Yeldan, E. (1996). Dilemmas of structural adjustment and environmental policies under instability: Post-1980 Turkey. *World Development, 24*, 373–393.
Capital Markets Board. (2004). 2003 *Annual report*. http://www.cmb.gov.tr/news/news.htm?tur=annualreport

Central Bank of Republic of Turkey. (2002). *2001 Annual report*. Ankara: TCMB.

Central Bank of Republic of Turkey. (2003). *2002 Annual report*. Ankara: TCMB.

Central Bank of Republic of Turkey. (2004). *2003 Annual report*. Ankara: TCMB.

Cizre, U., & Yeldan, E. (2002). Turkey: Economy, politics and society in the post-*crisis Era.* http://www.bilkent.edu.tr/~yeldane/umitcizre&yeldan_RIPE.pdf

Cobham, D., & Serre, J.M. (1996). *A characterization of the French financial system*. Department of Economics, University of St Andrews, Mimeographed.

Cobham, D., Cosci, S., & Mattesini, F. (1996). *The Italian financial system: Neither bank-based nor market-based*. Department of Economics, University of St. Andrews, Mimeographed.

Coleman, W. D. (1996). *Financial services, globalization and domestic policy change*. New York: St. Martin's Press.

Coleman, W. D., & Perl, A. (1999). Internationalized policy environments and policy network analysis. *Political Studies, 47*, 691–709.

Commission of the European Communities. (2004a). *Regular report on Turkey 's progress towards accession.* http://europa.eu.int/comm/enlargement/report_2004/pdf/rr_tr_2004_en.pdf

Commission of the European Communities. (2004b). Communication from the Commission to the Council and the European Parliament: Recommendation of the European Commission on Turkey's progress towards accession. http://europa.eu.int/comm/enlargement/report_2004/pdf/tr_recommandation_en.pdf

Corbett, J., & Jenkinson, T. (1997). *How is investment financed? A study of Germany, Japan, the United Kingdom and the United States*. The Manchester School of Economic and Social Studies. Manchester: Blackwell Publishing.

Demirag, I., & Serter, M. (2003). Ownership patterns and control in Turkish listed companies. *Corporate Governance, 11*, 40–51.

Demirguc-Kunt, A., & Levine, R. (2003). *Bank-based and market-based financial systems: Cross-country comparisons*. Washington, DC: World Bank Group.

Denizer, C. (1997). *The effects of financial liberalization and new bank entry on market structure and competition in Turkey*. Policy Research Working Paper Series no. 1839, Macroeconomics and Growth Development Research Group.

Dervis, K. (2001). *Statement by Mr. Kemal Dervis, Minister of State Press Conference Held on March 19, 2001*. http://www.treasury.gov.tr/bakan_basin_toplantisi_eng.htm

Dervis, K., & Robinson, S. (1978). *The foreign exchange gap, growth, and industrial atrategy in Turkey, 1973–1983*. World Bank Staff Working Paper no. 306. Washington, DC: The World Bank.

Deutsche Bank. (2004). Turkish Banks. 23 December.

Dyson, K. (2000). EMU as Europeanization: Convergence, diversity and contingency. *Journal of Common Market Studies, 43*, 645–666.

Economist. Europe: New man new hope? 24 March 2001.

Economist. Harsh medicine. 19 May 2001.

Economist. 9 November 2002.

Egilmez, M., & Kumcu, E. (2003). *Krizleri Nasil Cikardik?* Istanbul: Creative Yayincilik.

Eichengreen, B. (2002). Capitalizing on globalization. *Asian Development Review, 19*, 14–66.

Euromoney. April 1998.

Euromoney. April 2001.

Evrensel, A. (2004). IMF programs and financial liberalization in Turkey. *Emerging Markets Finance and Trade, 40*, 5–15.

Fort, J. L., & Hayward, P. (2004). *The supervisory implications of the failure of Imar bank.* Ankara: Commission of Inquiry, Treasury.

Freedom House. (2004). *Freedom in the World 2004: The annual survey of political rights and civil liberties.* Washington DC: Rowman and Littlefield Publishers.

Gelos, R. G., & Roldos, J. (2004). Consolidation and market structure in emerging market banking systems. *Emerging Markets Review, 5,* 39–59.

Gwartney, J., & Lawson, R. (2004). *Economic Freedom of the World: 2004 Annual Report.* Fraser Institute. www.freetheworld.com

Haas, P. M. (1992). Introduction: Epistemic communities and international policy coordination introduction. *International Organization, 46,* 1–35.

IMF. (1999). *Turkey-Letter of intent, 9 December.* http://www.tcmb.gov.tr/yeni/evds/yayin/imf/loi.html

IMF. (2001). *Turkey-Letter of intent Turkey, 26 June.* http://www.hazine.gov.tr/english/announce/imf/loi26jun.htm

IMF. (2002). *Turkey-Letter of intent, 28 January.* http://www.imf.org/External/NP/LOI/2002/tur/01/INDEX.HTM#loi

IMF. (2004a). *Turkey: Financial position in the Fund as of December 31, 2004.* http://www.imf.org/external/np/tre/tad/exfin2.cfm?memberKey1 = 980

IMF. (2004b). *Turkey. Letter of intent Turkey, 15 July.* http://www.imf.org/External/NP/LOI/2004/tur/02/

Kang, D. C. (2002). Bad loans to good friends: Money politics and the developmental state in South Korea. *International Organization, 56,* 177–207.

Kaplan, C. (2002). Open foreign positions for the banking sector. Paper presented to the *6th International Conference of Economics.* Ankara: Middle East Technical University.

Kingdon, J. W. (1995). *Agendas, alternatives, and public policies.* New York: Longman.

Mero, K., & Valentinyi, E. (2003). *The role of foreign banks in five central and eastern countries.* Magyar Nemzeti: National Bank of Hungary, Mimeographed.

Moran, M. (2002). Politics, banks and financial market governance in the Euro-Zone. In: D. Kenneth (Ed.), *European states and the Euro: Europeanization, variation, and convergence* (pp. 257–278). Oxford: Oxford University Press.

Morgan Stanley. (2004). Turkey: Jingle All the Way. 21 December.

Onder, I., Turel, O., Ekinci, N., & Somel, C. (1993). *Turkiye'de Kamu Maliyesi, Finansal Yapi ve Politikalar.* Istanbul: Gokhan Matbaacilik.

Onis, Z. (2004). Turgut Özal and his economic legacy: Turkish neo-liberalism in critical perspective. *Middle Eastern Studies, 40,* 113–134.

Organization for Economic Cooperation and Development. (2002). *Economic survey – Turkey.* Paris: OECD Publications Service.

Organization for Economic Cooperation and Development. (2003). *Bank profitability statistics.* Paris: OECD Publications Service.

Organization for Economic Cooperation and Development. (2004). *Economic survey – Turkey.* Paris: OECD Publications Service.

Pagoulatos, G. (1999). European banking: Five modes of governance. *West European Politics, 22,* 68–94.

Pazarbasioglu, C. (2003). *Costs of EU accession: The potential impact on the Turkish banking sector.* http://www.cie.bilkent.edu.tr/banking.pdf

Rato de, R. (2004). *14.12.2004. Statement by IMF Managing Director on Turkey.* http://www.treasury.gov.tr/duyuru/basin2004/IMFBaskaniRato_Basinaciklamasi_English.pdf

Sener, N. (2004a). *Kod Adi: Atilla.* Istanbul: Guncel Yayincilik.
Sener, N. (2004b). *Uzanlar: Bir Korku Imporatorlugunun Cokusu.* Istanbul: Guncel Yayincilik.
SPO (State Planning Organization). 2004. *Pre-accession economic program.* http:// www.dpt.gov.tr/files/Pep30112004i.pdf
Tartan, H. (2003). *Hortumun Ucundakiler: Turkiye'de Batan Bankalarin Hikayesi.* Istanbul: Toplumsal Donusum.
Transparency International. (2004). *Corruption perceptions index 2004.* http://www.transparency.org/cpi/2004/cpi2004.en.html#cpi2004
Treasury. (2001). *Transition to the Strong Economy Program.* Ankara: Undersecretariat of Treasury. http://www.treasury.gov.tr
Treasury. (2004). *Hazine Kamu Borç Yönetimi Raporu [Treasury report on debt stock management].* http://www.treasury.gov.tr/duyuru/basin2004/ KBYR_Agustos2004.pdf
Turkiye Sermaye Piyasasi Araci Kuruluslari Birligi. (2004). *Avrupa Birligine Dogru Turkiye Sermaye Piyasalarinda Sorunlar ve Cozumler.* Istanbul.
Weiss, L. (1998). *The myth of the powerless state.* Ithaca, NY: Cornell University Press.
Weiss, L. (2003). *States in the global economy: Bringing domestic institutions back in.* Cambridge: Cambridge University Press.
World Bank. (2002). *Turkey: World Bank supports economic reform.* News Release no: 2002/ 284/ECA. Washington DC: The World Bank.
World Bank. (2004). *Turkey: World Bank approves third programmatic financial and public sector adjustment Loan, 17 June.* Washington DC: The World Bank.
Zysman, J. (1983). *Governments, markets and growth: Finance and the politics of industrial change.* Ithaca, NY: Cornell University Press.

PART C:
FINANCIAL INNOVATION AND LIBERALIZATION

THE DEVELOPMENT OF FINANCIAL DERIVATIVES MARKETS IN AN EXPANDED EU

Jing Chi and Martin Young

1. INTRODUCTION

Financial derivatives markets are a relatively new development globally. In the USA, the first commodity derivatives trading began in Chicago at the Chicago Board of Trade in 1849. However, the first financial derivatives trading did not begin until 1972, when the Chicago Mercantile Exchange began trading futures contracts on seven foreign currencies. These were the world's first official financial futures contracts. In Europe, the oldest financial derivatives market was the London International Financial Futures Exchange, or LIFFE, which began trading financial futures in 1982.

In terms of product offerings and development, the major markets of the USA and Europe started with currency and then interest rate products, with equity-based products coming into existence at a later date. In the USA, derivatives exchanges tend to be independent of other exchanges and specific financial derivatives products tend to be traded on more than one exchange. For example, the Chicago Board of Trade and the Chicago Mercantile Exchange operate separately from any cash market such as the New York Stock Exchange or NASDAQ, and both trade commodity and financial derivatives. In Europe, however, there is a more specialized approach developing with the two largest derivatives markets of Europe,

Emerging European Financial Markets: Independence and Integration Post-Enlargement
International Finance Review, Volume 6, 215–234
Copyright © 2006 by Elsevier Ltd.
ISSN: 1569-3767/doi:10.1016/S1569-3767(05)06009-7

Euronext-LIFFE and Eurex, both concentrating very much on financial derivative products. The smaller derivatives markets of Europe have a tendency to trade both financial and commodity derivatives.

While there is ongoing debate about the appropriate level of regulation required in both exchange-based and over-the-counter (OTC) derivatives trading, there can be no argument as to the importance of financial derivatives markets as part of a modern capital market structure. However, financial derivatives markets are invariably the last part of the capital market structure to develop in any country, and their viability tends to be very much a function of both specific and overall capital market size. If we consider the three major economic areas, or blocs that now exist, they have their differences and similarities. For the Americas, the USA remains totally dominant and has a highly developed capital market structure with financial derivatives trading being a very significant part of this. Canada, Brazil, Mexico, and Argentina have well-developed financial derivatives markets also, but these all tend to operate independently of each other. The situation in Asia is similar to some extent, although Japan does not dominate in Asia to the same degree as the USA does in the Americas. It could be argued that the Japanese capital markets need more deregulation before they will be as highly developed as those of the USA. While there have been a number of links developed between Asian financial derivatives markets and those of the USA and Europe, there has been little inter-Asian cooperation. In fact, financial derivatives markets, such as the Singapore Exchange Derivatives Trading, have tended to be strong competitors to the other Asian financial derivatives markets rather than partners. It should also be noted that for the largest Asian economy, China, there is currently no official financial derivatives exchange operating, although efforts are now underway to establish one. Also the establishment of a financial derivatives exchange in China will certainly be undertaken independently of any other Asian, or major global economy.

The European situation is different in many ways and these differences have been driven, to a large extent, by the much stronger drive for economic union that has been taking place there. As the European Union (EU) has developed and strengthened over time, the competition and cooperation between the capital markets of the EU members have changed. This has been particularly pronounced in the financial derivatives markets of the EU on account of the development of the single currency. For the financial derivatives markets in the EU member countries, country barriers have become less important and competition at the corporate level has intensified. In fact, the competitive environment faced by the financial derivatives markets of the EU members is now similar to that faced by the financial derivatives markets of the USA. For interest rate derivatives in particular, the market for short-term European interest rate derivatives products is now dominated by Euronext-LIFFE based out of London but part of the Euronext group, which includes the financial derivatives markets of Amsterdam, Brussels, Lisbon, and Paris. The market for long-term European interest rate derivatives products, on the other hand, is dominated by Eurex, a derivatives market that was formed by the merging of the DTB and the Swiss Options and Financial Futures Exchange (SOFFEX) in 1998. For an earlier discussion on the restructuring of the European stock and derivative exchanges see Jochum (1999).

On 1 May 2004, 10 more countries became members of the EU. These countries are Cyprus, the Czech Republic, Estonia, Hungary, Latvia, Lithuania, Malta, Poland, Slovakia, and Slovenia. An interesting question to ask is how the financial derivatives markets of Europe should continue to develop in this new environment of a greater EU. This is the focus of this chapter, which is organized as follows. Section 2 of this chapter examines the development of financial derivatives markets in the EU to date. Section 3 examines the current state of financial derivatives markets within the new EU member countries, and the other countries of greater Europe which remain outside of the EU. Section 4 discusses the financial markets within the new EU member countries, their current status, and the likely alliances that will be formed. Section 5 investigates the likely role of financial derivatives markets within the new EU member countries, appropriate product development, and the benefits to be gained through the development of financial derivatives trading in these countries. A suggested strategy is discussed for the continuing development of the financial derivatives markets of Europe. Section 6 concludes this chapter.

2. THE DEVELOPMENT OF FINANCIAL DERIVATIVES MARKETS IN THE EU

The USA was the first country to start using financial derivatives products when the Chicago Mercantile Exchange began trading futures contracts on seven foreign currencies in 1972. It was not until 10 years later that Europe started trading its first financial derivatives product. This happened when the LIFFE began trading financial futures in 1982.[1] After the LIFFE began operations, it was not long before other financial derivatives markets were established, led by the Scandinavian counties. In 1985, the Stockholm

Options Market (SOM) was founded. This was followed by the Finnish Options Market (FOM) and the Danish Options and Futures Market (FUTOP) in 1987, with trading getting underway in 1988. By the beginning of the 1990s, there were a number of derivatives markets operating in Europe, but they were, in general, newly formed and were very much country-specific markets.

Given the competitive environment in Europe in the 1980s, it was somewhat surprising that Western Europe's two other major financial centres at the time, France and Germany, lagged some distance behind the UK in introducing financial derivatives markets. The first to move was France with the establishment of the Marche a Terme International de France (MATIF). This derivatives-trading market was established in 1986 and started trading financial derivatives in the same year. Then in 1988, the DTB Deutsche Terminbörse (DTB) was established, although the trading of financial derivatives did not start in this market until 1990.

By the mid-1980s, it had become clear that financial derivatives had an important part to play in the capital markets of Europe and a number of other markets were set up. It was the EU members, or other Western European countries that led the way as can be seen from the following list: Switzerland, the SOFFEX in 1986; the Netherlands, Financiele Termijnmarkt Amsterdam N.V. (FTA) in 1987; Spain, Mercado Espanol de Futuros Financieros S.A. (MEFF) in 1989; Belgium, the Belgian Futures and Options Exchange (BELFOX) in 1990; Italy, Mercato Italiano Futures (MIF) in 1992, which was an interest rate derivatives exchange, and IDEM in 1994, which was an equity derivatives exchange.

These developments in financial derivatives markets in Europe from the mid-1980s through to the early 1990s were, as stated earlier, mostly country specific. Markets were established to cater for the needs of institutions and individuals operating within these countries wishing to take derivative-based positions using contracts where the underlying asset was normally domiciled in the country of the market within which they were operating. However, by the mid-1990s, the pending introduction of the Euro was starting to change the thinking as to how these markets might develop into the future. The Euro's introduction had two major impacts on financial derivatives markets. In the first instance, it greatly reduced the hedging requirements within those countries that would adopt the Euro and also made hedging against the Euro bloc countries simpler. The same applied for interest rates. Financial derivatives exchanges had to consider how they could retain market share in this environment and how vulnerable they would be to competition from financial derivatives exchanges in other EU countries that offered identical products. It was with interest rate products, in particular, where the strongest competition developed with two exchanges finally dominating, almost totally in this market. Euronext-LIFFE, which came out of a merger of the derivatives exchanges of London, Amsterdam, Brussels, Paris, and Lisbon, took over the short-term interest rate derivatives market from its London base, with the benchmark for short-term interest rate derivatives being Euribor (see Hajek, 2000). Eurex, which came out of a merger of the DTB Deutsche Terminbörse and the SOFFEX, took over the long-term interest rate derivatives market. Here the benchmark is the German Bund. In terms of volume, these two sets of financial derivatives products are by far the most actively traded, so with their trading now concentrated on two exchanges, this has had a major impact on the product offerings and turnover for other financial derivatives markets within the EU. Currency-based financial derivatives products are much less popular than the interest rate-based products, and where the other financial derivatives markets of the EU have managed to retain market share and build their businesses has been in the area of stock and stock index options and futures.

2.1. LIFFE, Euronext-LIFFE, and Eurex

When LIFFE began operations in 1982, it focused on providing products to help in the management of interest rate and currency risk. Contracts introduced in the first year of operation included a 3-month Eurodollar interest rate contract, a short Sterling interest rate contract, and four currency contracts on the Pound, Swiss Franc, Yen, and Deutschmark. The highly successful German Government Bund futures contract was introduced in 1988. By 1989, 3-month Euromark futures, 3-month European currency unit (ECU) futures, and bond options contacts had also been introduced. The products introduced by LIFFE over this time showed that the exchange intended to be a dominant player in the area of financial futures. LIFFE continued to introduce further interest rate and currency derivatives products through the 1990s. On account of this and through mergers with other derivatives exchanges within the UK, LIFFE became the second largest futures and options exchange in the world by 1997.

In 1997, LIFFE made a serious mistake by deciding to stay with its open-outcry trading system, believing this to be the fairest and most efficient way of executing business. In reality, technology had improved to such a degree by this time that screen-trading systems could be both more efficient in the executing of trades and more cost effective. More importantly, business could shift between market places almost instantaneously in an electronic environment. LIFFE's major competitor in the interest rate derivate market, the Deutsche TerminBörse, moved to screen trading ahead of LIFFE, and in doing so took the trading of the German Government Bund contract from the trading floor at LIFFE to their own screen-based trading platform. This event forced a rethink at LIFFE and the exchange then quickly moved to develop its own screen-trading system called LIFFE CONNECT® which was launched in November 1998 and has since proved highly successful. LIFFE saw considerable volume growth through 2000 and 2001, but never regained the German Government Bund business. Then as part of the financial integration that was occurring in Europe, a decision was made for LIFFE to merge with Euronext in 2002. Euronext itself had come out of a merger between Amsterdam Exchanges, Brussels Exchanges, and the ParisBourse in September 2000. London then became the hub for the interest rate derivatives business of Euronext.

When Euronext itself was established, the main focus of the new entity was on the equity market operation, even though each exchange's derivatives market was part of the same group. As a group, the derivatives side of the operation was very significant at the time, particularly for the Euronext Paris derivatives market. Euronext Paris traded 43.3 million interest rate derivatives contracts in 2000, mainly on account of substantial growth in the Euro Notional Bond futures contract. Before the merger with LIFFE, Euronext expanded further with the merger of Bolsa de Valores de Lisoa e Porto, or BVLP, into the group. The merger with LIFFE gave Euronext the opportunity to incorporate the derivatives side of its business into one clear entity and to also integrate the markets onto a single electronic-trading platform, namely LIFFE CONNECT®. The timetable for this trading integration was early 2003 for Brussels and Paris, with Amsterdam and Lisbon to follow in 2004. On 24 March 2003, Brussels commenced trading on LIFFE CONNECT®. This allowed for a substantial reduction in trading fees within the current highly competitive European derivatives markets. For the year 2002, Euronext-LIFFE traded a total of 697 million futures and options contracts for an underlying value of €183 trillion, making it the world's second largest derivatives exchange. In 2003, this volume was steady at around 695 million contracts.

This grouping of exchanges has proven to be most successful with the group accounting for almost 38 per cent of all financial derivatives-trading volume in Europe for 2003. Within Euronext-LIFFE, the London operation concentrates very much on the interest rate derivatives, while the other four exchanges focus on individual equity and equity index derivatives products. Most volume for these four exchanges comes from equity index futures and options based on the home stock market. For Euronext Amsterdam this is the AEX; for Euronext Brussels, the BEL20; for Euronext Paris, the CAC40; and for Euronext Lisbon, the PSI20. This combination of cooperation and division of operation could well be the best way forward for derivatives markets in a greater EU.

Eurex, a German, Swiss joint venture came about through the merger of the DTB Deutsche Terminbörse, the German Options and Futures Exchange, and SOFFEX in 1998. DTB Deutsche Terminbörse was established in 1988 with the trading of financial futures commencing in 1990. SOFFEX was established in 1986 and also started trading financial futures in 1990. These two exchanges started working together in December 1996 when they decided to create a joint trading and clearing platform. They had seen, earlier than most, the need to create a derivatives market large enough to compete effectively in the ever more integrated Europe. The larger market would have a greater range of products, higher liquidity, and lower costs. In May 1998, the combined derivatives operations changed their name to Eurex and commenced trading on Eurex software.

Eurex has made a number of attempts to expand within Europe through alliances with other derivatives exchanges, but these attempts have been mostly unsuccessful although Eurex participants do operate both throughout and outside of Europe, as is the case with Euronext-LIFFE. Of more success has been the development of a relationship with the Chicago Board of Trade. Despite the setbacks with European alliances, Eurex has now become the world's largest derivatives market in terms of number of contracts traded. On a number of contracts traded basis, Eurex traded more than 40 per cent more than that traded by Euronext-LIFFE for 2003. On a value basis, however, Euronext-LIFFE trades significantly more than that traded by Eurex. This is driven by the fact that Euronext-LIFFE dominates the short-term interest rate market while Eurex dominates the longer-term interest rate market.

In terms of interest rate derivatives products, the almost total domination of these two exchanges in their respective areas is interesting. Even with an extended EU and more countries joining the Euro single currency, there may not be sufficient room for any more serious players to join them in this market long term. This is not to say that there is no scope for new interest rate products to be developed for trading on these exchanges, however, given the ever-changing nature of the financial investment marketplace (see Clare & Oozeer, 2001). While other EU derivatives exchanges have traded interest rate derivatives products in the past, at this time the only other European exchange that can still be considered active in interest rate derivatives products is the OMX Stockholm Exchange. Volumes for all short-term interest rate futures contracts traded in Europe in 2003 were as follows: Euronext-LIFFE, 185.1 million; Eurex, 0.5 million; and OMX Stockholm, 4.9 million. Volumes for all long-term interest rate derivatives products traded were: Euronext-LIFFE, 12.9 million; Eurex, 512.2 million; and OMX Stockholm, 1.8 million.

2.2. Other EU Financial Derivatives Exchanges Pre-2004

As stated above, in terms of interest rate derivatives, the only other EU financial derivatives exchange of significance now is OMX Stockholm. In fact, OMX Stockholm is the next largest derivatives exchange in the EU after Eurex and the Euronext group of exchanges with approximately 4 per cent of all financial derivatives-trading volume in Europe for 2003. Like Euronext-LIFFE and Eurex, OMX Stockholm has had a strategy of building alliances with other exchanges, and this strategy has helped the exchange to remain a major player in the financial derivatives marketplace. In 1989, the exchange established an international dimension after the setting up of the OM London Exchange to manage demand for Swedish financial products internationally. Since 1997, Norwegian equity and interest rate derivatives have been traded and cleared through the OM exchanges. In 2002 there were two developments of significance. Progress was made on the alliance of the Nordic region exchanges, the Copenhagen Stock Exchange, Iceland Stock Exchange, Stockholmbörsen, and Oslo Børs (NOREX). A major aim of this alliance was to have all exchanges trading on the same electronic system. The other important development was the move by OM, the Swedish operator of Stockholmbörsen, to form a joint venture with the London Stock Exchange. The purpose of this was to start a new derivatives exchange, EDX London, to trade equity-based derivatives products.

Then, most significantly, in 2003 OM HEX was formed with the merger of OM and HEX, creating an integrated Nordic and Baltic market. The OM HEX or OMX exchanges include Stockholm, Helsinki, Riga, Tallinn and, since 2004, Vilnius. Of the old HEX exchanges, Finland was the most significant and traded approximately 2 million financial derivatives contracts in 2003. These were almost all equity-based products, however. Other market participants of similar size were Austria's ÖTOB derivatives market and Denmark's FUTOP market, which operates under the Copenhagen Stock Exchange. These exchanges traded 1.4 and 0.8 million financial derivatives contracts, respectively, in 2003 and again these were equity-based products.

Of more significance is the ADEX market in Athens, which started operations in 1999. Its major growth in financial derivatives products has again been in stock index futures and options and stock options, though the market does still transact some interest rate derivatives business. Approximately 4.9 million financial derivatives contracts were traded in 2003 giving the exchange close to 0.3 per cent of the European financial derivatives market for that year.

The final two established EU member country derivatives exchanges that should be mentioned here are those of Italy and Spain with approximately 1 and 1.7 per cent European financial derivatives market share, respectively. Two financial derivatives exchanges developed in Italy. The first, MIF, started operating in 1992 and traded only interest rate derivatives products including a range of Government bond and interest rate futures and options and Euribor futures. The other exchange is IDEM, the Italian Exchange for equity derivatives. In 1998, both exchanges came under the control of Borsa Italiana, the Italian Exchange. The interest rate derivatives market has not traded since 2002, and now all financial derivatives products traded on the Italian Exchange are equity based. During the 2003 year a total of approximately 17.7 million contracts were traded on this exchange.

Like Italy, Spain originally developed two financial derivative exchanges: MEFF Renta Variable for equity derivatives and MEFF Renta Fija for interest rate derivatives. These exchanges started trading financial derivatives in 1990 and then came under one holding company, MEFF Sociedad Holding, in 1991. In September 1999 the management of the two entities was combined into one unit for greater efficiency. This was a necessary move as once again the equity derivative business has grown as the interest rate derivative business has declined. Now almost all trading activity is in equity-based financial derivatives though there is still a very small amount of trading in a long-term interest rate derivative, Bono 10. For the 2002 year, total trading activity on MEFF was approximately 41.4 million contracts of which 47,000 contracts were bond futures. In 2003, trading activity dropped to 30.4 million contracts of which just 1,300 were bond futures. For a fuller discussion on the development of the derivative markets of Europe see Young (2004).

3. OTHER EUROPEAN AND NEW EU MEMBER FINANCIAL DERIVATIVES MARKETS

Of the 10 new entrants to the EU of May 2004, three countries are part of the OM HEX group being Estonia, Latvia, and Lithuania. As a block, these countries are a significant part of OM HEX and with EU membership one can expect growth in financial derivatives activity coming from the financial institutions, corporations, and individual investors of these countries. Two of the 10 new entrants have well-established financial derivatives markets of their own. These are the Warsaw Stock Exchange of Poland and the Budapest Stock Exchange of Hungary. Hungary also has the Budapest Commodity Exchange, which provides an active market in currency derivatives.

The Warsaw Stock Exchange has a derivatives arm that started operating in January 1998. This market trades stock futures, equity index futures and options, and exchange rate futures, though by far the bulk of volume is with the equity index futures. In 2003, the Warsaw Stock Exchange traded approximately 4.4 million contracts accounting for 0.24 per cent of total financial derivatives turnover in Europe. The Budapest Stock Exchange started derivatives trading in 1995 and although there has been trading in interest rate derivatives in the past, this is now a very minor part of their business. The main activity is in equity- and currency-based products. The Budapest Stock Exchange traded approximately 2.6 million contracts in 2003, a little over half that of the Warsaw Stock Exchange.

Two other countries within Europe have derivatives markets of significance. In Norway, the Oslo Stock Exchange trades stock and equity index futures and options. In 2003, approximately 3.4 million contracts were traded. Of more and growing significance is the Russian Trading System (RTS) Stock Exchange based in Moscow. RTS launched its own derivatives trading in 2001 after reaching an agreement with the St Petersburg Stock Exchange, which had successfully run its derivatives trading up until that time. RTS Stock Exchange has a very active market in stock and equity index derivatives as well as a small market in currency derivatives. Contracts traded for 2003 amounted to 33.8 million, or 1.85 per cent of the European financial derivatives market. Russia has the Moscow Interbank Currency Exchange (MICEX) which trades stock, equity index, and exchange rate futures also. Table 1 shows the trading statistics for financial derivatives within Europe for all exchanges that are members of the IOMA/IOCA for 2003.

4. THE FINANCIAL MARKETS OF THE NEW EU MEMBER COUNTRIES

While increasing the number of EU members from 15 to 25 is a substantial increase in number terms, it is important to keep this expansion in

Table 1. Financial Derivatives Market Turnover Within Europe for the 2003 Trading Year for all Exchanges that are Members of the IOMA/IOCA ('000).

Country	Market	Equity	STIR	LTIR	F/X	Total
EU members						
Austria	Wiener Borse	1,392.6				1,392.6
Belgium	Euronext Brussels	969.1				969.1
Denmark	FUTOP	768.9				768.9
Finland	OM HEX	2,007.3				2,007.3
France	Euronext Paris	277,486.9				277,486.9
Germany[a]	Eurex	452,732.8	504.6	512,156.8		965,394.2
Greece	ADEX	4,767.3		66.3	74.2	4,907.8
Italy	IDEM	17,732.0				17,732.0
The Netherlands	Euronext Amsterdam	79,262.4			2.5	79,264.9
Portugal	Euronext Lisbon	849.3				849.3
Spain	MEFF	30,399.1		1.4		30,400.5
Sweden	OMX Stockholm	65,462.9	4,890.9	1,783.6		72,137.3
UK	Euronext-LIFFE	54,003.4	262,919.7	12,878.7		329,801.8
New EU members						
Hungary	Budapest Stock Exchange	983.5	0.1		1,627.8	2,611.4
Poland	Warsaw Stock Exchange	4,378.9			6.1	4,385.0
Other Europe						
Norway	Oslo Bors	3,386.9				3,386.9
Russia	RTS	33,738.0			24.5	33,762.5

Note: The Eurex market includes both the German and Swiss derivatives exchanges.
Source: IOMA Derivatives Market Survey (2003); World Federation of Exchanges (2004).
[a]Eurex trading data does not distinguish between German and Swiss-based trades. The Swiss component is therefore included in the data for Germany.

perspective on a population and gross domestic product (GDP) basis. The potential for growth in both GDP and capital market activity through this expansion is clearly very substantial. From Table 2, it can be seen that, on a GDP basis in purchasing power parity (PPP) terms, the expansion is only just over 9 per cent. On a population basis the expansion is a much greater 19.7 per cent as the GDP per capita in the new entrant countries is less than half that of the old. However, if EU membership for the new entrants can lead to GDP levels approaching those of the existing members over time, the growth potential is clearly substantial. The size differences are even more pronounced in terms of financial market activity. The stock market capitalization of the new EU member countries is currently less than 1 per cent

Table 2.   A Comparison of New and Existing EU Member Countries in Terms of Population, GDP on a PPP Basis, and Financial Derivatives Market Activity.

Country	Population (millions)	GDP on PPP (USD)	GDP per Capita	Share of European Financial Derivatives Market
EU members				
Austria	8.1	245.3	30,000	00.08
Belgium	10.3	299.1	29,100	00.05
Denmark	5.4	167.2	31,100	00.04
Finland	5.2	142.2	27,400	00.11
France	60.4	1,661.0	27,600	15.19
Germany[a]	81.8	2,271.0	27,600	52.83
Greece	10.6	213.6	20,000	00.27
Ireland	3.9	116.2	29,600	
Italy	57.5	1,550.0	26,700	00.97
Luxembourg	0.5	25.0	55,100	
The Netherlands	16.1	461.4	28,600	04.34
Portugal	10.4	181.8	18,000	00.05
Spain	40.2	885.5	22,000	01.66
Sweden	8.9	238.3	26,800	03.95
UK	59.8	1,666.0	27,700	18.05
Total EU	379.1	10,123.6	26,704	97.60
New EU members				
Czech Republic	10.2	161.1	15,700	
Cyprus	0.8	16.0	18,500	
Estonia	1.4	17.4	12,300	
Hungary	10.0	139.8	13,900	00.14
Latvia	2.3	23.9	10,200	
Lithuania	3.6	40.9	11,400	
Malta	0.4	7.0	17,700	
Poland	38.6	427.1	11,100	00.24
Slovakia	5.4	72.3	13,300	
Slovenia	2.0	36.8	19,000	
Total new EU	74.7	942.3	12,614	00.38
Totals	453.8	11,065.9	24,385	97.98

Note: The German financial derivatives market share includes all Eurex trades.*Source:* CIA – The World Fact Book (2004); IOMA Derivatives Market Survey (2003); and World Federation of Exchanges (2004).

[a]Eurex trading data does not distinguish between German and Swiss-based trades. The Swiss component is therefore included in the data for Germany.

that of the existing member countries. For the 2003 year, financial derivatives contracts traded in the new EU member countries was just 7.0 million compared to 1,783.1 million for the existing member countries, or less than half of 1 per cent. With converging GDP levels and general economic integration, one might expect financial market activity to also be similar on a per capita basis over time. Clearly, therefore, there is substantial growth potential for financial market activity in the new EU member countries as well. The interesting question to ask is how this growth can be best managed and within what type of financial market structure. Specifically, how should the markets for financial derivatives products be developed within the new EU member countries?

As can be clearly seen from the previous discussion, a single European currency has changed the overall makeup of the financial derivatives markets of the EU member countries over the last 5 years in particular. Where there has been commonality, financial derivative trading has migrated to just one or two exchanges. This has most clearly been the case with interest rate derivatives. In the case of currency derivatives, their need has diminished significantly within the EU as the advent of the single currency has either eliminated, or at least greatly reduced currency risk among EU member countries. While none of the new EU member countries are currently part of the Euro, the intention is that all will join the Euro over time. Initially it was hoped that all would join the Euro by 2010, but it is now thought that only Estonia, Latvia, Lithuania, and Slovenia will be ready by that time. It can be noted, however, that the currencies of Estonia, Lithuania, and Cyprus currently operate under a Euro-peg while the currency of Latvia operates under an SDR-peg.

In the shorter term, it may be possible for countries of the size of Poland, Hungary, and the Czech Republic to develop an interest rate derivatives market independently of other exchanges, but this would definitely only be shorter term. The same applies to currency derivatives. Currently the Budapest Stock Exchange in Hungary has a reasonably active currency derivatives market, and even after joining the Euro there could be a market niche to provide currency derivatives for cross rates between the Euro and currencies of other major European economies outside the Euro, but this market will also be very competitive and will more likely shift to the home country of the cross rate. For the new EU member countries, the most obvious area for financial derivatives market growth is in the area of stock and equity index derivative products.

Before discussing the market for stock and equity index products in detail, which will be presented in Section 5, it is worth noting the types of blocs that might develop either within or between the new EU member countries. Note that the blocs being considered here relate primarily to equity market blocs, as only Poland and Hungary have any sort of active financial derivatives market at this time. One bloc is already in place. This is between Estonia, Latvia, and Lithuania through their membership of OM HEX. With Sweden now part of OM HEX, this grouping looks set to establish itself as a real, if very much junior, competitor to Eurex and Euronext-LIFFE in terms of the financial derivatives markets of Europe. The Baltic country's membership of this group should be very advantageous to them and from their viewpoint this gives them a significant opportunity to further develop stock and equity index derivatives products based around the major listed corporations of their home countries. The blocs that may form within or around the seven other new EU entrants are not so easy to determine.

As at the end of 2003, the market capitalization of the stock markets of these seven countries amounted to approximately 81.6 billion USD, with Hungary and Poland accounting for approximately 51 billion of this total. While the numbers are relatively small at the moment, the growth potential is obviously substantial. Growth in the stock markets will naturally lead to growth in stock and equity index-based derivatives products. Given the potential, other EU exchanges have been considering their own strategic alliances also (Table 3).

Apart from Slovakia, the Mediterranean exchanges of Malta and Cyprus are currently the smallest of the group and on account of their locations may well continue to operate independently of other exchanges. Also given their size and prospects for growth, financial derivatives products based on their respective equity markets may not be particularly viable, though one would still expect there to be some demand from financial institutions investing at least a portion of their funds into these markets. From a location and historical ties viewpoint, a relationship between the Athens Exchange and Cyprus and the Italian or London Stock Exchange and Malta would be a possibility, though there is no official indication of any such relationships developing to date.

More has been happening in relation to the other five exchanges. In the first instance, they are in the same general Central-Eastern European region and have, for a number of years, been discussing their common future. They have worked together on the calculation of the CESI regional index, for example. Despite the fact that they do have this history of working together, an alliance of the five has not developed. This may be because there was no clear leader among them to instigate the process of unification. Recent privatizations within these exchanges have now opened up the market to

Table 3. Relative Sizes of the EU Member Country's Stock Markets as on 31 December 2003.

Country	Stock Market Capitalization (USD)	Share of EU Total Capitalization (USD)
EU members		
Austria	55.5	0.58
Belgium	263.8	2.76
Denmark	136.6	1.43
Finland	166.3	1.74
France	1,913.4	20.05
Germany	1,212.4	12.70
Greece	85.0	0.89
Ireland	78.3	0.82
Italy	690.8	7.42
Luxembourg	24.5	0.26
The Netherlands	833.2	8.73
Portugal	96.5	1.01
Spain	816.0	8.55
Sweden	359.6	3.77
UK	2,725.0	28.55
Total EU	9,456.9	99.09
New EU members		
Czech Republic	14.8	0.16
Cyprus	4.6	0.05
Estonia	3.6	0.04
Hungary	15.8	0.17
Latvia	0.7	0.01
Lithuania	0.8	0.01
Malta	1.8	0.02
Poland	35.2	0.37
Slovakia	2.6	0.03
Slovenia	6.8	0.07
Total New EU	86.7	0.91
Totals	9,543.6	100.00

Source: Individual stock exchange statistical reports.

possible mergers that will be based on corporate expediency rather than historical ties. The first major move in this direction has come with the 50.2 per cent purchase of the Budapest Stock Exchange by an Austrian consortium that could well lead to a consolidation of the Vienna and Budapest Exchanges. It is also possible that the Warsaw Stock Exchange may join this group. The Chairman of the Budapest Exchange has commented on a potential offer being made to the Warsaw Stock Exchange for joint shareholding to be established between Vienna, Budapest, and Warsaw. The Warsaw Stock Exchange, however, is also considering other options with the London Stock Exchange, Euronext, Deutsche Bourse, and OM HEX.

The Exchanges of the Czech Republic and Slovakia have been more concerned with ensuring their credibility as part of the EU stock exchanges rather than forging alliances to date. Both are relatively small and could possibly benefit through joint cooperation. It is also a strong possibility that the two markets could become part of an Austrian, Hungarian, Polish alliance in due course. The last stock exchange to consider, the Ljubljana Stock Exchange of Slovenia looks destined to move in a different direction. This exchange sees itself as being part of the South-Eastern Europe capital markets rather than the Central-Eastern European grouping. The exchange has been instrumental in developing a portal for the information integration of the stock exchanges of South-Eastern Europe, namely Sarejevo, Banja, Luka, Skopje, Belgrade, Varazdin, Podgorica, and Ljubljana itself. The Stock Exchange of Montenegro is also considering joining this grouping.

Overall, however, one thing is certain. Mergers and alliances among the financial exchanges of Europe will continue to occur as the EU itself continues to expand. For the development of financial derivatives markets, strong stock markets will be a prerequisite, as it is in the area of stock and equity index derivatives that the greatest potential for growth exists for those markets outside of Eurex and Euronext-LIFFE.

5. FINANCIAL DERIVATIVES MARKET DEVELOPMENT WITHIN THE NEW EU MEMBER COUNTRIES

Europe now has a clear history of derivatives markets being taken over by cash markets or developing out of the cash market. The only real exceptions to this have been LIFFE in London, though this is now part of the Euronext group, and OM in Sweden. It should be noted that this is quite different from the US experience where the derivatives markets have traditionally always been quite separate from the cash markets. With the new EU member countries, the same situation will almost certainly hold. Both the Warsaw and Budapest Exchanges have their own derivatives arms and the expansion of financial derivatives trading in other new EU member countries will almost certainly follow the same route. As screen trading now almost totally dominates financial derivative markets on account of its efficiency and cost advantages, any new derivatives exchange will be electronic based. Note that the cost advantage relates to the raw cost of executing an order. There is some debate as to whether or not electronic trading leads to lower liquidity costs than for an open-outcry system (Ulibarri & Schatzberg, 2003).

It does seem unlikely that any new financial derivatives market will develop within the 10 new EU member countries except possibly in the case of the Czech Republic and Slovenia. The Prague Stock Exchange has looked previously at developing a financial derivatives market and if it does retain its independence, this is a likely outcome. In the case of Slovenia, if the Ljubljana Stock Exchange is successful in building a grouping of South-Eastern European exchanges, a natural development within that grouping would be the establishment of a financial derivatives exchange. It is most likely that all stock exchanges of the EU bloc will either have their own derivatives arm or have access to a derivatives exchange in the not too distant future. This has certainly been the case with the pre-2004 EU member countries.

In terms of products offered by these exchanges, equity index derivatives products or exchange traded fund derivatives are the fastest growing derivatives products globally (see Goldfinger, 2004), and have the most promise for the derivatives markets of, or aligned with, the new EU member countries. Table 4 gives a breakdown of the trading activity of the financial derivatives markets of the pre-2004 EU member countries. It can be clearly seen that, outside of Euronext-LIFFE and Eurex, by far the most popular product is the equity index derivatives. The larger the equity market behind the index or the more internationalized the market is, the greater interest there is in such a product.

In order to find a market niche, those operating the financial markets of the new EU member countries need to think carefully as to the appropriate equity indices for derivatives products. It is interesting to note that some major financial derivatives markets have been successful in trading equity index derivatives on indices with constituents from outside their home market. Eurex has been a market leader in this area by introducing a derivatives product based on a European index being the Dow Jones Euro Stoxx 50, comprising of 50 of the largest companies in the EU. This product has been particularly successful trading 177.8 million futures and options contracts in 2003. This compares with 68.6 million contracts traded on Eurex for the German Stock Market index product, the DAX.

Table 4.   Stock and Equity Index Financial Derivatives Market Product
Volume for 2003 for the EU Member Country Financial Derivatives
Markets.

Country	Market	Single Stock Options	Single Stock Futures	Equity Index Options	Equity Index Futures	Main Equity Index Product
EU Members						
Austria	Wiener Borse	1,252.0	–	27.7	112.9	ATX
Belgium	Euronext Brussels	319.9	–	320.5	328.7	BEL 20
Denmark	FUTOP	142.4	0.3	8.4	617.8	KFX
Finland	OM HEX	332.2	1,675.0	–	0.1	–
France	Euronext Paris	174,487.3	–	73,668.1	29,331.5	CAC 40
Germany[a]	Eurex	188,239.8	–	108,504.3	155,988.7	DJES 50
Greece	ADEX	14.7	477.5	1,389.0	2,886.2	ASE 20
Italy	IDEM	7,924.1	468.1	2,505.4	6,834.5	MIB
Netherlands	Euronext Amsterdam	59,754.7	32.4	14,254.9	5,222.4	AEX
Portugal	Euronext Lisbon	12.3	622.6	–	214.4	PSI 20
Spain	MEFF	11,379.0	12,492.6	2,981.6	3,545.9	IBEX 35
Sweden	OMX Stockholm	43,098.8	1,424.9	6,371.4	14,567.9	OMX
UK	Euronext-LIFFE	10,108.1	6,349.2	15,745.1	21,801.0	FTSE100
Total EU		497,065.2	23,542.6	225,774.3	241,451.9	
New EU Members						
Hungary	Budapest Stock Exchange	0.8	618.3	–	364.4	BUX
Poland	Warsaw Stock Exchange	–	93.1	153.1	4,132.7	WIG 20
Total New EU		0.8	711.4	153.1	4,497.1	
Totals		497,066.0	24,254.0	225,927.4	245,949.0	

Note: The German financial derivatives market share includes all Eurex trades.
Source: IOMA Derivatives Market Survey (2003); World Federation of Exchanges (2004); and
individual derivatives exchange's statistical reports.
[a]Eurex trading data does not distinguish between German and Swiss-based trades. The Swiss
component is therefore included in the data for Germany.

The Euronext group has also tried some innovations in this area, though not as successfully as Eurex. Euronext-LIFFE trades four European equity index derivatives products on their market. First there are two FTSE indices set up in conjunction with Euronext-LIFFE. These are the FTSE Eurofirst 80 Index and the FTSE Eurofirst 100 Index. The 80 Index includes the 60 largest companies ranked by market capitalization in the FTSE Eurozone Index and 20 additional companies that are selected into the index based on their size and sector representation. The 100 Index is the same as the 80, but with 40 additional companies rather than 20. The other two European equity index derivatives products are based on the MSCI Euro Index and the MSCI Pan-Euro Index which include 112 and 230 European companies, respectively. From October 2003 to September 2004, 1.7 million futures and options contracts were traded by Euronext-LIFFE on these products.

The derivatives markets of, or aligned to, the new EU member countries need to consider the relevance of particular equity indices to their national, and the inter-European managed funds industry in particular. Where a derivatives market bloc has been formed, the strategic relevance of the bloc will be important. OM HEX, for example, is a logical bloc for the Baltic countries in particular, and a Baltic equity index is a logical product to market and offer derivatives on. The South-Eastern European Bloc that the Ljubljana Stock Exchange is supporting is another logical bloc, but there could be some difficulty with an Austrian, Hungarian, Polish bloc without Germany, so the development of a viable equity index which could support active derivatives trading could well be more difficult in this case.

6. CONCLUSION

In a modern capital market setting, financial derivatives markets are an important component to ensure a complete and efficient market environment. In the EU of pre-2004, most countries had their own financial derivatives markets, though in general these now trade mainly individual stock and equity index contracts. With a single currency throughout most of the pre-2004 EU, currency derivatives have become less important, but there has been substantial growth in interest rate derivatives, though this market activity is confined to just two major and one minor player. The major players are Eurex and Euronext-LIFFE and the minor player is OMX Stockholm. It is also of interest to note that interest rate derivative products have consolidated around the underlying benchmark assets being Euribor for the short-term rate and the German Bund for the long-term rate.

The 10 new entrants to the EU all have their own stock markets, but only two, Hungary and Poland, have financial derivatives markets and these are small but not insignificant. Both these derivative markets operate under their respective stock exchanges. Should any of the other new entrant countries develop a derivatives exchange, these also will most likely be developed by their respective stock exchanges. The most likely countries where this could happen are the Czech Republic, Slovakia, and Slovenia. The Baltic States are already part of the OM HEX group and Cyprus and Malta are probably too small to warrant a derivatives exchange.

Within the new entrant countries the main growth area for derivatives trading will be with equity index-based products and individual stock products. The exchanges or alliances of exchanges that develop should carefully consider the appropriate equity index mixes that will attract investors, with particular focus on the needs of the inter-European managed funds industry.

NOTE

1. Information relating to LIFFE, Euronext and Euronext-LIFFE, and Eurex, has been obtained from their respective press releases. Information on the stock and derivative markets of Europe has been obtained from the following market web sites: www.adex.ase.gr, www.aex.nl, www.ase.gr, www.bolsasymercados.es, www.borsaitalia.it, www.borzamalta.com.mt, www.bourse.lu, www.bse.hu, www.bsse.sk, www.cse.com.cy, www.cse.dk, www.deutsche-boerse.com, www.eurexchange.com, www.euronext.com, www.hex.com, www.ise.ie, www.ljse.si, www.londonstockexchange.com, www.oslobors.no, www.pse.cz, www.rts.ru, www.swx.com, www.wienerborse.at, www.wse.com.pl

REFERENCES

Clare, A. D., & Oozeer, M. C. (2001). Hedging sterling eurobond portfolios: A proposal for eurobond futures contract. *Applied Financial Economics*, *11*, 37–44.

Goldfinger, C. (2004). *Evolving instruments: What are we going to trade?* Discussion Paper 2004 European Financial Markets Convention, Frankfurt.

Hajek, J. (2000). The impact of the introduction of the Euro on the structure and the trade volume of the European derivatives exchanges. *Finance a Uver*, *50*, 406–420.

IOMA Derivatives Market Survey. (2003); World Federation of Exchanges (2004); Institute for Financial Markets, Futures and Options Fact Book (2004).

Jochum, C. (1999). Network economics and the financial markets – the future of Europe's stock exchanges. *Aussenwirtschaft*, *54*, 49–74.

Ulibarri, C. A., & Schatzberg, J. (2003). Liquidity costs: Screen-based trading versus open outcry. *Review of Financial Economics*, *12*, 381–396.

Young, M. (2004). Perspectives on European derivatives markets. In: J. A. Batten, T. A. Fetherston & P. G. Szilagyi (Eds), *European fixed income markets* (pp. 67–84). Wiley.

FINANCIAL LIBERALIZATION AND BUSINESS CYCLES: THE EXPERIENCE OF THE NEW EU MEMBER STATES

Lúcio Vinhas de Souza*

1. INTRODUCTION

Financial and capital liberalization can play a fundamental role in increasing growth and welfare. Typically, emerging or developing economies seek foreign savings to solve the inter-temporal savings-investment problem. On the other hand, current account surplus countries seek opportunities to invest their savings. To the extent that capital flows from surplus to deficit countries are well intermediated and put to the most productive use, they

*Corresponding author. This work was initially done while the author was a "Visiting Researcher" at the Research Center of the Deutsche Bundesbank. I would like to thank the comments of Kai Carstensen, Felix Hammermann, Heinz Herrmann, Giovanni Lombardo, Christian Pierdzioch, Franziska Schobert, Rainer Schweickert, Kiril Strahilov and George von Furstenberg, and the comments made during the Applied Econometric Association "Emerging Markets" Toledo meeting and during a "Lecture Series" seminar given at the Deutsche Bundesbank. Special thanks go to Harald Uhlig and Emanuel Mönch, who provided the original MATLAB programs used for the estimation of "Bry–Boschan" turning points. All the remaining mistakes are the exclusive responsibility of the author.

Emerging European Financial Markets: Independence and Integration Post-Enlargement
International Finance Review, Volume 6, 235–259
Copyright © 2006 by Elsevier Ltd.
ISSN: 1569-3767/doi:10.1016/S1569-3767(05)06010-3

increase welfare. Liberalization can, however, also be risky, as has been witnessed in many past and recent financial, currency and banking crises. It can make countries more vulnerable to exogenous shocks. In particular, if serious macroeconomic imbalances exist in a recipient country, and if the financial sector is weak, be it in terms of risk management, prudential regulation and supervision, large capital flows can easily lead to serious financial, banking or currency crises. A number of recent crises, like those in East Asia, Mexico, Russia, Brazil and Turkey (described, for example, in International Monetary Fund (IMF), 2001), and, to some extent, the Argentinean Crisis of late 2001, early 2002, have demonstrated the potential risks associated with financial and capital flows liberalization (Prasad et al., 2003).

Central Eastern Europe has a somewhat different experience, when compared to other emerging regions, concerning the financial liberalization process, as the process there seems to have been much less crisis-prone than elsewhere such as in Asia or Latin America. This may be at least partially because the current high degree of external and financial liberalization in these countries, beyond questions of economic allocative efficiency, must be understood in terms of the process of accession to the European Union (EU).

The EU integration process implies legally binding, sweeping liberalization measures – not only capital account liberalization, but investment by EU firms in the domestic financial services, and the maintenance of a competitive domestic environment, giving this financial liberalization process a strong external incentives (and constraints). Those measures were implemented parallel to the development of a highly sophisticated regulatory and supervisory structure, again based on EU standards. This whole process happened also with the EU's technical and financial support, through specific programs – like the PHARE one, for these formerly called Accession Countries (ACs), and the TACIS, for the former Soviet Union ones – and direct assistance from EU institutions, like the European Commission,[1] the European Parliament and the European Central Bank (also, on a very early stage of the transition process, the influence of the IMF in setting up policies and institutions in several countries in the region – an intervention widely considered to be haven been successful – was very important (Hallerberg, Vinhas de Souza, & Clark, 2002)).

Additionally, EU membership in the near future seems to act as an anchor to market expectations (de Souza & Hölscher, 2001), limiting the possibilities of self-fulfilling financial crises and regional contagion (Linne, 1999), which had the observed devastating effects in both Asia and Latin America (even a major event, like the Russian collapse of 1998, had very much reduced regional side effects). Several regional episodes of financial systems' instability did happen (Vinhas de Souza, 2002a, b), but none with the prolonged negative consequences observed in other regions (which was also due to the effective national policy actions undertaken after those episodes).

The main aim of this chapter is to expand the Kaminsky and Schmukler (2003) database (henceforth K&S) to include the 10 new EU ACs (Bulgaria, the Czech Republic, Estonia, Hungary, Latvia, Lithuania, Poland, Romania, Slovakia and Slovenia). In their original work, K&S built an extensive database of external and financial liberalization, which includes both developed countries and countries from emerging regions (but not from Eastern Europe). With that, they created different indexes of liberalization (capital account, banking and stock markets: see Table 1) and using them individually and in an aggregate fashion, test for the effects and causality of this process on financial and real volatility, for the existence of differences between regions, and for the effects of the ordering of the liberalization process. With the extended database built in this chapter, a similar set of regressions to enable comparability has been run for the 10 ACs, and the results are contrasted with those for the other regions included in the K&S original study.

One underlying hypotheses of this work is that the existing regulatory and institutional framework in Eastern Europe, plus a more sustainable set of macro policies, played an important role in enabling liberalization to largely deliver the welfare-enhancing outcomes that it is supposed to. Such an anchoring role of the EU in the ACs, through the process of EU membership and through the effective imposition of international standards of financial supervision and regulation, may indicate that, beyond multilateral organizations like the IMF and the Organization for Economic Cooperation and Development (OECD), a greater, pro-active regional stabilizing role in emerging markets by regional actors, for instance, the United States, or by some regional subgrouping, like Mercosur, may also be welfare enhancing for other emerging regions.

The remainder of this chapter is structured as follows. In Section 2, the constructed index and its components are presented and compared with K&S's original index. Section 3 introduces the relation between financial cycles and liberalization. Section 4 introduces the initial regression results building on the K&S compatible core regressions. Section 5 extends the analysis by considering institutional reform and EU accession. Section 6 presents a number of alternative specifications. The final section presents the conclusions.

Table 1. K&S Liberalization Index.

Capital Account Liberalization	Financial Sector Liberalization	Stock Market Liberalization
Criteria for Full Liberalization	**Criteria for Full Liberalization**	**Criteria for Full Liberalization**
Borrowing abroad by banks and corporations	*Lending and borrowing interest rates*	*Acquisition by foreign investors*
Banks and corporations are allowed to borrow abroad mostly freely. They may need to inform the authorities, but the authorization is granted almost automatically Reserve requirements might be in place but are lower than 10%. The required minimum maturity is not longer than 2 years	There are no controls (ceilings and floors) on interest rates.	Foreign investors are allowed to hold domestic equity without restrictions
And	*And*	*And*
Multiple exchange rates and other restrictions	*Other indicators*	*Repatriation of capital, dividends and interest*
There are no special exchange rates for either current account or capital account transactions. There are no restrictions to capital outflows	There are likely no credit controls (subsidies to certain sectors or certain credit allocations). Deposits in foreign currencies are likely permitted	Capital, dividends and interest can be repatriated freely within 2 years of the initial investment
Criteria for Partial Liberalization	**Criteria for Partial Liberalization**	**Criteria for Partial Liberalization**
Borrowing abroad by banks and Corporations	*Lending and borrowing interest rates*	*Acquisition by foreign investors*
Banks and corporations are allowed to borrow abroad, subject to certain restrictions. Reserve requirements might be between 10% and 50%. The required minimum maturity might be between 2 and 5 years. There might be caps in borrowing and certain restrictions to specific sectors	There are controls in either lending or borrowing rates (ceilings or floors)	Foreign investors are allowed to hold up to 49% of each company's outstanding equity. There might be restrictions to participate in certain sectors. There might be indirect ways to invest in the stock market, like through country funds
Or	*And*	*Or*
Multiple exchange rates and other restrictions	*Other indicators*	*Repatriation of capital, dividends and interest*
There are special exchange rates for current account and capital account transactions.	There might be controls in the allocation of credit controls (subsidies to certain sectors	Capital, dividends and interest can be repatriated, but typically not before 2 and

Table 1. (*Continued*)

Capital Account Liberalization	Financial Sector Liberalization	Stock Market Liberalization
There might be some restrictions to capital outflows	or certain credit allocations). Deposits in foreign currencies might not be permitted	not after 5 years of the initial investment
Criteria for No Liberalization	**Criteria for No Liberalization**	**Criteria for No Liberalization**
Borrowing abroad by banks and corporations	*Lending and borrowing interest rates*	*Acquisition by foreign investors*
Banks and corporations are mostly not allowed to borrow abroad. Reserve requirements might be higher than 50%. The required minimum maturity might be longer than 5 years. There might be caps in borrowing and heavy restrictions to certain sectors	There are controls in lending rates and borrowing rates (ceilings and floors)	Foreign investors are not allowed to hold domestic equity
Or	*And*	*Or*
Multiple exchange rates and other restrictions	*Other indicators*	*Repatriation of capital, dividends and interest*
There are special exchange rates for current account and capital account transactions. There might be restrictions to capital outflows	There are likely controls in the allocation of credit controls (subsidies to certain sectors or certain credit allocations). Deposits in foreign currencies are likely not permitted	Capital, dividends and interest can be repatriated, but not before 5 years of the initial investment

2. ESTIMATED INDEXES

The construction of the index for the ACs forms the core of this work. A comprehensive effort has been made to crosscheck the information collected from papers and publications with national sources. Below, I present the estimated monthly index for the period January 1990 to June 2003 (see Fig. 1). The base data for its construction was collected from IMF and European Bank for Reconstruction and Development (EBRD) publications, then exhaustively verified both with national sources and with works written about the individual countries and the region. This is an index that falls with liberalization, where maximum liberalization equals *one* and minimum *three* (in this sense, one could actually see it as an index of financial *repression*). As an additional robustness check, the year-end value of

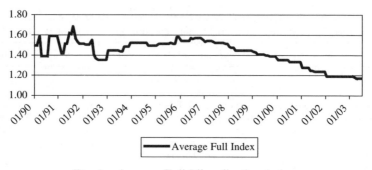

Fig. 1. Average Full Liberalization Index.

the index here constructed was regressed on the combined EBRD's yearly indexes of banking sector reform and non-banking financial sector reform. The results from a regression with the index constructed here on the LHS and the EBRD index on the RHS yield a coefficient of −0.60, and correlations among the individual country-specific index series range from –0.91 to –0.35.

As one may see from Fig. 1, the process of integration and liberalization was almost continuous throughout the 1990s and early 2000. The spikes in the full liberalization index in the early 1990s do not indicate reversals: They merely reflect the entry into the sample of the newly independent Baltic Republics. As former members of the Soviet Union, they "enter" the world as highly closed economies, but those countries introduced liberalization reforms almost immediately from the start. After this, a slight increasing trend, that does reflect a mild liberalization reversal, is observed, starting mid-1994 and lasting *until* early 1997, from when a continuous liberalization trend is observed: This reversal will be explained below. Noteworthy here is the fact that *virtually none* of the obvious candidates for a reversal of liberalization (the 1997 Asian Crisis, the collapse of the Czech monetary arrangement in 1997, the collapse of the Bulgarian monetary arrangement in 1996/1997, the 1998 Russian Crisis, the 1999–2001 oil price shocks – as all those economies are highly dependent of imported energy sources) seems to have driven these mild liberalization reversals.

Comparing the full index constructed here with the one constructed by K&S, for similar time periods, one may observe that the ACs start substantially below the average level of other emerging markets – that is they are more liberalized, but both the "entry" of the initially less liberalized former Soviet Republics, plus continuous liberalization efforts in the emerging markets' K&S set reverse this situation. A similar liberalization reversal trend in both the ACs and the emerging markets' set is observed from early 1994, but it is actually slightly stronger on the ACs sample, until its reversal in 1996. By the end of my sample, the ACs are clearly below the final value for the emerging set in K&S's sample (Fig. 2). This sort of remarkably fast pattern of the ACs' leap-frogging toward the best international practice is also observed in several types of institutional frameworks, like, for instance, monetary policy institutions and instruments (Vinhas de Souza & Hölscher, 2001): A process that virtually took decades for Western central banks was compressed in half a dozen years in them. Nevertheless, by the end of the sample, both emerging markets and ACs are still above the level of mature, developed economies.

Analyzing the individual components of the index (see Fig. 3), one may see that, abstracting again from the initial spikes in the index, which are, as

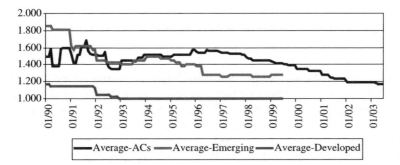

Fig. 2. Comparing the Liberalization Indexes.

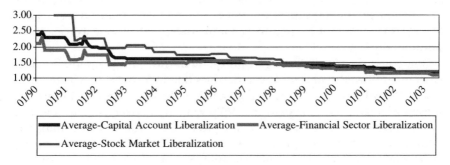

Fig. 3. Individual Components of the Liberalization Index.

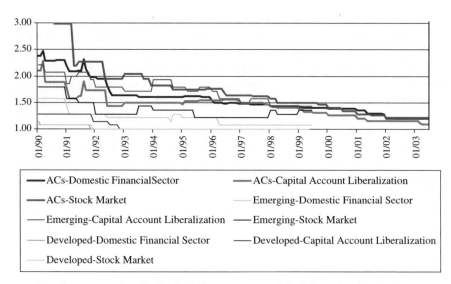

Fig. 4. Comparing Individual Components of the Liberalization Indexes.

explained above, caused by the addition of new countries to the sample, the 1994/1997 reversal of liberalization was essentially driven by the financial sector liberalization component. This was related, in most cases, to – and here it must be stressed that those were rather limited reversals – to the banking crises that plagued several countries in my sample in the early to mid-1990s (Vinhas de Souza, 2004). Comparing now the individual components of the full index constructed here with the ones from K&S, again for emerging and mature economies, it becomes clear that the reversals observed in Fig. 2 were driven by different sources in the emerging set (increase in capital account restrictions) and ACs set (financial sector) (see Fig. 4). All the indexes for mature economies are, again as one would expect, substantially lower.

One could, in principle, aggregate the countries in my sample in three different groups: Rapid liberalizers (the ones that followed a "big bang" early approach, without major reversals: Bulgaria, Estonia, Latvia, Lithuania), consistent liberalizers (the ones that followed a more delayed path, but also without major roll backs the Czech Republic, Hungary, Poland) and cautious liberalizers (the ones whose liberalization path was either openly inconsistent or downright mistrustful: Romania, Slovakia, Slovenia) (Table 2).

Table 2. Values of the Full Index by Country.

	Bulgaria	Czech Republic	Estonia	Hungary	Latvia	Lithuania	Poland	Romania	Slovakia	Slovenia
Average index	1.17	1.21	1.53	1.81	1.21	1.35	1.68	2.05	1.93	1.92
Initial value of index	2.37	1.30	3.00	2.47	3.00	3.00	2.30	2.83	2.40	2.13
Final value of index	1.00	1.00	1.00	1.00	1.00	1.20	1.53	1.60	1.30	1.07

3. FINANCIAL CYCLES AND LIBERALIZATION

The financial cycle coding which is used by K&S defines cycles as at least 12-month strictly downward (upward) movement, followed by equally upward (downward) 12-month movements from the trough (peak) of a stock market index, measured in US dollars, as they should reflect returns from the point of view of an international investor. One must be warned that there are specific factors in the countries in my sample that may affect the effectiveness of a stock market index as an adequate proxy of financial cycles, at least for the sample considered here, namely (Vinhas de Souza, 2004), even in the largest ACs, market capitalization, as a gross domestic product (GDP) share was and remains rather low (at around 15 percent of GDP on average in 2003 – non-GDP weighted, far below the EU average of around 72 percent of GDP). Only in the Czech Republic, Estonia, Hungary and Slovenia is the average market capitalization above a 20 percent GDP share, while in Romania is below 1 percent in several years. Beyond that, these series have a rather limited time extension. As an alternative to K&S criteria, I use the Bry and Boschan (1971) non-parametric algorithm to determine the cyclical turning points (see appendix for its description). With this procedure I find 45 cycles, 22 upward and 23 downward, in all countries except Romania.

After this procedure, following K&S, I estimate their core regression, given by:

$$\text{amplitude}_i = \alpha X_i + \rho_1 d_i^{\text{r}} + \beta_1 d_i^{\text{sr}} + \lambda_1 d_1^{\text{lr}} + \varepsilon_i \tag{1}$$

where the variable amplitude is two series with the amplitudes of the downward or upward movement of a stock market index, calculated as the depth of the contraction (height of the expansion). Following K&S, this is estimated as the change between peak (trough) and the following trough (peak) of the cycle identified as above, and them as a percentage of the average value observed during this cycle for country i. X_i is a matrix of control variables (which includes the world real interest rate, here defined as the United States prime lending rate minus the consumer price index (CPI) inflation in time t, world output growth, here represented by a linear combination of the monthly log industrial production series for the United States, Germany and Japan, and domestic output growth, here proxied by the monthly log industrial production series for each country) with their average value during the cycle, while d_i^r is a dummy variable that equals one if the cycle occurs during "non-liberalized" periods, while d_i^{sr} is the "short-run" dummy that equals one if the cycle occurs shortly after liberalization and while d_1^{lr} is a "long-run" dummy that equals 1 if the cycle occurs a longer time after liberalization.

It is also important to be aware of some features concerning the industrial production indexes for my sample of countries. Beyond their short time span, they are affected by the so-called transition recession, that is the stylized pattern of post-reform growth of a transition economy is characterized by a sharp initial fall followed by recovery and growth (Bakanova et al., 2004). The opening up and the onset of market prices made some sectors uncompetitive virtually overnight. This, coupled with the traditional over-industrialization of the former centrally planned economies, plus the early collapse of their Eastward-biased trade linkages had substantial effects on the level and composition of their industrial output (in Lithuania, the most extreme case in my sample, for instance, the industrial production index lost almost 70 percent of its original value).

4. INITIAL ESTIMATION RESULTS

With the provisos above, I perform a heteroskedasticity-consistent ordinary least squares (OLS) estimation. The results are shown in Table 3. As one may see, the R^2 is relatively low and there are signs of heteroskedasticity. World output is significant in upward cycles with a positive sign, while the other variables in the control set are non-significant, and all have rather small point estimates. Concentrating on the coefficients of main interest to this analysis, the financial repression variable (represented by a dummy that equals 1 in periods without partial or full liberalization, and 0 otherwise) is significant in upward cycles, as are the short- and long-run dummies. Financial liberalization increases the amplitude of upward cycles by around 5.6 percent in the short run (the K&S estimate for emerging markets is 37 percent, and 51 percent in mature ones) and by 9.4 percent in the long run, when compared to the period of financial repression (the K&S estimate for emerging markets is a long run decrease of 25 percent, and of 10 percent in mature markets). On the other hand, crashes decrease with liberalization by 15 percent in the short run (in K&S, crashes in emerging markets increase

Table 3. Values of Heteroskedasticity-Consistent OLS Estimation.

Variables	Upward Cycle		Downward Cycle	
	Coefficient	Standard Error	Coefficient	Standard Error
World real interest rate	0.07	0.01	−0.04	0.02
World output	−0.03*	0.00	−0.00	0.01
Domestic output	0.00	0.00	0.00	0.00
Financial repression dummy	2.33***	1.25	0.68	0.81
Short-run liberalization dummy	2.46***	1.39	0.58	0.91
Long-run liberalization dummy	2.55***	1.36	0.51	0.88
	R^2: 0.35	DW: 1.36	R^2: 0.26	DW: 1.48

Note: Included observations: 22 (upward) 23 (downward). Constants not shown.
Significance levels at:
*1% and
***10%.

their amplitude by 28 percent in the short run, and decrease by 20 percent in mature markets), and by 25 percent in the long run (in K&S, crashes decrease by 12 percent in emerging markets and by 43 percent in mature markets in the long run), albeit the coefficients are not significant for the downward cycles.

Bearing in mind the limited number of observation, and the fact that the series were buffeted by country specific (for instance, transition itself, which happened in different moments for different countries, the banking crises mentioned above) and common shocks (the Asian, Russian and oil price shocks), which affect the significance of the results, one can preliminarily state that there are some signs that the K&S inference that financial liberalization has short-run costs for emerging markets is not observed in my ACs sample.

5. INSTITUTIONAL REFORM AND EU ACCESSION

The institutional underpinnings of the liberalization process are essential to the analysis performed here, as one of the aims of this work is to test if the EU institutional framework imposed by the accession process is what enabled them to derive the previous welfare-enhancing results from liberalization. K&S, in their work, represent the "quality of institutions" via a dummy series based on the monthly International Country Risk Guide (ICRG) "law and order" index, which assumes a value of 1 if the index is growing or at its maximum (the ICRG index itself has a maximum value of

6, with 3 granted to the "law" component and 3 to the "order" component). K&S also use information on insider trading laws and enforcement, taken from Bhattacharya and Baouk (2002). This work uses also the ICRG index, but not the data from Bhattacharya and Baouk, as the information in that paper doesn't fit neither the knowledge of this author concerning the level of legal enforcement in the sample of countries here used, nor with the conclusions of works like Reininger, Schardax, and Summer (2002). Therefore, a modified version of K&S (Eq. (2)) is estimated, as given by:

$$\text{amplitude}_i = \alpha X_i + \rho_1 d_i^r + \beta_1 d_i^{sr} + \lambda_1 d_1^{lr} + \tau_1 d_i^{L\&O} + \varepsilon_i \tag{2}$$

where the new variable $d_i^{L\&O}$ is the dummy based on the ICRG law and order index. The results are shown in Table 4. They do not change qualitatively or quantitatively and the new "law and order" dummy features only in upward cycles, but with a peculiar, albeit small, negative sign (i.e., it reduces expansions).

To specifically verify the hypothesis that the EU integration process was the main force driving the liberalization process, the same regression as was run with dummies for the periods after (i) the Europe Association Agreements were signed (EU_{ts}), (ii) the date of official application for EU membership (EU_a) and (iii) the date in which they entered into force (EU_t). The results are rather similar to the previous ones: Upward cycles significantly increase with liberalization and downward cycles decrease in the short run

Table 4.   Results of ICRG Law and Order Index.

Variables	Upward Cycle		Downward Cycle	
	Coefficient	Standard Error	Coefficient	Standard Error
World real interest rate	0.06***	0.03	−0.04	0.03
World output	−0.03*	0.01	−0.01	0.01
Domestic output	0.00	0.00	0.00	0.00
Financial repression dummy	3.08**	1.17	0.87	1.32
Short-run liberalization dummy	3.36**	1.31	0.76	1.37
Long-run liberalization dummy	3.25**	0.62	0.69	1.33
Law and order dummy	−0.25***	0.06	−0.28	0.78
	R^2: 0.45	DW: 1.32	R^2: 0.27	DW: 1.46

Note: Included observations: 22 (upward) 23 (downward). Constants not shown.
Significance levels at:
*1%,
**5% and
***10%.

(albeit with somewhat stronger estimated effects, specially for the EU$_t$ dummy regression), but they are only significant for the upward cycles on the regressions using a dummy for the date of official application for EU membership: It significantly *increases* them. Those are perhaps intuitive results, as one would expect some of the effects of the EU and law and order dummies to be captured by the liberalization dummies, but the assumption concerning the importance of the EU enlargement process is *not* confirmed.

6. BEYOND K&S: ALTERNATIVE ESTIMATION RESULTS

Given the potential shortcomings of the previous analysis, which are derived both from limitations on the original K&S framework and from the specific features of my dataset, a set of alternative specifications was also estimated. More specifically, other measures of *volatility*, both financial, real and nominal, were used as the LHS of the regressions below, namely, the standard deviation of (i) the stock market index, (ii) the industrial production index and (iii) the changes in the nominal exchange rate, in rolling variance time-windows of 2–6 months (following Vinhas de Souza, 2002a, b), as given in Eq. (3). The basic notion behind this is that liberalization and integration will affect, and in a more fundamental fashion, not just the cyclical, but also the overall real and nominal volatility of a given economy, albeit in a not unambiguous fashion (for instance, if financial integration leads to increased specialization, it could increase country-specific shocks (see Razin & Rose, 1994)).

$$\text{volatility}_i = \alpha X_i + \rho_1 I_i + \varepsilon_i \tag{3}$$

Here, the X_i matrix of control variables includes, beyond the world real interest rate, world output growth, domestic output growth, a domestic nominal exchange rate index (re-based to May 1998, as the other indexes), the level of the S&P 500 equity index (equally re-based to May 1998), the domestic stock market indexes, dummies for a float exchange rate regime, a hard peg regime, a sliding peg regime for the specific country/period per regime (following Vinhas de Souza, 2002a, b) and, finally, the variable I_i, for "index", which is either the full liberalization index or its three components. As the index is better seen as a measure of financial restriction, a positive sign will indicate that a increase in liberalization reduces volatility. The results for the 6-month variance window using the full sample, the most robust ones, are show in Table 5 (those results are from a fixed effects, heteroskedasticity-consistent estimation, deemed superior to a random effects one after a Hausman test).

Table 5. Full Sample Results for the 6-Month Variance Window.

Variables	Stock Market		Industrial Production		Nominal Exchange Rate	
	Coefficient	Coefficient	Coefficient	Coefficient	Coefficient	Coefficient
World real interest rate	0.0003	0.0002	0.02	0.02	0.003	0.00005
World output index	−0.004*	−0.004*	0.02	0.01	0.10*	0.1*
Domestic output index	−0.0004*	−0.0004*	0.01	0.01	0.004	0.005***
Nominal exchange rate index	0.00005	0.00001	0.002	0.02	−0.001	0.00001
Standard & Poor's index	0.01***	0.01**	−2.11**	−2.02**	0.42	0.53
Domestic stock market index	0.04*	0.05*	2.13**	2.55*	−1.21*	−0.83*
Float dummy	−0.005	0.01**	1.86*	1.56**	−3.12*	−2.87*
Hard peg dummy	−0.04*	−0.01	2.38*	2.48***	−3.75*	−3.09*
Sliding peg dummy	−0.02*	−0.0002	1.76*	1.78***	−3.32*	−2.92*
Full liberalization index	−0.01*	–	−1.31**	–	−0.38	–
Capital account liberalization	–	0.05*	–	1.59**	–	1.83*
Stock market liberalization	–	−0.03*	–	−0.66***	–	−0.75*
Financial sector liberalization	–	−0.02*	–	−2.03*	–	−0.91*
	R^2: 0.33	R^2: 0.37	R^2: 0.48	R^2: 0.48	R^2: 0.60	R^2: 0.60

Note: Included observations: 920 (stock market), 927 (industrial production) and 929 (nominal exchange rate). Constant and country terms not shown.
Significance levels at:
*1%
**5%, and
***10%.

As one might see, the R^2s are similar to those in the previous regressions, the coefficients of the control set are rather small, but mostly significant (in a result similar to (Vinhas de Souza, 2002a, b), and almost all exchange rate frameworks significantly reduce the volatility of the stock market and nominal exchange rate variables, but increase the one of the industrial production series). Concentrating our analysis on the liberalization index variables, the full index significantly *decreases* the volatility of both the stock market and the industrial production index, but the point estimate is only truly substantial for the industrial production series. When the index is disaggregated on its components, we can see that the capital account liberalization component, which has the highest point estimate of all components (bar the financial sector liberalization component on the industrial production regression) *increases* volatility, while the stock market and the financial sector components significantly decrease it. These results tend to remain the same using a post-1996 sample. The main changes with this shorter sample are that the stock market and the financial sector components become non-significant on the stock market regression.

Adding the EU dummies used in the previous section to the regression below shows that *all the three dummies reduce volatility significantly in most cases*, leaving the other coefficients broadly unaffected. Peculiarly, when one uses the "law and order" dummy, it is non-significant on the industrial production regressions, increases volatility significantly on the stock market ones and reduces it significantly on the exchange rate ones, while rendering the liberalization index (full and components) insignificant on the industrial production and exchange rate estimations. When this is used together with the EU dummies, these results remain, but only the EU_t and EU_a dummies are *always* significant, perhaps indicating the somewhat delayed effects of the accession process on the legal framework and enforcement.

From a more clear theoretical point of view, financial liberalization and integration should also enable a reduction of the volatility of consumption, as it would allow better international risk-sharing opportunities (see Obstfeld & Rogoff, 1998). Given that, I also estimated the regression above using three quarters standard deviation series of consumption, both private and total, that is including government consumption expenditures as a GDP share as the dependent variable. As this data is available only on a quarterly basis and for shorter time samples, the number of observations is substantially reduced. The results are in Table 6. As one might see, the R^2s are again somewhat small and now also all the point estimates are rather small. More importantly, almost all the liberalization index variables are now non-significant (a result similar to the one obtained by Kizys & Pierdzioch, 2004). The EU dummies

Table 6.   Results of Liberalization Index Variables for Shorter Time
Samples.

Variables	Private Consumption		Total Consumption	
	Coefficient	Coefficient	Coefficient	Coefficient
World real interest rate	−0006***	−0.0006***	−0.0012*	−0.0011**
World output index	−0.0016*	−0.0016*	−0.0017**	−0.0017**
Domestic output index	−0.0000	−0.0000	0.0000	−0.0000
Nominal exchange rate index	0.0001*	0.0001*	0.0001*	0.0001**
Standard and Poor index	0.0159***	0.0167**	0.0219***	0.0226**
Domestic stock market index	0.0274*	0.0258*	0.0357*	0.0337*
Float dummy	0.0164**	0.0075	0.0154	0.0065
Hard peg dummy	0.0267**	0.0191	0.0248	0.0168
Sliding peg dummy	0.0091**	0.0002	0.0072	−0.0018
Full liberalization index	0.0008	–	−0.0006	–
Capital account liberalization	–	−0.0111	–	−0.0131
Stock market liberalization	–	0.0121**	–	0.0119
Financial sector liberalization	–	−0.0082	–	−0.0074
	R^2: 0.31	R^2: 0.32	R^2: 0.25	R^2: 0.26

Note: Included observations: 218. Constant and country terms not shown.
Significance levels at
*1%,
**5% and
***10%.

are equally non-significant (bar the EU_{ts} dummy on the total consumption
regressions) and these results remain the same using a post-1996 sample.

All the regressions in this section were also estimated with squared terms
for the liberalization indexes, to try to capture eventual non-linear effects of
a liberalization process (or threshold effects). The changes on the coefficients are mostly marginal. Another robustness test was to estimate all the
regressions on this section using different time samples, to test for the stability of the coefficients across time (roughly, using the first and later halves
of the sample) and here, as one should expect, given the initial instability of
the time series, one does observes some significant differences. Concentrating on the *index variables*, for the stock market index, when using the aggregate index the sign and significance are roughly the same for the later
part of the sample, but the coefficient is three times larger in the earlier
sample, and when using the disaggregate indexes, all the components are
non-significant in later sample, and again have much larger point estimates
in the earlier sample, but with same signs and significance as in the initial

estimations presented in this section (one may see this as an indication that liberalization was more important in the initial, set-up phase, of those stock markets); for the *industrial production index*, when using the aggregate index, the variable is non-significant for the later part of the sample, but the coefficient is again much larger in the earlier sample (which may be seen as an indication that liberalization was, again, more important early in the process, when industrial restructuring took place), and when using the disaggregate index, the sign, scale and significance of the coefficients remain roughly the same in the later sample, but in the earlier sample only the financial sector liberalization (FSL) component is significant, with a larger point estimate; for the changes in the *nominal exchange rate*, neither the aggregate index nor the disaggregate indexes are significant in the earlier sample, while in the later sample *both* the aggregate and disaggregate indexes are now significant, with the same signs but larger point estimates (perhaps an indication that the liberalization process only affected exchange rates after a certain degree of macro stabilization was achieved); for *private and total consumption*, one does not observe major changes between the two time samples. All the results above remain roughly unchanged using both the two different time samples and the squared terms for the liberalization indexes. This provides another indication that the time variance observed in the series dominates the results.

7. CONCLUSION

The main aim of this chapter has been to extend the index developed by Kaminsky and Schmukler (2003), for a specific sample of countries, namely, the previously centrally planned economies from Central and Eastern Europe, most of which are now members of the EU, and to perform a similar analysis on them. Our results lend only weak support to the basic assumption of this study: A re-estimation of K&S's core regressions, using cycles defined by a Bry–Boschan (BB) algorithm that finds cyclical turning points, finds some signs that financial liberalization does generate benefits both in the short and in the long run, measured via the statistically significant extension of the amplitude of upward cycles and a statistically non-significant, reduction for downward cycles of stock market indexes. Some of those weaknesses are likely related to the shortness and specific features of the sample of countries used here. Importantly, these estimated results diverge from K&S, as in their work "emerging markets" experience a relative *short run* increase in the amplitude of downward cycles.

Another noteworthy feature is that only minor liberalization reversals, led by the financial sector component, were observed in the aggregate index. Also, those reversals do not seem to be driven by "contagion" from shocks in other emerging markets (like the Asian or Russian Crisis), but reflect country-specific shocks. When considering the individual components of the index separately, again signs of minor reversals in financial sector liberalization are observed, related to temporary reactions to the several banking crisis observed in the region.

Concerning the importance of institutions and of the EU accession, this chapter's initial assumption was that the mostly positive results above would come about due to the anchoring of expectation provided by the perspective of entry into the EU already by mid-2004 (or 2007, in the case of Bulgaria and Romania) for the countries here analyzed, and by the imposition of a more robust macro and institutional framework by the requirements of the accession process itself. Strong signs of this are *not* found in the K&S regressions, perhaps because the liberalization index itself captures the effects of the EU accession process.

Finally, using a different framework than K&S's to assess the effects of liberalization on financial, real and nominal volatility, most of the econometric results seem to support the previous ones, but they seem to indicate that the *capital account liberalization* is the element that most consistently and significantly increases volatility. One also observes significant time-varying effects on the coefficients, as one should expect, given the nature of the series used, but no non-linear effects of liberalization.

On balance, the majority of my econometric results seem to support *some* specific role for the EU enlargement process in reducing volatility.

NOTE

1. The views expressed here are exclusively those of the author and do not necessarily reflect the official views of the European Commission. All usual disclaimers apply.

REFERENCES

Bakanova, M., de Souza, V., Kolesnikova, I., & Abramov, A. (2004). Transition and growth in Belarus. In: G. Ofer & R. Pomfret (Eds), *Transition and long-term growth in the CIS* (pp. 57–75). Cheltenham, UK: Edward Elgar.
Bhattacharya, U., & Baouk, H. (2002). *The world price of insider trading.* Mimeographed.

Bry, G. & Boschan, C. (1971). *Cyclical analysis of economic time series: Selected procedures and computer programs.* NBER Technical Working Paper no. 20.

European Bank for Reconstruction and Development, *Transition Report*, London, UK, several years.

Hallerberg, M., Vinhas de Souza, L., & Clark, W. (2002). Monetary institutions and the politics of the macro-economy in EU accession countries. In: R. Linden (Ed.), *Norms and nannies: The impact of international organizations on Central and East European States* (pp. 341–368). Lanham, MD: Rowman and Littlefield.

International Monetary Fund. *Exchange rate arrangements and exchange rate restrictions*, Washington, DC, USA, several years.

Kaminsky, G., & Schmukler, S. (2003). *Short-run pain, long-run gain: The effects of financial liberalization.* IMF Working Papers, WP/03/34, IMF.

Kizys, R., & Pierdzioch, C. (2004). *Business cycle fluctuations and international financial integration.* IFW Working Paper Series no. 23/04, Kiel, Germany.

Linne, T. (1999). Contagion effects of central and east European currency crises. Discussion Paper 96. IWH, Halle, Germany.

Mönch, E., & Uhlig, H. (2004).*Towards a monthly business cycle chronology for the Euro area.* Mimeographed. Berlin: Humboldt University.

Obstfeld, M., & Rogoff, K. (1998). *Foundations of international macroeconomics.* Cambridge, MA: MIT Press.

Prasad, E., Rogoff, K., Wie, S., & Kose, A. (2003). *Effects of financial liberalization on developing countries: Some empirical evidence.* Mimeographed. IMF.

Razin, A., & Rose, K. (1994). Business cycle and volatility and openness: An exploratory cross-sectional analysis. In: L. Leiderman, & A. Razin (Eds), *Capital mobility: The impact on consumption, investment and growth* (pp. 48–75). Cambridge: Cambridge University Press.

Reininger, T., Schardax, F., & Summer, M. (2002). *Financial system transition in Central Europe: The first decade.* SUERF studies, no. 16, Vienna.

Vinhas de Souza, L. (2002a). *Integrated monetary and exchange rate frameworks: Are there empirical differences?* Tinbergen Institute Discussion Paper no 2002-054/2, The Netherlands.

Vinhas de Souza, L. (2002b). *Integrated monetary and exchange rate frameworks: Are there empirical differences?* Working Paper Series 2-2002, Bank of Estonia, Tallinn.

Vinhas de Souza, L. (2004). *Financial liberalization and business cycles: The experience of the new EU member states*, Deutsche Bundesbank. Discussion Papers Series no. 23/04, Frankfurt a.M., Germany.

Vinhas de Souza, L., & Hölscher, J. (2001). Exchange rates links and strategies of new EU entrants. *The Journal of European Integration, 231*, 1–28.

Vinhas de Souza, L., de Groot, A., van Eden, H., Romijn, G., & Ledrut, E. (1999). *EMU and enlargement: A review of policy issues, economic affairs series.* Working Paper ECON 117 EN. Directorate General for Research, European Parliament, Luxembourg.

APPENDIX

The BB Algorithm

Bry and Boschan (1971) developed a non-parametric algorithm to find peaks and troughs (i.e., "turning points") in individual time series. Their procedure consists of six consecutive steps. First, outliers are identified and replaced by corrected values. Second, troughs (peaks) are determined, from a 12-month moving average of the original series, for observations whose values are lower (higher) than those of the 5 preceding and the 5 following months. In case two or more consecutive troughs (peaks) are found, only the lowest (highest) is retained. Third, after computing a weighted moving average (a so-called "Spencer curve"), the highest and lowest points on this curve, within the ± 5-month neighborhood of the previously determined peaks and troughs, are selected. Fourth, the same procedure is repeated using a short-term moving average, with a number of lags included depending on an MCD ("months of cyclical dominance": Following Bry and Boschan (1971), the MCD is the "number of months required for the systematic trend-cycle forces to assert themselves against the irregular time series component", pp. 25) measure. Finally, in the neighborhood of these intermediate turning points, troughs and peaks are determined (obviously, in the time series modified as described above, not in the original ones).

A MATLAB program originally created by Mönch and Uhlig (2004) that finds such business cycle turning points according to the BB algorithm was used in this chapter. This program leaves out two features of the original procedure, namely the adjustment for outliers in the original time series and a priori choice of the MCD measure, set to 3. The results for the countries in my sample (all but Romania, for who the procedure did not identify any cycles, using a minimum cycle-phase length of 5 months) are shown in the figures below: The red dot represents the peak of the upward cycle (average duration: 19.3 months), the green one through of the downward one (average duration: 21.1 months) (Figs. A.1–A.9). One must note that the BB procedure is statistically demanding for such short series, and the fact that it effectively eliminates the early and final sections of the sample from the cyclical turning points' calculation makes the usable parts of the series even shorter.

As a side remark, the usage of this BB procedure on the industrial production series of the countries above, to proxy for GDP, as Mönch and Uhlig (2004) do for the euro area, shows that only the Czech Republic,

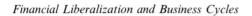

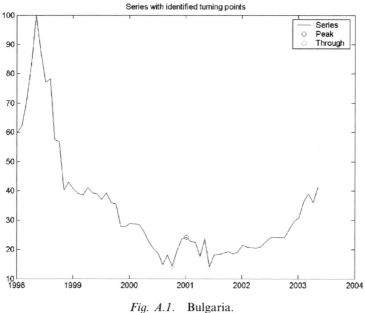

Fig. A.1. Bulgaria.

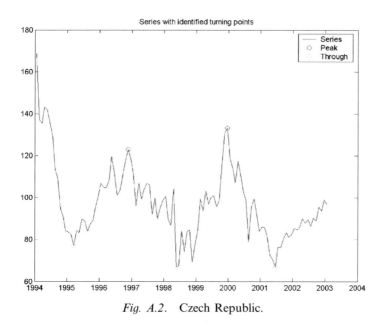

Fig. A.2. Czech Republic.

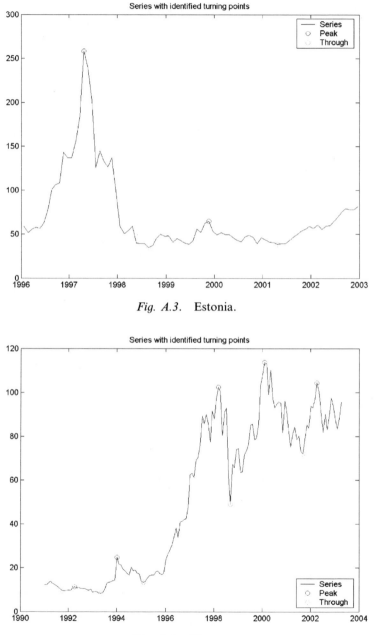

Fig. A.3.   Estonia.

Fig. A.4.   Hungary.

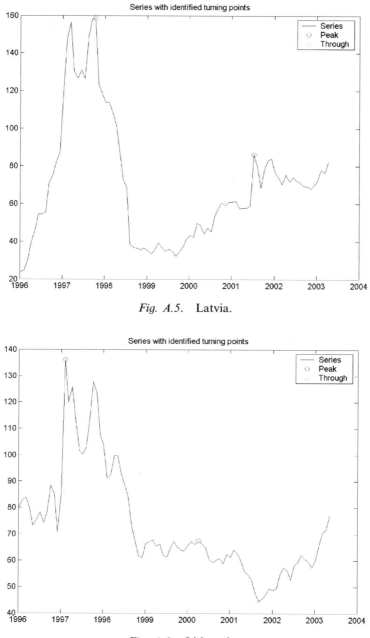

Fig. A.5. Latvia.

Fig. A.6. Lithuania.

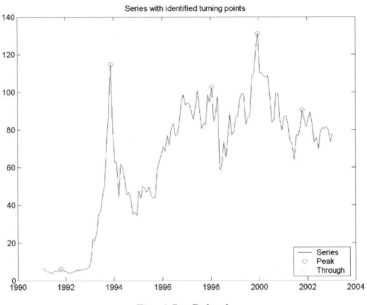

Fig. A.7.   Poland.

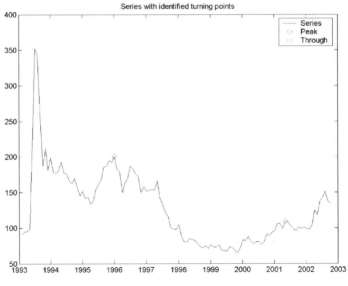

Fig. A.8.   Slovakia.

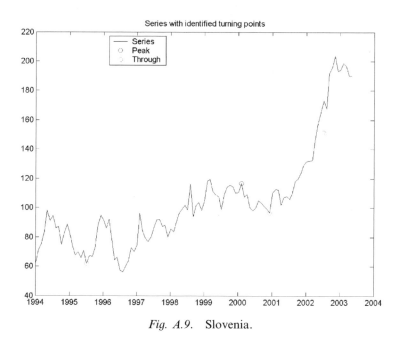

Fig. A.9. Slovenia.

Hungary and Slovenia – exactly the economies found by more traditional correlation studies (see, for instance, Vinhas de Souza, de Groot, van Eden, & Ledrut, 1999) to have greater GDP synchronization with the EU/euro area – have cycles within similar time frame, namely, a peak in February 1992, a trough in January 1993, as the *one* complete cycle found for the euro area by Mönch and Uhlig (2004).

COMMON FACTORS IN EURO-DENOMINATED EMERGING MARKET BOND SPREADS[1]

Patrick McGuire and Martijn Schrijvers

1. INTRODUCTION

The growth in euro-denominated bond debt issued by emerging market sovereigns picked up considerably after the Asian currency crises. However, while many emerging market governments now have outstanding euro-denominated issues, the market for this debt remains considerably smaller and less liquid than its US dollar counterpart. This has implications for both investors and sovereigns as they try to balance liquidity and cost of capital considerations against portfolio diversification and exchange rate movements. Broadly speaking, spreads on emerging market bonds across countries tend to move in tandem over time. This chapter takes an introductory look at the market for euro-denominated sovereign debt, and investigates the degree to which spreads on euro-denominated emerging market sovereign debt react to common forces. Following a similar analysis of the US dollar market in McGuire and Schrijvers (2003) (hereafter MS2003), we use principal factor analysis to determine the number of common factors that drive movements in spreads, and then seek to assign meaning to these factors through simple correlations with economic variables.

Emerging European Financial Markets: Independence and Integration Post-Enlargement
International Finance Review, Volume 6, 261–280
ISSN: 1569-3767/doi:10.1016/S1569-3767(05)06011-5

Like their US dollar counterparts, spreads on euro-denominated emerging market sovereign bonds tend to be correlated across countries. For example, for the sample of 15 emerging market borrowers described below, the average (across countries) correlation between the daily *movement* in each spread series with that of the J.P. Morgan Emerging Market Euro Bond Index Global (Euro EMBI Global) between end-2001 and mid-2004 was 0.4.[2] While spreads on some bonds, such as those of Korea, Hungary and China had relatively low correlations with the Euro EMBI Global, others, typically those issued by non-investment grade countries (e.g. Mexico, Argentina, Brazil and Turkey), had correlations that reached at least 0.5. From the portfolio manager's perspective, the underlying forces driving these spreads, and the degree of heterogeneity in spread movements, are key to achieving the appropriate degree of portfolio diversification. A necessary step in addressing the portfolio allocation decision is to determine both the number and the nature of the common sources of variation for each asset class. For example, a change in the global investing climate can influence investors' risk appetite, and hence be reflected in common movements in spreads across issuing countries.

We employ a principle factor analysis for a sample of 15 emerging markets that had euro-denominated sovereign bond issues outstanding during the 2001–2004 period, and provide tentative answers to the following questions. First, to what extent are movements in euro-denominated emerging market spreads driven by common forces? Second, how many distinct common forces drive their co-movement? Finally, what are these common forces? That is, can the underlying factors be interpreted in an economically meaningful way?

The results from this exercise are broadly similar to those for US-dollar-denominated emerging market sovereign bonds reported in MS2003, although important differences are apparent. As in the US dollar market, we find that common forces account for roughly one-third of the total variation in the daily movement of spreads for our primary sample of 15 emerging market issuers. Unlike in the US dollar data, however, this common portion of variation is driven by two significant common factors rather than one. Moreover, the two factors seem to capture common movements within different groups of bonds across the rating spectrum; the first common factor characterizes common variation in investment grade spreads, while the second does so for non-investment grade spreads. Both factors, to varying degrees, seem to reflect changes in investors' attitudes towards risk, as evidenced by their correlation with economic variables that are thought to reflect changes in risk premia.

The remainder of this chapter is organized as follows. In section 2, we provide some brief background material on the development of euro-denominated emerging market debt as an asset class. Section 3 lays out the methodology, with a brief review of factor analysis a description of the data sample. This is followed by our empirical analysis and a discussion of the results in section 4. Section 5 draws together the conclusions.

2. EURO-DENOMINATED BOND ISSUES: BACKGROUND

Relative to its US-dollar-denominated counterpart, the market for euro-denominated emerging market sovereign bond debt has been slower to materialize and remains less developed. Currently, the US-dollar-denominated debt market is approximately five times larger than the euro debt market (taking into account only liquid bonds). In aggregate, the market share of euro-denominated issues has remained relatively stable, at around 16 per cent since 2000, with a current market value of around €54 billion (Fig. 1(a)). If we take both liquid and non-liquid sovereign and corporate issuance into account, the share of euro-denominated bonds accounted for roughly 21 per cent of the total market in 2004.[3]

Growth in both the US-dollar- and euro-denominated debt markets was sparked by crises in emerging markets. US-dollar-denominated emerging

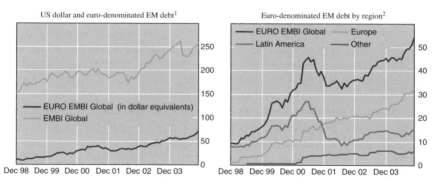

Fig. 1. Emerging Market Sovereign Bond Debt.
Note: [1]Amounts outstanding in billions of US dollars; euro-denominated in US dollars at markets rates. [2]Outstanding debt in billions of euros. *Source:* J.P. Morgan.

market sovereign bond issues took off in the beginning of the 1990s after the Mexican pesos crisis, when US dollar bank loans were restructured into collateralized bonds (so-called Brady bonds). By contrast, this event had little impact on the euro-denominated bond market. Instead, growth in this market was stimulated by the Asian currency crisis in the second half of the 1990s. Prior to 1997, the amount of emerging market euro-denominated bond debt was relatively modest, with less than €10 billion outstanding. The Asian currency crisis led to a significant rise in (US dollar) emerging market bond spreads, which prompted countries with large financing needs, mostly Latin American countries, to look for additional foreign capital in order to roll-over their amortizing foreign debt. In an attempt to broaden their investor base, countries initially began to issue Deutsch-mark- and yen-denominated bonds, and turned to euro-denominated issues in 1999. Indeed, outstanding euro-denominated debt of Latin American sovereigns was even higher than that of emerging European sovereigns until December 2001 (Fig. 1(b)). A significant part of the Latin American debt was purchased by European retail investors, concentrated mainly in Italy and Switzerland, who were attracted by the high coupons. At that time, a considerable spread differential between US-dollar- and euro-denominated debt instruments persisted because retail investors could not generally arbitrage these away through cross-currency swaps. Following the Argentine crisis in 2001, which severely depressed the value of Latin American debt, both European retail demand and Latin American euro-denominated issuance diminished. Currently, Latin American issuers account for nearly 30 per cent of the euro-denominated debt.[4]

Emerging European (and Turkish) sovereign issues have largely offset the fall in Latin American issuance.[5] This region currently accounts for roughly 60 per cent of the liquid euro-denominated bonds outstanding, with Poland, Hungary and Turkey being the largest issuers. Issuance has picked up after the introduction of the euro as it became easier for sovereigns to target the euro area investor base. The process of accession of eight Eastern European countries into the European Union (EU) in 2004, and the prospect that these countries may participate in exchange rate mechanism II (ERM-II) in the future, also contributed to the growth in euro issuance.[6] Although in general most bonds outstanding for Eastern European countries are still denominated in non-euro currencies, mostly dollars, the share of euro-denominated debt in total foreign currency issuance by Eastern European sovereigns increased rapidly, from 7 per cent in 1999 to 42 per cent by end-2004.

On balance, total issuance of foreign-currency-denominated debt by most Eastern European countries remains a relatively small share of their total debt. For example, currently 65 per cent of total Polish sovereign debt is domestic currency debt. The corresponding figures for Hungary and the Czech Republic are 75 and 90 per cent, respectively. While domestic currency issuance by emerging market sovereigns is often limited by under-developed capital markets and a lack of domestic demand, this does not seem to have been a constraint in most Eastern European countries. With the prospect of joining the euro area in the future, euro area investors have bet on yield convergence and purchased domestic currency bonds.[7] As a result, around 20 per cent of Polish domestic debt is currently foreign owned, up from 15 per cent 2 years ago and 10 per cent 4 years ago. This increased foreign demand allowed these governments to finance themselves in the domestic bond market at favourable interest rate levels, and without exchange rate risk. A second factor has been high foreign direct investment (FDI) inflows into these countries. Emerging economies with large current account deficits require relatively large inflows of foreign currency to stabilize their exchange rates. This is often obtained by issuing foreign-currency-denominated bonds. The prospect of entry into the EU and the subsequent access of EU countries to relatively cheap labour, stimulated FDI into Eastern Europe, especially in Poland and the Czech Republic. In the 2002–2004 period, FDI flows into Bulgaria, the Czech Republic and Slovakia were larger than their respective current account deficits, while FDI flows amounted to 90 per cent of Poland's current account deficit. This limited the need for sovereigns in these countries to issue in foreign currency.

Yields on euro-denominated bonds tend to be somewhat higher than their US dollar counterparts, reflecting (according to market participants) among other things the lower degree of liquidity for euro-denominated issues. Both volumes outstanding and trading volume are smaller for euro-denominated bonds in comparison with the US dollar market. Furthermore, investors in euro-denominated issues more often follow a "buy-and-hold" strategy, thereby reducing the free-floating volume in the market. However, spread differentials have fallen in recent years as arbitrage strategies have evolved and the customer base has become more sophisticated. Fig. 2 shows the average difference in (normalized) spreads in the last 3 months of 2004 between similar maturity euro- and US-dollar-denominated bonds. With the exception of Turkey and Russia, these differences are close to 0, or positive, indicating that, on average, euro-denominated bonds trade at a small discount to US-dollar-denominated paper.

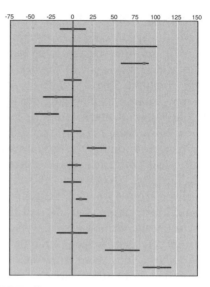

Turkey 9.625% '06 -TUR 06
Ukraine 10% '07 - UKR 07
Philippines 9.125% '10 - PHI 10
Mexico 8% '08 (DEM) -MEX UM S09
Russia 9.375% '05 (DEM) - RUS 05
Turkey 9.5% '11 - TUR 12
Mexico 5.375% '13 -MEX UM S13
Brazil 9.5% '11 -BRA 11
Bulgaria 7.5% '13 - BUL 15
Pemex 6.25% '13 - MEX PEMEX 14
South Africa 5.25% '13 - SOAF 12
Colombia 11.5% '11 - COL 12
Mexico 7.375% '08 - MEX UM S08
Venezuela 11.125% '11 - VEN 10
Brazil 12% '06 - BRA 06

Fig. 2.   Spread Differences in euro- and US-Dollar-Denominated Emerging Market Debt.

Note: The square indicates the 3-month average difference in spreads on comparable euro- and US-dollar-denominated bonds during the last quarter of 2004. The spreads of euro-denominated bonds are calculated by swapping all the separate cash flows into US dollars. The yield on this converted US-dollar-denominated bond is compared with the yield on US Treasury notes with the same maturity. Likewise, the yield on the US-dollar-denominated bond is compared with the yield on a same maturity US Treasury note. The horizontal lines indicate one standard deviation to the left and right of the 3-month average, and give an indication of the volatility of these spreads. *Source:* Deutsche Bank.

3. METHODOLOGY AND DATA

The search for common sources of variation has a long history in the asset pricing literature. Early work relied on analysis of the covariance matrix of securities to determine the common components driving returns. More recently, factor models of one form or another have become a standard tool to analyse security returns, although there remains considerable controversy over the number and the nature of the relevant factors.[8] In their paper on fixed income securities, Litterman and Scheinkman (1991) apply principal factor analysis to the returns on US Treasury notes, and find that three factors can explain a significant portion of the variation in returns across the term structure. They interpret these factors as representing the level of interest rates, the slope of the yield curve and the curvature of the yield curve.

The methodology used below is similar in spirit to Litterman and Scheinkman (1991), and follows closely the analysis in MS2003. In the first stage, we investigate the *number* of common forces that influence these spreads using principal factor analysis. This empirical technique also allows us to quantify the degree to which common forces, rather than idiosyncratic forces, influence spread movements. Simply put, factor analysis extracts the *common variation* in a set of correlated variables which is then used to form new data series (or factors) that "summarize" the original series. More concretely, factor analysis involves first calculating the variance–covariance matrix, R, of a set of variables, and then decomposing this matrix into common components, C, and idiosyncratic components, U:

$$R = C + U \tag{1}$$

$$C = c'_1 c_1 + c'_2 c_2 + \cdots + c'_m c_m \tag{2}$$

$$c_i = (f_{i1}, f_{i2}, \ldots, f_{im}) \tag{3}$$

Given an estimate of the diagonal matrix U, a factor is a series with the property that the partial correlation between any two observed variables, partialing out the factor, is 0. The matrix C can be decomposed into m component matrices, each of which is the outer product of a factor. The number of factors generated is, by construction, equal to the rank of C. However, only those factors that are important (in a way described below) are retained. In this sense, the common component of the total variation in the underlying data series captured by C can be "described" by a smaller set of vectors that (hopefully) can be interpreted in the second stage of analysis. In general, data series that are highly covariate need fewer common factors to explain a significant portion of their common variance.

Selection and interpretation of the factors are tackled in the second stage of analysis. It involves first selecting only those factors that account for a significant portion of the variation in the original set of variables. We use the Kaiser criterion, which retains only those factors that account for least as much of the total variance as at least one of the underlying data series. From here we turn to the more difficult problem of assigning economic meaning to the extracted factors. Since factor analysis is a purely statistical tool, it does not offer any guidance as to what the factors actually represent, making factor analysis an inherently subjective methodology. Our working hypothesis, guided primarily by the results in MS2003 for the

US-dollar-denominated bond spreads, is that the common factors loosely represent changes in investor risk tolerance. Our approach is to correlate the extracted factors with economic variables that are thought to capture changes in these tolerance levels.

Although spreads at issuance, which reflect the actual cost of capital, may be the most relevant for the issuer, investors arguably follow spreads in the secondary market more closely. Secondary market spreads, available with daily frequency, may reflect subtle changes in the global investing climate more accurately than lower-frequency, issuance-based data. As described above, the euro-denominated bond market emerged later, and until recently was tapped by fewer sovereign entities, than the US dollar market. Since factor analysis, by construction, requires a balanced panel, we face a stark trade-off between sample length and breadth. Only seven countries had outstanding euro-denominated issues in 1999; this increased to 16 by mid-2001. Thus, our primary data sample consists of the *changes in daily spreads* for 15 emerging markets for the period 1 August 2001 to 30 April 2004, a considerably shorter sample period than that considered in MS2003. These spreads are based on the country-specific components of the Euro EMBI Global index, the euro-denominated counterpart to the US dollar EMBI Global series.[9]

Spreads on sovereign debt issues differ significantly across the rating spectrum. Fig. 3 shows the difference in the average spread levels for investment grade and non-investment grade countries, as well as the greater average volatility of the non-investment grade debt. The spread on

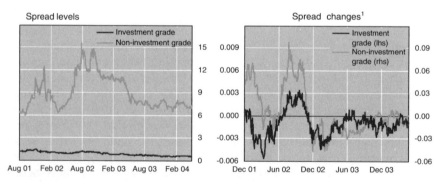

Fig. 3. Euro-Denominated Emerging Market Bond Spreads by Rating Class. *Note:* [1]Ninety-day moving average of the simple average across countries. Period of analysis is 1 August 2001 to 30 April 2004 (in percentages).

non-investment grade debt was, on average, 815 basis points higher than that on investment grade debt during the sample period. Similarly, the (absolute value of the) *daily change* in spreads on non-investment grade debt was, on average, 12 basis points higher than that on investment grade debt. Like their US-dollar-denominated counterparts, these differences across the rating spectrum were at their greatest between June 2002 and June 2003, reflecting the deteriorating situation in Argentina and Brazil during this period.

4. ANALYSIS AND INTERPRETATION

4.1. Common Variation and the Number of Factors

Factor analysis indicates that two significant factors drive the common portion of the variation in daily spread changes for the 15-country sample. This is somewhat surprising given that MS2003 found that only one common factor drives the common variation in spread movements for a larger sample of US-dollar-denominated bond spreads.[10] As argued below, these two common factors seem to capture the common variation in spreads at different ends of the rating spectrum. To the extent that this is true, the common factors, which by construction exclude idiosyncratic spread movements, may be useful in analysing the differential effect of macro-economic shocks on spreads.

Broadly speaking, the factor structure of euro-denominated spread movements is similar to that of their US dollar counterparts, although important differences are apparent. The first common factor explains roughly 73 per cent of the common variation in the underlying daily spreads, compared to 95 per cent for the *single* common factor in the US-dollar-denominated series. The second factor accounts for an additional 25 per cent of the overall common variation. Overall, however, the total common variation accounts for a relatively small share of the total variation in daily spread movements. As shown in Table 1, the average (across countries) "uniqueness", or the portion of total variation in each spread series *not* explained by the common factors, is 0.63, indicating that, on average, slightly more than one-third of the total variation in spreads is driven by common forces.

Even with two significant common factors, there remains considerable cross-country heterogeneity in spread movements. Table 1 lists the factor loadings, which are measures of the degree to which individual spreads move with each of the common factors, and the uniqueness measures for

Table 1. Factor Loadings, Uniqueness Measures and Country Ratings (Period of Analysis: 1 August 2001 to 30 April 2004).

Country	Factor 1 Loading	Factor 2 Loading	Uniqueness	Average Rating	Most Recent Rating
Argentina	0.136	0.105	0.970	76.3	Default
Brazil	0.013	0.765	0.415	4.6	BB–
China	0.462	–0.044	0.784	0.42	BBB+
Colombia	0.080	0.671	0.544	1.8	BB–
Croatia	0.768	0.199	0.370	0.613	BBB–
Hungary	0.474	–0.006	0.776	0.059	A–
South Korea	0.436	–0.096	0.801	0.27	A–
Mexico	0.379	0.709	0.354	0.82	BBB–
Malaysia	0.465	0.137	0.765	0.42	A–
Poland	0.688	0.060	0.524	0.55	BB+
Romania	0.519	0.486	0.494	8.79	BB+
Slovakia	0.673	0.176	0.516	0.698	BBB+
Turkey	0.096	0.452	0.787	16.69	BB–
Venezuela	0.078	0.470	0.773	17.95	B
South Africa	0.581	0.239	0.606	0.566	BBB
Average	0.390	0.288	0.632		

Note: The average rating for each country is an average (across the sample period) of the S&P foreign currency sovereign rating. Numerical values for these letter ratings are based on the historical default probabilities of corporate borrowers with the same letter rating. A state of default is given a value of 100 per cent.

each of the 15 countries. For only four countries (Brazil, Croatia, Mexico and Romania) do the common factors account for more than half the variation in the underlying spread series; that is, these countries' spreads load highly on (one or more of) the common factors and have relatively low uniqueness measures. Argentina, which defaulted on its foreign currency sovereign debt just after the start of the sample, has the highest degree of uniqueness, at 0.97, indicating that virtually none of the movement in Argentine spreads can be explained by variation which is common across the sample of emerging markets.

Closer analysis indicates a clear pattern across the rating spectrum. This pattern suggests that the two common factors capture, respectively, disparate movements in spreads for investment grade and non-investment grade countries. Fig. 4 presents the results of Table 1 after reordering the countries by their average rating.[11] A country is considered investment grade if it had a Standard & Poor's (S&P) rating of BBB– or above on its foreign-currency-denominated debt for at least half of the sample period. This yields

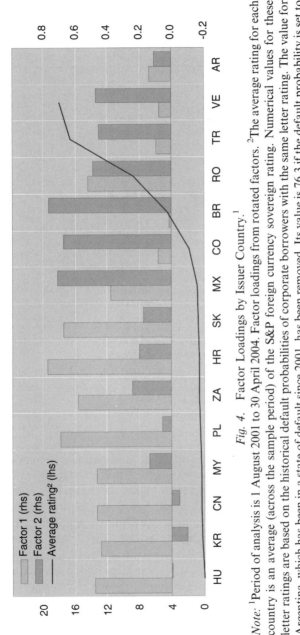

Fig. 4. Factor Loadings by Issuer Country.[1]

Note: [1]Period of analysis is 1 August 2001 to 30 April 2004. Factor loadings from rotated factors. [2]The average rating for each country is an average (across the sample period) of the S&P foreign currency sovereign rating. Numerical values for these letter ratings are based on the historical default probabilities of corporate borrowers with the same letter rating. The value for Argentina, which has been in a state of default since 2001, has been removed. Its value is 76.3 if the default probability is set to 100. *Abbrev.:* AR = Argentina; BR = Brazil; CN = China; CO = Colombia; HR = Croatia; HU = Hungary; KR = Korea; MY = Malaysia; MX = Mexico; PL = Poland; RO = Romania; SK = Slovakia; TR = Turkey; VE = Venezuela; ZA = South Africa.

Table 2. Correlation Between Common Factors and Economic
Variables (Period of Analysis: 1 August 2001 to 30 April 2004).

	Factor 1	Factor 2
Equity indices		
DAX	−0.1469*	−0.1589*
FTSE	−0.1280*	−0.2031*
S&P 500	−0.0531	−0.0941*
NASDAQ	−0.0456	−0.0991*
European corporate bond spreads		
BB	0.1270*	0.0906*
BBB	0.1399*	0.3078*
C	0.1038*	0.1321*
High yield	0.1846*	0.2214*
Euro interest rates		
3-month euribor	−0.0770*	−0.0711
2-year swap rate	−0.2476*	−0.1074*
10-year swap rate	0.0245	−0.0276
Slope of yield curve	0.0567	0.0015
US dollar interest rates		
US 3-month Treasury yield	−0.0436	−0.0208
US 2-year Treasury yield	−0.1361*	−0.0870*
US 10-year Treasury yield	−0.1433*	−0.0941*
Slope yield curve	−0.1141*	−0.0912*
Other measures		
Price of oil	−0.014	0.0495
US-dollar–euro exchange rate	0.043	0.0352
VDAX index	0.2244*	0.2017*

Note: All variables are in differences.
*Significance at the 5% level.

the 9 investment grade countries and 16 non-investment grade countries
which are listed in Table 2. Countries on the lower end of the rating spectrum (VE, TR, BR and CO) tend to load highly on the second factor, while
the better-rated countries (HU, MY, KR, SK, ZA, CN, PL and HR) load
more highly on the first factor. Romania, which has a *split rating* across the
rating agencies, loads relatively highly on both factors.[12] Mexico also loads
relatively highly on both factors possibly reflecting the fact that it was rated
non-investment grade for part of the sample period.[13] Argentina loads
highly on neither factor, again highlighting its special status since default in
November 2001.

One test which helps to clarify whether the two factors identified in the
pooled analysis actually represent differences across the rating spectrum is

to apply factor analysis separately to groups of investment grade and non-investment grade countries. If the two factors identified in the pooled sample characterize, respectively, the common movement in investment and non-investment grade spreads, we should expect that the common portion of variation in each individual rating group, when analysed in isolation, should be driven by a single common factor. Moreover, this common factor should be highly correlated with the corresponding factor from the pooled sample. Indeed, this appears to be the case. For both the investment and non-investment grade country groups, only one common factor passes the Kaiser criterion, and this single factor drives virtually all of the common portion of variation in daily spread changes (results omitted for brevity). Moreover, as shown in Fig. 5, the individual factors extracted from the smaller country samples are virtually identical to their counterparts from the pooled sample. This is taken as evidence that the two factors identified in the larger sample characterize differences across the rating spectrum. Moreover, the results here stand in sharp contrast to those for the US-dollar-denominated spread series, where the factor loadings on the single common factor did not seem to display any pattern across the rating spectrum. As shown in Fig. 5, the common factors move broadly together, but at times have opposite signs (e.g. mid-2003), indicating periods where investment grade and non-investment grade spreads diverged. The most striking feature is the greater variability in the non-investment grade factor, particularly during the period surrounding the Argentine default and the uncertainty surrounding the presidential elections in Brazil.

While differences in the degree of liquidity between investment grade and non-investment grade bonds could, in principle, be reflected in this factor structure, it seems unlikely in the current context. Latin American issuers, which tend to be at the lower end of the rating spectrum, historically had the largest issues in this market. More recently, analyst reports from commercial banks indicate that Brazilian, Mexican, Turkish, Hungarian, Polish and Venezuelan debt had the highest turnover in 2004. Clearly, there does not seem to be any discernable pattern between the available measures of liquidity and the underlying rating of the sovereign debt.

Differences in the investor base may help explain why common variation in euro-denominated spreads is split by rating class. Market participants indicate that a larger share of investors in euro-denominated debt have a buy-and-hold strategy, and thus a longer investment horizon, than do investors in US-dollar-denominated emerging market bonds (e.g. trading accounts). Consequently, it might be argued that these investors are less focused on temporary market movements and attach more value to changes

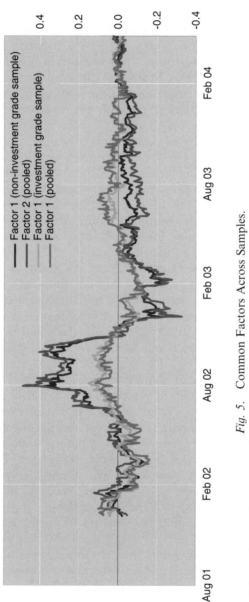

Fig. 5. Common Factors Across Samples.

Note: Ninety-day moving averages. The period of analysis is 1 August 2001 to 30 April 2004. Factors 1 (pooled) and Factor 2 (pooled) are the two retained factors from a principle factor analysis on the pooled data sample (with Bartlett scoring). Factor 1 (investment grade sample) and Factor 1 (non-investment grade sample) are the single common factors retained from separate analyses of investment grade and non-investment grade countries, respectively.

in long-term economic fundamentals. Since rating agencies claim that their ratings reflect economic fundamentals, rating differences across countries could, in principle, have more impact on the euro-denominated market than on the US-dollar-denominated market, where trading accounts seem to be more important.[14]

4.2. Assigning Economic Meaning

The above analysis suggested that movements in emerging market bond spreads are driven to some extent by two common components, but provided no guidance as to what economic forces might underlie these common sources of variation. This section explores this issue in search of an economically meaningful interpretation. By construction, the factors are *abstract* series that characterize the common variation in the daily spread movements. As such, it seems reasonable that they most likely to correspond to developments in the global economy, changes in the willingness of investors to incur risk, or common developments for emerging markets as a group. We analyse the simple correlation between the common factors and variables that are hypothesized to reflect these global trends. While it is impossible to identify *precisely* what the common factor represents, such an exercise may prove useful in determining which global trends tend to be the most important.

The focus is on variables that capture investor risk tolerance, since these proved to be the most highly correlated with the single common factor in US-dollar-denominated spread series. The economic variables used in the analysis below include the daily returns on equity indices (the DAX, FTSE, S&P 500 and the NASDAQ), long- and short-term euro area and US interest rates (and the slope of the euro area and US yield curves), spreads on euro-denominated corporate bonds across rating classes (B, BB, BBB, C and high yield), daily measures of market volatility (VDAX), the euro/dollar exchange rate and, finally, the price of oil (in US dollar).[15] All series are expressed as daily changes.

The common factors are significantly correlated with several of these variables. This can be seen in Table 2. This result is driven both by the high correlation between many of these variables themselves and by the fact that the common factors, by construction, represent a mixture of forces driving emerging market debt spreads. Overall, the analysis indicates a negative correlation between the common factors and euro area interest rate variables (levels), and as described below, a generally positive correlation between the factors and measures of risk tolerance.[16] Interestingly, the correlation between each factor and the slope of the euro yield curve is not significant, while their correlation with the slope of the US dollar yield curve is negative and significant. MS2003 found a negative correlation between the common factor in US-dollar-denominated bond spreads and the US dollar yield curve. It is often argued that the slope of the yield curve increases with rising investor optimism about future economic growth in the developed world. To the extent that this is true, the negative correlation between this slope variable and the common factor can be interpreted as the perceived benefit to emerging markets, particularly export-dependent countries, from improving economic performance in the developed world. The fact that there is a negative correlation between spreads and the US yield curve and not with the euro curve possibly indicates that developments in the US economy have more impact on global growth or are more a reflection of global economic growth than in the euro curve.

Many of the variables that correlate highly with the common factors are thought to be directly related to investors' risk tolerance. The correlation between the factors and the VDAX index and corporate bond spreads, in particular the spread on high yield corporate bonds, are relatively high and statistically significant. Moreover, the common factors are negatively correlated with equity market indices.[17] A rise in the return on the FTSE index, for example, is associated with declines in the common factors, and hence declines in spreads. To the extent that equity returns and changes in risk tolerance are linked, this negative relationship suggests that changes in investors' overall appetite for risk are a significant component of the common variation in emerging market spreads.

Do changes in investor risk tolerance influence the investment and non-investment grade factors in different ways? For example, macro-shocks that lead to changes in perceptions of future economic growth, risk aversion or risk appetite may have a larger effect on investor positions in lower-rated assets. Thus, to the extent that our variables capture changes in risk tolerance, a stronger correlation for the second factor, which best characterizes the common variation in non-investment grade spreads, seems reasonable. The evidence on this question is mixed. Overall, the second factor does seem to be more strongly correlated with many of these variables, although this pattern is far from precise. The second factor has a stronger (negative) correlation with each of the equity return indices, and is generally more highly correlated with changes in corporate bond spreads, particularly with spreads on lower-rated bonds.

5. CONCLUSION

Using principal factor analysis, we find that two common factors drive the common portion of variation in euro-denominated sovereign bond spreads for a sample of 15 emerging market countries. This stands in contrast to US-dollar-denominated spreads, which seem to be driven by a single common factor. The common factor accounts for, on average, one-third of the total variation in daily spread changes, indicating that idiosyncratic elements remain the most significant driver of spread movements.

The two factors seem to (respectively) characterize the common variation in investment grade and non-investment grade sovereign bond spreads. While any interpretation of the common factors is inherently subjective, those countries rated investment grade tend to load highly on the first factor, while non-investment grade countries load highly on the second. This interpretation is supported by separate analysis of countries grouped by rating class, which yields single common factors that are similar to those found in the pooled sample.

There is some evidence that these common factors reflect changes in investors' tolerance for risk. Although it is impossible to ascribe precise economic meaning to these common factors, the high correlation between them and high-frequency measures of risk tolerance suggests that the common variation in emerging market debt spreads is partially explained by changes in attitudes towards risk within the international investment community.

NOTES

1. The views expressed in this article are those of the authors and do not necessarily reflect those of the Bank for International Settlement (BIS) or De Nederlandsche Bank.

2. The corresponding figure for US-dollar-denominated bonds reported in MS2003 is 0.53. These statistics can be misleading because of differences in the weighting of countries in the various EMBI indexes. An alternative is to calculate the simple average of all the pairwise correlations between the series themselves. For euro-denominated bonds, this average correlation is 0.23 for the sample as a whole. This rises to 0.33 for investment grade countries and 0.30 for non-investment grade countries.

3. A liquid bond is defined here as having a minimum €500 million outstanding. Euro-denominated issues tend to be smaller than US-dollar-denominated issues and therefore more often classified as illiquid. Consequently, these issues are not in our sample. If all issues are taken into account, the market share of the euro-denominated issues is around 21 per cent.

4. The share of Latin America in the euro-denominated debt market can change considerably depending on whether Argentina's debt, which is in a state of default, is included. In this estimate, Argentine debt, valued at market rates, is nearly negligible. If the nominal amount outstanding is used, Argentina's market share rises to roughly 50 per cent for Latin America, pushing up the region's share of total debt outstanding.

5. Euro-denominated liquid issues by Asian sovereigns (primarily those in the Philippines and China) account for a relatively small 7 per cent of total outstanding euro-denominated issues.

6. Claessens, Klingebiel, and Schmukler (2003), in their study on macro-economic and institutional factors influencing government bond issues, find that the exchange rate regime and the anchor currency are significant determinants of the denomination of emerging market sovereign bond issues. In general, countries with a more flexible exchange rate regime have smaller foreign currency bond markets. Therefore, a move towards a fixed exchange rate regime (vis-à-vis the euro) could lead to an increase in issuance of euro-denominated bonds. Currently, Estonia, Lithuanian, Latvia and Bulgaria peg their currencies to the euro (and are member of the ERM-II based on the euro). Slovenia is an ERM-II member, and Hungary, Slovakia and Romania maintain a managed float against the euro. Only Poland and the Czech Republic still have a free float, but all countries have made the commitment to join the euro at a later stage.

7. Market participants expect interest rates to converge in a fashion similar to that which occurred during the introduction of the euro. At that time, the spreads on bonds issued by countries with relatively high domestic interest rates (e.g. Italy and Greece) quickly fell to their current level of less than 20 basis points. The demand for domestic currency bonds issued by the Eastern European countries is partially based on the expectation that the same convergence will take place once these countries join the euro. Market participants indicate that foreign demand for domestic paper has already compressed interest rates, and has supported the development of local bond markets in these countries.

8. At the heart of these factor models is the assumption that the returns on different securities will be correlated only through reactions to one or more of the specified factors. For equity returns, for example, the excess market return is the single factor in the standard capital asset pricing model (CAPM), although many have argued that equity returns are more appropriately modelled with multiple factors. See Fama and French (1992, 1993, 1996) for tests of the CAPM model. Ross's (1976) arbitrage pricing theory (APT) model shows that the systematic portion of equity returns can be expressed as a linear function of a set of "factors".

9. The Euro EMBI Global was initially compiled on 31 December 1998 by J.P. Morgan. It tracks the total return and spreads on euro-denominated debt instruments issued by emerging market sovereign and semi-sovereign entities. The spreads we use are duration weighted asset swap spreads comparing all the cash flows of the bond with the euro swap curve. Only straight fixed income instruments denominated in euros are included. For legacy currencies that have since joined the European Monetary Union (EMU), the amount outstanding for each issue is converted into euro using the fixed conversion rates. Differences in the average duration of each

country-specific component in the Euro EMBI Global may affect the degree to which each spread reacts to global shocks.

10. MS2003 found tentative evidence of a second common factor after 2001.

11. The average rating for a particular country is calculated as the average over the sample period. Numerical values for the S&P foreign currency sovereign debt ratings are based on the average historical default probabilities of corporate borrowers with the same letter rating. Using the most recent rating to rank countries yields similar results.

12. Fitch rates Romania as investment grade, while S&P and Moody's do not.

13. S&P has rated Mexico investment grade since February 2002.

14. According to market participants, one indication that investor bases may differ is that spread movements in the US dollar market seem to have an effect on spread movements in the euro-market with a lag of a few days. The lag in the reaction between the two markets is explained by the fact that the percentage trading accounts in the dollar market (e.g. banks and hedge funds which trade much more actively, and which tend to react to smaller changes in the market, than real money and retail investors) is higher in the US dollar market than in the euro-denominated market.

15. The corporate spread ratings are from S&P. The VDAX index is a market estimate of future volatility, and is derived form the implied volatility of options on the DAX index (assuming a constant 45 days remaining until expiration of the options). The slopes of the US and European yield curves are, respectively, the difference in yield on the 10-year and 3-month US Treasury bills, and the difference in the 10-year euro swap rate and the 3-month euro euribor fixing.

16. Whether emerging market bond spreads, either US-dollar- or euro-denominated, should be positively or negatively correlated with interest rates is unclear. MS2003 reported a negative correlation between US interest rates and the common factor in US-dollar-denominated emerging market bonds spreads. The negative relationship reported here is similar in size, but does not appear to be as robust. See MS2003 for discussion.

17. Changes in the discount factor (i.e. the degree of risk aversion) are thought to be responsible for a significant portion of the volatility in equity prices. See Cochrane (2001) for discussion.

REFERENCES

Claessens, S., Klingebiel, D., & Schmukler S. (2003). Government bonds in domestic and foreign currency: The role of macroeconomic and institutional factors. Centre for Economic Policy Research, Discussion Paper no. 3789, February.

Cochrane, J. (2001). *Asset pricing.* New Jersey: Princeton University Press.

Fama, E., & French, K. (1992). The cross-section of expected stock returns. *Journal of Finance, 47,* 427–465.

Fama, E., & French, K. (1993). Common risk factors in the returns on stocks and bonds. *Journal of Financial Economics, 33,* 3–56.

Fama, E., & French, K. (1996). The CAPM is wanted, dead or alive. *Journal of Finance, 49,*
   1579–1593.
Litterman, R., & Scheinkman, J. (1991). Common factors affecting bond returns. *Journal of*
   Fixed Income, 1, 54–61.
McGuire, P., & Schrijvers, M. (2003). Common factors in emerging market bond spreads. *Band*
   for International Settlements Quarterly Review, December, 65–78.
Ross, S. (1976). The arbitrage theory of capital asset pricing. *Journal of Economic Theory, 13.*

ROMANIAN FINANCIAL MARKETS[1]

Michael Skully and Kym Brown

1. INTRODUCTION

Romania was a centrally planned economy until 1990. Over 1950 to 1975 large-scale government investments were made into heavy industry and hence productivity increased. Performance was measured against required production quotas rather than quality products that could be exported (Bacon, 2004). Compared to most other Central and Eastern European countries, Romania had little prior experimentation with market practices, so when the change occurred it was even more significant (Bacon, 2004). Romanians initially enjoyed their new economic freedoms and imported consumables previously not permitted. Inflation increased and workers sought higher wages, with consequential negative effects on output (Daianu, 2004). The government also expended large amounts, particularly foreign exchange reserves, prior to elections. Meanwhile, supranationals, such as the International Finance Corporation (IFC), World Bank, International Monetary Fund (IMF) and European Bank for Reconstruction and Development (EBRD), all funded Romania's burgeoning market economy. In 1993, a pyramid-type scheme offering huge returns for money invested for 3 years blossomed and became so large it rivalled gross domestic product (GDP) at the time. Hence the 1990s was a period of instability despite efforts to transform the economy to market practices.

Emerging European Financial Markets: Independence and Integration Post-Enlargement
International Finance Review, Volume 6, 281–321
Copyright © 2006 by Elsevier Ltd.
All rights of reproduction in any form reserved
ISSN: 1569-3767/doi:10.1016/S1569-3767(05)06012-7

The Romanian financial system remains underdeveloped with banks providing the main mechanism for finance. Nevertheless, Romania's future is bright with accession to North Atlantic Treaty Organization (NATO) in 2004, and possibly European Union (EU) membership in 2007. However Romania must first have at least 2-year exchange rate stability, post-2007, for full membership (IMF, 2003). In line with the recently improved sentiment, Fitch upgraded Romania's rating to investment grade (BBB–) in November 2004. Moreover foreign investment is growing with US$3 billion invested in 2004, due predominantly to the US$1.5 billion privatisation of the petrochemical company Petrom.

Although macroeconomic fundamentals are currently in balance, inflation continues to threaten the economy. Particular features of this economy are the high levels of under-banking with many rural people having no access to banking services, and, as with other transitional states, the need to change the culture in relation to corporate governance, and related or politically directed lending. The latter is particularly important, as banking reform cannot be fully separated from reform of state enterprises (SEs). A number of state-owned banks (SOBs) have been privatised and foreign bank entry permitted. Given the population of 22.4 million people, and the limited financial development to date, Romania's financial sector offers considerable growth potential.

This chapter analyses Romania's financial markets by focusing on its banking, equity, investment funds, bonds and insurance markets. King and Levine (1993) note that once a certain level of financial development is achieved in a country, it serves a good indicator of future economic growth for the next 10–30 years. Hence an understanding of Romania's financial development, as a transition economy, is needed to predict its future prospects. The remainder of this chapter is as follows. Section 2 analyses the economy. Section 3 considers the financial institutions, the banks, credit co-operatives, leasing companies and insurance companies. Section 4 focuses on the capital markets including the various stock exchanges. Section 5 concentrates on the money and bond markets, including mutual funds and venture capital funds. Section 6 reports on recent developments with privatisation funds. Section 7 reports on about the futures and commodities exchange. Section 8 summarises this chapter and draws together the conclusions.

2. THE ECONOMY

Foreign investors are still concerned with inflation. Recent historical rates peaked in 1997 at 154.8 per cent (World Bank, 2005) but fluctuated

Table 1. Macroeconomic Indicators.

Series Name	Unit	1999	2000	2001	2002	2003
GDP at constant $ rate (January 2003)	US$ billion	16	24	35	45	56
GDP real growth rate	%	−1.2	2.1	5.7	5	4.9
Inflation rate	%	45.8	45.6	34.5	22.5	15.3
Budget balance (% of GDP)	%	−3.6	−4	−3.2	−2.6	−2.3
Unemployment (% of labour force)	%	11.5	10.5	8.6	8.1	7.2
Current account balance (% of GDP)	%	−3.6	−3.7	−5.5	−3.3	−5.8
International reserves	US$ billion	4	5	6	8	10
Domestic credit/GDP	%	17.8	13.9	12.2	13.0	15.8
Foreign assets (net)/GDP	%	7.5	11.5	14.6	15.6	13.3
Exchange rate US$/leu		15,332.9	21,692.7	29,060.9	33,055.5	33,200.1
Exchange rate EUR/leu		16,295.6	19,955.8	26,026.9	31,255.3	37,555.9

Source: The Economist Intelligence Unit. (2004). *Country Fact Sheet Romania*, December 9, EIU; IMF IFS statistics (accessed January 2005); the National Bank of Romania, *Monthly Bulletin Statistical Section*, December 2004.

throughout the 1990s.[2] As can be seen from Table 1, this had fallen to a more palatable 15.3 per cent by 2003. Also the various governments had to address rising external debt, trade and current accounts deficits, and budget deficits (Daianu, 2004). Domestic credit to GDP has tended to decrease accordingly, however, net foreign assets/GDP have increased. Hence there has been a move to foreign borrowings. The Romanian currency, the *leu* (*ROL*),[3] was devalued in 1996 and fixed prices for some energy/consumables dropped. The contraction in the economy (52.5 per cent in 1997) led to a reduction of credit available, which unfortunately affected small- and medium-state enterprises (SMEs) in the private sector, the most (61.3 per cent in 1997).

From the mid-1990s large enterprises found increasing difficulties in paying bills on time, and goods or services were often provided in lieu of cash, particularly for the energy industry. This was because energy providers were unable to cut services to non-payers due to specific legislation. These simply grew as "arrears" when payment could not be made. Furthermore firms due to be privatised could not have debts enforced by creditors. Finally the government itself began to accept non-monetary tax and utility payments, which spread the accepted usage of arrears and barter (IMF, 2004). Further privatisation was needed, but the credit squeeze did not provide a suitable environment.

Privatisations happened in earnest from 1996 to 2000 with over 1,100 firms privatised per year. By 2003 this had dropped to 310 firms (IMF,

2004). SMEs were easily privatised, whilst larger ones were more difficult given the consequences of mass unemployment. Many of the privatisations occurred through management–employee buyouts (MEBOs) which did not inject the same financial and cultural changes as with introducing new partners in the reform process (Asaftei & Kumbhakar, 2004). Concerns over the level of arrears continued with arrears measured at 39.7 per cent of GDP as of June 2003. Most of this debt was due to utilities and tax authorities, and notably not the banking sector. A juggernaut to the reform process, as of 2003, approximately 30 per cent of SEs were still unprofitable.

3. FINANCIAL INSTITUTIONS

3.1. The Banks

The banking system has undergone major restructuring in Romania's transition towards a market economy. Key elements have been the transformation of the National Bank of Romania (NBR) into a traditional central bank, and the development of a network of commercial banks. The Law on Banking Activity (Law no. 33/1991) and the NBR Statutes (Law no. 34/ 1991) established the legal framework for banking in Romania. In early 1998, the government adopted three laws that will enhance the NBR's independence: (1) the new Law on Banking Activity, which makes the central bank's supervisory role stronger; (2) the new NBR Statutes, that establish the NBR's independence in conducting monetary policy; and (3) the Bank Insolvency Law, which regulates bank insolvency and bankruptcy.

Banking has traditionally been reported as the main form of external finance available within Romania.[4] During the Communist regime the stock and bond markets did not exist. As with many transitional states there was one central bank, the NBR and a number of specialist banks. These operated as the main conduit of funds to the SEs.[5] This was done as directed by political directions and not necessarily based on credit scores or to the most efficient users of the funds. The specialist banks were developed in the areas of industry and infrastructure (Romanian Development Bank), foreign trade (Bancorex), agriculture (Agricultural Bank) and savings finance (Romanian Savings Bank – Casa de Economii si Consemnatiuni, CEC SA). Each type of bank operated in separate specialist areas, and hence no competition existed prior to December 1989 (Tsantis, 1997). Foreign banks were only permitted to undertake foreign exchange business with foreign firms operating in Romania.[6] In the non-bank financial sector credit cooperatives, credit unions and leasing companies also provided some limited competition.

The NBR shed its commercial bank activities by creating a new bank, the Romanian Commercial Bank, in 1990.[7] Also at that time the once specialist state banks became universal banks (Asaftei & Kumbhakar, 2004). The only domestic bank with previous foreign exchange experience was Bancorex, so Bancorex soon found up to 25 per cent of its staff hired by other banks. Bancorex and Banca Agricola had very high levels of bad debts by 1995, and Bancorex was merged with Banca Comerciala Romana in 1999 and Banca Agricola was sold to Raiffeisen Bank in 2001. Romania had 38 banks in 2003 (World Bank, 2005) with most of these established (or merged with others) in the 1990s except for Romanian Savings Bank – Casa de Economii si Consemnatiuni.[8]

The number of commercial banks increased from 5 in 1990 to 33 in 1996, of which 25 were Romanian entities and 8 were branches of foreign banks. Of the Romanian banks, 5 remained wholly state-owned (SOBs), 10 wholly private, and the remainder had a combination of state and private domestic and/or foreign capital. Another 9 foreign banks had representative offices in Romania. The Bank Privatization Law was enacted in May 1997. It stipulates that only reputable international financial institutions may acquire more than 20 per cent of a state-owned Romanian bank. The NBR's approval is mandatory for any purchases of more than 5 per cent of a bank's stock.

All commercial banks now operating in Romania have international correspondent relationships, and all are members of the NBR's domestic interbank payment system. Although this system has reduced float and payment clearance delays, inefficiencies remain but there are long-term plans for its full computerisations. As cheque accounts are largely unknown, most domestic remittances must be made either through the interbank payment system or in cash. To deal with bad and doubtful debts of large SOBs, an Asset Recovery Agency (AVAB) was established in 1998. In December 2000, the Agency was restructured and became the Office for the Recovery of Bank Assets (ORCB).

The Romanian banking system has good potential as demonstrated by comparing intermediation levels to neighbouring states. As shown in Table 2, the bank assets to GDP levels are extremely low at just 33 per cent for Romania whilst the EU average is 277 per cent. Correspondingly low figures are also reported for loans/GDP and deposits/GDP. Most Eastern European countries have depressed levels, but Romania is one of the lowest. Loans and deposits in relation to GDP also appear relatively small. Given

Table 2. Comparative Intermediation Levels of Romanian Banks
(2003).

	Assets EUR Billion	Assets/ GDP (%)	Loans/ GDP (%)	Deposits/ GDP (%)	Inhabitants/ Branch
Romania	15	33	16	26	7,800
Poland	114	61	28	41	3,900
Hungary	39	64	32	40	8,400
Czech Republic	80	130	40	64	6,000
EU average	n/a	277	120	96	1,900

Source: Danila, Nicolae (2004). *The Romanian banking sector – key issues and opportunities.*
Banca Comerciala Romana.

Table 3. Forecasted Intermediation Levels for Romanian Banking.

	2003	2004	2005	2006	2007	2008
Total lending to the private sector (US$ billion)	8.1	10.3	14.6	16.0	20.2	22.4
Total lending (% of GDP)	15.9	17.3	21.1	22.6	28.3	31.9
Bankable households ('000)	465.8	786.5	1,170.5	1,412.7	1,511.0	1,707.8
Bank deposits (US$ billion)	14.7	16.9	23.6	24.6	31.1	34.2
Banking assets (US$ billion)	18.9	22.8	29.9	32.1	38.5	41.7
Current-account deposits (US$ billion)	1.8	2.1	2.8	2.9	3.5	3.8
Time and savings deposits (US$ billion)	12.5	14.4	19.5	19.9	24.4	26.1
Loans/deposits (%)	47.1	52.0	53.9	56.5	57.2	58.0

Source: Economist Intelligence Unit. (2004). Country forecast summary, December.

the volatile inflation rates in the 1990s and high levels of rural inhabitants, a lower result could be expected. Nevertheless promoters of Romanian banking claim this low intermediation offers a large potential for foreign investors (see for instance, *The Banker*, 2003 or 2004). The positive prospects of Romanian banks are also echoed by forecasted figures that expect banking assets to more than double from 2003 to 2008 to US$41.7 billion (see Table 3).

At the beginning of the transition period in December 1999, all Romanian banks were SOBs. The bank reform process of a transition economy is often measured against the state ownership of the banking sector. Not only has Romania managed to privatise many SOB assets, but it has also encouraged foreign ownership. In 1999, the government still owned 70 per cent of banking assets, however this reduced to 41.8 per cent by 2003 (Clarke, Cull, & Shirley, 2004). If the last large state bank, Banca Comerciala Romana, is sold in 2005, then the government will only own 10 per cent of the banking assets (Economic Intelligence Unit (EIU), 2005). Hence Romania has performed well particularly given its late start in privatisation.

Foreign banks have therefore recently added Romania to their portfolio options. As of March 2004, most foreign banks in Romania were from the EU region, with Austrian banks owning 23 per cent of Romanian bank capital. Foreign European banks had a total of 53.8 per cent of assets while the USA (with largest interests outside Europe) had a 2.9 percent stake in Romanian banking assets (Popa, 2004). Table 4 shows that foreign banks have been taking a considerable share of Romanian banking assets. Nevertheless the SOBs continue to be more popular in collecting deposits or savings but do not have a corresponding lending rate. Foreign banks as of March 2003 owned 32.6 per cent of the banking assets. The entry of foreign banks has many proponents who cite advantages such as improved market efficiency due to new competition, new technology, better training for staff, use of appropriate credit checks and lack of total reliance on the local market especially in times of crisis for the host country (De Haas & van Lelyveld, 2004; Bonin, Hasan, & Wachtel, 2005; Drakos, 2003). Host country regulators often fear that they may lose control of the banking system, although they can provide rules as to the mode of entry, for example de novo, branch only, size of assets and lending restrictions (Pomerleano & Vojta, 2001; Crystal, Dages, & Goldberg, 2001).

Given the late reform of Romanian banks, there seems to have been little debate over the merits of foreign bank entry. Perhaps this was due to the country's economic problems and a desire to attract new foreign capital from every source possible. Alternatively, this may reflect a realisation that foreign bank entry would be one of the many structural reforms that would be required for EU accessibility. Foreign banks were able to enter from 1990, however none did until 1993. Daianu and Vranceanu (2003) note that transition economies tended to open up capital markets as "fast as possible" in the hope that financial resources would then be allocated to the most productive users within the economy. Connected lending distorted this process.

Next Romania's banks performance will be compared to Eastern European countries. Non-interest revenue to total revenue was quite high for Romanian banks at 49.82 per cent in 2002 (Table 5). This could be due to ownership of government bonds used to cover non-performing loans (NPLs). Banks traditionally make money by lending out depositor money. When the figure of non-interest revenue to total revenue is that high it indicates bank portfolios in areas other than loans. NPLs were as high as

Table 4. Romania: Financial Soundness Indicators, March 2003.

	Total	Romanian State Banks	Romanian Private Banks	Previously State Banks	Subsidiaries of Large International Banks	Other Foreign Banks	Foreign Bank Branches
Number of banks	39	3	4	3	2	19	8
Per cent of assets	100	41.2	3.2	22.9	9.5	15.7	7.4
Per cent of deposits	100	43.5	2.8	23.5	11.3	12.5	6.4
Per cent of loans	100	30.8	3.6	26.0	6.7	22.2	10.6

Source: IMF, Country Report. (2003). International Monetary Fund, Washington, DC, p. 11.

Table 5. Performance of Banking Systems.

Country	ROA (%)	ROE (%)	Non-Interest Revenue/ Total Revenue (%)	NPLs At % of Total Loans
Czech Republic	−0.24	−5.24	2.76	32.09
Estonia	1.50	9.20	33.90	2.70
Lithuania	0.13	1.32	27.90	12.47
Poland	0.99	13.48	n/a	13.7
Slovenia	0.79	7.76	4.04	5.6
Romania	0.00	0.00	49.82	35.39
Turkey	0.74	−14.54	8.78	4.69
Moldova	4.42	15.29	38.5	21.9

Source: Demirguc-Kunt et al. (2003), adapted from Tables 1 and 2.

71.7 per cent at the end of 1998, but reduced significantly to just 2.8 per cent by the end of 2001. Fries and Taci (2005) examined a sample of banks from 15 Eastern European countries. Romania reported low levels of cost efficiency at just 47 per cent. They concluded that macroeconomic stability and greater foreign bank entry were related to high-cost-efficiency levels thus supporting foreign entry.

The ratio cost to income has traditionally been a means of measuring bank performance. A result above 100 per cent indicates that banks earnings were unable to cover the costs adequately. From 1998 to 2003 the cost to income ratios for Romanian banks averaged nearly 80 per cent. In 1996 it spiked at over 120 per cent when the *leu* was sharply devalued. The world-wide average is 60.8 per cent (*The Banker*, 2002).[9] A large level portion of Romanian bank lending is in hard currency and for short terms. Therefore if the *leu* is devalued domestic borrowers will be greatly affected.

Corporate governance of banks is required to be reformed in all economies to aid the confidence that investors have in entrusting their money to the banking system. Demirguc-Kunt, Laeven, and Levine (2003) measured corporate governance of banks based on a series of questions to the regulator in many countries. Romania scored 10 out of a possible 12 on this basis, which is pleasing, however stated regulations or practices may not, infact, be enforced. Banking Law no. 58/1998 was amended December 2003 to align with EU Directives. In particular corporate governance requirements in relation to the separation of executives and board competencies were updated (Green, Murinde, & Nikolov, 2004). Reform in the bank accounting transparency needs further work. Consolidated accounts have been required since 2002 but to date, as reported on the BankScope database, most banks still report on an unconsolidated basis.

The NBR is responsible for supervising all commercial banks, and may establish rules and regulations to ensure their soundness, including setting minimum reserve requirements, solvency ratios, loan exposure limits and financial reporting requirements. A yearly on-site supervision regime is in place and a variation of the Capital, Assets, Management, Earnings and Leverage (CAMEL)-rating system is used to assess banks liquidity. A credit-rating bureau was established to maintain information on borrowers which was previously not available (Asaftei & Kumbhakar, 2004). Following Bank for International Settlements' (BIS) advice, capital adequacy requirement were increased from 10 to 12 per cent in 1998, whilst domestic reserve requirements increased from 10 to 30 per cent (Asaftei & Kumbhakar, 2004). In 2002, domestic reserve levels were reduced to 18 per cent and due to increasing foreign currency lending the reserve for these commitments increased to 25 per cent. Commercial banks are authorised to engage in a wide range of banking functions. They may take deposits, make loans, issue guarantees and letters of credit, trade securities and other financial instruments, provide depository and custodial services, and engage in other activities traditionally performed by large commercial banks. Banks may establish subsidiaries to engage in securities brokerage, trading and under-writing. With appropriate NBR licenses, they may also engage in foreign currency trading.

In March 1997, the NBR allowed all chartered banks in Romania, domestic or foreign, to act both as forex brokers and dealers. Banks may use their own daily forex rate, when buying or selling foreign currency. The NBR now calculates a weighted average for all forex rates set by the dealers, which is used for bookkeeping purposes.[10]

Romanian entities borrow funds from overseas. Some indication of the level can be gained by looking at developed country lending levels reported for Romania by the BIS. International assets of foreign banks reporting to the BIS have increased more the threefold in regard to Romania since 1998 from US$3.5 billion (end 1998) to US$12.2 billion. Assets could include loans provided or bank offices, for instance. This is similar to other Eastern European countries except Turkey, which is an Organization for Economic Cooperation and Development (OECD) member. Table 6 indicates which sectors of the economy are borrowing money internationally through the BIS reporting banks. For Romania only 25 per cent of the international borrowings are in domestic currency. The non-bank private sector had 57.8 per cent of the borrowings which again shows a good signal for banking

Table 6. Claims of Reporting Banks on Individual Countries, end June 2004.

Country	Total Foreign Claims (US$ Billion) (A + F)	Consolidated Cross-Border Claims in all Currencies and Local Claims in Non-local Currencies					Local Currency Claim (US$ Billion) (F)
		Total (A)	Sector % of Total				
			Banks (B)	Public Sector (C)	Non-Bank Private Sector (D)	Unallocated (E)	
Croatia	26.0	16.6	38.5	16.8	44.5	0.0	9.3
Czech Republic	67.5	17.4	10.3	11.5	62.6	0.1	50.0
Hungary	56.0	37.8	29.4	32.3	38.1	0.1	18.2
Poland	88.2	40.0	15.8	29.5	54.2	0.3	48.1
Romania	12.2	9.1	17.9	24.1	57.8	0.1	3.1
Russia	57.5	54.6	35.8	14.0	50.0	0.0	2.9
Slovakia	19.5	8.3	30.7	31.2	37.2	0.7	11.1
Turkey	41.7	38.2	24.0	21.9	53.8	0.0	3.5

Source: Bank for International Settlements (BIS). (2004). *Consolidated banking statistics*, second quarter, Table 8.

reform. It must be noted however; the increasing level of foreign bank ownership may preclude the reported Romanian banking sector borrowings given that a foreign bank may use home country funds.

As has been shown above, tremendous progress has been made on developing Romanian banking markets from fully state owned in 1989. More competition resulted from many new banks opening in the 1990s and the large influence of foreign-owned banks. Interest rates have declined from a lending rate of 55.4 per cent in 1998 to 24.8 per cent in September 2003 (EIU, 2005). The overall growth of the economy, together with the desire to align the banking system with EU Banking Directives for possible EU membership, has taken Romanian banking to new levels. As the exchange rate become more stable and inflation settles for a longer period, more investors and depositors will gain confidence in the banking system. Even with the growth of longer-term assets (such as mortgage finance) and financing requirements (such as corporate bonds), it signifies a move to market practices in the economy. An electronic payment system is to be implemented in 2005 which will make real-time payments possible.

3.2. Credit Cooperatives

Romania has a strong tradition of cooperatives which operate across a range of businesses. Savings and credit are no exception and credit cooperatives, known as popular banks, operate throughout the country. They provide a range of lending and other effectively banking services both directly and through centralised apex institutions. Those in rural areas may also provide soft loans in support of farm production programmes. Credit cooperatives became formally regulated in 1996 under the Credit Cooperatives Act. This supervision was nevertheless minimal and eventuated in the failure of the largest of these institutions, the Banca Populara Romana, in June 2000. New legislation resulted in 2000 which made the central bank their regulator. The NBR responded by forcing these institutions either to register as a normal bank or join together under a central umbrella or apex organisation that would in turn be responsible in part for their supervision as well as support. These networks require a strong capital base in order to obtain approval and this will rise to EUR 5 million by 2006. The popular banks within these networks, though, in return gain coverage to Romania's deposit insurance scheme. As of 2004, only one such network, a 565 popular bank network under the name Creditcoop, had received NBR approval but others were also under consideration.

In addition to more general credit cooperatives, there is also an active credit union movement in Romania. They are known as *caseles adjutor reciproac* or CARs. According to World Council of Credit Union figures, Romania's 26 CARs had a membership of 119,859 as of the end of June 2004.

3.3. Leasing Companies

Lease finance is increasingly popular in Romania and has grown at close to 30 per cent per annum. Local bank affiliated companies are the largest with perhaps 20 per cent of the market with another 15 per cent held by those affiliated with manufactures. The rest of the market is held by a large number of smaller independent firms. As of 2004, vehicle leasing comprised almost all of the business, but industrial equipment and real estate are expected to become more important. The average contract is for 5 years. As the market becomes more attractive, banks are more likely to become more active directly in this market.

3.4. Insurance Companies

As might be expected with a planned economy, the Romanian insurance industry was a state monopoly from 1952 to 1991. Then under Law no. 47/1991, the state insurance company ADAS, was split into two insurers, ASIROM and ASTRA, and new entry was permitted. The industry is now regulated by the Insurance Supervision Commission (Comisa de Supraveghere A Asigurarilor or CSA) under the Law nos. 136/1995 and 32/2000. Insurance companies may take the form of joint stock companies, mutual organisations, local subsidiaries or local branches of foreign insurers. The licensing is based on the type of insurance underwriter with a minimum capital of ROL 15 billion required for all general insurance (excluding compulsory insurance), ROL 30 billion for general insurance and ROL 21 billion for life insurance. Composite firms require the ROL 36 or 51 billion depending on the type of general insurance conducted. The Insurance Supervision Commission currently is working to harmonise its regulations in line with those of the EU by 2006.

At the end of 2004 there were 44 insurers authorised for business in Romania: 1 life insurer, 17 non-life insurers and 26 composite companies. In terms of non-life insurance, the formerly state-owned insurer, Asirom

Table 7. Insurance Companies in Romania, 1997–2002.

	1997	2000	2002
Insurance company total premiums (US$ billion)	0.2	0.3	0.5
Life insurance premiums (US$ billion)	0	0	0.1
Non-life premiums (US$ billion)	0.2	0.3	0.4
Insurance companies (number)	50	66	40

Source: Economist Intelligence Unit. (2003). Country Data, EIU.

shares the market leadership with the German affiliated, Allianz Tiriac. The Israeli affiliated, Omniasig ranks third and the other former state company Astra, fourth. In life insurance, the Dutch affiliated ING holds over half of the premiums with Arisom and IAG Life having a roughly 11 and 7 per cent, respectively, share. In terms of new business, the top five firms controlled 80 per cent of business sold. As elsewhere in the financial sector, Romania's insurance market has substantial growth potential (see Table 7). Only one in four Romanians have property insurance and only one in ten have a life policy.

3.5. Pension Funds

The Romanian State Pension Scheme has operated as a pay-as-you-go system where the current retirement benefits are paid from contributions from the current work force. While the benefits are paid with only some contributions from the government budget (e.g. in 1998 and 2002), an unfunded system is not a good long-term solution, particularly for a country with an aging population. This lack of any significant accumulation of funds similarly removes the potentially largest source of longer domestic funding from the capital market. Worse still, the surplus it has had was often invested in loans to state-owned enterprises and their repayment rates are not always good. As the IMF (2003, p. 21) noted, its "high contribution rate and the weak administration of collections, audit and enforcement have contributed to widespread evasion and thus a narrow contribution base." There is also substantial problem with arrears.

The Romanian system has also suffered from frequent unplanned, politically driven increases in its benefits payable. Retirement, for example, has often been made easier as a means of indirectly addressing unemployment problems. For example, for a brief period woman and men in supposedly "hardship occupations" could retire early with 20 and 25 years of work, respectively, at the age of 50 and 55 years. This means that the current 4.75 million Romanians receiving a pension are being supported by a 13 million potential workforce of which perhaps 1 million are unemployed.

Romania is reforming its previous national pension system over 2005 into a three-pillar one: the current public system, compulsory employer-based pension schemes and voluntary personal programmes. These reforms, which follow the Chilean model, are expected to boost the life insurance business as well as that for funds managers and the overall stock market. The reforms required are being funded by the EBRD.

In 2004, the Insurance Supervision Commission created a special pension funds department to regulate the private pension funds. According to the EIU (2005), voluntary occupational pension funds were to commence operations on 1 January 2005, and are expected to receive contributions from some 400,000 employees. As an incentive, these participants can deduct an amount equal to their contributions of up to EUR 200 per year as against their taxes as can their employers.

In early 2005, the government effectively increased pension entitlements by extending the current benefits on retirement to those retirees who had retired before 1989. This will place further fiscal pressure on the government as well as the state pension system. There are certainly limits on the amount that can be charged on existing workers. The payroll tax paid by employers in 2004 already stood at 49.5 per cent of nominal earnings in which 31.5 per cent represented the State Pension Scheme payment. Already an increasing number of employees now have been effectively out sourced into the informal sector in response.

4. THE CAPITAL MARKETS

This section addresses the key aspects of Romania's capital market. It commences with a discussion of its two stock exchanges, its government and corporate bond market, the mutual funds, privatisation funds, the futures and commodities exchanges, and the National Securities and Exchange Commission.

4.1. Stock Exchanges

The Romanian capital markets are regulated by the National Securities Commission (the Comisia Nationala a Valorilor Mobiliare or CNVM). The

CNVM was created in 1994 under Law no. 52/1994. These regulations were replaced in April 2002 with an emergency ordinance introduced to align Romanian practices with that of the EU. Law no. 525/2002 formalised these new arrangements and revitalised the National Securities Commission's powers. The CNVM commissioners are appointed for a 5-year term and can serve no more than two terms. They must meet normal "fit and proper" requirements and 5 years of experience as well as not be political party members. Today, the National Securities Commission (CNVM) is responsible the primary and secondary markets as well as mutual funds, clearing houses, share registries, securities dealers and fund managers.

The Romanian capital market has two main formal stock exchanges: the Bucharest Stock Exchange (BSE), an over-the-counter exchange, and the Romanian Association of Securities Dealers Automated Quotation (RASDAQ) market. The BSE is the larger of the two with a market capitalisation of ROL 395,433.8 billion in January 2005 compared with ROL 86,467.9 billion for the RASDAQ. The difference in turnover volume was even greater with the BSE's being about seven times more. There were moves in progress in early 2005 to merge the two exchanges. As the IMF (2003, p. 19) complained, the "equity market capitalisation is insufficient to justify the coexistence of two independent exchanges and ensure the sustainability of functioning capital markets over the long run."

4.1.1. The BSE

The BSE was established on 22 June 1995 and commenced trading on 20 November 1995. Its initial activities were fairly limited. With just six listed companies, all trading was conducted during once-a-week, 2-h-trading session. As the market grew, the trading periods expanded and so trading became daily, and a new electronic system was introduced in 1999 to facilitate both higher volumes and a wider range of securities. Trading now includes equities, debt securities, rights and warrants.

The BSE operates through a computerised order-driven system, which automatically matches the buy and sell orders provided by its members through online remote terminal connections. The BSE serves as the counterparty on all trades and handles the related clearing and settlement system, too. The electronic system nets the position of each broker with respect to money and shares. So on $T + 3$, the broker's net funding positions (positive or negative) are cleared, through the National Romanian Bank, with the BSE and the securities electronically settled accordingly. The BSE operates three official stock indexes. The first, the Bucharest Exchange Trading Index (the BET) is comprised of the top 10 most actively traded tier-one listed stocks. It was introduced on 22 September 1997. The second, the Bucharest Exchange Trading Composite Index (BET-C) covers all listed firms excluding the five SIFs (see Privatisation funds, Section 6) and has operated since 17 April 1998. The third, the BET-FI also covers all firms but includes the five SIFs.

The BSE divides its listings into two groups: a base or second tier and a first tier. There is also a special transparency plus tier status that both base and first-tier firms can achieve through an adherence of the corporate governance code and the operation of a web site in English and Romania for disclosure purposes. A base-tier listing requires the company have a share capital worth at least lei equivalent of EUR 2 million, and to have issued its securities under a public offering and have had them registered with the National Securities Commission. The securities themselves must be freely transferable. The company must complete the appropriate listing documentation and fee payment as well as agree to comply with the BSE's disclosure requirements, and have their annual accounts audited by an external independent auditor. A first-tier listing must meet all of the base-tier requirements, plus a number of additional requirements. For example, the firm must have a share capital the equivalent of at least EUR 8 million, have been in operation for at least 3 years and have been profitable for the last 2 years. The firm's management must also be considered to be competent and have integrity. In addition, at least 15 per cent of its issued shares must be held by at least 1,800 non-employee shareholders each with a minimum nominal value of at least ROL 100,000.

As shown in Table 8, the BSE's listings grew rapidly over the 1990s, but then dropped sharply in 2001 as a large number of firms were delisted due to mergers and takeovers. These listings, however, may somewhat overstate the BSE's actual position. As the IMF (2003, p. 6) recommend, the BSE should "enforce listing requirements and de-list inactive companies on the stock exchange." Market capitalisation has also grown rapidly and as shown in Table 9, more than doubled over 2004. The turnover similarly doubled over the same period. These activity and listing figures, however, may give a slightly misleading impression as the 10 top listed companies accounted for over 80 per cent of market capitalisation. Similarly, World Bank (2005, p. 17) calculated that 81 per cent of BSE trading is in the shares of the five SIFs, two banks and Petrom. Likewise, while these companies often have 1000 of shareholders, institutional investors, particularly the SIFs, accounted for most of trading activity. This reflects the "free float" on most BSE listed shares. Many listed companies, for example, are still substantially state owned. Local and foreign institutional investors then

Table 8.   BSE Listing, 1995–2004.

Year	Number of Listings		
	Tier 1	Tier 2	Total
1995	0	9	9
1996	0	17	17
1997	13	63	76
1998	21	105	156
1999	26	101	157
2000	22	92	114
2001	19	46	65
2002	19	46	65
2003	18	44	62
2004	17	43	60
2005*	17	44	61

Source: Bucharest Stock Exchange. (2004). Annual Report 2004 (in Romanian), p. 5.
*As at January 2005.

Table 9.   BSE Trading Statistics, 1995–2004.

Year	Number of Trades	Total Turnover (EUR Million)	Market Capitalisation (EUR Million)	Turnover Ratio (%)
1995	379	760	98,500	
1996	17,768	3,880	59,800	6.19
1997	609,651	240,520	624,900	72.51
1998	512,705	184,800	392,620	36.94
1999	415,045	84,067	313,001	20.17
2000	496,887	93,244	450,512	21.31
2001	357,577	148,544	1,361,079	15.82
2002	689,184	222,426	2,646,438	10.43
2003	440,084	268,641	2,991,017	9.59
2004	644,839	598,072	8,818,832	10.29

Source: Bucharest Stock Exchange. (2005). *General Statistics.* http://www.bse.com, accessed January 2005.

often hold major portions of the shares that remain. Hence the liquidity is tight for most listed companies. The major exceptions are the SIFs which are owned mainly by individual investors and so effectively have a 100 percent free float.

4.1.2. The RASDAQ Market

The RASDAQ market was created in September 1996 to provide an additional marketing vehicle for Romania's massive privatisation programme. It commenced trading on 25 October 1996 utilising a nationwide computerised system created with the support of the US National Association of Securities Dealers (NASD). RASDAQ's ability to offer remote locations equal access to transactions, handle a large volume of transactions and operate with market makers all made it particularly effective means for the State Ownership Fund (SOF) to sell off its residual shareholdings in privatised firms. The trading system, run by a wholly owned subsidiary RASDAQ SRL, is actually comprised of three markets: a regular secondary securities market for stocks and bonds; a primary public offer market for new floats; and an electronic auction system through which the SOF can sell its residual stock holdings.

The RASDAQ's less restrictive listing requirements also made it more suited for these newly privatised firms. As a result, close to 4,000 companies listed on the RASDAQ. However there is only active market in perhaps 10–15 per cent of them. The quality of some of these firms also must be questioned. As the OECD (2001, p. 9) commented on the RASDAQ, "a vast number of these companies are de facto insolvent, with no prospects for their shares being traded." It suggested that the removal of these non-performers would benefit the overall market and there has been a significant drop in numbers, accordingly. There was once over 5,000 listings.

The Romanian Association of Securities Dealers (ANSVM) sets the consumer protection guidelines and trading rules for the RASDAQ, and is overseen by the government's National Securities Commission (CNVM). The CNVM also conducts regular market surveillance to ensure fair trading practices. While over 200 stockbrokers are RASDAQ members, the top 10 most active firms handle some 90 per cent of the turnover. The National Securities Clearing, Settlement and Depository Company (SNCDD) provides the clearing, settlement and depository system from RASDAQ listed securities. Since 1998, it has been recognised by the US Securities and Exchange Commission as an eligible foreign custodian.

The RASDAQ listing requirements were modified accordingly and so by 2003, there were three listing categories: a first-tier, second-tier and base listing. The base listing has the least requirements. The firm must be registered as a public company; have at least 100 shareholders; hold a social capital of at least EUR 100,000; and have a CNVM authorised, independent share registry. It must also pay the appropriate processing fee, submit its last financial statements, show its board approval of the listing, and complete a

Table 10.   RASDAQ Listing, Capitalisation and Turnover, end
November 2004.

	Number of Companies	Market Capitalisation (US$ Million)	Turnover Value (US$ Million)
Category I listings	11	200.15	43.57
Category II listings	17	252.29	5.68
Category base	3,971	2,334.14	118.86
Total	3,999	2,786.58	168.11

Source: RASDAQ Monthly Bulletin, December 2004, pp. 6, 8 and 10.

number of forms. The second-tier status is more demanding. It requires all of the above but has a higher social capital requirement of EUR 0.5 million. It also requires the firm have at least a EUR 2.5 million in business turnover, and that the total holdings by shareholders with less than a 5 percent shareholding exceeds 10 per cent of the total shares. The first tier is the most selective with a requirement for the firm to have first shown a profit in at least one of its last 2 years; have a business turnover of at least EUR 4.5 million, assets of at least EUR 4.5 million, a social capital of at least EUR 1 million; and the total holdings of shareholders with less than 5 per cent of the shares outstanding should exceed 15 per cent of total number of shares. As shown in Table 10, the base category is the most popular and accounts for all but 28 of the RASDAQ's 3,999 listings. Base trading also is the most important but the more actively traded companies are typically listed in the other two categories.

5. THE MONEY AND BOND MARKETS

5.1. Money Market

As in most countries, the Romanian money market is where securities with initial maturities of less than 1 year are traded. It is also where financial institutions manage their liquidity positions via the interbank market. Romanian government Treasury bills (T-bills) are the dominant money market instrument with a maturity from 30 to 364 days. At one time, their average maturity on issue was for 6 months or less but 364 days T-bills are now the most commonly issued. They are used to cover budget deficits. As shown in Table 11, these bills outstanding reached a peak in 2002. These securities are

Table 11. T-Bills in Romania, 1996–2003.

	1996	1997	1998	1999	2000	2001	2002	2003
T-bills (US$ million)	944	793	1,371	1,084	1,263	1,512	1,780	1,300
T-bills/domestic Public debt securities (%)	70	42	56	29	44	52	55	33
Nominal T-bill yields (%)	45.3	62.4	62.0	54.8	33.5	30.9	22.2	18.0
Yields less CPI (%)	6.5	−92.5	2.9	9.0	−12.2	−3.6	−0.3	3.9

Note: CPI – Consumer Price Index.
Source: Compiled from Tables 13 and 14 in Capital Markets and Non-bank Financial Institutions in Romania, p. 21.

generally sold at a discount from face value with the difference between the purchase price and the maturity value providing the de facto interest payment for holding the securities. Their importance is enhanced by the lack of commercial paper (companies are seemingly not allowed to issue it) or other short-term money market securities as well as (again see Table 11) their high nominal rates of interest and low perceived risk.

5.2. Bond Market

The bond market in Romania is comprised of government bonds, municipal bonds, corporate bonds and, finally, though not yet in operation, potentially mortgage bonds. The Romanian government has been an active issuer of government bonds. These are sold on the primary market by the NBR through auctions or public subscriptions. As can be seen by comparing Tables 11 and 12 government initially made more use of bills than bonds but this position changed in 1999.

In addition to domestic issues, the Romanian government has also conducted a number of overseas issues. These became more feasible when in February 1996, Romania received reasonable credit ratings from credit-rating agencies; Standard & Poor's for example gave it a BB– rating. In addition to the Euromarket, Romania had a US$520 million Samurai bonds issue in Japan. Given Romania's own financial problems in the late 1990s, it suspended additional raisings. Foreign currency denominated debt raisings resumed overseas in November 2000. Also in 2000, T-bills in ROL and foreign currency began with the former offering higher interest rates than bank deposits, which improved the level of intermediated funds within the economy (Bichi & Antohi, 2002). In 2002, its 10-year euro issue had an

Table 12.   Domestic Government Bonds, 1996–2003.

	1996	1997	1998	1999	2000	2001	2002	2003
Domestic government bonds outstanding (US$ million)	410	1,088	1,087	2,669	1,580	1,375	1,443	2,204
Number of transactions	n/a	n/a	n/a	n/a	19,572	27,815	32,362	23,850
Total traded volume (US$ billion)	n/a	n/a	n/a	n/a	13.2	15.7	15.9	9.8

Source: World Bank (2005).

initial margin of 395 basis points over the Bunds benchmark. As the reform has made Romania more attractive to investors, more recent secondary trading has seen this margin drop to close to 100.

5.3. Municipal Bonds

As shown in Table 13, Romania had 18 municipal bonds on issue. The local municipal government issues these securities with their credit standing based on that municipality's revenue streams rather than any other guarantees and are generally considered more secure than any corporate debt issues. They are issued in the form of a floating rate note (FRN) with the interest rate adjusted by 200–300 basis points margin over the 3-month Bucharest Interbank Offered Rate (BUBOR). Three years is roughly the most common initial maturity but there have been some slightly longer issues. These issues are mainly directed towards institutional investors with the most common minimum denomination of ROL 1 million each. The total issue size has ranged from ROL 5 billion to ROL 150 billion with ROL 15 billion to ROL 30 billion the most common. Each of these issues is listed on the BSE. As shown in Table 14, these bonds have not been actively traded. This position started to improve in 2004.

   In September 2004, the Bucharest city council announced plans for its first Eurobond issue which would raise up to EUR 500 million. It would be the first overseas raising by a municipal government. As with the domestic issues, the proceeds will be used for infrastructure development. In terms of investors, the fixed interest market attracts mainly institutions investors. The financial investment funds (SIFs), for example, are major purchasers of municipal debt securities. Besides their relative safety, SIFs are required to

Table 13. Romanian Municipal Bonds 2004.

Charasteristics	Total Issue Value (ROLBillion)	Bond's Face Value (ROL Thousands)	Annual Coupon Rate (%)	Issue Date	Maturity
Predeal municipal bonds	7,500	750	19	01/11/2002	14/04/2006
Sebes municipal bonds	10,000	250	20	17/12/2002	18/12/2004
Bacau municipal bonds	35,000	200	18	17/12/2002	23/05/2005
Tg. Mures municipal bonds	20,000	200	18	18/12/2002	27/05/2005
Timisoara municipal bonds	100,000	340	18.8	03/07 2003	02/06/2005
Oradea municipal bonds	100,000	1,000	17.98	22/05/2003	05/05/2006
Bistrita municipal bonds	15,000	400	18.7	03/07/2003	25/11/2005
Alba-Iulia municipal bonds	24,000	750	19	21/10/2003	28/04/2006
Arad municipal bonds	65,000	666	14	12/08/2003	16/07/2006
Câmpulung Muscel municipal bonds	10,000	400	17.5	04/09/2003	22/12/2005
Deva municipal bonds	58,000	800	19	15/09/2003	24/08/2008
Logoj municipal bonds	6,000	500	19	05/11/2003	26/10/2005
Slobozia municipal bonds	15,000	50	19	25/03/2003	11/05/2005
Giurgiu municipal bonds	12,046	500	19.5	14/08/2003	14/08/2005
Aiud municipal bonds	5,000	375	20	06/08/2003	29/07/2005
Tg. Mures municipal bonds	30,000	700	19	13/02/2004	15/07/2006
Sebes municipal bonds	15,000	850	18	21/04/2004	15/03/2007
Oradea municipal bonds	150,000	1,500	21	24/06/2004	25/05/2010
Cluj-Napoca municipal bonds (second issue)	30,000	400	18.31	24/12/2003	15/06/2005

Source: Bucharest Stock Exchange, *Monthly Bulletin*, December 2004, p. 18.

Table 14.   Municipal and Corporate Bonds.

Year	Number of Trades	Number of Bonds Traded (Volume)	Turnover (EUR)	Number of Bond Issuers	Number of New Listings of Bond Issues
2001	5	45	173	2	2
2002	10	59,050	238,705	4	2
2003	39	187,870	4,556,257	10	8
2004	1,116	530,466	71,266,813	22	16

Source: Bucharest Stock Exchange, *General Statistics.* http://www.bvb.ro, accessed January 2005.

pay out any dividends they receive to their shareholders but this rule does not apply to fixed interest income.

5.4. Corporate Bonds

The corporate bond is one of the least developed components of Romania's financial sector. Initially, Romania businesses obtained their money from the government and the banking system. So there was no need for additional funding. They were also restricted in issuing corporate bonds due to the provisions of the local company's legislation. This limits the total amount of corporate debt on issue less than an amount equal to 75 per cent of the firm's subscribed nominal share value (paid-up capital). Similarly on the demand side, foreign investors were restricted from purchasing these debt securities until 1998.

Thus the corporate bond market in Romania has only just started operations. The first issue, by a real estate developer, S.C. Impact SA, happened in February 2003. It had a 3-year maturity with a total issue size of ROL 49 billion. The second issue was actually by a bank, the BRD Groupe Societe Generale, and for considerably more, ROL 500 billion. As shown in Table 15, other financial institutions have found this market attractive for medium-term funding. No doubt some slightly longer maturities will eventuate as the market develops. Those banks with foreign bank shareholders would seem particularly well placed to help in this extension process. They might also obtain quicker approval from the regulator. The attractiveness of bank issuers to investors is also apparent as normal corporate issues typically must either have insurance or a bank guarantee in order to attract subscribers.

Table 15. Romanian Corporate Bonds 2004.

Characteristics	Total Issue Value (ROL millions)	Bond's Face Value (ROL Million)	Annual Coupon Rate (%)	Issue Date	Maturity
Impact corporate bonds	49,800	US$30.24535	5.93	28/02/2003	17/02/2005
Raiffeisen Bank corporate bonds	1,380,000	5	16.44	04/06/2004	04/06/2007
BRD Groupe Societe Generale corporate bonds	500,000	25	18.61	20/04/2004	21/03/2007
BCR leasing corporate bonds	75,000 EUR 1.8	1 EUR 24.4553	6.0	01/04/2004	16/03/2007
TBI leasing corporate bonds	24,500 EUR 0.64	n/a EUR 0.658	6.5	15/09/2003	01/08/2006
Finanbank corporate bonds	410,000	10	18	05/11/2004	05/11/2007

Source: Bucharest Stock Exchange, *Monthly Bulletin,* December 2004, p. 18.

In addition to domestic issues, there is considerable interest in foreign currency denominated corporate debt issues. It should first be noted, though, that the Impact issue and others did not actually result in investors taking a position in local currency even though the debt was seemingly ROL denominated. Instead, the actual interest and principal payments in ROL were adjusted by a formula tied to the US dollar. Real offshore issues, as of 2004, are still limited in size to an amount equal to 75 per cent of issuer's paid-up share capital issuer like local issues, but must also first obtain approval from the NBR; its hard currency approval requires considerable justification.

Another drawback to the corporate bond market has been the BSE's listing requirements for bonds. They require that at least 30 per cent of the bonds listed be held by at least 1,000 investors. Furthermore, each of these 1,000 investors must hold at least ROL 300,000 worth of these securities and constitute in total at least 50,000 bonds. This places a considerable marketing challenge on any potential issuer.

5.5. The Secondary Mortgage Market

Romania does not have a secondary mortgage market as yet but there is certainly interest in establishing one. Previously Romanian housing was largely state owned. With the move to a market economy, however the sale of government-owned housing to the public was approved in 1990 and extended to that owned by SEs in 1992. As a result home ownership has become popular and the banks have found mortgage finance a new growth area. The foreign-owned banks have been particularly active in mortgage lending, and the rates and maturities have improved accordingly with a limited number of 20–25-year loans are now possible.

As a means to encourage more mortgage lending, the government with the help of the EBRD has been working to develop this market and several foreign specialist mortgage banks, particularly from Germany, commenced operations in Romania over 2003–2004. The World Bank's IFC has also been active indirectly through a foreign funded venture capitalist firm, the Romanian American Enterprise Fund. This entity created a housing finance subsidiary, the RoFin Mortgage Loan Company. With a capital of ROL 1,200 billion, it is by far the largest private mortgage company. Besides supporting the growth and availability of mortgage finance, this venture is expected to refinance its loan portfolio via mortgage securitisation. Securitisation of residential mortgages has worked well in other countries and might help form the basis of a longer-term debt market in Romania, too.

At present, a major drawback to securitisation is the lack of a standard contract within mortgage finance. The RoFin together with the foreign banks is expected to show leadership in formulating the necessary infrastructure for this to take place. Successful securitisation of course also requires a more uniform approach in lending standards, documentation, land title and ownership transfers. Actions available to lenders in the case of default also need to be made straightforward. The Canadian government has provided technical assistance to address these issues, and a "securitisation and mortgage bond regulatory package" was int-oduced in parliament accordingly in 2004. The changes will also ensure the Romanian legislation is more in keeping with others in the EU.

5.6. Mutual Funds

The Romanian mutual fund industry developed earlier than the rest of the capital market but operated rather differently than in most markets. Rather than stocks, the early funds lent out their funds through small commercial loans. So they were more quasi-banks than even a traditional money market fund. The rates offered were nevertheless attractive and so the public was pleased to invest. Unfortunately, the industry then afforded little regulatory protection and so investors experienced some significant losses through the failures of some early schemes. Of these, Caritas is probably the most famous. Caritas was created in 1992 with assets of ROL 100,000. The founder, Ioan Stoica, promised initial investors a return of eight times their investment after 3 months. Initially, only residents of Cluj could invest, but this was liberalised so that within the first 5 months, some 1.2 million Romanians were depositors and even some foreigners had found ways to invest, too. Like other initially successful de facto Ponzi or pyramid schemes, Caritas' inflows were soon exceeded by its outflows. When it finally collapsed in 1993, Caritas had attracted perhaps as much as US$200 million from the public. Caritas was certainly not the only such scheme, and between 1990 and 1994 some estimate more than 100 such funds were operating in Romania. An excellent account of this period can be found in Verdery (1995).

The government responded to the Caritas collapse with improved legislative controls but ironically the next major collapse, that of SAFI/FMOA, resulted directly from one of these changes. The CNVM had noted substantial differences in the way mutual funds calculated their net asset backing or share value, and so had moved to standardise the practice. When reporting under the new system, some funds showed surprisingly lower figures and substantial withdrawals resulted in April 2000. SAFO/FMOA was one of the funds unable to survive the resulting liquidity crunch. One might have thought after two major failures that the regulatory structure would have been modified to avoid any additional problems. Unfortunately, the industry experienced yet a third major failure, that of the National Investment Fund (the Fondula Nationale de Investitii or FNI). The FNI was established in 1995 and soon grew to have some 300,000 retail investors. Besides high interest rates, the investors were also attracted by the fact that the then state savings bank was a 20 percent shareholder and more importantly it had issued a guarantee over the FNI's liabilities. So unlike a traditional Romanian mutual fund, this one appeared to offer both high returns and, via the state savings bank, a de facto government guarantee. Unfortunately, when the guarantee arrangement expired in 2000, the state savings bank elected not to renew it. Interestingly, there is some question as to whether this really changed the risk. The government had claimed as it had not approved the state savings banks, the guarantee had not been legally binding. Investors responded with a massive withdrawal of funds in April 2000. The subsequent collapse the National Investment Fund, according to World Bank (2005, p. 13), resulted in most of its 300,000 investors losing an estimated US$100–150 million.

Local mutual funds in Romania still suffer from the reputation effect of these three major collapses. As Pogonaru and Apostol (2000) commented, mutual funds responded to their problems of the 1990s by shifting "the bulk of their investments from equities to the money market and strove to attract capital from institutional investors." As a result, they have become much more conservative and have a portfolio more in keeping with a money market fund than a diversified investment vehicle. This has seemingly proved more attractive to investors. As shown in Table 16, the number of investors and their average participation increased over 2001 to 2003. In 2003, 22 such funds were in operation of which, as shown in Table 17, Simfonia is the most important. In addition to the government, most industry members are also part of a self-regulatory organisation, the National Union of Collective Placement Organisations (UNOPC).

As of late 2003, the CNVM's Collective Investment Scheme Directorate regulated 25 open-end investment companies (mutual funds), 3 venture capital funds and 18 funds management companies. In addition to the domestic mutual funds, a number of foreign-managed investment funds are

Table 16. Open-End Investment Funds in Romania.

Indicators	2001	2002	2003
Number of open-end investment funds	27	23	22
Number of investors	49,296	65,445	63,407
Participation titles (thousand pieces)	5,151	21,518	19,162
Total net assets (ROL billion)	495	992	937
Average investment/investor (ROL billion)	10.1	15.1	14.7

Source: Romanian National Securities Commission. Annual Report 2003, p. 4.

also active investors in the Romanian market. The so-called "country funds" are perhaps the most interesting. As the name suggest, these foreign funds are supposed to invest all of their capital into a specific country. As shown in Table 18, these funds are created by primarily foreign fund managers who then raise money from clients outside of Romania for local investment.

In addition to country funds, there is also what are known as "regional funds" which in this case focus on their investments typically within East Europe. Some of these together with their respective fund manager are listed in Table 19. Unfortunately, these regional funds found it difficult to invest much Romanian shares so these holdings are relatively low in comparison with other countries.

5.7. Venture Capital Funds

Venture capital in Romania is controlled under Government Ordinance no. 20/1998. In addition to the three domestic venture capital firms regulated by the CNVM, a number of foreign venture capitalist firms may also invest foreign funds into local private equity opportunities. Much of these funds were attracted to the potential opportunities afforded under Romania's privatisation programmes. Some examples of the major funds and their managers are shown in Table 20. In addition, several of the SIFs are also establishing venture capital affiliates.

One of the largest fund is the Romanian American Enterprise Fund. It was established in 1993 with financial support of US$61 million from the USAID. It has since provided some US$130 million in equity and US$25 million in loans to some 1,650 small-to-medium Romanian enterprises.

Table 17. Open-End Investment Funds in Romania (ROL Million).

Name	New Asset Value
Active Dinamic	1,682
Allegro	1,512
ARDAF	1,910
Armonia	47
BCR Clasic	111,745
BCR Dinamic	31,685
Capital Plus	38,573
FCE	63,331
FMPR	3,195
FON	6,048
Fortuna Classic	54,761
Fortuna Gold	4,324
Integro	43,703
Inter Capital	6,973
Napoca	22,873
Plus Fidelity	1,531
Retcon*	911
Simfonia 1	356,194
Stabilo	4,692
Tezaur	11,215
Transilvania	150,197
Vanguard Protector	20,001
Total	937,072

Source: Romanian National Securities Commission. Annual Report 2003, Annex 12.
*As of 21 August 2003, whilst others as of 31 December 2003.

Table 18. Selected Romania Country Funds.

Fund	Fund Manager
Broadhurst Investors	New Century Holdings
Romania Post Privatisation Fund	GED Capital Development
Romania Investment Fund	Capital SA
Romanian Growth Fund	Global Euro Asia Management
Romanian Investment Company	Foreign and Colonial
SG Romania Fund	Societe Generale

Source: Expanded from Pogonaru, F., & Apostol, C. (2000). *Romanian capital markets: A decade of transition.* RECP Working Paper no. 9, October, p. 21.

Table 19. Foreign Regional Funds.

Fund	Fund Manager
AIG New Europe Fund	AIG
Black Sea Fund	Global Finance
Balkan Fund	Global Finance
Coop Central European Fund	Julius Baer
Central European Growth Fund	Credit Suisse
DB Osteuropa Fund	Deutsche Bank
East European Development Fund	Invesco
Eastern European Trust	Pictet Asset Management
Framlington East Europe Fund	Framlington
Pictet Targeted Fund Eastern Europe	Pictet
Raiffeisen Osteuropa Fund	Reiffeissen
Vontobel Eastern European Fund	Vontobel

Source: Updated and expanded from Pogonaru, F., & Apostol, C. (2000). *Romanian capital markets: A decade of transition.* RECP Working Paper no. 9, October, p. 21.

Table 20. Venture Capital Funds in Romania.

Fund	Fund Manager
Romanian Post Privatisation Fund	GED Capital Development
Romanian American Enterprise Fund	Romania Capital Advisors
Danube Fund	Southeastern Europe Management
Oressa Ventures	Self-Managed

Source: Pogonaru, F., & Apostol, C. (2000). *Romanian capital markets: A decade of transition.* RECP Working Paper no. 9, October, p. 22.

6. PRIVATISATION FUNDS

As mentioned earlier, Romania did not initially experiment with the private sector to the extent of the other Eastern European states. So when the government decided to privatise its business holdings, it was faced a much more significant challenge as result. In terms of the process, the Privatisation Law no. 15/1990 provided the basis on which the government separated the SEs from those that would be commercialised and those that would not. First some 6,280 state-owned enterprises legally converted into commercial firms. Then these firms were divided between those that would continue initially as SEs and those that would be privatised. Interestingly, the former comprised just slightly less than half of the overall assets.

The actual ownership of those firms to be privatised under Privatisation Law no. 58/1991 was then transferred so that the newly created SOF owned 70 per cent and one or more of five regional-based, Private Ownership Funds (POFs) owned the remaining 30. The SOFs and POFs could also sell their shareholdings via a public offering, through an auction or by direct sale. The latter was initially the most successful. These sales were to foreign investors, typically major multinational companies, or employee associations via MEBOs.

The SOF was created by the Romanian parliament to privatise the Romanian government's industrial, agricultural and financial enterprises. It was supposed to sell at least 10 per cent of its initial shareholdings each year and be in a position to dissolve itself within 7 years. As mentioned, the SOF was intended to liquidate its holdings within 7 years. Unfortunately, as only a small portion of its holdings had been sold, further action was required and host regulatory changes resulted. This allowed the sale of a number of companies in previously protected sectors, particularly of the larger SEs, among other changes. In 2000, the SOF was reconstructed into a new body, the Authority for Privatisation and Management of State Ownership (APAPS). This in turn was merged with the government's Banking Asset Recovery Agency (AVAB) to form the Authority for State Asset Recovery (AVAS). This body has since been responsible for the privatisation of those assets still held by the Romanian government. At the end of 2004 AVAS held shares in some 1,066 companies. Of these, 527 are set to be privatised, 509 foreclosed or liquidated, and 30 companies to be merged into other existing state bodies.

The POFs were also government entities but their role in privatisation was more to distribute their shareholdings to individuals than to raise cash. This could be via staff buyouts, public offerings to the general public or selected sales of large parcels to outside investors. They initially operated as creatures of the state with their seven member boards appointed by the parliament, but after 5 years were to be converted into private sector styled mutual funds.

The POFs were intended to offer some 10 per cent of their holdings via public offerings with the remainder through MEBOs. This was in part because the transfer of shares to employees generally entailed substantial discounts in the pricing as well as other benefits. The employees did not own the shares directly but rather through an employees' association. They then had to repay any money used to purchase the shares within 3–5 years.

As might be expected, each POF was generally allocated shares in those SEs located within their respective region but this was not always the case.

Those firms that were in "critical industries" (ones in need of national restructuring) and those with monopoly status (banks and insurance), for example, were distributed equally across the five POFs. The results was that each POF received shares in some 1,100–1,300 companies. Due to their regional economic differences, however each POF had a slightly different industry focus within its portfolio. POF Moldova, for example, had a significant number of textile and clothing firms within its portfolio (see Table 21) whereas POF Oltenia's portfolio contain substantial holdings in electronics companies.

With the ownership moved from the government to these entities, the next step was to distribute these holdings to the general public. This was done by distributing a Certificate of Ownership (CO) in each of the five POFs to every Romanian citizen over 18 years. These certificates could then be sold for cash to other Romanians, exchanged for shares in specific companies owned by the respective POF via a public offering, or converted into normal shares in the POF when it became a mutual fund. The latter was effectively the default position should the CO holder take no specific action.

Despite some initial success, the privatisation programme had not achieved its perceived objectives and so new legislation, the Accelerating Privatization Law no. 55/1995 was initiated. It formed the basis of Romania's mass privatisation programme and yet another distribution of vouchers to Romanian citizens known this time as Privatisation Coupons. These gave the holder the right to purchase shares in the some 4,000 companies still to be privatised or the ability to take additional shareholdings in the then POFs. It also allowed companies themselves to exchange up to 60 per cent of their shares (held by the SOF) for coupons. They did not relate to the POF's 30 per cent. If the above seems somewhat confusing, it was even more so for the investing public and the companies involved. In 1996, further legislation, special Law no. 133/1996, moved to transform the POFs as

Table 21. The Private Ownership Funds.

Name	Region	Initial Industry Emphasis
POF Banat Crisana	Western	Wood processing, non-ferrous metals
POF Moldova	Eastern	Textile and clothing
POF Transylvania	Central	Naval transport, fishing tourism
POF Muntenia	Southern	Glass, ceramics, construction materials, cosmetics, pharmaceuticals
POF Oltenia	Southern	Electronics, footwear and leather

Source: Adapted OECD. (2001). *Corporate governance in Romania* (pp. 48—49). Paris: OECD.

planned into mutual funds. This meant the existing exchangers finally received their shares. The new entities, though, also had to finalise their arrangements with their past coupon holders in respect to any past dividend entitlements.

The POFs formally became Financial Investment Funds (SIFs) in 1997 and were listed on the BSE in November 1999 with some 9 million shareholders each. They may be equated to closed-end mutual funds, but their fund management skills were hampered by the quality of their initial share portfolio of allocated state companies. As Pogonaru and Apostol (2000) observed the SIFs were facing "problems created by their initial portfolio structure, burdened with over-valued stocks of many ineffective companies, by the poor management of the controlled companies, and by lack of disclosure." In an effort to create a more useful share portfolio, the SIFs tried to sell their holdings in both small companies (with high administrative costs compared to the potential benefit) and loss making firms. So in 2000, SIF Banat Crisana still held shares in 724 firms while SIF Olentia had only 301. Even within these numbers the management approach differed. SIF Muntenia, for example, retained a number of companies where it held more than 50 per cent control whereas SIF Moldova seems to avoid portfolio positions of control.

Though listed on the stock exchange and supposedly private, the SIFs remain very much creatures of the state with many directors still politically connected. One SIF, for example, had 7 of its 11 directors who were members of parliament. This position was made worse by the fact that SIF shareholders are limited in their voting rights to 0.1 per cent of the shares regardless of their shareholding; a restriction expected to be removed in 2005. As all formerly SEs that were privatised needed to be listed on a stock exchange as part of the process, this considerably expanded the number and quality of listed companies, mostly on the RASDAQ. Besides expanding the number of listed firms and shareholders, the process also created six significant institutional investors (the SOF and five POFs). As major holders of local shares, these entities became major players in the local stock exchange and together with other institutional investors dominate local trading. Their holdings also allowed them to nominate their representatives on the board of directors, and so they became even more powerful institutions.

While Romania's privatisation was a success in that it disbursed the shareholdings over a country's population, this dispersion is now actually a problem. As the OECD (2001, p. 9) noted, "this ownership structure makes it almost impossible to monitor management or controlling interests, resulting in very poor treatment for minority shareholders." This dispersion has also discouraged institutional investors taking positions in many privatised companies. Due to the large number the shareholders holding relatively small number of shares, a broker would need to merge a considerable number of small individual holdings in order to create a reasonable size parcel of shares. This need for consolidation initially resulted in almost an industry of its own as many holders were largely unaware of their holdings and so needed to be contacted directly before they would sell. As of 2005, the five SIFs have been among the better long-term investments on the BSE. They have each paid dividends now for several years but nevertheless still sell below their net asset backing, as shown in Table 22.

7. FUTURES AND COMMODITIES EXCHANGES

The Romanian Commodities Exchange opened in Bucharest in December 1992. Similar exchanges were established subsequently in other cities. Some of these include: the Agricultural and General Commodities Exchange of Arad, Commodities Exchange of Brasov, Commodity Exchange of Timisoara, Grain Exchange of Braila, Maritime and Commodities Exchange of Constant, Moldavia Commodity Exchange, Sibiu Monetary, Financial and Commodities Exchange, Transilvanian Commodity Exchange of Cluj-Napoca and the Wood Exchange of Piatra Neamt. These exchanges and their related brokerage companies and business centers signed a cooperation agreement in Bucharest in May 1995. This is now reflected in the Romanian Commodities Exchange Union. Almost all commodities exchanges have started to develop various types of futures contracts, although the volume of transactions has been limited. The two most important in respect to the capital markets are the Romanian Commodities Exchange and the Sibiu Monetary, Financial and Commodities Exchange.

The Romanian Commodities Exchange is the oldest of Romania's commodity exchanges. It handles both a computerised auction system for physical commodities and, more recently, financial derivatives. The latter include futures and options contracts on the ROL against the US dollar and against the euro, the US dollar against the euro, and on future interest rates via the Bucharest Offered Lending Rate (BUBOR) 3-month index. The ROL/dollar-related contracts are by far the most important and constitute 94 per cent of the turnover. Its total turnover value in 2003 stood at ROL 108,793 million.

The Sibiu Monetary, Financial and Commodities Exchange was established in December 1994 and commenced operations in July 1997. It is

Table 22.   Financial Investment Companies: Selected Statistics, 2004.

Name	Total Asset Value (ROL Billion)	Total Market Value (ROL Billion)	% of BSE Capitalisation	Price Earnings Ratio (%)	Dividend Yield (%)
SIF 1 Banat Crisana Arad	5,968.0	4,555.4	1.33	13.21	5.78
SIF 2 Moldova Bacau	5,122.1	3,763.3	1.10	9.60	7.05
SIF 3 Transilvania Brasov	77,200.9	5,679.1	1.66	16.12	4.04
SIF 4 Muntenia Bucuresti	5,202.8	4,680.8	1.37	12.51	7.26
SIF 5 Olenia Crajova	8,648.5	5,047.4	1.48	17.50	4.25

Note: The SIF is Romania for Societatai de Investili Financaire. While legally they do not have a number in their corporate name, they are commonly called only by this number, such as SIF 1.
Source: Bucharest Stock Exchange, *Monthly Bulletin*, December 2004, pp. 11, 13 and 15

Romania's first financial futures and options exchange. Initially it operated with a trading floor but moved to electronic trading in June 2000. This system is accessed via the Internet and so can serve its 28 member brokerage firms anywhere in Romania. In 2005, the Sibiu Monetary, Financial and Commodities Exchange offered both futures and option contracts on the US dollar, euro and Japanese yen, each against the Romanian ROL; the US dollar against the euro; the BUBOR interest rate level; wheat; and individual contracts on the share prices of each of SIFs, SNP Petrom SA and Banca Transilvania. All trading is cleared through the member-owned Romanian Clearing House. As with other futures markets, the clearing house serves as the counterparty for each transaction reducing settlement risk and facilitating novation.

8. SUMMARY AND CONCLUSIONS

In conclusion, just as its economy, the Romanian banks and capital market has made considerable progress over the last decade. With the banking sector, Government ownership levels have declined and foreign bank ownership has expanded. Lending to the private sector increases each year and is expected to double from 2003 to 2007. The intermediation levels however are still well below average EU levels. Banks have been concentrating more on consumer financing, however business banking remains important. Credit cards usage has grown exponentially with up to 5 million users in 2003, which was a 25 percent increase on 2002 (EIU, 2004).

The government's efforts to reform the sector include the so-called "A Strong Capital Market" programme in mid-2004 which was designed in three stages. The first was to encourage the trading of government securities, the creation of a mortgage bond market and the privatisation of additional large SEs. The second was intended to merge the existing exchanges and otherwise improve the capital market's infrastructure. Finally, the third was directed at developing pension funds.

Improvements can be characterised on the supply side with that of the companies themselves and on the purchase side with the investors and the infrastructure. More funds are formally used in the economy due to the privatisation process whereby previously state-owned assets have been sold. The privatisation process, however, is not yet complete and a number of potentially attractive listed companies still remain in state hands rather than on the stock exchange. Agricultural farms for instance were state owned during the socialist period, and now can be privately owned. Although mortgage backed securities and securitisation do not yet exist, such developments will lead to more funds being available. On the purchase side of the investment equation could be the potential growth of the pension and mutual funds, venture capital funds and FICs. In addition Romanians are underinsured and this market is also set to rise. Pension funds need to be accumulated to provide more funds for investment, although this is difficult at the state level where current monies received are used to pay current retirees. Mutual funds which used to act as quasi-banks have recently tended to invest conservatively in government securities (after a spate of failed investor schemes in the early 1990s) and could potentially expand their asset portfolios to include more stocks.

On the macroeconomic front, the inflation rate for 2005 is hoped to be just 7 per cent, which is certainly an improvement on the extreme levels experienced in the 1990s. The macroeconomic instability of the 1990s made investors nervous whilst market-based systems emerged. Early 2005, Romania was under discussions with the IMF to liberalise its capital account further with a plan for non-residents to be granted access to short-term bank deposits by 10 April 2005. Nervousness remains over the potential ability of foreigners to destabilise macroeconomic stability with such a move as domestic interest rates are high. The *leu* is expected to appreciate in value as a result. In the meantime the informal market remains significant and Euromoney (1 April 2001) once reported claims that some 50 per cent of GDP is not visible.

In addition as part of the reform process and particularly with the alignment to EU principles, improvements have been made in corporate governance and disclosure rules, although it is noted that corruption remains a persistent problem. As the World Bank (2005, p. xiii) commented, "improving corporate governance remains a prerequisite to financial sector development in Romania and in particular to capital markets development." The rules regarding the roles and responsibilities of directors and management need much improvement and the financial disclosure remains fair below international standards. Further to this World Bank (2005, p. 2) concluded, "despite the recent adoption of a corporate governance code, corporate governance lags significantly behind OECD principles." More regulation may result in both overlap and overkill. For instance, the high levels of capital required for banks, is like a tax on the banks and prevents them from investing the money with higher returns.

In 2005, the Romanian government announced plans for significant changes in the taxation system with personal and corporate tax rates of 18–40 and 25 per cent, respectively, cut to a single flat tax of 16 per cent. Besides stimulating the economy, the lower rates and their supposed simplicity was intended to attract those in the informal sector to report their activities. In early 2005, the Romanian government also announced that it would increase its capital gains tax from 1 to 10 per cent in April 2005 in line with IMF recommendations.

In January 2005, the Romanian parliament debated a move to join Romania's three regulatory bodies: the NBR, CSA and CNVM, to cover the banks, insurance companies and the securities market within the one regulator entity. But despite a number of recent improvements, "a number of deficiencies still remain in the institutional, legal and regulatory framework for capital markets" (World Bank, 2005, p. 2). The challenge remains once Romania joins the EU to integrate with the single EU wholesale market and open up to the EU retail market. Tax, legal and governance systems will need to be in line with EU standards.

Minority shareholders need further protection. Together with the diffuse shareholder structure of the Romanian companies resulting from the mass privatisation programme, minority shareholders were left unprotected from the abuses of majority shareholders. Also accounting standards need to be overhauled to align with international practice. It is difficult to make direct comparisons with firms in other countries due to differing practices. Inventories, for instance, have been measured through the weighted average cost method, which has meant operating costs were reported low in inflationary periods. Also provisioning of doubtful debts and obsolete tangible assets is allowed, but companies seldom use it adding to the confusion over firms' true position.

Romania's financial markets are continuing the development process with the added incentive to possibly join EU financial markets. The 1990s were characterised by instability due fundamentally to macroeconomic shocks in inflation and exchange rates. More recent reforms appear promising and financial markets are being aligned with EU standards. Pension reform is imperative however and remains a threat with an aging population. Perhaps the government could invest some monies from current budgets into pension schemes for future payments even though the current pay-as-you-go system does not provide adequate cover. Foreign investment will be further aided by Romania's eligibility to follow the OECD Declaration on International Investment and Multinational Enterprises achieved in December 2004. Provided Romania attains EU membership, financial market development is expected to expand much further and faster due to more competitive pressures from EU counterparts.

NOTES

1. We would sincerely like to thank Surica Rosentuler, Ramona Merce and Corina Ciobanu for helpful comments
2. Verdery (1995) reports inflation in 1993 at 300 per cent.
3. The leu will be revalued on 1 July 2005 at the value of 1 new leu (RON) for 10,000 old lei (ROL). The size of the notes will be similar to the size of euros so ATMs will not need to be upgraded provided EU accession occurs.
4. According to World Bank (2005, p. 9), Romanian businesses fund some 72 per cent of new investment from internal sources and retained earnings, 11 per cent from bank loans, and 5 per cent from family and friends.
5. The Ministry of Finance (MOF) was responsible for collecting state revenues.
6. Foreign banks before 1989 included: Chemical or Manufacturers Hanover, Soceiete Generale Banque Franco-Roumaine, Frankfurt Bucharest Bank (Tsantis, 1997).
7. Note that in 2003 the Romanian Commercial Bank was the largest bank in Romania with assets close to US$6 billion, 297 branches and over 13,000 employees in 2003 (BankScope database).
8. Listed banks include Banca Transilvania SA, Banca Comerciala Carpatica SA and BRD Groupe Societe Generale SA and Eurom Bank SA (BankScope database).
9. The current account was almost halved in 1998 to avoid a default on balance of payments. This led to further depreciation of the *leu* in 1998 and increased inflation to 55 per cent in 1999.
10. The US dollar has frequently been traded for the ROL (75 per cent) (Bichi & Antohi, 2002). With EU alignment now more imperative this will no doubt change.

REFERENCES

Asaftei, G., & Kumbhakar, S. C. (2004). Development and efficiency of banking in a transitional economy: The case of Romania. Presented at the *Australian Banking and Finance Conference*. Sydney, 15–17 December.

Bacon, W. (2004). Economic reform. In: H. F. Carey (Ed.), *Romania since 1989: Politics, economics and society* (pp. 373–390). Lanham: Lexington Books.

Bichi, C., & Antohi, C. (2002). Romania's financial sector in transition and on the road to EU accession. In: C. Thimann (Ed.), *Financial sectors in EU accession countries* (pp. 189–206). Frankfurt: European Central Bank.

Bonin, J. P., Hasan, I., & Wachtel, P. (2005). Bank performance, efficiency and ownership in transition economies. *Journal of Banking and Finance, 29*, 31–53.

Clarke, G. R. G., Cull, R., & Shirley, M. (2004). Empirical studies of bank privatisation: Some lessons. *The International Society for New Institutional Economics (ISNIE) Conference*. Institutions and Economic and Political Behavior, *8th annual conference*, September 30 to October 3, 2004, Tucson, Arizona, USA.

Crystal, J. S., Dages, B. G., & Goldberg, L. S. (2001). Does foreign ownership contribute to sounder banks in emerging markets? The Latin American experience. In: R. Litan, P. Masson & M. Pomerleano (Eds), *Open doors: Foreign participation in financial systems in developing countries* (pp. 217–266). Washington, DC: Brookings Press.

Daianu, D. (2004). Fiscal and monetary policies. In: H. F. Carey (Ed.), *Romania since 1989: Politics, economics and society* (pp. 391–417). Lanham: Lexington Books.

Daianu, D., & Vranceanu, R. (2003). *Opening the capital account of transition economies: How much and how fast*. William Davidson Working Paper no. 511, September.

De Haas, R., & van Lelyveld, I. (2004). Foreign bank penetration and private sector credit in Central and Eastern Europe. *Journal of Emerging Market Finance, 3*, 125–151.

Demirguc-Kunt, A., Laeven, L., & Levine, R. (2003). *The impact of bank regulations, concentration, and institution on bank margins*. World Bank Working Paper no. 3030, April.

Drakos, K. (2003). Assessing the success of reform in transition banking 10 years later: An interest margins analysis. *Journal of Policy Modelling, 25*, 309–317.

Economic Intelligence Unit (EIU) (2004). *Executive briefing Romania*. London: Economic Intelligence Unit.

Economic Intelligence Unit. (2005). *Executive briefing Romania*. London: Economic Intelligence Unit.

Fries, S., & Taci, A. (2005). Cost efficiency of banks in transition: evidence from 289 banks in 15 post-communist countries. *Journal of Banking and Finance, 29*, 55–81.

Green, C. J., Murinde, V., & Nikolov, I. (2004). The efficiency of foreign and domestic banks in Central and Eastern Europe: Evidence on economies of scale and scope. *Journal of Emerging Market Finance, 3*, 175–205.

King, R. G., & Levine, R. (1993). Finance and growth: Schumpeter might be right. *Quarterly Journal of Economics, 108*, 717–737.

OECD. (2001). *Corporate governance in Romania*. Paris: OECD.

Pogonaru, F., & Apostol, C. (2000). *Romanian capital markets: A decade of transition*. Romanian Centre for Economic Policies, RCEP, Working Paper no. 9, October.

Pomerleano, M., & Vojta, G. J. (2001). What do foreign banks do in emerging markets? An institutional study. The World Bank, International Monetary Fund and Brookings

Institution, *3rd annual financial markets and development conference*, April 19–21, New York.

Popa, C. (2004). Banking on Romania. Presented at the Romanian Banking System presentation, Bucharest, May 10, National Bank of Romania.

The Banker. (2003). Romania supplement, April.

The Banker. (2004). Romania supplement, April.

Tsantis, A. (1997). Developments in the Romanian banking sector. In: *OECD proceedings, the new banking landscape in Central and Eastern Europe: Country experience and policies for the future* (pp. 167–216). Paris: Organisation for Economic cooperation and Development.

Verdery, K. (1995). Faith, hope and caritas in the land of the pyramids: Romania, 1990 to 2000. *Comparative Studies in Society and History, 37*, 625–669.

World Bank. (2005). *Capital markets and non-bank financial institutions in Romania: Assessment of key issues and recommendations for development*. World Bank Working Paper no. 45.

PART D:
EQUITY MARKET INTEGRATION

CONDITIONAL CONTEMPORANEOUS CORRELATIONS AMONG EUROPEAN EMERGING MARKETS

Seppo Pynnönen[1]

1. INTRODUCTION

The biggest enlargement of the European Union (EU) took place in May 2004 when 10 new countries (Cyprus, Czech Republic, Estonia, Hungary, Latvia, Lithuania, Malta, Poland, Slovakia, and Slovenia) joined the union, increasing the number of member states from 15 to 25. Of these newcomers, eight are former Eastern European countries with transition to Western-type market economies. These emerging markets provide increasingly growing investment opportunities and international diversification options for fund managers and individual investors. Well-known features of emerging equity markets are high returns, high volatility, and low correlation with developed markets. Bekaert and Harvey (2002) find that this correlation is on average increasing, particularly for those emerging markets that have liberalised their financial markets. Mateus (2004) finds similar results with EU access countries for recent years. Additional features of emerging markets are sparse data, low liquidity, and large price changes due to political changes or market crashes (e.g. Hwang & Pedersen, 2004).

Emerging European Financial Markets: Independence and Integration Post-Enlargement
International Finance Review, Volume 6, 325–351
Copyright © 2006 by Elsevier Ltd.
ISSN: 1569-3767/doi:10.1016/S1569-3767(05)06013-9

Volatility and contemporaneous correlation are the attributes in the diversification process. Until the 1980s, volatility was usually modelled as a constant, although it was long known to the investment community that speculative series tend to exhibit volatility clustering across time (e.g. Mandelbrot, 1963; Fama, 1965). Nevertheless, there was no successful empirical method to model this phenomenon until Engle (1982) introduced the idea of autoregressive conditional heteroscedasticity (ARCH). This new idea started a new era in research on volatility and even higher moments' characteristics in equity markets (for excellent reviews, see Engle & Bollerslev, 1986; Bollerslev, Chou, & Kroner, 1992; Bera & Higgins, 1993).

Volatility clustering is now widely accepted as a stylised fact, and researchers have more recently started questioning the constancy of the other parameters like CAPM beta and (contemporaneous) correlations between stocks (Bollerslev, Engle, & Wooldridge, 1988; Christodoulakis & Satchell, 2002; Engle, 2002; Tse & Tsui, 2002). Indeed, it was found early that contemporaneous correlations particularly between international markets are unstable over time (e.g. see Makridakis & Wheelwright, 1974; Koch & Koch, 1991). Furthermore, King and Wadhwani (1990), Longin and Solnik (1995), Solnik, Boucrelle, and Fur (1996), and Ramchand and Susmel (1998) find that correlations among international markets tend to increase during unstable periods. Ramchand and Susmel (1998) address the relationship between high volatility and correlation. With the switching ARCH technique, they find that correlations between the USA and other world markets are 2–3.5 times higher when the US market is in a high-volatility state as compared to the low-volatility state. Longin and Solnik (2001), however, argue that correlation is not related to market volatility per se but to the market trend, and they argue that the correlations tend to increase especially with negative returns, and hence the negative tail-distribution deviates much from the normal distribution. Consequently, they infer that correlation tends to increase in bear markets but not in bull markets. This casts serious doubt whether diversification works when it is most needed.

Regarding earlier studies of European emerging markets, Mateus (2004) found by visual inspection of rolling correlations that the European access country correlations with the major European markets have increased during last years. Voronkova (2004) finds further that the Central European markets (Czech Republic, Hungary, and Poland) display equilibrium relations with their mature counterparts (France, Germany, UK, and USA). Hwang and Pedersen (2004) evaluate asymmetric risk measures in modelling emerging market equities, and conclude that risk and asset management in emerging markets involves customised approaches across regions. Knif and

Pynnonen (2006), Knif, Kolari and Pynnonen (2005) extend the analysis by examining the dependence of the correlations directly on the level of prevailing uncertainty measured in terms of volatilities and some other potential factors. Their results indicate like the earlier papers that contemporaneous correlation is time varying, but also highly persistent, and particularly that the contemporaneous correlations are dependent on global market volatility.

Using the methodology suggested in Knif et al. (2005), this chapter extends the analysis to cover European emerging markets, and investigates the time variability of contemporaneous correlation between the emerging markets and their relations to the leading European Economies and the world leading market of the USA. As discussed above, typical characteristics of the emerging markets are low correlations with the developed markets, high volatilities, and high return autocorrelations. In terms of these characteristics the results of the paper show that Estonia, Latvia, Lithuania, Slovakia, Slovenia obviously share these features, while the Czech Republic, Hungary, and Poland form another group that could be judged as being semi-developed markets in the sense that they are more correlated with each other and are also more correlated with the major European markets.

The remainder of this chapter is organised as follows. In Section 2 the methodology is briefly introduced. Section 3 describes the sample data and gives preliminary summary statistics. In Section 4 the empirical results are given, and Section 5 concludes the study.

2. CORRELATION AND VOLATILITY

The conditional correlation of (return) series u_t and v_t is defined as:

$$\rho_{uv,t} = \frac{\text{cov}_t(u, v)}{\sqrt{\text{var}_t(u)\text{var}_t(v)}} \tag{1}$$

where the subscript indicates the predicted entity given information up to time point t–1. For example, $\text{var}_t(u) = E_{t-1}[u_t - E_{t-1}(u_t)]^2 = E\left[(u_t - E(u_t|\Psi_{t-1}))^2|\Psi_{t-1}\right]$ with Ψ_{t-1} indicating the available information up to time t–1. In terms of the covariance, we get:

$$\text{cov}_t(u, v) = \rho_{uv,t}\sqrt{\text{var}_t(u)}\sqrt{\text{var}_t(v)} \tag{2}$$

In the simple case where the correlation is time invariant, Eq. (2) shows that time varying covariance must change in a fixed proportion to the product of the time varying standard deviation. In order to investigate the stylised fact that correlation tends to increase under uncertain episodes, Knif et al. (2005) suggest dealing with a generalised conditional covariance:

$$\text{cov}_{t,a,b}(u,v) = c_t \sigma_{u,t}^a \sigma_{v,t}^b \tag{3}$$

where $\sigma_{u,t} = \sqrt{\text{var}_t(u)}$, $\sigma_{v,t} = \sqrt{\text{var}_t(v)}$, and c_t is a coefficient which may be time varying and depend on some additional variables. Hence parameters a and b determine the importance of each standard deviation's relative contribution to the covariance, and if both a and b are larger than one, the correlation is an increasing function of the volatilities.

Dividing both sides of Eq. (3) by the conditional standard deviations we get:

$$\rho_{uv,t} = c_t \sigma_{u,t}^\alpha \sigma_{v,t}^\beta \tag{4}$$

where $\alpha = a-1$ and $\beta = b-1$. If the correlation is independent of the level of volatilities then $\alpha = \beta = 0$. Given estimates of the correlations and standard deviations one can in principle estimate Eq. (4) with non-linear techniques. However, technical difficulties may arise because the left-hand side is restricted by definition between -1 and $+1$, whereas the right-hand side is not restricted in an econometric specification. In order to linearise the problem and make both sides unrestricted, Knif et al. (2005) suggest to make a generalised logit transformation such that:

$$\log\left(\frac{1 + \rho_{ij,t}}{1 - \rho_{ij,t}}\right) = \omega_t + \gamma_i \log(\sigma_{i,t}) + \gamma_j \log(\sigma_{j,t}) \tag{5}$$

in which both sides are now balanced in the sense that they can assume all real values. In addition this transformation guarantees that $|\rho_{ij,t}| < 1$. The intercept term ω_t may include other variables like autoregression (AR) terms, time trends, and foreign volatilities, or some economic variables. From Eq. (5) one immediately sees that if the correlation is not dependent on the levels of volatilities the coefficients γ_i and γ_j are zero. A positive sign of the coefficient indicates increasing correlation with the volatility, and a negative sign indicates that the returns tend to even divert with increasing volatility (further discussion and its estimation details are given in Knif et al., 2005).

The volatilities in Eq. (5) are specified as GARCH processes. In order to capture asymmetry we utilise the Threshold GARCH (TGARCH) for which the TGARCH(1,1) is of the form:

$$\sigma_t^2 = \alpha_0 + \alpha e_{t-1}^2 + \delta e_{t-1}^2 D_{t-1} + \beta \sigma_{t-1}^2 \tag{6}$$

where $D_{t-1} = 1$ if $e_{t-1} < 0$ and 0 otherwise. A positive δ indicates the presence of leverage-type asymmetry.

3. DATA AND INITIAL ESTIMATES

The analysis utilises daily close-to-close log-index returns from the eight European emerging markets including Czech Republic (PXGL),[2] Estonia (TALSE),[3] Hungary (BUX),[4] Latvia (RSEDJ),[5] Lithuania (LITNG),[6] Slovakia (SAX),[7] and Slovenia (SPI-20).[8] In addition the major European stock markets of Germany (DAX) and the UK (FTSE-100), and the world leading market of the USA (SP500) are included to the analysis to investigate their role in the mutual correlations of the emerging markets. The series started on 3 June 1996 and ended on 21 September 2004, except for Latvia and Lithuania for which the series began on 1 February 1997 and 3 April 1997, respectively. Index quotations for national holidays are replaced by the index value of the previous trading day resulting to $n = 2,146$ daily observations (Latvia 1,974 and Lithuania 1,928 due to the shorter available sample periods). The data is obtained mainly from the Global Financial Data Inc (www.globalfindata.com).

Table 1 reports basic demographic, macroeconomic, and stock exchange summary statistics for these markets accompanied with major European economies of German and UK, and the world largest economy of the USA. Estonia, Latvia, Lithuania, Slovakia, and Slovenia are small countries with population ranging from Estonia's 1.4 million to Slovakia's 5.4 million. Poland is obviously the largest with close to 39 million inhabitants. Czech Republic and Hungary are about the same size with approximately 10 million people. Typically the purchasing power parity (PPP) adjusted gross domestic product (GDP) per capita ranges from 35 to 57 per cent of that of Germany (27.4 thousand USD) or UK (26.9 thousand USD), and about from 27 to 43 per cent of that of the USA (36.5 thousand USD) with the exception of Slovenia whose PPP corrected GDP per capita is about 72 per cent of that of Germany.

The largest market capitalisation in terms of domestic shares listed in the main list of the country is Poland with 47 billion EUR compared to Germany's 798 billion EUR or USA's 12,696 billion USD. The next biggest are Czech Republic (29 billion EUR) and Hungary (18.3 billion USD). The others are considerably smaller, Latvia and Slovakia being the tiniest with market capitalisation only 1 billion EUR (as of October 2004). The turnover statistics (as of 2003) of Table 1 reveal that they are relatively smallest for Estonia, Latvia, Lithuania, Slovakia, and Slovenia, being in most cases

Table 1. Demographic, Economic, and Stock Exchange Statistics for European Emerging Markets and World Leading Markets.

Country	Population 2003 (mn)[a]	GDP (PPP, 2003) (bn USD)	GDP per capita (PPP, 2003) (USD)	GDP growth 1990–2001 (% p.a.)	Domestic Market Capitalisation as of 25 Oct 2004 (bn EUR)[b]	Turnover 2003 (bn EUR)[a]	Number of Listed Shares as End of Sept 2004[a]
Czech Republic	10.2	160	15,669	1.2	29.35	34.91	82
Estonia	1.3	17	12,190	0.2	3.87	0.49	13
Hungary[b]	9.9	144	14,574	1.9	18.34	8.60	50
Latvia	2.3	23	9,683	-2.2	1.05	0.12	12
Lithunia	3.4	38	11,036	-2.2	5.10	0.17	43
Poland	38.6	421	10,854	3.7	47.30	17.81	215
Slovakia[c]	5.4	72	13,363	2.1	1.03	0.41	14
Slovenia[d]	2.0	39	19,618	2.9	5.02	0.46	29
Germany[e]	82.5	2,256	27,351	1.5	798.27	2,277.25	684
UK[f]	59.3	1,606	26,929	2.7	1,386.84	1,876.92	2311
USA[g]	294.0	10,626	36,520	3.4	12,696.30	9,692.32	2747

[a]As of 25 October 2004.
[b]Market capitalisation as of 30 September 2004 in billion EUR, turnover in billion USD.
[c]Market capitalisation as of 31 December 2003.
[d]Shares on official list. Market capitalisation and turnover as of 30 September 2004.
[e]All German exchanges, market capitalisation as of 31 August 2004.
[f]UK listed, capitalisation and turnover in billion GBP, capitalisation as of 30 September 2004.
[g]NYSE, market capitalisation as of 30 September 2004 in billion USD, turnover in billion USD.

one-tenth of the market capitalisation. These indicate illiquidity which is typical to emerging markets.

The daily index returns are defined by log-differences as:

$$r_t = 100 \times \log(I_t/I_{t-1}) \tag{7}$$

where log is the natural logarithm and I_t is the index value of day t. Table 2 reports sample statistics for the returns. Generally, the sample period is characterised by a small positive daily mean return between 0.01 and 0.07 per cent for all other but Latvia and Lithuania for which the averages are slightly negative. Daily standard deviations range from 1.13 to 1.92 per cent or 18 to 31 per cent annual volatility which are about the same on the developed markets. All returns including developed markets are obviously leptokurtic, and most exhibit negative skewness. The exceptions are Slovenia with positive skewness, and USA and Lithuania with statistically non-significant skewnesses.

Table 3 reports contemporaneous correlation for the sample period. With few exceptions the correlations are positive. There are three clearly identifiable groups in the correlations: (Czech Republic, Hungary, Poland), (Estonia, Latvia, Lithuania, Slovakia, Slovenia), and (German, UK, USA). Czech Republic, Hungary, and Poland have pretty high mutual correlations of 0.556 (Czech Republic, Hungary), 0.415 (Czech Republic, Poland), and 0.605 (Hungary, Poland). Furthermore they are moderately correlated with the leading Western markets, particularly German and UK, for which the correlations are ranging from 0.337 to 0.419. Thus these markets do not have in this sense typical features of low correlations among themselves and developed markets. As noted in Bekaert and Harvey (2002), although it is not necessary that market integration leads to higher correlation, it usually is high among integrated markets. Consequently in this sense these three markets are getting more and more strongly integrated to the developed world capital markets. The second group of Estonia, Latvia, Lithuania, Slovakia, and Slovenia have the typical characteristics attributed to emerging markets. That is, as seen from Table 3, low mutual correlations and low correlations with developed markets. Only Estonia is correlated statistically significantly (mostly borderline) at the 5 per cent level[9] with the others in the group and the European developed markets. Even in this case the correlations are obviously low, ranging between 0.008 and 0.153. The third group consists of the developed markets with high mutual correlations, the highest being 0.718 between Germany and UK. The correlations with the USA are a bit lower: 0.418 (Germany, USA) and 0.501 (UK, USA).

Table 4 reports the individual autoregressive moving average (ARMA)–TGARCH specifications as given in (6). We have excluded some obvious

Table 2. Descriptive Statistics for National Daily Index Returns.

	CZE	HUN	POL	EST	SLO	SLV	LAT	LIT	US	UK	GER	WLD
Mean	0.022	0.013	0.017	0.059	0.002	0.069	-0.013	-0.025	0.024	0.010	0.021	0.015
Std deviation	1.241	1.402	1.917	1.958	1.384	1.130	1.921	1.381	1.213	1.200	1.710	0.927
Excess kurtosis	1.915	4.551	4.720	19.306	8.480	51.250	12.442	6.019	2.674	2.220	2.259	2.180
Skewness	-0.186	-0.369	-0.152	-1.113	-0.291	1.527	-0.926	0.039	-0.077	-0.169	-0.205	-0.140
Range	12.897	17.562	27.870	34.443	21.979	30.546	26.326	16.619	12.687	11.789	16.427	9.385
Minimum	-7.077	-9.459	-14.161	-21.577	-11.484	-11.613	-14.538	-7.383	-7.114	-5.885	-8.875	-4.825
Maximum	5.820	8.103	13.709	12.867	10.495	18.933	11.789	9.235	5.573	5.904	7.553	4.561
Count	2,146	2,146	2,146	2,146	2,146	2,146	1,974	1,928	2,146	2,146	2,146	2,146

Sample period of daily returns covers July 1996 to September 2004, except for Latvia and Lithuania that start on February 1997 and April 1997, respectively.

	CZE	HUN	POL	EST	SLO	SLV	LAT	LIT	US	UK	GER	WLD
Volatility	19.7	22.3	30.5	31.1	22.0	18.0	30.6	22.0	19.3	19.1	27.2	14.7
χ^2 (excess kurtosis)	327.9	1,851.7	1,991.7	33,325.8	6,429.8	234,860.6	12,731.6	2,910.4	639.4	440.6	456.5	424.8
P-val (excess kurtosis)	0.000	0.000	0.000	0.000	0.000	0.000	0.000	0.000	0.000	0.000	0.000	0.000
χ^2 (skewness)	12.43	48.58	8.30	443.29	30.22	834.30	282.29	0.49	2.10	10.19	14.97	7.01
P-val (skewness)	0.000	0.000	0.004	0.000	0.000	0.000	0.000	0.485	0.148	0.001	0.000	0.008
Jarque–Bera (JB)	340.3	1,900.3	2,000.0	33,769.1	6,460.0	235,694.9	13,013.9	2,910.9	641.5	450.8	471.5	431.8
P-val (JB)	0.000	0.000	0.000	0.000	0.000	0.000	0.000	0.000	0.000	0.000	0.000	0.000

Note: Daily index returns in the sample period 3 July 1996 to 21 September 2004 (Latvia starting in 2 February 1997 and Lithuania starting in 2 April 1997) are defined as differences in log-prices, $r_t = 100 \times (\log(I_t) - \log(I_{t-1}))$. Returns for national holidays are replaced by zeros. CZE: Czech Republic; HUN: Hungary; POL: Poland; EST: Estonia; SLO: Slovakia; SLV: Slovenia; LAT: Latvia; LIT: Lithunia; GER: Germany; WLD: Financial Times World Index.

Table 3. Contemporaneous Index Return Correlations Between National Market Returns.

	CZE	HUN	POL	EST	SLO	SLV	LAT	LIT	UK	GER	US	WLD
CZE	1											
HUN	0.556	1										
POL	0.413	0.605	1									
EST	0.135	0.191	0.189	1								
SLO	0.016	0.032	–0.001	0.008	1							
SLV	0.067	0.161	0.096	0.058	–0.009	1						
LAT	0.066	0.079	0.050	0.136	–0.016	0.017	1					
LIT	0.087	0.123	0.058	0.158	0.007	0.032	0.102	1				
UK	0.373	0.337	0.394	0.112	0.025	0.046	0.015	0.046	1			
GER	0.339	0.346	0.419	0.125	0.014	0.044	–0.006	0.017	0.718	1		
USA	0.200	0.156	0.203	0.031	0.019	–0.021	0.010	–0.039	0.418	0.501	1	
WLD	0.319	0.346	0.366	0.110	0.028	0.016	0.029	0.026	0.660	0.688	0.862	1
Average[a]	0.225	0.259	0.243	0.114	0.010	0.049	0.045	0.059	0.248	0.252	0.148	

Notes: Daily index returns in the sample period 3 July 1996 to 21 September 2004 (Latvia starting in 2 February 1997 and Lithuania starting in 2 April 1997) are defined as differences in log-prices, $r_t = 100 \times (\log(I_t) - \log(I_{t-1}))$. Returns for national holidays are replaced by zeros. For abbreviations to country names refer to footnote of Table 2.
[a]World market is excluded from the marketwise averages.

outliers from some of the series. Usually these had only an impact on skewness and kurtosis, but did not materially change the estimation results. The uppermost panel indicates that in most cases the returns of the emerging markets exhibit first-order autocorrelation. Latvia is an exception, where ARMA specification proved not to fit at all into the series, although the standardised residuals show strong autocorrelations. A reason for this is that in the Latvia return series there are lots of peaks as indicated in Fig. 1. So the series is pretty erratic, particularly in August 2001, which makes usual time series models not fitting the data. In 2001 Riga Stock Exchange adopted a new Enforcement Note on Securities, which fully complies the respective EU directives and requirements of the Nordic stock exchanges. As a consequence lists were restructured, which may have had some influence on stock general index. The 11 September 2001 impact is discernible in the index, but not that dramatic compared with the turbulence in latter half of August. The 11th September variation remained between ±6 per cent range.

For Slovenia and Lithuania the serial correlation is of ARMA(1,1) type, although some serial dependency may still be left behind particularly for Slovenia. There is no discernible autocorrelation in the returns of the major

Table 4. Conditional Variance Estimates for the Index Returns.

	CZE	HUN	POL	EST	SLO	SLV	LAT	LIT	UK	GER	US	WLD
Constant	0.048	0.029	0.037	0.075**	-0.014	0.042*	0.027	-0.010	0.001	0.041	0.011	0.011
Std error	0.025	0.030	0.035	0.029	0.028	0.018	0.025	0.034	0.020	0.027	0.021	0.019
AR(1)	0.143***	0.134***	0.048*	0.220***		0.178*		0.695**				
Std error	0.023	0.024	0.024	0.029		0.078		0.087				
MA(1)						0.195**		-0.566**				0.206***
Std error						0.076		0.099				0.021
Variance equation												
Constant	0.034***	0.023	0.046**	0.027*	0.186*	0.030***	0.285***	0.191***	0.016***	0.042***	0.029***	0.011***
Std error	0.009	0.013	0.016	0.013	0.086	0.008	0.057	0.039	0.005	0.012	0.007	0.003
ARCH(1)	0.082***	0.018	0.046***	0.099***	0.093*	0.353***	0.474***	0.207***	0.013	0.040*	-0.021	-0.009
Std error	0.021	0.011	0.013	0.031	0.049	0.085	0.093	0.047	0.504	0.020	0.014	0.010
ARCH(1)<0	0.040	0.039*	0.032	0.038	-0.016	0.025	0.079	0.065	0.100***	0.096***	0.168***	0.126***
Std error	0.032	0.020	0.018	0.093	0.047	0.104	0.165	0.069	0.023	0.027	0.028	0.024
GARCH(1)	0.879***	0.949***	0.925***	0.889***	0.822***	0.665***	0.508***	0.661***	0.930***	0.895***	0.918***	0.932***
Std error	0.016	0.018	0.013	0.035	0.067	0.047	0.060	0.039	0.011	0.016	0.016	0.011
Diagnostic statistics												
$Q(5)\ z$	4.649	3.840	7.034	12.079	3.290	9.674	20.196	5.258	10.024	1.387	3.935	4.348
P-val (Q(5) z)	0.325	0.428	0.134	0.017	0.510	0.022	0.001	0.154	0.075	0.926	0.559	0.361
$Q(5)\ z^2$	6.596	8.383	4.061	1.888	0.973	11.672	4.597	8.260	6.258	7.849	6.034	8.063
P-val (Q(5) z^2)	0.159	0.079	0.398	0.756	0.914	0.009	0.467	0.041	0.282	0.165	0.303	0.089
Skewness	-0.034	-0.056	0.101	0.252	-0.799	-0.331	-0.077	0.088	-0.324	-0.254	-0.355	-0.278
P-val (skewness)	0.525	0.288	0.056	0.000	0.000	0.000	0.162	0.115	0.000	0.000	0.000	0.000
Excess kurtosis	1.256	2.865	1.078	15.890	8.744	3.566	4.818	2.221	0.793	0.567	4.281	1.211
P-val (excess kurtosis)	0.000	0.000	0.000	0.000	0.000	0.000	0.000	0.000	0.000	0.000	0.000	0.000
Jarque–Bera (JB)	141.3	734.9	107.6	22,590.5	7,061.6	1,175.9	1,923.6	398.9	93.7	51.9	191.8	158.9
P-val (JB)	0.000	0.000	0.000	0.000	0.000	0.000	0.000	0.000	0.000	0.000	0.000	0.000
Outliers removed			2				3	3				
N	2,145	2,145	2,143	2,145	2,145	2,145	1,984	1,925	2,145	2,145	2,145	2,145

Notes: Standard errors are estimated using Bollerslev–Wooldridge (1992) robust procedure. Daily index returns in the sample period 3 July 1996 to 21 September 2004 (Latvia starting in 2 February 1997 and Lithuania starting in 2 April 1997) are defined as differences in log-prices, $r_t = 100 \times (\log(I_t) - \log(I_{t-1}))$. Returns for national holidays are replaced by zeros. For abbreviations to country names refer to footnote of Table 2.
Significant at
*5%,
**1%, and
***0.1% level.

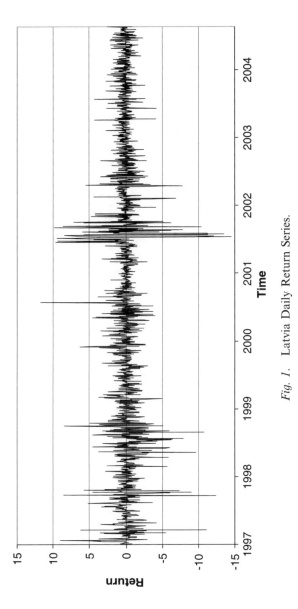

Fig. 1. Latvia Daily Return Series.

European markets or the USA. Thus the results fully support those found in other emerging market studies (e.g. see Bekaert et al., 1998). It is notable that the world market index returns have a strongly statistically significant moving average MA(1) autocorrelation. The middle panel of Table 4 reports the TGARCH estimation results. In each market the GARCH structure is evident. However, unlike the developed market no statistically discernible asymmetry can be found from the European emerging markets. In the case of Hungary the asymmetry component is just borderline statistically signif-icant (*P*-value 0.047). Finally the lower panel of Table 4 reports relevant diagnostic statistics of the ARMA–GARCH residuals. As discussed above, the ARMA estimates did not indicate any statistical significance in the Latvian returns, although there is strong autocorrelation in the residuals. In the same manner Estonia and Slovenia have some autocorrelation in the residuals. In numerical terms, however, these are small (the first-order residual autocorrelation for Estonia is 0.045 and for Slovenia 0.040), but become statistically significant due to the large number of observation. In the case of the developed markets no discernible autocorrelation can be found in the returns. In addition the TGARCH proves to capture statis-tically adequately the second-order dependencies in the returns.

Table 5 reports the contemporaneous correlations of the volatilities (square roots of the estimated GARCH series). The pattern of the correlation matrix is pretty much identical to that of the return correlations. Again Czech

Table 5.   Correlations of GARCH Volatilities.

	CZE	HUN	POL	EST	SLO	SLV	LAT	LIT	UK	GER	US	WLD
CZE	1											
HUN	0.640	1										
POL	0.512	0.863	1									
EST	0.218	0.610	0.662	1								
SLO	−0.019	0.053	0.045	0.090	1							
SLV	0.235	0.306	0.329	0.282	−0.079	1						
LAT	0.161	0.256	0.267	0.252	−0.047	0.091	1					
LIT	0.239	0.422	0.428	0.417	−0.006	0.191	0.260	1				
UK	0.453	0.464	0.330	0.151	0.069	0.298	0.123	0.115	1			
GER	0.369	0.422	0.298	0.170	0.002	0.352	0.165	0.161	0.889	1		
USA	0.569	0.557	0.397	0.192	0.005	0.374	0.139	0.168	0.801	0.737	1	
WLD	0.516	0.572	0.396	0.230	0.022	0.316	0.145	0.181	0.856	0.830	0.914	1
Average[a]	0.338	0.459	0.413	0.304	0.011	0.238	0.167	0.240	0.369	0.356	0.394	

Note: For abbreviations to country names refer to footnote of Table 2.
[a]World market is excluded from the marketwise averages.

Republic, Hungary, and Poland share fairly high mutual volatility correlations and are moderately correlated with the major Western volatilities, whereas Estonia, Latvia, Lithuania, Slovakia, and Slovenia have noticeably smaller correlations among themselves and with all other markets. Again the three developed markets are mutually highly volatility correlated, and have high correlations with the world market volatility. Consequently, the sample statistics of Tables 4 and 5 indicate that the developed markets have high co-movements both in returns and volatilities, while the emerging markets, particularly Estonia, Latvia, Lithuania, Slovakia, and Slovenia, have much lower degree of co-movement in both returns and volatilities among themselves and with the developed markets. The next section presents results regarding time variability of the correlation.

4. CONTEMPORANEOUS CORRELATIONS

Before estimating the correlation models, let us look at some preliminary tests on the time variability of the correlations. Assuming in Eq. (1) that the variables u_t and v_t have zero means, the standardised series, $\varepsilon_{u,t} = u_t/\sigma_{ut}$ and $\varepsilon_{v,t} = v_t/\sigma_{vt}$, are i.i.d $(0,1)$, and the conditional correlation (1) can be written as:

$$\rho_{uv,t} = E_{t-1}(\varepsilon_{u,t}\varepsilon_{v,t}) \tag{8}$$

In an analogous manner with preliminary ARCH testing (Engle, 1982) a Lagrange Multiplier (LM) statistic can be used as a preliminary check for the time variability of the contemporaneous correlations. For the purpose define the auxiliary regression:

$$z_t = \beta_0 + \sum_{j=1}^{q} \beta_j z_{t-j} + e_t \tag{9}$$

where $z_t = \varepsilon_{u,t}\varepsilon_{v,t}$ and e_t is a residual term. Computing the R-square of the regression gives an LM statistic TR^2, where T is the number of observation. The asymptotic distribution of the LM statistic under the null hypothesis of no serial dependency is $\chi^2(q)$. Another popular test is the Ljung–Box (LB, Ljung & Box, 1979) statistic:

$$Q_{LB}(q) = T(T+2) \sum_{j=1}^{q} \tau_j^2/(T-q) \tag{10}$$

SEPPO PYNNÖNEN

where τ_j is the jth autocorrelation of z_t. Again $Q_{LB}(q)$ is asymptotically $\chi^2(q)$ distributed if the series is white noise. In our case both of these test gave virtually the same results. We report only the LB statistics.

Table 6 reports LB statistics for the time variability of the contemporaneous correlations up to the first five lags. The preliminary results indicate time variability of Czech Republic particularly with Poland, and possibly with UK and Germany. Similarly the test suggests time variability in the correlations of (Hungary, Slovenia), (Hungary, USA), (Poland, UK), (Estonia, Latvia), (Slovenia, Germany), and in the developed market pairs of (German, UK) and (German, USA).

In order to investigate more closely the time variability and drivers of the contemporaneous correlation we use the following general specification of Eq. (5) for the markets i and j:

$$y_{ij,t} = x_t \beta_{ij} + c_t \eta_{ij} \tag{11}$$

where $y_{ij,t} = \log[(1 + \rho_{ij,t})/(1 - \rho_{ij,t})]$, x_t is a vector including the constant term and log-volatilities, c_t includes possible additional variables, like ARMA terms.

As found in the previous section, the returns and volatilities are highly correlated particularly between the developed markets, which suggest that there are common factors behind them. The high correlation may cause

Table 6. LB Test Statistics with Five Lags for Testing Time Variation of Contemporaneous Correlations.

	CZE	HUN	POL	EST	SLO	SLV	LAT	LIT	UK	GER
HUN	4.2									
POL	28.5***	4.1								
EST	8.7	2.4	6.2							
SLO	5.7	2.0	1.1	4.8						
SLV	1.1	17.1**	6.1	4.5	4.0					
LAT	3.1	8.4	3.7	12.7*	8.1	7.1				
LIT	8.0	7.9	3.1	3.8	5.6	3.9	9.0			
UK	14*	2.4	12.2*	5.0	5.2	9.9	7.3	5.1		
GER	13.7*	10.3	3.8	7.5	19.2**	9.2	10.3	2.4	12.8*	
USA	4.7	13.5*	10.1	4.6	5.6	5.5	9.0	8.6	7.8	18.7**

Note: For abbreviations to country names refer to footnote of Table 2.
Designate statistical significance at
*5%,
**1%, and
***0.1% level, respectively.

multicollinearity problem in estimating Eq. (11). Consequently we simplify Eq. (11) by using only the world market volatility in the developed market equations. We also include the previous day world return into the equations to designate the response of the co-movement of the countries to the world markets. Thus Eq. (11) for developed–developed market correlations (USA/UK, USA/Germany, UK/Germany) is specified as:

$$y_{ij,t} = \omega + \beta_{w,v} \log(h_{w,t}) + \beta_{w,r} r_{w,t-1} + \beta_{AR} y_{ij,t-1} \tag{12}$$

for a developed–emerging market correlation (j = emerging market) as:

$$y_{ij,t} = \omega + \beta_{j,v} \log(h_{j,t}) + \beta_{w,v} \log(h_{w,v})$$
$$+ \beta_{w,r} r_{w,t-1} + \beta_{AR} y_{ij,t-1} \tag{13}$$

and for a emerging–emerging market correlation as:

$$y_{ij,t} = \omega + \beta_i \log(h_{i,t}) + \beta_i \log(h_{j,t})$$
$$+ \beta_{w,v} \log(h_{w,t}) + \beta_{w,r} r_{w,t-1} + \beta_{AR} y_{ij,t-1} \tag{14}$$

where $h_{w,t}$ is the world index return TGARCH volatility, $r_{w,t}$ is the world index return, and $h_{i,t}$ and $h_{j,t}$ are local market return TGARCH volatilities. The AR term ($y_{ij,t-1}$) is introduced to the model only if needed. The parameters are estimated with the two-step maximum likelihood of the same type as given in Engle (2002) (details are given in Knif et al., 2005).

Tables 7–10 report the estimation results of the correlation models (12)–(14). Table 7 presents the developed market dependencies on the global (world index) conditional volatility and the previous day return.[10] The results of Table 7 indicate that the global volatility is significant in each contemporaneous correlation with positive coefficient. This shows that the contemporaneous correlation tends to be higher when world markets are globally more volatile. The previous day world index return is also statistically significant with positive coefficients in all but the UK/German correlation. Thus the next day correlations are directly related to the previous day index change such that the previous day negative returns tend to decrease the next day correlation and positive returns increase it. Earlier studies have found that the contemporaneous correlation increases with market drops (e.g. Longin & Solnik, 2001). This is not necessarily in contradiction with the findings of this chapter, because we have the previous period market movement in the equation. The first-order autoregressive coefficient is also highly statistically significant in each equation. The positive high AR coefficients suggest strong persistence in the correlations. Finally, the multivariate LB tests indicate that there is no discernible time variation left in the residuals.

Table 7. Dependence of Mutual Correlations Between US, UK, and Germany on the Changes of World Volatility and Asymmetric Shock.

	US/UK			US/GER			UK/GER		
	Coeff	Std error	P-val	Coeff	Std error	P-val	Coeff	Std error	P-val
Constant	0.504	0.108	0.000	0.604	0.166	0.000	0.465	0.173	0.007
World volatility	0.117	0.058	0.042	0.391	0.107	0.000	0.236	0.098	0.016
World return (t–1)	0.386	0.089	0.000	0.366	0.106	0.001	0.073	0.064	0.254
AR(1)	0.487	0.111	0.000	0.496	0.143	0.001	0.741	0.096	0.000
Diagnostic statistics	Stat	P-val		Stat	P-val		Stat	P-val	
QM(2)	1.234	0.872		0.674	0.955		3.935	0.415	
QM(5)	15.835	0.465		12.945	0.677		22.182	0.137	
Observations	2,143			2,143			2,143		

Notes: The estimated equation is of the form Eq. (12). The sample period covers daily observations from 4 July 1996 to 21 September 2004. QM(2) and QM(5) are multivariate LB statistics at lags 2 and 5, respectively (Hosking 1980; Knif et al., 2005).
For abbreviations to country names refer to footnote of Table 2.

Table 8 reports the results of correlations between the developed markets and the emerging markets group of Czech Republic, Hungary, and Poland that have the highest emerging market mutual correlations and are most strongly correlated with the developed markets (Table 3). The estimated equation is Eq. (13) where the local volatility is the emerging market GARCH volatility. The world volatility is statistically significant in all but the USA/Poland, UK/Czech Republic, Germany/Czech Republic, and Germany/Poland correlations. All coefficient estimates are positive indicating that the global volatility again tends to increase the correlation of these emerging markets with the developed markets. The local volatilities are statistically significant in the emerging market correlations with the two European leading markets (some cases are borderline), but not in the correlations with the USA. Again, the coefficients are positive suggesting that under volatile emerging market periods their returns tend to follow increasingly the European leading markets. Finally, contrary to the developed market correlations, the world previous day index return is generally not statistically significant in the correlations. USA/Poland is the only exception and USA/Czech Republic is on the borderline. The multivariate LB tests indicate that the models capture the first-order time variation in all series. However, there may be some longer-order dependencies particularly in the USA/Poland and UK/Poland equations. Table 9 reports the results of the developed market correlations with the rest of the emerging markets. As

Table 8. Dependence of Mutual Correlations Between Developed and Emerging Markets of Czech Republic, Hungary, and Poland on the Changes of World Volatility and World Asymmetric Shock.

	US/CZE (v_2)			US/HUN (v_2)			US/POL (v_2)			UK/CZE (v_2)			UK/HUN (v_2)			UK/POL (v_2)		
	Coeff	Std error	p-val	Coeff	Std Error	p-val	Coeff	Std error	p-val	Coeff	Std error	p-val	Coeff	Std error	p-val	Coeff	Std error	p-val
Constant	0.184	0.030	0.000	0.403	0.109	0.000	0.355	0.102	0.001	0.028	0.014	0.043	0.583	0.085	0.000	0.595	0.102	0.000
Local volatility (v_2)	0.047	0.082	0.711	-0.032	0.247	0.899	0.215	0.142	0.129	0.061	0.018	0.001	0.438	0.223	0.050	0.447	0.138	0.001
World volatility	0.226	0.085	0.008	0.398	0.203	0.049	0.217	0.153	0.155	0.008	0.014	0.570	0.546	0.180	0.002	0.349	0.138	0.011
World return ($t-1$)	0.132	0.067	0.049	0.167	0.103	0.107	0.246	0.104	0.018	0.019	0.030	0.527	0.090	0.084	0.283	0.062	0.088	0.482
AR(1)	0.592	0.105	0.000	—	—	—	—	—	—	0.950	0.019	0.000	—	—	—	—	—	—
Diagnostics	Stat		p-val	Stat		p-val	Stat		p-val	Stat		p-val	Stat		p-val	Stat		p-val
QM(2)	8.910		0.063	8.190		0.085	8.868		0.064	4.382		0.357	3.275		0.513	8.432		0.077
QM(5)	22.84		0.118	26.05		0.053	30.73		0.015	21.68		0.154	21.38		0.164	34.32		0.005
Observations	2,143			2,143			2,143			2,143			2,143			1,970		

	GER/CZE (v_2)			GER/HUN (v_2)			GER/POL (v_2)		
	Coeff	Std error	p-val	Coeff	Std Error	p-val	Coeff	Std error	p-val
Constant	1.043	0.231	0.000	0.623	0.077	0.000	0.202	0.091	0.026
Local volatility (v_2)	1.048	0.331	0.002	0.389	0.213	0.068	0.272	0.135	0.045
World volatility	0.284	0.269	0.292	0.465	0.164	0.004	0.117	0.070	0.094
World return ($t-1$)	-0.099	0.092	0.283	0.007	0.097	0.942	0.010	0.058	0.862
AR(1)	-0.748	0.347	0.031	—	—	—	0.616	0.160	0.000
Diagnostics	Stat		p-val	Stat		p-val	Stat		p-val
QM(2)	4.276		0.370	5.118		0.275	5.346		
QM(5)	14.61		0.553	15.57		0.483	19.61		0.238
Observations	2,143			2,143			2,143		

Note: Estimation results of Eq. (13). The sample period covers daily observations from 4 July 1996 to 21 September 2004. QM(2) and QM(5) are multivariate LB statistics at lags 2 and 5, respectively (Hosking, 1980; Knif et al., 2005). The standard errors are robustified with White (1980) heteroscedasticity correction.

Table 9. Dependence of Mutual Correlations Between Developed and Emerging Markets of Estonia, Slovakia, Slovenia, Lithuania, and Latvia on the Emerging Local Volatility, Global Volatility, and Global Return Changes.

	US/EST (v_2)			US/SLO (v_2)			US/SLV (v_2)			US/LAT (v_2)			US/LIT (v_2)		
	Coeff	Std error	p-val	Coeff	Std error	p-val	Coeff	Std error	p-val	Coeff	Std error	p-val	Coeff	Std error	p-val
Constant	0.142	0.064	0.026	0.022	0.006	0.000	-0.004	0.073	0.942	0.078	0.104	0.451	0.082	0.110	0.453
Local volatility (v_2)	-0.032	0.080	0.690	-0.005	0.023	0.815	0.107	0.085	0.204	-0.083	0.322	0.797	-0.680	0.354	0.054
World volatility	0.117	0.144	0.418	0.056	0.036	0.115	0.077	0.143	0.590	0.318	0.321	0.322	0.356	0.354	0.314
World return ($t-1$)	-0.047	0.119	0.694	0.124	0.049	0.011	0.041	0.093	0.660	-0.062	0.081	0.445	-0.071	0.095	0.458
AR(1)	-	-	-	0.790	0.073	0.000	-	-	-	-	-	-	-	-	-

Diagnostics	Stat	p-val		Stat	p-val		Stat	p-val		Stat	p-val		Stat	p-val	
QM(2)	4.310	0.366		2.006	0.735		6.513	0.164		9.912	0.042		18.198	0.001	
QM(5)	21.04	0.177		10.67	0.828		16.86	0.395		23.15	0.110		36.32	0.003	
Observations	2,143			2,143			2,143			1,970			1,925		

	UK/EST (v_2)			UK/SLO (v_2)			UK/SLV (v_2)			UK/LAT (v_2)			UK/LIT (v_2)		
	Coeff	Std error	p-val	Coeff	Std error	p-val	Coeff	Std error	p-val	Coeff	Std error	p-val	Coeff	Std error	p-val
Constant	0.454	0.061	0.000	0.009	0.101	0.932	0.142	0.058	0.014	0.033	0.082	0.688	0.164	0.073	0.024
Local volatility (v_2)	-0.179	0.080	0.024	0.178	0.305	0.560	0.051	0.097	0.597	0.115	0.268	0.667	-0.189	0.243	0.437
World volatility	0.457	0.130	0.000	0.149	0.158	0.346	0.098	0.091	0.282	0.160	0.273	0.559	0.381	0.273	0.163
World return ($t-1$)	-0.104	0.100	0.300	0.059	0.102	0.563	-0.075	0.064	0.241	-0.039	0.085	0.648	-0.006	0.095	0.951
AR(1)	-	-	-	-	-	-	-	-	-	-	-	-	-	-	-

Diagnostics	GER/EST (v₂)		GER/SLO (v₂)		GER/SLV (v₂)		GER/LAT (v₂)		GER/LIT (v₂)	
	Stat	p-val	Stat	p-val	Stat	p-val	Stat	p-val	Stat	p-val
QM(2)	4.340	0.362	1.506	0.826	3.183	0.528	10.721	0.030	20.143	0.000
QM(5)	22.28	0.134	15.33	0.501	26.47	0.048	27.43	0.037	48.82	0.000
Observations	2,143		2,143		2,143		1,970		1,925	

	GER/EST (v₂)			GER/SLO (v₂)			GER/SLV (v₂)			GER/LAT (v₂)			GER/LIT (v₂)		
	Coeff	Std error	p-val	Coeff	Std error	p-val	Coeff	Std error	p-val	Coeff	Std error	p-val	Coeff	Std error	p-val
Constant	0.433	0.063	0.000	−0.099	0.101	0.330	0.124	0.051	0.015	0.263	0.158	0.097	−0.004	0.131	0.973
Local volatility (v_2)	−0.149	0.093	0.111	0.313	0.282	0.267	0.143	0.058	0.014	−0.402	0.261	0.124	0.112	0.224	0.617
World volatility	0.409	0.180	0.023	−0.071	0.149	0.634	0.057	0.068	0.399	0.766	0.304	0.012	−0.221	0.254	0.385
World return ($t-1$)	−0.093	0.103	0.364	−0.087	0.099	0.378	−0.086	0.098	0.381	−0.041	0.094	0.661	0.055	0.096	0.568
AR(1)	–	–	–	–	–	–	–	–	–	–	–	–	–	–	–

Diagnostic statistics	GER/EST (v₂)		GER/SLO (v₂)		GER/SLV (v₂)		GER/LAT (v₂)		GER/LIT (v₂)	
	Stat	p-val	Stat	p-val	Stat	p-val	Stat	p-val	Stat	p-val
QM(2)	3.345	0.502	1.099	0.893	3.543	0.471	20.143	0.000	19.447	0.001
QM(5)	18.255	0.309	8.010	0.949	19.395	0.249	48.815	0.000	37.463	0.002
Observations	2,143		2,143		2,143		1,970		1,925	

Notes: The estimated equation is of the form Eq. (13). The sample period covers daily observations from 4 July 1996 to 21 September 2004, except for Latvia and Lithuania for which the starting dates are 3 February 1997 and 7 April 1997, respectively. QM(2) and QM(5) are multivariate LB statistics at lags 2 and 5, respectively (Hosking, 1980; Knif et al., 2005). The standard errors are robustified with White (1980) heteroscedasticity correction.

For abbreviations to country names refer to footnote of Table 2.

Table 10. Dependence of Mutual Correlations Between Emerging Markets on Local and Global Volatilities and Global Return Changes.

	CZE (v_1)/HUN (v_2)			CZE (v_1)/POL (v_2)			HUN (v_1)/POL (v_2)			CZE (v_1)/EST (v_2)			CZE (v_1)/SLO (v_2)			CZE (v_1)/SLV (v_2)		
	Coeff	Std error	p-val	Coeff	Std error	p-val	Coeff	Std error	p-val	Coeff	Std error	p-val	Coeff	Std error	p-val	Coeff	Std error	p-val
Constant	1.081	0.099	0.000	0.633	0.112	0.000	1.824	0.146	0.000	0.530	0.074	0.000	0.060	0.086	0.486	0.170	0.066	0.010
Local volatility (v_1)	0.275	0.244	0.260	0.976	0.177	0.000	0.276	0.316	0.382	0.010	0.203	0.962	-0.366	0.175	0.037	-0.024	0.165	0.883
Local volatility (v_2)	0.059	0.276	0.832	0.060	0.176	0.733	-0.727	0.278	0.009	0.238	0.098	0.015	0.305	0.244	0.213	-0.035	0.092	0.701
World volatility	-0.011	0.223	0.961	-0.020	0.186	0.913	0.835	0.197	0.000	0.650	0.150	0.000	0.341	0.167	0.041	0.216	0.161	0.180
World return ($t-1$)	0.004	0.106	0.973	-0.139	0.114	0.226	0.019	0.100	0.849	0.066	0.093	0.479	0.021	0.089	0.811	0.022	0.075	0.771
AR(1)	—			—			—			—			—			—		
Diagnostics	Stat	p-val		Stat	p-val		Stat	p-val		Stat	p-val		Stat	p-val		Stat	p-val	
QM(2)	7.44	0.114		14.64	0.005		6.34	0.175		5.54	0.236		2.92	0.572		6.36	0.174	
QM(5)	26.67	0.045		26.95	0.042		11.99	0.744		21.22	0.170		15.06	0.520		19.27	0.255	
Observations	2,143			2,143			2,143			2,143			2,143			1,970		

	CZE (v_1)/LAT (v_2)			CZE (v_1)/LIT (v_2)			HUN (v_1)/EST (v_2)			HUN (v_1)/SLO (v_2)			HUN (v_2)/SLV (v_2)			HUN (v_1)/LAT (v_2)		
	Coeff	Std error	p-val	Coeff	Std error	p-val	Coeff	Std error	p-val	Coeff	Std error	p-val	Coeff	Std error	p-val	Coeff	Std error	p-val
Constant	0.093	0.083	0.265	0.086	0.063	0.170	0.730	0.097	0.000	0.092	0.116	0.430	0.345	0.088	0.000	0.124	0.165	0.450
Local volatility (v_1)	-0.226	0.156	0.146	0.275	0.197	0.162	-0.301	0.271	0.266	0.184	0.174	0.290	0.321	0.209	0.125	0.615	0.367	0.094
Local volatility (v_2)	0.172	0.098	0.079	0.041	0.076	0.586	-0.172	0.102	0.090	0.190	0.303	0.532	0.118	0.091	0.196	0.018	0.119	0.877
World volatility	0.247	0.167	0.140	0.062	0.174	0.723	0.795	0.159	0.000	0.158	0.184	0.392	0.571	0.159	0.000	0.527	0.261	0.044
World return ($t-1$)	-0.059	0.089	0.509	0.024	0.083	0.030	0.090	0.084	0.736	0.035	0.075	0.640	0.068	0.091	0.453	0.288	0.083	0.001
AR(1)	—			—			—			—			—			-0.585	0.193	0.002
Diagnostics	Stat	p-val		Stat	p-val		Stat	p-val		Stat	p-val		Stat	p-val		Stat	p-val	
QM(2)	9.89	0.042		17.51	0.002		4.16	0.385		3.44	0.487		5.01	0.287		12.72	0.013	
QM(5)	25.09	0.068		39.88	0.001		19.83	0.228		13.91	0.606		15.79	0.468		25.57	0.060	
Observations	1,972			2,143			2,143			2,143			2,143			1,925		

Panel 1

	HUN (v_1)/LIT (v_2)			POL (v_1)/EST (v_2)			POL (v_1)/SLO (v_2)			POL (v_1)/SLV (v_2)			POL (v_1)/LAT (v_2)			POL (v_1)/LIT (v_2)		
	Coeff	Std error	P-val	Coeff	Std error	P-val	Coeff	Std error	P-val	Coeff	Std error	P-val	Coeff	Std error	P-val	Coeff	Std error	P-val
Constant	0.160	0.088	0.069	0.689	0.117	0.000	-0.009	0.144	0.952	0.013	0.108	0.902	0.098	0.151	0.517	0.155	0.117	0.182
Local volatility (v_1)	0.208	0.230	0.365	-0.389	0.195	0.045	-0.097	0.164	0.554	0.357	0.159	0.025	0.253	0.206	0.219	0.028	0.184	0.881
Local volatility (v_2)	0.037	0.099	0.705	0.051	0.101	0.617	0.114	0.279	0.684	0.032	0.084	0.707	0.008	0.110	0.942	-0.053	0.086	0.536
World volatility	-0.089	0.223	0.691	0.434	0.169	0.010	-0.248	0.170	0.754	0.312	0.128	0.015	0.010	0.201	0.962	0.094	0.206	0.648
World return ($t-1$)	0.036	0.086	0.675	-0.146	0.104	0.162	-0.008	0.080	0.040	-0.093	0.101	0.360	0.088	0.098	0.366	-0.013	0.095	0.892
AR(1)	—			—			—			—			—			—		
Diagnostics	Stat	P-val		Stat	P-val		Stat	P-val		Stat	P-val		Stat	P-val		Stat	P-val	
QM(2)	18.96	0.001		7.82	0.098		4.62	0.329		7.95	0.093		16.62	0.002		34.52	0.000	
QM(5)	49.69	0.000		24.48	0.080		17.89	0.330		21.92	0.146		28.86	0.025		61.82	0.000	
Observations	2,143			2,143			2,143			2,143			1,970			1,925		

Panel 2

	EST (v_1)/SLO (v_2)			EST (v_1)/SLV (v_2)			EST (v_1)/LAT (v_2)			EST (v_1)/LIT (v_2)			SLO (v_1)/SLV (v_2)			SLO (v_1)/LAT (v_2)		
	Coeff	Std error	P-val	Coeff	Std error	P-val	Coeff	Std error	P-val	Coeff	Std error	P-val	Coeff	Std error	P-val	Coeff	Std error	P-val
Constant	-0.043	0.095	0.652	0.232	0.075	0.002	0.116	0.128	0.366	0.326	0.067	0.000	0.079	0.089	0.376	0.169	0.101	0.095
Local volatility (v_1)	0.040	0.082	0.630	-0.109	0.077	0.159	0.092	0.121	0.448	-0.163	0.100	0.103	0.122	0.273	0.655	-0.461	0.277	0.097
Local volatility (v_2)	0.301	0.287	0.294	0.117	0.093	0.209	-0.039	0.211	0.853	0.144	0.160	0.368	0.208	0.069	0.003	-0.100	0.098	0.307
World volatility	0.328	0.132	0.013	0.206	0.116	0.076	-0.309	0.209	0.140	0.245	0.132	0.064	0.118	0.115	0.307	0.167	0.145	0.249
World return ($t-1$)	0.053	0.091	0.562	-0.135	0.076	0.073	0.042	0.101	0.679	0.058	0.106	0.586	0.133	0.070	0.057	-0.092	0.082	0.262
AR(1)	—			—			—			—			—			—		
Diagnostics	Stat	P-val		Stat	P-val		Stat	P-val		Stat	P-val		Stat	P-val		Stat	P-val	
QM(2)	2.04	0.728		9.53	0.049		13.34	0.010		19.88	0.001		5.03	0.284		18.45	0.001	
QM(5)	13.80	0.614		38.31	0.001		28.78	0.025		44.38	0.000		14.97	0.527		37.30	0.002	
Observations	2,143			2,143			1,970			1,925			1,970			1,925		

Panel 3

	SLO (v_1)/LIT (v_2)			SLV (v_1)/LAT (v_2)			SLV (v_1)/LIT (v_2)			LAT (v_1)/LIT (v_2)		
	Coeff	Std error	p-val	Coeff	Std error	p-val	Coeff	Std error	p-val	Coeff	Std error	p-val
Constant	-0.094	0.094	0.317	0.154	0.074	0.038	0.046	0.070	0.508	0.121	0.065	0.064
Local volatility (v_1)	0.579	0.288	0.044	0.116	0.088	0.188	-0.133	0.111	0.230	0.152	0.099	0.124
Local volatility (v_2)	-0.126	0.086	0.145	-0.145	0.090	0.107	-0.049	0.113	0.664	-0.037	0.095	0.697
World volatility	0.150	0.119	0.207	0.074	0.144	0.607	0.143	0.163	0.381	0.131	0.155	0.399

Table 10. (Continued)

	SLO (v_1)/LIT (v_2)			SLV (v_1)/LAT (v_2)			SLV (v_1)/LIT (v_2)			LAT (v_1)/LIT (v_2)		
	Coeff	Std error	p-val	Coeff	Std error	p-val	Coeff	Std error	p-val	Coeff	Std error	p-val
World return (t−1)	0.000	0.091	0.998	−0.189	0.074	0.011	−0.089	0.086	0.302	−0.107	0.158	0.500
AR(1)	–	–	–	–	–	–	–	–	–	–	–	–
Diagnostic statistics	Stat	p-val		Stat	p-val		Stat	p-val		Stat	p-val	
QM(2)	17.86	0.001		12.22	0.016		18.70	0.001		8.14	0.087	
QM(5)	43.75	0.000		26.72	0.045		42.91	0.000		21.57	0.158	
Observations	2,143			2,143			2,143			2,143		

Notes: The estimated equation is of the form (14). The sample period covers daily observations from 4 July 1996 to 21 September 2004, except for Latvia and Lithuania for which the starting dates are 3 February 1997 and 7 April 1997, respectively. QM(2) and QM(5) are multivariate LB statistics at lags 2 and 5, respectively (Hosking, 1980; Knif et al., 2005). The standard errors are robustified with White (1980) heteroscedasticity correction.

For abbreviations to country names refer to footnote of Table 2.

found in Table 3, these markets have the lowest unconditional correlations with all other markets. This seems to be generally the case also with the conditional correlations. There are few exceptions like UK/Estonia and Germany/Estonia, where the world market volatility is statistically significant. In the UK/Estonia correlation the local (Estonian) volatility is significant and negative, suggesting that it reduces the return co-variation. The multivariate LB statistics also indicate that there is no additional time variation in any of the series. The exceptions are pairs where Latvia and Lithuania are involved. The problems with these series lie in their erratic behaviour that is not captured adequately by the univariate ARMA–GARCH processes.

Finally, Table 10 reports the sole emerging market correlation results. In each equation both of the local volatilities are included in addition to the world volatility and world previous day return. Structuring the results according to the correlation blocks in Table 3, we find that in the group of the highest emerging market correlations of the Czech Republic, Hungary and Poland, Hungary/Poland seem to be sensitive to world market volatility while the Czech Republic/Poland correlation is sensitive to local (Czech Republic) volatility. The Czech Republic/Hungary correlation also seems to be independent of local and global volatility factors, and hence essentially time invariant. These results are consistent with the preliminary tests of Table 6 suggesting that in this group only the Czech Republic/Poland correlation is time variant. The multivariate LB test on the residuals remains, however, highly statistically significant. Nevertheless, the univariate LB test given in Eq. (10) gets values $LB(1) = 0.216$ (*P*-value 0.642) and $LB(5) = 10.8$ (*P*-value 0.055) suggesting that the possible dependencies are of some other type than time varying correlation.

The next block in Table 3 consists of correlations between the Czech Republic, Hungary, and Poland with Estonia, Slovakia, Slovenia, Latvia, and Lithuania. All these unconditional cross-correlations are small, being below 0.20, and mostly below 0.10. Table 6 suggests that only the Hungary/Slovenia correlation might be time varying. However, the more structured analysis of Table 10 reveals that there are a number of other pairs that should be time varying via time varying volatilities. The world market volatility is statistically significant in Czech Republic/Estonia, Czech Republic/Slovakia, Hungary/Estonia, Hungary/Latvia, Poland/Estonia, and Poland/Slovakia correlations. In all but Hungary/Latvia, the coefficient is positive. In the Czech Republic/Estonia, Czech Republic/Slovenia, and Poland/Estonia correlations, one of the local volatilities is statistically significant. In each case, the global world volatility has a positive sign and the local volatility a negative sign. This indicates again that increasing global uncertainty tends to increase the return co-variation, whereas local volatility reduces the return co-variation. In the Poland/Slovenia correlation, the sign of the local volatility (Polish volatility) is positive, which might indicate that an increased volatility in a larger neighbouring market can raise the common return behaviour. Except for some occasional cases, the previous day's global world market return is not statistically significant in the correlations.

The last block consists of mutual correlations between the unconditionally least correlated markets of Estonia, Slovakia, Slovenia, Latvia, and Lithuania. The results are reported in the fourth and fifth panels of Table 10. Table 6 suggests that the Estonia/Latvia correlation is time varying. However, the fourth panel of Table 10 shows that none of the explanatory variables are statistically significant in the equation. In this as in most other cases with the Latvian correlation, the multivariate LB test shows serial dependency in the residuals. We consequently conclude that the serial dependency is of some other type than time varying contemporaneous correlation.

Although Table 6 does not indicate any other time variable correlations in this group, the fourth panel of Table 10 suggests that the Estonia/Slovakia correlation depends on global volatility with a positive coefficient. Table 3 on the other hand shows that the Estonia/Slovakia unconditional correlation is statistically zero. This particular case demonstrates that even if the unconditional correlation is zero, the conditional correlation may at times be non-zero depending on global conditions. In all, the general picture in this group is that the conditional correlations are usually zero, and mostly do not depend on global market conditions like the developed market correlations.

5. SUMMARY AND CONCLUSION

In this chapter we have analysed the dependence of contemporaneous return correlations of European emerging markets on local and global volatilities. The markets included were Check Republic, Estonia, Hungary, Latvia, Lithuania, Poland, Slovakia, and Slovenia. The major European developed markets of Germany and UK as well as the USA were included in the analysis as references. On the basis of the strength of the unconditional contemporaneous correlations, the markets clustered into three groups: the developed markets as one block; the largest emerging markets of Czech Republic, Hungary, and Poland as a second block; and Estonia, Latvia, Lithuania, Slovakia, and Slovenia as a third block. In this last group, the unconditional correlations are low both mutually and with the other two groups. The volatilities, however, are clustering on all markets. The major difference between the developed and the emerging markets in this respect is the asymmetry which is clearly present in the developed market volatilities and, without one borderline exception, missing from the emerging market conditional volatilities. Otherwise the results of the study indicate that among the developed markets, the increasing world conditional volatility and the previous day's return have a direct impact on the next day contemporaneous correlation. World volatility has a similar increasing influence on the contemporaneous correlations between the largest European emerging markets of Czech Republic, Hungary, and Poland with the developed markets of Germany, UK, and the USA. This indicates that emerging markets tend to be also part of the world economy and sensitive to the global risk trends. The world market return on the other hand does not show up statistically significant in these correlations. The role of the local emerging market volatility does not have an equally unambiguous role as the global volatility in the correlation equations. An a priori hypothesis would have been that local volatility should reflect foremost local uncertainty, and hence should weaken the mutual correlations. The estimation result remains, however, in this respect rather inconclusive, for the signs, when statistically significant, are in some cases positive and in some cases negative. Finally, in those cases where the unconditional correlations are low, the conditional correlations are also low. There are, however, some interesting exceptions, like Estonia/Slovakia, for which the unconditional correlation is statistically zero while the conditional correlation could occasionally deviate from zero depending on world market volatility.

NOTES

1. This chapter was prepared while the author was a Senior Scientist at Academy of Finland, and working as a Visiting Researcher at the Finance Department of the Mays Business School at Texas A&M University. The funding the Academy of Finland is gratefully acknowledged. Also the financial support from Jenny and Antti Wihuri Foundation is gratefully acknowledged. I also want to thank Mays Business School Finance Department for the great support and facilities.

2. PX 50, the Prague official Stock Exchange index which is a price index excluding dividends (see www.pse.cz/obchodovani/index_px50.asp, as of 27 October 2004).

3. TALSE is Tallinn Stock Exchange capital weighted return index including dividends (for a detail description, see http://files.hex.ee/oigusaktid/en_talse.pdf, as of 27 October 2004).

4. BUX is the official index of Budapest Stock Exchange capital weighted return index including dividends (for a detailed description, see www.bse.hu > Trading > Indices, as of 27 October 2004).

5. RSEDJ is Dow-Jones Riga Stock Exchange Index calculated in USD.

6. LITNG is the National Stock Exchange of Lithuania (NSEL) global stock index which includes all shares quoted on the NSEL.

7. SAX is a capital weighted index including dividends and other revenues.

8. SPI-20 is Ljubljana Stock Exchange Index which is market capitalisation weighted price index including 15 most liquid shares traded in Ljubljana Stock Exchange (for more details, see www.ljse.si/StrAng/Trading/Indices/inSBI20.htm, as of 27 October 2004).

9. From the t-statistic

$$t = \frac{r\sqrt{n-2}}{\sqrt{1-r^2}}$$

$$|r| < \frac{t_{\alpha/2}}{\sqrt{t_{\alpha/2}^2 + n - 2}}$$

with $\alpha = 0.05$, $n = 2,146$ we get $t_{0.025} = 1.96$, and correlations (on absolute value) less than 0.042 are statistically insignificant.

10. We also tested the possible asymmetric effect by including to the equation previous day negative shock. The results are not reported here, but the negative shock was not statistically significant in any of the equation.

REFERENCES

Bekaert, G., Erb, C. B., Harvey, C. R., & Viskanta, T. E. (1998). Distributional characteristics of emerging market returns and asset allocation. *The Journal of Portfolio Management* (winter), 102–116.

Bekaert, G., & Harvey, C. R. (2002). Research in emerging market finance: Looking to the future. *Emerging Market Review, 3*, 429–448.

Bera, A. K., & Higgins, M. L. (1993). ARCH models: Properties estimation and testing. *Journal of Economic Surveys, 4*, 305–362.

Bollerslev, T., & Wooldridge, J. F. (1992). Quasi-maximum likelihood estimation and inference in dynamic models with time-varying covariances. *Econometric Reviews, 11*, 143–172.

Bollerslev, T., Engle, R. F., & Wooldridge, J. M. (1988). A capital asset pricing model with time-varying covariances. *Journal of Political Economy, 96*, 116–131.

Bollerslev, T., Chou, R. Y., & Kroner, K. F. (1992). ARCH-modeling in finance: A review of the theory and empirical evidence. *Journal of Econometrics, 52*, 5–59.

Christodoulakis, G. A., & Satchell, S. E. (2002). Correlated ARCH (CorrARCH): Modelling the time-varying conditional correlation between financial asset returns. *European Journal of Operational Research, 139*, 351–370.

Engle, R. F. (1982). Autoregressive conditional heteroscedasticity with estimates of the variance of the United Kingdom inflations. *Econometrica, 50*, 987–1007.

Engle, R. F. (2002). Dynamic conditional correlation: A simple class of multivariate generalized autoregressive conditional heteroskedasticity models. *Journal of Business and Economic Statistics, 20,* 339–350.

Engle, R. F., & Bollerslev, T. (1986). Modeling the persistence of conditional variances. *Econometric Reviews, 5,* 1–50.

Fama, E. F. (1965). The behavior of stock market prices. *The Journal of Business, January,* 39–105.

Hwang, S., & Pedersen, C. S. (2004). Asymmetric risk measures when modelling emerging market equities: Evidence for regional and timing effects. *Emerging Markets Review, 5,* 109–128.

King, M., & Wadhwani, S. (1990). Transmission of volatility between stock markets. *The Review of Financial Studies, 3,* 5–33.

Knif, J., & Pynnonen, S. (2006). Volatility driven stock return correlation dynamics. *Managerial Science* (forthcoming).

Knif, J., Kolari, J., & Pynnonen, S. (2005). *What drives correlation between stock market returns? International evidence.* University of Vaasa, Working paper.

Koch, P. D., & Koch, T. W. (1991). Evolution of dynamic linkages across daily national stock indices. *Journal of International Money and Finance, 10,* 231–251.

Ljung, G., & Box, G. (1979). On a measure of lack of fit in time series models. *Biometrika, 66,* 265–270.

Longin, F., & Solnik, B. (1995). Is the correlation in international equity returns constant: 1960–1990? *Journal of International Money and Finance, 14,* 3–23.

Longin, F., & Solnik, B. (2001). Extreme correlation of international equity markets. *Journal of Finance, 56,* 649–676.

Makridakis, S. G., & Wheelwright, S. C. (1974). An analysis of the interrelationships among the major world stock exchanges. *Journal of Business Finance and Accounting, 1,* 195–216.

Mandelbrot, B. (1963). The variation of certain speculative prices. *Journal of Business, October,* 394–419.

Mateus, T. (2004). The risk and predictability of equity returns of the EU accession countries. *Emerging Market Review, 5,* 241–266.

Ramchand, L., & Susmel, R. (1998). Volatility and cross correlation across major stock markets. *Journal of Empirical Finance, 5,* 397–416.

Solnik, B., Boucrelle, C., & Fur, Y. L. (1996). International market correlation and volatility. *Financial Analysts Journal, 52,* 17–34.

Tse, Y. K., & Tsui, A. K. C. (2002). A multivariate generalized autoregressive conditional heteroscedasticity model with time-varying correlations. *Journal of Business and Economic Statistics, 20,* 351–362.

Voronkova, S. (2004). Equity market integration in central European emerging markets: A cointegration analysis with shifting regimes. *International Review of Financial Analysis, 13,* 633–647.

White, H. (1980). A heteroscedasticity-consistent covariance matrix estimator and direct test for heteroscedasticity. *Econometrica, 48,* 817–838.

THE LINKS BETWEEN CENTRAL, EAST EUROPEAN AND WESTERN SECURITY MARKETS [☆]

Roy Kouwenberg and Albert Mentink

1. INTRODUCTION

Over the last few years, Central and East European economies have become more integrated with the West European economy. In general, these economies have become more market-oriented and restrictions on foreign investment have been relaxed. An important step in this development was the admission of eight East European countries to the European Union (EU) in 2004. As the economic ties between Western, Central and Eastern Europe strengthen, one would naturally expect the financial markets to follow suit and become more integrated as well. A good example is the historical case of the Italian and German government bond markets: Before 1999 these two markets differed markedly in terms of credit quality and price volatility, but since the creation of the Euro zone in 1999 they have become highly similar.

[☆]The authors would like to thank Tjeert Keijzer, Roelof Salomons and Sandor Steverink for their help in constructing the dataset. Views expressed in this chapter are the authors' own and do not necessarily reflect those of AEGON Asset Management NL. All errors remain the responsibility of the authors.

Emerging European Financial Markets: Independence and Integration Post-Enlargement
International Finance Review, Volume 6, 353–381
Copyright © 2006 by Elsevier Ltd.
All rights of reproduction in any form reserved
ISSN: 1569-3767/doi:10.1016/S1569-3767(05)06014-0

As the security markets in Europe integrate, an important issue is whether West European investors can still gain diversification benefits from investments in the stock and bond markets of Central and Eastern Europe. In this chapter we try to answer this question, and we focus on how the West, Central and East European security markets are linked with each other, both in the short term and in the long term.[1] In contrast to earlier research, we do not analyze the stock markets or the government bond markets in these regions separately. Rather we analyze both markets and their interaction. We think it is important to analyze bond and stock markets at the same time because most investors tend to hold a diversified stock–bond portfolio. Furthermore, we include the volatility of these markets in our analysis.

We calculate correlations between the security market returns to measure short-term links. A low return correlation coefficient among markets is often considered as a sign of potential diversification benefits, and an opportunity for portfolio risk reduction based on modern portfolio theory of Markowitz (1952) and others. However, markets that are seemingly unrelated in the short term can share a common long-term trend, which limits the scope for potential risk reduction for long-term investors (e.g., pension funds). We, therefore, apply the well-known Johansen (1991) cointegration test and the Granger (1969) causality test to assess the long-term links between security markets.

Our data set consists of the S&P/IFC stock market indices and the Lehman Brothers euro-denominated government bond indices for the region Western Europe,[2] three Central European countries, namely the Czech Republic, Hungary and Poland, and two East European countries, Russia and Turkey. The stock market total returns cover the time period February 1997 to November 2004, on a weekly basis. The euro-denominated government bond market total returns cover the shorter time period October 2001 to November 2004, again on a weekly basis (data for the Czech Republic is not available).

One of our main findings is that there are clear links between stock markets of Western Europe and Central and Eastern Europe, but there still is ample opportunity for risk reduction through portfolio diversification. The maximum short-term return correlation is 51 percent, between Poland and Western Europe. We find no evidence of a long-term cointegration relationship between the stock markets. Moreover, the Granger (1969) tests show that no stock market clearly leads all other stock markets. For the euro-denominated government bond markets, the picture is completely different: The short-term return correlation between Western Europe and two Central European countries, Poland and Hungary, is 90 percent or more. Diversification of euro-denominated government bond portfolios is still possible through investments in the Russian and Turkish markets though, as the short-term correlation of these below investment grade markets with Western Europe is 27 percent or less. Granger (1969) causality tests reveal that no bond market leads all other bond markets. Finally, we find the best opportunities for diversification in stock–bond portfolios: The short-term correlation between Western European stocks and bonds is –55 percent in our sample period from October 2001 to November 2004. We find similar negative correlations for the stock–bond relationship in Hungary and Poland.

The rest of this chapter proceeds as follows. Section 2 briefly reviews related literature and explains the contribution of this chapter. Section 3 describes the Johansen (1991) cointegration test and the Granger (1969) causality test. Next, in Section 4, our stock market data are described. Both tests are implemented and their results are discussed. Section 5 follows the same steps as Section 4 for the government bond market data, while Section 6 addresses the links between stock markets and bond markets. Finally, Section 7 summarizes this chapter.

2. RELATED LITERATURE

Dockery and Vergari (2001) analyze the cointegration between three Central European stock markets: the Czech Republic, Hungary and Poland and two West European stock markets: Germany and the United Kingdom for the time period 1991–1995, on a weekly basis. They apply the Johansen (1991) cointegration test and find that the three Central European stock markets are cointegrated with the two West European stock markets. Gilmore and McManus (2002) study the relationship between the stock markets of the Czech Republic, Hungary and Poland, and of the United States. They apply the Johansen (1991) cointegration test and investigate Granger causality among the markets, using a dataset that spans the time period July 1995 to August 2001. Their results show that there does not exist a long-term return relationship between these countries, except that the Hungarian stock market Granger causes the Polish market.

Syriopoulos (2004) applies a Johansen (1991) cointegration test to the returns of the Central European stock markets, the Czech Republic, Hungary, Poland and Slovakia, and Germany and the United States. His sample covers the time period 1 January 1997 to 20 September 2003, with daily frequency. He finds moderate to high correlations between Germany, the Czech Republic, Hungary and Poland, ranging from 0.32 to 0.82, save for the correlation between Germany and the Czech Republic: 0.01. Further, he finds evidence for one stationary long-term relationship between these stock markets. Yang, Kolari, and Sutanto (2004) also apply the Johansen (1991) cointegration test to the United States and a large sample of emerging markets: African, Asian, Latin American and European (Greece). Their sample period extends from January 1985 to December 2001, on a monthly basis. They conclude that significant economic crisis events can alter the cointegration relationship between the countries. During crisis periods the evidence in favor of cointregration becomes stronger (e.g., during the 1997 Asian crisis).

Smith (2002) studies the correlations and cointegration between the developed bond markets of the United States, Canada, the United Kingdom, Germany, France and Japan. The results show that the return correlations between most of these bond markets are decreasing. The cointegration tests indicate, however, that common factors drive these markets. Lucey, Kim, and Wu (2004) analyze the dynamic links between the government bond markets of the Czech Republic, Hungary and Poland, and Belgium, France, Ireland, Italy, the Netherlands and Germany. They apply Haldane and Hall's Kalman filtering approach and a bivariate EGARCH model, using the MSCI government bond indices of the countries. They find that there are strong links between the Euro zone countries, but these strong links do not exist between the bond markets of the Euro zone countries and the three Central European countries: the Czech Republic, Hungary and Poland.

Connolly, Stivers, and Sun (2004) focus on the daily return comovements of stocks and bonds within the United States, Germany and the United Kingdom, and stock return comovements across these countries for the time period 1992–2002. They use the implied volatility from stock options as a state variable that influences the correlation between stocks and bonds. They find that both the security returns within these countries and the stock returns across countries do move together and that implied volatility has a significant impact on the sign of the stock–bond correlation. Chan and Kim (2004) implement Johansen's (1991) cointegration test, the Granger (1969) test and a price discovery measure using stock prices, credit default swap spreads (cds) and bond spreads for the time period March 2001 to May 2003. They analyze the following emerging markets: Brazil, Bulgaria, Colombia, Mexico, the Philippines, Russia, Turkey and Venezuela. They find cointegration between Russian cds and bond spreads, but they do not find this relationship for Turkish cds and bond spreads. For most countries no cointegration exists between stock and bond markets.

In this chapter we focus on the link between the West European security markets and the major emerging markets in Central and Eastern Europe.

Our contribution to the literature is that we study both stock markets and bond markets in this chapter and we consider the link between stock and bond markets. Related papers like Dockery and Vergari (2001), Gilmore and McManus (2002), Lucey et al. (2004) and Syriopoulos (2004) focus on either the stock market or the bond market separately. Most investors hold a diversified portfolio of stocks and bonds, and for this reason we think it is of importance to investigate the short-term correlations and the potential long-term relationships between stocks and bonds. Furthermore, we analyze the links between the return volatility of these markets. As Europe is in a constant process of unification and economic integration, it is also important to update earlier research with more recent data.

3. TESTS

3.1. The Johansen Cointegration Test

Low return correlation between security markets is often considered as sufficient evidence of potential for portfolio diversification. However, as pointed out by Kasa (1992) amongst others, it is important to check as well if there is a stable long-term relationship between security prices in different markets. If such a cointegration relationship exists, then the potential for diversification might be overstated by the short-term return correlation matrix.

We apply the standard Johansen (1991) cointegration test to check for long-term relationships between time series of total return security market indices. First, we need to establish that the levels of the total return indices are non-stationary: For this purpose we apply the augmented Dickey–Fuller (ADF) test and the Phillips–Perron (PP) test. Let y_t represent a $(k \times 1)$ vector of non-stationary I (Eq. (1)) index level time series. Next, a vector autoregression (VAR) model of order p is estimated:

$$y_t = A_1 y_{t-1} + \cdots + A_p y_{t-p} + \varepsilon_t \tag{1}$$

We can rewrite the VAR model as follows:

$$\Delta y_t = \Pi y_{t-1} + \sum_{i=1}^{p} \Gamma_i y_{t-i} + \varepsilon_t \tag{2}$$

where $\Pi = \sum_{i=1}^{p} A_i - I$, $\Gamma_i = -\sum_{j=i+1}^{p} A_i$.

If the matrix Π has rank 0, then no combination of the k time series in y_t is stationary and hence, there are no cointegration relationships between the variables. If the coefficient matrix Π has rank $r < k$, then there exist $(k \times r)$ matrices α and β, each with rank r, such that $\beta' y_t$ is stationary and $\Pi = \alpha \beta'$. The number of cointegration relationships is r and each column of β contains the coefficients of one cointegration equation. If the matrix Π has rank k, then all the k time series in y_t are stationary.

Johansen's (1991) method tests the restrictions imposed by cointegration on the unrestricted VAR. We use the trace test statistic, which tests the null hypothesis that the number of cointegration relationships is less than or equal to r against a general alternative. If the test statistic is greater than the critical value, then the null hypothesis that there are r cointegrating vectors is rejected in favor of the alternative that there are more than r.

3.2. The Granger Causality Test

Another way of looking at the links between the security market returns R and return volatility V is the Granger (1969) causality test. This test reads:

$$x_{1,t} = \alpha + \sum_{j=1}^{n} \beta_j x_{1,t-j} + \sum_{j=1}^{n} \gamma_j x_{2,t-j} + \varepsilon_t \qquad (3)$$

where α, β_j and γ_j are regression coefficients, $x_{i,t}$ is the total (excess) security return or volatility of a country in week t, $x_{1,t} \neq x_{2,t}$, $i = 1$, 2, $t = 1$, 2, $\ldots$, $T - 1$, T and $T = 164$ (bonds) or 407 (stocks). We define return as the first difference of the logarithm of the total return price index and volatility as the standard deviation of (maximal) five daily returns in a trading week, ending on a Friday.

The null hypothesis states that $x_{2,t}$ does not Granger cause $x_{1,t}$ in Eq. (3): $H_0 : \gamma_1 = \cdots = \gamma_n = 0$. For example, we examine whether the West European stock return "Granger causes" the Hungarian bond volatility, and vice versa. If the null hypothesis cannot be rejected and the coefficient(s) are significantly different from zero then West European stock returns indeed Granger causes the Hungarian bond volatility. Under the null hypothesis, the test statistic follows a F-distribution with n numerator degrees of freedom and $T - (2 \times n + 1)$ denominator degrees of freedom.

Granger (1969) tests provide a simple way of testing whether one security market leads (all) other security markets. In the extreme case that one security market Granger causes all other markets, the prospect of portfolio diversification from the perspective of an investor in this dominant market could be limited if the other markets eventually all react in a similar manner to a shock in the dominant market. We apply both the Johansen's (1991) cointegration test and the Granger (1969) causality test to examine the long-term links between the Western, Central and Eastern European security markets.

4. STOCK MARKET RESULTS

We employ end-of-the-week data of the FTSE Europe index, measured in euro, to represent the developed stock markets of Western Europe. The FTSE Europe index is a value-weighted total return index. The legacy currencies are converted into euros for the period 7 February 1997 to 31 December 1998 using the fixed euro-legacy currency exchange rates.

Among the emerging countries, we focus on three Central European countries, namely the Czech Republic, Hungary and Poland, and two East European countries, Russia and Turkey. The stock markets of these five countries are large enough to invest in for international investors according to the standards of the IFC. We use weekly data of the S&P/IFC investable (IFCI) total return stock indices, measured in euro, for the time period 7 February 1997 to 26 November 2004. The starting date of the sample follows from the fact that the Russian stock market weekly data are only available as of 7 February 1997. The full sample consists of 407 weekly return observations for each stock market. We choose a weekly frequency to capture the links between the stock market within a relatively large sample of observations, without having to worry about the impact of different time zones, the different opening hours of exchanges and day-of-the-week effects (these issues affect daily data).

First we analyze the properties of the individual stock markets returns. Table 1 shows a brief statistical summary of the weekly stock returns in euro. The table shows that the mean total return is positive in each market, save for Poland. The return distributions are all negatively skewed as the mean return is smaller than the median, with one exception: The stock market return of Turkey has a comparable mean and median. The maximum and minimum returns, and the standard deviation of the returns are higher in Russia and Turkey than in the other countries. The minimum return in Turkey in particular is exceptionally large: −73.12 percent. The null hypothesis of a normal return distribution is rejected at all regular confidence levels using a Jarque–Bera test.

The short-term links between the six stock market total returns in euro are measured using correlations. Table 2 reports the correlation matrix of the

Table 1. Summary Statistics of the Total Returns of the S&P/IFC Stock Markets Indices.

	WE	CZ	HU	PL	RU	TU
Mean (%)	0.12	0.15	0.20	−0.03	0.18	0.04
Median (%)	0.21	0.41	0.26	0.16	0.30	0.03
Maximum (%)	12.18	17.58	14.43	14.38	45.68	37.27
Minimum (%)	−9.86	−15.68	−34.27	−24.56	−35.25	−73.12
Standard deviation (%)	2.65	3.78	4.63	4.64	8.43	8.84
Jarque–Bera test P-value	0.00	0.00	0.00	0.00	0.00	0.00

Notes: All figures in euros. WE: Western Europe; CZ: the Czech Republic; HU: Hungary; PL: Poland; RU: Russia; TU: Turkey, using 407 weekly observations.
Source: IFC.

Table 2. Correlation Matrix of the Total Returns of the S&P/IFC Stock Market Indices.

	WE	CZ	HU	PL	RU	TU
WE	1.00					
CZ	0.38	1.00				
HU	0.50	0.54	1.00			
PL	0.51	0.53	0.58	1.00		
RU	0.47	0.40	0.48	0.44	1.00	
TU	0.32	0.30	0.38	0.32	0.34	1.00

Notes: All figures in euros. WE: Western Europe; CZ: the Czech Republic; HU: Hungary; PL: Poland; RU: Russia; TU: Turkey, using 407 weekly observations.
Source: IFC.

weekly returns for the full sample period, that is from 7 February 1997 to 26 November 2004. From this table we see that all correlations are positive. The return correlations between the Czech Republic, Hungary and Poland are relatively large, compared to others in the table. However, as the maximum correlation is only 58 percent, there still appears to be quite some potential for diversification by spreading an investment portfolio among these markets. Further, the correlations between the emerging Central and East European markets on the one hand and the developed West European market on the other hand are also moderate (the highest return correlation is 51 percent, namely between Western Europe and Poland). We will further analyze the potential long-term links among these markets in Subsections 4.1 and 4.2 below.

4.1. The Johansen Cointegration Test

We first test whether these time series have a unit root using the ADF and the PP test. As the graphs of the stock market indices do not show a clear trend, we use a test equation with a constant and without a trend. Table 3 shows the test results. We cannot reject the null hypothesis of a unit root at the 5 percent significance level for all stock indices, except for Poland. The graph of the log of the Polish IFCI index is displayed in Fig. 1 to illustrate the apparent stationarity of the series and the absence of a unit root.

Table 4 displays the results of the Johansen (1991) cointegration test for the presence of a stationary relationship between the stock markets of Central and Eastern Europe and the developed West European markets. We first run bivariate cointegration tests for the relationship between Western Europe and each developing stock market separately. Next we test for the existence of long-term relationships among the Central and East European stock markets. Finally, we test for cointegration relationships between all markets, including Western Europe. The Polish stock market is excluded

Table 3. ADF and the PP Tests for the Presence of a Unit Root in the Time Series of the Logarithm of the S&P/IFC Total Return Stock Market Indices.

	Lags	Regression with Intercept	
		ADF	PP
WE	0	−2.30	−2.32
CZ	3	−0.74	−0.46
HU	2	−1.92	−1.79
PL	2	−3.27**	−3.09**
RU	1	−1.32	−1.44
TU	0	−2.17	−2.25

Notes: All figures in euros. WE: Western Europe; CZ: the Czech Republic; HU: Hungary; PL: Poland; RU: Russia; TU: Turkey, using 407 weekly observations.

The second column shows the number of lagged first differences that were used to remove serial correlation from the residuals of the ADF-test regression (based on Ljung & Box (1979) Q-statistics).

Significance levels at; *1%, **5% and ***10%.

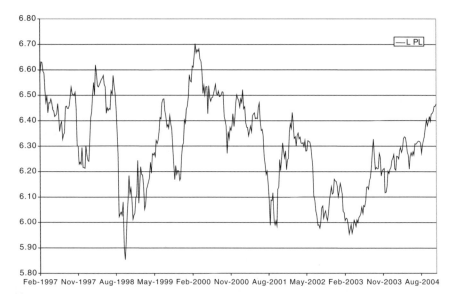

Fig. 1. Logarithm of the S&P/IFC Total Return Stock Market Index for Poland (Label: L PL), Using Weekly Data from 7 February 1997 to 26 November 2004.

from all cointegration test, as for this series we reject the null hypothesis of a unit root in favor of a stationary process. For each test we use a VAR model specification without a constant (no linear trend in the data) and assuming cointegration equations with a constant, but without a trend. This specification was selected a priori, as the graphs of the stock market indices do not show a clear trend. The results are robust to a change in the specification of the VAR model.

The results in Table 4 show that in each case the null hypothesis of no cointegration relationship cannot be rejected. Hence, we do not find evidence for stationary relationships between the (log-)price levels of the Central, East and West European stock markets. Given the moderate levels of short-term return correlation between these markets in Table 2, it now seems appropriate to conclude that West European stock portfolios can be diversified by investing in the Central and East European stock markets under consideration. Regardless of the continuing process of EU integration and enlargement, it appears that the stock markets of Central and Eastern Europe still had their own particular dynamics in the sample period and were quite loosely related to the West European stock market. Gilmore and McManus (2002) investigate the relationship between Central European

Table 4. Johansen (1991) Cointegration Test for the Presence of a Stationary Relationship between the Time Series of the Logarithm of the S&P/IFC Total Return Stock Market Indices.

Stock Markets Included	Lags in VAR	Null Hypothesis	Trace Statistic	10% Critical Value***	5% Critical Value**	1% Critical Value*
CZ, WE	1	$r \leqslant 0$	7.74	17.98	20.26	25.08
		$r \leqslant 1$	0.57	7.56	9.16	12.76
HU, WE	1	$r \leqslant 0$	8.19	17.98	20.26	25.08
		$r \leqslant 1$	1.90	7.56	9.16	12.76
RU, WE	1	$r \leqslant 0$	9.05	17.98	20.26	25.08
		$r \leqslant 1$	1.30	7.56	9.16	12.76
TU, WE	1	$r \leqslant 0$	15.79	17.98	20.26	25.08
		$r \leqslant 1$	3.35	7.56	9.16	12.76
CZ, HU, RU, TU	1	$r \leqslant 0$	33.75	50.53	54.08	61.27
		$r \leqslant 1$	9.55	32.27	35.19	41.20
		$r \leqslant 2$	4.06	17.98	20.26	25.08
		$r \leqslant 3$	0.61	7.56	9.16	12.76
CZ, HU, RU, TU, WE	1	$r \leqslant 0$	54.88	72.77	76.97	85.34
		$r \leqslant 1$	28.55	50.53	54.08	61.27
		$r \leqslant 2$	10.62	32.27	35.19	41.20
		$r \leqslant 3$	4.53	17.98	20.26	25.08
		$r \leqslant 4$	0.74	7.56	9.16	12.76

Notes: Figures in euros. WE: Western Europe; CZ: the Czech Republic; HU: Hungary; RU: Russia; TU: Turkey, using 407 weekly observations.
The second column shows the number of lagged terms in the VAR model, selected based on the Schwartz criterium. The third column shows the null hypothesis, which puts an upper bound on the number of cointegration relationships r. The fourth column shows the trace test statistic. The critical levels in the last three columns are based on MacKinnon, Alfred, and Michelis (1999).
Significance levels at; *1%, **5% and ***10%. The Polish stock market is excluded from the Johansen (1991) tests, as the time series is stationary (i.e., not integrated of order 1).

stock markets and the United States stock market as well: They also do not find evidence for long-term cointegration relationships with the United States.

4.2. The Granger Causality Test

Next, we examine the links between the six stock markets total returns and volatilities with the help of the Granger (1969) causality test, as described in Section 3.2. In Table 5 the first left hand column Granger causes the first row, with $n = 1$. For example, the volatility of the Czech Republic, Poland and Turkey together Granger cause the return of Western Europe. Total returns and volatility seem to be related to some extent within Europe as about half (68 out of the 132) of the Granger causality tests are significant at a level of 10 percent or less. No security market return Granger causes all other returns. So, for a euro investor there is room for portfolio diversification across these countries. Furthermore, the number of return and volatility Granger causalities are the same, indicating that both return and volatility roughly contain the same amount of information. After increasing the number of time lags, n, to 2 and 3, the pattern in Table 5 remains essentially the same.[3]

5. BOND MARKET RESULTS

We turn from the stock markets to the government bond markets of the six countries that are also analyzed in Section 4.1. First we look at S&P's long-term foreign currency sovereign credit ratings during the time period October 2001 to November 2004.[4,5] Table 6 reports the ratings. We select those West European countries with the highest credit rating: AAA. The three Central European countries are all investment grade, where Poland has the lowest credit rating (BBB+). The two East European countries, Russia en Turkey, are non-investment grade. The credit rating of Russia improved from B to BB and the credit rating of Turkey improved from B− to B+ in our sample period.

Now, we turn to the government bond markets total returns. Similar to the investable stock market indices of S&P/IFC, we use clear, rule-based bond indices with transparent pricing that can be replicated by bond investors. The Lehman Brothers Euro-Aggregate Treasury-Aaa index represents the return of euro-denominated bonds of the 12 sovereign countries

Table 5. Granger (1969) Causality Tests for the S&P/IFC Total Return Stock Market Indices.

	WE Return	WE Volatility	CZ Return	CZ Volatility	HU Return	HU Volatility	PL Return	PL Volatility	RU Return	RU Volatility	TU Return	TU Volatility
WE Return		*		**	***	**		*		***	**	
WE Volatility				**		*		*	**	***		*
CZ Return	*	**			**	**		*		**	**	**
CZ Volatility		*			***		*	*			***	*
HU Return		***								*	***	
HU Volatility				*		***			***			***
PL Return	***	***							*	**		
PL Volatility				**	**	**				**		**
RU Return			**	*		*		*		*		*
RU Volatility				**		*					***	***
TU Return							**	**				*
TU Volatility	*	*		***			**	**				

Notes: Figures in euros. WE: Western Europe; CZ: the Czech Republic; HU: Hungary; PL: Poland; RU: Russia; TU: Turkey, using 407 weekly observations.

Source: IFC.

Significance levels at; *1%, **5% and ***10%.

Table 6. S&P's Long-Term Foreign Currency Sovereign Credit Ratings.

Country	S&P Long-Term Credit Rating
WE	AAA
CZ	A–
HU	A–
PL	BBB+
RU (date: mm-yy)	B, B+ (12-01), BB– (07-02), BB (12-02)
TU (date: mm-yy)	B–, B(07-03), B+ (10-03)

Notes: WE: Western Europe; HU: Hungary; PL: Poland; RU: Russia; TU: Turkey, during the time period October 2001 to November 2004.
Sources: Bloomberg L.P., S&P.

participating in the Economic Monetary Union (EMU) for the period 10 October 2001 to 26 November 2004.[6,7,8] These indices are market-weighted and we use end-of-the-week closing prices, just as the equity data.

For the Central European bond markets we use the total return, measured in euro, of the Lehman Brothers Euro-Aggregate indices for Poland and Hungary, during the period 10 October 2001 to 26 November 2004, with weekly frequency.[9,10] The index requirements of Central Europe correspond to those of Western Europe. Finally, we use the total returns in euro of the Lehman Brothers Pan-European Emerging Markets for Russia and Turkey during the same time period.[11] Please note that the government bonds included in these four indices are denominated in euro (or a legacy currency, such as the German Mark), that is a foreign currency for the issuing countries. Hence, from the perspective of a West European investor these bond indices involve very little or no foreign exchange rate risk.

Table 7 reports a statistical summary of the weekly total bond returns. Most statistical properties of the West and Central European bond markets are comparable: Positive mean, negatively skewed return distribution and the returns are not normally distributed at the 5 percent level of significance. The East European mean is also positive and higher than in Western and Central Europe, the return distribution is more symmetric, but not normally distributed. East European maximum, minimum and standard deviation attain more extreme values than the West and Central European values, with the exception of the return standard deviation of Turkey.

The correlations between these total bond returns are displayed in Table 8. All correlations are positive. As expected, the correlations between the investment grade markets (i.e., Western Europe, Hungary and Poland) are very high, ranging between 0.90 and 0.95. Therefore, we analyze their

Table 7. Summary Statistics of the Total Returns of the Lehman Brothers Euro-Denominated Bond Market Indices.

	WE	HU	PL	RU	TU
Mean (%)	0.12	0.14	0.16	0.24	0.32
Median (%)	0.17	0.18	0.23	0.22	0.31
Maximum (%)	1.19	1.51	1.68	2.16	3.72
Minimum (%)	−1.32	−1.31	−1.95	−3.07	−6.90
Standard deviation (%)	0.51	0.54	0.68	0.63	1.18
P-value Jarque–Bera test	0.00	0.02	0.02	0.00	0.00

Notes: WE: Western Europe; HU: Hungary; PL: Poland; RU: Russia; TU: Turkey, using 164 weekly observations.
Source: Lehman Brothers, Inc.

Table 8. Correlation Matrix of the Total Returns of the Lehman Brothers Euro-Denominated Bond Market Indices.

	WE	HU	PL	RU	TR
WE	1.00				
HU	0.95	1.00			
PL	0.92	0.90	1.00		
RU	0.27	0.25	0.36	1.00	
TR	0.13	0.17	0.24	0.34	1.00

Notes: WE: Western Europe; HU: Hungary; PL: Poland; RU: Russia; TU: Turkey, using 164 weekly observations.
Source: Lehman Brothers, Inc.

excess returns as well below. The return correlation between Russia and Turkey is 34 percent, lower than among their investment grade counterparts. The correlations between the investment grade countries and the non-investment grade countries are much lower as well, with a maximum of 36 percent. We conclude that from the perspective of a West European bond investor, no apparent diversification benefits can be gained from investing in the euro-denominated government bond markets of Hungary and Poland. The two East European bond markets, Russia and Turkey, on the other hand still provide ample opportunity for diversification based on the low return correlation with Western Europe (27 percent and 13 percent, respectively).

5.1. Euro Excess Returns

As shown above the total returns of Western and Central Europe are highly correlated. Consequently we now focus on the excess return, defined as the return of the indicated index over the corresponding government benchmark, here the AAA German government bond total return index (Lehman Brothers, Inc.) For the sake of completeness we include the Central European excess returns as well. Table 9 reports that the mean excess returns are always positive, the excess return distributions are symmetric, save for Turkey, and not normally distributed. Turkey also has the highest maximum, the lowest minimum and the largest standard deviation.

Table 10 shows that all excess returns, which can be considered as the realized compensation for taking credit risk, are negatively correlated with the total returns of the AAA West Europe index. The negative relation is stronger in case of Eastern Europe than Central Europe. Further, the excess return correlation between Hungary (HU) and Poland (PL) is positive. The same applies to Eastern Europe. Finally, the Poland excess return is also moderately correlated with Eastern Europe countries.

5.2. The Johansen Cointegration Test

We first test whether the logarithm of the total return euro-bond indices (i.e., euro-denominated bonds and returns measured in euro) have a unit root using the ADF and the PP test. The logarithm of each total return bond index displays a clear increasing trend due to reinvested coupon payments

Table 9. Summary Statistics of the Excess Returns of the Lehman Brothers Euro-Denominated Bond Market Indices.

	HU	PL	RU	TU
Mean (%)	0.02	0.03	0.14	0.20
Median (%)	0.02	0.02	0.12	0.14
Maximum (%)	0.71	0.96	1.71	3.43
Minimum (%)	−0.26	−2.08	−2.68	−5.51
Standard deviation (%)	0.12	0.25	0.53	1.05
P-value Jarque–Bera test	0.00	0.00	0.00	0.00

Notes: HU: Hungary; PL: Poland; RU: Russia; TU: Turkey, using 164 weekly observations.
Source: Lehman Brothers, Inc.

Table 10. Correlation Matrix of the Total Returns of the Lehman Brothers Euro Bond Market Indices.

	WE	HU	PL	RU	TR
WE	1.00				
HU	−0.01	1.00			
PL	−0.06	0.19	1.00		
RU	−0.12	0.05	0.34	1.00	
TR	−0.13	0.03	0.31	0.32	1.00

Notes: WE: Western Europe, and the excess returns of the Lehman Brothers euro-denominated bond market indices of HU: Hungary; PL: Poland; RU: Russia; TU: Turkey, using 164 weekly observations.
Source: Lehman Brothers, Inc.

and declining interest rates during the sample period. For this reason we use a unit root test equation with a constant and a trend. Table 11 shows the results. We cannot reject the null hypothesis of a unit root at the 5 percent significance level for all bond market indices.

Table 12 displays the results of the Johansen (1991) cointegration test for the presence of a stationary relationship between the euro bond markets. We run bivariate cointegration tests for the relationship between Western Europe and each developing bond market separately. Next we test for the existence of long-term relationships among the Central and East European bond markets. Finally, we test for cointegration relationships between all markets, including Western Europe. For each test we use a VAR model specification with constant (linear trend in the data) and assuming a cointegration equation with a constant and a trend. This specification is selected as the graphs of the logarithm of the total return indices all show a clear trend (see Franses (2001)).

The results show that the null hypothesis of no cointegration relationship cannot be rejected in each case. Hence, we do not find evidence for stationary relationships between the logarithm of the total return euro bond indices. Given the relatively high level of short-term return correlation between the euro-denominated bond indices of Western and Central Europe in Table 8 (in excess of 90 percent), it is quite surprising to find no evidence of a long-term relationship. There are three potential explanations for this finding. First, the short-term changes in the bond markets are highly correlated, but these markets do not share a common long-term trend. Second, the relatively small number of observations (165 weekly returns) leads to a low-test power, making it difficult to reject a false null hypothesis. Third,

Table 11.   ADF and PP Tests for the Presence of a Unit root in the Time
Series of the Logarithm of the Lehman Brothers Euro-Denominated
Total Return Bond Market Indices.

	Lags	Regression with Trend and Intercept	
		ADF	PP
WE	0	−2.02	−2.03
HU	0	−2.74	−2.80
PL	0	−2.12	−2.18
RU	1	−2.78	−2.81
TU	1	−2.56	−2.36

Notes: WE: Western Europe; HU: Hungary; PL: Poland; RU: Russia; TU: Turkey, using 165
weekly observations.
The second column shows the number of lagged first differences that were used to remove serial
correlation from the residuals of the ADF-test regression (based on Ljung & Box (1979) Q-
statistics).
Significance levels at; *1%, **5% and ***10%.

there are structural breaks in the long-term relationship during the sample
period and as a result the VAR model is misspecified.[12]

5.3. The Granger Causality Test

Table 13 can be interpreted analogously to Table 5. From this table, with
$n = 1$, we observe that the number of significant test results is low compared
to the stock markets, only about 10 percent of all tests. Return and volatility
of the three countries with the lowest credit rating, Poland, Russia
and Turkey, have the most impact on the two other countries and themselves. This implies that there is no leading bond market in this sample and
all information seem to be absorbed at the same time across all markets. Increasing the number of lags to 2 and 3, the Turkish return and
volatility become a function of returns and volatilities of more security
markets.

We repeat the Granger (1969) tests for the West European total returns
and the Central and East European excess returns. Comparing Tables 13
and 14 the conclusion remains the same: No bond market leads all other
markets and only a limited number of test is significant.

Table 12. Johansen (1991) Cointegration Test for the Presence of a Stationary Relationship between the Logarithm of the Lehman Brothers Euro-Denominated Total Return Bond Market Indices.

Bond Markets Included	Lags in VAR	Null Hypothesis	Trace Statistic	10% Critical Value	5% Critical Value	1% Critical Value
HU, WE	1	$r \leq 0$	14.75	23.34	25.87	31.15
		$r \leq 1$	3.41	10.67	12.52	16.55
PL, WE	1	$r \leq 0$	13.86	23.34	25.87	31.15
		$r \leq 1$	5.47	10.67	12.52	16.55
RU, WE	1	$r \leq 0$	12.68	23.34	25.87	31.15
		$r \leq 1$	3.73	10.67	12.52	16.55
TU, WE	1	$r \leq 0$	14.04	23.34	25.87	31.15
		$r \leq 1$	3.99	10.67	12.52	16.55
HU, PL, RU, TU	1	$r \leq 0$	34.58	60.09	63.88	71.48
		$r \leq 1$	17.92	39.76	42.92	49.36
		$r \leq 2$	8.32	23.34	25.87	31.15
		$r \leq 3$	3.90	10.67	12.52	16.55
HU, PL, RU, TU, WE	1	$r \leq 0$	64.23	84.38	88.80	97.60
		$r \leq 1$	35.92	60.09	63.88	71.48
		$r \leq 2$	21.62	39.76	42.92	49.36
		$r \leq 3$	10.45	23.34	25.87	31.15
		$r \leq 4$	4.28	10.67	12.52	16.55

Notes: WE: Western Europe; HU: Hungary; PL: Poland; RU: Russia; TU: Turkey, using 165 weekly observations. The second column shows the number of lagged terms in the VAR model, selected based on the Schwartz criterium. The third column shows null hypothesis, which puts an upper bound on the number of cointegration relationships r. The fourth column shows the trace test statistic. The critical levels in the last three columns are based on MacKinnon, Alfred, and Michelis (1999).

Table 13. Granger (1969) Causality Tests for the Lehman Brothers Euro-Denominated Total Return Bond Market Indices.

	WE Return	WE Volatility	HU Return	HU Volatility	PL Return	PL Volatility	RU Return	RU Volatility	TU Return	TU Volatility
WE return										
WE volatility										
HU return										
HU volatility										
PL return	***									
PL volatility	***		**							
RU return					**			**		
RU volatility										
TU return							*	*		
TU volatility		***							***	**

Notes: WE: Western Europe; HU: Hungary; PL: Poland; RU: Russia TU: Turkey, using 164 weekly observations.
Source: Lehman Brothers, Inc.
Significance levels at; *1%, **5% and ***10%.

Table 14. Granger (1969) Causality Tests for the Total Returns of the Lehman Brothers Euro Bond Market Index of WE and the Excess Returns of the Lehman Brothers Euro-Denominated Bond Market Indices of HU and PL, RU and TU, Using 164 Weekly Observations.

	WE	HU	PL	RU	TU
WE					***
HU			**		
PL	***				**
RU	***				
TU			*	*	

Notes: WE: Western Europe; HU; Hungary; PL: Poland; RU: Russia; TU: Turkey.
Source: Lehman Brothers, Inc.
Significance levels at; *1%, **5% and ***10%.

6. STOCK AND BOND MARKET RESULTS

Sections 4.1 and 5.1 analyze the characteristics of the stock and bond market data separately. Here, we compare both security markets and investigate the potential links, using the same data. We start with the correlation matrix of the security returns for the time period 10 October 2001 to 26 November 2004. We leave out the Czech Republic, as explained in Section 5.

Table 15 shows that correlation between West European stock and bond returns is negative, as expected. The magnitude of the negative correlation coefficient is surprisingly large (–55 percent), however. As stock–bond correlations are notoriously instable (see, e.g., Connolly et al. (2004)) and the sample period is relatively short, it seems unlikely that the stock–bond correlation will remain at such a low in the future. However, it appears quite safe to can conclude that West European bonds provide a very good diversification opportunity for West European stock market investors. The stock–bond correlation in the investment grade Central European markets is also negative: –16 percent for Hungary and –18 percent for Poland, respectively.

The non-investment grade East European countries show positive correlations between stock and bond returns: +8 percent for Russia and +38 percent for Turkey. The positive stock–bond correlation for the two countries with low credit ratings can be explained well by the fact that bonds become more similar to equity in case of financial distress (see Merton,

Table 15. Correlation Matrix of the Stock and Bond Total Return Indices.

	WE Stocks	WE Bonds	HU Stocks	HU Bonds	PL Stocks	PL Bonds	RU Stocks	RU Bonds	TU Stocks	TU Bonds
WE stocks	1.00									
WE bonds	-0.55	1.00								
HU stocks	0.39	-0.19	1.00							
HU bonds	-0.50	0.95	-0.16	1.00						
PL stocks	0.50	-0.27	0.53	-0.22	1.00					
PL bonds	-0.53	0.92	-0.13	-0.90	-0.18	1.00				
RU stocks	0.42	-0.25	0.35	-0.22	0.35	-0.25	1.00			
RU bonds	-0.12	0.27	0.13	0.25	0.18	0.36	0.08	1.00		
TU stocks	0.22	-0.03	0.29	-0.02	0.32	0.00	0.08	0.09	1.00	
TU bonds	0.11	0.13	0.20	0.17	0.22	0.24	0.13	0.34	0.38	1.00

Notes: WE: Western Europe; HU: Hungary; PL: Poland; RU: Russia; TU: Turkey, using 164 Weekly Observations.
Sources: IFC and Lehman Brothers, Inc.

1974). Further, West and Central European bond returns are always negatively correlated with all stock markets returns, save for the zero correlation between Polish bonds and Turkish stock, whereas the East European bond returns are positively correlated with all stock markets (except for the negative correlation between Russian bonds and West European stocks). Based on the correlation matrix, it appears that investments grade euro-denominated bonds provide much better diversification opportunities for West European stock market investors (and vice versa of course) than investments in the stock markets of Central and Eastern Europe, or investments in the two non-investment grade bond markets.

6.1. The Johansen Cointegration Test

For the test of long-term relationships between stock and bond markets we use data from the period 10 October 2001 to 26 November 2004, that is, 164 weekly observations, as the bond market total return series are available from 10 October 2001. We first test for the presence of a unit root in the time series of the logarithm of the total return stock indices over the shorter sample period. We find that each series cannot reject the null hypothesis of a unit root at the 5 percent significance level, including the series for the Polish stock market.[13]

Table 16 displays the results of the Johansen (1991) cointegration test for the presence of a stationary relationship between the bond and stock markets. We run bivariate cointegration tests for the relationship between the stock market and bond market of each country separately. We then test for the existence of long-term relationships among all Central and East European stock and bond markets. Finally, we include the West European stock and bond markets in the joint test. For each test we use a VAR model specification with constant (linear trend in the data) and assuming a cointegration equation with a constant and a trend. This specification is selected a priori as the graph of the logarithm of most series shows a clear trend during the sample period since October 2001.

The results show that the null hypothesis of no cointegration relationship cannot be rejected in each case. We do not find evidence of a long-term relationship between stocks and bonds in each of the markets. This finding is in line with the relatively low level of short-term return correlation between bond and stock markets, reported in Table 15. We also do not find a cointegrating vector among the combined stock and bond markets of Western, Central and Eastern Europe.

Table 16. Johansen (1991) Cointegration Test for the Presence of a Stationary Relationship between the Time Series of the Logarithm of the Stock and Bond Market Total Return Indices.

Bond and Stock Markets Included	Lags in VAR	Null Hypothesis	Trace Statistic	10% Critical Value	5% Critical Value	1% Critical Value
WE	1	$r \leqslant 0$	13.53	23.34	25.87	31.15
		$r \leqslant 1$	3.99	10.67	12.52	16.55
HU	1	$r \leqslant 0$	9.39	23.34	25.87	31.15
		$r \leqslant 1$	2.12	10.67	12.52	16.55
PO	1	$r \leqslant 0$	13.43	23.34	25.87	31.15
		$r \leqslant 1$	3.54	10.67	12.52	16.55
RU	1	$r \leqslant 0$	21.48	23.34	25.87	31.15
		$r \leqslant 1$	6.69	10.67	12.52	16.55
TU	1	$r \leqslant 0$	11.77	23.34	25.87	31.15
		$r \leqslant 1$	4.12	10.67	12.52	16.55
HU, PO, RU, TU	1	$r \leqslant 0$	170.57	181.16	187.47	199.81
		$r \leqslant 1$	113.64	144.87	150.56	161.72
		$r \leqslant 2$	81.27	112.65	117.71	127.71
		$r \leqslant 3$	54.19	84.38	88.80	97.60
		$r \leqslant 4$	31.82	60.09	63.88	71.48
		$r \leqslant 5$	20.29	39.76	42.92	49.36
		$r \leqslant 6$	10.18	23.34	25.87	31.15
		$r \leqslant 7$	4.23	10.67	12.52	16.55
HU, PO, RU, TU, WE	1	$r \leqslant 0$	240.81	265.63	273.19	287.88
		$r \leqslant 1$	182.39	221.37	228.30	241.73
		$r \leqslant 2$	136.05	181.16	187.47	199.81
		$r \leqslant 3$	103.17	144.87	150.56	161.72
		$r \leqslant 4$	74.84	112.65	117.71	127.71
		$r \leqslant 5$	51.83	84.38	88.80	97.60
		$r \leqslant 6$	34.76	60.09	63.88	71.48
		$r \leqslant 7$	23.29	39.76	42.92	49.36
		$r \leqslant 8$	13.27	23.34	25.87	31.15
		$r \leqslant 9$	5.52	10.67	12.52	16.55

Notes: WE: Western Europe; HU: Hungary; PL: Poland; RU: Russia; TU: Turkey, using 164 weekly observations.

The second column shows the number of lagged terms in the VAR model, selected based on the Schwartz criterium. The third column shows null hypothesis, which puts an upper bound on the number of cointegration relationships r. The fourth column shows the trace test statistics. The critical levels in the last three columns are based on MacKinnon, Alfred, and Michelis (1999).

6.2. The Granger Causality Test

Table 17 reports the results of the Granger (1969) causality tests of the stock and bond markets, save for the Czech Republic, for the time period October 2001 to November 2004. The interpretation of this table follows that of Tables 5 and 13. From the original table we skip those rows[14] and columns[15] that do not contain any significant test result. We find again that no security market return clearly leads the others. The volatility of the West European equity market significantly depends on Hungarian, Polish, Turkish and its own bond market. This may follow from the fact that West European companies have large investments in these countries, but the time lag of 1 week is somewhat surprising as the stock market is usually considered quite efficient. Again, increasing the number of time lags does not really change Table 17.

7. SUMMARY AND CONCLUSIONS

Over the last few years, Central and East European economies have become more integrated with the West European economy. An important step in this development was the admission of eight East European countries to the EU in 2004. As the security markets in Europe integrate, an important issue is whether West European investors can still gain diversification benefits from investments in the stock and bond markets of Central and Eastern Europe? In this chapter we try to answer this question and we focus on how the West, Central and East European security markets are linked with each other, both in the short term and in the long term. In contrast to earlier research we do not analyze the stock markets or the government bond markets in these regions separately, but we analyze both markets and their interaction. We think it is important to analyze bond and stock markets at the same time, as most investors tend to hold a diversified stock–bond portfolio. Furthermore, we include the volatility of these markets in our analyses.

We calculate correlations between the security market returns to measure short-term links. We also apply the Granger (1969) causality test, which includes lagged returns. To assess the potential long-term links between security markets, we use the well-known Johansen (1991) cointegration test and the Granger (1969) causality test. Our data set consists of the stock markets and the euro-denominated government bond markets of the region Western Europe, three Central European countries, namely the Czech Republic,

Table 17. Granger (1969) Causality Tests for the Stock and Bond Market Total Returns of WE and the Excess Returns of HU and PL, RU and TU, Using 164 Weekly Observations.

	WE EQ Volatility	WE B Return	WE B Volatility	HU EQ Volatility	HU B Return	PL B Return	RU B Return	RU B Volatility	TU EQ Volatility	TU B Return	TU B Volatility
WE EQ volatility				*					*		*
WE B return	*		***						***		
WE B volatility	***										
HU B return	*										
HU B volatility	*										
PL B return	**	***			**			**			
RU B return		***		**					***		
RU B volatility											
TU EQ volatility	*						*	**		**	
TU B return	**		***			**		*		***	**
TU B volatility	*								*		

Notes: WE: Western Europe; HU: Hungary; PL: Poland; RU: Russia; TU: Turkey, using 164 weekly observations. EQ: equity; B: bond.

Sources: IFC and Lehman Brothers.

Significance levels at; *1%, **5% and ***10%.

Hungary and Poland, and two East European countries, Russia and Turkey. The stock market total returns cover the time period February 1997 to November 2004, on a weekly basis. The euro-denominated government bond market total returns cover the shorter time period October 2001 to November 2004, again on a weekly basis (data for the Czech Republic is not available).

One of our main findings is that there are clear links between stock markets of Western Europe, and Central and Eastern Europe, but still there is ample opportunity for risk reduction through portfolio diversification. The maximum short-term return correlation is 51 percent, between Poland and Western Europe. We find no evidence of a long-term cointegration relationship between the stock markets. Moreover, the Granger (1969) tests show that no security market dominates all other security markets. For the euro-denominated government bond markets, the picture is completely different: The short-term return correlation between Western Europe and two Central European countries, Poland and Hungary, is 90 percent or more. Diversification of euro-denominated government bond portfolios is still possible through investments in the Russian and Turkish markets though, as the short-term correlation of these below investment grade markets with Western Europe is 27 percent or less. Granger (1969) tests show that no bond market leads all other bond markets. Finally, we find the best opportunities for diversification in stock–bond portfolios: The short-term correlation between Western European stocks and bonds is –55 percent in our sample period from October 2001 to November 2004. We find similar negative correlations for the stock–bond relationship in Hungary and Poland.

NOTES

1. For a description of the European Bond Market, see Batten, Fetherston, and Szilagyi (2004).

2. We treat the Western European stock (bond) markets as a single market, due to their high level of integration (see, e.g., Yang, Min, and Li (2003) amongst others).

3. The numbers are available from the authors upon request.

4. We thank Bloomberg L.P. for the data.

5. Currency and period follow from the available bond data as shown in Table 6.

6. We thank Lehman Brothers, Inc. for the data.

7. The rules of the Lehman Brothers Euro-Aggregate Index are: "The Lehman Brothers Euro-Aggregate Index consists of bonds issued in the Euro or the legacy currencies of the 12 sovereign countries participating in the Economic Monetary Union (EMU). All issues must be investment grade rated, fixed-rate securities with at least 1 year remaining to maturity. The Euro-Aggregate Index excludes convertible securities, floating rate notes, perpetual notes, warrants, linked bonds and structured

products. German Schuldscheine (quasi-loan securities) are also excluded because of their trading restrictions and unlisted status, which results in illiquidity. The country of issue is not an index criterion, and securities of issuers from outside the euro zone are included if they meet the index criteria. The minimum outstanding amount for all bonds in the index is €300 million equivalent. The exchange rates among the 11 EMU currencies were fixed up to 1 January 1999. Lehman Brothers uses both issue and issuer ratings by Moody's Investors Service and S&P's Ratings Group to determine if a bond is investment grade (Baa3/BBB– and above) and, therefore, eligible for inclusion. If both Moody's and S&P provide a rating for a security, the lower of the two ratings is used. If neither exists for a security, then an issuer rating is applied. Once again, the lower of the two ratings is used. If the issue and issuer are found to be unrated by both major rating services, then the unrated bond issue does not participate in the index." (Lehman Brothers, Inc.)

8. The start date follows from the fact that the East European bond returns time series start at that date.

9. The Chech Republic issued a government bond denominated in Euro in June 2004 (Bloomberg L.P.).

10. At this moment J.P. Morgan also focuses on foreign currency bonds in their emerging bond markets indices.

11. "This index includes only fixed-rate bonds (excluding Brady bonds) of emerging market countries with over 1 year to maturity, denominated in Euro (or legacy currencies), British pounds (GBP), Danish krone (DKK), Swedish krona (SEK) or Norwegian krone (NOK). Issues must have sovereign ratings of either Baa3 or lower by Moody's or BBB– or lower by S&P and have a par amount outstanding equivalent to at least €300 million. Defaulted corporate bonds are removed from the index at the end of the month, while defaulted sovereign bonds remain in the index until they are restructured, deceased, exchanged or put away."

12. A regime-switching model is well suited to capture structural breaks. However, we think that the sample of bond market data available is too short to estimate such a model effectively.

13. Results not reported to save space, but available upon request.

14. Headers: WE Equity Return, HU Equity Return, HU Equity Volatility, PL Equity Return, PL Equity Volatility, PL Bond Volatility, RU Equity Return, RU Equity Volatility and TU Equity Return.

15. Headers: WE Equity Return, HU Equity Return, HU Bond Volatility, PL Equity Return, PL Equity Volatility, PL Bond Volatility, RU Equity Return, RU Equity Volatility and TU Equity Return.

REFERENCES

Batten, J. A., Fetherston, T. A., & Szilagyi, P. G. (Eds) (2004). *European fixed income markets money, bond, and interest rate derivatives*. New York: John Wiley & Sons, Inc.

Chan, J. A., & Kim, Y. S. (2004). *Equity prices, credit default swaps and bond spreads in emerging markets*. IMF Working Paper, IMF.

Connolly, R., Stivers, C., & Sun, L. (2004). *Commonality in the time-variation of stock–bond and stock–stock return comovements*. Working Paper, University of North Carolina at Chapel Hill, NC, USA.

Dockery, D., & Vergari, F. (2001). An investigation of the linkages between European Union equity markets and emerging capital markets: The East European connection. *Managerial Finance, 27*, 24–39.

Franses, P. H. (2001). How to deal with intercept and trend in practical cointegration analysis? *Applied Economics, 33*, 577–579.

Gilmore, C. G., & McManus, G. M. (2002). International portfolio diversification: US and Central European equity markets. *Emerging Markets Review, 3*, 69–83.

Granger, C. W. J. (1969). Investigating causal relationships by econometric models and cross-spectral methods. *Econometrica, 37*, 424–438.

Johansen, S. (1991). Estimation and hypothesis testing of cointegration vectors in gaussian vector autoregressive models. *Econometrica, 59*, 1551–1580.

Kasa, K. (1992). Common stochastic trends in international stock markets. *Journal of Monetary Economics, 29*, 95–124.

Ljung, G., & Box, G. (1979). On a measure of lack of fit in time series models. *Biometrika, 66*, 265–270.

Lucey, B. M., Kim, S. J., & Wu, E. (2004). Dynamics of bond market integration between existing and accession countries. Working Paper, University of New South Wales, Australia.

MacKinnon, J. G., Alfred, A. H., & Michelis, L. (1999). Numerical distribution functions of likelihood ratio rests for cointegration. *Journal of Applied Econometrics, 14*, 563–577.

Markowitz, H. M. (1952). Portfolio selection. *Journal of Finance, 7*, 77–91.

Merton, R. C. (1974). On the pricing of corporate debt: The risk structure of interest rates. *Journal of Finance, 2*, 449–470.

Smith, K. L. (2002). Government bond market seasonality, diversification, and cointegration: International evidence. *Journal of Financial Research, 35*, 203–221.

Syriopoulos, T. (2004). International portfolio diversification to Central European stock markets. *Applied Financial Economics, 14*, 1253–1268.

Yang, J., Min, I., & Li, Q. (2003). European stock market. *Journal of Business Finance and Accounting, 30*, 1253–1276.

Yang, J., Kolari, J. W., & Sutanto, P. W. (2004). On the stability of long-run relationships between emerging and US stock markets. *Journal of Multinational Financial Management, 14*, 233–248.

THE RELATIONS BETWEEN EMERGING EUROPEAN AND DEVELOPED STOCK MARKETS BEFORE AND AFTER THE RUSSIAN CRISIS OF 1997–1998

Brian M. Lucey and Svitlana Voronkova[1]

1. INTRODUCTION

After the collapse of communist and socialist regimes at the beginning of 1990s, a number of Central and Eastern European (CEE) economies started their journey into capitalism by establishing private property and capital markets. As a result, a number of stock markets have since been established in the region. Since then, they have displayed considerable growth in size and degree of sophistication, and they have attracted the interest of academics for a number of reasons. *First*, these markets provide a possibility to re-examine existing asset-pricing models and pricing anomalies in the conditions of the evolving markets. Market efficiency of the CEE markets is tested in Ratkovicova (1999) and Gilmore and McManus (2001); a version of the CAPM is tested in Charemza and Majerowska (2000); Mateus (2004) explores the predictability of European emerging market returns within an unconditional asset-pricing framework while the January-pricing anomaly is

Emerging European Financial Markets: Independence and Integration Post-Enlargement
International Finance Review, Volume 6, 383–413
Copyright © 2006 by Elsevier Ltd.
ISSN: 1569-3767/doi:10.1016/S1569-3767(05)06015-2

studied in Henke (2003). *Second*, in the light of growing interdependencies between world equity markets due to enhanced capital movements, numerous studies have investigated the extent to which emerging European stock markets are integrated with global markets, and the extent to which they are subjects to global shocks (Gelos & Sahay, 2000; Gilmore & McManus, 2002; Scheicher, 2001). Among the CEE markets, those of the Vysegrad countries (Poland, Hungary and the Czech Republic) have attracted most of the attention of the academics due to their economies faster growth relative to their regional counterparts (Slovakia, Slovenia, Bulgaria, Croatia and Baltic countries), in addition to political stability and their (successfully realized) prospects of joining the European Union (EU).

The repercussions of the Russian currency and debt crises for world stock markets have been extensively discussed in the literature (see, among others, Baig & Goldfain, 2000; Gelos & Sahay, 2000; Hernández & Valdés, 2001; Dungley, Fry, Gonzales-Hermosillo, & Martin, 2003). However, as far as we are aware, no studies have been done on linkages shared by the Russian market after 1998. This lack of research is surprising. Russia is the largest among the CEE stock markets in terms of market capitalization, and the Russian economy remains important for the Eastern European region. Although trade links have declined significantly since the collapse of the Soviet Union, Russia still remains an important trading partner for the Vysegrad countries, as well as a source of significant direct investment in the region (Jochum, Kirschgässner, & Platek (JKP), 1998; UNCTAD, 2004a, b, c). *Third*, a number of studies have shown that the nature of market linkages is time-varying (Bekaert & Harvey, 1995, 1997). Gelos and Sahay (2000) suggest that "… *the reaction of the more advanced financial markets in the region around the time of the Russian ruble collapse suggests that further financial market liberalization, … and integration may result in higher future financial market comovements*". Thus the aim of this chapter is to investigate and document the changing role of the Russian stock market for the CEE markets and to explore whether its importance for the regional markets has changed after the 1998 crisis. This chapter also explores its linkages with the developed markets (US, UK, European Monetary Union (EMU) and Japan), with a special emphasis on the post-crisis period.

Increasing integration of equity markets and capital markets in general can be expected to have three broad sets of implications if the integration spurs greater development of the financial sector (see Pagano, 1993). *First*, the attractiveness of international portfolio diversification will weaken as returns are equalized across countries. *Second*, the more complete are the world's capital market, the more robust will be the economies of individual states. *Third*, household savings rates will consequently change over time. The former two outcomes are in general seen to have positive effects on economic growth while the latter is more uncertain.

International portfolio diversification is justified only if there are gains from it. With increasing integration of international equity markets, the diversification benefits will tend to decline as the correlations become increasingly positive and strengthen. This concept has been well known for at least several centuries, and has been quantified and modeled since at least the early years of the 20th century. Goetzmann, Li, and Rouwenhorst (2000) demonstrate using over 150 years of capital market history that a few key facts keep emerging. *First*, the periods when diversification benefits tend to be of the highest potential (with low correlations between international indices) tend also to be periods that present investors with the greatest difficulty in diversifying. These tend to be periods of war and significant international tension. *Second*, the periods that have the highest correlations (and thus the lowest diversification benefits) are during the turn of the 19th century, during the Great Depression and during the late 20th century, which tend to be periods when markets are generally bearish in tendency. Thus, the *third* finding that diversification benefits are non-constant and may be least available when they are most needed. Interestingly, it is not clear why these shifts in correlations and linkages occur over the long run. Roll (1992) proposes Ricardian specialization, Heston and Rouwenhorst (1994) suggest that national cultures and economic predilections dominate industrial explanations, while Chen and Knez (1995) and Korajczyk (1996) suggest that lack of integration drives the issue, without addressing why this integration has not occurred.

The structure of this chapter is as follows. The next section presents literature review on the linkages displayed by Russian stock market. Section 3 provides a brief overview of the development of the Russian stock markets since its re-establishment in 1991, including the events of the Russian crisis of August 1998 and its implications for the Russian stock market. Section 4 presents data and methodology used in the study. Section 5 discusses empirical results and Section 6 provides conclusions.

2. RUSSIAN EQUITY MARKET INTEGRATION

Studies that shed light on co-movements of Russian and international stock prices are not plentiful and usually analyze Russia along with other CEE markets. The conclusions of these studies do not necessarily conform to each other, due to differences in sample period, data frequency, stock market indices used and adjustment procedures applied to the indices used. Probably one of the earliest studies is that of Linne (1998). This study sought to investigate whether newly established Eastern European markets (Russia, Poland, Hungary, the Czech Republic and Slovak Republic) display any long relationships within the group, and with mature markets (Germany, UK, France, Italy, Switzerland, US and Japan). The data set consisted of local stock market indices expressed in USD, at weekly frequency, over the period from 1991 to 1997. The results suggest that during the sample period none of the two most important Russian stock market indices displayed linkages with any of the analyzed markets. Among the CEE markets only Poland displayed co-movements with the world portfolio proxied by the MSCI-World Index. By contrast, the Slovakian stock market showed cointegration relations with all mature stock markets. The author concludes that at that period CEE markets were mostly driven by domestic factors. This chapter, however, does not attempt to provide explanations of the country-specific patterns of the long-run linkages.

Röckinger and Urga (2001) explored integration of the four emerging stock markets over the period from 1994 to 1997 using an extended Bekaert and Harvey (1997) model for conditional volatility with time varying parameters. Apart from valuable information about the extent and strength of financial integration provided by the time-varying parameters, the advantages of this approach are the following. *First*, accounting for GARCH structure of the residuals, it allows to establish the nature of the GARCH effect in case of the emerging markets (leverage versus liquidity hypotheses). *Second*, the model incorporates a latent factor, which accounts for information beyond stock market indices. The study uses daily data for the most important local stock market indices expressed in USD. The results suggest that the Russian stock market differs from the other three markets with regard to sources of shocks spillovers. The USA and Germany are important sources of shock spillovers in case of Russia. Czech Republic and Polish stock returns seem to reflect movements in the UK and not in the USA. Both Czech Republic and Hungarian stock returns were mostly influenced by German market movements, although in case of Hungary the impact has declined, whereas for Czech Republic it increased. This chapter, however, does not comment on the importance of regional shocks for the CEE countries.

JKP (1998) pointed out the importance of political and economic events in Russia for CEE economies (Hungary, Poland and the Czech Republic). As an example, although by the end of 1997 CEE markets had largely recovered from the losses incurred due to the Asian crisis, they underwent further losses as domestic Russian economic conditions worsened over the first half of 1998. Therefore in their analysis the authors take into account the timing of events in Russia when analyzing the impact of the crisis on the extent of predictability and co-movements between CEE markets and between these markets and the US stock market. Assuming a time-varying pattern of market co-movements, JKP distinguish between pre-crisis and crisis periods. Basing on the results of the principal component analysis and Hansen and Johansen (1993) tests of the constancy of cointegration vector, they set the latter from September 1, 1997 to September 21, 1998. They find considerable differences both in short- and long-term linkages between the markets. In line with the evidence for developed markets (Longin & Solnik, 1995) they find significant increase in the values of daily correlations during the crisis period between market returns and absence of cointegration vectors for any of the markets. Before the crisis period the Russian stock market shared bivariate cointegration relations with Hungarian and the US markets, which are no longer detected in the crisis period. JKP explain the absence of cointegration after the crisis by the dominance of the short-run adjustments over the long-run dynamics. Results of the variance decomposition show that before the crisis 95 percent of the variance in the Russian stock market was explained by itself after 5 days. During the crisis period the share of foreign markets in explaining variance increased from 5 to 20 percent. In both periods most of the impact was due to movements in US markets, with the Polish stock market exerting the smallest impact on fluctuations in the Russian stock market.

Gelos and Sahay (2000) explore financial spillovers due to various external crises on CEE foreign exchange and stock markets. They find increasing financial market integration since 1993, measured by the change in (unadjusted) stock return correlations. The increase is especially significant around the Russian crisis, which corresponds to the JKP finding. Gelos and Sahay find strong evidence of shock transmission from Russian to CEE markets, especially to the Hungarian one (compare with JKP, 1998, finding above). Russian stock returns appear to Granger-cause returns in these markets, which did not seem to be the case before the crisis. They also document evidence that negative shocks in Russia have stronger effect on other emerging markets than positive ones. A similar study by Baele, Crombez, and Schoors (2003) notes that EU equity shocks have increased influence on CEE after 1998, but that the Russian market remains segmented from EU influences.

Jithendranathan and Kravchenko (2004) conclude albeit using a simple regression analysis at the stock level that Russian equities are more integrated in the aftermath of the 1998 crisis. Finally, Hayo and Kutan (2004) analyzed the impact of US stock returns on Russian stock and bond markets (along with other factors such as oil prices and political news), within a GARCH framework. The study covers the period between 1995 and 2001. The papers findings echo that of Röckinger and Urga (2001) suggesting US stock returns tend to Granger-cause Russian stock returns. Also, higher US returns seem to be associated with lower volatility on the Russian stock market. The paper also points to the link between increased financial liberalization and increased impact of the US returns. Therefore the Hayo and Kutan (2004) study implies a time-varying pattern in the US–Russia relation; however, as opposed to Röckinger and Urga (2001), they utilize a static GARCH model. Finally, Fedorov and Sarkissian (2000) examine the issue of integration at the industry level, finding the not surprising result that integration with the world market proxy is greater the larger and more internationally orientated (through trade) is the typical industry firm.

3. THE RUSSIAN STOCK MARKETS

Since published literature on emerging European stock markets usually analyses Russia along with a number of CEE countries, it typically does not provide much information on the organization and development of the Russian stock market. This section aims to fill this gap. Table 1 presents the basic statistics for the CEE markets; recent developments of Polish, Czech Republic and Hungarian markets are analyzed in detail in Schröder (2001).

Table 1. CEE Stock Markets as of December 2003.

Indicator	Russia	Poland	Hungary	Czech Republic
Market capitalization, million USD	72,210	28,849	12,988	25,122
Value of share trading, 2003, million USD		9,662	8,269	9,187
Number of listed securities	207	203	49	65
Local index, December 2003	RTS	WIG	BUX	PX 50
		20,820.07	9,379.99	659
Local index, % change 2002–2003	57	44.9	20.3	43
Market capitalization as % of the GDP	22	14	17	

Source: World Federation of Stock Exchanges (http://www.world-exchanges.org), Prague Stock Exchange (www.pse.cz).

3.1. Organization of the Russian Stock Market

There are a number of stock exchanges in Russia. In terms of value most stock trading takes place through MICEX (Moscow Interbank Currency Exchange) or RTS (Russian Trading System). RTS, where trading is in USD is dominated by international investors, while Russian traders are concentrated in MICEX (Grigoriev & Valitova, 2002). The Moscow Stock Exchange was traditionally a market for shares of Gazprom, the Russian gas monopoly. There are also a number of regional stock exchanges; however, their share in stock trading is negligible in comparison with those of MICEX and RTS (see appendix for details).

3.2. The RTS Stock Exchange (RTS)

The RTS Stock Exchange, formerly RTS, was established in the middle of 1995 by leading brokerage companies to organize single regional markets. It is the first and biggest electronic trading floor in Russia, organized using trading technologies provided by NASDAQ. Initially RTS operated as an over-the-counter (OTC) market, with settlement in foreign currency only. Nowadays RTS includes the following markets: RTS Classic market (quote-driven) and RTS Order-driven stock market; FORTS (futures and options trading with ruble settlement); RTS Bonds (bonds trading); RTS Board (the system used for indicative quotation of securities not listed on the RTS); NQS Bills (the system used for indicative quotation of bills issued by Russian companies) (www.rts.ru). The Classic market remains the main venue for trading by foreign and domestic investors. The Order-driven stock market, established in 2002 in cooperation with Sankt-Petersburg Stock Exchange, aims to develop the ruble stock market segment of RTS. This is an important venue for trading of shares of Gazprom and shares of other 200 companies (RTS, 2002).

The official index of the RTS was first calculated on September 1, 1995. It is a market value-weighted index of capitalization of shares on the RTS quoting lists. RTS index is calculated basing on the data from the RTS Classic market. Since March 1999 RTS index is calculated not only in USD, but also in Russian rubles. A key feature of the RTS is that trading is concentrated in a small number of companies representing oil and energy sectors. For example, in 2002 shares of six companies (RAO, UES (United Energy Systems), LUKoil, Surgutneftegaz, Yukos and Tatneft) accounted

Table 2. Key Indicators for RTS Stock Exchange.

	1995	1996	1997	1998	1999	2000	2001	2002	2003
Market capitalization, billion USD	–	–	–	–	32.4	35	69.2	92.9	72.2
Value of stock trading, billion USD	0.22	3.54	15.6	9.3	2.4	5.8	4.9	4.6	6.1
Average daily turnover, million USD	–	–	62.7	36.9	9.5	23.3	19	18	24
Number of listed securities	–	–	324	369	358	391	368	247	312
Stock exchange index: RTS	82.92	200.50	396.41	58.9	175.3	143.3	256.8	359.1	567.3
RTS, % change to previous year	−17	129	98	−86	194	−20	96	34	57

Source: RTS Annual Reports, various issues.

for 72 percent of RTS turnover; that is in the short term, dynamics of the RTS index is determined by the market leaders. Companies from energy, oil and telecommunication industries account for more than 60 percent of RTS capitalization.

The RTS is a dynamically developing exchange. By 1999 RTS accounted for about half of the trading volume of the Russian stock market, competing with MICEX. The exchange seeks to expand the range of stocks and other instruments, and improve clearing and settlement procedures. In 2002 RTS introduced a market for futures and options, FORTS, although the Austrian Derivatives Exchange had introduced futures and options on RTS as early as 1997. Key indicators of RTS development are presented in Table 2 and discussed in the following sub-sections in the context of the events of the crisis and post-crisis period.

3.3. MICEX

MICEX started security trading in March 1997 (FCS, 1997). It is another leading Russian trading floor, where trades are held in stocks of 150 Russian companies, including blue chips RAO UES, LUKoil, Rostelekom and Mosenergo. Total market capitalization is 150 billion USD. The year 2001 saw a drastic increase in MICEX turnover, as opposed to RTS saw a decline in its trading in that year. In 2002 the volume of transactions in MICEX reached 70 billion USD (www.micex.ru). MICEX calculates the MICEX Composite Index (market value-weighted index of shares included in MICEX quotation lists) and MICEX10 (arithmetical average of price changes for 10 most liquid stocks), available since September 22, 1997 and January 6, 1998.[2]

3.4. Development of the Russian Stock Market

The crisis in Russian financial markets of 1997–1998 is usually divided into three periods: October 1997 to January 1998, March to May 1998 and July to August 1998 (IET, 1999; FCS, 1999). During the period of October 1997, RTS was characterized by an increase in trading volume and number of the participants, and the RTS Index displayed an impressive 94 percent growth. However, positive tendencies in the stock market were taking place against the background of poor fundamentals of the Russian economy (budget crisis, vulnerability of the banking system and high value of short-term government liabilities relative to the values of the reserves of the Central Bank (IET, 1999), aggravated by instability in international financial markets, in particular, by the events in the South Asian markets in 1997. The latter are seen as those that stipulated the timing of the Russian crisis. As Buchs (1999) elegantly puts it: "... *if the timing as well as the speed of the Russian crisis were definitely linked to the East Asian ... events, the underlying vulnerability of Russia was a serious problem which no investor could ignore*".[3] Under these circumstances, foreign investors that started close monitoring of the economy fundamentals initiated selling government and corporate bonds. Increased demand for foreign currency triggered a sharp decline of the reserves of the Central Bank.[4] These events were reflected in a falling stock market: by January 1998 the RTS Index had plummeted by 50 percent.

In March to May 1998 there followed a further 20 percent decline in stock market prices. The government crisis, a worsening deficit of the balance of payments and issue of new debt induced foreign investors to continue selling Russian securities. Despite financial aid provided by International Monetary Fund (IMF) and International Bank for Reconstruction and Development (IBRD) in July, further decline in prices of the Russian securities took place. The crisis of the Russian banking system provided an additional reason. Russian banks, facing increased claims from the foreign lenders, were induced to sell securities to maintain their currency reserves.[5] As a result, a new wave of price declines took place. On August 17, 1998 the Russian central bank allowed the ruble to devalue. During August to September 1998 the RTS Index fell by almost 70 percent.

3.5. Post-crisis Development

By 1999 international interest in the Russian stock market was very low, reflected in record-low levels of trading activity, which had fallen by 84 percent since 1997. Low turnover created pre-conditions for the speculative growth of the market that amounted to 194 percent and made RTS the fastest growing market in the world. In the next year, despite the fastest growth of Russian economy since the start of the reforms, the performance of the stock market was disappointing: RTS declined by 20 percent. This reflected primarily a decline in price of the Russian blue chips, mostly oil companies depending heavily on the dynamics of the oil prices. However, improving macroeconomic and political situation helped to revive the interest of investors and boost turnover, which more than doubled in 2000 (IET, 2001). During 2001–2003 the Russian market grew, in contrast to the slowdown in the US and EU economies, and financial and political instability in Latin American emerging markets. In 2002 RTS grew by one-third. In 2003 the political risks of investing in Russian market became important again against the background of the conflict between Yukos and government that resulted in imprisonment of the Head of the Company M. Khodorkovsky. The market reacted with a 25 percent decline during October 2003.[6] However, the overall results of the year were positive due to remarkable increase in prices of the blue chips, stipulated by high oil prices. Growth of some of the leading companies exceeded 100 percent (Norilskij Nikel, 220 percent; Mosenergo, 114 percent; RAO UES, 112 percent).

4. DATA AND METHODOLOGY

4.1. Data

Several equity market indices currently exist for Russia. The most widely recognized ones are the RTS Index, the NAUFOR Official Index and the MT Index calculated by the *Moscow Times* newspaper. Other indices include the AK&M Information Agency and Commersant Newspaper Indices, with Creditanshtalt-Grant, Russian Brokerage House and CS First Boston all also producing variants of indices. In this chapter we use MSCI Indices, dollar denominated, on a daily frequency. The indices analyzed are those for Russia, EMU countries, UK, USA, Japan, Hungary, Czech Republic and Poland. The choice of data reflects a desire to analyze co-movements of the Russian market both with the developed markets and local markets. The data run from December 31, 1994 to October 14, 2004. We use MSCI Indices as they are designed to be directly comparable across national exchanges, compiled on a value-weighted basis of freely investible shares. As such they represent here a data set that is significantly different to the most of the previous studies and are we believe more directly comparable than those used by other studies (Fig. 1).

Shown in Table 3 are the basic descriptive statistics of the returns of the indices, and in Table 4 the correlation matrix of the returns data. All data in the sample are found to be I(1) in levels of the indices and I(0) in returns using the conventional unit root testing procedures of Dickey–Fuller and Phillips–Perron.

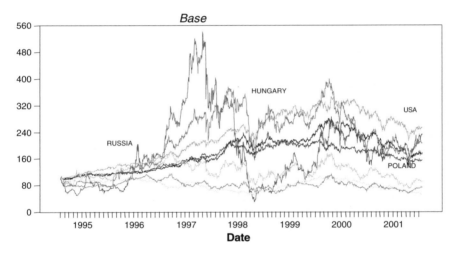

Fig. 1. MSCI Indices Russia, CEE and Developed Markets.

Table 3. Basic Descriptive Statistics (% Returns Data), 1994–2004.

	EMU	UK	USA	Russia	Poland	Hungary	Japan	Czech Republic
N	2,555	2,555	2,555	2,555	2,555	2,555	2,555	2,555
Minimum (%)	−5.84	−5.27	−6.97	−28.10	−11.59	−19.01	−7.16	−7.39
Maximum (%)	5.72	5.26	5.61	24.22	9.02	13.00	12.27	6.76
Mean (%)	0.03	0.02	0.03	0.07	0.02	0.06	−0.02	0.03
Standard deviation (%)	1.23	1.09	1.14	3.42	1.96	1.96	1.48	1.52
Skewness	−0.1775	−0.1810	−0.1200	−0.3309	−0.1105	−0.5793	0.2593	−0.1349
Kurtosis	2.2533	2.2708	3.2349	8.0672	2.5049	9.9245	3.2632	2.0393

Table 4. Correlation Matrix (% Returns Data), 1994–2004.

	UK	USA	Russia	Poland	Hungary	Japan	Czech Republic
EMU	0.7665	0.4259	**0.3097**	0.3397	0.3984	0.2152	0.3743
UK		0.3722	**0.2576**	0.2730	0.3090	0.1749	0.2927
USA			**0.1574**	0.1278	0.1387	0.0664	0.1168
Russia				**0.2730**	**0.3326**	**0.1336**	**0.2585**
Poland					0.4081	0.2216	0.3329
Hungary						0.2047	0.3569
Japan							0.1764

4.2. Johansen Cointegration Tests and VECM Modeling

We are concerned to capture in any modeling both the short- and the long-run relationships that may arise. We initially examine the data for cointegration under the Johansen approach. Where we find cointegrating vectors, the parameters of these vectors are then set as constraints in a Vector Error Cointegration Model. This allows us to derive, while addressing long-run equilibrium relations, the short-run dynamics of the system using impulse response functions (IRFs) and variance decomposition analysis (VDA). We analyze the data in the entire period (December 31, 1994 to October 14, 2004), and in three sub-periods: before 1997, during the 1997–1998 crises period and from 1999 onward. Thus we first separate the crisis and tranquil periods by exogenously defining the duration of these periods, relaying on the market events described earlier. Since imposing the break dates exogenously may not necessarily reflect the true dynamics of the adjustment process, we proceed with a methodology that allows us to estimate the break dates from the data, Gregory–Hansen residual-based cointegration test.

4.3. Gregory–Hansen (1996) Residual-Based Cointegration Test

Results of Monte Carlo experiments (Campos, Ericcson, & Hendry, 1996; Gregory & Hansen, 1996) show that when a shift in parameters takes place standard tests for cointegration (like the one of Engle & Granger, 1987) may lose power and falsely signal the absence of equilibrium in the system. A number of tests of unit roots under structural stability are available. In this chapter we use the Gregory–Hansen (1996) test. The Gregory–Hansen test assumes the null hypothesis of no cointegration against the alternative hypothesis of cointegration with a single structural break of unknown timing. The timing of the structural change under the alternative hypothesis is estimated endogenously. Gregory and Hansen suggest three alternative models accommodating changes in parameters of the cointegration vector under the alternative. A *level* shift model allows for the change in the intercept only (C):

$$y_{1t} = \mu_1 + \mu_2\varphi_{t\tau} + \alpha'y_{2t} + e_t \quad t = 1, \ldots, n \quad (1)$$

The second model accommodating a trend in data also restricts shifts only to the change in *level with a trend* (C/T):

$$y_{1t} = \mu_1 + \mu_2\varphi_{t\tau} + \beta t + \alpha'y_{2t} + e_t \quad t = 1, \ldots, n \quad (2)$$

The most general specification allows for changes both in the *intercept and slope* of the cointegration vector (R/S):

$$y_{1t} = \mu_1 + \mu_2\varphi_{t\tau} + \alpha'_1 y_{1t} + \alpha'_2 y_{2t}\varphi_{t\tau} + e_t \quad t = 1, \ldots, n \quad (3)$$

The dummy variable, which captures the structural change, is represented as:

$$\varphi_{t\tau} = \begin{cases} 0 & t \leq [n\tau] \\ 1 & t > [n\tau] \end{cases} \quad (4)$$

where $\tau \in (0, 1)$ is a relative timing of the change point. The trimming interval is usually taken to be $(0.15n, 0.08n)$, as recommended in Andrews (1993). The models (1)–(3) are estimated sequentially with the break point changing over the interval $\tau \in (0.15n, 0.85n)$. Non-stationarity of the obtained residuals, expected under the null hypothesis, is checked by augmented Dickey–Fuller (ADF) and Phillips–Perron (PP) tests. Setting the test statistics (denoted as ADF* (Za*, Zt*)) to the smallest value of the ADF (Za, Zt) statistics in the sequence, we select the value that constitutes the strongest evidence against the null hypothesis of no cointegration.

4.4. The DCC–GARCH Approach

We also use the recent dynamic conditional correlation (DCC) specification of multivariate GARCH models (Engle, 2002) to model the main series for which we find significant relationships. Unlike the previous methodologies we analyze the multivariate relationships using returns of the indices. Arising from the Gregory–Hansen and the Johansen–Juselius approach we identify the variables that are related in long-term equilibrium and then model these using the multivariate GARCH model. We use a parsimonious approach, describing the mean and variances as both autoregressive moving average (ARMA)(1,1) processes. This is strictly ad hoc. The data are modeled as a DCC–GARCH(1,1) process, within a four variable system. The major advantage of this formulation is that while it preserves the main features of standard multivariate GARCH models it allows for explicit time variation in the conditional covariance (and correlation) matrix. The extraction of the conditional time-varying correlations allows us to examine the short-run dynamics of the series that are linked by a long-run relationship. It also allows to trace the effects attributed to the sequence of crisis events that took place throughout the sample.

5. RESULTS

We examine the data over the entire period and over three sub-periods as shown above. We use two techniques, as discussed, the Johansen multivariate method and the Gregory–Hansen approach. We show the results for the Johansen approach in Table 5 and the Gregory–Hansen approach in Tables 6–8. We show in Table 9 the variance decomposition for the four periods. Two distinctly different stories emerge from these methods.

5.1. Johansen Multivariate Cointegration Test, VARs and IRFs Results

A number of features arise from a Johansen analysis over the entire period (Table 5). Johansen cointegration tests based on a lag length of 2^7 indicates

Table 5. Johansen Cointegration Tests.

	Trace = 0	Trace = 1	Trace = 2	Max = 0	Max = 1	Max = 2
Overall	105.3236	70.10955	44.59244	35.21407	25.51711	17.36702
Pre-crisis	151.1522	92.27682	63.73410	58.87537	28.54272	24.35854
Crisis	151.1522	92.27682	63.73410	58.87537***	28.54272	24.35854
Post–crisis	179.8941***	125.3571*	78.32393	54.53705***	47.03316**	26.91778

Notes: Table shows the results of a Johansen–Juselius multivariate cointegration test. Null hypothesis is that of a specified or maximum number of cointegrating relationships (trace and max statistics, respectively).
Significance levels at
*10%,
**5% and
***1%.

Table 6. Gregory–Hansen Cointegration Tests: Overall Period.

Variables	Model	ADF	Break Point/Date	PP Zt	Break Point/Date	PP Za	Break Point/Date
Russia – EMU	C	-2.62	0.157	-2.39	0.155	-12.73	0.155
Russia – EMU	C/T	-5.24**	0.351 (08/06/98)	-5.06**	0.349 (01/06/98)	-49.81**	0.349 (02/06/98)
Russia – EMU	C/S	-2.73	0.335	-2.63	0.334	-14.86	0.336
Russia – UK	C	-2.79	0.157	-2.56	0.155	-14.44	0.155
Russia – UK	C/T	-4.99*	0.359 (06/07/98)	-4.85*	0.349 (01/06/98)	-45.44*	0.349 (01/06/98)
Russia – UK	C/S	-2.96	0.329	-2.90	0.329	-18.07	0.335
Russia – USA	C	-2.65	0.157	-2.38	0.155	-12.54	0.155
Russia – USA	C/T	-5.74***	0.359 (06/07/98)	-5.53***	0.349 (01/06/98)	-57.87***	0.360 (09/07/98)
Russia – USA	C/S	-2.63	0.157	-2.52	0.234	-12.71	0.234
Russia – Japan	C	-2.28	0.157	-2.17	0.849	-9.42	0.155
Russia – Japan	C/T	-3.86	0.359	-3.74	0.360	-28.33	0.360
Russia – Japan	C/S	-2.60	0.296	-2.41	0.294	-12.79	0.294
Russia – EMU, UK, USA	C	-4.80	0.500	-5.15*	0.509	-52.63*	0.509
Russia – EMU, UK, USA	C/T	-6.01**	0.359 (06/07/98)	-5.86**	0.360 (09/07/98)	-64.43**	0.360 (09/07/98)
Russia – EMU, UK, USA	C/S	-5.29	0.515	-5.52	0.509	-60.29	0.509
Russia – All developed markets	C	-5.34*	0.516	-5.49*	0.509	-59.66**	0.509
Russia – All developed markets	C/T	-5.99**	0.359 (09/07/98)	-5.95**	0.369 (11/08/98)	-65.54***	0.369 (11/08/98)
Russia – All developed markets	C/S	-5.27	0.524	-5.84	0.513	-67.37	0.513
Russia – Poland	C	-3.35	0.652	-3.43	0.652	-22.46	0.652
Russia – Poland	C/T	-4.20	0.360	-4.08	0.360	-33.63	0.360
Russia – Poland	C/S	-3.60	0.649	-3.59	0.637	-25.71	0.636
Russia – Hungary	C	-2.36	0.606	-2.29	0.293	-10.49	0.293
Russia – Hungary	C/T	-4.47	0.359	-4.31	0.360	-37.23	0.360
Russia – Hungary	C/S	-2.45	0.304	-2.36	0.299	-11.13	0.299
Russia – Czech Republic	C	-3.09	0.157	-2.86	0.155	-16.42	0.155
Russia – Czech Republic	C/T	-3.85	0.359	-3.69	0.360	-27.14	0.360
Russia – Czech Republic	C/S	-3.07	0.157	-2.84	0.155	-16.22	0.155
Russia – All CEE markets	C	-3.16	0.659	-3.12	0.653	-19.65	0.65
Russia – All CEE markets	C/T	-5.31**	0.360	-5.21	0.349	-51.87	0.35
Russia – All CEE markets	C/S	-4.78	0.336	-4.79	0.337	-45.55	0.33

Notes: Model specifications for the bivariate cointegration relationship: C – level shift (change in constant); C/T – level shift with trend (model with a linear trend and change in constant only); C/S – regime shift (model with change in both constant and slope). Critical values are taken from Gregory and Hansen (1996).

Significance levels at

*10%,

**5% and

***1%.

Table 7. Gregory–Hansen Cointegration Tests: Pre-crisis Period 30/12/1994 to 31/07/1998.

Variables	Model	ADF	Break Point/Date	PP Zt	Break Point/Date	PP Za	Break Point/Date
Russia – EMU	C	-2.59	0.429	-2.47	0.850	-14.19	0.850
Russia – EMU	C/T	-3.37	0.207	-3.47	0.200	-24.38	0.200
Russia – EMU	C/S	-4.10	0.774	-4.08	0.768	-28.06	0.768
Russia – UK	C	-3.48	0.845	-3.53	0.850	-23.26	0.850
Russia – UK	C/T	-3.27	0.850	-3.36	0.850	-20.92	0.850
Russia – UK	C/S	-3.49	0.771	-3.52	0.769	-23.45	0.769
Russia – USA	C	-2.86	0.847	-2.90	0.849	-14.69	0.849
Russia – USA	C/T	-2.86	0.398	-2.85	0.398	-17.07	0.398
Russia – USA	C/S	-3.55	0.670	-3.48	0.679	-20.69	0.679
Russia – Japan	C	-2.87	0.429	-2.53	0.424	-14.16	0.421
Russia – Japan	C/T	-2.81	0.848	-2.73	0.558	-16.79	0.558
Russia – Japan	C/S	-3.15	0.667	-3.10	0.694	-19.75	0.694
Russia – EMU, UK, USA	C	-3.71	0.842	-4.02	0.199	-28.24	0.186
Russia – EMU, UK, USA	C/T	-4.29	0.369	-4.27	0.363	-33.99	0.363
Russia – EMU, UK, USA	C/S	-4.63	0.768	-4.88	0.393	-44.30	0.393
Russia – All developed markets	C	-3.80	0.394	-4.01	0.199	-28.19	0.199
Russia – All developed markets	C/T	-4.42	0.569	-4.28	0.363	-34.70	0.568
Russia – All developed markets	C/S	-4.78	0.768	-5.04	0.393	-46.74	0.393
Russia – Poland	C	-2.87	0.429	-2.56	0.424	-14.36	0.642
Russia – Poland	C/T	-2.72	0.832	-2.55	0.850	-12.95	0.804
Russia – Poland	C/S	-3.03	0.541	-2.76	0.540	-17.13	0.543
Russia – Hungary	C	-3.18	0.845	-3.04	0.850	-21.38	0.839
Russia – Hungary	C/T	-3.28	0.838	-3.12	0.839	-22.53	0.839
Russia – Hungary	C/S	-3.28	0.786	-3.32	0.688	-24.12	0.688
Russia – Czech Republic	C	-3.78	0.379	-3.27	0.382	-21.26	0.382
Russia – Czech Republic	C/T	-2.72	0.848	-2.57	0.382	-14.26	0.382
Russia – Czech Republic	C/S	-3.01	0.363	-3.01	0.395	-19.32	0.395
Russia – All CEE markets	C	-3.33	0.817	-3.18	0.816	-23.87	0.816
Russia – All CEE markets	C/T	-3.37	0.817	-3.21	0.816	-24.18	0.816
Russia – All CEE markets	C/S	-4.44	0.837	-4.23	0.836	-35.97	0.836

Notes: For abbreviations, refer to footnote of Table 6.
Significance levels at *10%, **5% and ***1%.

Table 8. Gregory–Hansen Cointegration Tests: Post-crisis Period 01/08/1998–14/10/2003.

Variables	Model	ADF	Break Point/Date	PP Zt	Break Point/Date	PP Za	Break Point/Date
Russia – EMU	C	-2.94	0.510	-2.86	0.507	-16.43	0.507
Russia – EMU	C/T	-4.83**	0.848 (05/11/03)	-4.99**	0.846 (31/10/03)	-40.90	0.848
Russia – EMU	C/S	-3.36	0.427	-3.42	0.426	-23.99	0.426
Russia – UK	C	-2.91	0.843	-2.78	0.841	-15.18	0.841
Russia – UK	C/T	-4.78**	0.847 (03/11/03)	-4.92**	0.846 (31/10/03)	-39.57	0.846
Russia – UK	C/S	-2.84	0.246	-3.04	0.248	-18.78	0.248
Russia – USA	C	-3.07	0.508	-2.98	0.529	-17.78	0.529
Russia – USA	C/T	-5.80***	0.848 (05/11/03)	-5.85***	0.846 (31/10/03)	-48.72**	0.846 (31/10/03)
Russia – USA	C/S	-3.80	0.424	-3.74	0.425	-26.19	0.425
Russia – Japan	C	-3.63	0.502	-3.62	0.502	-24.99	0.502
Russia – Japan	C/T	-5.88***	0.846 (31/10/03)	-5.94***	0.846 (31/10/03)	-50.73***	0.846 (31/10/03)
Russia – Japan	C/S	-3.67	0.502	-3.67	0.483	-25.51	0.502
Russia – EMU, UK, USA	C	-5.09**	0.841	-6.09***	0.830	-69.23***	0.830
Russia – EMU, UK, USA	C/T	-7.32***	0.574	-7.36***	0.519	-53.14***	0.591
Russia – EMU, UK, USA	C/S	-7.29***	0.604 (01/05/02)	-8.04***	0.602 (26/04/02)	-110.63***	0.602 (26/04/02)
Russia – All developed markets	C	-5.35*	0.843	-6.26***	0.830	-72.44***	0.830
Russia – All developed markets	C/T	-7.61***	0.549	-7.52***	0.542	-84.11***	0.542
Russia – All developed markets	C/S	-7.25***	0.604 (01/05/02)	-8.01***	0.602 (26/04/02)	-109.75***	0.602 (26/04/02)
Russia – Poland	C	-3.42	0.457	-3.49	0.450	-24.19	0.450
Russia – Poland	C/T	-4.85**	0.200 (28/10/99)	-4.80*	0.217 (06/12/99)	-41.80	0.217
Russia – Poland	C/S	-3.66	0.446	-3.74	0.447	-27.54	0.447
Russia – Hungary	C	-3.84	0.270	-3.76	0.266	-28.34	0.266
Russia – Hungary	C/T	-4.58	0.218	-4.50	0.150	-36.98	0.217
Russia – Hungary	C/S	-4.56	0.293	-4.64	0.291	-42.49*	0.291 (22/05/00)
Russia – Czech Republic	C	-1.44	0.248	-1.19	0.849	-3.70	0.245
Russia – Czech Republic	C/T	-4.66	0.568	-4.41	0.568	-38.97	0.568
Russia – Czech Republic	C/S	-1.57	0.827	-1.41	0.823	-4.19	0.823
Russia – All CEE markets	C	-3.89	0.823	-3.82	0.823	-29.41	0.823
Russia – All CEE markets	C/T	-5.27	0.456	-5.13	0.462	-51.80	0.462
Russia – All CEE markets	C/S	-4.32	0.743	-4.34	0.575	-37.60	0.575

Notes: For abbreviations, refer to footnote of Table 6.
Significance levels at
*10%,
**5% and
***1%.

Table 9. Variance Decompositions: 10-Day Horizons, % Terms.

Period	RU	CZ	HU	JP	PL	UK	USA	EMU
Overall								
1	100.00	–	–	–	–	–	–	–
2	97.56	0.12	0.08	0.06	0.00	0.03	2.02	0.13
3	97.02	0.15	0.12	0.08	0.00	0.03	2.42	0.18
4	96.73	0.16	0.14	0.09	0.00	0.03	2.63	0.22
5	96.53	0.17	0.15	0.09	0.00	0.02	2.78	0.25
6	96.37	0.18	0.15	0.09	0.00	0.02	2.90	0.29
7	96.24	0.19	0.15	0.10	0.00	0.02	2.99	0.32
8	96.11	0.19	0.15	0.10	0.00	0.02	3.08	0.35
9	96.00	0.20	0.15	0.10	0.01	0.02	3.15	0.39
10	95.88	0.20	0.15	0.10	0.01	0.02	3.22	0.42
Pre-crisis								
1	100.00	–	–	–	–	–	–	–
2	99.94	0.00	0.00	0.01	0.00	0.03	0.00	0.01
3	99.80	0.01	0.00	0.04	0.01	0.09	0.02	0.04
4	99.59	0.01	0.00	0.07	0.02	0.19	0.03	0.09
5	99.33	0.02	0.00	0.11	0.02	0.31	0.06	0.14
6	99.03	0.03	0.00	0.15	0.03	0.45	0.09	0.21
7	98.69	0.04	0.01	0.20	0.04	0.61	0.13	0.28
8	98.31	0.05	0.01	0.25	0.05	0.79	0.17	0.37
9	97.92	0.06	0.01	0.30	0.06	0.98	0.22	0.46
10	97.50	0.08	0.02	0.34	0.07	1.18	0.27	0.55
Crisis								
1	100.00	–	–	–	–	–	–	–
2	93.83	0.05	0.40	0.34	0.01	0.18	4.62	0.57
3	93.69	0.16	0.26	0.93	0.03	0.37	4.00	0.56
4	93.40	0.19	0.19	1.29	0.02	0.60	3.82	0.49
5	93.31	0.22	0.15	1.47	0.02	0.74	3.65	0.43
6	93.25	0.24	0.13	1.58	0.01	0.84	3.56	0.39
7	93.20	0.25	0.13	1.66	0.01	0.91	3.49	0.35
8	93.16	0.26	0.13	1.73	0.01	0.95	3.43	0.32
9	93.12	0.27	0.16	1.79	0.01	0.99	3.38	0.29
10	93.08	0.27	0.19	1.84	0.01	1.02	3.33	0.27
Post-crisis								
1	100.00	–	–	–	–	–	–	–
2	98.60	0.02	0.00	0.04	0.01	0.06	1.23	0.05
3	98.19	0.02	0.01	0.07	0.03	0.07	1.57	0.05
4	98.02	0.01	0.01	0.09	0.04	0.09	1.69	0.04
5	97.90	0.01	0.01	0.12	0.05	0.11	1.76	0.03
6	97.80	0.02	0.01	0.14	0.06	0.13	1.81	0.03
7	97.68	0.03	0.01	0.17	0.06	0.15	1.85	0.03
8	97.57	0.05	0.01	0.20	0.07	0.17	1.89	0.03
9	97.44	0.08	0.01	0.24	0.08	0.19	1.92	0.04
10	97.31	0.12	0.01	0.27	0.09	0.21	1.94	0.05

Notes: RU: Russia; CZ: Czech Republic; HU: Hungary; JP: Japan; PL: Poland.

an absence of cointegrating vectors. This, if correct, would have important finance implications. The first is that there is no long-run stable relationship between the various equity markets. As a consequence, there are potential gains from international diversification, the series all moving separately with no shared common stochastic trend.

This evidence is relatively unusual. Although earlier studies on cointegration that used bivariate Engle–Granger approach have found little evidence in favor of cointegration, the later chapters that used the more sophisticated Johansen multivariate approach generally found stronger evidence of integration. To the former group belong works of Kasa (1992) that finds a single cointegrating vector indicating low levels of integration, Arshanapalli and Doukas (1993) that document similar results for world market. Gallagher (1995) finds no evidence of cointegration between Irish and either German or UK equity markets. Studies that, like the present analysis, have used Johansen multivariate approach find stronger evidence of integration. Some evidence of integration is found in Chou, Ng, and Pi (1994) for the G7 countries, Hung and Cheung (1995) for the Asian markets, Kearney (1998) for Irish and European markets, Gilmore and McManus (2002) for US–Central European markets, and Ratanapakorn and Sharma (2002) and Manning (2002) for Southeast Asian, European and US markets. This is not unanimous, however, with Kanas (1988), Chan, Gup, and Pan (1997) and Allen and Macdonald (1995) finding evidence of segmentation.

Having found no long-term relationship, we proceed to a vector autoregression (VAR) without the need to impose error correction terms. We order the data based on the contemporaneous correlation between the equity indices, giving the ordering shown. Based on block exclusion tests we find that all variables apart from EMU and Czech Republic have an impact on Russia. An examination of the residual correlation matrix indicates that there is strong remaining correlation between the variables, and thus while IRFs can be derived we cannot, except in the case of Russia–Japan, ascribe the resulting shocks to the perturbed series. For the Japan case we find that a positive shock in Japan leads to a rapid and sustained drop in the Russian market return of 0.4 percent (Fig. 2).

Examining the pre-crisis period, December 1994 to December 1996, we again find no long-run relationship present in the data, again indicating that over that period there would have been diversification benefits from investing in the area (see Table 5). There is a different order implied in the VAR model than that for the overall period. In common with the findings for the entire period, we find, based on block exogeneity tests, that all series apart from EMU and Czech Republic have an impact on Russia.

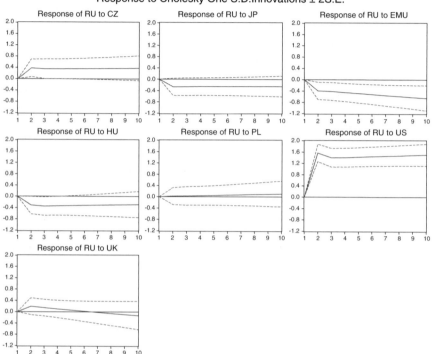

Response to Cholesky One S.D.Innovations ± 2S.E.

Fig. 2.   IRFs for the Overall Period, 30/12/1994 to 14/10/2004.

Apart from Poland the residuals are uncorrelated with the Russian market, and so we can examine IRFs. The evidence from the IRFs is mixed with regard to the markets. Local CEE markets provide little stimulus to the Russian market, while it responds strongly positively to rises in US and EMU markets, and falls against UK and Japanese markets (Fig. 3).

During the period around the Russian and Asian crises, defined as 1997–1998 here, we find emerging some evidence of long-run relationships (see Table 5). During the crisis period we find a single cointegrating vector, between Russia and Japan, emerging. This provides some evidence of weak international integration. However, after the crisis period, while there is increased evidence of integration, with two cointegrating vectors, Russia is not bivariatly correlated with any of the other variables. Again we find that

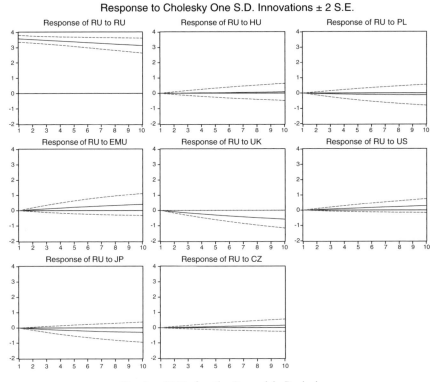

Response to Cholesky One S.D. Innovations ± 2 S.E.

Fig. 3. IRFs for the Pre-crisis Period.

all variables, apart from Czech Republic and EMU, have a significant impact on Russia. The strong correlations evident between the majority of the variables, apart from Russia–Japan and Russia–Czech Republic, renders interpretation of the IRFs uncertain. Again, the response to the Japanese market is negative, consistently overall, while the response to the EMU is mixed, starting negative and then rising to end positive. The evidence is that, consistently, the Russian market responds negatively to shocks in the Japanese and positively to shocks from the USA with mixed responses to UK and EMU markets, and negligible responses to local markets (Poland, Czech Republic and Hungary) (Fig. 4).

Therefore the evidence from Johansen cointegration tests suggests that the Russian equity market remains segmented from the world equity markets. With the exception of the crisis period there was and remains a benefit

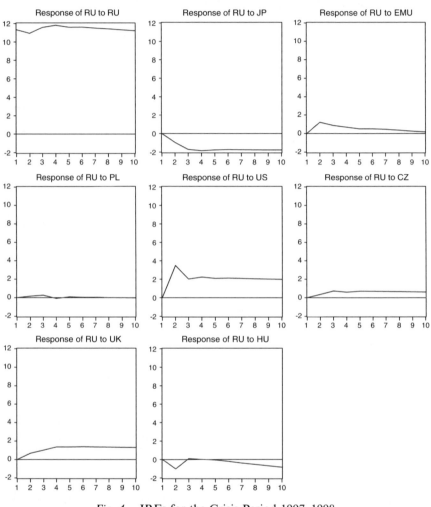

Fig. 4. IRFs for the Crisis Period 1997–1998.

to international diversification by including holdings of Russian equities for the investors of the other countries examined. Even within a VAR system we find that the market has remained relatively isolated. In particular, Russian equities remain segmented from the EMU markets.

5.2. Gregory–Hansen Test Results

Turning, however, to the Gregory–Hansen approach, we find a different situation as regards long-run relationships. For the Russian market the test indicates the presence of a number of bivariate cointegration relations with major markets. In particular, we find that the Russian market was cointegrated with the EMU, UK and USA, albeit with a break in the relationship. In the multivariate setting a break is found in the cointegration vector for Russia and two groups of the developed markets (including and excluding Japan). Overall we find a number of unique break points. These are all in the period June to August 1998, corresponding exactly to the etiology of the crisis. The breaks detected were 01/06/98, 02/06/98, 08/06/98, 06/07/98, 09/07/98, 11/08/98. The final break point was therefore set at 31/7/98, to allow for the gradual adjustment. These results lead us to suggest that despite the serious impact on world markets of the Asian crisis of 1997 we find no evidence here that this crisis had an immediate effect on the stability of relationships between Russia and developed or regional markets.

Using 31/7/98 as the break point in Tables 7 and 8 we show the results of further Gregory–Hansen analyses. In the "pre-crisis" period, up to 31/7/98, we find no evidence of bivariate cointegration relations between the Russian market and any other market or group of markets (Table 7). This corresponds to the results of Johansen cointegration tests showing that the Russian stock market remained isolated until 1997. In the "post-crisis" period, defined relying on Gregory–Hansen test results as 01/08/98 to 14/10/04, we find evidence of bivariate cointegration relations for all four developed markets, again however with a break (Table 8). This break holds both individually and as a group. In the multivariate setting a break is found in the cointegration vector for Russia and two groups of the developed markets (including and excluding Japan). We also find, for the first time, some evidence of increased integration with regional economies, the Gregory–Hansen techniques showing evidence in favor of cointegration with Poland, and very weak evidence for cointegration with Hungary. Therefore Gregory–Hansen test results strengthen weak evidence in favor of increased integration of the Russian stock market provided by the Johansen tests. The test suggests that the long-run market co-movements have strengthened after the crisis; the test thus indicates the importance of the Russian crisis for the dynamics of the long-run relationships between the Russian and developed stock markets (Fig. 5).

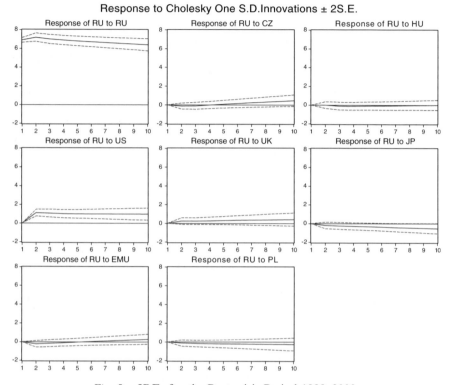

Fig. 5. IRFs for the Post-crisis Period 1999–2003.

5.3. DCC–GARCH Results

Whether the pattern of the short-run interdependencies between the Russian and major developed markets has been affected in a similar manner is examined by means of the DCC–GARCH model. The correlations are derived from a quadrivariate ARMA(1,1)–DCC–GARCH(1,1) model estimated over the 1995–2001 period. Shown in Fig. 6 are the estimated daily conditional correlations between Russia and the main developed markets.

The marked change in the pattern of conditional correlations in the Summer of 1997, at the time of the Asian crisis, is evident. We can see from Fig. 6 that during the period of the Asian crisis correlations with the major equity indices rose dramatically by mid-1997, especially those with the EMU markets. In the second half of 1997, as the crisis was unfolding, the strength

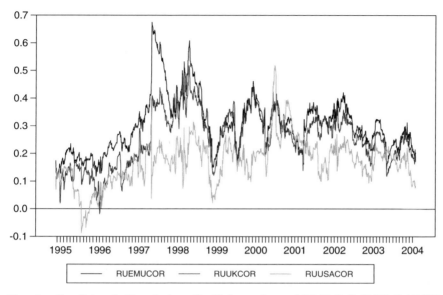

Fig. 6. Conditional Correlation Coefficients from ARMA(1,1)–DCC-GARCH (1,1) Model.

of the short-term dependencies weakened reflected in falling conditional correlations, especially in the cases of the UK and EMU; correlations with the USA remained relatively stable. Interestingly, correlation with the USA has remained the lowest of the three correlation series. A second rise in conditional correlations with EMU and UK followed in the first half of 1998, coinciding with the first phase of the Russian crisis. This rise in the extent of short-term relationship preceded the break in the long-term relationships in August 1998 point indicated by the Gregory–Hansen test. Toward the end of 1999, as the crisis was evolving, we again observe a sharp decline in the intensity of the co-movements as the events in the domestic market started to dominate influences from abroad. Simple visual inspection of Fig. 6 suggests the presence of three periods with differing patterns of the conditional correlations: before 1997 (upward trend, low volatility), 1997–1998 (with two major peaks in the series) and since 1999 (no distinct trend, high volatility; higher levels than before 1997). The evidence from conditional correlations provides an indirect support to our exogenous division of the sample in the three sub-periods used in Section 1 in Chapter 4. The DCC analysis suggests, not surprisingly, that short-term interdependencies between the Russian and the developed stock markets underwent major changes in the 1997–1998 period and have been generally strengthening afterward.

5.4. Variance Decomposition Results

Shown in Table 9 are variance decompositions, showing the percentage of forecast errors, over a 10-day period, that are attributable to each series. The table reports results using exogenous break point to separate crisis period. However, the results using the break points suggested by Gregory–Hansen approach lead to the same conclusions.

An interesting feature that emerges from Table 9 is the changing role of the EMU markets as a source of volatility of the Russian stock market. Whereas movements in the European markets played an important role for the Russian stock market during the crisis, their importance dropped significantly afterwards, therefore leaving the USA a dominant source of influence on the Russian market, albeit the dominance of the latter has also fallen post-crisis. During the crisis another dominant market appeared to be the Japanese one. Post-crisis, we find that shocks in EMU or local markets, play little role in determining changes in the Russian market.

6. CONCLUSION

We have examined the relationship between Russian, developed markets, and other CEE equity markets over the 1995–2004 period. During this period the Russian crisis of 1997–1998 had major impacts on equity markets worldwide. Using traditional Johansen multivariate cointegration approaches and examining IRFs from vector-error correction models we find that the extent of the relationship differs markedly before and after the Russian crisis of 1998. However, further examination, using the Gregory–Hansen approach, indicates that the effect of the Russian crisis is more complex, and that the Russian market shows significantly more evidence of integration with developed markets since, albeit the extent of interdependencies differs in case of the US and European markets. The USA remains the dominant market from which shocks impact on the Russian market A DCC–GARCH model indicates that the conditional relationships between the Russian market and the main developed markets is, as shown by the Gregory–Hansen approach, shifting. No clear effect of the Asian crisis is evident from our analysis, with the DCC measures showing it to have had a major effect, the Gregory–Hansen tests, not.

NOTES

1. Research assistance of Thomas Lagoarde Segot and Terhi Jokipii is gratefully acknowledged. We also wish to thank the participants in the IIIS Workshop in International Financial Integration, in particular Patrick Geary, Thomas Flavin and Margaret Hurley. We also acknowledge the support of the Irish Government through the Programme for Research in Third Level Institutions.

2. See Grigoriev and Valitova (2002) for the analysis of the relationship between RTS and MICEX indices as well as impact of oil and gas prices on their dynamics.

3. The Asian crisis of the late Summer of 1997 saw the meltdown of East Asian currencies that led to further speculative attacks on East Asian financial system components including equity markets, and further spread to the Latin American exchanges. We thus have in our sample two interlinked crises closely following each other that may emerge as potential sources of instability in the relationships.

4. Buchs (1999) points out that financial linkages between emerging markets in form of substantial amounts of Russian and Brazilian Government debt by Korean banks and Russian short-term bonds (GKO) by Brazilian banks, served as a contagion channel in the course of Asian crisis. Komulainen (1999) indicate another reason behind the spillover effect, namely decline in prices for the row materials stipulated by the decreased demand in Asia.

5. See Ippolito (2002) for the excellent review of the state of the Russian banking system during and after the crisis.

6. See *The Economist* (2004) about the reaction of the Russian stock market on the development of the Yukos case. RTS plummeted despite soaring oil prices after the rumors about the Yukos bankruptcy strengthened.

7. In all cases and sub-periods we found that a lag of 2 was appropriate for VAR analyses, based on the Hannan-Quinn and Schwartz criteria. Except for Poland in the pre-crisis period we find, using ADF tests, that the data are I(1).

REFERENCES

Allen, D., & Macdonald, G. (1995). The long run gains from international equity diversification; Australian evidence from cointegration tests. *Applied Financial Economics*, *5*(1), 33–42.

Andrews, D. W. K. (1993). Tests for parameter instability and structural change with unknown change point. *Econometrica*, *61*, 821–856.

Arshanapalli, B., & Doukas, J. (1993). International stock market linkages: Evidence from the pre- and post-October 1987 period. *Journal of Banking and Finance*, *17*(1), 193–208.

Baele, L., Crombez, J., & Schoors, K. (2003). *Are Eastern European equity markets integrated? Evidence from a regime-switching shock spillover model*. Working Paper, Ghent University.

Baig, T., & Goldfain, I. (2000). *The Russian default and the contagion to Brazil*. IMF Working Paper no. WP/00/160.

Bekaert, G., & Harvey, C. R. (1995). Time-varying world market integration. *Journal of Finance, 50*, 403–444.

Bekaert, G., & Harvey, C. R. (1997). Emerging equity market volatility. *Journal of Financial Economics, 43*, 29–78.

Buchs, T. D. (1999). Financial crisis in the Russian Federation: Are the Russians learning to tango? *Economics of Transition, 7*, 687–715.

Campos, J., Ericcson, N. R., & Hendry, D. F. (1996). Cointegration tests in the presence of structural breaks. *Journal of Econometrics, 70*, 187–220.

Chan, K., Gup, B., & Pan, M. (1997). International stock market efficiency and intregration: A study of 18 countries. *Journal of Business, Finance and Accounting, 24*(4), 803–813.

Charemza, W. W., & Majerowska, E. (2000). Regulation of the Warsaw stock exchange: The portfolio allocation problem. *Journal of Banking and Finance, 24*, 555–576.

Chen, Z., & Knez, P. (1995). Measurement of market integration and arbitrage. *Review of Financial Studies, 8*, 287–325.

Chou, R., Ng, V., & Pi, L. (1994). *Cointegration of International Stock Market Indices*. IMF Working Papers.

Dungley, M., Fry, R., Gonzales-Hermosillo, B., & Martin, V. (2003). *Unanticipated shocks and systemic influences: The impact of contagion in global equity markets in 1998*. IMF Working Paper no. WP/03/84.

Engle, R. F. (2002). Dynamic conditional correlation: A new simple class of multivariate GARCH models. *Journal of Business and Economic Statistics, 20*, 339–350.

Engle, R. F., & Granger, C. W. (1987). Cointegration and error correction: Representation, estimation and testing. *Econometrica, 55*(1), 251–276.

FCS. (1997). Annual Report 1997, in Russian. www.fcsm.ru

FCS. (1999). Annual Report 1999, in Russian. www.fcsm.ru

Fedorov, P., & Sarkissian, S. (2000). Cross-sectional variations in the degree of global integration: The case of Russian equities. *Journal of International Financial Markets, Institutions and Money, 102*, 131–150.

Gallagher, L. (1995). Interdependencies among the Irish, British and German stock markets. *Economic and Social Review, 26*(2), 131–147.

Gelos, G., & Sahay, R. (2000). Financial market spillovers in transition economies. *Economics of Transition, 91*, 53–86.

Gilmore, C. G., & McManus, G. M. (2001). Random-walk and efficiency tests of Central European markets. Paper prepared for presentation at the *European Financial Management Association Conference 2001*, Lugano, Switzerland.

Gilmore, C. G., & McManus, G. M. (2002). International portfolio diversification: US and Central European equity markets. *Emerging Markets Review, 3*, 69–83.

Goetzmann, W., Li, L., & Rouwenhorst, K. G. (2000). *Long-term global market correlations*. Yale ICF Working Paper no. 00-60.

Gregory, A. W., & Hansen, B. E. (1996). Residual-based tests for cointegration in the models with regime shifts. *Journal of Econometrics, 70*(1), 99–126.

Grigoriev, L., & Valitova, L. (2002). Two Russian stock exchanges: Analysis of relationships. *Russian Economic Trends, 113*, 44–53.

Hansen, H., & Johansen, S. (1993). *Some tests for parameter constancy in cointegrated VAR-models*. Mimeographed.

Hayo, B., & Kutan, A. M. (2004). *The impact of news, oil prices, and global market developments on Russian financial markets*. The William Davidson Institute Working Paper no. 656.

Henke, H. (2003). *Tax-loss selling and window-dressing: An investigation of the January effect in Poland*. Working Paper, European University Viadrina.

Hernández, L. F., & Valdés, R. O. (2001). What drives contagion: trade, neighborhood, or financial links? *International Review of Financial Analysis, 10*, 203–218.

Heston, S. L., & Rouwenhorst, K. G. (1994). Does industrial structure explain the benefits of international diversification? *Journal of Financial Economics, 36*, 3–27.

Hung, B., & Cheung, Y. (1995). Interdependence of Asian equity markets. *Journal of Business, Finance and Accounting, 22*, 281–288.

IET. (1999). Russian Economy in 1998. Tendencies and Perspectives in Russian. www.iet.ru

IET. (2001). Russian Economy in 2000. Tendencies and Perspectives in Russian. www.iet.ru

Ippolito, F. (2002). *The banking sector rescue in Russia*. BOFIT Working Paper no. 12.

Jithendranathan, T., & Kravchenko, N. (2004). *Integration of Russian equity markets with the world equity markets – effects of the Russian financial crisis of 1998*. Working Paper, University of St Thomas.

Jochum, C., Kirschgässner, G., & Platek, M. (1998). A long-run relationship between Eastern European markets? Cointegration and the 1997/98 crisis in emerging markets. *Weltwirtschaftliches Archiv, 1353*, 454–479.

Kanas, A. (1988). Linkages between the US and European equity markets: Further evidence from cointegration tests. *Applied Financial Economics, 8*, 607–614.

Kasa, K. (1992). Common stochastic trends in international stock markets. *Journal of Monetary Economics, 29*(1), 95–124.

Kearney, C. (1998). Causes of volatility in a small integrated stock market: Ireland 1975–1994. *Journal of Financial Research, 21*(1), 85–105.

Komulainen, T. (1999). *Currency crisis theories – some explanations for the Russian case*. BOFIT Discussion Papers no. 1.

Korajczyk, R. (1996). A measure of stock market integration for developed and emerging markets. *The World Bank Economic Review, 10*(2), 267–289.

Linne, T. (1998). *The integration of the Central and Eastern European equity markets into the international capital markets*. Working Paper no. 1/1998, Institut für Wirtschaftsforschung Halle.

Longin, F., & Solnik, B. (1995). Is the correlation of international equity returns constant: 1960–1990? *Journal of International Money and Finance, 141*, 3–26.

Manning, N. (2002). Common trends and convergence? South East Asian equity markets, 1988–1999. *Journal of International Money and Finance, 21*(2), 183–202.

Mateus, T. (2004). The risk and predictability of equity returns of the EU accession countries. *Emerging Markets Review, 5*, 241–266.

Pagano, M. (1993). Financial markets and growth: An overview. *European Economic Review, 37*, 613–622.

Ratanapakorn, O., & Sharma, S. C. (2002). Interrelationships among regional stock indices. *Review of Financial Economics, 11*(2), 91–108.

Ratkovicova, M. (1999). *Driving factors of efficiency of CEE capital markets*. CASE-CEU Working Paper Series, Warsaw.

Röckinger, M., & Urga, G. (2001). A time-varying parameter model to test for predictability and integration in the stock markets of transition economies. *Journal of Business and Economic Statistics, 191*, 73–84.

Roll, R. (1992). Industrial structure and the comparative behaviour of international stock market indices. *Journal of Finance, 47,* 3–41.

RTS. (2002). Annual Report, in Russian. www.rts.ru

Scheicher, M. (2001). The comovements of the stock markets in Hungary, Poland and the Czech Republic. *International Journal of Finance and Economics, 6,* 27–39.

Schröder, M. (Ed.) (2001). *The new capital markets in Central and Eastern Europe.* Berlin, Heidelberg, New York: Springer-Verlag.

The Economist. (2004). That sinking feeling, June 5, 2004.

UNCTAD. (2004a). FDI country profiles: Poland. http://www.unctad.org/Templates/Page.asp?intItemID = 3198&lang = 1

UNCTAD. (2004b). FDI country profiles: Czech Republic. http://www.unctad.org/Templates/Page.asp?intItemID = 3198&lang = 1

UNCTAD. (2004c). FDI country profiles: Hungary. http://www.unctad.org/Templates/Page.asp?intItemID = 3198&lang = 1

FURTHER READING

FCS. (1998). Annual Report 1998, in Russian. www.fcsm.ru.

FCS. (2001). Annual Report 2001, in Russian. www.fcsm.ru.

FCS. (2002). Annual Report 2002, in Russian. www.fcsm.ru.

IET. (2000). Russian Economy in 1999. Tendencies and Perspectives in Russian. www.iet.ru

IET. (2002). Russian Economy in 2001. Tendencies and Perspectives in Russian. www.iet.ru

IET. (2003). Russian Economy in 2002. Tendencies and Perspectives in Russian. www.iet.ru

IET. (2004). Russian Economy in 2003. Tendencies and Perspectives in Russian. www.iet.ru

RTS. (1997). Annual Report, in Russian. www.rts.ru

RTS. (1998). Annual Report, in Russian. www.rts.ru

RTS. (1999). Annual Report, in Russian. www.rts.ru

RTS. (2000). Annual Report, in Russian. www.rts.ru

RTS. (2001). Annual Report, in Russian. www.rts.ru

RTS. (2003). Annual Report, in Russian. www.rts.ru

APPENDIX

Russian Stock Exchanges

RTS Stock Exchange (www.rts.ru)
Moscow Interbank Curency Exchange (www.micex.ru)
Moscow Stock Exchange (www.mse.ru)
Sankt-Petersburg Stock Exchange (www.spbex.ru)
Rostov Currency and Stock Exchange (www.rndex.ru)
Nizhny Novgorod Stock and Currency Exchange (www.nnx.ru)
Kazan Board of Security Trade (www.kbst.ru)
Ekaterinburg Stock Exchange (www.ese.ru)
Siberian Interbank Currency Exchange (www.sice.ru)
Ural Regional Currency Exchange (www.urvb.ru)

TRADING VERSUS NON-TRADING RETURNS: EVIDENCE FROM RUSSIA AND THE U.K.

Uri Ben-Zion and Niklas Wagner[1]

1. INTRODUCTION

Overnight risk is of particular interest for many market participants including traders who provide liquidity to the market, but also to market participants with longer investment horizons who want to determine whether a given risk–return tradeoff can justify possible intermediate portfolio hedging transactions. Overnight risk may in particular play a highly significant role in emerging markets, given that information is incorporated into prices at a slower rate and liquidity may hinder a quick unwinding of portfolio positions.

In this study we examine the trading day versus overnight non-trading returns for the Russian and the U.K. stock market. We use data for the FTSE100 index, which represents London as a mature European benchmark market. For Russia we use data from the Russian Trading System (RTS) Stock Exchange in Moscow, an emerging European exchange. Daily returns are converted to Euro during the period January 1, 1999 to December 31, 2000, a period during which the Russian market was subject to substantial political and economic policy uncertainty. Russia has played a central role in the opening of the eastern European economies since the start

Emerging European Financial Markets: Independence and Integration Post-Enlargement
International Finance Review, Volume 6, 415–427
Copyright © 2006 by Elsevier Ltd.
ISSN: 1569-3767/doi:10.1016/S1569-3767(05)06016-4

of the transition process in the late 1980s. Up to the end of the year 1999, Russia was under the political regime of President Jelzin. The subsequent regime under President Putin was established at the beginning of 2000 as a result of political developments that led to early presidential elections. The impacts of liberalization and the opening of the economy during the late Jelzin and the early Putin regime also had large impacts on the Moscow Exchange. Our empirical findings are useful in explaining the effects of transition from emerging to mature stock market status, and they shed light on how emerging markets can potentially improve the investment opportunities for foreign investors.

Our empirical results for both markets indicate that expected returns per unit of time are higher during non-trading periods, which further suggests the existence of an overnight risk premium. This premium does not seem to be only attributable to volatility risk, however, because the risk of large price drops for both markets appears to be much higher overnight. The results for Russia in particular are in line with this observation, while being even more pronounced. The Russian emerging market offers relatively high average returns during non-trading hours. Also, the RTS index exhibits time series dependence such that overnight close-to-open returns positively correlate with the subsequent close-to-close trading day returns. Our examination of trading versus non-trading variance per hour ratios in turn shows that relatively more return variability is given during trading hours in the U.K. than in Russia. In other words, volatility stays relatively high overnight in Russia, while it tends to shrink in the mature U.K. market.

This chapter adds to previous studies on returns and volatility during trading and non-trading hours. Examples are the seminal paper by French and Roll (1986) and more recent work such as Zdorovtsov (2003). Related market microstructure research on non-trading periods is by Cao, Ghysels, and Hatheway (2000). The remainder of the chapter is structured as follows. Section 2 introduces the dataset, defines the trading and non-trading returns used in the examination and discusses the relevant trading times. Section 3 outlines our empirical analysis and discusses the results. The conclusions are contained in Section 4.

2. THE DATASET AND RETURN DEFINITIONS

Our joint dataset reflects the view of a continental European investor who may have invested in the U.K. equity market as represented by the FTSE 100 stock index and in the Russian equity market as represented by the RTS stock index. Daily returns are converted to Euro during the period January 1, 1999 to December 31, 2000. The dataset is collected from three sources. The Russian market data are collected from the Russian RTS Stock Exchange in Moscow (www.rts.ru). The data for the FTSE 100 index are obtained from Datastream, Thomson Financial, London. Given are daily opening and closing prices for both markets. For simplicity, an approximate exchange rate adjustment is done via one exchange rate per day, where the exchange rate quotes are taken from Olsen and Associates, Zurich (www.oanda.com). Removing holidays, Moscow yields $T = 501$ daily close-to-close sample return observations while London yields $T = 504$ sample observations.

For trading time information we refer to the local stock exchanges. The trading times for Moscow and London are as follows. The Moscow Stock Exchange is open from 11 a.m. to 6 p.m. ($+3$ GMT), which yields 7 h during exchange open-to-close, $h_{oc} = 7$ (h). The London Stock Exchange has trading hours between 8:00 a.m. to 4:35 p.m. (± 0 GMT). Consequently, we have $835/60$ h during exchange open-to-close for London, $h_{oc} = 8\,35/60$ (h). Note that both markets operate in parallel while Moscow closes 1 h and 35 min earlier than London.

Given the above dataset, we calculate daily logarithmic returns from open and closing prices which are transferred to euros. Daily close-to-close returns,

$$R_{t,cc} = \ln P_t - \ln P_{t-1} \qquad (1)$$

are measured over time intervals of 24 h or over 24 h plus the number of intermediate exchange holidays (weekends and public holidays) times 24 h. As such the close-to-close time span is:

$$h_{cc} = 24 + 24\,\#\text{holidays (h)} \qquad (2)$$

where the number of intermediate exchange holidays is: $\#\text{holidays} = 0, 1, 2, 3, \ldots$ The close-to-close returns can be split up into non-trading[2] returns (i.e. overnight returns), which may include exchange holidays, $R_{t,co}$, and trading day returns, $R_{t,oc}$, which are determined during stock exchange opening hours, h_{oc}. We have:

$$R_{t,cc} = R_{t,co} + R_{t,oc} \qquad (3)$$

Hence, the number T of close-to-close returns $R_{t,cc}$ for each market equals the number of calendar days minus one and minus the number of exchange holidays, as denoted by "#holidays". The number of non-trading returns $R_{t,co}$ equals T, and the number of trading day returns $R_{t,oc}$ equals $T+1$. As

Table 1. Trading Times and Average Overnight Trading Times in
Hours for Russia (RTS) and the U.K. (FTSE) during the Sample Period
January 1, 1999 to December 31, 2000.

	h_{co}	h_{oc}	h_{cc}
RTS	27.9	7.0	34.9
FTSE	26.0	8.6	34.6

with the close-to-close returns, non-trading returns may span different time
intervals. The time span of their measurement again depends on the number
of intermediate exchange holidays. We have:

$$h_{co} = 24 - h_{co} + 24 \text{ #holidays (h)} \qquad (4)$$

For our dataset as described above, we can now calculate average time
spans over which returns were measured in the given sample period, January
1, 1999 to December 31, 2000. Out of $T = 501$ observations, Russia exhibits
396 regular overnight returns. The number of days with one, two (typical
weekends), three and four intermediate holidays is 1, 89, 11 and 4, respectively. For the U.K. we have 401 regular overnight returns and the number
of days with intermediate holidays is 0, 92, 6 and 5, respectively. Given these
numbers, we can calculate the average time spans for the close-to-close and
the close-to-open returns in our sample.

The results for both markets, Russia and the U.K., are summarized in
Table 1. The average time spans in hours for the overnight returns show
that, due to weekends and exchange holidays, close-to-close returns span on
average much longer periods than 24 h. In fact in our sample, Russia has an
average time span of 34.9 h over which close-to-close returns are measured,
the U.K. has an average time span of 34.6 h. In Table 1 and in the following
we denote the average times by the symbols h_{co} and h_{cc} as introduced above.

3. ANALYSIS OF TRADING AND NON-TRADING PERIODS

In this section, we study the characteristics of trading and non-trading period returns. We would like to learn more about how returns relate to time,
trading, volatility as well as risk for mature markets and Russia as a market
in transition. The analysis is straightforward in that we apply simple graphical tools and descriptive sample statistics in order to derive our results.

3.1. Joint Distribution of Trading and Non-trading Returns

A graphical representation of our return data is given in Figs. 1 and 2. We jointly plot the close-to-open, the open-to-close and the resulting close-to-close returns. Fig. 1 shows the results for Russia and Fig. 2 for the U.K. As the figures indicate, the joint distribution of the returns for both markets shows structural differences. While the returns in Fig. 2 for the U.K. are quite evenly spread, the returns in Fig. 1 shows asymmetry. Large positive close-to-close returns in Russia hardly ever occur once the overnight return is negative. The same holds for large negative close-to-close returns which tend to occur under given negative overnight returns.

These findings are also supported by a correlation analysis in Table 2. The correlations between trading day and close-to-close returns are high for both markets what we would expect from the fact that that they overlap during the last h_{oc} trading hours. However, the correlation between the overlapping close-to-close returns and the preceding overnight close-to-open return is positive and much more substantial for Russia than for the U.K. A sample correlation of 0.71 for the RTS versus 0.10 for the FTSE indicates a much higher persistence in RTS returns, which may relate to asynchronous

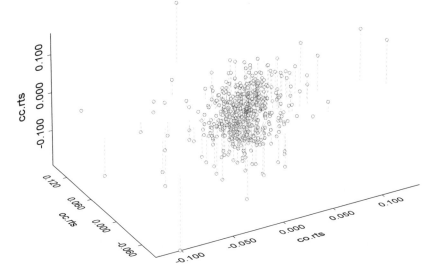

Fig. 1. Plot of Close-to-Open, Open-to-Close and Resulting Close-to-Close Returns for Russia (RTS).

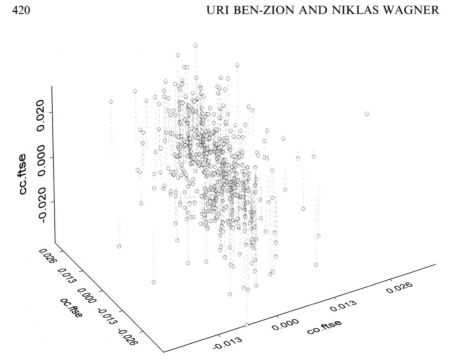

Fig. 2. Plot of Close-to-Open, Open-to-Close and Resulting Close-to-Close
Returns for the UK (FTSE).

Table 2. Sample Correlations Between Overnight, Trading Day and
Close-to-Close Returns in Russia (RTS) and the U.K. (FTSE); Period
January 1, 1999 to December 31, 2000 with 501 and 504 Daily
Observations, Respectively.

	RTS			FTSE		
	$R_{t,co}$	$R_{t,oc}$	$R_{t,cc}$	$R_{t,co}$	$R_{t,oc}$	$R_{t,cc}$
$R_{t,co}$	1	0.03	0.71	1	0.09	0.10
$R_{t,oc}$		1	0.73		1	0.99
$R_{t,cc}$			1			1

trading and market liquidity. This persistence is also documented by a
higher time series correlation in daily close-to-close returns; first order sample autocorrelation is significantly positive for the Russian market (value of
0.172) and insignificant for the U.K. (value of 0.0289). There is no evidence

of predictability from overnight to trading day returns in both markets (see the estimated correlations in Table 2).

3.2. Univariate Distributions of Trading and Non-trading Returns

In order to characterize the univariate properties of the returns we consider the descriptive statistics. Table 3 reports minimal, maximal and average returns as well as their sample standard deviation, skewness and kurtosis.

The statistics in Table 3 indicate that much of the mean daily close-to-close returns is due to the overnight returns for both markets. The sample standard deviation is lower for overnight returns than for trading day returns. The higher risk of the Russian market is also demonstrated by the larger range between minimal and maximal sample returns. The return distributions on a close-to-close basis show negative skewness for both markets. Excess kurtosis statistics tend to be highest for the overnight returns.

Further evidence on the univariate distributional and tail properties of the various returns is given by the quantile/quantile plots (QQ-plots) in Figs. 3 and 4. In these plots, the quantiles of the empirical distribution functions of the returns are plotted against the theoretical quantiles of a normal distribution function with identical sample mean and variance. Given that the distributions match, all plotted quantiles should tend to lie on a straight line as indicated in the plots.

Whereas some increased variability is expected in the corner parts of the plots of Figs. 3 and 4, there should not be a systematic bias in the deviation

Table 3. Sample Summary Statistics for Overnight, Trading Day and Close-to-Close Returns for Russia (RTS) and the U.K. (FTSE); Period January 1, 1999 to December 31, 2000 with 501 and 504 Daily Observations, Respectively.

	RTS			FTSE		
	$R_{t,co}$	$R_{t,oc}$	$R_{t,cc}$	$R_{t,co}$	$R_{t,oc}$	$R_{t,cc}$
Minimum	−0.1242	−0.0920	−0.1929	−0.0249	−0.0389	−0.0389
Maximum	0.1382	0.1540	0.1556	0.0368	0.0315	0.0315
Mean	0.001529	0.000138	0.001667	0.000371	0.000074	0.000111
Standard deviation	0.0249	0.0255	0.0362	0.0058	0.0116	0.0135
Skewness	−0.1245	0.3285	−0.1361	0.2609	−0.1487	−0.1353
Excess kurtosis	5.687	3.374	2.528	4.035	0.071	0.290

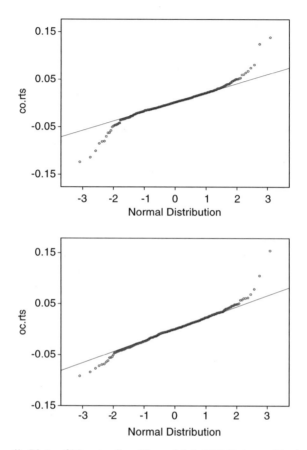

Fig. 3. Quantile Plots of Non-trading (Overnight) RTS Returns (Top) and Trading Day RTS Returns (Bottom) Each Against Quantiles of the Normal Distribution Function.

from the plotted straight line. As a matter of fact, only the FTSE trading period returns do not exhibit such systematic bias, while all other return distributions exhibit small and large returns more frequently than we would expect under the normal distribution. The Russian market shows fat-tailed returns for non-trading as well as trading returns where the non-trading returns deviate more from normality. This is also indicated by the sample kurtosis statistics in Table 3. The results suggest that for the London exchange fat-tailedness is induced via the non-trading periods (Fig. 4 top)

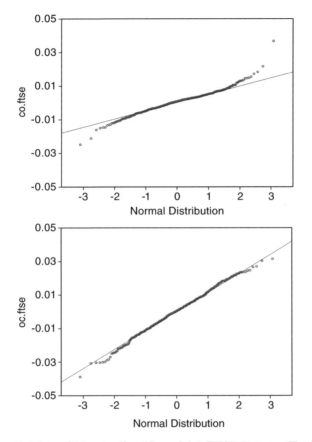

Fig. 4. Quantile Plots of Non-trading (Overnight) FTSE Returns (Top) and Trading Day FTSE Returns (Bottom) Each Against Quantiles of the Normal Distribution Function.

while the trading period returns (Fig. 4 bottom) are thin-tailed and show marginal excess kurtosis (see Table 3).

3.3. Rescaled Return and Risk Relations for Trading and Non-trading Returns

The statistics in Table 3 indicate that much of the mean daily close-to-close returns is due to the overnight returns for both markets. We analyze in the following, whether this difference is due to different time spans over which returns are measured. Furthermore, we ask whether different levels of risk per unit time as measured by return volatility can account for such difference.

Our rules for annualizing returns and return variance are as follows. First the measured return is rescaled to the standard daily close-to-close basis. Then the annualization takes place based on the assumption that there are approximately 250 exchange trading days per calendar year. As such the following relations apply:

$$E_{\text{ccpa}}(R_{\bullet\bullet}) = \frac{\hat{\mu}_{\bullet\bullet}}{h_{\bullet\bullet}} h_{\text{cc}} \cdot 250 \tag{5}$$

$$Var_{\text{ccpa}}(R_{\bullet\bullet}) = \frac{\hat{\sigma}^2_{\bullet\bullet}}{h_{\bullet\bullet}} h_{\text{cc}} \cdot 250 \tag{6}$$

Here, $\bullet\bullet \in \{oc, co, cc\}$ (i.e. all our defined return measures) may be considered. The subscript "ccpa" indicates that the annualized measure rescaled to the close-to-close basis. Given these annualized measures of expected return and risk, we may calculate return/risk measures per unit time as:

$$p_{\bullet\bullet} = \frac{E_{\text{ccpa}}(R_{\bullet\bullet})}{\sqrt{Var_{\text{ccpa}}(R_{\bullet\bullet})}} \tag{7}$$

The results on the annualized per unit time mean returns, standard deviations, $\sqrt{Var_{\text{ccpa}}(R_{\bullet\bullet})}$, and return/risk ratios are plotted in Table 4. A striking result is that the overnight return per unit time is much higher than the trading day return for the RTS index, while the difference is small for the FTSE. However, once risk is accounted for, the overnight return/risk ratios are very similar for both markets.

In order to characterize trading versus non-trading return variance per unit time, we may form variance ratios. We denote the ratio of estimated trading versus non-trading variances per unit time as:[3]

$$q_{\text{occo}} = \frac{\hat{\sigma}^2_{\text{oc}}/h_{\text{oc}}}{\hat{\sigma}^2_{\text{co}}/h_{\text{co}}} \tag{8}$$

The results for this ratio as given in Table 4 indicate that, relative to trading day volatility, overnight volatility in Russia is not at a substantially lower level as it is the case for the mature benchmark market. Hence, the ratio for Russia is much lower than that for the U.K. and the effect of higher trading versus non-trading volatility is weaker for Russia as an emerging market.

Table 4. Annualized Means and Standard Deviations for Overnight, Trading Day and Close-to-Close Returns As Well As Return/Risk Ratios and Variance Ratios for Russia (RTS) and the U.K. (FTSE); Period January 1, 1999 to December 31, 2000 with 501 and 504 Daily Observations, Respectively.

	RTS			FTSE		
	$R_{t,\text{co}}$	$R_{t,\text{oc}}$	$R_{t,\text{cc}}$	$R_{t,\text{co}}$	$R_{t,\text{oc}}$	$R_{t,\text{cc}}$
E_{ccpa} (%)	47.80	17.25	41.68	11.70	9.42	11.13
Standard deviation$_{\text{ccpa}}$ (%)	44.00	89.91	57.19	10.59	36.88	21.31
P	1.09	0.19	0.73	1.10	0.26	0.52
q_{occo}	–	4.174	–	–	12.095	–

4. CONCLUSION

The question addressed in the present contribution is concerned with the risk–return relation for equity markets during trading versus non-trading periods. It is of interest to market participants such as short-term traders as well as long-term investors, which levels of equity market compensation they can expect during trading hours versus overnight (and exchange holiday) periods when there is no possibility to trade in response to the arrival of new information. Our empirical results for both markets indeed indicate that expected returns per unit time are higher during such non-trading periods and that an overnight (per unit time) risk premium exists.

We study return to volatility ratios and find evidence that overnight risk as well as return may be relatively high for an emerging market such as Russia. Despite such differences between the mature U.K. and the emerging Russian market, taking volatility risk into account, both markets reveal a similar return to risk ratio for the trading period as well as for the non-trading period. The trading to non-trading volatility ratio is much lower for Russia, which coincides with a relatively high overnight return volatility as compared to the U.K. Finally, we point out that the overnight risk premium for both markets, although not fully attributable to volatility, may well be due to the risk of large price drops which appears much higher during overnight periods, especially for Russia. Hence, while both markets appear to reward overnight risk, what may seem as an anomaly at first sight, does not necessarily seem to violate the notion of market efficiency. Future research could address in greater detail whether a fair risk–return tradeoff is given during trading versus non-trading periods.

In addition, our diagnostics for both markets indicate that overnight shocks unrelated to trading may in part be responsible for what is called "fat-tailedness" in equity market returns. This is an interesting finding since a vast literature following Clark (1973) including the model extension by Ané and Geman (2000) shows that different levels of trading activity may induce fat tails. Hence, non-normality in daily close-to-close asset returns may persist in empirical studies even if we account for variables such as volume or the number of trades. In sum, we believe that the analysis of trading versus non-trading return periods has not yet obtained sufficient interest, while it bears a fruitful empirical research potential towards our understanding of trading, the transmission of information into prices and the formation of asset price illiquidity premiums.

NOTES

1. up> The authors thank Bea Chipchinsky for helpful suggestions and Christine Sangl for valuable research assistance. Uri Ben-Zion is with Ben Gurion University and Technion, Israel. Niklas Wagner is with Munich University of Technology, Germany.

2. There might be some debate stemming from the question as to whether we should prefer the term "overnight" or "non-trading" returns for the close-to-open returns, especially once the recent emergence of after hours trading is considered; for a study (e.g. see Barclay & Hendershott, 2003). We still use the term "non-trading" in order to indicate the important difference to trading day returns (i.e. so-called "non-trading" returns) result under no, or only marginal, trading activity.

3. We do not go into details here. Note that, given appropriate assumptions, the asymptotic distributions of such variance ratios may be derived as normal limiting distributions (e.g. see Lo & MacKinlay, 1999). In an extension of our analysis it may also be fruitful to further distinguish the results on the close-to-open returns according to regular and weekend or holiday overnight returns (see also Section 2).

REFERENCES

Ané, T., & Geman, H. (2000). Order flow, transaction clock, and normality of asset returns. *Journal of Finance, 55*, 2259–2284.

Barclay, M., & Hendershott, T. (2003). Price discovery and trading after hours. *Review of Financial Studies, 16*, 1041–1073.

Cao, C., Ghysels, E., & Hatheway, F. (2000). Price discovery without trading: Evidence from the Nasdaq pre-opening. *Journal of Finance, 55*, 1339–1365.

Clark, P. K. (1973). A subordinate stochastic process model with finite variance for speculative prices. *Econometrica, 41*, 135–155.

French, K., & Roll, R. (1986). Stock return variances: The arrival of information and the reaction of traders. *Journal of Financial Economics, 17*, 5–26.

Lo, A. W., & MacKinlay, A. C. (1999). *A non-random walk down Wall Street*. Princeton: Princeton University Press.

Zdorovtsov, V. (2003). *Firm-specific news, extended-hours trading and variances over trading and non-trading periods*. Working Paper, University of South Carolina.

PART E:
FDI AND ENLARGEMENT

FOREIGN DIRECT INVESTMENT IN EMERGING AND TRANSITION EUROPEAN COUNTRIES

Steven Globerman, Daniel Shapiro and Yao Tang

1. INTRODUCTION

Many of the emerging and transition economies in Central and Eastern Europe (CEE) have been building their economies largely on the infrastructure inherited from Communist times. It is widely recognized that much of the infrastructure in both the private and public sectors must be replaced if those economies are to achieve acceptable rates of economic growth and participate successfully within the broader European Union (EU) economic zone (The Economist, 2003). Upgrading infrastructure includes the likely importation of technology and management expertise, as well as substantial financial commitments. In this regard, inward foreign direct investment (FDI) is a particularly important potential source of capital for the emerging and transition European economies (ETEEs). FDI usually entails the importation of financial and human capital by the host economy with measurable and positive spillover impacts on host countries' productivity levels (Holland & Pain, 1998a). The ability of ETEEs to attract and benefit from inward FDI should therefore be seen as an important issue within the broader policy context of how these countries can improve and expand their

Emerging European Financial Markets: Independence and Integration Post-Enlargement
International Finance Review, Volume 6, 431–459
Copyright © 2006 by Elsevier Ltd.
All rights of reproduction in any form reserved
ISSN: 1569-3767/doi:10.1016/S1569-3767(05)06017-6

capital infrastructure, given relatively undeveloped domestic capital markets and scarce human capital.

The focus of this chapter is on the direct investment process in ETEEs.[1] In particular, we are interested in the relationship between political and economic governance, and flows of inward and outward direct investment for ETEEs. Previous research has suggested that good governance is particularly important for promoting FDI in developing countries (Globerman & Shapiro, 2002). One might expect this to be also true for ETEEs. Nevertheless, the importance of governance to the direct investment process might be conditioned by specific attributes of emerging economies in Europe. In particular, the legacy of Communism in many of those economies might strengthen the importance of public sector governance attributes as influences on the direct investment process, since informal private sector networks of trust and established reputations for honest dealing are arguably lacking compared to countries with longer legacies of private ownership and market transacting (Slangen, van Kooten, & Suchanek, 2004). On the other hand, for those ETEEs that have joined the EU, the importance of governance attributes at the national level might be mitigated by formal and informal governance institutions that exist at the EU level including, for example, national treatment provisions for companies based in EU-member countries that apply to all EU members. Even countries that have not yet joined the EU might be expected to condition the treatment of private investment with a view towards being accepted into the EU. Thus, while de jure public sector governance might be seen as relatively poor, de facto governance might be relatively good. These latter considerations suggest that measured governance attributes per se might be less important influences on the direct investment process in ETEEs than in comparable developing countries located elsewhere. Therefore, a specific focus of the chapter is whether and how the relationship between governance and inward and outward direct investment differs for ETEEs compared to other European countries, as well as to developing countries outside Europe.

Our chapter makes a number of contributions to the relevant literature. First, it explores the determinants of both inward and outward FDI for ETEEs. Previous studies have focused exclusively on the determinants of inward FDI. Second, the sample of ETEEs is larger than in other studies that have focused on the direct investment process in transition European countries. We also include more recent years than most other available studies. Third, our study explicitly compares the determinants of FDI in ETEEs with alternative samples of developed and, perhaps more interesting, other developing countries. This comparison adds a potentially important perspective on whether and how the basic determinants of FDI differ between ETEEs and other developing countries. Fourth, we seek to identify whether there are differences in the FDI process within our sample of ETEEs. In seeking to identify the determinants of inward and outward FDI, as well as in comparing and contrasting results across different sub-samples of countries and regions, particular attention is paid to measures of governance and institutional change, including privatization. In this respect, our study is distinguished by yet another difference from earlier studies. Specifically, we use a relatively broad measure of governance compared to other investigations of the direct investment process in emerging European countries. This measure, available for a broad sample of countries worldwide, permits us to evaluate explicitly cross-country differences in the impact of governance on capital flows.

This chapter proceeds as follows. Section 2 presents an overview of FDI in ETEEs against the background of FDI flows in Europe as a whole, as well as in other emerging economies. Section 3 discusses measures of governance for ETEEs and reviews studies of the determinants of FDI in those countries. A model of inward and outward direct investment is specified in Section 4, and the estimation results are presented and discussed in Section 5. A summary and conclusions are provided in the final section with particular reference to policy implications for ETEEs.

2. OVERVIEW OF FDI IN ETEEs

Net capital flows in Eastern Europe and the former Soviet Union built up rapidly during the 1980s, reaching around US$5 billion per annum in the second half of the decade. These flows largely took the form of commercial bank loans and trade finance, often through official lending. With the fall of the Berlin Wall in 1989, the countries of Central Europe embarked on programs of liberalization and privatization with a subsequent increase in private capital inflows (Lankes & Stern, 1998).[2] In particular, direct equity investment flows to Eastern Europe and the former Soviet Union more than doubled between 1989 and 1990, and then increased a further tenfold between 1990 and 1993. In 1997, direct investment equity flows to the region were approximately US$12 billion compared to around US$4 billion in 1993. As a share of total capital inflows, direct equity investment increased consistently from around 12 percent in 1990 to around 20 percent in 1997 (Lankes & Stern, 1998).

Observers acknowledge that the growth in FDI in the transitional economies was impressive in the early post-restructuring period, although the level of inward FDI was arguably low compared to that in other developing economies, particularly in East Asia (Lansbury, Pain, & Smidkova, 1996). On average, over the period 1991–1993, FDI inflows to the transitional countries accounted for about 2.5 percent of total world inflows compared to 30.5 percent for developing countries overall; however, FDI flows to the transitional economies increased in the post-1990 period, such that the share of FDI flows going to CEE countries as a share of total inflows to developing countries increased from 0.9 percent in 1990 to 10.7 percent in 1995 before decreasing to 8.9 percent in 1999 (Altomonte & Guagliano, 2003).

The distribution of inward FDI among transitional European countries has been highly concentrated within a relatively few countries. Specifically, over the period 1990–1994, over 70 percent of FDI was channeled to the Central European economies (Czech Republic, Hungary and Poland). Over the period 1990–1999, these three countries accounted for cumulated FDI inflows amounting to 79 percent of total FDI into CEE. Most FDI into the Central European economies originated in Germany and France. For example, over the period 1994–1998, Germany accounted for around 40 percent of the total value of inward FDI, while France accounted for around 10.5 percent. Overall, EU countries accounted for around 70 percent of the total FDI recorded (Altomonte & Guagliano, 2003). In the former Soviet Republics, the USA has been the single largest home country for inward FDI.

More recent patterns of FDI into emerging European countries are summarized in Section 1 where we report total FDI (in millions of current US dollar), total gross domestic product (GDP; in billions of current US dollar) and the ratio of inward FDI to GDP for our sample of ETEEs averaged over the period 1995–2001. Over the full sample period, Poland is the single absolute largest recipient of inward FDI with the Czech Republic and Russia being the next absolute largest recipients. However, Poland and especially Russia are far from being the most FDI-intensive host economies when nominal FDI flows are deflated by nominal GDP levels. Indeed, in our sample of ETEEs, only Turkey has a lower ratio of FDI/GDP than Russia, while Malta has the highest ratio notwithstanding the small absolute amount of FDI going to Malta. The Czech Republic is noteworthy inasmuch as it enjoys a relatively high ratio of FDI/GDP, as well as relatively large inflows of FDI over the sample period. Perhaps the main point to highlight in Table 1 is the continued dominance of Central Europe (Poland, Czech Republic and Hungary) as recipients of inward FDI, notwithstanding

Table 1. FDI and GDP in ETEE Countries (US$).

Country	FDI (Million)	GDP (Billion)	FDI/GDP (%)
Albania	88.29	3.14	2.74
Belarus	192.29	13.06	1.46
Bulgaria	535.86	12.08	4.37
Croatia	915.71	19.76	4.63
Cyprus	138.57	8.95	1.55
Czech Republic	3,604.86	54.69	6.61
Estonia	347.14	4.80	7.03
Hungary	2,378.00	47.03	5.09
Latvia	342.43	6.10	5.75
Lithuania	402.43	9.74	3.87
Macedonia, FYR	128.00	3.85	3.59
Malta	377.71	3.47	10.71
Moldova	81.29	1.53	5.50
Poland	6,410.29	157.75	3.99
Romania	1,019.14	37.27	2.68
Russian	2,916.29	318.68	0.96
Slovak Republic	755.71	20.43	3.73
Slovenia	254.86	18.92	1.35
Turkey	1,197.57	184.59	0.70
Ukraine	574.00	39.21	1.49

Source: Authors' calculations from United Nations Conference on Trade and Development (UNCTAD) in various years.

the liberalization and reform undertaken by other ETEEs including Russia. Thus, the three countries collectively account for somewhat over 55 percent of the total FDI reported in Table 1.

The average ratio of FDI/GDP (expressed as a percentage) over the period 1995–2001 is reported for our sample of ETEE countries, as well as for a number of other regions, in Table 2. The purpose is to provide a basis for evaluating the relative attractiveness of the ETEE countries to foreign direct investors. By and large, ETEE countries were relatively successful in attracting inward FDI given the sizes of their economies. Specifically, the FDI/GDP share was generally higher in the ETEEs than in all countries (Total) with the "out-performance" being particularly notable in the post-1997 period. Whereas the FDI/GDP measure was higher in the Association of South-East Asian Nations (ASEAN) countries than in the ETEE countries from 1995 to 1997, the reverse was true in the post-1997 period. Indeed, relative to the sizes of their domestic economies, the ETEE group attracted more FDI than did China over the period 1998–2001. On the other hand, the FDI/GDP measure was higher in non-ETEE Europe, as well as in the

Table 2.   FDI/GDP (%) in ETEE and Other Regions.

	Countries	1995	1996	1997	1998	1999	2000	2001
ETEE	20	2.48	2.49	2.93	4.02	4.63	5.38	5.28
Non-ETEE Europe	17	1.66	1.70	2.16	4.47	5.69	7.73	4.04
OECD	28	2.19	1.99	2.56	4.10	5.58	7.66	4.22
Non-OECD	133	2.43	2.44	3.68	4.15	4.19	3.57	3.69
ASEAN	9	3.54	4.31	4.79	3.94	3.61	3.21	2.66
China	1	5.12	4.92	4.92	4.62	4.07	3.78	4.04
Total	161	2.39	2.36	3.48	3.48	3.48	4.28	3.78

Source: Authors' calculations from United Nations Conference on Trade and Development (UNCTAD) in various years.

entire Organization for Economic Cooperation and Development (OECD), than in the ETEE sample for all but the most recent year post-1997.

In summary, our sample of ETEE countries became progressively more attractive host locations for foreign direct investors relative to other developing regions of the world in the period 1998–2001. At the same time, there is a fair amount of heterogeneity among our sample of ETEE countries with respect to their attractiveness to foreign investors. In the remainder of this chapter, we attempt to explain the differences in the foreign direct investment experiences of our sample focusing on both inward and outward foreign direct investment (FDI and FDO, respectively).

3. DETERMINANTS OF DIRECT INVESTMENT IN ETEEs

Empirical studies focusing on the direct investment process in emerging European countries are relatively limited in number. In part, this presumably reflects the fact that several of these countries, such as Croatia and Latvia, have only recently experienced a significant growth in inward direct investment. It might also reflect a view that the experiences of emerging European countries are unlikely to be different from those of other countries, including non-European emerging countries.

Virtually all studies of FDI into ETEEs highlight the importance of governance as a factor conditioning the FDI process. In broad terms, governance encompasses laws, regulations and public institutions that determine the extent of economic freedom in a country, the security of private property rights, the costs to the private sector of complying with government regulations and legislation, the competence and efficiency of the civil service in carrying out state activities that, in turn, affect the efficiency of private sector enterprises, the transparency of the legal system and the honesty of government officials (Slangen et al., 2004; Globerman & Shapiro, 2002; Laporta et al., 1999). The basic presumptions are that good governance is characterized by economic freedom, secure property rights, an honest and efficient public sector, a minimum of "dead-weight" regulations and re-strictions on trade, and transparency in government, and that both FDI and domestic investment are directly encouraged by good governance regimes. Furthermore, good governance should promote successful economic performance, and the latter should indirectly encourage FDI by increasing the scope for profitable business activities.

A number of studies document the broad importance of governance to the FDI process in ETEEs. For example, Holland and Pain (1998a, b, 2000) find that the level of inward investment in Eastern Europe is significantly and negatively related to a constructed indicator of country risk based on the principal component of four separate series: GDP growth, inflation, the ratio of foreign exchange reserves to import values and the average country score across all the transition indicators published annually by the European Bank for Reconstruction and Development (EBRD). The EBRD assigns transition economies in Europe a ranking based on nine separate categories according to how far they have progressed toward the standards of indus-trialized countries. The categories cover the legal framework, corporate governance, trade and competition policies, as well as the extent of priva-tizations. Barrell, Holland, and Pain (2000) estimate an equation for inward FDI in the Visegrad economies where country risk is similarly defined from the first principal component of inflation growth and the transition ranking by the EBRD. FDI inflows are negatively and significantly related to the country risk estimate.

Other studies employ more specific measures of governance. Hellman, Jones, and Kaufman (2002) find that corruption reduces FDI inflows for a sample of transition economies. Carstensen and Toubal (2003) use a mac-roeconomic risk ranking found in Euromoney to estimate a panel data model of the determinants of FDI into CEE countries. The less risky the country by the Euromoney ranking, the more attractive is the country for FDI.

In summary, a number of studies identify the importance of governance as a determinant of inward FDI flows in transition economies in Europe. Similar governance measures are used in the various studies, most typically the risk rankings prepared by the EBRD or Euromoney.[3] In this respect, the studies explore the influences on FDI of what might be broadly identified as potential risks surrounding the legal security of property rights and potential risks surrounding the security of the macroeconomic environment; however, available econometric studies ordinarily focus on one or the other. In this regard, Lankes and Venables' (1996) survey of senior managers of western manufacturing companies that were either planning, or had already undertaken, FDI projects in transition economies is noteworthy. Among other things, they find that regulatory and legal risks, as well as risk from macroeconomic instability tend to be important considerations for managers in choosing whether to invest in transition economies.[4] The inference one might draw is that any measure of governance used in statistical models of the direct investment process in ETEEs should be fairly broad in order to encompass the relevant set of risks considered by foreign managers.

A variable related to governance that has also been identified as an important determinant of FDI is privatization. For example, Holland and Pain (1998b) identify the privatization process as one of the key determinants of the level of direct investment in the early years of transition. Specifically, for 11 European economies for the period 1992–1996, they find that indicators of privatization are positively related to levels of inward FDI. Carstensen and Toubal (2003) also find that the level of privatization plays an important role in determining the flows of FDI into a sample of CEE countries over the period of the 1990s.

The impacts of governance and privatization are not necessarily uniform across transition economies. In this regard, Qian (1999) argues that some transitional institutions may be more effective than others at any given time, as removing any one particular distortion may be counter-productive in the presence of other distortions. Russia offers an illustration of this "second-best" principle. Specifically, the policies of mass privatization and capital account convertibility in Russia created incentives for "asset-stripping" and capital flight because they were implemented at a time when reforms to the judiciary and the enforcement of property rights had barely begun (Barrell et al., 2000). Thus, a faster pace of privatization might not encourage a net increase in inward FDI to the extent that other aspects of governance are unfavorable.

The nature of privatization also conditions the FDI experiences of individual countries. In particular, the more open privatization sales are to foreign investors, the stronger the expected relationship between the extent of measured privatization and inward FDI in any transition economy.[5] In this regard, the presence of a local stock exchange might also play a significant role in conditioning inflows of FDI. Specifically, a relatively liquid stock exchange can facilitate takeovers of local firms by foreign investors. This mode for FDI is likely to be more important, the greater the prominence of international mergers and acquisitions (M&A) in the FDI process.

Existing studies of inward FDI to ETEEs also identify a number of factors that are featured as standard independent variables in numerous studies of the FDI process in developed countries, as well as in other parts of the developing world.[6] One such variable is the size of the host country measured usually by GDP or, sometimes, by total population. Market size measures such as total real output (Holland & Pain, 1998a) or total population (Altomonte & Guagliano, 2003) have been found to be positively related to inward FDI in samples of transition European countries.

A second general variable is the "openness" of the host economy to trade. Conceptually, trade and FDI can be either substitutes or complements. Specifically, to the extent that inward FDI is strongly motivated by host country barriers to trade, the reduction or elimination of those barriers might have the primary effect of discouraging inward FDI flows while encouraging the repatriation of retained earnings by established foreign-owned companies. On the other hand, to the extent that multinational companies increasingly engage in geographic specialization of production and intra-firm trade (so-called vertical specialization), host countries that are more integrated through trade with their regional neighbors are likely to be more attractive to multinational companies as locations for specific value-chain activities, ceteris paribus, and therefore more likely to attract inward FDI. Carstensen and Toubal (2003) and Lansbury, Pain, and Smidkova (1996) find that lower tariffs and/or greater trade integration with Central European countries promotes inward FDI in emerging European countries.

Relative labor costs and attributes of the workforce such as skill and educational levels are sometimes included as independent variables in FDI equations. In principle, lower relative labor costs and a more highly educated and skilled workforce should encourage inward FDI, all other things constant;[7] however, the empirical performance of such variables has been mixed, at best. Specifically, wage rates and related variables are not consistently statistically significant in FDI models. In part, this is because labor costs are an incomplete measure of unit costs, and measured levels of formal education may not accurately identify labor productivity differences across countries given different national educational standards and differences in "on-the-job" training and education across countries. While several studies of emerging Europe find that lower relative labor costs and a more educated workforce encourage inward FDI, this is not uniformly the case for all emerging countries.

A country's exchange rate regime has also been featured as an independent variable in FDI models. The broad finding of various empirical models is that volatile exchange rates tend to discourage inward FDI (Globerman & Shapiro, 1999). Again, however, this finding is not uniform across all studies. Nevertheless, it could imply that emerging European countries that have adopted, or plan to adopt, the euro as their national currencies will be disproportionate beneficiaries of inward FDI flows. More generally, attention has been focused on whether a country's membership in a regional free trade area affects FDI flows into that country. Beyond affecting the degree to which a country is integrated into regional trade patterns, free trade agreements such as the North American Free Trade Area (NAFTA) also reduce direct and indirect barriers to inward FDI. Joining a free trade agreement might therefore be expected to promote inward FDI flows, and evidence for NAFTA and the EU generally supports this expectation, although the results are sensitive to the sample time period, as well as the mix of industries in the sample.[8]

To our knowledge, there are no econometric studies of FDO involving ETEEs. One might imagine that FDO is the "mirror image" of FDI. That is, the factors that encourage increased inward FDI discourage FDO. In fact, as Globerman and Shapiro (1999) argue, the conditions that encourage inward FDI are also conducive to the formation and growth of internationally competitive domestically owned firms. Ultimately, successful domestic firms will undertake outward FDI. Hence, given time, one might expect to observe the same factors that encourage increased FDI also promote increased FDO. Whether sufficient time has transpired for this phenomenon to be observed for ETEEs is ultimately an empirical question.

4. MODELING DIRECT INVESTMENT INFLOWS AND OUTFLOWS

Our empirical strategy is to specify and estimate a series of equations to identify the cross-country determinants of direct investment inflows (FDI) and outflows (FDO), and to compare the results using different country sub-samples. Specifically, we estimate a general model for a sample that includes all countries, and for sub-samples that include all emerging and transition economies (ETEW), all-European countries (EUROPE) and ETEE. We also augment the European model to include euro-specific variables.

For the general model, we extend the parsimonious specification of FDI and FDO flows developed in Globerman and Shapiro (2002, 2003a). Thus, we estimate equations of the general form:

$$\text{Ln FDI}_{it} = \beta_0 + \beta_1 \text{ Ln GDP}_{it-1} + \beta_2 \text{ growth GDP}_{it-1}$$
$$+ \beta_3 \text{ governance index}_{it} + \beta_4 \text{ Im exp}_{it-1}$$
$$+ \beta_5 \text{ stock}_{it-1} + \beta_6 \text{ privatization}_{it}$$
$$+ \beta_7 \text{ oil}_i + \beta_8 \text{ China}_i + \beta_9 Xi + \varepsilon_{it} \qquad (1)$$

$$\text{Ln FDO}_{it} = \beta_0 + \beta_1 \text{ Ln GDP}_{it-1} + \beta_2 \text{ growth GDP}_{it-1}$$
$$+ \beta_3 \text{ governance index}_{it} + \beta_4 \text{ Im exp}_{it-1}$$
$$+ \beta_5 \text{ stock}_{it-1} + \beta_6 \text{ privatization}_{it}$$
$$+ \beta_7 X_i + \varepsilon_{it} \qquad (2)$$

The variables and their expected signs are summarized in Table 3 and are discussed below. The X variable represents a vector of factors specific to Europe in general, and the emerging and transitional markets of Europe in particular. The two equations are for the most part similar. We have

Table 3. Expected Signs of Explanatory Variables.

Variable	Inbound FDI	Outbound FDO
GDP	+	+
GDP growth	+	−
Governance index	+	+
Ratio of imports to exports	+, −	+, −
Stock market capitalization	+	+
Privatization	+	−
Oil producer	+	Not included
China	+	Not included
EU member[a]	+	+
Future EU member[a]	+	?
Euro currency[a]	+	+
Regional dummy variables[a]	See text	See text

[a]These variables are included only in the Europe equations. EU members, defined as at 2001 are: Austria, Belgium, Denmark, Finland, France, Germany, Greece, Ireland, Italy, The Netherlands, Portugal, Spain, Sweden and UK. Future EU members are: Bulgaria, Croatia, Cyprus, Czech Republic, Estonia, Hungary, Latvia, Lithuania, Malta, Poland, Romania, Slovak, Slovenia and Turkey. EMU member are: Austria, Belgium, Finland, France, Germany, Greece, Ireland, Italy, The Netherlands, Portugal and Spain. Regional dummy variables are defined for two categories: the CEFTA countries adjacent Europe (Czech Republic, Hungary, Poland, Slovakia and Slovenia) and the Baltic countries (Estonia, Latvia and Lithuania).

elsewhere suggested, with supporting evidence that direct investment inflows and outflows are to a large extent symmetrical (Globerman & Shapiro, 1999, 2002). The presumption is that capital outflows may be stimulated by many of the same factors that encourage capital inflows. For example, superior governance encourages inward flows, as well as increased capital investment more generally. In particular, successful firms created through the domestic investment process are likely to invest abroad as world-class multinational companies. In effect, superior governance encourages capital investment and the expansion of businesses that, in turn, stimulates increases in both inward and outward FDI. In specifying the list of independent variables, we draw upon both previous studies of aggregate FDI flows as well as the recent studies that have focused on FDI flows within Europe and the ETEE, as discussed in the previous section.

We control for the size of the economy and its rate of growth. Country size is measured by the logarithm of GDP. Large market size is expected to attract FDI because of economies of scale in production and distribution for products sold in the host market. In addition, larger markets may be associated with agglomeration economies that lower costs for all producers in that market. These advantages conceptually enhance the attractiveness of a country to foreign investors. At the same time, multinational companies headquartered in large domestic economies are more likely to undertake outward FDI to the extent that location in a large domestic economy conveys firm-specific advantages upon those companies, possibly related to agglomeration efficiencies. For these reasons, we expect that GDP is positively associated with both capital inflows and capital outflows.

The growth of GDP is included to capture potential future economic opportunities and the existence of economic rents. Specifically, rapid economic growth can contribute to disequilibria in input and output markets that create above average profit potential for investors who identify the opportunities and possess the resources to exploit those opportunities. We therefore expect growth to be positively related to FDI, but negatively related to FDO, because a growing economy not only attracts investors from abroad, but it also encourages domestic firms to invest locally.

The overall governance environment of the host and home economies can be expected to affect both FDI and FDO flows. In previous work, we discuss the importance of what we call governance infrastructure as a determinant of FDI and FDO (Globerman & Shapiro, 2002, 2003a). Governance infrastructure refers to a country's political, institutional and legal environment, as well as to the policies that accompany them. Well-governed host countries can expect to attract more inward FDI compared to other countries that offer less attractive environments for private investment. However, well-governed countries can also be expected to spawn companies with the capabilities to be competitive in foreign markets (Bris & Cabolis, 2004). Hence, governance should also be positively related to FDO.

The governance infrastructure measure that we employ is a broad composite index that encompasses a wide diversity of country-specific factors, including political risk, macroeconomic and regulatory policies, rule of law and the extent of corruption. The governance index is sufficiently comprehensive that it accounts for a number of specific variables often included in studies of this kind.[9] Importantly, it is available for a broad cross-section of countries. We expect that countries with strong governance structures will attract capital, and will also be capital exporters. It is important to note that the impact of governance on capital flows may not be the same for all countries. In particular, it is likely that the marginal effects of governance improvements will be stronger for countries whose "stock" of governance infrastructure is relatively low. That is, there may be diminishing returns to governance (Globerman & Shapiro, 2002). For this reason, we report estimates of Eqs. (1) and (2) for sub-samples of both emerging market countries, whose governance infrastructure is generally weak, and developed market economies, whose governance infrastructure is generally strong.

Previous studies have identified factors such as per capita GDP, physical infrastructure and human capital as determinants of FDI inflows. We do not include such variables in our specification because they are highly correlated with governance infrastructure. This is not surprising since these measures, particularly per capita GDP, are also measures of development outcomes that result from good governance (Globerman & Shapiro, 2002).

As noted previously, trade and FDI can be either complements or substitutes. As a consequence, we include a measure of openness to trade (imports + exports/GDP) in the FDI equation. The estimated coefficient will be positive in the FDI equation if FDI and trade are complements, and negative if they are substitutes. We include the same variable in the FDO equation for similar reasons.

It has been documented that, especially in recent years, the majority of aggregate FDI flows are associated with cross-border M&A activity (Kang & Johansson, 2000; Letto-Gillies, Meschi, & Simonetti, 2001; Chen & Findlay, 2002). Of the potential variables that make entry via M&A mode more attractive, the most obvious are those associated with greater liquidity and efficiency of capital markets. We use the ratio of stock market capitalization to GDP as a measure of stock market liquidity, and we expect that higher ratios should encourage greater cross-border M&A activity and therefore FDI (Di Giovanni, 2004; Rossi & Volpin, 2003). Likewise, liquid stock markets should make it easier for companies to raise financial capital that can be used, in turn, to acquire foreign companies. In short, we would expect both FDO and FDI to be positively related to stock market liquidity.[10]

An additional variable that should be directly related to inward FDI via acquisitions is the degree of privatization activity in the host country. Privatization initiatives create a pool of potential acquisition targets or merger partners for foreign firms, and privatization should therefore be positively to FDI activity. In addition, countries pursuing privatization may also engage in more general liberalization policies that encourage capital inflows. To the extent that privatization activities also create more opportunities for domestic firms to invest in the home economy, they may limit FDO. As a consequence, we include this variable in the FDO equation with an expected negative sign.

Finally, we include dummy variables for major oil-producing countries and for China in FDI equations. Other things constant, one might expect the availability of oil exploration and production targets to encourage FDI, especially given the fact that those targets are frequently in emerging countries that lack domestic firms with the technology to engage in efficient and effective oil exploration and production. In the case of China, while it is not a major focus of oil exploration, substantial publicity has attended large recent FDI inflows to China, particularly given the fact that China's governance infrastructure is not strong. Thus, it is possible that China is receiving more FDI than would be forecast by the model. We believe that this may be so primarily because a substantial amount of FDI in China has been undertaken by firms owned by Chinese expatriate families resident in countries that are themselves characterized by weak governance infrastructures (Thailand, Malaysia and Indonesia). Shapiro, Gedajlovic, and Erdener (2003) have argued that expatriate Chinese family firms have developed particular skills in operating in environments with weak governance infrastructure. These advantages, together with their cultural familiarity, may have resulted in capital inflows to China exceeding what our basic model would forecast. The variables above are included in all equations for all sub-samples (except, obviously, the China variable when China is not in the sample). However, we also include a number of variables that are specific to Europe, and are only included in the Europe sub-samples. These variables are dummy variables indicating EU membership, future EU membership, and membership in the European Monetary Union (EMU). All of these variables are expected to increase FDI. Specifically, EU and EMU membership facilitate market access and reduce transaction costs associated with variable exchange rates, both resulting in increased FDI. For the same reason, they should also increase FDO.

Critical to our analysis is the variable for future EU membership. This variable, defined as of 2001, defines countries that were accepted into the EU at a later date. In fact, there are two such groups of accepted members, those that entered in 2004 and those who will enter after 2004. Separate dummy variables for each category did not improve or change the results in any way and so we report results using only a single variable. Our hypothesis is that the "halo effect" of potential EU membership increased the FDI flows into those countries beyond the amount predicted by other measures, particularly de jure standards of governance. In other words, these countries may benefit from the anticipated protections provided by EU membership in ways that are not measured by other included variables, including governance. Although symmetrical arguments may apply to FDO, it is not immediately apparent why future membership in the EU would enhance capital outflows.

Evidence from the studies discussed above suggests that one cannot expect the same factors to affect all ETEE countries in the same way. In particular, a country's previous history of trade and investment, proximity to other long-standing EU members, and the length of time under a Communist political regime may all be factors in explaining capital inflows and outflows. As a consequence, and based on previous studies, we distinguish among different groups of ETEE countries with specific respect to differences in the impacts of EU membership on direct investment flows. In particular, we distinguish between countries that were formerly Communist, and those that were not. We further break down the former category into two additional categories, based on geography and previous history. The first group is comprised of three Baltic countries (Latvia, Lithuania and Estonia), whose proximity to the Scandinavian countries may increase their capital inflows and outflows. The second group is comprised of the five countries that belonged to the Central Europe Free Trade Association (CEFTA) and are adjacent to EU members (Czech Republic, Hungary, Poland, Slovakia and Slovenia).[11]

Previous evidence and experience suggests that the parsimonious specifications employed in this study are successful in modeling FDI and FDO flows (Globerman & Shapiro, 2002, 2003a, b). Our specifications exclude a number of country-level variables often included in other studies (per capita

GDP, labor costs, tax rates), albeit with mixed results. The exclusions are either because relevant variables are unavailable for a sample as large as ours (e.g., corporate tax rates), or because they are correlated with one of the included variables (e.g., per capita GDP is highly correlated with governance). Furthermore, Kaufmann (2003) has argued that governance is more important to FDI than are specific indicators of macroeconomic and exchange rate stability.

We have also not included any variables that specifically identify a country's legal regime. Legal regimes have been shown to be important determinants of the general investment climate, and therefore of FDI and FDO, through their effects on shareholder and property rights (LaPorta, Lopez-de-Silanes, Shleifer, & Vishny, 1998, 2000; Beck, Demirguc-Kunt, & Levine, 2003; Globerman & Shapiro, 2003a, b). However, for the European sample of interest to us, the vast majority of countries use a civil law system. In addition, there is evidence that stock market liquidity is in part a reflection of the legal system (Beck et al., 2003) and is also associated with stronger shareholder protection (LaPorta, Lopez-de-Silanes, Shleifer, & Vishny, 1997, 2000). Thus, the stock market capitalization term indirectly reflects the role of the legal system. In addition, Kaufmann (2003) argues that the broad measure of governance employed here is more statistically robust than measures of legal systems in models of investment behavior, and supporting evidence is found in Globerman and Shapiro (2005). As noted above, the impact of common law might be indirect, in any case, through its influence on the growth of domestic capital markets. Similarly, a common measure of investor protection, defined as the interaction of an index of shareholder rights with an index of the rule of law (LaPorta et al., 1998; Pistor, Raiser, & Gelfer, 2000; Johnson, Boone, Breach, & Friedman, 2000), is excluded because it was not available for the full sample of countries and because it was correlated with the governance index ($r = 0.69$).

Definitions of the variables we use and their sources are provided in Table 4. The FDI/FDO data were compiled for the period 1995–2001, for a sample of 138 countries, resulting in 928 pooled observations. The remaining series were compiled to overlap the same time period for the same countries. Where possible, we lagged the independent variables by 1 year in order to minimize problems of endogeneity. In fact, the governance data were available only for the years 1996, 1998 and 2000. Therefore, we extrapolated these values in order to obtain observations for the missing years. The stock market capitalization data were also not available for all years and were similarly extrapolated. The privatization data were not available on an annual basis, and so the average value of the ratio of

Table 4. Variables, Definitions and Data Sources.

Variable	Definition	Source
FDI (inflows)	Foreign direct investment inflows, annual, 1995—2001	UNCTAD, *World Investment Report*, various years
FDO (outflows)	Foreign direct investment outflows, average 1995–2001	UNCTAD
GDP	Nominal GDP, 1994–2000, measured in natural logarithms	IMF, *World Economic Outlook Database*, 2003
GDP growth	Logarithmic growth rate; the difference between log of current and previous year GDP	IMF
Governance index	Sum of six governance indicators (government effectiveness, political instability, rule of law, graft and corruption, voice and accountability, and regulatory burden). Available for 1996, 1998 and 2000.	Kaufmann et al. (2003)
Import and export intensity	Ratio of imports + exports to GDP, 1994—2000	IMF
Stock market capitalization	Ratio of stock market capitalization to GDP, 1995—1999	Beck, Demirguc-Kunt, & Levine (1999)
Privatization	Average ratio of privatization revenues to GDP, for either 1988–1998 or 1990—2000	Brune, Garrett, & Kogut (2004), OECD (2002)

Note: UNCTAD: United Nations Conference on Trade and Development; IMF: International Monetary Fund.

privatization revenues to GDP was used. Since the data were obtained from different sources, the years over which the data were averaged is not the same for each country.

As we use four different sub-samples of countries in our estimation, we do not present a correlation matrix. However, it should be noted that some of the independent variables are often quite highly correlated. Nevertheless, even the highest correlation coefficient (between the governance index and stock market capitalization, $r = 0.65$) is not that high when compared to the R^2 values for the estimated equations (reported below). In addition, we calculated the variance inflation factor (VIF) for each variable (Greene, 2003). No VIF exceeded 2.5, indicating that, in general, multicollinearity is not likely a concern.

5. ESTIMATION RESULTS

In this section, we report regression results focusing first on inflows of foreign direct investment and then outflows. Our primary interest is in comparing the estimated results of the FDI model for the ETEE countries with similar models using different samples of countries and regions as references. The FDI results are reported in Table 5. The estimates are obtained using generalized least squares (GLS) random effects estimation. Although the data are pooled, some of the variables are time invariant (China-, oil- and EU-related variables). Thus, fixed effects estimation was not a possible alternative.

We first present the results obtained by estimating a basic model for the sample of ETEE. These results (Column 1) indicate that the only statistically significant variables are market size (Ln GDP), and the governance index. Thus, our broad measure of governance does matter for these countries, a result consistent with previous studies discussed earlier where governance was measured differently. However, we find no evidence that trade openness, privatization or stock market liquidity have any effect on direct investment capital inflows to ETEE countries. Since our purpose is to situate these results in various contexts, we next present the results obtained from estimating the same model with different samples of countries and regions. Results for other samples are reported in Columns (2)–(4). When comparing estimation results for the ETEE model with results for other samples, we find similarities and important differences. In general, the coefficient on the governance term is higher for the sample of emerging and transition economies (Column 3) than for all countries and for all Europe.[12] Thus, when developed market economies are included in the sample as in Columns (2) and (4), the estimated governance coefficient is lower. This is consistent with the hypothesis that there are diminishing returns to governance (Globerman & Shapiro, 2002), and that emerging and transition economies benefit more on the margin from improvements in their governance stocks than do more developed market economies.[13] In this sense, however, the ETEE countries do not resemble other emerging economies since the governance coefficient in the former is lower (Columns 1 and 3). This suggests that the effective stock of governance may be higher in ETEE countries than in other emerging markets.

Stock market liquidity is not an important determinant of FDI flows in any sample, except the sample including all countries. This is perhaps not surprising for emerging markets in Europe or elsewhere, since stock markets in these countries are relatively small and illiquid. In addition, firms are

Table 5. FDI Results.

	(1) Emerging and Transition Europe	(2) World	(3) Emerging and Transition World	(4) All Europe	(5) All Europe	(6) All Europe
Log GDP	0.848***	0.787***	0.846***	0.910***	0.898***	0.864***
	(0.132)	(0.065)	(0.080)	(0.081)	(0.099)	(0.107)
Growth GDP	0.069	0.314	0.269	0.055	0.015	0.010
	(0.394)	(0.230)	(0.254)	(0.371)	(0.380)	(0.372)
Governance	0.503**	0.565***	0.627***	0.367**	0.299*	0.309*
index	(0.252)	(0.151)	(0.196)	(0.167)	(0.167)	(0.177)
Trade	0.004	0.004*	0.003	0.009***	0.009***	0.009***
	(0.003)	(0.002)	(0.003)	(0.003)	(0.002)	(0.003)
Privatization	−0.012	0.027*	0.037**	−0.070	−0.015	−0.019
	(0.025)	(0.014)	(0.017)	(0.016)	(0.016)	(0.017)
Stock market	−0.002	0.004**	0.001	0.001	0.002	0.002
capitalization	(0.003)	(0.002)	(0.003)	(0.002)	(0.002)	(0.002)
China		2.560**	2.735**			
		(1.188)	(1.243)			
Oil	−0.079	−0.272	−0.801**	0.0142	0.284	0.544
	(0.819)	(0.332)	(0.408)	(0.428)	(0.478)	(0.478)
Future EU (former Communist)					0.804*** (0.312)	
Future EU (CEFTA)						0.958** (0.429)
Future EU (Baltic)						0.806* (0.456)
Future EU (other former Communist)						0.826* (0.441)
Future EU (non-Communist)					−0.001 (0.440)	0.077 (0.489)
EU					0.936* (0.512)	0.609* (0.437)
EMU					−0.599 (0.440)	
Intercept	2.929***	2.370***	2.216***	2.178***	1.843***	1.899***
	(0.580)	(0.298)	(0.342)	(0.446)	(0.467)	(0.484)
Adjusted R²	0.71	0.65	0.48	0.82	0.85	0.85
Countries	20	138	112	36	36	36
Observations	140	928	746	252	252	252

Notes: Values in parentheses are standard errors.
Coefficients are obtained by GLS random effects estimation. All equations include unreported time dummy variables. The R^2 reported here is computed in the usual ordinary least squares (OLS) fashion.*Significance at*
*10% levels,
**5% and
***1%

more likely to be family owned, or closely held (LaPorta et al., 1998), and this would mitigate M&A activity by foreign firms. It is of interest to note, however, that the relevant term is positive and statistically significant in the world sample, but not in the all-Europe sample. This result is difficult to explain, although it should be pointed out that the relevant t-statistic is typically above unity in the Europe equations.

The trade term is not statistically significant in either the ETEE or ETEW samples, but it is positive and statistically significant in both the World and all-Europe equations. This suggests that in emerging and transition markets, FDI mainly services the domestic market, whereas in the developed economies it is more likely to be related to rationalizing the value chain associated with increased intra-industry trade specialization. In this regard, the ETEE countries appear little different from other emerging and transition economies.

One notable difference between the ETEE sample and the ETEW samples is identified with respect to the privatization variable. Specifically, we find that privatization is, positively and statistically, significantly related to FDI for both the world and ETEW samples, but not for ETEE, or for Europe as a whole. This is likely because the most important privatizations in the ETEE occurred before the start of our sample period. In particular, major privatizations occurred in the early 1990s in Hungary, Poland, the Czech Republic and Russia, whereas our sample begins in 1995. Nevertheless, the different impacts of privatization distinguish ETEE countries from other developing countries.

We included a dummy variable for oil-producing countries in the expectation that such countries would attract FDI. This turns out not to be the case for any sample. Indeed, for the ETEW sample, the relevant coefficient is negative and statistically significant. We believe that this result reflects the presence of Middle-Eastern oil-producing countries in the ETEW sample. The oil resources of these countries are to a large extent government owned, and there are fewer opportunities for FDI than in developed countries with oil resources. The negative coefficient might also reflect, in part, unmeasured characteristics of Middle-Eastern countries that negatively affect FDI flows and that are not captured by other included variables.

The China dummy variable was included to capture unmeasured characteristics of that economy that might encourage FDI, despite its relatively poor governance infrastructure. In fact, we find that the relevant coefficient is positive and statistically significant in both samples where China is present. Indeed, the magnitude of the "China effect" is very strong. The coefficients are both above 2.5, which may be compared with the world FDI mean of 5.4 and the ETEW mean of 4.7 (measured in natural logs).

An important feature of our results is that we were unable to identify a similar "location" effect, positive or negative, for the ETEE sample, or components of it. When we included in the ETEW equation a dummy variable for ETEE countries, or a dummy variable for those ETEE countries that have been accepted to the EU, the relevant coefficients were never statistically significant. Relative to other emerging and transition economies, there is no indication that ETEE countries have any unmeasured characteristics that either attract or repel FDI. In particular, there is no evidence from this sample (Eq. (2)) of a "halo effect" that attracts FDI to future EU members.

In order to investigate this issue further, we added specific variables to the all-Europe model. These results are reported in Columns (5) and (6) of Table 5. In Column (5), we add dummy variables for EU members, future EU members, and members of the EMU. In the case of future EU members, we further distinguished between former Communist countries and others. Arguably, if the prospect of joining the EU augments the benefits of good governance, as captured by our governance variable, the benefits are particularly marked for former Communist regimes where existing stocks of "non-measurable" governance attributes are relatively low. Put differently, the prospect of joining the EU might be seen as "locking in" governance improvements captured in our governance variable, and this locking in has particular value in former Communist regimes that may be seen by foreign investors as especially prone to backsliding on political and economic reforms.[14]

As can be seen, the future EU coefficient for the former Communist countries is positive, and statistically significant, suggesting that relative to other ETEE that are neither EU members, nor future EU members, future EU members have unmeasured advantages when they are former Communist countries.[15] Conversely, future EU membership for non-Communist ETEEs in our sample (Malta, Cyprus and Turkey) does not promote increased FDI. This result is suggestive of a halo effect associated with EU membership for former Communist countries.

It might be noted that the EU term is also positive, and statistically significant, albeit at only 90 percent. However, its effect is stronger when the EMU term, which is never statistically significant, is omitted. The EU effect may reflect the higher GDP per capita of its members, and in fact these two variables are positively correlated ($r = 0.69$). If so, it would also explain the relatively weaker performance of the governance term in Column (5), since governance and per capita GDP are also highly correlated ($r = 0.82$).

Finally, we further disaggregated the future members of the EU that were formerly Communist by geography, and in particular we isolate the countries that were adjacent or close to EU-member states (Baltic states, CEFTA states and others). These results are reported in Column (6), where it can be seen that there is some advantage to future EU membership for all formerly Communist states, but the strongest advantage accrues to the CEFTA states. We attribute this to both the effects of CEFTA itself, as well as to the fact that the CEFTA countries included in this category are adjacent to EU-member states. Thus, distance does matter in attracting FDI.

The FDO results are reported in Table 6. It should be noted that because a relatively large number of countries reported no outbound FDI, the equations are estimated using random effects TOBIT estimation. For these equations, we report as a goodness of fit criterion the correlation between FDO and its fitted value (Wooldridge, 2002, p. 529). The specifications for the FDO equations are for the most part symmetrical in specification to the FDI equations.[16]

Empirically, the FDO results are both similar to, and different from, the FDI results.[17] There is considerable empirical symmetry arising from the positive and significant effects on outflows arising from market size and governance, the two most important determinants of inflows. For all samples, large markets and strong governance infrastructures promote capital outflows. However, there is an important difference between the FDI and FDO results with respect to the impact of governance on ETEE countries. Relative to the World, and to Europe, the ETEE governance coefficient is larger when no Europe-specific dummy variables are employed (compare Columns 1, 2 and 4). The same is true of the ETEW coefficient (compare Columns 2–4). Thus for emerging markets anywhere, and for ETEE countries in particular, the impact on FDO of an increase in governance is more strongly positive, other things equal. Moreover, when a dummy variable for the ETEE countries was regressed on the residuals for the ETEW equation, the resulting coefficient was negative and statistically significant.[18] Thus, given governance and other characteristics, ETEE countries are characterized by less direct investment capital outflow than other emerging and transition economies.

In addition, unlike the FDI equations, none of the Europe-specific variables are statistically significant. In particular, the future EU status of both former Communist countries is statistically insignificant (Column 5). The same is true for the non-Communist future EU members, although the relevant t-statistic is well-above unity. Hence, there is little to distinguish one ETEE country or region from another with respect to FDO, with the

Table 6. FDO Results.

	(1) Emerging and Transition Europe	(2) World	(3) Emerging and Transition World	(4) All Europe	(5) All Europe	(6) All Europe
Log GDP	1.586***	1.208***	1.106***	1.323***	1.277***	1.326***
	(0.157)	(0.064)	(0.074)	(0.094)	(0.130)	(0.162)
Growth GDP	0.372	0.161	−0.053	0.712	0.802	0.742
	(0.838)	(0.443)	(0.486)	(0.777)	(0.825)	(0.818)
Governance	2.433***	1.732***	1.930***	1.898***	1.794***	1.757***
index	(0.331)	(0.144)	(0.184)	(0.236)	(0.593)	(0.353)
Trade	0.020***	0.008***	0.007***	0.013***	0.009*	0.009*
	(0.020)	(0.002)	(0.003)	(0.004)	(0.005)	(0.005)
Privatization	−0.105***	−0.041*	−0.066***	−0.019	−0.020	−0.015
	(0.027)	(0.022)	(0.018)	(0.038)	(0.032)	(0.034)
Stock market	0.014***	0.002	0.005*	0.008***	0.008***	0.008**
capitalization	(0.004)	(0.002)	(0.003)	(0.003)	(0.003)	(0.004)
Future EU (former Communist)					−0.283 (0.503)	
Future EU (CEFTA)						−0.594 (0.835)
Future EU (Baltic)						0.344 (0.984)
Future EU (other former Communist)						−0.514 (0.785)
Future EU (non-Communist)					0.996 (0.676)	0.968 (0.781)
EU					0.460 (1.112)	0.190 (0.729)
EMU					0.132 (0.989)	
Intercept	−3.847***	−2.225***	−1.918***	−3.064***	−2.566***	−2.622***
	(0.789)	(0.374)	(0.427)	(0.608)	(0.731)	(0.852)
R^2	0.46	0.71	0.41	0.83	0.84	0.84
Countries	20	138	112	36	36	36
Observations	140	927	745	252	252	231

Notes: Values in parentheses are standard errors. Coefficients are obtained by TOBIT random effects estimation. All equations include unreported time dummy variables. The R^2 is the square of the sample correlation coefficient between the dependent variable and its fitted value.
Source: Wooldridge (2002, p. 529).Significance levels a*t*
*10%.
**5% and
***1%

possible exception of Malta, Cyprus and Turkey. Thus, there is little evidence of any European halo effect that encourages FDO.

Another difference between the FDI and FDO results is the coefficient for the trade variable, which is positive and statistically significant in all samples reported in Table 6. Thus, for the most part, FDO and trade are complements. The privatization coefficient is negative and statistically significant in the ETEE and ETEW samples in Table 6, as expected, although this seems inconsistent with finding a statistically insignificant coefficient for privatization in the FDI equation for ETEE countries. Finally, stock market liquidity tends to promote FDO in both emerging and developed Europe.

It is perhaps surprising to note that the stock market capitalization term is not statistically significant in the world equation, although it is significant in the ETEE (and all-Europe) equations. However, it might be noted that capital outflows from Western Europe during the latter half of the 1990s were especially noteworthy and that the majority of those outflows took the form of M&A activity (Globerman & Shapiro, 2003b, 2005).

6. SUMMARY AND CONCLUSIONS

This chapter addresses the recent history of FDI and FDO for a relatively large sample of emerging and transition European countries. In particular, it identifies and assesses the major determinants of direct investment patterns including the empirical importance of a broad measure of institutional and economic governance.

By and large, the determinants of foreign direct investment for our sample of European countries are similar to those for other developing countries and, indeed, for developed countries as well. In short, governance matters. Indeed, governance is relatively more important for developing European countries than for developed European countries. Joining the EU, or even the prospect of joining the EU, promotes inward FDI (a halo effect), although this phenomenon particularly characterizes the former Communist countries. We interpret this result as suggesting the potential importance of a locking in effect with respect to governance. That is, political integration into developed Europe provides longer-term assurances to foreign investors that institutional changes undertaken by transition economies will not be reversed.[19] This finding has particular significance for developing economies that might be contemplating EU membership.

Findings with respect to the influence of trade intensity and privatization may reflect the time period of our sample. For example, trade intensity and the adoption of the euro do not appear to affect inward FDI flows to emerging European economies. This may be the case because inward FDI in those economies, at least for our sample period, was largely concerned with serving local buyers. As such, the importance of trade openness and the costs of trading, including costs associated with managing foreign exchange risks, may increase in the future as foreign investors increasingly utilize emerging European countries as bases for specialized value-chain activities. The unimportance of privatization in our sample might reflect the fact that most major privatizations for our ETEE countries took place prior to our sample time period. Nevertheless, there is still scope for privatization to re-emerge as an empirically relevant determinant of FDI in future periods.

There are some important differences in the determinants of inward and outward direct investment. For example, FDO from ETEEs, but not FDI, is promoted by trade intensity and stock market liquidity. More importantly, it would appear that there is no halo effect for FDO. Indeed, given their governance and other characteristics, ETEE countries export less capital than would be forecast by the regression equation for other emerging markets. Future EU membership does not promote in any way the export of capital. Thus, the "lock-in" effect associated with prospective EU membership that promotes FDI does not apparently work in reverse. This result remains a puzzle, but may be explained by the fact that in the ETEE countries, the level of governance is low relative to the EU, and so relatively few firms with the potential to invest abroad emerge at all. Thus, when capital flows from high governance countries, it typically seeks high governance hosts (where high governance can include the protection afforded by extra-national bodies). However, the reverse is not true. Low levels of local governance in the domestic market results in fewer firms with the capacity to invest abroad, and these deficiencies are not compensated for by extra-national institutions. Put otherwise, local institutions matter.

It is still true that good governance promotes both FDI and FDO. This observation should not be seen as diminishing the overall economic benefits of governance infrastructure. Specifically, increased FDO should not be seen as a "cost" of good governance. Rather, it should be seen as part of a process that promotes international specialization of production and trade with the associated efficiency gains that economists traditionally associate with economic specialization. Finally, the importance of formal political integration into a regional trade group is the finding perhaps most worthy of being highlighted. The experience of emerging Europe suggests that important benefits to transition countries from formally joining a regional group of developed countries may be associated with enhanced confidence on the part of foreign investors that host government commitments to good governance will prove durable.

NOTES

1. ETEEs in our sample are identified in Table 1. The exclusion of other emerging European countries was dictated by considerations of data availability; however, our sample includes virtually all of the countries that would be considered ETEE geographic space.

2. Liberalization and institutional change in the former Soviet Union Republics, including Russia, did not commence until after the break-up of the Soviet Union in 1991.

3. Claessens, Oks, and Polastri (1998) focus on capital inflows to transition economies over the period 1992–1996 using a "reform index" constructed by the World Bank based on criteria similar to those used by the EBRD.

4. Lankes and Stern (1998) also make this point.

5. Lansbury et al. (1996) distinguish between two basic forms of privatization. They identify the first as the "standard" method which involves direct sales to "strategic investors" and provides a source of cash revenues to governments. The second is identified as the "transitional" method which involves the restitution of property and voucher privatization, the primary purpose of which is to re-establish private property rights.

6. Comprehensive reviews of the empirical literature on the overall determinants of FDI flows can be found in Dunning (1993) and Caves (1996).

7. Lankes and Venables (1996) qualify this assertion by distinguishing between FDI projects whose primary function is to serve local and regional markets, and those aimed at exporting outside the region. Factor cost considerations are likely to be of substantially greater importance for the latter types of FDI investments than the former. For their sample of 17 emerging countries, including a number of former Soviet Republics, they find that market seeking is the dominant form of FDI.

8. In this regard, Lansbury et al. (1996) argue that the perceived risks of investment within Central European emerging economies may have been reduced by an expectation that they would eventually integrate fully with Western Europe. Altomonte and Guagliano (2003) identify "agglomeration economies" within the European region as a factor contributing to increased FDI in emerging Central and Eastern European economies.

9. The governance index we use was first developed by Kaufmann, Kraay, and Zoido-Lobaton (1999a, b), and recently expanded upon and updated by Kaufmann, Kraay, and Mastruzzi (2003). They estimate six separate indices (which we will refer to as KKM indices) including measures of political instability, rule of law, graft, regulatory burden, voice and political freedom, and government effectiveness. The indices have been estimated (using an unobserved components model) employing 31 different qualitative indicators from 13 different sources, including BERI, DRI/McGraw-Hill, the Heritage Foundation, the World Bank, the World Economic Forum and the Economist Intelligence Unit. The indices are highly correlated with each

other such that it is very difficult to use them all in a single equation (Globerman & Shapiro, 2002). We therefore created an aggregate measure that is the sum of the six measures. We also created an aggregate index calculated as the first principal component of the six measures, but this does not change the results. The data are available at: http://www.worldbank.org/wbi/governance/datasets.htm#dataset

10. Stock market liquidity may be important for broader reasons. The ability of firms to raise capital in liquid capital markets could also facilitate their ability to make other types of foreign investments besides acquisitions of foreign companies. This would reinforce the positive relationship between FDO and stock market liquidity.

11. CEFTA also included Romania, which is not adjacent to any EU country.

12. The ETEW countries are defined as non-OECD members. Israel, Hong Kong and Singapore are also excluded from the sample.

13. The degree of diminishing returns may not be strong. When a squared governance term is included in the world sample, it is negative, as expected, but not quite statistically significant.

14. At the time of writing, the Russian government's treatment of that country's largest oil company was raising concerns about the reliability of property rights guarantees in Russia.

15. The omitted category also includes Norway and Switzerland, but exclusion of these countries from the sample does not change the results.

16. Note that the FDO equations do not include the China dummy, since there was no a priori reason to do so. When included, the variable was not statistically significant.

17. Note that TOBIT coefficient estimates are not directly comparable to the GLS coefficient in the FDI equations because the marginal effects are different for the two estimation methods (Greene, 2003, p. 764). In order to compare the marginal effects of each variable, the TOBIT coefficients must be adjusted to account for the probability that a non-zero outcome is observed.

18. This result is unreported and is available from the authors upon request. Recall that a similar procedure in the FDI case resulted in a coefficient that was not statistically significant.

19. A similar locking-in effect has been suggested to be a major benefit of Mexico's accession to the NAFTA.

REFERENCES

Altomonte, C., & Guagliano, C. (2003). Comparative study of FDI in Central and Eastern Europe and the Mediterranean. *Economic Systems, 27*, 223–246.

Barrell, R., Holland, D., & Pain, N. (2000). Openness, integration and transition: Prospects and policies for economies in transition. Prepared for *International Economics Study Group 25th Annual Conference*, Isle of Thorns, Sussex, September, Mimeographed.

Beck, T., Demirguc-Kunt, A., & Levine, R. (1999). *A new database on financial development and structure*. World Bank Policy Research Working Paper 2146. Washington, DC: The World Bank.

Beck, T., Demirguc-Kunt, A., & Levine, R. (2003). Law and finance: Why does legal origin matter? *Journal of Comparative Economics, 31*, 653–675.

Bris, A., & Cabolis, C. (2004). *Adopting better corporate governance: Evidence from cross-border mergers.* New Haven Conn.: Yale School of Management, Mimeographed.

Brune, N., Garrett, G., & Kogut, B. (2004). The International Monetary Fund and the global spread of privatization, *IMF Staff Papers, 51,* 195–219.

Carstensen, K., & Toubal, F. (2003). *Foreign direct investment in Central and Eastern European countries: a dynamic panel analysis.* Kiel, Germany: Kiel Institute for World Economies, Mimeographed.

Caves, R. E. (1996). *Multinational enterprise and economic analysis.* Cambridge: Cambridge University Press.

Chen, C., & Findlay, C. (2002). *A review of cross-border mergers and acquisitions in APEC.* Canberra: The Australian National University, Mimeographed.

Claessens, S., Oks, D., & Polastri, R. (1998). *Capital flows to Central and Eastern Europe and the former Soviet Union.* Washington, DC: The World Bank, Policy Research Working Paper 1976, Mimeographed.

Di Giovanni, J. (2004). What drives capital flows? The case of cross-border M&A activity and financial deepening. *Journal of International Economics, 65,* 127–149.

Dunning, J. H. (1993). *Multinational enterprises and the global economy.* Wokingham, England: Addison-Wesley Publishing Company.

The Economist. (2003). A survey of EU enlargement. November 22, 3–16.

Globerman, S., & Shapiro, D. (1999). The impact of government policies on foreign direct investment: the Canadian experience. *Journal of International Business Studies, 30,* 513–532.

Globerman, S., & Shapiro, D. (2002). Global foreign direct investment flows: The role of governance infrastructure. *World Development, 30,* 1898–1919.

Globerman, S., & Shapiro, D. (2003a). Governance infrastructure and US foreign direct investment. *Journal of International Business Studies, 34,* 19–39.

Globerman, S., & Shapiro, D. (2003b). Assessing recent patterns of foreign direct investment in Canada and the United States. In: Richard Harris (Ed.), *North American linkages: Opportunities and challenges for Canada* (pp. 281–312). Calgary: University of Calgary Press.

Globerman, S., & Shapiro, D. (2005). Assessing international mergers and acquisitions as a mode of foreign direct investment. In: L. Eden & W. Dobson (Eds), *Governance, multinationals and growth.* London: Edward Elgar.

Greene, W. H. (2003). *Econometric analysis* (5th ed.). Upper Saddle River, New Jersey: Prentice-Hall.

Hellman, J., Jones, G., & Kaufman, D. (2002). *Far from home: Do foreign investors import higher standards of governance in transition economies?* Washington, DC: The World Bank, Mimeographed.

Holland, D., & Pain, N. (1998a). *The diffusion of innovations in Central and Eastern Europe: A study of the determinants and impact of foreign direct investment.* London, UK: National Institute of Economic and Social Research, Mimeographed.

Holland, D., & Pain, N. (1998b). The determinants and impact of foreign direct investment in the transition economies. In: V. Edwards (Ed.), *Convergence or divergence: Aspirations and reality in Central and Eastern Europe and Russia.* Buckingham: Centre for Research into East European Business, University of Buckingham.

Holland, D., & Pain, N. (2000). *On the road to the market: The prospects for growth in Central Europe.* London: National Institute for Economic Research, Mimeographed.

Johnson, S., Boone, P., Breach, A., & Friedman, E. (2000). Corporate governance in the Asian financial crisis. *Journal of Financial Economics, 58*, 141–186.

Kang, N. H., & Johansson, S. (2000). *Cross-border mergers and acquisitions: Their role in industrial globalization.* STI Working Papers 2000/1. Paris: OECD, Mimeographed.

Kaufmann, D. (2003). *Governance redux: The empirical challenge.* World Bank Policy Research Department Working Paper. Available at: http://www.worldbank.org/wbi/governance/pubs/govredux.html

Kaufmann, D., Kraay, A., & Zoido-Lobaton. (1999a). *Aggregating governance indicators.* World Bank Working Paper no. 2195. Available at: http://www.worldbank.org/wbi/governance

Kaufmann, D., Kraay, A., & Zoido-Lobaton. (1999b). *Governance matters.* World Bank Working Paper no. 2196. Available at: http://www.worldbank.org/wbi/governance

Kaufmann, D., Kraay, A., & Mastruzzi, M. (2003). *Governance matters III: Governance indicators for 1996–2002.* World Bank Policy Research Department Working Paper. Available at: http://www.worldbank.org/wbi/governance

Lankes, H. P., & Stern, N. (1998). *Capital flows to Eastern Europe and the former Soviet Union.* London: European Bank for Reconstruction and Development. Working Paper no. 27, Mimeographed.

Lankes, H. P., & Venables, A. J. (1996). Foreign direct investment in economic transition: The changing pattern of investments. *Economics of Transition, 4*, 331–347.

Lansbury, M., Pain, N., & Smidkova, K. (1996). Foreign direct investment in Central Europe since 1990: An econometric study. *National Institute Economic Review, 158*, 104–114.

LaPorta, R., Lopez-de-Silanes, F., Shleifer, A., & Vishny, R. (1997). Legal determinants of external finance. *Journal of Finance, 52*, 1131–1150.

LaPorta, R., Lopez-de-Silanes, F., Shleifer, A., & Vishny, R. (1998). Law and finance. *Journal of Political Economy, 101*, 678–709.

LaPorta, R., Lopez-de-Silanes, F., Shleifer, A., & Vishny, R. (1999). The quality of government. *Journal of Law, Economics and Organization, 15*, 222–279.

LaPorta, R., Lopez-de-Silanes, F., Shleifer, A., & Vishny, R. (2000). Investor protection and corporate governance. *Journal of Financial Economics, 58*, 3–27.

Letto-Gillies, G., Meschi, M., & Simonetti, R. (2001). *Cross-border mergers and acquisitions: Patterns in the EU and effects.* London: South Bank University, Mimeographed.

OECD (2002). Recent privatization trends in OECD countries. *Financial Market Trends, 82*(June).

Pistor, K., Raiser, M., & Gelfer, S. (2000). *Law and finance in transition economies.* EBRD Working Paper no. 48, February.

Qian, Y. (1999). Institutional foundations of China's market transition. Paper presented at *World Bank annual conference on development economics.* Washington, DC.

Rossi, S., & Volpin (2003). *Cross-country determinants of mergers and acquisitions.* Discussion Paper no. 3889. London: Centre for Economic Policy Research.

Shapiro, D., Gedajlovic, E., & Erdener, C. (2003). The Chinese family firm as a multinational enterprise. *International Journal of Organizational Analysis, 11*, 105–122.

Slangen, L., van Kooten, C., & Suchanek, P. (2004). *Institutions, social capital and agricultural change in Central and Eastern Europe.* The Netherlands: Wageningen University, Mimeographed.

Wooldridge, J. M. (2002). *Econometric analysis of cross section and panel data.* Cambridge: MIT press.

FOREIGN DIRECT INVESTMENT, STOCK EXCHANGE DEVELOPMENT, AND ECONOMIC GROWTH IN CENTRAL AND EASTERN EUROPE

Yusaf H. Akbar, Heather Elms and Tej S. Dhakar

1. INTRODUCTION

Understanding economic development in the transition economies of Central and Eastern Europe (CEE) requires an analysis of investment in these economies. Previous analyses, however, have focused primarily if not singularly on the role of foreign direct investment (FDI; Akbar & McBride, 2004; Clague & Rausser, 1992; Uhlenbruck & De Castro, 2000). This focus follows that of regional policy-makers, who heavily encouraged FDI through acquisition or greenfield investments (Frydman, Rapaczynski, & Earle, 1993). These policy-makers, however, additionally established stock exchanges in each of their countries. There are now at least 24 operating stock exchanges in CEE and the countries that previously made up the former Soviet Union and the former Yugoslavia.[1] The role of the development of these local stock exchanges in the development (LSED) of local economies (primarily through foreign portfolio investment) has not yet been

Emerging European Financial Markets: Independence and Integration Post-Enlargement
International Finance Review, Volume 6, 461–472
ISSN: 1569-3767/doi:10.1016/S1569-3767(05)06018-8

systematically examined, nor has it been linked explicitly to the role of FDI. Finally, the role of local companies' listings on foreign exchanges (FSEL) has not been examined in tandem with the role of FDI or LSED (for an examination of the relationship between FDI, LSED, and FSEL, however, see Claessens, Klingebiel, & Schmukler, 2001).

We provide that examination here, and suggest the links between FDI, LSED, and FSEL in the development of these economies. The link we suggest is sequential, in that initial economic development is primarily associated with FDI. As opportunities for FDI decrease over time, however (primarily because of the lessening availability of potential acquisitions, but also given saturation in the greenfield arena), further economic development depends primarily on LSED and FSEL. Thus we propose a positive but non-monotonic relationship between FDI and economic development, a positive and monotonic relationship between LSED and economic development, and between FSEL and economic development, and a sequential association between these relationships.

2. BACKGROUND

2.1. FDI and Economic Development

There is a broad literature that focuses on the impact of FDI on economic development in developing and transition countries (e.g., King & Váradi, 2002; Konings, 2001; Krkoszka, 2001; Economic Commission for Europe, 2001; Barrell & Holland, 2000; Havrylyshyn et al., 2000; Barrell & Pain, 1997; Balasubramanyam, Salisu, & Sapsford, 1996; Borensztein, Gregorio, & Lee, 1995). This specialized literature is supported by a more general literature on sources of economic growth (e.g., Durlauf & Quah, 1999; Temple, 1999).

Both literatures point to the positive impact of FDI on the economic development of recipient economies, and relate that impact to two main effects. First, inward FDI upgrades the existing stock of physical and human capital in the recipient economy, thereby enhancing microeconomic efficiency. Through access to new technologies and management practices, and by producing goods and services that embody foreign knowledge, spillovers occur in the domestic economy, as local firms, forced by competitive pressures, adopt the technologies demonstrated by foreign firms. Foreign firms may also provide technical assistance to customers and local upstream and downstream firms who are part of their supply chain. This microeconomic effect contributes to macroeconomic growth. Second, increasing incomes from employment generated by FDI lead to increased consumption and reinvestment in the capital stock, thereby further enhancing economic growth.[2]

Initially, FDI was a remarkable success story for CEE. The privatization of state-owned enterprises (SOEs), increasing consumer demand, and the prospects of European Union (EU) membership drove a process that led to huge flows of inward FDI from multinational enterprises (MNEs) from the EU, North America, and East Asia. Small economies such as the Czech Republic and Hungary during the 1990s were able to attract FDI per capita in excess of 5,000 USD per annum (Akbar & McBride, 2004).

By 2002, the World Bank was reporting in Hungary, for example, that the "corporate sector is now largely owned and controlled by foreigners as a result of the now-completed privatization program" (World Bank, 2002). As the privatization process, and thus the availability of potential acquisitions wound up, and as greenfield potential evaporated due to increased factor costs in CEE, the surge of FDI seen in the 1990s appeared to have slowed by 2002–2003. It is now widely accepted by policy-makers, and aid and development organizations, that the future capital base and innovative potential of CEE economies are most likely to come from private sector capital formation, and thus the development of these countries' stock exchanges.

2.2. LSED and Economic Development

It is widely accepted that strong public securities markets are associated with economic development (Federation of Euro-Asian Stock Exchanges, 2003; Levine & Zervos, 1998; Atje & Jovanovic, 1993; Greenwood & Jovanovic, 1990). This relationship materializes as effective and robust domestic financial infrastructures enable emerging markets to integrate successfully into global financial systems, offering local firms access to international capital markets from which to avail themselves of capital necessary for firm growth, but not locally available. Well functioning stock markets additionally channel investment funds to the most productive companies, or "best users", focusing investment on those firms most likely to contribute to economic and social development (Goldsmith, 1969, p. 400), and facilitate investment in longer run, development enhancing, projects, by reducing the disincentives associated with such projects (by enabling investors to sell their stake even before the project matures (Levine & Zervos, 1998)).

However, while a positive relationship between stock market and economic development is generally accepted and theoretically well argued, empirical evidence on *any* association between stock market and economic development remains limited – Levine and Zervos (1998) offer a similar critique – and there exist arguments suggesting instead a *negative* relationship. Shleifer and Vishny (1986), for example, argue that greater liquidity encourages shareholders to shirk on their monitoring role, allowing them to easily sell their shares rather than incurring monitoring costs, and focusing the market on punishment rather than prevention of non-productivity enhancing activity, the former being a potentially less effective method.

Systematic studies of CEE stock exchanges remain particularly limited (the two perhaps most cited, recent empirical studies of the relationship between stock exchange and economic development: Atje and Jovanovic (1993) and Levine and Zervos (1998) do not include these exchanges[3]), and anecdotal evidence is mixed. The number of publicly traded companies in each of the countries remains small, and total market capitalization and trading volumes remain low and concentrated in a few issuers. Although the World Bank rated Hungarian capital markets as relatively large and successful, for example, the Budapest Stock Exchange's market capitalization remains at only about 20 percent of gross domestic product (GDP), versus more than 50 percent in developed countries, and three companies (*Matav*, the previously entirely state-owned telecommunications monopoly; *MOL*, the previously entirely state-owned monopoly oil and gas company; and *OTP*, the previously entirely state-owned monopoly savings bank) accounting for 66 percent of market capitalization and a similar amount of trading volume (World Bank, 2002).

The reasons for the thus far limited development of Economic Commission for Europe (ECE) stock exchanges are many. Following the German traditional corporate governance model, firms tend to turn to the banks for financing, rather than to the market. Using Hungary as an example again, banks provide 75 percent of corporate finance (World Bank, 2002). Additionally, because most of the money on the market is that of international institutional investors (e.g., only 2 percent of the Hungarian population invests on the Budapest Stock Exchange), the disclosure demands (additionally including increased demands by the exchanges themselves, which have resulted in many cases with the exchanges experiencing more de-listings than listings over recent years) of going on the market discourage firms and their executives, used to the opacity of the previous economic regime, from doing so.

Policy-makers recognize, however, the need to develop their stock exchanges, and have begun to institute various programs meant to do so. Most of all have adopted Corporate Governance Guidelines to address continuing concern about the strength of corporate governance mechanisms and processes. These guidelines in many cases focus in particular on the rights of minority shareholders, as another characteristic of publicly traded CEE firms is that they tend to remain dominated by majority shareholders, who in the past have proved disrespectful of minority shareholder rights. Some countries, for example, Hungary, have developed campaigns both for the public, encouraging them to invest in the stock market, and for potentially listable firms, encouraging them to go to the market for capital (e.g., the Budapest Stock Exchange has developed an IPO Club of 25 member firms moving towards listing).

The relationship between local companies' listings of shares on international exchanges and economic development appears to be the least researched relationship of the three we examine. Claessens et al. (2001) examine relationship between FDI, LSED, and FSEL, suggesting that FDI is positively correlated with stock market capitalization and value traded, and that FDI is further positively correlated with the degree to which capital raising, listing, and trading migrates to international financial centers. They do not, however, explicitly examine the relationship between these three forces and economic development, or their sequential relationship.

3. TESTING THE RELATIONSHIP BETWEEN FDI, LSED, AND ECONOMIC DEVELOPMENT

While anecdotal or case study research on this topic continues to offer important information on processes and linkages, we additionally offer a systematic and theoretically and empirically rigorous study of the relationships between FDI, LSED, FSEL and economic development. We examine a cross-country, longitudinal study of the association between levels of economic development in CEE countries on the one hand and FDI, LSED, and FSEL on the other. In our initial analysis, we test the following hypotheses:

Hypothesis 1. The relationship between FDI and economic development is positive.

Hypothesis 2. The relationship between LSED and economic development is positive.

However, following the arguments described above, future analyses will also include tests of the following hypotheses as shown in Fig. 1.

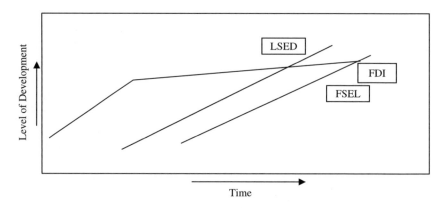

Fig. 1. Our Final Hypotheses: Evolution of FDI, LSED, FSEL, and Level of Development Over Time.

4. METHODOLOGY

4.1. Sample and Measures

Our data come from the World Bank's World Development Indicators
(WDI) on-line. This database includes traditional measures of FDI (e.g.,
acquisition versus greenfield), LSED (e.g., number of companies listed,
market capitalization as a percent of GDP, trading volume), and economic
development (e.g., economic growth, productivity growth, capital accumulation) for the 24 countries/stock exchanges we examine (countries are listed
in Note 1) from 1960 to 2002. As it does not yet include data on local
companies' FSEL, we do not include that empirical analysis here. We followed two key articles on the link between LSED and development (Atje &
Jovanovic, 1993; Levine & Zervos, 1998) in our selection of measures,
although we did utilize alternative measures as noted.

Given the relatively short history of FDI and stock markets in CEE
countries, we were faced with scarcity of data, especially on stock market
development. Therefore, we chose the following data for our analysis:

- *GDP annual percent growth*: We used this data as a measure of the economic development of the CEE countries. This data was available for as
  long as 42 years for Hungary and only 7 years for Serbia and Montenegro.
- *FDI as percent of GDP*: We used this data as measure of the FDI infused
  into each of the CEE countries. This data was available for as long as 17
  years for Hungary and only 7 years for Serbia and Montenegro.

- *Market capitalization as percent of GDP*: We used this data as an indicator of the level of stock market development in each of the CEE countries. This data was available for as long as 12 years for Hungary and for as little as 2 years each for Azerbaijan and Kyrgyz Republic.

Scarcity of data especially on stock market development limited our analysis severely. We, therefore, first looked at countries for which we had many years of data on all three measures (GDP, FDI, and market capitalization). Those countries were Hungary and Poland, with 12 years of data on all three variables. We then combined 11 countries for which we had data for the period 1995–2002 on all three measures (GDP, FDI, and market capitalization) for an aggregate study of CEE countries.

5. RESULTS

Hungary is one of the two countries for which we had data on all three measures (GDP, FDI, and market capitalization) for 12 years. Hungary received significant FDI during the 1990s, which exceeded more than 30 percent of GDP in some years. FDI came down to a more modest level of 20 percent of GDP in 2001 and 2002. As we can also see, the market capitalization of listed companies as a proportion of GDP moved in tandem with GDP growth. We found the correlations reported in Table 1. The correlations show that FDI was not significantly associated with GDP growth, but that LSED, as measured by the market capitalization of listed companies, *was* significantly associated with GDP growth. These correlations provide evidence in support of Hypothesis 2, but not in support of Hypothesis 1, at least in the case of Hungary.

Poland is the country in addition to Hungary for which we had data on all three measures (GDP, FDI, and market capitalization) for 12 years. Poland

Table 1. Hungary 1991–2002.

	FDI, Net Inflows (% of GDP)	GDP Growth (Annual %)
GDP growth (annual %)	–0.0756	
Market capitalization of listed companies (% of GDP)	–0.249	0.689*

*Correlation is significant at 0.05 level.

too received significant FDI during the late 1990s, which came close to 20 percent of GDP in some years. FDI came down to a more modest level of 15 percent of GDP in 2001 and 2002. These correlations suggest that neither FDI nor LSED, as measured by market capitalization of listed companies, was significantly associated with GDP growth in Poland. However, LSED was significantly associated with FDI. Thus, in case of Poland, the correlations do not support either Hypothesis 1 or 2 (Table 2).

We then combined data on the 11 CEE countries (Bulgaria, Croatia, Czech Republic, Hungary, Latvia, Lithuania, Poland, Romania, Russian Federation, Slovak Republic, and Slovenia) for which we had data available for the 8-year period 1995–2002 on all three measures (GDP, FDI, and market capitalization). We computed averages on all three measures for these countries. All 11 countries received an increasing amount of FDI over the period 1995–2002, to a maximum of 18 percent of GDP in 2002. Table 3 reports the correlations.

These correlations, based on limited data (8 years), do not demonstrate significant associations between either FDI or LSED with GDP growth. Thus, the aggregation of data for the 11 CEE countries included does not support either Hypothesis 1 or 2. The aggregated data, do, however, suggest a positive relationship between FDI and LSED for these 11 CEE countries, as did our analysis for Poland alone. Our future analyses will examine the sequential nature of this relationship, following Hypothesis, as well as the monotonicities between FDI, LSED, and FSEL, respectively, and economic development, hypothesized in Hypothesis, as well as the simple positive relationship hypothesized between FSEL and economic development hypothesized in Hypothesis.

Our current analyses and results remain limited for the following reasons. There remains missing data for the countries and time periods we examined. This limitation is compounded by the paucity of available measures of relevant variables. Moreover, since much of the phenomenon we examine has

Table 2.   Poland 1991–2002.

	FDI, Net Inflows (% of GDP)	GDP Growth (Annual %)
GDP growth (annual %)	0.553	
Market capitalization of listed companies (% of GDP)	0.807*	0.576

*Correlation is significant at 0.01 level.

Table 3. Correlations for 11 East European Countries for the Period
1995–2002.

	FDI, Net Inflows (% of GDP)	GDP per Capita Growth (Annual %)
GDP per capita growth (annual %)	0.361	
Market capitalization of listed companies (% of GDP)	0.758*	−0.044

*Correlation is significant at 0.05 level.

occurred over a period of less than 20 years, we are constrained longitudinally. All three constraints are indicative of the widespread problem concerning statistical research on CEE.

From a conceptual viewpoint, there are issues with respect to both the FDI and LSED variables we examined that warrant further research. For FDI, there may be a lag between an FDI decision and its actual impact on economic growth. On an enterprise level, this is intuitively explained by making reference to a decision to greenfield a facility, and the lead time required before production can start. The lag in this relationship may explain the lack of a clear statistical relationship in our study. Further analyses could incorporate explicit time lags on the FDI–economic development relationship in order to capture the true relationship.

Regarding our analysis of local stock market development, we found a positive and statistically significant relationship to economic development in the Hungarian case, and a statistically insignificant relationship in the Polish and more general case. As our conceptual discussion indicated, the development of local stock exchanges is not the sole indicator of the role of stock markets and their contribution to economic development in the region. Many of the region's most actively traded stocks are traded both on local and international exchanges. MOL, one of Hungary's largest companies, for example, is traded both on the Budapest Stock Exchange and on the New York Stock Exchange (NYSE), as well as London's stock exchange automated quotations system (SEAQ). However, local companies are not only listing on the large international exchanges (BorsodChem, Hungary's leading chemical manufacturer), but recently decided to list on the Warsaw Stock Exchange. In order to truly understand the forces behind development in the region, local companies' FSEL must be addressed, conceptually – as we have – but also empirically, as we hope to do in a future analysis.

6. CONCLUSIONS

Previous studies of economic development in the CEE countries have focused on the positive association between FDI and development. We argue that these studies, while providing important insights, neglect the following issues: (i) the current phenomenon of decreasing FDI in these countries, and thus a here-hypothesized non-monotonicity in this relationship; (ii) the role of LSED in economic development, though policy-makers in these countries are increasingly focused on this role; and (iii) the role of FSEL, which we have addressed conceptually but not empirically. The preliminary results and findings of this study begin to offer a more comprehensive and uptodate characterization of the relationship between investment and economic development, and in doing so, offer explanation and direction to these policy-makers in appropriate policies regarding FDI, LSED, and FSEL as well as explanation and direction to scholars regarding the results of previous studies, and future studies which need to be done.

NOTES

1. In CEE, in Bulgaria (the Bulgarian Stock Exchange, BSE), the Czech Republic (Prague SE), Estonia (Talinn SE), Hungary (Budapest SE), Latvia (Riga SE), Lithuanian (NSEL), Poland (Warsaw SE), Romania (Bucharest SE), Slovakia (Bratislava SE), Slovenia (Llubljana SE); in the former Soviet Union, in Armenia (Yerevan SE), Belarus (BSE), Georgia (GSE), Kazakhstan (KASE), Kyrgystan (Kyrgy SE), Moldava (MSE), Russia (RSE), Tajikistan (TSE), Ukraine (UKRSE), and Uzbekistan (Tashkent SE); in the former Yugoslavia (not including the EU accession states listed above as CEE, in Croatia (Zagreb SE), Macedonia (MSE), Montenegro (MSE), and Serbia (Belgrade SE).

2. Notwithstanding, research suggests that while the overall impact of FDI has been largely positive, there have been important redistributive consequences (e.g., Kiss, 2003; Sinn & Weichenrieder, 1997).

3. Atje and Jovanovic (1993) include 40 countries: Egypt, Nigeria, A. Africa, Zimbabwe, India, Israel, Japan, Jordan, Republic of Korea, Malaysia, Philippines, Singapore, Taiwan, Thailand, Austria, Belgium, Denmark, France, Germany, Greece, Italy, Netherlands, Norway, Portugal, Spain, Sweden, United Kingdom, Canada, Jamaica, Mexico, United States, Argentina, Brazil, Chile, Colombia, Peru, Uruguay, Venezuela, Australia, and Indonesia. Levine and Zervos (1998) include those, minus A. Africa and Uruguay, and nine more, Finland, Turkey, Luxembourg, Morocco, New Zealand, Hong Kong, Pakistan, Cote d'Ivoire, and Bangladesh, as well as non-stock market data for 31, Bolivia, Botswana, Cameroon, Central African Republic, Costa Rica, Dominican Republic, Ecuador, Ethiopia, Ghana, Guatemala, Guyana, Haiti, Kenya, Lesotho, Liberia, Madagascar, Malawi, Mauritania, Mauritius, Nicaragua, Niger, Paraguay, Rwanda, Senegal, Somalia, Sri Lanka, Tunisia, Uruguay, Zaire, and Zambia.

REFERENCES

Akbar, Y., & Brad McBride, J. (2004). Multinational enterprise strategy, Foreign direct investment and economic development. The case of Hungary. *Journal of World Business, 39*, 89–105.

Atje, R., & Jovanovic, B. (1993). Stock markets and development. *European Economic Review, 37*, 632–3640.

Balasubramanyam, V. N., Salisu, M., & Sapsford, D. (1996). Foreign direct investment and growth in EP and IS countries. *Economic Journal, 106*, 92–106.

Barrell, R., & Holland, D. (2000). Foreign direct investment and enterprise restructuring in Central Europe. *Economics of Transition, 8*, 477–505.

Barrell, R., & Pain, N. (1997). Foreign direct investment, technological change and economic growth within Europe. *Economic Journal, 107*, 70–86.

Borensztein, E., Gregorio, J., & Lee, J. W. (1995). *How does foreign direct investment affect economic growth?* NBER Working Paper no. 5057.

Claessens, S., Klingebiel, D., & Schmukler, S. L. (2001). *FDI and stock market development: Complements or substitutes?* Working Paper, University of Amsterdam and World Bank.

Clague, C., & Rausser, G. (1992). *The emergence of market economies in Eastern Europe.* Cambridge, MA: Blackwell.

Durlauf, S., & Quah, D. (1999). The new empirics of economic growth. In: J. Taylor & M. Woodford (Eds), *Handbook of macroeconomics* (pp. 235–308). Amsterdam: Elsevier Science.

Economic Commission for Europe. (2001). Economic growth and foreign direct investment in the transition economies. *Economic Survey of Europe, 1*(1), 185–226.

Federation of Euro-Asian Stock Exchanges. (2003). *Best practices for the development of stock exchanges in transition economies.* Working Paper.

Frydman, R., Rapaczynski, A., & Earle, J. (1993). *The privatization process in Central Europe.* Budapest: Central European University Press.

Goldsmith, R. (1969). *Financial structure and development.* New Haven: Yale University Press.

Greenwood, J., & Jovanovic, B. (1990). Financial development, growth, and the distribution of income. *Journal of Political Economy, 98.*

Havrylyshyn O. et al. (2000). Growth experience in transition countries 1990–1998. IMF Occasional Paper no. 184.

King, L., & Váradi, B. (2002). Beyond manichean economics: Foreign direct investment and growth in the transition from socialism. *Communist and Post-Communist Studies, 35*, 1–21.

Kiss, J. (2003). System changes, export-oriented growth and women in Hungary. *Europe–Asia Studies, 55*, 3–38.

Konings, J. (2001). The effects of foreign direct investment on domestic firms: Evidence from firm-level panel data in emerging economies. *Economics of Transition, 9*, 619–634.

Krkoszka, L. (2001). *Foreign direct investment financing of capital formation in East and Central Europe.* EBRD Working Paper no. 67.

Levine, R., & Zervos, S. (1998). Stock markets, banks and economic growth. *American Economic Review, 88*, 537–558.

Shleifer, A., & Vishny, R. (1986). Large shareholders and corporate control. *Journal of Political Economy, 96*, 461–488.

Sinn, H. W., & Weichenrieder, A. J. (1997). Foreign direct investment, political presentment and the privatization process in Eastern Europe. *Economic Policy, 10*, 177–210.

Temple, J. (1999). The new growth evidence. *Journal of Economic Literature, 37*, 112–156.

Uhlenbruck, K., & De Castro, J. (2000). Foreign acquisitions in East and Central Europe: Outcomes of privatization in transitional economies. *Academy of Management Journal, 43*, 381–402.

World Bank. (2002). *Report on the observance of standards and codes: Hungary*. Washington, DC: World Bank.

THE IMPACT OF EU
ENLARGEMENT ON FDI FLOWS

Kálmán Kalotay[1]

1. INTRODUCTION

In the enlarged European Union (EU) with 25 members, the free movement of capital, coupled with the free movement of goods and services should be a major direct attraction for both intra-EU and external foreign direct investment (FDI) inflows. EU membership does not, however, lead to a linear increase in FDI inflows as many analysts suggest (ECE, 2001). With EU accession, the structure of FDI may change substantially (Hunya, 2000; Dyker, 2001). Activities based on the existence of closed domestic markets (e.g. food and beverages) and on cheap labour (e.g. assembly activities) might be reduced, or even closed down, giving way to more knowledge-intensive activities in the new EU member countries (Kalotay, 2004a). FDI in the new EU member countries is not yet on an uninterrupted growth path. In the pre-accession phase (1995–2003), the relative importance of new EU members in global FDI flows when compared to that of the "old" members of the EU, was actually *shrinking*. Thus, if new members want to use FDI as one channel for catching up, they have to reverse this trend and increase their inward FDI quite rapidly.

This chapter explores why the potential of the new EU members has not been realised to date. It documents that compared to the opportunities, FDI inflows and outflows of the new members have so far been small and

Emerging European Financial Markets: Independence and Integration Post-Enlargement
International Finance Review, Volume 6, 473–499
Copyright © 2006 by Elsevier Ltd.
ISSN: 1569-3767/doi:10.1016/S1569-3767(05)06019-X

slow-growing. In other words, favourable circumstances do not automatically translate to more FDI. This issue is the main focus of this chapter. The chapter is structured as follows. In Section 2, we set the context for the analysis. In Section 3, we present the developments with regard to FDI inflows and outflows. The untapped FDI potential of the new EU members is analysed in Section 4, and this is followed by a discussion of the new members' productivity advantages in Section 5, including factors such as the free movement of goods and services, taxation issues and future monetary union. We also discuss the possibility of FDI diversion at this point. In Section 6, we consider the possibility of a pan-European division of labour. We outline the important policy challenges in Section 7, and we draw together our conclusions in the final part, Section 8.

2. THE CONTEXT

In May 2004, the membership of the EU increased from 15 to 25 countries. Since the signature of the treaty of Rome in 1957 by its six founding members, the EU had never accepted such an unprecedented number of new members. And, with the exception of the integration of the new German Länder in 1991, this was the first time that the territory of the EU was extended beyond the former Iron Curtain. The enlargement of the EU is not yet necessarily complete. At least four countries are officially recognized as candidates for membership. Two of them, Bulgaria and Romania are already in the phase of negotiating the terms of their accession, and Croatia may follow suit in 2005. Nevertheless, it is not likely that any future enlargement will bring in as many new members as recently.

The enlarged EU will have economic power comparable with that of other major integrated groupings worldwide such as the North American Free Trade Area (NAFTA) and the Association of South-East Asian Nations (ASEAN). Enlargement has increased the population of the EU from 377 to 451 million (+ 74 million). This is higher than the population of NAFTA (413 million), although still less than that of the very populous ASEAN (521 million). The gross domestic product (GDP) of the enlarged EU increased only slightly, from US$7.9 trillion to US$8.2 trillion (+ US$0.3 trillion only), due to the relatively low GDP per capita of the new members. But income levels are expected to rise fast in the enlarged EU, making it possible to close the gap on NAFTA, which, with a combined GDP of US$11 trillion, is today ahead of the enlarged EU. (As for the ASEAN, the total GDP of that developing country group remains under US$1 trillion.)

Compared to its peers, the EU possesses a major qualitative advantage: Its integration processes are deeper and more comprehensive than those of the NAFTA and the ASEAN. The EU is a customs and (potentially) economic union, with free movement of people (after a transition period), capital, goods and services. Compared with that, the NAFTA is only a free trade area, although it has side agreements on environment and labour. As for ASEAN, it is a de facto preferential trade area.

3. FDI INFLOWS AND OUTFLOWS

The 10 countries that joined the EU on 1 May 2004 have so far neither diverted significant FDI flows away from the 15 older members of the Union, nor improved their FDI position significantly relative to the older members. Over most of the late-1990s and early 2000s, the combined inflow of the 10 new EU member countries remained considerably lower than the inflows of individual EU-member countries such as France and Germany, and, more recently, Ireland and Spain (see Table 1). Since the mid-1990s, the FDI in-

Table 1. FDI Inflows of New EU Members in International Comparison, 1995–2004 (Billion US Dollars).

Country/Group	1995	1998	2000	2001	2002	2003	2004ᴾ
New EU members	12.2	16.8	20.6	18.6	22.9	11.8	18
Of which:							
Czech Republic	2.6	3.7	5.0	5.6	8.5	2.6	4
Hungary	5.1	3.8	2.8	3.9	2.8	2.5	4
Poland	3.7	6.4	9.3	5.7	4.1	4.2	5
Slovakia	0.3	0.7	1.9	1.6	4.1	0.6	1
Memorandum items:							
World	335.7	690.9	1,388.0	817.6	678.8	559.6	597
EU-15	114.6	249.9	671.4	357.4	374.0	295.2	242
Of which:							
France	23.7	31.0	43.3	50.5	48.9	47.0	26
Germany	12.0	24.6	198.3	21.1	36.0	12.9	−11
Ireland	1.4	8.6	25.8	9.7	24.5	25.5	19
Spain	6.3	11.8	37.5	28.0	35.9	25.6	14
New EU member countries per EU-15 (%)	10.7	6.7	3.1	5.2	6.1	4.0	7.4

Source: Author's calculation, based on the UNCTAD, FDI/TNC database.
ᴾProjections.

flows of the 10 countries that joined the EU in 2004 accounted for a fraction of the inflows of the EU 15 – a mere 4 per cent in 2003, declining from a high of 10.7 per cent in 1995. Projections for 2004 suggest a strong recovery of FDI in new EU members (Table 1). That fact, combined with an expected decline in the EU-15 can result in a return to the relative level of 1998 (7 per cent). However, it remains to be confirmed if the recovery in the new EU members will remain sustainable in the longer run. While part of the low FDI inflows in the early 2000s can be explained by short-term factors such as the completion of the large privatization deals (first in Hungary, then in Poland, and more recently in the Czech Republic and Slovakia), the gap between actual and potential FDI in the 10 new members is too large to be explained by such factors alone.

To a certain degree, the low and slow-growing level of FDI in the new members may also be due to its shift towards services. Service-related FDI inflows into the new EU members have indeed followed the general trend of growth in services (in GDP, employment and FDI) worldwide and in Europe itself. What is unique to new EU members – with the exception of the two smallest countries: Cyprus and Malta – is that prior to their transition from centrally planned economies, which began only a decade and a half ago, services were neglected. This complicated the transition and growth process. In many service industries, the need for investment, technological upgrading, building of market-related skills and improvement of management practices has resulted in an intensive use of inward FDI as a tool to meet those requirements in the short or medium term. Moreover, nowadays, the composition of FDI in the new EU member countries is not just gradually shifting away from manufacturing towards services, but also within services, from network industries privatized in earlier years towards business services.[2] And the latter tend to be less large-scale and less capital intensive than the former. In other words, even if the number of new FDI projects is increasing in the new EU members, their combined value does not necessarily grow.

One of the main reasons why FDI has not yet increased so fast in the new EU members may be related to the nature of FDI, especially the sunk costs of already existing projects. Sunk costs create high inertia for locational choices. New locations are considered only if firms envisage large new ventures and, even in that case, they have to consider the trade-off between the synergies and relative security of old locations compared to the lower costs offered by new ones.

In line with the above, the low level of FDI in new EU member countries – as far as flows originating in the EU are concerned – is also due to a lack of vigorous home-country measures in the 15 older member countries of the EU and at the level of the Union. Due to the perception that new countries are a threat to jobs at home, no older member country has so far suggested a programme of outward FDI promotion to increase investment in new member countries. On the contrary: Firms envisaging an expansion in the new member countries could potentially face an informal pressure of the public opinion, trade unions and political leaders at home. The gradual introduction of structural and cohesion funds in the new members (see below) can further handicap the efforts of the new members to attract FDI.

In FDI outflows, the underperformance of new EU members compared to the "old" ones is even more pronounced than in FDI inflows. The combined share of the 10 new members has remained under 1 per cent since the mid-1990s (Table 2). With the exception of Hungary in 2003, the FDI outflows of individual new member countries have never exceeded the US$1 billion benchmark. Put simply, they are not in the same league as the leading EU source countries of outward FDI (France, Germany, the Netherlands and the United Kingdom; see Table 2).

In the light of the nascent stage of capitalism in new EU members – with the exceptions of Cyprus and Malta – the low level of outward FDI is not surprising. One also has to consider the additional fact that even when capitalism building was on the political agenda, no critical role was attributed to outward FDI in the process. Hence while immediately after transition had started, trade liberalization became the first vehicle of reintegration, followed by inward FDI from the mid-1990s, outward FDI was at most a tolerated phenomenon for most of the time.

The structural patterns (industries, countries of destination) of outward FDI from the new EU members confirm the nascent status of those investments. Recent evidence points to a geographical concentration on lower-income neighbouring countries, especially those with which they have traditionally close business links. For example, Slovenian firms target former Yugoslavia (Jaklič & Svetličič, 2003). Within that general pattern, there are some country-by-country differences: An overwhelming majority of outflows and outward stocks of Estonia, in addition to those of Slovenia, target the close neighbourhood (UNCTAD, 2001, pp. 37, 252). Neighbours are also a dominant destination for Czech Republic firms, and are sizeable for Hungary. On the other hand, Latvia is an exception, with minimal outward FDI stock in the Baltic neighbourhood.

In some countries such as Estonia, Hungary and Poland, an important part of outward FDI is carried out by foreign affiliates. The leading outward investing Estonian banks, for example, are foreign owned: Hansapank is

Table 2.   FDI Outflows of New EU Members in International
Comparison, 1995–2003 (Billion US Dollars).

Country/Group	1995	1998	2000	2001	2002	2003
New EU members	0.14	1.05	1.07	1.08	1.26	3.11
Of which:						
Cyprus	0.03	0.07	0.20	0.22	0.30	0.35
Hungary	0.06	0.32	0.62	0.37	0.27	1.58
Poland	0.04	0.32	0.02	−0.09	0.23	0.39
Slovenia	−0.01	−0.01	0.07	0.14	0.09	0.30
Memorandum items:						
World	358.2	687.2	1186.8	721.5	596.5	612.2
EU-15	159.7	415.4	806.2	429.2	351.2	337.0
Of which:						
France	15.76	48.61	177.45	86.77	49.43	57.28
Germany	39.05	88.82	56.56	36.85	8.62	2.56
The Netherlands	20.18	36.67	75.63	47.97	34.55	36.09
United Kingdom	43.56	122.82	233.37	58.86	35.18	55.09
New EU member countries per EU-15 (%)	0.1	0.3	0.1	0.3	0.4	0.9

Source: Author's calculation, based on the UNCTAD, FDI/TNC database.

owned by Sweden's Swedbank and Ühispank by Sweden's SEB (Kilvits &
Purju, 2001, p. 255). Outside Estonia, the most salient example is the invest-
ment of Hungary's Matáv, majority controlled by Deutsche Telekom, into
Maktelekom (TFYR Macedonia), carried out at the end of 2000. Another
case is an investment by German–Austrian controlled Dunapack (Hungary)
into Romania. Similarly, the Czech Republic affiliate of Germany's RWE
Entsorgung has invested in Romania, and Swedish-owned Czech Pramet in
Bulgaria (UNCTAD, 2001, p. 119).

A further element confirming the nascent stage of outward FDI is Central
and Eastern Europe (CEE) is the fact that, at least in some countries (Czech
Republic, Estonia and Poland) services industries (especially trading and
banking) dominate. This is apparently different from the sequence of outward FDI from developed countries where manufacturing firms are usually
the first outward investors (Stare, 2002). All in all outward FDI is rather a
long-term development concern for new EU member countries. In the immediate future, they will more likely focus on inward FDI. For that reason,
the rest of this chapter will focus on issues related to inward FDI, reflecting
also its pre-eminence in the international economic relations of new EU
member countries.

4. THE UNTAPPED FDI POTENTIAL OF NEW EU MEMBERS

Low inward FDI in new the EU members suggests a large untapped FDI potential as well as a need for concerted policy efforts between home and host countries to speed up the integration of the new EU member group into the enlarged EU, and its economic catching up with the 15 old members. The 10 new members had developed and improved the key ingredients that would make them a major attraction for FDI within the enlarged EU partly during their early transition from centrally planned to market economies, and partly during the accession negotiations. Within the enlarged EU, the new members offer both competitive production costs and relatively low fiscal burdens (see discussion below). Parallel with accession negotiations, huge amounts were invested into improving the physical infrastructure – and that effort is expected to continue after joining the EU.

In the countries that joined the EU in May 2004, full membership of the Union affected various factors, mostly institutional, that directly or indirectly influence FDI flows. They are discussed below.

4.1. Political Framework and International Treaties

The new EU members have gained full rights to participate in the political decision-making mechanisms of the EU, including the Council of Ministers, the Commission and the European Parliament. This enables them to better influence all decisions concerning the political, social and economic environment for FDI. The new EU members have also become subject to the various treaties signed previously by the EU-15. Accordingly, they have had to adjust their bilateral investment treaties (BITs) and double taxation treaties (DTTs) with third partners to comply with EU standards and norms. On balance, by further increasing stability and predictability, that adjustment will have improved the attractiveness of new EU member countries.

4.2. The Acquis Communautaire

The new EU members have committed themselves to adopting the full body of EU law (the so-called *acquis communautaire*). The *acquis communautaire* improves the business environment and the attractiveness of accession countries (Dyker, 2001, p. 1007; ECE, 2001, p. 192; Hunya, 2000, p. 21). On the other hand, its application (e.g. concerning environmental protection and labour standards) may increase the cost of doing business in the new EU member countries.

The ambiguous impact of the *acquis communautaire* on business in general, and FDI in particular, is the result of the philosophical compromise between a more liberal and a more *dirigiste* interpretation of what a common market means (Tupy, 2003). A pragmatic approach to the question cannot deny the need for a minimum level of technical standards, consumer protection rules, environmental standards, competition policy and workplace standards. The new EU members, however, face two dilemmas in this respect. On the one hand, it is not easy to define the border line between necessary and excessive regulations. On the other hand, countries at different levels of development may have different views of what a necessary minimum should be. Generally speaking, the wealthier countries tend to require stricter standards. Moreover, less-developed members possess less institutional capabilities to effectively assimilate and adopt the ever increasing body of the *acquis* (Blažek, 1999, p. 181; Dyker, 2001, p. 1008). As a consequence, in the dynamics of the enlarged EU, new members are expected to advocate less stringent rules and more flexibility in their applications, while old members may argue for the contrary.

4.3. Free Movement of Goods and Services

The accession countries became full members of its customs union and the single market, and could start benefiting from the freedom of movement for goods, services, capital and labour (with the exception of the free movement of people to which transition periods apply). In terms of intra-EU transportation, logistical and administrative costs, this offers a major locational advantage to FDI targeting new EU members (Barry, 2004, p. 757; Hunya, 2000, p. 21; Tupy, 2003, p. 2). Furthermore, restrictions on the migration of persons from East to West encourage firms to increase their presence in the East, which is the source of cheaper labour.

4.4. EU Funds

The new EU members became participants in the EU budget. On balance, the amounts of net transfers are expected to be limited (see Table 3 and Tupy, 2003, p. 3), given the transition period of 10 years before new members can

Table 3. Net Transfer of EU Funds to New Members, 2004–2006 (Million euros and Percentage).

| | Nominal Net | | | |
| | Transfers[a] | | Real Transfers[b] | |
Country	€ Million	% of GDP	€ Million	% of GDP
Czech Republic	778	0.3	−97	0.0
Estonia	504	2.1	271	1.0
Hungary	1,374	0.6	772	0.3
Latvia	831	3.0	498	1.6
Lithuania	1,353	2.7	405	0.7
Poland	6,997	1.2	3,119	0.5
Slovakia	831	0.8	264	0.2
Slovenia	244	0.3	−100	−0.1
Total	13,130	1.0	5,332	0.4

Source: Author's calculation, adopted from Morgan (2004, p. 16).
[a]Based on the official data of the European Commission.
[b]Estimated on the basis of the absorption rates of PHARE funds in 1990–2002.

gain full access to all regional aid and the record of limited absorptive capacities for EU funds (Blažek, 1999, p. 182). The EU member countries are entitled to 25 per cent of the Common Agricultural Policy funds and 30 per cent of the Regional Development funds available to current EU members. Subsequently, those shares will increase by 10 per cent per annum until they reach the level of 100 per cent by around 2014 (UNCTAD, 2003, p. 79, fn. 43). Moreover, these transfers are not expected to be used for direct FDI promotion, but they will help to improve the physical and human infrastructure in the new EU members.

4.5. Monetary Union

In due course, the new EU members will join the Economic and Monetary Union (EMU) and adopt the euro. On the positive side, this will reduce currency and exchange risks for firms operating in the new member countries. On the negative sign, joining the EMU will require limiting the autonomy of exchange rate management as a tool to keep production costs competitive, and this could potentially lead to an overvaluation of national currencies.

Beside the challenge of establishing and strengthening the institutional framework of the single currency (Blažek, 1999, p. 181), the new EU members have to carefully evaluate the arguments for and against introducing the euro as soon as possible. Until then, ample room remains for further productivity increases in the new EU member countries, a fixed exchange rate, caused by a premature adoption of the euro, would allow relative price adjustments only through inflation in non-tradable goods, which would then affect the competitiveness of exportable goods. According to Dyker (2001, p. 171), EMU membership could even push new EU countries into recession.

There is room for containing the appreciation of the real exchange rate, because it is caused only partly by natural phenomena such as the Balassa–Samuelson effect (Égert, Drine, Lommatzsch, & Rault, 2003). If only the Balassa–Samuelson effect (Balassa, 1964; Samuelson, 1964) were responsible for the difference between inflation rates and devaluation in new EU members, the upward pressure on domestic prices should originate in the non-tradable goods sector, in which productivity grows much slower than that of the fast modernizing export sector. That would then result in wage increases in all sectors. However, a study on nine CEE countries (Égert et al., 2003) has found that increases in the prices of tradable goods have significantly contributed to inflation and currency appreciation. This is a trend that could be potentially contained.

Despite the short-term constraints to FDI in new EU members, there is reason for optimism in the medium and longer term. It is expected that, despite the lack of policy support, investors will substantially increase their presence in the new EU member countries because it makes business sense. By 2014, the transition period for regional and structural funds provided to new members will be over, and the new EU member countries will be entitled to the same assistance as older members. It may also transpire that awareness about the interdependence of welfare in the two parts of the enlarged EU will increase. If perceptions change, home countries may give a second thought to the idea of promoting FDI in the new members.

5. THE NEW MEMBERS' PRODUCTIVITY ADVANTAGE

Policy harmonization through EU membership has its own limitations. There are no commonly agreed policies in areas such as wages or most aspects of taxation. This lack of agreement reflects the different interests of the member countries, largely due to the diversity in their levels of development, economic structures and development objectives.

5.1. The Relative Wage Advantage

In terms of wages (see Table 4) and related policies, there have always been long-standing differences between the more-developed, higher-wage members, and the less-developed, lower-wage members. With the accession of the 10 new countries, discrepancies in wages have further increased. In 2001, the average wage level of the EU-15 was more than three times higher than that of the 10 new member countries. Adjusted to productivity, the new EU member countries offer major labour cost advantages, especially compared to some Mediterranean EU members (Greece and Portugal). The only exception is Poland whose average national productivity is low due to weak competitiveness in agriculture. The value added per €1,000 in labour costs in Polish

Table 4. Gross Monthly Average Salary in Selected Economies, Adjusted to Productivity, 1999–2002 (Euros and Percentage).

| Country | Gross Monthly Average Salary | | | | Productivity[a] | Productivity/ Salary (EU-15 = 100%) |
	1999	2000	2001	2002	2000	2000
Average of the EU-15[b]	1,923	2,127	2,191	–	42.5	100
Of which:						
Greece	1,160	1,227	1,286	1,357	19.4	79
Portugal	–	1,052	1,112	–	10.0	48
Spain	1,297	1,326	1,372	1,425	26.1	98
New EU members[c]	381	410	460	–	11.7	117
Of which:						
Czech Republic	*343*	*379*	*430*	*510*	10.9	144
Estonia	*282*	*303*	*328*	–	8.3	137
Hungary	314	348	408	489	11.1	160
Latvia	*257*	*277*	*280*	–	–	–
Lithuania	251	270	300	–	–	–
Poland	442	*471*	626	598	9.3	99
Slovakia	260	299	320	382	9.2	154
Slovenia	*895*	*935*	*988*	*1 041*	21.3	114
EU candidates	115	132	146	153	–	–
Of which:						
Bulgaria	111	120	127	132	–	–
Romania	*120*	*144*	*165*	*174*	–	–

Source: Author's calculation, based on http://europa.eu.int/comm/eurostat/; www.dree.org/elargissement (data in italics); and Stephan, 2003, p. 10 (for productivity data).
[a]Value added per €1,000 labour costs, national average.
[b]EUROSTAT estimate. Data for Austria, Ireland and Italy are not available.
[c]Average productivity is based on data for the Czech Republic, Estonia, Hungary, Poland, Slovakia and Slovenia only.

agriculture is only €2.6 (Stephan, 2003, p. 76). If only manufacturing and services were counted, Poland would have productivity levels similar to those of the other accession countries. These findings confirm similar findings reported in previous studies (e.g. Domański, 2001; Hardy, 1998; Hunya, 2001).

Combined with a favourable fiscal environment (see below) and access to EU funds used partly to finance infrastructure development, the competitive wage levels of the new EU member countries are a major factor in attracting efficiency-seeking FDI. Such FDI could help accelerate growth, needed for them to catch up with current EU members. More specifically, the productivity advantage in the new EU member countries has manifested a general two-way relationship with inward FDI. On the one hand, the productivity gains of the past decade have been to a large degree derived from inbound FDI (Hunya, 2000, p. 12; Kalotay, 2001, p. 272). This is in line with the mainstream literature on global FDI patterns which emphasize the productivity advantages of foreign affiliates over local forms (see Akbar & McBride, 2004; Blomström & Sjöholm, 1999; Djankov & Hoekman, 2000), although the spillover effects of such FDI may be limited (see Hardy, 1998). On the other hand, productivity is a key determinant of FDI.

5.2. The Balassa–Samuelson Effect

Wages will remain competitive in new EU member countries only if they do not increase faster than productivity. Developments in this area are difficult to forecast. With the gradual opening up of EU-15 labour markets and expected higher GDP growth, wages may start to increase rapidly in the new EU member countries. As mentioned above, currency appreciation can also contribute to a partial erosion of wage advantages in new EU members.

There is some evidence (see Table 5) that since the end of 2000 the national currencies of three countries with large productivity advantages towards the end of the millennium – the Czech Republic, Hungary and Slovakia – have appreciated, reducing, although not fully eliminating their relative advantages. In case of further real appreciations of the national currencies participating in the EMU, to remain competitive, investors may move their labour-intensive production activities to countries with even lower wages such as Bulgaria, Romania or Ukraine. The hope of new EU countries in this respect is that with fast economic development, productivity will increase more rapidly than wages. In addition, they may gradually specialize in higher value-added production processes or business functions (see below).

Table 5. The Balassa–Samuelson Effect in New EU Member Countries, 2001–June 2004.

Countries/ Territories	Change in Exchange Rate Against € (%)	Change in Consumer Price (%)	Change in Real Exchange Rate Against € (%)
Euro-zone	–	9.2	–
Cyprus	−1.3	10.8	0.1
Czech Republic	10.5	45.9	47.6
Estonia	0.0	15.8	6.0
Hungary	6.9	26.6	23.9
Latvia	−14.0	14.4	−10.0
Lithuania	7.8	1.7	0.3
Malta	−5.1	7.8	−6.3
Poland	−15.1	10.9	−13.9
Slovakia	10.1	27.6	28.6
Slovenia	−11.6	25.3	1.5

Source: The author's calculation, based on national statistics and eurostat data.

5.3. Taxation

Part of the adjustment of national development policies in general, and FDI policies in particular, to EU enlargement in the new member countries comes in the form of adjusting their fiscal systems to the new realities of international competition. This was done because even within the EU, member countries enjoy a high degree of autonomy in setting their corporate tax rates according to their development priorities (Tupy, 2003, p. 1). For example, countries wishing to attain high GDP growth rates at least partly with the involvement of inward FDI, may set their tax rates relatively low in order to stimulate the reinvestment of earnings into production. In turn, countries with higher GDP per capita, lower growth rates and large social safety nets may maximize fiscal revenues by setting their rates relatively high.

In the EU of 25 members, the diversity of national priorities is well reflected in the differences of corporate tax rates. Ireland, for example, has one of the lowest corporate tax rates in international comparison.[3] After the wave of tax reductions at the beginning of 2004, the majority of new EU member countries also belong to this category (with the notable exceptions of Malta, the Czech Republic and Slovenia; see Table 6). These findings are based on an international comparison of corporate taxes made for a sample of 75 economies (69 jurisdictions reported in the "KPMG's Corporate Tax

Table 6.   Corporate Tax Rates in Selected Economies, 1 January 2004
(%).

Country	Rate	Country	Rate
EU-15	*30.8*	*New EU members (9)*	*19.8*
Austria	34.0	Cyprus	10/15
Belgium	34.0	Czech Republic	28.0
Denmark	30.0	Estonia	0/26[a]
Finland	29.0	Hungary	16.0
France	34.3	Latvia	15.0[a]
Germany	38.3	Lithuania	15.0[a]
Greece	30.0	Malta	35.0
Ireland	12.5	Poland	19.0
Italy	37.3	Slovakia	19.0
Luxembourg	30.4	Slovenia	25.0[a]
The Netherlands	31.8	Memorandum:	
Portugal	27.5	*Other developed countries (9)*	*31.9*
Spain	35.0	*Developing economies (37)*	*30.0*
Sweden	28.0		
United Kingdom	30.0		

Source: Author's calculation, based on "KPMG's Corporate Tax Rates Survey – 2004" (http://
www.kpmg.co.uk/pubs/taxrates_04.pdf).
[a]Information collected directly by UNCTAD.

Rates Survey — 2004"[4] plus information for six more countries collected by
UNCTAD to make the comparison complete: Bulgaria, Estonia, Latvia,
Lithuania, Malta and Slovenia).

In a worldwide comparison, the high-tax EU member countries such as
Germany and Italy compare with other developed countries such as the
United States and Japan. However, there are some high-tax economies in
developing South Asia, too (India, Pakistan and Sri Lanka). In turn, the
low-tax new EU member countries compare with some selected emerging
locations such as Chile and Hong Kong (China) and Ireland. The corporate
tax rates of other CEE countries (not shown in the table) are either comparable with those of EU member countries (e.g. 19.5 per cent in Bulgaria,
20.3 per cent in Croatia), or slightly higher (25 per cent in Ukraine and
Romania, 24 per cent in the Russian Federation). Moreover, in two of these
five countries (Bulgaria and Ukraine), the rate was reduced in 2004.

These numbers suggest that the corporate tax policies of the new EU
members and other CEE countries are in line with their level of development
and development objectives. In the first group, it may be also interpreted as
one of the measures to compensate for the relatively high costs of adopting

the EU's regulatory standards and to deal with the consequences of the consensus-driven compromise deals about the application of cohesion policies (UNCTAD, 2003, p. 79, fn. 43). At the end, the improved competitiveness of firms located in the enlarged EU benefits both old and new members alike.

A comparison of corporate tax rates and the balances of central government budgets in the EU-25 (see Table 7) belies the fears that too low taxes, or a lowering of them, would lead to a destabilization of national budgets, and that low-tax countries would survive only from transfers coming from high-tax countries. Among the older members of the EU, for example, Ireland has a budget surplus, despite the fact that it has the lowest corporate tax rate in the group. In the accession group, the same applies to Estonia. Conversely, France and Germany, from the group of older members, are beyond the 3 per cent Maastricht criterion of fiscal deficit, despite their high-corporate taxes. In the group of new members, the Czech Republic combined a record high fiscal deficit with the second highest corporate tax rate in 2003. As a result of these relationships, the correlation between corporate tax levels and fiscal balances in the EU-25 is slightly negative. In other words, countries with higher corporate taxes tend to have higher budget deficits. Finally, a simple comparison of tax rates is not sufficient for

Table 7. Corporate Taxes and Fiscal Balances of Central Government in the EU-25, 2003 (Percentage and Per cent of GDP).

Economy	Corporate Tax Rate	Fiscal Balance	Economy	Corporate Tax Rate	Fiscal Balance
Austria	34.00	−1.3	Latvia	19.00	−1.8
Belgium	33.99	0.3	Lithuania	15.00	−1.7
Cyprus	10/15	−6.3	Luxembourg	30.38	−0.1
Czech Republic	31.00	−12.9	Malta	35.00	−9.7
Denmark	30.00	1.5	The Netherlands	31.75	−3.2
Estonia	0/26	2.6	Poland	27.00	−4.1
Finland	29.00	2.3	Portugal	33.00	−2.8
France	34.33	−4.1	Slovakia	25.00	−3.6
Germany	39.58	−3.9	Slovenia	25.00	−1.8
Greece	30.00	−3.2	Spain	35.00	0.3
Hungary	18.00	−5.9	Sweden	28.00	0.7
Ireland	12.50	0.2	United Kingdom	30.00	−3.2
Italy	38.25	−2.4			
Correlation	−0.13				

Source: Same as Table 5, and Eurostat (for fiscal balances).

assessing the relative tax burdens imposed by different governments. The method of computing the profits to which the tax rates will be applied (the tax base) should also be taken into account.

5.4. FDI Diversion?

In Western European public opinion, it has become an almost commonplace assertion that CEE countries are attracting away FDI from the "old" members of the EU. To what degree is this perception right? How frequent and large are the cases of *délocalisation* to the CEE countries? To what degree are perhaps relocations towards other regions such as Asia lumped into the same phenomenon? One has to ask also why the widespread perception about job losses in the old EU is so strong. The location of FDI projects is not a simple win/lose game. The locations not chosen for a given activity can still have major business links with new projects (and thus create additional jobs). Thirdly, as the case of the food industry indicates, reorganization itself is a two-way street: Projects can be relocated from new EU member countries to older EU members if the latter offer better agglomeration advantages. Three elements of a classical case of FDI diversion (Dunning & Robson, 1988; Baldwin, Forslid, & Haaland, 1996), missing from the FDI inflows of new EU member countries, are as follows:

(1) The inflows of the new EU members are too small compared to old members (4 per cent, Table 2). Therefore, even if *all* of their inward FDI had been of a "diverting" type, they would not have been massive enough to explain any major fluctuation in the inflows of the latter.
(2) There is no evidence to date of relocations of a large scale (Domański, 2001). The known cases have affected a very small number of workers in both groups (Kalotay, 2004a).
(3) There is no evidence of large FDI projects in new EU member countries that would have chosen a Western European location if enlargement had not taken place. In the automobile industry, for example, in the most important new projects (Toyota/PSA in the Czech Republic, PSA in Slovakia, Hyundai/KIA in Slovakia), EU enlargement was a pre-condition for considering a European location, and Western Europe was not even listed/short-listed for the projects (UNCTAD, 2004).

There is a further caveat to the current discussion on FDI diversion to new EU member countries. Such an analysis usually compares the current volume of FDI in individual EU member countries with a counter-factual situation under which no enlargement had taken place. From that perspective, what counts is the volume of flows. If the current volume were lower than the counter-factual volume, one would speak about FDI diversion. However, this interpretation is not necessarily correct once one returns to the Vinerian concepts of *trade* creation versus trade diversion (Viner, 1950), from which the concepts of FDI creation version diversion are derived. A key test to determine whether changes in trade flows are of a creating or diverting nature is their link with efficiency. If the volume of trade remains unchanged, but a more efficient location replaces a less efficient one, it is considered to be trade creation. This is so because, from a dynamic perspective, an improvement in global efficiency will lead to trade expansion in the longer one, even if the static impact is zero (with both winners and losers). This is probably the most precious Ricardian heritage of Viner.

If the efficiency test is applied to FDI, even cases of relocation, or of competing out projects, are of the FDI creating nature, on condition that the winner location is more efficient than the losing one. This is exactly the case of new EU member countries, which derive their competitiveness from a better relative productivity (when adjusted to wage levels).

6. TOWARDS A PAN-EUROPEAN DIVISION OF LABOUR?

EU enlargement offers large opportunities and poses major challenges for firms already established in the EU or planning to enter the area. Transnational corporations (TNCs) have to adapt their strategies to the new regulatory environment of location Europe (Akbar, 2003). The opportunities and challenges follow the standard impact (expansion, reorganization and rationalization) of integration groupings (Barrell & Pain, 1997). But given the *ampleur* of EU enlargement and the degree of differences between old and new members, the element of uncertainty in predicting the exact impact is large.

One also needs to differentiate between incumbent firms (locally and foreign owned alike) already operating in any of the EU-25 countries, and newcomers planning to establish themselves in the EU. Firms planning a major expansion of activities, too, show characteristics similar to newcomers. In the incumbent group, the expansion of the customs union is expected to lead to a gradual and continuous reorganization, and consolidation of activities. In this process, any location in the EU-25 is a potential winner of loser, independently of the fact that it is in an "old" or "new" member country. For newcomers, the main issue is where to locate their facilities. As explained above, in this respect the new member countries offer, for the time being, major cost and productivity advantages. As for firms from outside the EU, they are likely to locate increasingly their efficiency- and EU-market-seeking new FDI in new EU member countries (Hunya, 2000, pp. 23–24). For them, the considerations of sunk costs and home country pressure may be less relevant. In turn, they can imitate the strategy of such firms as Flextronics (Singapore) that have started using new EU member countries as an export platform replicating the global strategy of production experimented in locations such as China on a regional scale.

The opportunities and challenges also depend on the motivations for investment. For market-seeking investors (e.g. in food, beverages and tobacco, financial services (Akbar, 2003), retail trade and telecommunications; see Table 8), the enlargement of the EU area provides an important opportunity to increase sales and do more business, especially in the longer term, when the purchasing power and income of new members start to increase significantly. However, in the immediate future, restructuring and reorganization, prompted by fiercer competition in the wake of disappearing trade barrier may be a dominant force in those manufacturing industries and tradable services industries (Dyker, 2001, p. 1004). That may explain, for example, the rationalization of the food, beverages and tobacco industries of the new EU members.

For efficiency-seeking investors, for example, in the automotive industry, the electronics manufacturing industry in the broad sense, or, more recently, the shared services and call centres (Table 8), more competitiveness is the main benefit of EU enlargement, at least in the short and medium term. For the time being, they are likely to stop expanding in old EU members and continue expanding in new EU countries. However, they may increasingly find out that new EU members are no longer the right location for activities based on cheap unskilled labour (Hunya, 2000, p. 21). Those activities may be expected to move either to the new frontier of the EU (Southeast Europe and the Commonwealth of Independent States/CIS), or to South-East Asia. It also remains to be confirmed to what degree the productivity advantage of new EU members will be preserved after the entry of these countries into the euro zone.

Strategic-asset-seeking FDI is still in a nascent stage in new EU member countries. It is taking place mostly in information technologies (IT) and research and development (R&D), and in three countries: the Czech Republic, Hungary and Poland (Table 8). In these areas, the competitiveness offered by new EU members seems to be significant at the long term, especially if they

Table 8. Examples of Expansion Strategies of TNCs in New EU Member Countries, 2002–2004.

Sector	Market-Seeking (National or Regional) Strategy	Efficiency-Seeking (Export-Platform) Strategy	Strategic-Asset-Seeking Strategy
Manufacturing	*Automotive:* Poland (in part)	*Apparel:* Estonia, Latvia, Lithuania	
	Building materials: Poland, Hungary, Slovakia	*Automotive:* Czech Republic, Hungary, Slovakia, Poland (in part)	
	Chemicals: Czech Republic, Poland	*Electronics:* Czech Republic, Hungary, Slovakia	
	Food, beverages and tobacco: Poland, Slovakia, Slovenia, Latvia, Estonia	*Machinery:* Czech Republic, Slovakia	
	Metallurgy: Poland	*Pharmaceuticals:* Poland, Slovenia	
	Paper and packaging: Poland	*Wood and furniture:* Estonia, Latvia	
Services	*Financial services:* All but Slovenia	*Logistics:* Hungary, Poland	*IT:* Hungary, Poland, Czech Republic
	Retail trade: Hungary, Hungary, Poland, Czech Republic, Latvia	*Shared services and call centres:* Czech Republic, Hungary, Poland	*R&D:* Czech Republic, Hungary, Poland
	Telecommunications: All but Slovenia *Utilities:* Hungary, Czech Republic, Slovakia		

Source: Author's collection.

succeed in catching up with the science, technology and innovation capacities of old members. The challenge is how to catch up and benefit from such FDI as quickly as possible. In the short and medium term, the old members of EU are likely to attract the bulk of FDI in that area.

In the area of knowledge-based services, the laggard status of the new EU member countries is evident not just in comparison with the locations in the Asia and Pacific (such as India and China) that are the global magnets of such activities but also in comparison with the EU-15 and North America. One of the reasons, as mentioned above, is also the very nature of those activities, which do not require large investment to be able to provide services (such as, for example, infrastructure services). While the number of cases has been rather limited so far, the experience of those firms that located business services in the new EU member countries has been positive. Potentially, the arrival of knowledge-based services, first to Budapest, and to Prague, both in 2002, is the most marked change of FDI patterns in middle-income accession countries. The move to FDI based on higher labour skills makes the EU-accession countries direct competitors with other emerging locations and older EU members simultaneously.

Strategic-asset-seeking FDI is nevertheless potentially important for development because of its indirect contribution to host countries' economic structures. Knowledge-based services serve as inputs to other activities as they indirectly affect the efficiency and competitiveness of the whole economy. Additionally, FDI in those services enables the transfer of more advanced managerial, marketing and organizational skills and expertise, which have been so far deficient in the new EU members. R&D, which is perhaps the oldest form of services going offshore, when allied to manufacturing, can not only help improve the product but can also generate new spillover effects. As a result, it pays to encourage overseas firms to engage in R&D and network it with local private and public research institutions. The networks could enhance human capital and knowledge, which is an essential input into the development process. It is also necessary to enhance the teamwork and managerial skills of talented work force for them to undertake team-based projects at home.

6.1. Implications for the Pan-European Division of Labour

An overall question related to all FDI in the EU is how the realities of increased competition would affect decisions to relocate activities from old to new EU member countries. As mentioned above, it seems that pure relocations remain an infinitely small part of the FDI universe (Domański, 2001). Restructuring and rationalization, leading to changes in the division of labour between the two groups of countries are more likely to dominate FDI flows.

If adjustment to EU membership is successful, it will affect FDI all over the European continent. All accession countries except Bulgaria and Romania are upper-middle-income or high-income (Slovenia) countries. All South-East European and CIS countries but Croatia are lower middle-income countries. This may lead to an increase in FDI in services and higher corporate functions in accession countries, in part attracted from current EU members and third countries (Kalotay, 2004b). EU enlargement offers opportunities to South-East European and CIS countries, because assembly type manufacturing may shift to them from higher cost-accession countries. New EU member countries may become major sources of skill-intensive assets, combining their advanced education with competitive production costs. This trend is in variance with earlier expectations about a largely unchanged FDI pattern in new EU member countries after accession (see Dyker, 2001, p. 1015). In this integrating European continent, market size and market growth will increasingly denote the enlarged EU as a whole, providing benefits mostly to new member countries, particularly those with limited domestic purchasing power.

The emerging specialization of FDI between the accession and non-accession countries does not yet follow a "flying-geese" pattern. The basic idea of the "flying-geese" paradigm, developed for the case of TNC-led growth by Kojima (1973), is that, as host countries industrialize and go through industrial upgrading and learning in an open-economy context, the type of FDI flowing from home countries changes in character towards higher skills; in turn, simpler activities will gradually flow out from relatively advanced host countries to newcomer host countries. This process reinforces the basis for, and the benefits from, trade (see UNCTAD, 1995, pp. 258–260). Labour-intensive activities relocated from accession countries now go more to developing Asia (especially China) than to lower-income CEE countries. And the low outflows of FDI from accession countries limit the scope for restructuring to non-accession countries.

It may be argued that this type of division of labour is far from being accomplished because of the inherited structures of the past, in addition to the policy-related reasons mentioned above. As for the first factor, until the 1990s, most of the current EU-accession countries slated to join in 2004 were not on the production map. Middle-income functions were undertaken in some of the relatively lower-income members of the EU (e.g. Spain, Portugal,

Greece), and most of the labour-intensive production in Turkey or in the Southern Mediterranean. With the changes during the 1990s, and for that reason, the accession countries of 2004 increasingly started attracting first, labour-intensive, then middle-income functions. Low-income CEE was originally a latecomer but became a magnet for labour-intensive production in the late 1990s. One may argue that most of the CEE countries are in this sense in a catch-up phase.

As for policy obstacles to a new geography, one may mention protectionist pressures in the incumbent EU members, calling for the retention of departing production (e.g. textile and footwear). For the new EU members, the nature of that pressure may change from open to less formal measures. In turn, for the rest of CEE, the fact of being outside the EU increases the probability of administrative protectionism applied against them. This may be only partly counterbalanced by improvements in the business environment. Moreover, in that area, too, problems in the accession countries which are undergoing a forced march towards applying the *acquis communautaire* are less acute than in the rest of CEE.

7. POLICY CHALLENGES

In the new EU members, the need to upgrade public administration to the requirements of EU membership created an unprecedented challenge. In this respect, it is sufficient to recall the complexities of administering the structural and cohesion funds that some of the investment promotion agencies (CzechInvest, Enterprise Estonia, Latvian Development Agency) will be required to deal with. In line with the adoption of the *acquis*, EU-accession countries had to harmonize their FDI regimes with EU regulations. Examples of non-conforming FDI instruments are Slovakia's special incentives for foreign investors and Hungary's 10-year tax holidays granted only to large investors. Both countries changed their investment incentives in 2002 to conform to EU rules, while seeking to provide a framework no less favourable for investors.

The accession countries have to learn how to make the best use of the facilities now available to them for promoting investment, such as EU regional development funds (which are more limited than those for actual EU members). The accession countries also have to develop the institutional framework to administer and properly channel the variety of funds available from European Community sources for assisting economic development. Originally designed for high-income countries, these funds require sophisticated administrative capabilities. Reaching similar levels of public administration in the short time left until accession will test human and financial resources (Blažek, 1999; Dyker, 2001). In addition, the task is to modernize FDI promotion policies and measures. Only by doing so they can get the most from efficiency-seeking FDI.

In all economic activities, but in strategic-asset-seeking ones, in particular, the main challenge for both policy makers and implementing agencies such as investment promotion agencies, is to attract more FDI, and if possible, containing the highest value added possible. To what degree the new EU member countries can cooperate with each other in this area, given the fact that, often, they are each other's competitors for the same projects? While full harmonization is not feasible, some ways may be suggested to reduce the potential for a race-to-bottom competition. An important element in this partial cooperation and harmonization may be the fact that they have joined the EU and would in principle apply the same rules on subsidies and government assistance.

The priority areas of economic policies in which action is required if new EU countries wish to attract higher value-added FDI include infrastructure (especially in the area of information and communication technology), and skills and education. These are important for all types of economic activities. For R&D projects, governments need to consider investment policies to be part of broader efforts at developing the innovation system. Thus, science and technology, education labour market, fiscal and regional policies assume importance. For various business services, the transportation infrastructure is key. In all these areas, the policy advocacy role of investment promotion agencies is crucial. They have to indicate to policy makers the problems investors face and suggest ways to deal with them.

Some of the investment promotion agencies such as the CzechInvest, ITD Hungary, TIPO Slovenia, are providing direct incentives such as grants, subsidies and tax holidays to attract FDI in higher value-added services. On the other hand, Estonia provides no specific incentives but tries to attract FDI in general with a favourable fiscal regime and corporate taxation. There is no definitive answer to the question of how effective incentives have been. It seems that for a project to be attracted into a given location, the basic conditions should be right and competitive. In that respect, incentives cannot compensate for the lack of basic preconditions. On the other hand, if all conditions are very similar (which they often are), the choice between short-listed locations may be influenced by the incentives package. It is also argued that foreign investors see the existence of incentives as an additional sign of commitment by the host location. Interestingly, the Czech Republic recently overhauled its incentives system to make it more conducive to FDI in services.

Another aspect of the incentives discussion relates to the use of those instruments to direct FDI projects to less-developed locations within a host country. In such a case, selective incentives are offered to foreign investors only if they choose a priority area. The results have so far been mixed. It seems that especially in business services and R&D, access to skills, as well as transportation and telecommunications infrastructure and quality of life, available in the metropolitan areas, have been overwhelming concerns, making regional incentives ineffective. It was suggested hence that host countries striving for a more balanced distribution of quality FDI need to address infrastructure needs, even if that is difficult and time-consuming.

8. CONCLUSIONS

This chapter has examined some of the implications of EU membership for inward FDI in the new member countries. In a nutshell, in the pre-accession period, those flows proved to be disappointingly low, despite the obvious productivity advantage of the countries. That situation is expected to change gradually from 2004 onwards, on condition that the advantages of the new member countries are not annulled by either an overvaluation of their national currencies, or by protectionism in the "old" EU member countries.

In a broader perspective, a new division of labour between the three Europes – the "old" EU, the New EU and other CEE countries – is more likely to emerge than competition for the same investment projects or, for that matter, massive relocation. This emerging division of labour across the integrating European continent improves the efficiency of operations in Europe as a whole. For example, for Flextronics, the existence of R&D in Austria and Germany makes sense only if complemented by some manufacturing operations in CEE (especially Hungary and to some degree in Poland); if production were to move to other continents, so would R&D (UNCTAD, 2003, p. 79, fn. 36). In other words, because "EU enlargement is not a zero sum game in which the new member states will compete against current incumbents for a fixed pool of FDI" (Barry, 2003, p. 189), changes in FDI flows to different parts of Europe can potentially benefit all of them, and not just one group at the expense of another.

Potentially, outward FDI may become yet another source of competitiveness and catching up for new EU member countries. At this point of time, however, the TNCs of the new EU member countries tend to be small in number and size. It may also well be that their deepening integration into the corporate networks of the EU area and the globe will take place through teaming up with, or partly being controlled by, the largest TNCs of the "old" EU members. That would further exacerbate the phenomenon of indirect FDI. In the longer term, however, if catching up turns out to be successful, new EU members may also become home countries of an increasing number of "independent" TNCs.

NOTES

1. The views expressed in this chapter are those of the author and do not necessarily reflect the opinion of the United Nations. The author is particularly grateful to Vinod K. Jain (University of Maryland University College, Adelphi, MD, United States), who initiated the panel on "Central and Eastern Europe: Opportunities and Challenges of EU Accession" at the Academy of International Business Annual Meeting in Stockholm, Sweden, on 10–13 July 2004, where the original ideas of this study were first presented. He is also indebted to Tatiana Kostova (University of South Carolina, Columbia, SC, United States), who chaired the panel meeting, and to co-panellists Tomasz Mroczkowski (American University, Washington, DC, United States) and Francis J. Skrobiszewski (Hungarian-American Enterprise Fund, Washington, DC, United States) for their comments and suggestions. The issues described in this study have undergone heated discussions with colleagues at the *World Investment Report* team in Geneva, Switzerland, from which the author has benefited substantially. All the remaining errors are the full responsibility of the author.
2. See the proceedings of the UNCTAD/KOPINT-DATORG/ITDH Workshop on FDI in Services in Central and Eastern Europe: Trends, Impact and Government Policies, held in Budapest, 4–6 March 2004.
3. http://www.kpmg.co.uk/pubs/taxrates_04.pdf.
4. See Note 3 above.

REFERENCES

Akbar, Y. H. (2003). *The multinational enterprise and EU enlargement: The effects of regulatory convergence*. London: Palgrave.
Akbar, Y. H., & McBride, J. (2004). Multinational enterprise strategy, foreign direct investment and economic development: The case of Hungary. *Journal of World Business, 39*, 89–105.
Balassa, B. (1964). The purchasing power parity doctrine: A reappraisal. *Journal of Political Economy, 72*, 584–596.
Baldwin, R. E., Forslid, R., & Haaland, J. I. (1996). Investment creation and investment diversion in Europe. *The World Economy, 19*, 635–659.

Barrell, R., & Pain, N. (1997). Foreign direct investment, technological change, and economic growth within Europe. *Economic Journal, 107*, 1770–1786.

Barry, F. (2003). EU accession and prospective FDI flows to CEE countries: A view from Ireland. In: Deutsche Bundesbank (Ed.), *Foreign direct investment in the real and financial sector of industrial countries, Deutsche Bundesbank conference*, 3–4 May 2002, Eltville am Rhein.

Barry, F. (2004). Enlargement and the EU periphery: Introduction. *The World Economy, 27*, 753–759.

Blažek, J. (1999). Regional development and regional policy in CEECs in the perspective of the EU Eastern enlargement. In: Martin Hampl (Ed.), *Geography of societal transformation in the Czech Republic* (pp. 181–207). Department of Social Geography and Regional Development: Charles University, Prague.

Blomström, M., & Sjöholm, F. (1999). Technology transfer and spillovers: Does local participation with multinationals matter? *European Economic Review, 43*, 915–923.

Djankov, S., & Hoekman, B. (2000). Foreign investment and productivity growth in Czech enterprises. *The World Bank Economic Review, 14*, 49–64.

Domański, B. (2001). Poland: Labour and the relocation of manufacturing from the EU. In: H. Grigor Gradev (Ed.), *CEE Countries in EU companies' Strategies of Industrial Restructuring and Relocation* (pp. 21–49). Brussels: European Trade Union Institute.

Dunning, J. H., & Robson, P. (Eds) (1988). *Multinationals and the European Community*. Oxford: Basil Blackwell.

Dyker, D. A. (2001). The dynamic impact on the Central–Eastern European economies of accession to the European Union: Social capability and technology absorption. *Europe–Asia Studies, 53*, 1001–1021.

Economic Commission for Europe (ECE). (2001). Economic growth and foreign direct investment in the transition economies. *Economic Survey of Europe 2001 no. 1*. United Nations, New York and Geneva, United Nations publication, Sales no. E.01.II.E.14, 185–226.

Égert, B., Drine, I., Lommatzsch, K., & Rault, C. (2003). The Balassa–Samuelson effect in Central and Eastern Europe: Myth or reality? *Journal of Comparative Economics, 31*, 552–572.

Hardy, J. (1998). Cathedrals in the desert? Transnationals, corporate strategy and locality in Wrocław. *Regional Studies, 32*, 639–652.

Hunya, G. (2000). Central Europe catching-up through FDI? In: G. Hunya (Ed.), *Integration through foreign direct investment: Making Central European industries competitive* (pp. 8–27). Cheltenham and Northampton: Edward Elgar.

Hunya, G. (2001). Uneven competitiveness of industries in the wake of foreign penetration of advanced economies in transition. *Transnational Corporations, 10*(2), 35–66.

Jaklič, A., & Svetličič, M. (2003). *Enhanced Transition Through Outward Internationalization: Outward FDI by Slovenian firms*. Aldershot, Hampshire: Ashgate.

Morgan, J. P. (2004). *EU enlargement: Opportunities grasped by the east, missed by the west*. JPMorgan Research, New York, 27 April. Available at www.morganmarkets.com

Kalotay, K. (2001). The contribution of foreign direct investment to transition revisited. *The Journal of World Investment, 2*, 259–276.

Kalotay, K. (2004a). The European flying geese: New FDI patterns for the old continent? *Research in International Business and Finance, 18*, 27–49.

Kalotay, K. (2004b). A macro look at Central and Eastern Europe and EU enlargement. Presentation at the *Panel on Central and Eastern Europe: Opportunities and challenges of EU accession*, Academy of International Business 2004 Annual Meeting, Stockholm, Sweden, 10–13 July.

Kilvits, K., & Purju, A. (2001). Estonian direct investment abroad: Sources, targets and adjustment to conditions. In: Kari Liuhto (Ed.), *East Goes West: The internationalization of Eastern enterprises* (pp. 233–264). Lappeenranta: Lappeenranta University of Technology.

Kojima, K. (1973). A macroeconomic approach to foreign direct investment. *Hitotsubashi Journal of Economics, 14*(1) (June), 1–12.

Samuelson, P. A. (1964). Theoretical notes on trade problems. *Review of Economics and Statistics, 46,* 145–154.

Stare, M. (2002). Service sector internationalisation via OFDI: Comparative analysis of Czech Republic, Estonia, Hungary, Poland, Slovenia. Presentation at the Workshop on *EU-integration-driven investment networking: Outward foreign direct investment of candidate countries,* Bled, Slovenia, 11 May.

Stephan, J. (2003). Evolving structural patterns in the enlarging European division of labour: Sectoral and branch specialisation and the potentials for closing the productivity gap. *Sonderheft no. 15/2003.* Institut für Wirtschaftsforschung, Halle. http://www.iwh-halle.de/d/publik/sh/SH%205%2003.htm.

Tupy, M. L. (2003). EU enlargement: Costs, benefits, and strategies for Central and Eastern European countries. *Policy Analysis no. 489.* Washington, DC: Cato Institute.

United Nations Conference on Trade and Development (UNCTAD). (1995). *World Investment Report 1995: Transnational corporations and competitiveness.* United Nations, New York and Geneva, United Nations Publication, Sales no. E.95.II.A.4.

United Nations Conference on Trade and Development (UNCTAD). (2001). *World Investment Report 2001: Promoting linkages.* United Nations, New York and Geneva, United Nations Publication, Sales no. 01.II.D.12.

United Nations Conference on Trade and Development (UNCTAD). (2003). *World Investment Report 2003: FDI policies and development: National and international perspectives.* United Nations, New York and Geneva, United Nations Publication, Sales no. E.03.II.D.8.

United Nations Conference on Trade and Development (UNCTAD). (2004). *World Investment Report 2004: The shift toward services.* United Nations, New York and Geneva, United Nations Publication, Sales no. E.04.II.D.33.

Viner, J. (1950). *The Customs Union Issue.* New York: Carnegie Endowment for International Peace.

ABOUT THE AUTHORS

Yusaf Akbar is Associate Professor of International Business at the Southern New Hampshire University, United States. His teaching and research interests are in foreign direct investment, public policy and strategy, and his geographical area interests are in East and Central Europe. He has published widely in peer-reviewed journals including *Journal of World Business, Thunderbird International Business Review and World Competition*. Yusaf has been Visiting Professor at various schools around the world, including the American University in Bulgaria, ESSCA, the KMBS, the MIB School of Management-Trieste, and Thunderbird.

Caner Bakir is Assistant Professor in the Department of International Relations at Koc University, Turkey. Caner holds a Ph.D. from Monash University, Australia. His current research interests include financial and monetary governance, government–business relations and international political economy. He is a member of the editorial board of the *International Encyclopedia of Public Policy: Governance in a Global Age*. Recent articles have appeared in the *Australian Journal of Political Science*, the *Australian Journal of Politics and History*, the *Journal of Australian Political Economy*, among others.

Jonathan Batten is Professor of Management (Finance) at Macquarie University, Sydney, Visiting Professor of Finance at Aarhus School of Business, Denmark, Honorary Professor Faculty of Arts, Deakin University, Melbourne and Research Associate in the Institute for International Integration Studies at Trinity College, Dublin. He is co-editor of *Research in International Business and Finance*. Jonathan has published work in many journals, including *The Journal of Business Ethics, The Journal of International Business Studies*, the *International Review of Financial Analysis* and *Physica A*. He has recently co-edited a volume, *European Fixed Income Markets: Money, Bond and Interest Rate Derivatives*, as part of the Wiley Finance series.

Uri Ben-Zion is a professor in the Department of Economics of Ben Gurion University in Beer Sheva, Israel. His current research areas include behavioral and empirical finance, as well as applied economics. Uri is a fellow of the Institute for the study of Labor in Bonn (IZA) and the Center for Financial Studies in Frankfurt (CES) and held visiting positions in many academic and public institutions, including the University of Pennsylvania, City university of New York, Monash University, University of Frankfurt, University of Osaka, the World Bank and the International Monetary Fund. He also served as a consultant to the Bank of Israel and to firms in Israel and worldwide. Uri has published in many leading journals, including the *American Economic Review*, the *Journal of Finance*, the *Review of Economics and Statistics, Public Choice*, and *Management Science*.

Kym Brown is Assistant Lecturer at Monash University in Australia. Currently researching Asian bank efficiency, Kym's research interests predominantly relate to banking at the macro level and financial depth analysis. Further interests include the performance of Islamic banking and developing markets.

Jing Chi is Senior Lecturer in the Department of Finance, Banking and Property, Massey University, New Zealand. Jing worked in Huatai Securities Company in China for 2 years, responsible for IPOs and M&A, and as an analyst at the London Stock Exchange. Jing received her Ph.D. from the University of Reading in England in 2003. Her academic publications and research interests are in the area of Chinese IPOs, corporate finance, financial derivatives, and financial markets.

Tej Dhakar is Professor and Chair of the Department of Quantitative Studies and Operations Management at the Southern New Hampshire University, United States. His teaching interests are in quantitative methods and operations management. Current and recent research areas include the impact of financial markets on economic development in Eastern Europe and the impact of NAFTA integration on member states. He has published in many journals including *Computers and Operations Research* and *Communications in Statistics.*

Heather Elms is Assistant Professor of Strategy and Ethics and Director of the Center for the Social Foundations of Business at the Central European University Graduate School of Business. Her research and teaching interests are in Strategy and Business Ethics, especially as it relates to corporate governance. Prior to coming to CEU, Professor Elms taught at the University of Florida.

Steven Globerman is the Kaiser Professor of International Business at Western Washington University. He holds a Ph.D. in economics from New York University and has published and consulted extensively on the causes and consequences of foreign direct investment.

Dalia Grigonytè has been a Research Fellow at the Center for European Integration Studies, University of Bonn. Her research area covered fiscal and exchange rate policies in Central and Eastern European countries, particularly the impact of tight exchange rate arrangements on fiscal discipline in small open economies.

Nico Groenendijk is Jean Monnet Professor of European Economic Governance and Director of Research, Centre for European Studies, University of Twente, The Netherlands. He has published on the political economy of taxation, corruption, fiscal federalism, EU tax harmonization and on budgetary control within the EU. His current research interests include the application of neo-institutional economics to multi-level governance issues within the EU. He is member of the editorial board of the *Journal of European Political Economy*.

Kálmán Kalotay has been a member of the UNCTAD team preparing the World Investment Reports since 1996. Previously, he worked on monetary and financial cooperation issues at UNCTAD (1990–1996) and taught at the Corvinus University, Budapest, Hungary (1983–1990), from where he also received his Ph.D. in economics. Kálmán has served as editor of the *Transnational Corporations Journal* (1996–2004), and has published extensively on foreign direct investment in economies in transition.

Colm Kearney is Professor of International Business in the School of Business Studies, and Research Associate in the Institute for International Integration Studies at Trinity College, Dublin. He holds Masters degrees in Economics from the University of Essex and the University of Western Ontario, and his Ph.D. degree in economics is from the University of Warwick. Prior positions include Professor of Finance and Economics at the

University of Technology Sydney, and Professor of Economics at the University of Western Sydney. He has published widely in the area of international finance. His homepage is at www.internationalbusiness.ie

Roy Kouwenberg is Assistant Professor in the School of Management at the Asian Institute of Technology in Thailand. Roy received a Ph.D. degree in Finance from Erasmus University, Rotterdam in 2001 and is a CFA charterholder. Previously, Roy worked at the University of British Columbia as a postdoctoral fellow and as a quantitative analyst at the equity department of AEGON Asset Management in The Hague. Roy's research reflects his interest in asset pricing, optimization and empirical finance. His work has appeared in various journals, including the *Review of Economics and Statistics*, the *Journal of Economic Dynamics and Control* and *Operations Research.*

Brian Lucey is Lecturer in Finance in the School of Business at Trinity College Dublin, Ireland, and a Research Associate of the Institute for International Integration Studies at the University. He holds a BA in economics from Dublin, an MA in International Integration from the National University of Ireland, and his Ph.D. in Finance is from the University of Stirling in Scotland. Prior to joining academia, Brian worked in the Central Bank of Ireland. He has published widely in the area of empirical finance.

Orazio Mastroeni is Principal Economist at the European Central Bank in Frankfurt, in charge of the operational team managing the Eurosystem's assets for refinancing operations. He graduated in Economic Sciences at the University of Rome and took a Masters Degree in International Finance in the UK. Prior to joining the ECB, he served in the Banca d'Italia as a financial economist. He is currently Secretary of the "Eurosystem Policy Committee on the Single List of collateral". He has published a number of articles in financial journals, books and in ECB publications, on monetary policy implementation, and the Eurosystem's collateral framework.

Patrick McGuire has worked as an economist at the Bank for International Settlements in Basel, Switzerland, since 2002. Prior to this, he completed his Ph.D. in economics at the University of Michigan, with research focused on the Japanese financial system. Patrick spent several years living in Japan, most recently as a visiting scholar at METI. His current research efforts are broadly focused on financial stability issues, with a specific interest in the international banking market, emerging market financing, and hedge fund activity.

Albert Mentink holds Master's degrees in both Economics and Econometrics from the University of Groningen. Since 1997, he has been working at AEGON Asset Management in The Hague, The Netherlands, where he is currently head of Quantitative Research. His research interests focus on topics in the fields of interest rate, credit and liquidity risk of corporate bonds. His work has been published in various academic journals, including the *Journal of Banking and Finance* and the *Journal of Derivatives.*

Ilko Naaborg is to complete his Ph.D. degree in economics at the SOM Research School at the University of Groningen. His research is focussed on foreign banks in Central and Eastern Europe. Topics include the determinants, modes and processes of foreign bank entry, and the relative performance of foreign banks. Recent articles have been published in the *Journal of Emerging Market Finance* and the *European Journal of Finance.* Other publications are in the field of hedge funds and financial intermediation in EU Accession Countries.

Seppo Pynnönen is Professor of Statistics in the Department of Mathematics and Statistics at the University of Vaasa in Finland. His current research interest is in empirical finance covering areas like information transmission across stock markets, the determinants of credit risk of corporate bonds, common features in stock returns and stock market responses on news. He has published in *Applied Economics, Applied Financial Economics, European Journal of Operational Research, Journal of International Financial Markets, Institutions & Money, International Review of Financial Analysis, Journal of Asian Pacific Economy, Management International Review,* and other refereed journals and edited books of collected papers. He is also an associate editor of *Research in International Business and Finance.*

Bert Scholtens is Professor in the Department of Finance at the University of Groningen, the Netherlands. He teaches and researches in the areas of portfolio management, credit risk analysis, and corporate governance. Another research interest is corporate social responsibility and socially responsible investing. He has published in the *Journal of Banking and Finance, Journal of Investing, Research in International Business and Finance, Journal* *of Fixed Income, Ecological Economics, Journal of Alternative Investments, Journal of Performance Measurement*, among others.

Martijn Schrijvers is an economist and portfolio manager at the Financial Markets Division of De Nederlandsche Bank, where he manages the euro-fixed income portfolio and analyses developments in the financial markets. He has Master degrees in General Economics and Development Economics from the Erasmus University of Rotterdam. His previous positions at De Nederlandsche Bank include advising on and the implementation of monetary policy, and as policy advisor on international affairs.

Daniel Shapiro is the Dennis Culver EMBA Alumni Professor in the Faculty of Business Administration at Simon Fraser University, Vancouver. He obtained his Ph.D. from Cornell University. He teaches and researches in the areas of business strategy, international business and business economics. Recent articles have appeared in the *Strategic Management Journal*, the *Journal of International Business Studies*, the *Academy of Management Journal*, the *Industrial and Corporate Change*, the *Journal of Strategic Management Education*, and the *Journal of Business Research*, among others.

Michael Skully is Professor of Banking at Monash University in Australia. He came to Monash in 1992 from the University of New South Wales. He has published widely in the areas of financial institutions and corporate finance. His publications include the book on Merchant Banking in Australia, co-author of Management of Financial Institutions; and the general editor of the Handbook of Australian Corporate Finance. His current research interests include banking and banking efficiency in developing and transitional economies, operational risk and corporate governance.

Yao Tang received his BA degree in international trade from Beijing Second Foreign Language Institute, his MA degree in economics from Simon Fraser University, Canada, and is now completing his Ph.D. degree in the Department of Economics at the University of British Columbia, Canada. Yao is working on both theoretical and empirical problems in macroeconomics and international economics.

Lúcio Vinhas de Souza is currently the officer responsible for Belarus and Russia at the DG-ECFIN of the European Commission. He is also a member of the Managing Board of the UACES (University Association of Contemporary European Studies), and an Associate Fellow of the Institute for World Economics (IfW) and of the United Nations University Centre for Comparative Regional Integration Studies (UNU-CRIS). He formerly held positions of Economist at the IfW in Germany and at the United Nations Secretariat, and worked as a Visiting Fellow/Visiting Researcher at the ECARES-Free University of Brussels and at the Central Banks of Germany and Estonia. He also worked as a consultant for the European Parliament, and in World Bank, European Union and USAID projects. His most recent research deals with the macroeconomic issues of "transition" economies, mainly related to the monetary aspects of the Accession of Eastern European countries to the European Union and with trade and monetary policy questions applied to Western CIS countries. He was also a guest editor of the *Journal of Comparative Economics* and a co-editor of the *Journal of European Affairs*. He has a considerable list of publications in several different languages.

Svitlana Voronkova is Lecturer in Finance in the School of Business Studies at Trinity College, Dublin and a Research Fellow at the Institute for International Integration Studies, Trinity College, Dublin. She received her Ph.D. degree from the European University, Viadrina in Germany in 2004, being a scholar of Stiftungsfond Deutsche Bank im Stifterverband für die Deutsche Wissentschaft. Svitlana has published in the *Journal of Business Finance and Accounting*, the *International Review of Economics and Finance*, and the *International Review of Financial Analysis*.

Niklas Wagner is Assistant Professor of Finance at Munich University of Technology. He received his Ph.D. degree in Finance from Augsburg University, Germany, and held postdoctoral visiting appointments at the Haas School of Business, University of California, Berkeley, and at Stanford GSB. His research interests cover the areas of applied financial econometrics including portfolio optimization, risk management, trading strategies, and applications in behavioural finance. Niklas' industry background is in quantitative asset management with HypoVereinsbank AG, Munich, and with Munich Financial Systems Consulting.

Richard Werner is Professor of International Banking at the School of Management, University of Southampton, UK. Previously he was tenured Assistant Professor of Economics at Sophia University, Tokyo, and Marie

Curie Fellow at the Institute of Economics and Statistics, University of Oxford. Richard received his training in economics at the London School of Economics, University of Oxford and Tokyo University. He has been visiting researcher or scholar at the Bank of Japan, the Japanese Ministry of Finance and the Japan Development Bank. Richard has been senior consultant to the Asian Development Bank and many of the world's largest institutional investors. He was selected 'Global Leader for Tomorrow' by the World Economic Forum in Davos in January 2003.

Martin Young is Associate Professor of Finance in the College of Business at Massey University, New Zealand. Prior to this he spent four years as a Senior Fellow at the Nanyang Business School in Singapore. Martin has wide experience working within financial markets and was a member of the New Zealand Stock Exchange for many years. Recent academic publications and research interests are in the areas of derivative usage, returns momentum and market structure.

Peter Zajc is Assistant Professor at the Faculty of Economics, University of Ljubljana in Slovenia. Upon completion of his graduate studies at the Kiel Institute for World Economics, Peter completed his Ph.D. degree in economics at the University of Ljubljana. His research interests lie in the areas of banking sector restructuring and bank efficiency, with a focus on Central and Eastern Europe.

AUTHOR INDEX